Mastering the Internet and HTML

Ibrahim Zeid
Northeastern University

Prentice Hall
Upper Saddle River, NJ 07458

Library of Congress Cataloging-in-Publication Data available

Editor-in-chief: *Marcia Horton*
Publisher: *Alan Apt*
Acquistion editor: *Petra Recter*
Editorial/production supervision: *Rose Kernan*
Managing editor: *David George*
Executive managing editor: *Vince O'Brien*
Cover design: *Heather Scott*
Manufacturing buyer: *Pat Brown*
Editorial Assistant: *Sarah Burrows*
Assistant vice president of production and manufacturing: *David W. Riccardi*
Art manager: *Xiaohong Zhu*
Marketing manager: *Jennie Burger*

©2000 Prentice-Hall, Inc.
Upper Saddle River, New Jersey 07458

The author and publisher of this book have used their best efforts in preparing this book. These efforts include the development, research, and testing of the theories and programs to determine their effectiveness. The author and publisher make no warranty of any kind, expressed or implied, with regard to these programs or the documentation contained in this book. The author or publisher shall not be liable in any event for incidental or consequential damage in connection with, or arising out of, the furnishing, performance, or use of these programs.

Product names mentioned herein are the trademarks or registered trademarks of their respective owners.
Netscape Navigator, Netscape Communicator, Netscape Composer, Microsoft Internet Explorer, Windows, Paint, Winamp, ws_ftp32, wintel32, winzip, Apache, SnagIt, Adobe Photoshop, Adobe Illustrator, Mapedit, Paint Shop Pro, ThumbsPlus, WebEdit PRO, WebImage, WS FTL LE, Lview, GoldWave, CoolEdit, Macromedia, SoundEdit Pro II, Sound catcher, Sox, Kamboo! Factory, Synchrome's Maestro V, Acoustica, Sound Forge, Sound Recorder, Indeo video, Active Movie, Maplay 32, VMPEG, Media Player, CoffeeCup, HotDog Pro, HotMetal Pro, FrontPage, Page Mill, AOLserver, Domino, CommerceServer, Enterprise Server, Java Web server, Personal Web Server, Internet Information Server, NCSA HTTPD, Netscape Enterpirse Server, Oracle Web Application Server, and MicroServer.

Printed in the United States of America
10 9 8 7 6 5 4 3 2 1

ISBN 0-13-908005-8

Prentice-Hall International (UK) Limited, *London*
Prentice-Hall of Australia Pty. Limited, *Sydney*
Prentice-Hall Canada Inc., *Toronto*
Prentice-Hall Hispanoamericana, S.A., *Mexico*
Prentice-Hall of India Private Limited, *New Delhi*
Prentice-Hall of Japan, Inc., *Tokyo*
Prentice-Hall (Singapore) Pte. Ltd., *Singapore*
Editora Prentice-Hall do Brasil, Ltda., *Rio de Janeiro*

To my wife and children,
who have given me their
unconditional love, support,
and encouragement.

Elaine Pan

2001/3/7.

Contents

Preface

The explosion of the Internet and the World Wide Web is beyond any imagination. Even with this explosion, the Internet and its related applications are not near their peak yet. The Internet growth is expected to continue in the future. The Internet has been impacting all aspects of our lives and all segments of societies all over the world. All segments of populations use the Internet on daily basis. Students and educators at elementary, middle, high, and vocational schools have their computers connected to the Internet. At the college level, the use of the Internet is even more pervasive. Both community colleges and universities are indulged in using the Internet in course work, research, and marketing. Moreover, the commercial segment of our society is more heavily involved in using the Internet. Many companies already have Web masters, sites, and pages with the goal of becoming e-commerce leaders. It is because of this impact and potential that this book is written.

The purpose of this book is to present the fundamental concepts of the Internet and its HTML scripting tools in a generic framework with enough depth and breadth. These concepts and tools are supplemented with examples, tutorials, as well as problems to provide students and readers with hands-on experience so that they can master the concepts. The book strikes a delicate balance between subject depth and breadth on one hand, and between generic an practical aspects of the Internet on the other hand. Regarding depth and breadth, the book covers the basic topics about the Internet and its effective use in daily tasks such as e-mail and searching, and all aspects of client-side HTML. Regarding generic and practical aspects, the book always relates the generic concepts to their use in technology, software, and practical applications. For example, the book covers the generic concepts behind Internet browsers. It then covers the details of the two popular browsers today, Netscape Communicator® and Microsoft Internet Explorer®. Another example is the use of HTML editors. After covering all generic aspects and tags of

HTML, the book presents some of the commonly used HTML editors such as Netscape Composer®, and relates its user interface to the generic HTML tags.

This book strives to build a new "mental model" in the reader's mind to deal with the Internet successfully. This new model shows the reader how to deal with the fast changing and dynamic nature of the Internet. For example, Web sites come and go. URLs change all the time. Instead of memorizing the maze of the World Wide Web, the book shows how to effectively use existing search and navigation tools of the Internet.

This book fills an important need in the market. The market needs a book that meets the demand of students, instructors, and professionals alike. Students need a book that explains the subject matter in a simple, yet comprehensive and coherent way with enough examples and hands-on tutorials. Students need a book that gets right to the point. As a matter of fact, this book mirrors the nature of surfing the Web. If surfers do not find what they want in a Web page in 30 seconds, they move on to another one. If a Web site does not offer visitors concentrated services and information, it loses them. This book offers concentrated knowledge to its readers so that they find what they want very quickly.

Instructors need a book that provides them with abundant topics to choose from. More importantly, they need a book that provides examples, tutorials, and problems. Many Internet courses, whether academic or professional, are taught in a lab setting. Many of the Internet topics are inherently lab and hands-on oriented. With this book, instructors can offer their courses in a lecture/lab format. During a lab session, the instructor may choose to get the students to do the examples, the tutorials, or the exercises. The instructor may also use the summary section at the end of each chapter as the basis for, say, a Microsoft Power Point® presentation for teaching purposes.

Professionals need a book that they can use for self-teaching purposes due to the demand on their times. They also need a book that provides them with solutions to specific questions they may have during developing Web sites and Web pages. With this book, professionals can tap into the summary and the FAQs (frequently asked questions) sections for quick consultation. Many of the questions in the FAQs sections of the book are questions of past students and professionals who used the material of this book in the past before its publication.

The book is organized into two parts. Part I covers the effective use of the Internet. It begins with an overview of the Internet and the World Wide Web, followed by the methods used to connect to the Internet. The Internet browsers are covered. We focus on the two major browsers: Netscape Communicator (version 4.7) and Microsoft Internet Explorer (version 5.0). Internet access tools and resources are covered followed by navigation tools and search engines. Part II discusses, in details, HTML (hypertext markup language) and Web page design and development. Client-side HTML is covered, with enough coverage of server-side HTML to make the book readers fully understand the client-side HTML.

This book enjoys may unique and distinguishing features. It is structured and organized in a logical way with two integrated parts. It is written in an easy-to-follow and direct style. It covers all the important topics with enough depth and breadth. It provides both generic and practice-oriented material. Each chapter has few unique features: overview, examples, tutorials, FAQs, summary, and problems. The overview and the summary serve as a quick reference for readers and instructors. The examples and tutorials are designed to be done in a lab setting, as a part of a course, using PCs running Microsoft Windows® 95, 98, 2000, or NT. Mac® computers or Unix workstations may also be used. They provide hands-on experience for readers, students, and instructors. The FAQs section has many useful practical questions. These questions are not a reformulation of material already covered in the chapter. They are different and add a new knowledge and material in a very concise way to the chapter.

The problems section is divided into two parts: exercises and homework. The exercises are very specific and well-defined. They can be used in a lab where class time is limited. Thus, instructors have three options to provide students with hands-on experience. They can use either the examples and tutorials, the exercises, or both. Students can follow the examples and tutorials until they gain experience. If there is time left in the class, they can do the exercises on their own. The homework problems are designed to be more extensive and some of them are open-ended in nature as students have more time outside the classroom to do them. A solution manual of both the exercises and homework problems accompanies this book.

The material in this book can be used in various ways. As a textbook, it could be used for undergraduate and professional courses. The material in the book could be covered in one three-hour semester, or one four-hour quarter undergraduate course. Or, it could be covered in a 20 or 30-hours professional course. the book could also be used in intensive seminar courses. A three or four-day seminar course is adequate. It is preferred that courses using the book have lab sessions with them. The lab environment typically consists of PCs, a browser, and a text or HTML editor. The book is also ideal for teach-yourself or self-study mode. Any Internet enthusiast can use it.

To write a book in the very rapidly changing Internet and World Wide Web field is a very challenging endeavor an individual can undertake. The book design and organization has taken this observation into consideration. The book has been divided into two integrated parts which can be updated or expanded easily in the future to reflect new trends. This is important for the book users and readers.

I am indebted to all the people who helped directly and indirectly to make this book idea a reality. I would like to thank the following reviewers for their valuable comments, suggestions, and advice throughout the project: Floyd LeCureux of California State University at Sacramento, Harold Grossman of Clemson University, Rayford Vaughn of Mississippi State University, and Scott Henninger of University of Nebraska, Lincoln. There is no doubt that their suggestions have bettered this book.

I would like to thank all my students and colleagues who contributed to this book in many ways through seminars, discussions, and courses. Special thanks are due to the following former students who gave me their generous permission to use their work in this book: Debra Buchanan, Ted Catino, John Doyle, Roger Eames, Linda Haviland, Regina Lagakos, Stephanie Rogers, David Shadmon, Suzanne Sigman, and Donna Waugh.

Thanks are due to the Prentice Hall staff for their patience and professional help. Mr. David Ostrow introduced the book manuscript to Mr. Alan Apt who directed the book project at the beginning. The help and support of Alan were crucial to publishing this book. The valuable experience and vision of Petra Recter, senior acquisitions editor, has permitted the successful completion of the manuscript. Her e-mail messages, phone calls, and visits kept the project moving. Her coordination of the review process ensured the reception of valuable feedback in a timely manner. I would also like to thank Rose Kernan, the production editor, for managing all the production phases of the book, and keeping the production schedule under control. The developmental edit conducted by Nick Murray has greatly improved the readability of the book. The copy editor, Bill Salvatore of Write With Inc., has done a great job in reading the manuscript carefully to maintain the consistency of the writing style. Jennie Burger, marketing manager, has done a great job promoting the book already. Many thanks are also due Sarah Burrows, Eileen Clark, Toni Holm, and Xiaohong Zhu for their valuable help.

Last, but not least, very special thanks are due to my family and friends who supported me from start to finish with their love, support, and encouragement, which are greatly appreciated.

Ibrahim Zeid
Boston

Effective Use of the Internet

This part covers the essentials of the Internet. The main goal of this part is to develop what we call a "mental model" to effectively deal with the Internet as an infinite source of information. Unlike traditional sources of knowledge such as libraries, the Internet has two unique characteristics for the information it holds: randomness and fluidity. The World Wide Web (WWW), the largest segment of the Internet, consists of a collection of Web pages (sites) that are randomly organized; thus the name Web. There is no master catalog index of these pages. These pages keep changing over time whether they disappear, become obsolete, or change content. Chasing these pages becomes a formidable task. To deal effectively with this medium of the Internet and the WWW, this part of the book organizes the Internet and WWW into a coherent set of basic concepts and topics that help users and surfers of the Internet to develop the mental model. The part begins with **chapter 1** which gives an overview of the Internet and provides definitions of some of its jargon. **Chapter 2** discusses the hardware and software requirements to connect to, and use the Internet. The chapter covers the various methods of connecting to the Internet, especially the dial-up connection used by many homes and PCs. **Chapters 3 and 4** are dedicated to the topic of browsers and how to use them. They cover the details of the functions and tools offered by the two most popular browsers: Netscape Communicator (Chapter 3) and Microsoft Internet Explorer (Chapter 4). **Chapter 5** discusses useful tools of the Internet such as newsgroups, FTP, and Telnet. It also shows how to install and use related software and shareware. The last chapter, **Chapter 6**, presents the available search tools and techniques in depth, including search engines, metasearch engines, smart browsing, and Web portals.

CHAPTER 1

Overview of the Internet

T his chapter provides an overview of the Internet, to help the reader to understand its structure and communications. After reading this chapter, the reader should be able to know the relationship between the Internet and the World Wide Web, a brief history of the Internet, how it works, who owns it, what is on it, what you do while surfing it, and where it is going.

1.1 Introduction

The Internet has been acknowledged as the most revolutionary discovery since xerography or electricity. The Internet has already been changing our lives and the way we communicate or conduct business. Many of us send e-mail messages back and forth to friends, colleagues, customers, clients and/or relatives all over the world. The Internet provides an instant way of communication (electronic mail — or e-mail for short), faster than fax and overnight mail. There are so many news groups, chat rooms, and organizations that already exist. You can meet people on the Internet as well. Home or Web pages are cluttering the Internet. Today, there exist Yellow Pages books for the Internet. There is no doubt that this medium of communication will dominate and will surpass any other medium. The Internet had more users in its first five years than the telephone did in its first thirty years, and e-mail already outnumbers regular mail by a ten to one ratio.

While it is exciting to hear and read about the Internet, it often confusing to put all its related pieces together. The Internet, Intranets, Extranets, World Wide Web, surfing the net, web browsers and navigators, and search engines are but some of the terms we hear everyday. This chapter attempts to put this terminology into perspective, to facilitate using this exciting medium of communication.

1.2 The Internet and the World Wide Web

The Internet is all about diverse computers and programs working together seamlessly. The Internet is a network of networks. Think of it as a very-high-speed highway system that connects many regions; it is known as the information superhighway. It is a giant network (web) of computers, located allover the world, that communicate with each other. This giant network consists of other networks. These networks include various federal networks, a set of regional networks, campus networks, and foreign networks. A network may include, in addition to computers, various devices such as printers and disk drives. The computers and these devices are connected by some communications channel in such a way that all users can have access to the resources found in the network. The channel is typically a copper telephone wire or a fiber-optic cable. It can also include high-speed wireless microwave and satellite connections.

The definition of the Internet should not mean much to the end user. The user wants to do something useful, such as running a program, accessing a Web site, or downloading a specific file. An end user should not worry about how the Internet is put together. A good analogy is the telephone system; it, too, is a network. Phone companies such as AT&T, MCI, Sprint, and others are all separate corporations running pieces of the telephone system. They worry about how to make it all work together; all you have to do is dial the number you want. If it was not for the cost, dealing with any of these companies should not be of concern to you.

You only begin to worry when a problem occurs and you cannot complete your phone calls. The company that owns the part of the phone system causing your problem should fix it. Different phone companies can talk to each other, to fix the problem as soon as possible. But each phone company or carrier is responsible for fixing problems within its own part of the system. The same is true for the Internet. Each network has its own operations center. These centers can talk to each other and know how to resolve problems. A given site has a contract with one of the Internet's networks that keeps your site up and running. If something goes wrong, the company that operated that network should fix it. If it is not their problem, they will pass it along.

Currently, the Internet's driving force is the World Wide Web (WWW, or W3). The Web is the section of the Internet that features multimedia capabilities (i.e., has video, audio, images, graphics, and text). The Web began to take off after graphical Web viewers (called browsers) were developed in 1993. The Web has quickly become a vast network of data, news, shopping guides, promotional materials, periodicals, and interest-group home pages, displayed in colors, often with audio and video output. As presented in the second part of the book, hypertext markup language (HTML) allows Web site creators to link their home pages directly to other pages, including remote sites anywhere on the Web, with each page accessed by a mouse click. To find Web sites, users can use search programs (known as search engines), as covered in chapter 6.

The Internet now links millions of powerful server computers in every part of the world, allowing millions of users access to thousands of sites. Web users can print data and download computer programs, send electronic messages to others with e-mail addresses, and set up their own pages for whatever purpose. Companies, universities, government agencies and individuals throughout the world now maintain pages on the Web, and the demand for Web access is increasing PC (personal computer) use. Many U.S. households currently have IBM, IBM-clone, or Mac computers equipped with modems.

The Internet is a unique medium of information and communication when compared to such traditional media as libraries. Information in libraries is organized in books that are classi-fied and shelved in order according to a standard classification system. Each library has a cata-log or an index system that readers can search manually or online to find a book. Readers can search by using a book title, an author, or a subject. When a reader checks out a book, it recorded by the librarian. When the book is returned, it is re-shelved in the same location it was checked from.

Unlike traditional libraries, where information is indexed, information on the Internet is not indexed or organized at all. There are no catalogs, index systems, or classification system. Information is organized in Web pages (HTML documents). Using the library model of storing books, the Internet can be thought of as a very big open field with books (Web pages) piled ran-domly at the center of that big field. The question that the Internet user may ask is, how can I find what I want? Or how can I search for what I need? The answer is much simpler than one could think: Simply use a search tool. There are many search tools that are covered in Chapter 6. The most popular tool is search engines, such as Yahoo, Lycos, and so forth. Here the reader types a search string and the search engine returns the Web pages that match the string (usually known as hits). In an effect, this process is similar to searching by subject in the traditional library search.

The conclusion to draw from the above analogy is that we need to use a different "mental" model when it comes to dealing with information on the Web. At the heart of this model are the dynamic nature and the randomness of the information. Thus, one should tend not to memorize Web sites and titles, but, instead, to learn how to search for information effectively, as covered in Chapter 6. As a matter fact, some Web sites that one might know at one time may disappear later in the future or change their address, or new and better Web sites may become available in the future. It is usually a good practice to use a search tool and perform a fresh search to update and complement the existing results of a past search.

1.3 History of the Internet and the World Wide Web

This section provides a brief history of the Internet. For further information, the reader can use a search engine and use a search string such as "history of the Internet". The early research on the concept of the Internet as we know it today began in 1962 in the Advanced Research Project Agency (ARPA; known then as DARPA) within the Department of Defense (DoD). The main idea was to study the feasibility of communication using packets rather than circuits. This concept is what fueled computer networking. The Internet of today was born, as a result of this research, in 1969, when ARPA established ARPAnet, in an effort to connect together the U.S. Defense Department network. In 1969, four computer clients were connected together via

ARPAnet. To use ARPAnet, a computer packs data into Internet protocol (IP) packets and labels them with the correct address. The packets are then sent through ARPAnet to a receiving computer. In 1972, ARPAnet was demonstrated successfully at the International Computer Communication Conference. During this year, also, e-mail was invented.

Much of the time during the 1970s was spent on researching the idea of open-architecture networking. Ethernet was developed by Xerox during this period, also. With ARPAnet and Ethernet, the U.S. was able to develop a working network, and the academic and research users had access to it. A variety of networks was soon developed in the late 1970s and early 1980s, including CSNET, USENET, and BITNET. They pushed the use of the Internet. Internet developers in the U.S. and Europe, responding to market pressures, began to put IP software onto every type of computer. This practice accelerated the spread of the Internet. At about the same time, Ethernet local area networks (LANs) were developed. LAN technology kept developing until 1983, when desktop workstations became available and local networking exploded. These workstations came with UNIX, including IP networking software that provided workstations the ability to talk to each other instead of talking to a single large timesharing mainframe computer per site. Users wanted to connect their entire LANs to the ARPAnet. Many companies and organizations started building private networks using the IP protocol.

NSFnet was one of the important networks that developed in 1980s. Nascent was created in 1986 by the National Science Foundation (NSF) to connect five supercomputer centers at major universities. NSFnet was built using the ARPAnet IP protocol, as a result of collaboration between NSF and ARPA IAB (Internet Activities Board). NSFnet selected TCP/IP as its communication protocol. NSFnet divided the U.S.A. into five regions. Each region has a supercomputer center as a hub or gateway for it. Universities and organizations belonging to a region connect to the designated center via a regional network. Because of the overloading of these centers in 1987, the NSFnet was upgraded with faster telephone lines and more powerful computers.

By 1990, NSFnet replaced ARPAnet, with a well-developed set of regional and metropolitan area networks feeding into the NSF backbone. Now the backbone network is operated and maintained by commercial vendors such as IBM and MCI. The regional networks and service providers such as America Online (AOL) and others connect to the backbone. Private and institutional networks feed into these nets. Today, the Internet is accessible by many users.

NSFnet's major objective was to serve educational, research, and government networking needs. In 1991, the CIX (Commercial Internet Exchange) Association was formed by Internet service providers to commercialize the Internet and establish the legitimate uses of the Internet for business and profit purposes.

Also in 1991, two key technologies were adopted: WAIS and Gopher. WAIS (wide-area information service) was developed by Thinking Machines Corporation to provide a userfriendly easy-to-use user interface to search the Internet and its related databases. Gopher was another search program developed at the University of Minnesota to help users search the Internet in a simple, consistent manner. The program is menu-driven and hierarchical.

PCs, becoming a major platform in the 1980s, helped promote the widespread use of the Internet. LANs became available from major players in the market such as Novell. These LANs were connected to Ethernet, allowing PCs to connect to the Internet. PCs at home could access the Internet via modems and telephone lines.

In 1989, the World Wide Web was conceived by Berners-Lee of the European Laboratory for Particle Physics, or CERN (an acronym for the group's original name in French), in Geneva, Switzerland. By the end of 1991, CERN released a line-oriented browser, but the actual explosive growth of the Web started when the first graphically-oriented browser, Mosaic, was developed at the National Center for Supercomputing Applications (NCSA) at the University of Illinois at Urbana-Champaign (UIUC) in 1992. The Web offered a client/server-based, distributed retrieval system using hypertext markup language (HTML). The second part of the book covers HTML and its applications in details. The terms *the Web* and *the Internet* are often used interchangeably today, because the Web has quickly become the predominant way of navigating the Internet. This happened because the Web supports documents with all multimedia elements: text, graphics, colors, images, and sounds. In addition, the tools needed to use the Web, such as browsers and search engines, are fairly easy to use. With the wide use of the Web, an organization called the World Wide Web Consortium (W3C) has taken the responsibility for evolving the various protocols and standards related to the Web.

1.4 Transmission across the Internet

The best way to understand how the Internet works is to think of mail delivery via a postal service. The postal service has its network of offices, its hardware (mail trucks, cars, sorting machines, etc.), and its distribution system, consisting mainly of letter carriers. Similarly, the Internet has its network of computers, its hardware (computers, routers, telephone lines, etc.), and its software needed to distribute the data from one location to another. Figure 1.1 shows the Internet hardware.

As shown in figure 1.1, the basic idea of communication via the Internet is to have two remote sites or computers connected together via a network (LAN or WAN) or a transmission line (wires, telephone voice systems, thick/thin coax cables, twisted pairs, or fiber optics). Figure 1.1 shows four networks (1 - 4), five routers (R1 - R5), one modem (M), and four computers (A-D). The four networks resemble the Internet. They could be LANs (local area networks), WANs (wide area networks), regional networks, national networks, or international networks. The networks are connected to each other via the routers. Computers A, C, and D are connected to the Internet via dedicated lines such as TV cables or T1 lines. Computer B is connected to the Internet via a modem and a typical telephone line. The dedicated and the telephone lines are equivalent to postal trucks and cars. They move the data from one place to another. The routers are the postal substations. They decide about how to route the data transmitted through the network lines. They find the shortest and best way to deliver the data (e.g., e-mail messages). The routers utilize sophisticated routing software and algorithms.

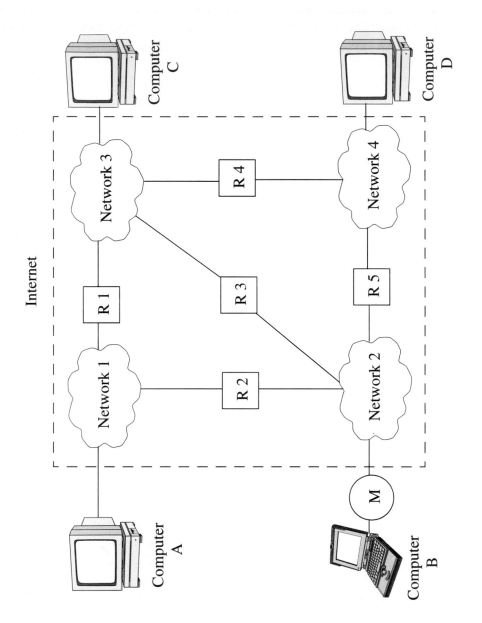

Figure 1.1 The Internet.

How does the Internet know where data is coming from and going to? It obviously needs the addresses of the sending and receiving destinations. It gets them via the Internet software. The Internet uses a communication protocol called TCP/IP (transmission control protocol/Internet protocol). TCP/IP can be viewed as the Internet rules, similar to the postal service rules. The postal service rules are to enclose a letter in an envelope, address the envelope with both sending and receiving addresses, seal the envelope, affix the stamp, and finally drop it in the post office or the mail box. TCP rules are as follows: TCP breaks the data to be transmitted, say an e-mail message, into chunks (called TCP packets) of a maximum size of 1500 bytes each, numbers the chunks sequentially, puts each chunk into a TCP envelope, places the TCP envelope inside an IP envelope, and passes the IP envelope to the network for shipping. Once you have something in an IP envelope, the network can carry it through the telephone lines and/or the fiber-optic cables. Similarly to a post office envelope, an IP envelope has the IP addresses of both the sender and the recipient. At the receiving end, TCP software collects the envelopes, extracts the data packets and puts them into the correct order. Once the data is recovered in the proper order, TCP passes it to the application, such as an e-mail program. Figure 1.2 shows the Internet software.

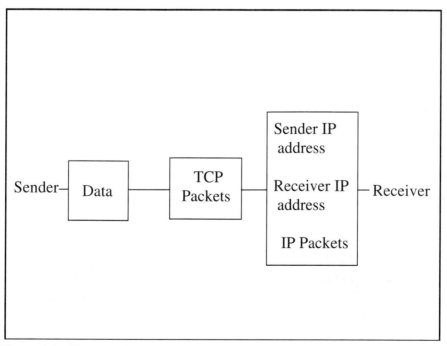

Figure 1.2 Transmission across the Internet.

A particular sender or receiver address is part of an address scheme used by the Internet and its TCP/IP protocol. TCP/IP uses a separate, logical address that guarantees that a host machine or a node in the network has a unique address. A TCP/IP address, known also as an IP address, is a 32-bit number. A typical IP address is 129.10.1.13. While numbers are convenient for machines, they are not for human beings. We would rather deal with names. Therefore, we use names for addresses, and the TCP/IP uses its DNS (domain name system) application to provide name-to-address translation. For example, ftp.netscape.com corresponds to 198.95.249.66 IP address. Obviously, it easier and more logical to use names as Internet addresses. The IP addresses are the ones used to send the IP Packets shown in figure 1.2 across the Internet.

1.5 Uniform Resource Locators (URLs)

The name that corresponds to an IP address in the DNS is known as a URL or an Internet name. A URL identifies a node on the Internet uniquely. The Internet DNS follows a standard format to assign a URL (IP address) to any of its nodes. To many of the Internet users or surfers, a URL corresponds to a Web site. To a Web developer, a URL corresponds to a Web page. Thus, one can think of a URL as either a Web site or a Web page. When a user types a URL in a browser window, the browser sends a request to the Web site of the URL. In turn, the Web server of the Web site sends the Web page as a response to the browser request. Chapter 3 covers this communication in more detail. In most cases, URLs are case-sensitive (i.e. uppercase and lowercase letters are different).

A URL (an IP address) usually consists of several domains (usually less than 5) separated by periods. As an example, the College of Engineering at Northeastern University has the IP address coe.neu.edu. This address has three domains: coe, neu, and edu. As a general rule, the sizes of the domains in an address get more general from left to right; i.e., the College of Engineering is part of Northeastern University which, in turn, is part of the education world. For international use, the domain in the far right of an IP address is the country code, e.g. 'au' for Australia, 'uk' for England, etc. Thus, in general, the format of a URL (an IP address) may look as follows: p1.p2.....d.ttt.cc, where —

p1.p2.: parts of an organization tree, e.g., dept1.coe. That tree organization can be as deep as needed. For example, dept1 may have groups, and each group may have subgroups for both faculty and students. In this case, we keep adding different domains separated by periods; i.e., p1.p2.p3.p4. The top domain of the tree is usually www. For example, we have www.neu.edu and www.dell.com for Northeastern University and Dell Computer Corporation respectively.

d: the organization name; e.g., neu, harvard, mit, sun, ibm, dell, etc.

ttt: top-level domain. It is usually three characters long. The most common top-level domain names used are the following:

.com: commercial institution or service provider;

.edu: educational institution;

.gov: government institution or agency;

.org: nonprofit organization;

.net: network service provider;

.mil: U.S. military;

.cc: country code. This code identifies countries or geographical zones. While the country code, 'us', is optional for the United States, it is mandatory for other countries. Here are sample codes: at (Austria), au (Australia), nz (New Zealand), ca (Canada), ch (Switzerland), dk (Denmark), es (Spain), fr (France), de (Germany), gr (Greece), jp (Japan), uk (United Kingdom), se (Sweden), and ie (Republic of Ireland). Country codes are defined in the ISO-3166 standard.

1.6 E-mail Addresses

The foregoing naming scheme is extended by the Internet to assign e-mail addresses to its users. Each node, computer, or user on the Internet has a unique e-mail address. This is like a social security number. Often, e-mail addresses use the "username@DNS-domain" format. The username could be a combination of the first and last names, or any other fictitious names or IDs. Some users use the first letter of their first name followed by a period or an underscore and their last names, e.g., p.smith or p_smith for, say, Paul Smith. Others use their last names only. The author's e-mail address is zeid@coe.neu.edu. In general, an e-mail address can be represented in one of the following ways:

username@organization.extension;

username@organization.extension.country-code;

username@organizational-unit.organization.extension;

username@server.organization.extension.country-code.—

here, username is the e-mail name of the sender or the recipient; organization is the sender or recipient organization; organizational-unit (server) is also optional; extension is the type of organization used in the address (same as the top-level domain ttt described above); country-code is the international domain name.

There are many available Web-based e-mail services offered by many Web sites. They are all free. Two major free e-mail services are *hotmail*, offered by Microsoft (www.microsoft.com), and Yahoo (www.yahoo.com) mail services. Getting an e-mail address requires the user to sign on. The procedure is simple and allows the user to use a username and a password.

1.7 Intranets and Extranets

Since the explosion of the Internet, many related new technologies have evolved. Most notably, Intranets and extranets are now common terms we hear everyday, similar to "the Internet". These terms bring confusion with them. What is an Intranet or an Extranet? And how they differ from the Internet?

The underlying concept for the Internet, Intranets, and Extranets is the same. They are all networks using the same hardware and software covered in section 1.4. The main differences come in their geographical domains and in the level of security they use. Figure 1.3 shows the three types of networks. An Intranet is a network that is contained within an organization; i.e., it is an internal or private network. Organizations, such as companies, use Intranets to share information across departments and widespread offices. As with the Internet, Intranets connect heterogeneous computer hardware, including servers, workstations, PCs, etc. Because Intranets provide company-wide (intracompany) access to the secret information of the entire company, such an Intranet must be protected from outside intruders. Thus, it is typical for companies to

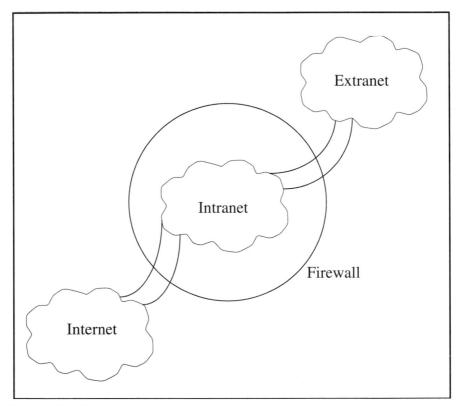

Figure 1.3   The Internet, Intranet and extranet.

install firewalls around their Intranets to prevent public access to company secrets. A firewall is a term that refers to special hardware and software that protect the Intranet from outside unauthorized access by other networks such as the Internet.

An Extranet is a network outside an organization, yet it has access to the organization Intranet. An Extranet facilitates intercompany relationships. Extranets typically link companies and businesses with their customers, suppliers, and partners over the Internet. Extranets provide secure links via advances in network security. An Extranet may be viewed as an intermediate network between the Internet and the Intranet.

1.8 Owners of the Internet

No one person or organization owns the Internet as a whole. If the Internet is a network of networks, we expect many owners for these networks. This is similar to the highway system and roads. Roads go from one town to another, from one state to another. Each town or a state owns and maintains the portion of the road or highway in its jurisdiction. For the Internet, every network attached to the Internet is owned by its governing organization. For example, NSF owns NSFnet, and the American Telephone and Telegram (AT&T) company owns its national network. Universities, corporations, and governments all have their own internal networks. They also have policies and rules for how to use them. Universities, corporations, and individuals must also pay for the cost of connecting to a national Internet service provider such as AT&T, in addition to the costs of their own networks.

The rules and guidelines for using the Internet depend on every organization. For example, most service providers inform their customers that they are not allowed to send illegal or obscene material via their networks. This is important to the providers, who could be held liable for material that passes through their networks.

If there are so many owners of the Internet, who makes it work in harmony? Or who runs it? Every network of the Internet must follow its rules. These rules are set by ISOC (the Internet SOCiety). The ISOC meets regularly to discuss changes to the way the Internet works. These meetings sometimes lead to meetings of the IAB (Internet Architecture Board). These two groups discuss the details of the network operation, such as how IP addresses are assigned or how IP packets are interpreted. These rules enable all the networks connected to the Internet to talk to each other.

1.9 Contents of the Internet

What is on the Internet? This question is similar to asking what you can do in life. While the question is very difficult, the answer is very simple: everything. The Internet use is really up to individuals' imaginations. However, a broad division of what is on the Internet may follow the division of the common top level domain names used in IP and e-mail addresses (.com, .edu, .gov, .org, .net, .mil). Thus, the types of use of the Internet are commercial, education/research, government, non-profit, service providers, and military. Within each group, there are many users, organizations, and activities. On the basis of the type of use, the corresponding network traffic is routed properly. This affects the fee for using the Internet. Commercial use is generally more expensive than education/research use, because the former is not subsidized and the latter is. An organization that wishes to use the Internet must tell the service provider the type of use, which affects the access fee.

Research and education networks form a large portion of the Internet. There are many sites and companies offering Web content for K–12 school education. Online service providers such as AOL offers content for kids and parents together. In terms of research, all levels of academic institutions and research laboratories have Web sites that offer all sort of information, from admissions, to department and faculty profiles, to recent research results.

What is allowed on the Internet follows the traditional rules of copyrights and ethics. When you ship something to someone (especially in another country), you need to be aware of property rights. Security is the most important issue when it comes to Internet ethics. We have heard about break-ins and viruses. If you have a dial-up modem, anyone can dial the number and try to break in. Once you are on the Internet, the general address of your network is easily found, and an intruder would only have to try several host numbers before stumbling onto an active one.

1.10 Activities on the Internet

What you can do on the Internet is controlled by information exchange. You can do an enormous number of things on the Internet, but most activities fall into five broad categories:

1. Sending and receiving e-mail. This is often the first thing Internet users do when they log in to their accounts. Many systems have an announcement feature that informs you as soon as you log in if you have unread e-mail. E-mail is fast, convenient, and addictive. Once you start using it, you get hooked on it. We cover e-mail in more details in chapter 4.

2. Transferring files between computers. This is the next most popular activity on the Internet after e-mail. FTP (file transfer protocol) is the command used to transfer files from one computer to another across the Internet. The command FTP allows you to list the contents of a directory, change directories, view files, and transfer them to your computer from any computer in the world that is on the Internet. We cover FTP in more details in Chapter 4.

3. Participating in discussion groups. These discussion groups allow people with a common interest to share their views and thoughts on certain issues. Two forms of discussion groups are common on the Internet: mailing lists and Usenet news groups. Public mailing lists are usually managed by Listserv software (list server) and organized on BITNET (a network of IBM mainframes). If a member of a group wants to send everyone else a message about a topic, he/she could address it to the list server. The computer would then explode (or redirect) the message to all the members on the mailing list. To belong to a mailing list, you simply subscribe to this list, i.e., someone adds your e-mail address to the list. You then receive an e-mail copy of everything sent to the list server. You reply to the entire list as you reply to ordinary e-mail from a person. Usenet (known as *net news* or just *news*) is similar in concept to mailing lists.   The big difference is that Usenet messages are not automatically e-mailed to you. To read Usenet messages, you must connect to a computer (news server) that has the news, and you must use a special software application (news reader). You can read all the news or only selected messages. Usenet is similar to discussion groups encountered on bulletin board systems (BBSs). We cover discussion groups and newsgroups in more details in chapter 4.

4. Searching (surfing the net) for information. This is the most exciting and frustrating activity you can do on the Internet. It is exciting because you can find things of interest to you by venturing into cyberspace with neither direction nor goal, and enjoy whatever serendipity brings your way. It is frustrating because you can spend days hunting for what you are looking for. Many search engines exist to try to guide and facilitate searching the Internet. We cover search engines in more details in chapter 5.

5. Conducting e-commerce. Electronic commerce is one of the most popular activities on the Web. E-commerce is one of the fastest-growing segments of the Internet. The biggest advantages of shopping online are the prices, the selection and the convenience. Online shopping is less expensive because it eliminates the conventional overhead encountered in renting stores and having personnel running them. Instead, online shopping uses large warehouses or distributors who store goods ready for shipping as soon as an online order is placed. As a result of these large warehouses or distributors, online shoppers have a wide variety of goods and products to choose from. The convenience of online shopping is in its availability 24 hours a day, 7 days a week. Online shopping also has drawbacks. For example, many people may not want to buy clothes over the Internet, while other may not want to use their credit card numbers online.

1.11 Internet Future

It is always difficult and dangerous to predict the future. One will have a very hard time predicting totally new concepts. However, it is a little easier predicting the future by extending current technology. The new Internet technology is to merge the Internet, cable television, and telephone services over one big wire, with a wireless offshoot part of the mix as well. Here are some emerging trends.

1. Faster communication links. Technically, this means we need more bandwidth to transmit information through the Internet. The higher the bandwidth, the faster the communication on the Internet. Broadband, or high-speed, connections are important to the future of the Internet, delivering high-quality video and audio to Internet users demanding richer content. By using cable television lines or dedicated wires carrying digital signals, broadband technologies attain speeds up to 150 times faster than traditional systems. That gain translates into faster download times for Web pages as well as video, sound, and graphics files; however, the effect of this new technology may diminish soon. As broadband increases, so will the desire of users to download large video, sound, and graphics files. Soon, the users may complain again of not having enough bandwidth. The push and pull between bandwidth and use is expected to continue, as we always want more.

High-speed networking technologies are being developed. Wide area network (WAN) technologies are of great interest to the Internet community. The WAN technologies include asynchronous transfer mode (ATM), Frame Relay, and integrated service digital network (ISDN). These should replace the existing packet-switching technologies. An ATM switch operates at the speed of 100 megabits per second (Mbps) or faster. A Frame Relay runs at speeds between 4 and 100 Mbps. In practice, however, Frame Relay subscribers use 1.5 Mbps or 56 kilobits per second (Kbps) connections. An ISDN connection operates at a speed of 128-144

Kbps. The cutting-edge search for more bandwidth is focused on developing gigabit technologies that require fiber-optic media. These technologies may be expensive today; however, when these technologies are used, the Internet will be able to deliver full-motion, full-screen, high-resolution video (better than TV quality). This is what is behind Web TV. The TV and the PC become one set. These technologies will also be able to provide interfaces to virtual realities where you can interact with an artificial world. These applications and services should dwarf the already staggering capabilities and resources provided by today's Internet.

Two of the current initiatives that will greatly influence the future of today's Internet are NGI (Next Generation Internet) and Internet2. The NGI initiative is led by the federal government, the Internet2 initiative program by U.S. universities. Both NGI and Internet2 were established in October 1996, and they are working together in many areas. For example, the Internet2 program is working on an NSF merit-based High Performance Connections program. Briefly, the NGI project was established with the goal of connecting 100 institutions at 100 times the speed of the current Internet, and 10 institutions at 1000 times the speed of the current Internet. The Internet2 project is a collaborative effort by over 120 universities to develop advanced Internet technologies and applications. The target next-generation applications for both projects include health care, national security, distance learning, digital libraries, video teleconferencing, virtual laboratories, and manufacturing. Internet2 and NGI are not intended to replace the current Internet. Instead, they will complement it.

2. Wireless Communication links. In addition to the broadband Internet connections, wireless connections are becoming increasingly important. The forefront research and technology are focusing on enabling users and surfers to connect to the Internet from any place, and away from the traditional mode of using desktop computers. Thus, road warriors can connect to the Internet and go online anytime anywhere, from their laptops, cell phones, pagers, had-held palm computers, and other cordless devices. Many major Web sites, such as AOL and Yahoo, have developed versions of their Web sites to fit wireless devices' smaller screens, and narrower bandwidth. In addition, some service providers have launched wireless Web services in some cities. Some people think that WWW should take a new meaning; that is Worldwide Wireless Web.

3. More services and service providers. Many communications giants (such as AT&T, Sprint, MCI, and WilTel) and regional Bell operating companies (such as Bell, PacTel, Bell Atlantic, Bell South, etc.) provide Internet services.

4. More and better access. As broadband connections, which provide Internet users with high-speed access, become more available, users become connected in to the Internet 24 hours a day to eliminate dial-up connections and busy signals. Online music offerings should help fuel the broadband demand as more users insist on the ability to listen to CD-quality songs on the Internet.

There are several broadband technologies. Cable access TV (CATV) companies are becoming Internet providers. These cable companies already own technologies like ATM, Frame Relay, and even T-1 telephone lines. Small, compact dish receivers are emerging as a wireless alternative to cable. They will provide mobile (portable) Internet services. Also, ISDN communications systems are available. ISDN is the international standard for transmitting voice, video, and data over digital lines. Another competing technology is DSL (Digital Subscriber Line). These technologies are covered in chapter 2 of the book. The future of broadband technology is essentially shaping up as a two-horse race between cable and DSL.

1.12 Book Scope and Approach

This book focuses on developing the client-side skills of Internet and World Wide Web users, in two parts. The first part covers the basic topics about the Internet, its browsers, its resources (such as Telnet and FTP), and its effective use in daily tasks such as e-mail, searching and surfing, downloading and uploading files, and participating in newsgroups.

The second part builds on the background gained in the first part and covers HTML, to enable readers develop their own Web sites and write their own HTML code. After presenting all the HTML tags, chapter 17 in this part presents HTML editors as a tool to automate and speed the writing process of HTML code. While this book is focusing on client-side aspects of the Internet and HTML, it is compelling to cover just enough about server-side processing of HTML forms in chapter 18. This is important to show the full cycle of writing and using forms, which are a very important element of Web pages and HTML. The coverage in this chapter is presented from a client-side point of view. We use the Apache server. We install it on the client PC. Thus, we use the PC as a client and server at the same time. Moreover, we do not get into any details of setting up the server environment, securing, and optimizing, as all these topics are out of the scope of the book.

The approach taken in this book to fulfill its scope is simple, and has the following features:

1. **Cover concepts, followed by tools and hands-on practice.** The book consistently covers the basic and generic concepts of every subject to create a frame of reference in the reader's mind. Once the reader understands the "big picture", it presents specific software tools, examples, tutorials, and hands-on practice. For example, the book presents browsers in a generic way, then detailed coverage of both Netscape Communicator and Microsoft Internet Explorer (MS IE).

2. **Use available freeware and shareware.** All the software tools used and covered in this book are either freeware (software distributed for free) or shareware (software free for a trial period). This makes it easy for every reader to have and use the software. The book also tries to minimize the separate software programs required for the book, to make it easy to use in a lab or at home. The software required for this book is a browser, and an HTML editor. The book uses both Netscape Communicator and MS IE as browsers.

3. **Provide examples, tutorials, and problems.** The book has examples, tutorials, and problems. They are designed to be done in a lab setting as part of a course, or at home on a PC.

Examples focus on one concept at a time. Tutorials combine all the concepts in the chapter into one comprehensive application, to illustrate real-life solution. Problems are divided into exercises and homework. Exercises are specific, well-defined questions that can be used when class time is limited. Homework problems are designed to be more extensive and sometimes open-ended.

4. **Provide a FAQs section in each chapter.** This section provides a handy resource of quick answers to many of the questions that readers may encounter as they use the book material and its software tools.

5. **Provide a summary section in each chapter.** This section is intended as a quick reference for when readers need to refer to the chapter material quickly.

1.13 Book Organization

The book is organized to reflect the main concepts and ideas of the Internet and the World Wide Web. The book presents strategies that are effective in using the Internet on a daily basis: at a classroom, at work and/or at home. Some of the organizational highlights include the tutorial, FAQs, and homework sections in each chapter. These sections are full of concentrated knowledge and a hands-on approach that help the students and readers to grasp the concepts easily. The appendices at the end of the book provide the reader with a source for definitions of many terms encountered throughout the book, HTML tags, and hexadecimal codes for various colors.

The book is in two major parts. Part I covers the effective use of the Internet. This part should be beneficial to both experienced and novice users of the Internet. For experienced users and students, the book will help them solidify their understanding and use of the Internet and its tools. For beginners, the book will enable them to gain the background they need to start using the Internet effectively. Chapter 1 provides a framework for understanding the Internet. It covers how transmission across the Internet takes place. It explains how the Uniform Resource Locators (URLs) identify every node and computer on the Internet. It also explains how e-mail addresses and domain names are formed. The concepts of Intranets, extranets, and firewalls are also covered in chapter 1.

Chapter 2 focuses on Internet connections and on the different connection speeds. The most common method of connecting to the Internet is a dial-up connection. The chapter covers in a step-by-step fashion how to create and use a dial-up connection. Once you are connected, Chapters 3 and 4 explain in detail how to use Web browsers to surf and navigate the Internet and the Web. Chapters 3 and 4 cover the Netscape Communicator and Microsoft Internet Explorer, respectively. Each chapter shows how to download, install, configure, and use the browser. The main browser tasks, such as navigation, e-mail, bookmarks, and address books, are covered.

Chapter 5 covers the details of three useful Internet access tools. They are newsgroups, FTP, and Telnet. FTP allows users to download (upload) files to (from) a client computer from (to) an Internet server. Telnet allows users to connect to a remote site.

Chapter 6 focuses on navigating the Internet via many widely used search engines. Other search tools, such as metasearch engines, smart browsing, Web portals, and channels are also covered.

Part II of the book builds on the background established in Part I. Once the reader has a good understanding of the Internet and how it works, Part II covers the details of HTML, of how it works, and of how it is used to develop Web pages that make up the landscape of the World Wide Web. This part looks at all the possible multimedia elements of a Web page and covers the details of the corresponding HTML tags. In addition, it covers the basic principles of Web page design and layout.

Chapter 7 lays the foundation of HTML, its definition, its markup, and its hyperlinks. It also covers the structure of an HTML document, the text tags, the hyperlink tag, and the ISO character sets. Chapter 8 covers the various types of lists and their corresponding tags. Chapter 9 covers the use of colors in Web pages and of the color tags. Chapter 10 covers images, their use in Web pages, and the image tags. The concept of image (clickable) maps and the related tags are covered in Chapter 11. Sound, video, and their tags are discussed in Chapter 12 and 13, respectively.

HTML forms are an important and popular concept that provides an easy way to conduct e-commerce on the Internet. Chapter 14 discusses forms, the complete set of elements that makes up a form, and the form tags. Chapter 15 covers HTML frames, and their tags. Chapter 16 introduces tables, their use, and their tags.

Chapters 7 – 16 cover the creation of a web page. They show how to use individual HTML tags to write and generate HTML code manually. Chapter 17 covers in details HTML editors. These editors allow Web authors to generate HTML automatically. Thus, these editors act as an automation tool for developing Web pages. Understanding all the HTML tags is a prerequisite to using these HTML editors efficiently.

The last chapter in this book, Chapter 18, covers CGI scripting. The main focus of this book is client-side HTML, but chapter 18 is important in helping readers understand the relationship between client-side and server-side HTML. The coverage in Chapter 18 focuses on the client side of CGI scripting.

1.14 Tutorials 指南

In this tutorial, we just explore the Internet without worrying about any technical details. Here are several things you can do (screen captures are included for illustrations).

1.14.1 Surf the Shareware Sites

There are many useful software tools that you can find and download on a trial basis for 30 days. If you like a software program, you can register for a fee to use it on permanent basis (i.e. purchase a license to use it). The main shareware site is www.shareware.com. Here are the steps to follow (assuming your computer is connected to the Internet and has a browser):

1. Type www.shareware.com in the browser URL bar (figure 1.4).

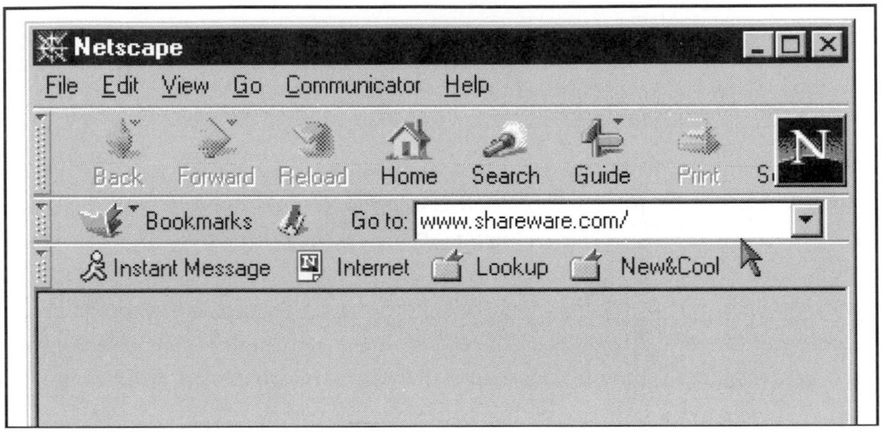

Figure 1.4   Type the name of the Web site.

2. Type, say, *screen capture* as the name of shareware you'd like to download (figure 1.5), and then click "Search". This search finds screen capture programs that allow you to capture windows.

Figure 1.5   Type the name of the shareware program.

3. Click one of the hyperlinks (program name) that are returned by the shareware search engine (figure 1.6). The first link is the latest version of the shareware you are looking for.

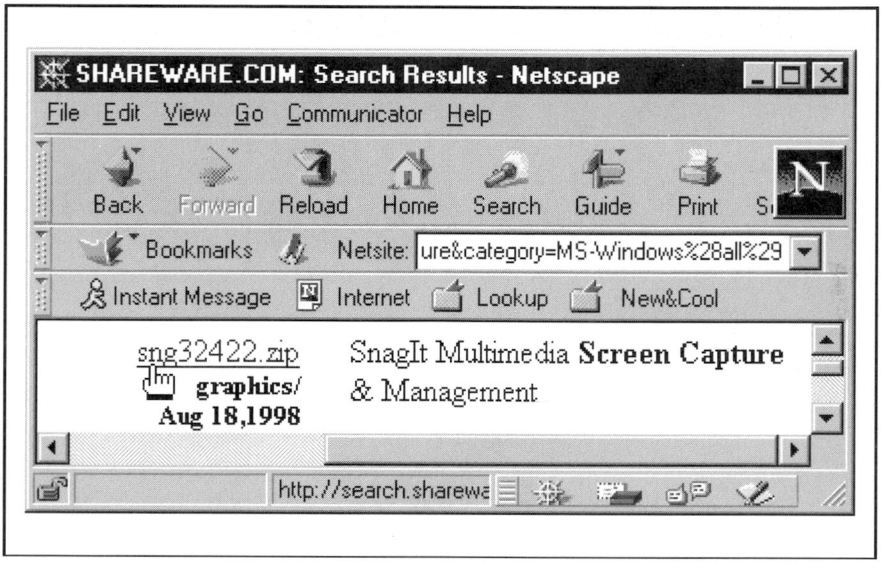

Figure 1.6   Click the hyperlink of the desired program.

4. Choose a site to download from (figure 1.7). Before downloading, make sure you specify the directory (folder) where you want to save the downloaded file. Also, make sure you remember the file name.

Figure 1.7   Click the hyperlink to download.

5. After the download is complete, go to the directory where the file is, and install it by double clicking it and following the instructions. When the installation is complete, a shortcut is created (figure 1.8). As part of the installation, you need to unzip the file. All shareware files are zipped to reduce their sizes and, in turn, the time needed to download them. You may need an unzip program such as WINZIP. If you do not have WINZIP on your computer, download it from, www.shareware.com and install it first, before downloading other shareware.

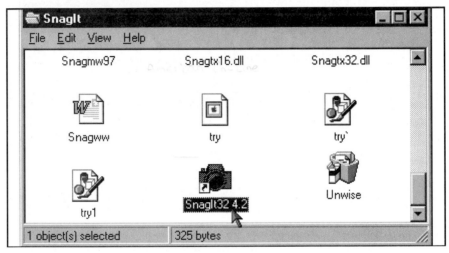

Figure 1.8   Double click the shortcut to run the program.

6. Now you are ready to use the screen capture program. When you double-click the short-cut shown in figure 1.8, the program window shown in figure 1.9 is displayed. Most of screen capture programs allow you to capture a window, part of the desktop, or the entire desktop. To capture part of the desktop, you define a rectangle that surrounds the region you want to capture. Some programs also allow you to capture the contents of the clipboard.

Another shareware site is www.download.com. Repeat this tutorial to investigate it.

1.14.2 Search the Internet

Visit the www.search.com site to find most of the available search engines. Search for more information on this chapter's topics: e.g., history of the Internet (sec. 1.3). Here are the steps to follow:

1. Type *www.search.com* in the browser URL bar.

2. Click the arrow where it says "choose your weapon" to get a list of search engines you can choose from.

3. Type the string or the topic you want to search for in the "search for" field.

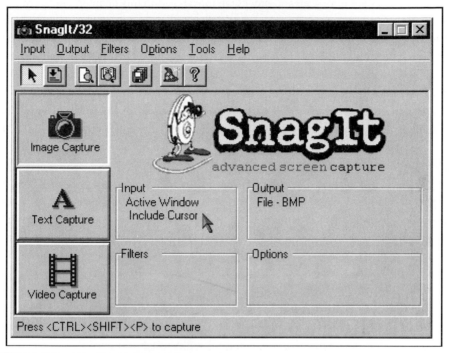

Figure 1.9 Use the screen capture program.

1.14.3 Send an e-mail Message

Use the Netscape mailer facility to send e-mail messages from your computer lab or from home. Most likely, you already know how to send e-mails. Just remember, you normally need a valid account on a computer to be able to send e-mail messages. Sometimes, computers in labs are not set up to allow e-mail.

1.15 FAQs

Each chapter has a FAQs (Frequently Asked Questions) section. This section answers the most commonly asked questions related to the chapter material. If you wnat to contribute to the FAQs sections in this book, please e-mail the author at zeid@coe.neu.edu. Credit will be given to you in this section.

Q: Is the Internet free? Who pays when I am connected to a site in, say, Australia?

A: You pay in the form of an access fee to your service provider. However, your service provider usually provides you with a phone number that is local to you.

Q: What can I do to find more information on some of the chapter topics — such as history of the Internet, the future of the Internet, NGI, and Internet2, to name a few?

A: Following the Internet mental model we introduced in this chapter, you simply use one of your favorite search engines, and type the string or the topic you want to search about. This produces a lot of new and interesting information. Do not memorize names of Web sites; they may change or become obsolete, or new and better ones may become available on the same topic.

Q: What is a digital city?

A: It is an area that is part of the AOL (America Online) user interface. It provides information, such as restaurants and local activities, about cities throughout the world. It is a good source for those travel a lot.   *American On-Line*

Q: What is a POP?

A: *POP* is term that stand for *point of presence*. It is an access point with an IP address to the Internet. Service providers have many POP locations in various geographical locations, to allow customers to connect to the Internet via local phone calls. With these POPs come phone numbers that are local. For example, AOL and TIAC service providers provide their customers with phone numbers in their local areas to allow them to connect to their networks. POP also may stand for Post Office Protocol. For example, POP3 is a popular mail-server type. We cover e-mail in more detail in Chapters 3 and 4.

Q: How can I find the directory (folder) to which a file was downloaded?

A: Quite often, you rush to save a file you are downloading without paying attention to the directory (folder) it is saved into. You then start to realize that you need the directory name to access the file to unzip it. The file name is usually xxx.zip, where xxx is any name. If you know the file name, use a search tool on your computer to locate it on your hard disk. For example, if you have Windows 95, 98, or 2000, Click Start -> Find -> Files or Folders, choose the disk partition you want to search (default is C:), type the file name, and click Find. If you also forgot the file name, use the wild card as a name, i.e. *.zip. Here you search for all file names with the ".zip" extension type.

Q: How can I find people and friends on the Internet?

A: There are many tools you can use, including search engines and Web sites. Try this Web site: http://www.switchboard.com.

Q: What is the difference between shareware and freeware?

A: Shareware is software that is distributed for free on trial basis for a period of time, usually 30 days. The user may purchase a copy of the shareware at the end of the trial period. Freeware, on the other hand, is software that is offered free, at no cost on permanent basis. Freeware is copyrighted, and you cannot use it in any of your own software development without permission from its developer.

Q: Why does a shareware I downloaded and installed not work correctly?

A: Downloading a file could result in a corrupted .zip file. For example, only part of the file may be downloaded for one reason or another, or, say, the modem connection during downloading could be bad. In this case, you need to uninstall the shareware, download it again, unzip it, and reinstall. Advice: Always write down the size (usually in kbytes) of the shareware program you are about to download. After downloading is complete, compare the size of the downloaded file with the size you wrote down. If they are equal, you know this is a good start.

Q: What is some of the basic shareware I need for the Internet?

A: Your needs will grow as you use the Internet more and more. As a good start, you need a screen capture program and WINZIP. While most PCs have a *print screen* key on the keyboard, users may still need a screen capture program to capture only one window or a part of the screen. You can download both from www.shareware.com and install on your hard drive. They are small programs. You need to install WINZIP first. Other shareware you may need depend on your specific activities. For example, if you work with graphics and images extensively, you may need Paint Shop (creates graphics) and Mapedit (editor for clickable maps).

Q: Why do some zipped files need WINZIP to unzip and others do not?

A: Zipped files fall into two types: self-extracting and non-self-extracting. A zipped file that belong to the first group can be unzipped by simply double clicking it. Such a file unzips and installs itself. Examples include Netscape and Java software. Non-self-extracting files require a zip program such as WINZIP. To find out whether a file needs WINZIP, double click it. If it needs it and you have not yet installed it on your hard drive, your computer will ask you to choose an application program.

Q: How can I find definitions for much of the Internet-related jargon?

A: The Web site www.whatis.com has many of the common definitions. It has an index, ordered A-Z. If you want to know what an Extranet is, click the letter E in the index. This provides you with a listing of the words that begin with the letter E in alphabetical order. Click any of the words, e.g., Extranet, to get the definition. Another Web site that is considered an online encyclopedia is www.webopaedia.com. This site is more like a search engine. When you type a keyword, say extranet, you receive its definition.

Q: How do I know whether a domain name is already used?

A: The Web site www.whois.net can help you find out. When you type the domain name, say sun.com, you receive the answer. If the domain name is already registered, the Web site will offer you some suggestions on how to find an available name.

1.16 Summary

Introduction

•The Internet provides a means of instant communication via such tools such as e-mail, newsgroups, chat rooms, and e-commerce.

The Internet and the World Wide Web

•The Internet is a network of networks analogous to a very-high-speed highway system that connects many regions.

•The World Wide Web (WWW or W3) is the largest segment of the Internet. It began to take off after graphical Web viewers called browsers were developed in 1993.

•The Web supports all multimedia capabilities (text, colors, graphics, images, audio, and video) in an easy and simple way.

•Unlike traditional libraries, information on the Internet is heterogeneous, random, dynamic, and unorganized.

•Information on the Internet is contained in Web pages (HTML documents).

•Users (surfers) of the Internet need to adopt a new "mental" model to search the Internet. This model is different from the one used to search traditional libraries. Surfers of the Internet use search tools (such as search engines) to find what they are looking for on the Internet.

History of the Internet and the WWW

•The Web was conceived by Berners-Lee of the CERN Center in 1989.

•The actual explosive growth of the Web is attributed to the release of the first graphically-oriented browser, Mosaic, by the NCSA Center at the University of Illinois at Urbana-Champaign in 1992.

•The roots of the Internet go back to the 1960s. Here is the sequence of development: ARPAnet (1960s) => CSNET, USENET, BITNET, NSFnet (1970s, 1980s) => World Wide Web (1990s).

Transmission across the Internet

•The Internet uses a communication protocol called TCP/IP to deliver information from one site to another.

•The TCP/IP software breaks information to be delivered into TCP/IP packets (similar to traditional letters), bundles them together, labels them with the sender's and receiver's IP addresses (similar to traditional envelopes), and sends them to the receiver's IP address.

•On the receiving end, the TCP/IP software unpacks the TCP/IP packets (similar to opening an envelope), connects them together to reconstruct the original document (such as an e-mail message), and makes it available to the receiver to use with an application program (such as an e-mail tool to read e-mail messages).

•TCP/IP software can locate a Web site by using its IP address (such as 129.320.897.37) or its URL (such as www.neu.edu). Humans prefer URLs over IP addresses.

•TCP/IP uses its DNS (domain name system) application to provide name-to-address translation to convert a URL to an IP address.

Uniform Resource Locators (URLs)

• Users access Web sites by typing their URLs in the browser's URL location toolbar.

• A URL (an IP address) usually consists of several domains (usually less than 5) separated by periods. The most common top-level domain names used are the following six:

.com: commercial institution or service provider;

.edu: educational institution;

.gov: government institution or agency;

.org: nonprofit organization;

.net: network service provider;

.mil: U.S. military.

E-mail Addresses

• E-mail addresses use the username@DNS-domain format. In general, an e-mail address can be represented in one of the following ways:

username@organization.extension;

username@organization.extension.country-code;

username@organizational-unit.organization.extension;

username@server.organization.extension.country-code.

Intranets and Extranets

• The underlying concept for the Internet, Intranets, and Extranets is the same. They are all networks using the same hardware and software. The main differences come in their geographical domains and the level of security they use.

• An Intranet is a network that is contained within an organization; it is an internal or private network. Companies installs firewalls around their Intranets to prevent public access to company secrets. A firewall is special hardware and software that protects the Intranet from outside unauthorized access by other networks such as the Internet.

• An Extranet is a network that is outside an organization, but yet has access to the organization Intranet. Extranets typically link companies and businesses with their customers, suppliers, and partners over the Internet. Extranets provide secure links by using advances in network security. An Extranet may be viewed as a network intermediate between the Internet and the Intranet.

Owners of the Internet

• No one person or organization owns the Internet as a whole. If the Internet is a network of networks, we expect many owners for these networks. This is similar to the highway system and roads.

Contents of the Internet

•The Internet and the World Wide Web have everything one could imagine.

•The contents of the Internet are subject to the traditional rules of copyrights and ethics.

Activities on the Internet

•The activities that surfers can do on the Internet are limited only by their imaginations. Broad categories of activities include sending and receiving e-mail, transferring files between computers, participating in discussion groups, searching (surfing the net) for information, and e-commerce.

Future of the Internet

•The future of the Internet should bring faster communication links via broadband connections, wireless communication links, more services and service providers, and more and better access.

PROBLEMS

Exercises

1.1   Browse the Internet and find some of your favorite sites.
1.2   If you do not have WINZIP or a screen capture program, download and install it on your computer.
1.3   Find more details about both the history and the future of the Internet.

Homework

1.4   Browse the Internet and find three of your favorite sites. Document the following for each site:
   (a)   The full Web site (URL)
   (b)   The site category (entertainment, computers, jobs, careers, etc.)
   (c)   What does the site offer?
   (d)   Sample printouts.
1.5   You need to write a report about the U.S. Civil War. How can you search the Internet for information?
1.6   Your next-door neighbors asked you to help them to find information on the Internet about London, because they plan to vacation there. How can you help them?
1.7   A child needs to study for a test on European geography. The child has ruined the map brought from school. It is the night before the test. Everyone is panicking. How can you help the child?

Connecting to the Internet

T his chapter discusses the various methods available for connecting to and accessing the Internet. It begins by covering the popular client/server model, which forms the core of modern computing. It also covers both the online service providers and the Internet service providers and the differences between them. It then presents both the hardware and the software needed to connect to the Internet. The various types of connections *Goal!* are presented. More emphasis is placed on the dial-up connection, because this is the most popular means of connecting homes to the Internet. This chapter shows how to create a PPP connection, for Windows, for home access to the Internet. The procedure for both versions of Windows is the same.

2.1 Introduction

①You need both hardware and software to connect to the Internet. ②Connecting to the Internet is based on the well-known client/server model used in distributed computing. In this model, multiple computers (known as the clients) are connected to a central computer (known as the server or the host) via a network (Internet, Intranet, Extranet, or any other LAN or WAN). In a ③ client/server model, network applications are either client-side or server-side, as shown in figure 2.1. The client-side (or client, for short) application runs locally on the client computer and remotely accesses server-side (or server, for short) applications. A client application usually initiates communication with a server; a server application is always waiting in a stand-by mode to make contact with a client.

④ For connecting from home for personal use, the hardware is typically a PC (and a modem if needed). For commercial use by companies and large organizations, the hardware is typically a mix of PCs and workstations, supported by dedicated servers. These servers handle the net-

⑤ Many ISPs exist. Choosing one depends on many factors such as connection speed, monthly fee, etc.

29

not quite right

work traffic among the PCs and workstations, and that between the company computers and the Internet. In many cases, companies use Intranets, extranets, and firewalls in their connections, as discussed in Chapter 1. The software is TCP/IP and a browser. Users who have computer background can set up their connections by working with TCP/IP software, including SLIP/PPP. Users who do not want to get involved at this level usually subscribe into an online service that does all the setup work for them and makes the Internet connection transparent to them.

Unix only

Microsoft generly

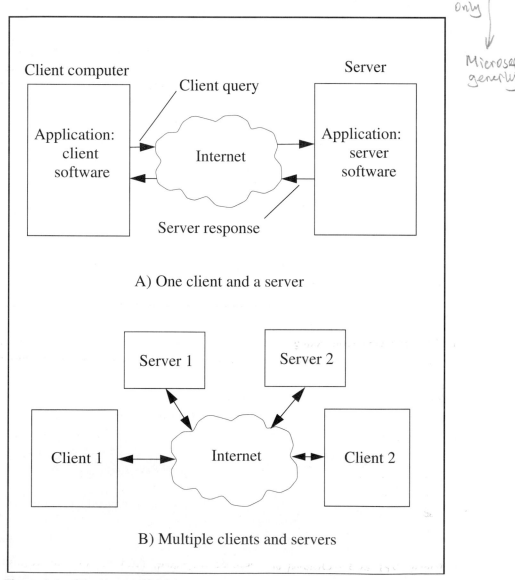

Figure 2.1   Client/server model.

There are two groups of providers to access the Internet. The first group is known as the online service providers. This group serves the end-user dial-up Internet-connectivity market. This group offers extensive online information to end users in addition to Internet access. Sample commercial online services are AOL and the Microsoft Network (MSN). The second group is known as the Internet service providers (ISPs). This group offers businesses direct Internet connections, as well as dial-up access for individual and home users. This group includes AT&T WorldNet, Concentric Network, EarthLink Sprint Total Access, IBM Internet Connection, MCI Internet, MindSpring Enterprises, NetCom, Prodigy Internet, SpryNet, and UUnet (Unix to Unix network).

There is one main difference between online service providers and ISPs. While both groups offer a connection to the Internet, online service providers offer much content with the connection. Each online service provider creates its own content. Each also provides a connection to the Web. Take the example of AOL. It provides its subscribers with news, sports, finance, and so forth. With ISPs, you have to surf the Internet on your own and find the content you need. This could be time-consuming for some users. If one can think of the Internet as a city, the online service provider would be its directory. Once you remove the directory, you are "on your own" finding your way around the city. ISPs do not provide much content. You have to find it yourself.

⑤ The choice of an online service provider or an ISP depends largely on the particular needs of the user. It is out of the scope of this book to compare online service providers or ISPs, but the following general guidelines should help to choose one:

1. The maximum connection speed. Many online service providers and ISPs provide different modem speeds. Section 2.4 covers the various types of Internet connections and their related speeds. The faster the connecting speed is, the faster it is to download Web pages and deliver and receive large e-mails.

2. Dial-up access. Connecting to the Internet via a dial-up connection may be frustrating to the user if the phone lines are busy, especially at peak daily usage times (e.g., during the evening hours).

3. 800-number help line. This is handy for new users, who typically may require handholding during the first several days or weeks of using the ISP services. for new users.

4. Software. Some providers, such as AOL, have their own user interfaces that their customers can use. One may then ask, how easy is it to use the software? Does it run fast? Does it offer personal control? Can the user block selected junk mail and newsgroups?

5. Service rates. Many providers do not charge setup fees. However, a variety of rates exist. These rates are dynamic and keep changing with time. A small monthly fee may exist for a limited usage. After the allotted monthly hours, an additional hourly fee starts to kick in. Other rates for unlimited use exist. Some rates include access to Web and newsgroup services.

6. Search tools and Web services. While most of surfing and searching the Web is done via search engines (see chapter 5), service providers may have their own custom search tools. In addition, many service providers offer their customers Web-page construction and free hosting, of any additional charges.

7. Technical support. Support may come in many ways, including online, e-mail, phone, Usenet (see chapter 4), and user training. The technical support hours are important — is it available for only limited hours of the day?

8. Trial accounts. These accounts are available for users who have not made up their minds fully. A common example is AOL. It offers 50, 100 , or more free hours of connection to the Internet.

9. Installation and orientation. In many cases, installation is as simple as using a floppy disk or a CD-ROM.

10. Discussion groups and forum. This is an important factor. One of the main uses of the Internet is the exchange of information in this rapidly changing world. Many national and international issues of interest to the public are frequently discussed on the Internet, in forums and other venues. AOL, for example, has many chat rooms that allow you to send written messages to others in the room by clicking a button.

2.2 Connection Requirements

The required hardware and software to connect to the Internet is very common and affordable for many users, both personal and commercial. The continually falling prices of hardware make the price/performance ratio of computers very attractive. The client-side software is mostly a browser and the TCP/IP protocol. The browser is usually free, and the TCP/IP is part of the operating system.

2.2.1 Hardware

is the internet works and computers.

⊿ The hardware required for connecting to the Internet depends on whether it is for the client side or the server side. Assuming that there is a network in place to connect to the Internet backbone, the client-side hardware is a PC and the server-side hardware is a server. The server would require configuration. There is always a Web master who manages the server. For the client side, no special requirements are needed for the PC, except that it have a modem connection. Typically, today's PCs have plenty of memory (RAM) and hard disk.

2.2.2 Software

△ The software required to connect desktop computers to use the Internet is the TCP/IP and a browser. At the heart of Internet communication are the LANs/WANs and the TCP/IP software. The TCP/IP is the communication protocol. It is part of the OS. Windows and Unix OSs have it. Including TCP/IP as part of the OS makes it much easier for users to configure Internet connections on their computers, as is shown in the tutorial section at the end of this chapter.

TCP/IP software includes three components: TCP protocol, IP protocol, and Winsock protocol. TCP/IP protocol provides a method for delivering data packets through the Internet from on location to another, as is covered in section 1.4. Winsock (Windows socket) protocol allows Windows-based PCs to be connected to the Internet. The protocol became available in 1993. Before that, it was difficult to make the connection. Winsock protocol, in a sense, made Windows-based Internet products from various vendors compatible, so that a client program from one vendor would be compatible with the networking products of any other. Winsock is an application-programming interface that is generally built into TCP/IP software.

The communication between the TCP/IP software and the Internet users occurs via browsers. The browser is the main user interface that users navigate the Internet with. While the browser software is usually free to download for client use (individual users), server use normally requires licensing it. Browsers allow users to perform a variety of various tasks, from sending e-mail messages to searching the Web and downloading information. If the user has an ISP that has its own user interface, such as AOL, the user would not need a browser. These types of interfaces allow the user to get access to the plain Internet if needed. The major browsers are two, Netscape Communicator and Microsoft Internet Explorer. Both browsers are covered in chapters 3 and 4, respectively.

△ A commercial connection requires PCs, workstations, servers, and a dedicated network

2.3 Managing Host Names via the Domain Name System (DNS)

As discussed in chapter 1, each Web site, server, or node on the Internet has a unique address called the IP address. An IP address is a 32-bit integer represented by four 8-bit numbers written in base 10 and separated by periods. For example, an IP address of a Web site could be 198.465.327.80. Similar to a house address, this IP address is assigned to only this particular Web site.

We have two concerns with these IP addresses: remembering and assigning them. An IP address as a bunch of numbers is difficult to relate to. It would be better if we could replace these numbers by something logical. For example, one could more easily remember a company name than a code for it. Thus, on the one hand, computers can deal only with numbers, and, on the other, humans like logical names. The best solution to this conflict is to map the numbers to names. This process creates distributed name/address directory. The Domain Name System or Service (DNS) is application software that translates names to IP addresses and vice versa, by using a technique called reverse look-up. There are DNS servers that maintain lists of domain name/IP address correspondences. If a client types a Web site as www.neu.edu, the DNS server converts it into an IP address, locates the node of the site, and connects the client to the site. This conversion is sometimes known as DNS host name resolution. If the node (e.g., a server) corresponding to a certain IP address is down, or the IP address is incorrect, no communication takes place between the client and the node.

Assigning IP addresses is managed and controlled by national and international organizations. Each node on the Internet is assigned a unique IP address that cannot be assigned to any read !!

other entity in the future. It is similar to a registered trademark. There is a company in the United States called Network Solutions Inc. in Herndon, VA that has a contract with the federal government to run and administer the computer system that controls the IP addresses as well as the .com, .net, and .org domain names. Network Solutions charges companies $100 and individuals $35 a year to have an IP address. It is the responsibility of Network Solutions to ensure that these IP addresses are unique.

With the explosive growth of the Internet, the IP addresses using the top-level domain names (.com, .net, and .org) are running out. Some companies applied for large chunks of these addresses in anticipation of this shortage. There have been proposals to create new domains — for example, web, .shop, .firm, .rec, .xxx — to be administered by a for-profit or nonprofit business. These proposals are still under discussion, and the consensus is to have the domains controlled by a nonprofit organization.

Based on this consensus, the U.S. federal government has decided to end its management of the name and address system by creating an international nonprofit corporation, ICANN (Internet Corporation for Assigned Names and Numbers), based in California and run by a board of 19 members from around the world. The board of ICANN, selected by the U.S. Commerce Department, takes over most of the running of the Internet, particularly the entire system of assigning and managing IP addresses and domain names, such as those ending with .com, .net, etc. ICANN is currently operational.

Under the new system, ICANN and Network Solutions work together. ICANN oversees the numerical addresses system and 11 "root server" computers that list all the IP addresses and their corresponding names (URLs). Network Solutions, meanwhile, maintains a database of all Internet sites in the popular .com, .net, and .org top-level domains. Network Solutions also sends frequently updated copies of its database to the root servers.

In addition to Network Solutions, other companies are now allowed to sell IP addresses to individuals, organizations, and companies. Five such companies are AOL, www.register.com, CORE (a Swiss-based consortium of registrars of 23 countries), Trans Telecom, and Milburn IT Australian registrar. Other companies, such as AT&T may also sell IP addresses in the future, once they are granted permissions by ICANN. Network Solutions charges these companies wholesale prices. This is similar to the telephone industry, where AT&T, for example, charges other phone companies wholesale prices for phone numbers. This could accelerate the sale of IP addresses to the point that they could become like phone numbers.

2.4 Types of Connections

Access to the Internet requires a service provider, whether at the personal or the corporate level. If you are interested in connecting to the Internet, an Internet connection may already be available to you for free, through your employer, if you are willing to perform some investigation. This saves you the monthly fee you have to pay to the service provider. The free way, as usual, may not be the most convenient to connect to the Internet. You have to rely on friends and others for help to find your way, to download free software, to configure the connecting software, to set up the connection, and to make sense of and understand what is going on. If you want to save yourself these headaches, you can simply subscribe to a service provider, who does the legwork for you and makes your Internet connection transparent to you and simple. It may not, however, be a bad experience to go through the process of creating and understanding your own connection, as this should help you to know your provider's setup and terminology.

Once an online service provider or an ISP is chosen, the user needs a connection to connect to the provider's server to access the Internet. Two methods exist to connect to the server: dedicated, and dial-up (dial-in). Other methods, such as using shell accounts, are obsolete and are not covered here; as they are seldom used since the existing advances in computer hardware and software. Selecting the type of Internet connection depends on your needs. Each method of connection lets you perform most of the basic functions, such as surfing the Web, sending and receiving e-mail, and using FTP and Telnet sites. The major differences between a dedicated and a dial-up connection are the access speed and the monthly fee. The former is always faster and more expensive. In general, businesses use the dedicated method of connection, individuals at households use the dial-up connection.

2.4.1 Dedicated Internet Access

This is the easiest, fastest, and most convenient connection to access the Internet. It is a hardwire connection, as opposed to a dial-up connection. The PC or the workstation is connected to a LAN port directly. The PC or the workstation has a network card (e.g., Ethernet card) to make the connection possible. The port could be in an office or in a lab. Corporations and large institutions/universities (call them sites) usually have this type of connection. In this case, the site leases a dedicated telephone line at a speed of choice from a commercial provider. The provider places a routing computer (a router) at the site for taking communications from the site and sending them to their final destinations. All site computers can be connected to the router via a LAN. The LAN is the responsibility of the site. Once the site is up and running, the provider is responsible for only the router and the telephone line.

How fast are these dedicated telephone lines or connections? Two of the existing technologies are T1 and T3 connections. A T1 line provides a bandwidth of 1.5 million bits per second. A T3 line has a bandwidth of 45 Mbps (45 megabits or 45 million bits per second). A bandwidth of 45 Mbps means that a T3 line transmits 45 million bits of data, voice, and video per second. A T1 line uses 24 64 Kbps channels (24×64 Kbps = 1.5 Mbps) to deliver its data throughput. A T3 line uses 672 64 Kbps channels (the equivalent of 28 T1 lines). The channels of a T line can be divided or allocated between data, video, and voice depending on a company's needs. A T1 line provides enough speed for a small company that has a Web server that gets more than 1500 hits a month. A T3 line is good for a large company with an active Web site that gets more than 25,000 hits per month. A T1 line cost includes installation fees and a monthly fee that depends on the traffic (number of bits) that goes through the line. A T3 line costs much more than a T1 line, because it can handle much more traffic.

Dedicated access offers the most flexible connection. Each computer is a full-fledged Internet member, capable of performing any network function. Another advantage is the dial-up capability. Some sites allow their employees to dial in from home via a modem and PC and connect to the Internet. An interested employee needs a computer account. In this case, the home connection is free (except for the cost of the phone call, if it is long distance). These sites provide some guidelines into how to set up the home connection, as we explain in section 2.5. This connection requires a SLIP/PPP account.

Dedicated Internet access is ideal if the site plans to use the Internet heavily, 24 hours a day, 7 days a week, for activities such as e-commerce or for using intensive technologies such as real-time audio, Internet phone, Internet video conferencing, and so forth. Companies and organizations use this type of connection to connect their Intranets and Extranets to the Internet. Dedicated connections provide a wide range of access speeds: from 56K to T1, T3, or ISDN. (See section 2.4.2 below). Dial-ups to a dedicated site usually face as an issue the speed of their modems. The modem speed is the bottleneck for dial-ups.

Dedicated Internet connections come with overhead costs. First, this method of connection is expensive, especially if it is a high-speed line. Second, security is a very major concern. Without implementing strict security measures, a corporate network could be vulnerable to outside piracy. Without security, the full promise and the potential of e-commerce cannot be realized. Most e-commerce security tools use encryption technology. Third, in-house technical expertise is required to set up the connection, configure it, and maintain/update it.

2.4.2 Dial-up and Home Connection

A dial-up connection typically uses a PC, a modem, and a phone line to connect to the Internet via a phone call. The PC must have TCP/IP software installed on it and a configured PPP connection. The dial-up connection is the method most widely used to connect homes to the Internet. Any family member can go online by dialing a phone number to connect to the Internet through a service provider, whether an online provider or an ISP. It does not take too much effort to make a home PC Internet-ready. The TCP/IP software is part of the OS (such as Windows). Configuring a PPP connection is systematic and is shown in the tutorial section of this chapter.

Different types of modems exist (see below). What most people refer to as just "a modem" is an analog modem. In this book, when we say a modem, we mean an analog modem. A modem is used to transfer data from one location to another through phone lines. On the sending end, the modem converts the digital information into sound (analog) waves that can be transmitted through the phone lines or wires. Thus, the modem acts as a modulator. On the receiving end, the modem performs the opposite operation; it converts the sound waves back to digital information. Here, the modem acts as a demodulator. The name modem, therefore, originates from the words "*mo*dulator" and "*dem*odulator".

The main bottleneck for dial-up users is the access speed. Downloading uploading Web pages with much graphics, animation, and sound content is very slow when using modem speeds. Access speeds are directly dependent on the wires that make up the telephone system.

双 绞线

They are typically twisted-pair copper wires. These wires are not the ideal medium for moving data at high speeds. As a result, telecommunication companies, such as Cisco, Lucent Technologies, and Northern Telecom, as well as telephone and cable television companies, have been competing fiercely to upgrade transmission methods and speeds. Sprint Telephone Company has developed a digital network called SprintPC that can transmit voice and data. With one phone line, home users can still make their phone calls as usual and connect to the Internet via faster modems.

The battle for faster dial-up connections has resulted in many technologies and ways to access the Internet. Here is a list of the available technologies for dial-up users to connect to the Internet:

1. Telephone modems (analog modems). This is the most common and least expensive way to connect to the Internet, but it is also the slowest. The fastest modem speed today is 56K; i.e., the modem can transmit 56,000 bits of data per second. Slower modem speeds, 28.8K and 14.4K, exist. The slower the modem speed, the longer it takes to download Web pages. Modems use existing phone lines. Most home PCs come with a 56k modem. All 56K modems use the ITU V.90 analog modem speed standard that was reached on February 6, 1998 in Geneva, Switzerland by most major modem manufacturers, such as 3COM/USR and Rockwell. For tens of millions of people, using a V.90 modem will be the way to connect to the Internet for the foreseeable future. They provide narrowband connections.

2. DSL and ADSL modems. Digital Subscriber Line (DSL) and asynchronous DSL (ADSL) is a technology that allows Internet users to tap into the Internet over an ordinary phone line, at speeds significantly faster than those of the existing V.90 modems. DSL and ADSL modems are installed inside PCs, similarly to V.90 modems. DSL technology uses existing phone lines. A DSL modem takes an electronic signal and splits it so that a single phone wire can transmit voice (regular phone calls) and data (Internet content) simultaneously. A DSL modem uses the same speed for download and upload. An ADSL modem splits the bandwidth so that more is dedicated to download. Thus, ADSL modems allow faster download than upload. Using DSL and ADSL modems means that a family member can chat on the phone or fax a document while another member in the same house can surf the Internet using the same phone line. DSL and ADSL modems eliminate the need to dial up; the computers are always connected around the clock, 24 hours a day, 7 days a week. Speeds of DSL and ADSL modems range from 160K bits to 1.5Mb per second with plans for 7.1 Mbps. Phone companies are the logical users of the DSL technology because it enables them to compete with cable companies that offer fast access to the Internet via the cable modems. Phone companies may use two rates to charge their customer: one rate for voice and another rate for data. The rate for voice is per minute and the rate for data is per Kbyte of downloaded information. Or phone companies can simply charge their customers a monthly flat rate and charge only for phone calls as they currently do. DSL and ADSL modems allow the user the freedom to choose an ISP; cable modems do not.

3. Cable modems. Cable television wire holds an advantage over telephone wire. The former has a higher bandwidth than the latter. Thus, cable television wires, made of coaxial

cable!? one

cables, can be adapted to transfer data at access speeds as high as 10 Mbps. The cable companies charge monthly fees for using cable modems. Cable companies may charge installation fees as well. With cable modems, the cable company becomes one's ISP. This eliminates the choice of an ISP. Dial-up users who are interested in using cable modems should check with their local cable companies to make sure that the service exists in their area or neighborhood. Only two-thirds of households are connected to cable networks in the U.S.A.

4. ISDN lines (digital modems). ISDN (Integrated Services Digital Network) lines transmit data, voice, and video over the same telephone lines. Transmission speed is up to 128 Kbps. An ISDN line is a digital line. Thus, it requires a different modem (known as digital modem) or adapter installed at home. ISDN lines are able to use telephone lines because telephone lines transmit phone calls in a digital form until the last connection between the home phone and the telephone line, where the call is converted into analog form. The monthly fee for an ISDN line depends on its speed and use. In addition, there may be installation fees and a charge for the adapter (several hundred dollars). Before thinking of installing an ISDN line, dial-up users must check whether their service providers support ISDN lines. If they do not, the ISDN line will not do them any good.

5. B-ISDN lines. This is broadband ISDN (the above ISDN is known as narrowband ISDN). B-ISDN lines use fiber optics instead of the twisted-pair copper wires. B-ISDN is much faster than ISDN. B-ISDN technology is still in development. *incorrect!*

6. Satellite. A satellite-based Internet access uses a satellite dish to receive data at an average speed of 300 Kbps. A satellite Internet connection requires a special receiver, a PC adapter card, and special software. Each one of these components has a price associated with it, in addition to a monthly fee. The advantage of satellite-based Internet connection is to allow rural areas and the developing world, where phone lines are rare or nonexistent, to access the Internet.

7. The wireless connection (cellular modems). This method of connection is used to connect a laptop computer to the Internet through a cellular modem. This alleviates the need to plug the laptop into a wall socket. Users can check their e-mail while on the road, in a boat, in a plane, etc. While this method seems exciting, individual users seldom use it because it is slow and expensive. While connected, the modem may transfer data no faster than 9600 bits per second over a cellular phone line, thus costing a lot just to check your e-mail. To try to bring the cost down, the cellular phone companies have developed a replacement for the TCP/IP protocol. The new protocol is called CDPD (cellular digital packet data). The packets used by CDPD are IP packets encrypted for security purposes. This technique allows cellular phone companies to charge customers by packets transferred and not by the minute of connection. While you may be connected for 5 minutes of airtime, you may have used only two minutes to download or send packets. To use CDPD, you need a special CDPD telephone called MES (mobile end system) and a special CDPD account. This type of telephone is fairly expensive. Prices should come down with time. The wireless connection is designed for short bursts of information. For example, police can use CDPD to check license plate numbers from their cruisers. Fuel oil companies can use it to dispatch their delivery trucks. Visiting nurses may also use it. For now, and until the prices of CDPD come down, you can use your traditional cellular telephone and a PC card.

2.5 Point-to-Point Dial-up Connection

All the Internet dial-up connections via a modem and a telephone line require a serial line interface protocol (SLIP) or point-to-point protocol (PPP) account. Whether you establish the connection yourself or through your service provider, it is beneficial that you know basically how to set up the connection and configure the software. In this section, we provide a framework to establish a SLIP/PPP connection and explain some basics and terms commonly used. The tutorial in section 2.6 shows the SLIP/PPP procedure for Microsoft Windows.

2.5.1 Point-to-Point

SLIP and PPP are the protocols that allow connecting two hosts, say, your PC and an Internet server, over a direct link such as a telephone connection. Your PC becomes a host on the network. If you do not have a SLIP or PPP connection, your PC will have to connect to a host as a dumb terminal and communicate with the network via this host. This is a slow and inconvenient way of communication. SLIP came into use in the mid-1980s. Compressed SLIP (CSLIP) was specified in 1990. It improves the SLIP performance. SLIP has its drawbacks. The most noticeable is that it is slow, because it sends only one bit at a time. It does not support all types of networks — only IP networks.

The PPP protocol was introduced in 1992 to address most of SLIP's shortcomings. It allows the user to specify the network protocol — whether it is IP or not. It can negotiate connection parameters as well as compression, and it can protect against transmission errors. It is also more popular in WANs than in LANs. PPP connection is most commonly used today.

2.5.2 Winsock

Winsock is the Windows Sockets API (Application Programming Interface). It allows Windows to work with the Internet. It contains information that Windows itself needs to work with TCP/IP to perform Internet tasks. Once you have Winsock working, you can then run client programs like Netscape and communicate with the Internet through your PPP connection. Winsock is now part of Windows. Windows comes with built-in TCP/IP and networking support to make establishing and using a PPP connection much easier. (See section 2.6).

2.5.3 Logging in to a PPP Account

You need a PPP account to be able to use the PPP connection you have created. Your service provider provides you with the account and its information. The provider gives you a phone number, a username, and a password. With this information, you can log in to your service provider server or network by using the PPP connection. This connection makes the entire Internet available to you at home. The phone call you make to connect to the Internet may be a local call to you, and, depending on your phone billing plan, the call may not add any extra charge to your phone bill. To minimize or eliminate charges for phone calls during connection time, all service providers have POPs (point of presence) in may regions of the country. Once connected, you can surf the net, download Web pages, read and send e-mail, chat with friends, etc.

2.6 Tutorials

The main goal of this tutorial is to enable you to configure and establish you own PPP connection using Windows.

2.6.1 Configuring a PPP Connection in Windows

The online help function of Windows provides a list of the steps required for creating a PPP connection (Windows calls it Dial-UP Networking). In this book, "click" means to click with the left mouse button once. Also, the names of buttons, menus, menu items, windows, file names, and other, similar elements are shown in Courier font throughout the book, to distinguish them from other text. To access this online documentation, follow the following steps:

1. Double click the My Computer icon on the desktop.
2. Click the Help menu on the menu bar of the My Computer window.
3. Click the Help Topics menu item.
4. Type Internet as the word(s) you want to find.
5. Click Connecting to the Internet using Dial-Up Networking.
6. Click Quick Overview.

The quick overview lists the Microsoft steps that are needed to create and use a PPP connection. In step 6 above, if you click Getting an Internet account instead of Quick overview, you get the details of each Microsoft step. The actual procedure to create a PPP connection is documented in this tutorial. We here create a PPP connection called NU. The procedure consists of the following steps:

A. Obtain a PPP account from your service provider. Whether your service provider is your employer, an online service such as AOL, or an ISP, the provider should set up a PPP account for you and provide you with a phone number (for step C below), a username, and a password. You need this account to log in to the provider server and eventually to the Internet.

B. Install Dial-Up Networking component if needed. Double click the My Computer icon on the desktop. If you see the Dial-UP Networking icon, move to step C below. Otherwise, install it as follows. The screen captures are shown below. The mouse cursor (shown as an arrow in the screen captures) is positioned next to the icon or item the reader needs to click to follow the sequence.

1. Double click the Control Panel icon (figure 2.2).

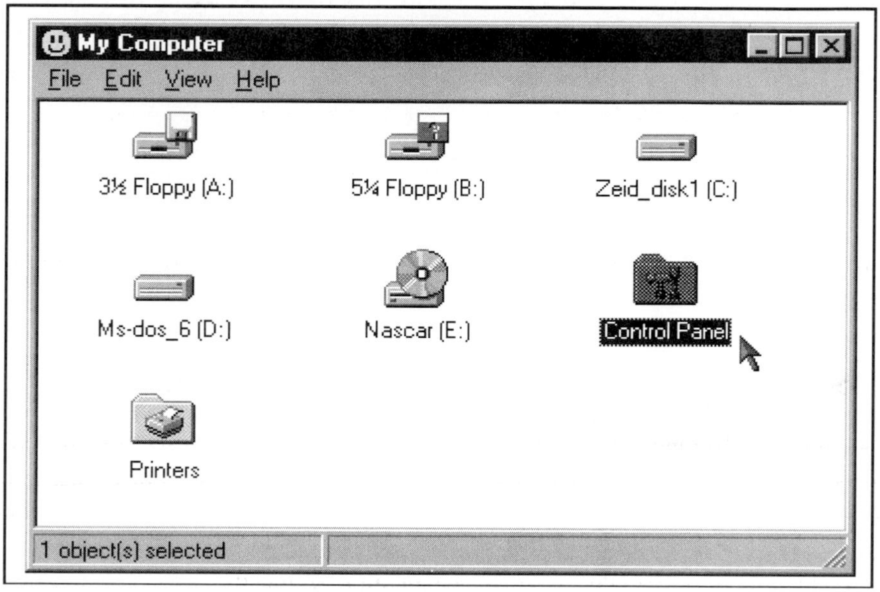

Figure 2.2   Open the Control Panel folder.

2. Double click Add/Remove Programs (figure 2.3).

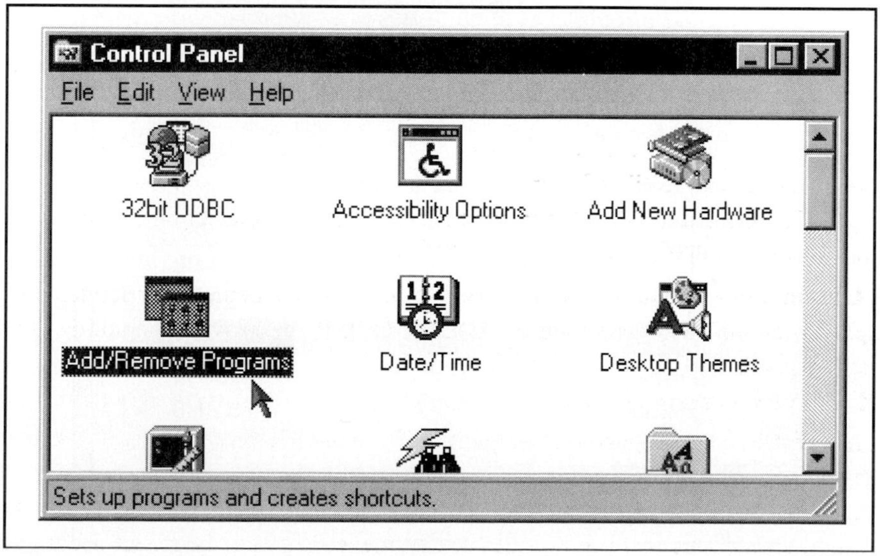

Figure 2.3   Run the Add/Remove program.

3. Click the Windows Setup tab (figure 2.4).

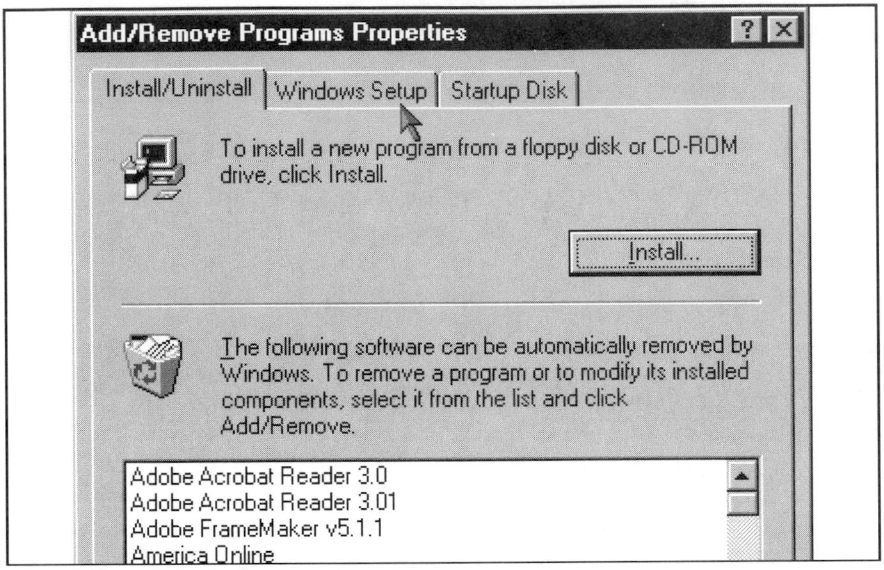

Figure 2.4   Display the components of Windows.

4. Click Communications, followed by Details (figure 2.5).

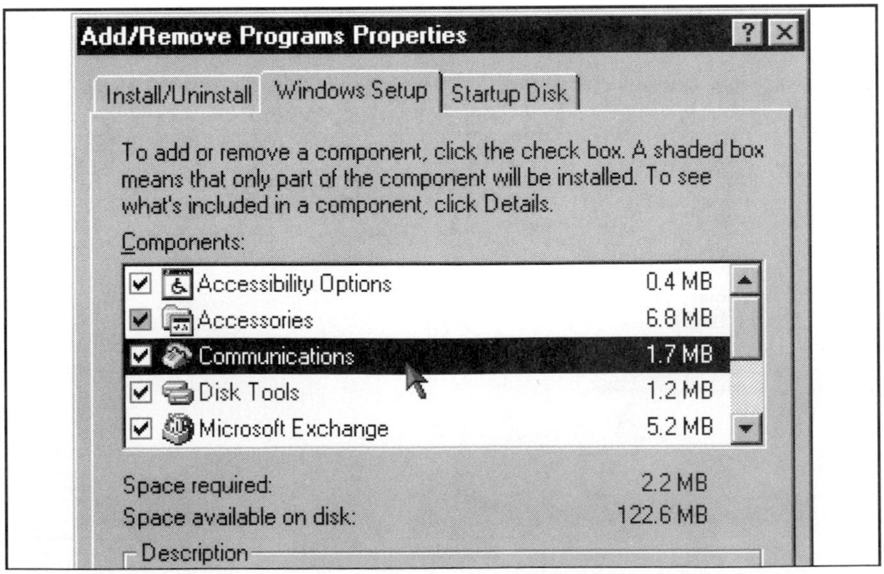

Figure 2.5   Access the Dial-Up Networking component of Windows.

5. Click Dial-Up Networking, followed by OK (figure 2.6).

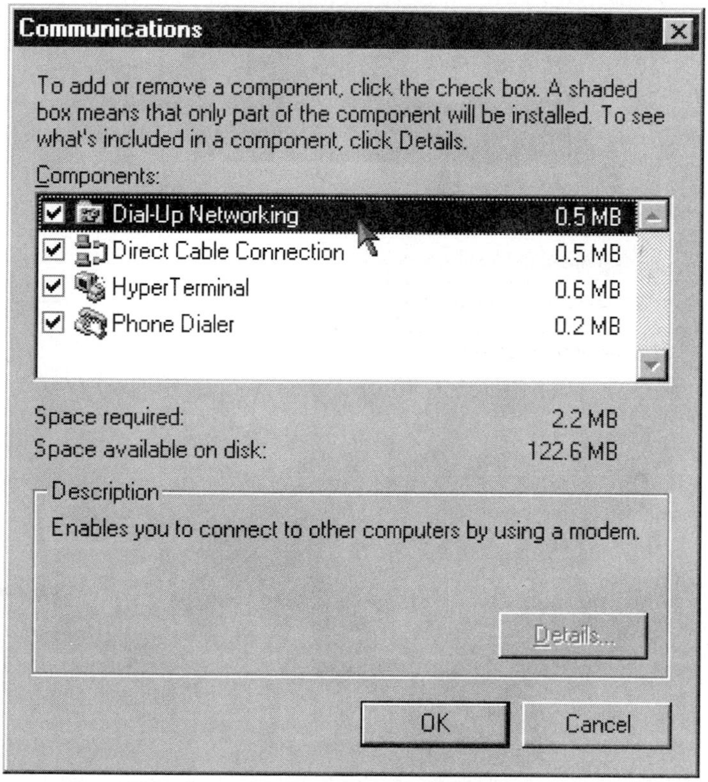

Figure 2.6 Enable the Dial-Up Networking Component.

6. Click OK (figure 2.7).

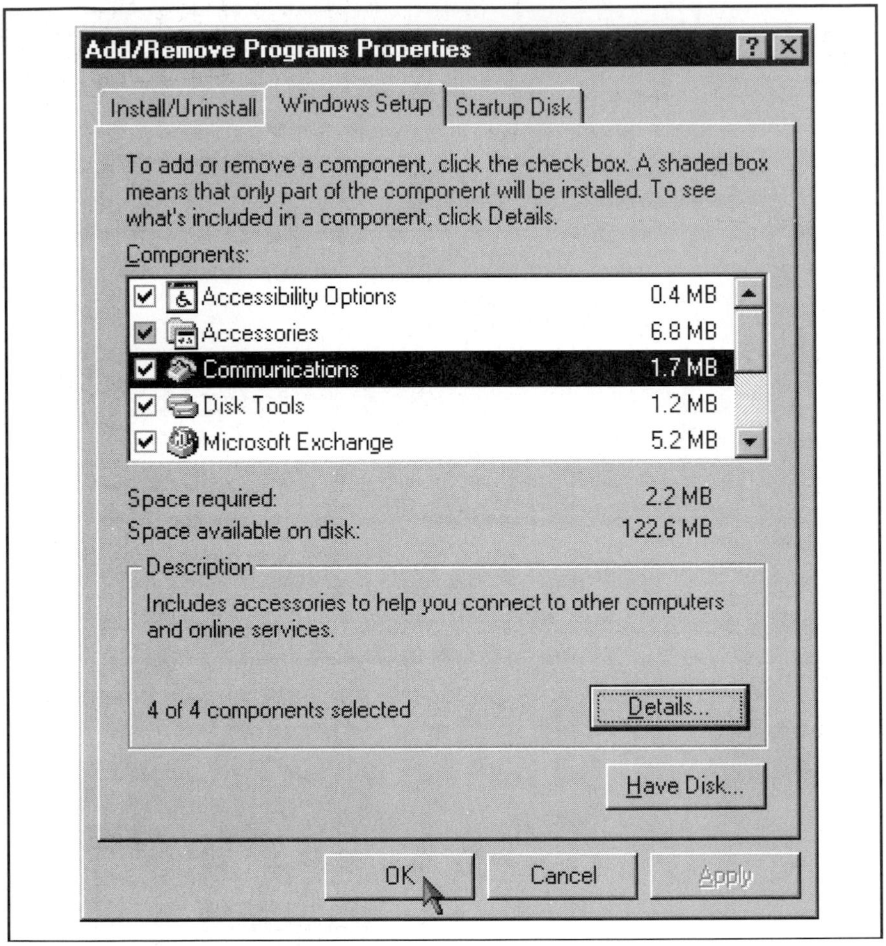

Figure 2.7   Finish installing the Dial-Up Networking component.

You should now see the Dial-Up Networking icon in the My Computer window (folder). When this icon is opened, it has the Make New Connection icon that is used to create the new connection we want.

C. Configure the modem for the new connection. You need the communication port (usually COM1), the modem speed and type, and the phone number. Once you configure the modem, an icon called My Connection (or any name you chose for the new connection) is created in the Dial-Up Networking window. Use the following sequence to input the modem information.

1. Double click the `Dial-Up Networking` icon (figure 2.8).

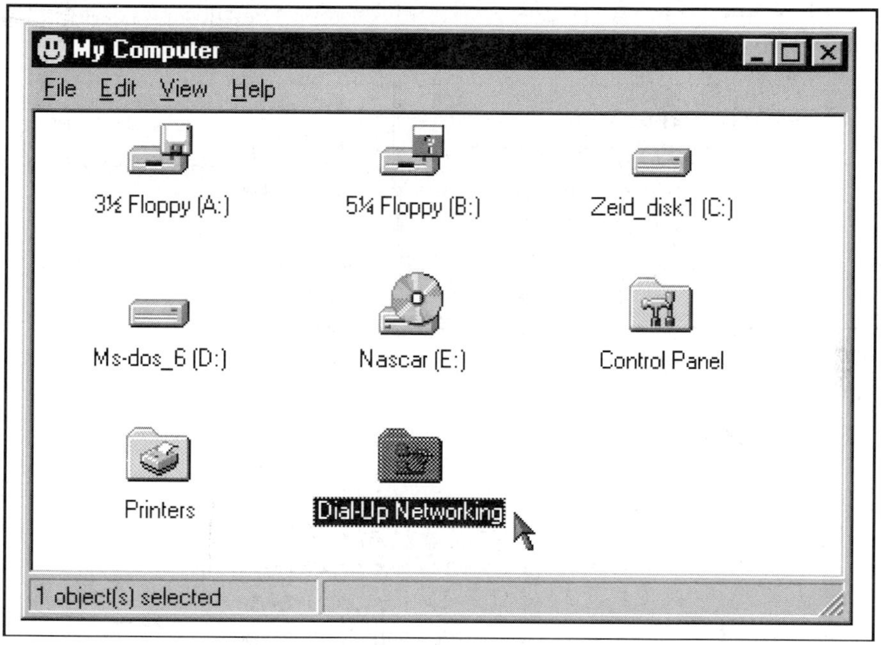

Figure 2.8   Begin creating the NU PPP connection.

2. Double click the `Make New Connection` icon (figure 2.9).

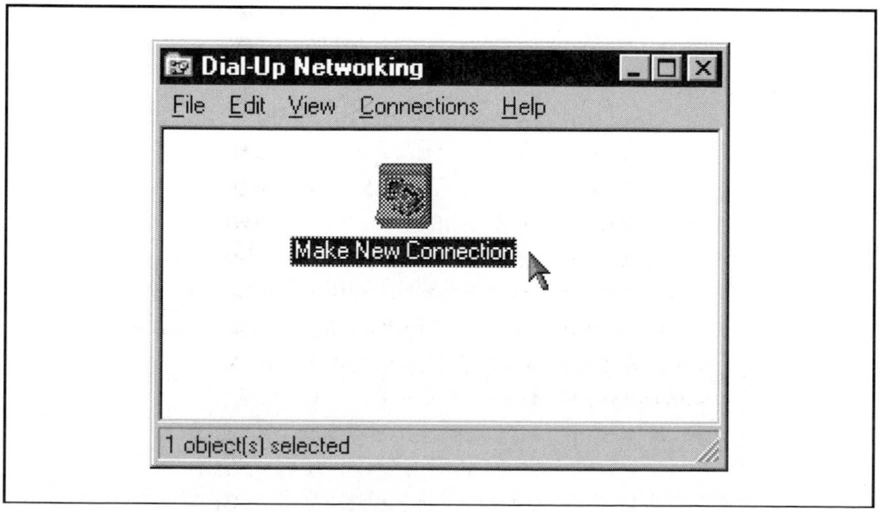

Figure 2.9   Use this master connection.

3. Replace the name `My Connection` by NU, and click the `Configure` button (figure 2.10).

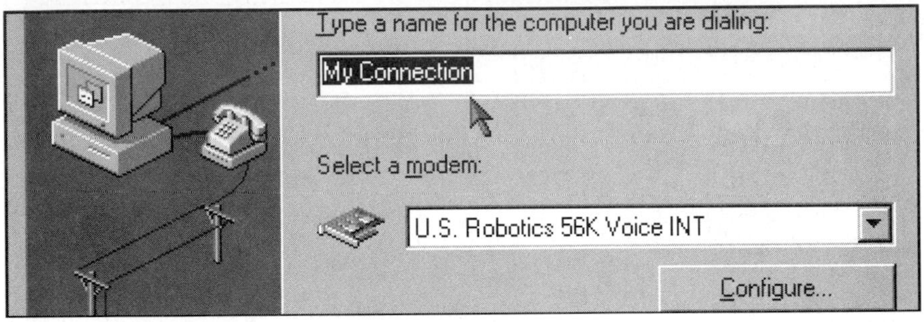

Figure 2.10   Type the connection name.

4. Change the communication port and the maximum speed, if needed (figure 2.11). Click OK.

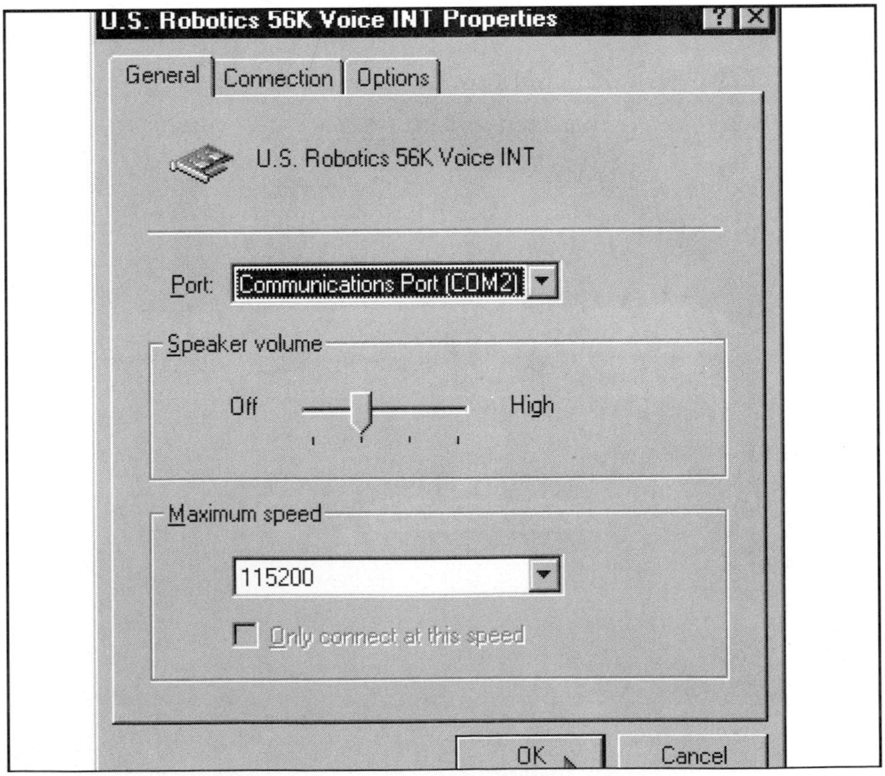

Figure 2.11   Select the modem port and speed.

5. Click the `Next` button (figure 2.12).

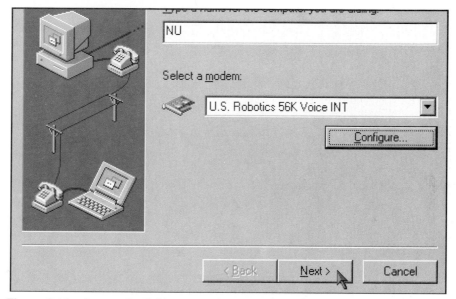

Figure 2.12   Access the field to enter the service provider telephone number.

6. Type the phone number of your service provider, and click `Next` (figure 2.13).

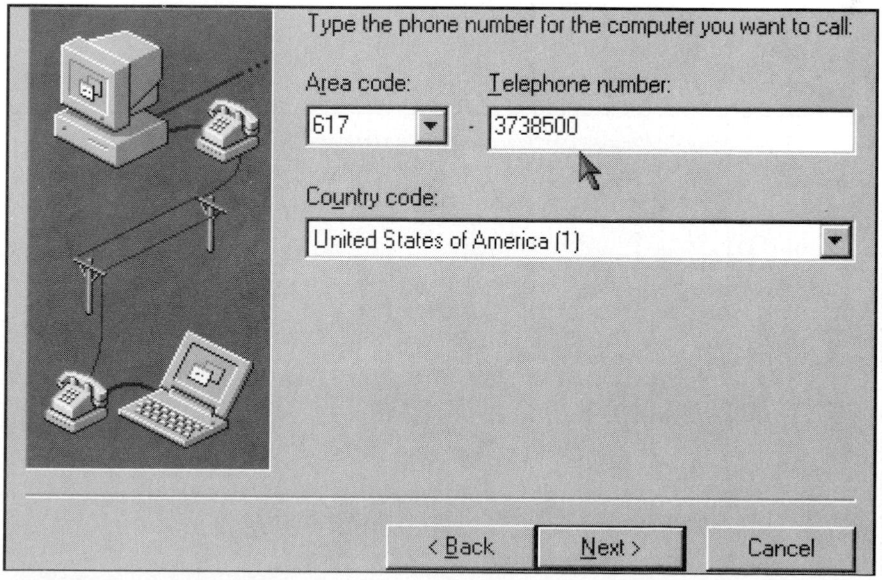

Figure 2.13   Enter the telephone number of the service provider.

7. Click the Finish button (figure 2.14).

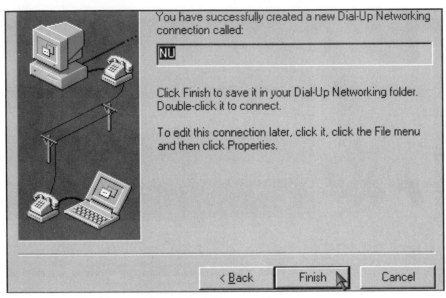

Figure 2.14   End the creation of the NU connection.

D. Set the server and TCP/IP protocol; Here we choose the PPP server and the TCP/IP. Following is the sequence for this step.

1. Click right on the NU icon, then click Properties (figure 2.15).

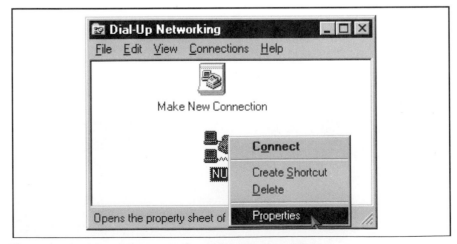

Figure 2.15   Access the properties of the NU connection.

2. Click the `Server Type` button (figure 2.16).

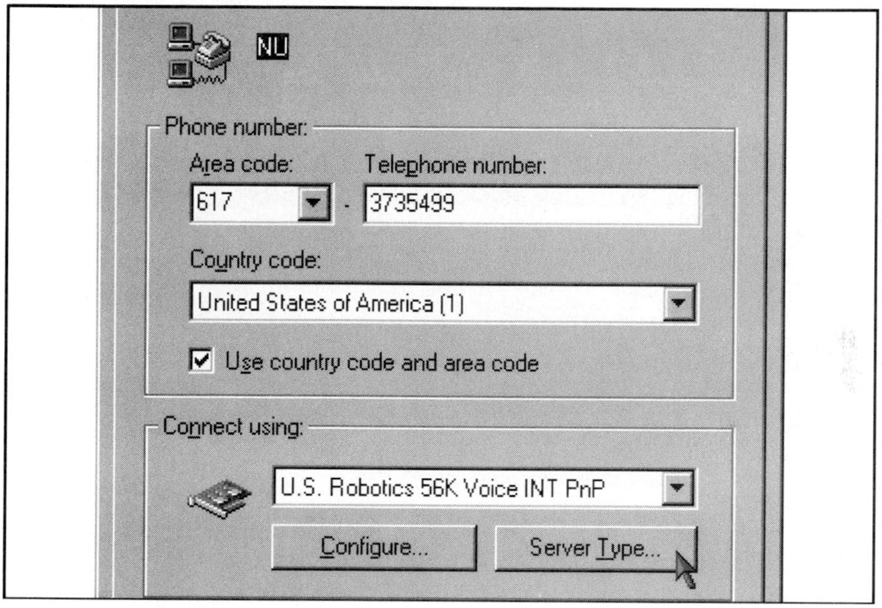

Figure 2.16 Set up the server.

3. Choose `PPP` for Type of Dial-Up Server (figure 2.17).
4. Enable `Enable software compression` (figure 2.17).
5. Enable `TCP/IP` (figure 2.17).
6. Click the `TCP/IP Settings` button (figure 2.17)

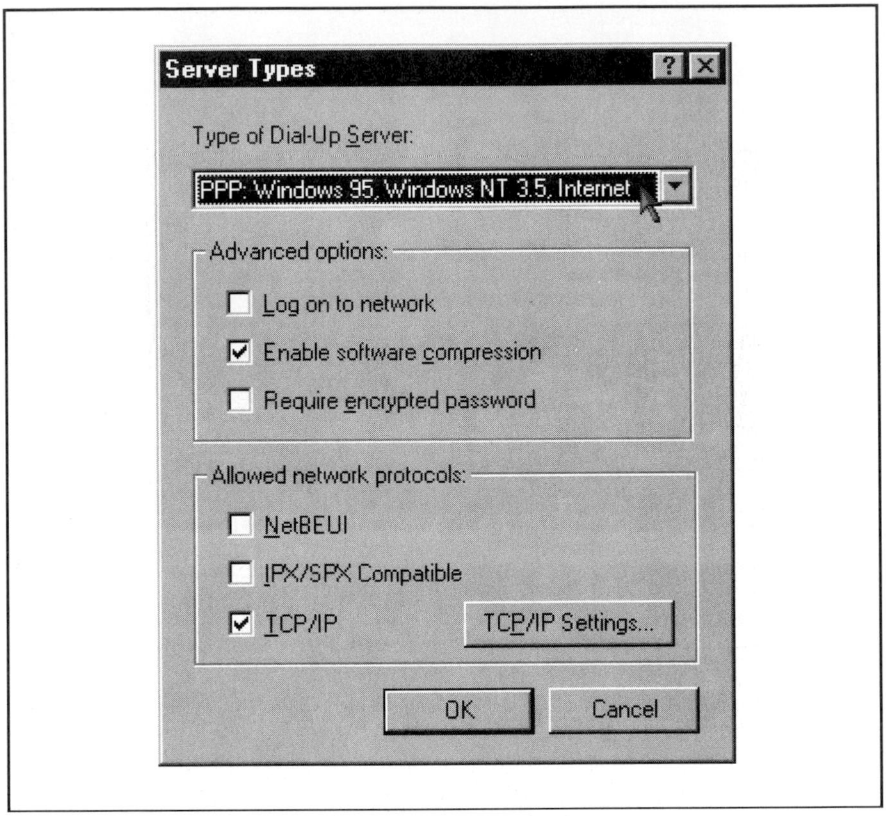

Figure 2.17   Specify the type of server.

7. Choose `Server assigned IP address` (figure 2.18).
8. Choose `Server assigned name server addresses` (figure 2.18).
9. Enable `Use IP header compression` (figure 2.18).
10. Enable `Use default gateway on remote network` (figure 2.18).
11. Click `OK` (figure 2.18).

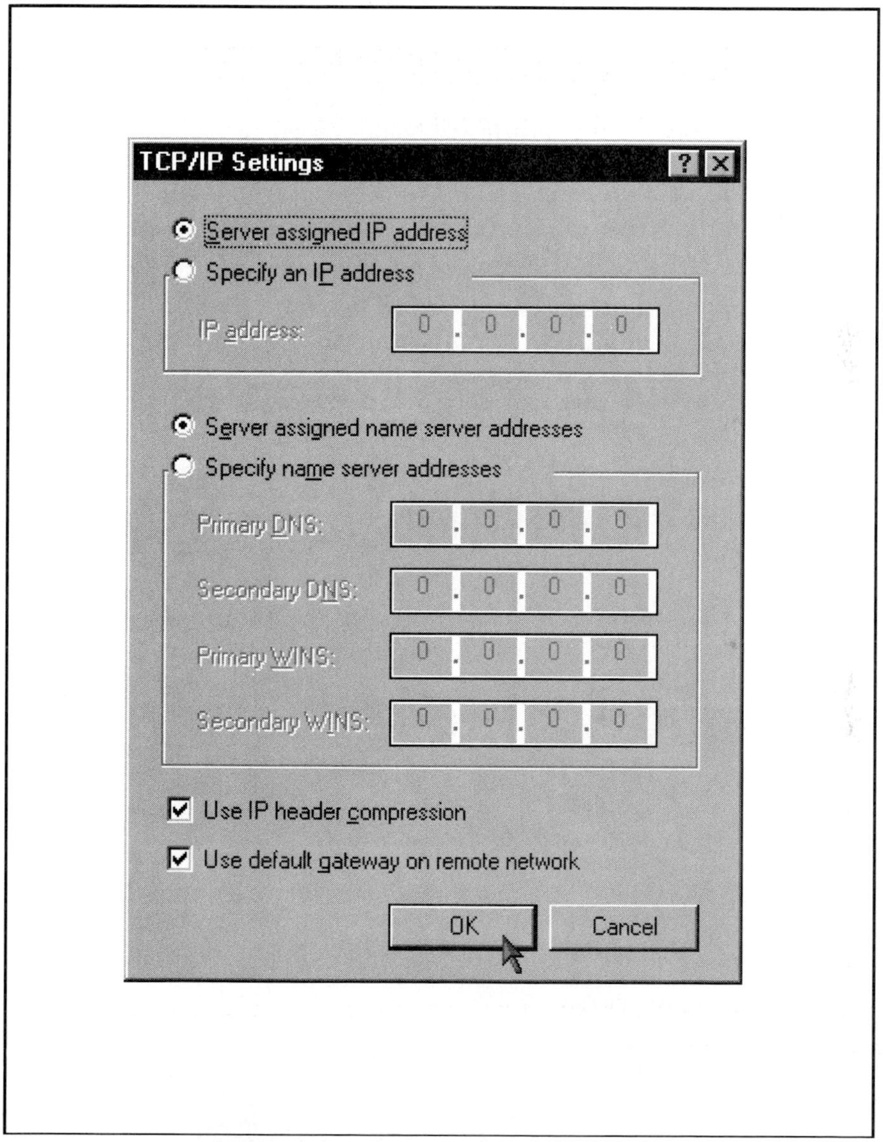

Figure 2.18 Choose the TCP/IP settings.

12. Click OK (figure 2.19).

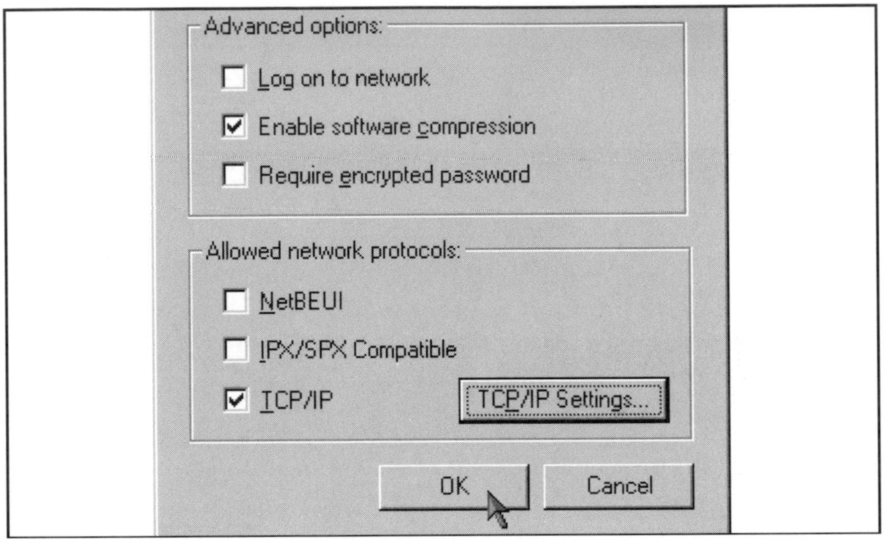

Figure 2.19   Finish setting the TCP/IP protocol.

13. Click OK (figure 2.20).

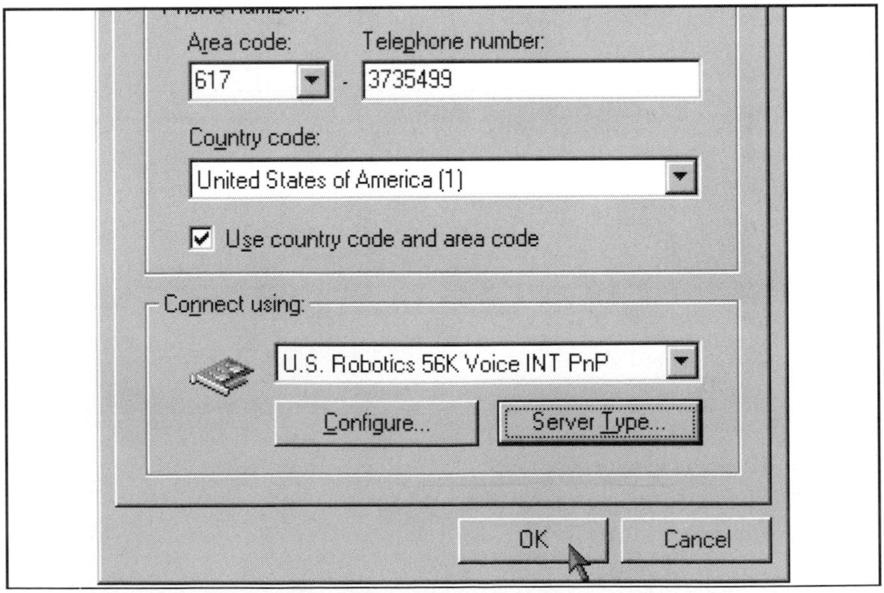

Figure 2.20   Finish setting the Dial-UP Server.

14. Double click the Control Panel icon.
15. Double click the Network icon (figure 2.21).

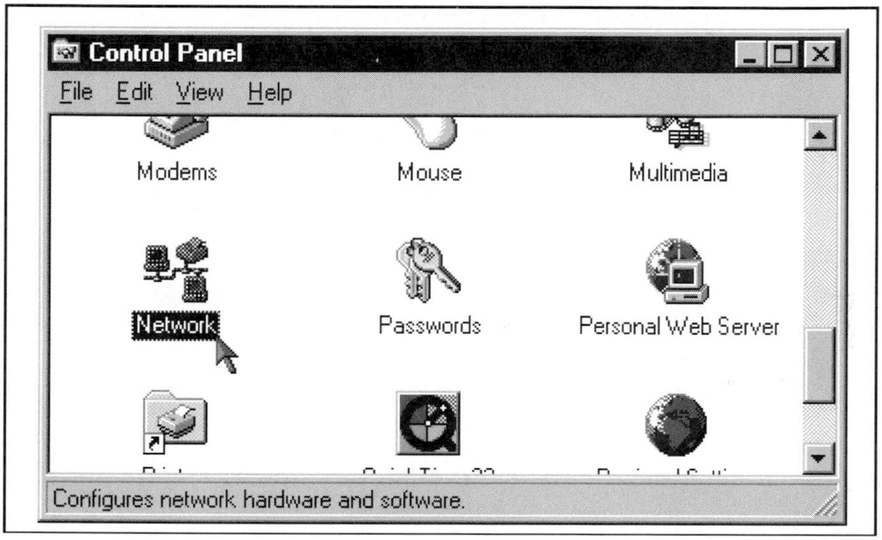

Figure 2.21   Begin to access the DNS configuration.

16. Select the TCP/IP component (figure 2.22).
17. Click the Properties button (figure 2.22).

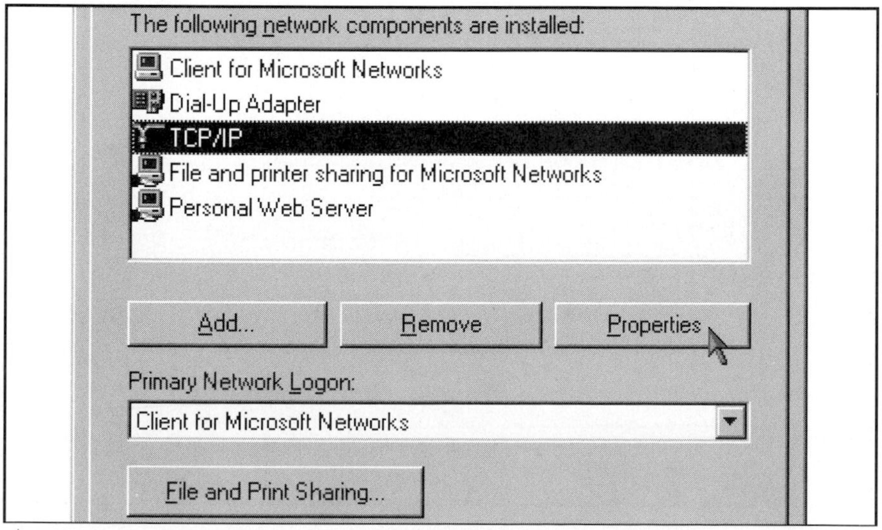

Figure 2.22   Access the properties of TCP/IP.

18. Click the DNS Configuration tab (figure 2.23).

19. Click Enable DNS (figure 2.23).

20. Type a name — for example, MyNode — for Host (figure 2.23).

21. Type a DNS IP address (obtained from your service provider) (figure 2.23).

22. Click Add (figure 2.23).

23. Click OK (figure 2.23).

24. Click OK.

25. Follow the system response.

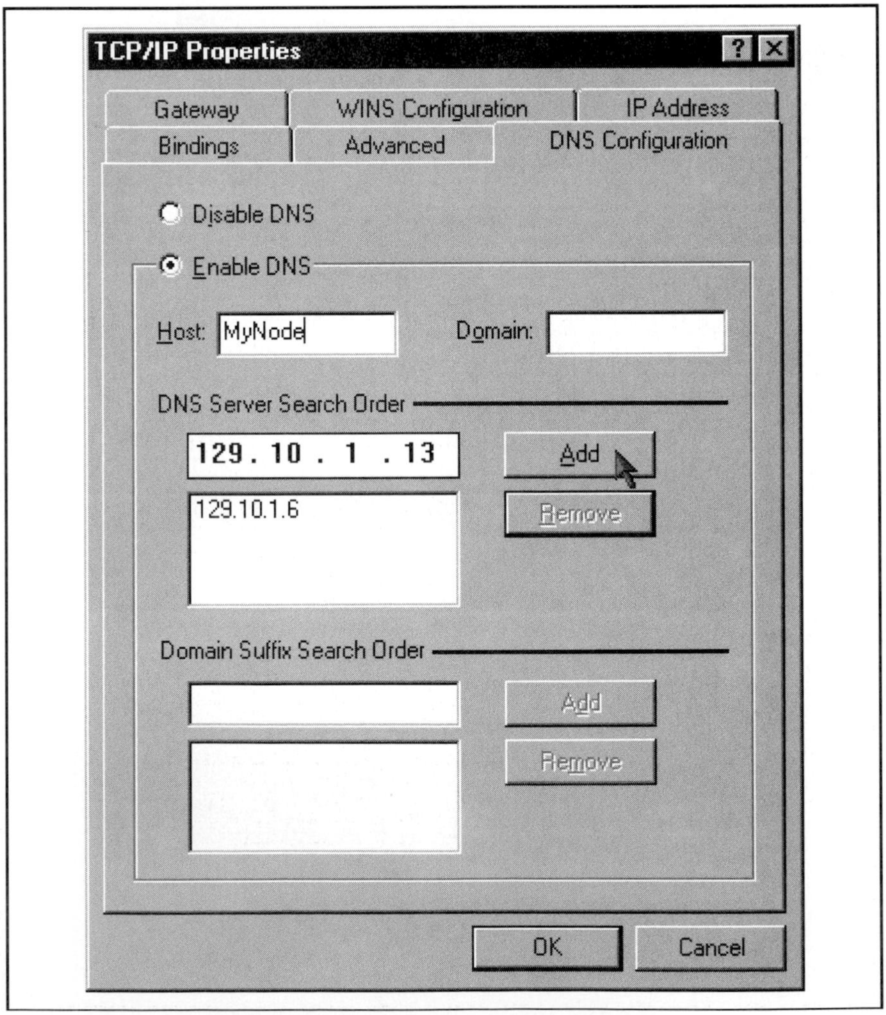

Figure 2.23   Input DNS information for your PPP connection.

E. Activate a post-dial terminal window. You need to bring up a post-dial terminal window after dialing, to type the server type (PPP), your username, and the password. Without this window, you cannot log in to your account. Here is the sequence to add to activate this window.

1. Right click the NU icon, then click Properties (figure 2.15).

2. Click the Configure button (figure 2.24).

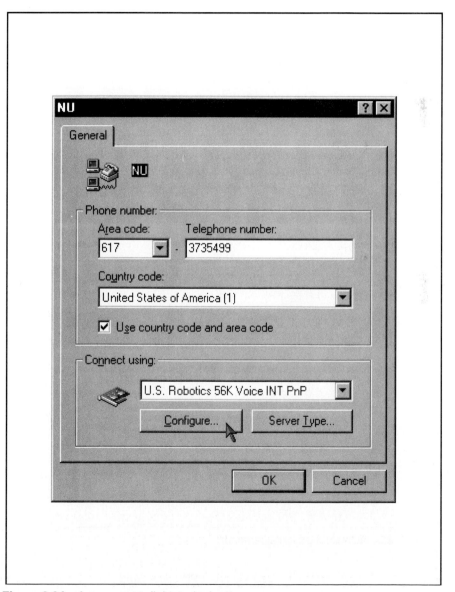

Figure 2.24   Access post-dial terminal set up.

3. Click the `Options` tab (figure 2.25).

4. Enable `Bring up terminal window before dialing` (figure 2.25).

5. Enable `Display modem status` (figure 2.25).

6. Click `OK` (figure 2.25).

7. Click `OK`.

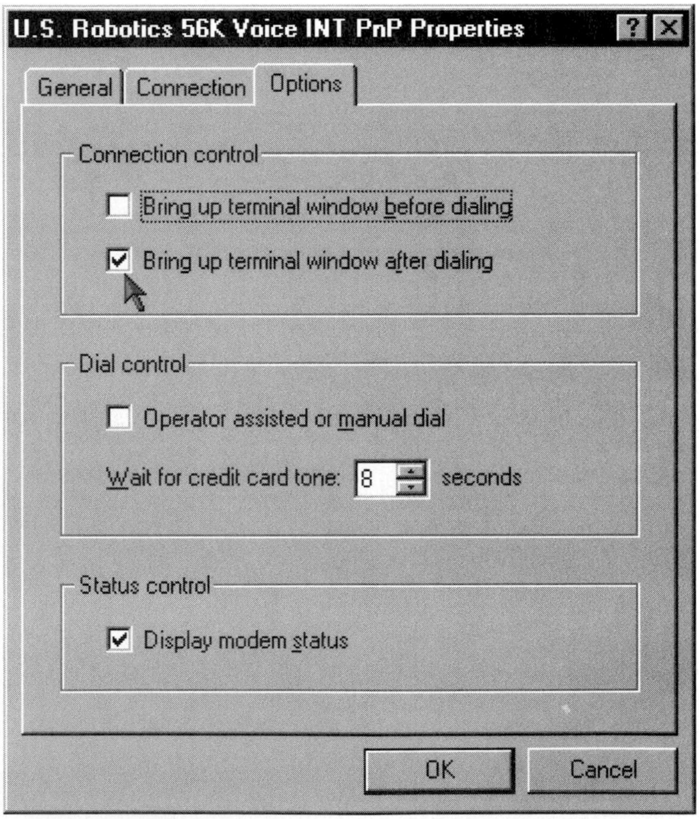

Figure 2.25   Activate a post-dial terminal.

Now, you have successfully created the NU PPP connection, and you are ready to try it. One more issue you need to be aware of is call waiting. If you have call waiting, your connection gets disconnected if someone tries to call you while you are online. To disable call waiting, follow this sequence.

1. Double click the NU connection (figure 2.26).

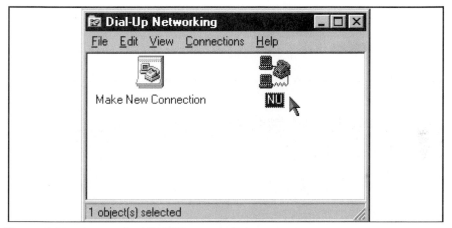

Figure 2.26 Access the NU PPP connection.

2. Click the Dial Properties button (figure 2.27).

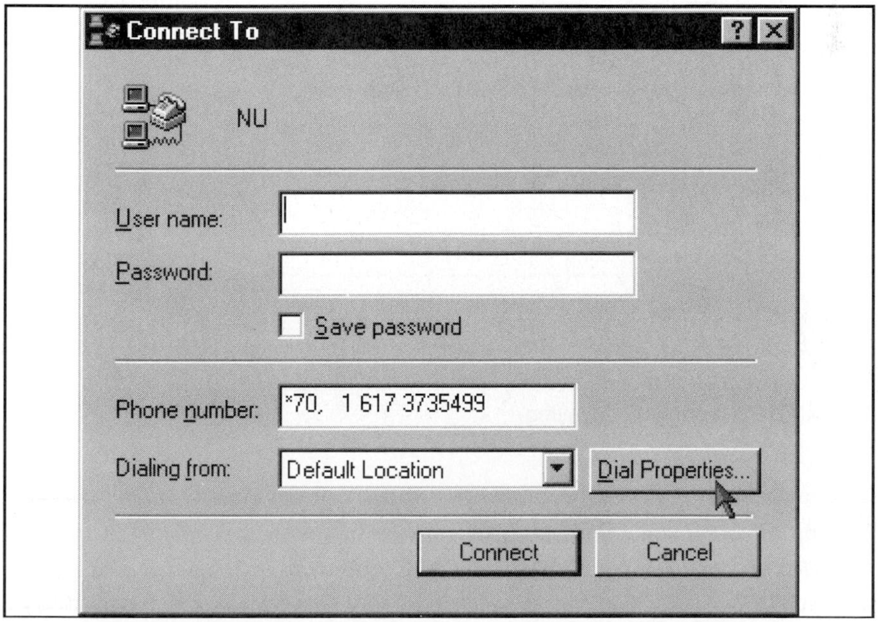

Figure 2.27 Begin to disable call waiting.

3. Enable "This location has call waiting. To disable it, dial".

4. Select "*70," (figure 2.28).

5. Click OK (figure 2.28).

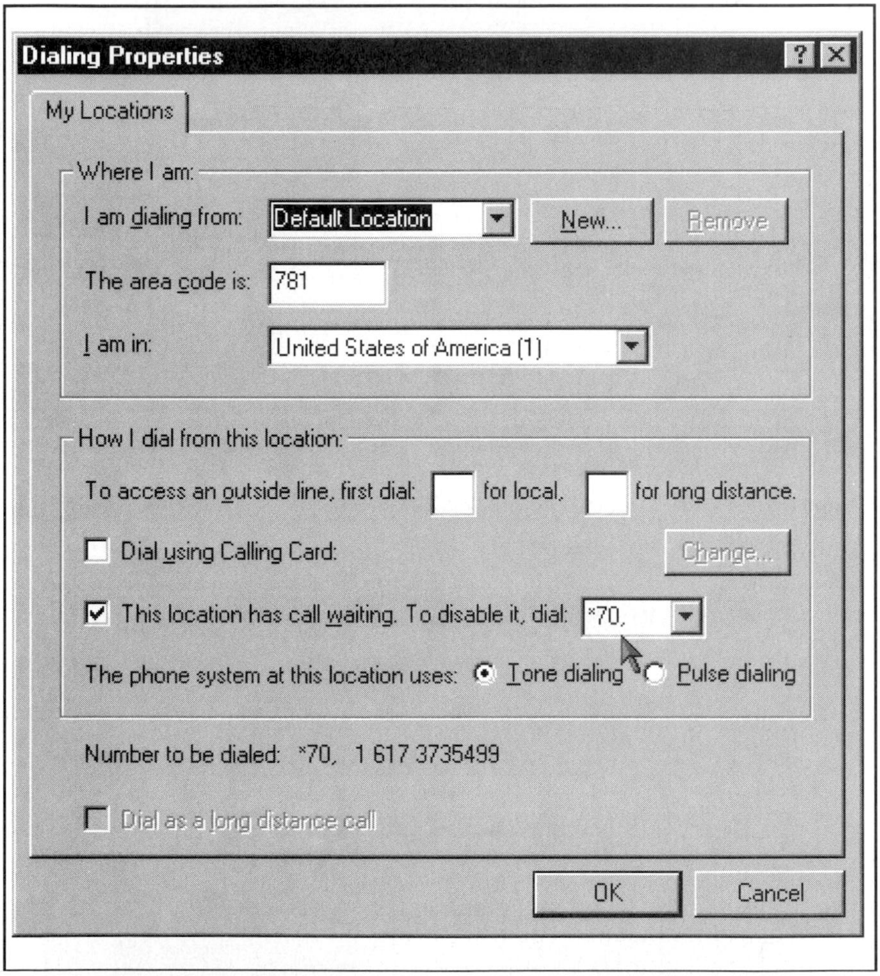

Figure 2.28   Disable call waiting.

You can create as many connections as you like. You can delete existing connections and recreate them. We recommend that you take a closer look at the menus of the menu bar of the Dial-Up Networking window. For example, if you want to delete an existing connection, highlight it by clicking its icon. Click the File menu from the menu bar, then Delete from the menu, and follow the system prompts.

2.6.2 Using a PPP Connection in Windows

It is fairly simple to use the PPP connection you created in tutorial 2.6.1. Follow the following sequence.

1. Double click the NU icon (figure 2.29).

2. Click the Connect button (a post-dial window is displayed) (figure 2.29). When a connection is established, the PC OS displays the post-dial window shown in figure 2.30).

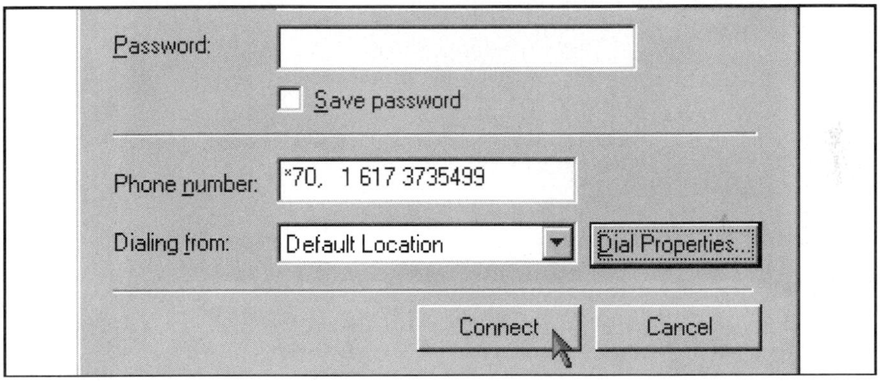

Figure 2.29   Use the NU PPP connection.

3. Type PPP (figure 2.30).

4. Type your username (figure 2.30).

5. Type your password (figure 2.30).

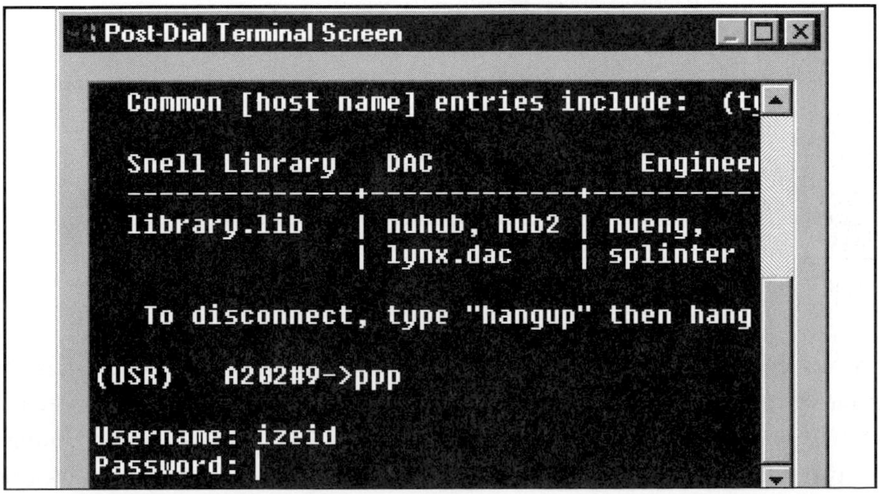

Figure 2.30   Log in to your service provider.

6. Click the Continue button (figure 2.31).

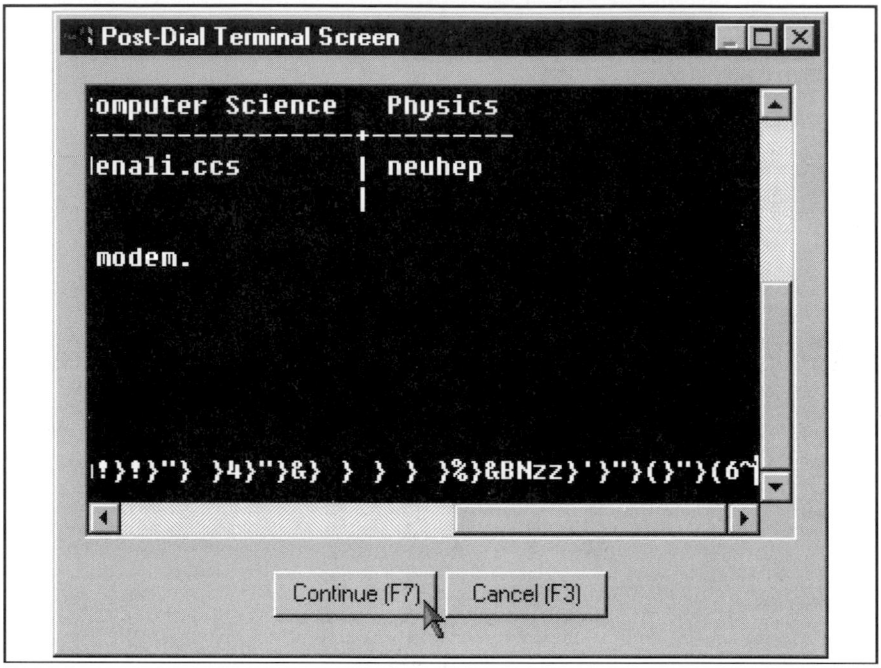

Figure 2.31   Open the NU PPP connection.

Your PC will try to establish a connection with your service provider's server. Once connected, you can surf the Internet. You need a browser. When you run the browser, it finds the PPP connection automatically. When you request a Web site, the browser will find it and connect you to it. See Chapter 3 for more details on browsers and how to use them. After you are done browsing, you simply disconnect the connection by clicking a "Disconnect" button. Note that the sequence to log in to your service provider may be different, but the basic idea should remain the same.

2.7 FAQs

Each chapter has a FAQs (Frequently Asked Questions) section. The section answers the most commonly asked questions related to the chapter material. If you would like to contribute to the FAQs sections in this book, please e-mail the author at zeid@coe.neu.edu. Credit will be given to you in this section.

Q: How can I publish on the Internet? Is my PC with a PPP connection enough?

A: You cannot publish on the Internet using a PPP connection. You need a permanent Internet DNS name, e.g., www.xxx.yyy, for the Internet community to access your Web page with. Some online service providers or ISPs provide their users with Web addresses for free. In general, you need a computer with a permanent DNS address and a dedicated Internet connection. If you do not have this environment, you can lease a Web space from any provider. Many providers offer leasing services. They host, manage, and maintain your Web site.

Q: What can I do to learn more about T1 and T3 lines?

A: While this textbook is not a communication text, interested readers may obtain much more knowledge about T1 and T3 lines (and others) by searching the Internet. Use your favorite search engine (see chapter 3) and use such search strings as "T1 and T3 telephone lines", "cost of T1 and T3 lines", etc.

Q: How can I configure a PPP connection for a Mac computer?

A: A Mac computer needs the same elements as a PC to create a PPP connection. It needs a modem and TCP/IP software. The software you need is OT (Open Transport) and PPP. OT is the TCP/IP for the MAC. There are several versions of PPP software, e.g., FreePPP, MacPPP, and Apple's OT/PPP. MacPPP is reliable. The general steps to create a Mac PPP connection are: to obtain the software, to install PPP, and to configure PPP. For more details, use a search engine, and search for such strings as "Mac PPP", "Mac TCP/IP", and "Mac Open Transport."

Q: Can I use the Internet as a telephone?

A: Yes. Your modem and PPP connection is all you need as hardware. In addition, you need software to allow you to speak in real-time over the Internet. Some software is free. The way it works is similar to a modem. The software converts your sound into digital data that is transmitted as TCP packets to the other person's location. These packets are then converted back to sound. The quality of sound is comparable to that of a regular phone. There may be slight delays for bad PPP connections. Some software allows you and the other person to speak at the same time (known as full duplex). Other software allows only one person to speak at a time (known as half duplex). Some software also allows multicasting, i.e., you can speak to several individuals at the same time (call it audio conferencing). The Internet phone can be used across platforms. A PC user may call a Mac or Unix user. Moreover, you can use your computer to call someone who has a regular phone. There are several telephone software programs. Samples are Netphone and Internet Phone for Macs, CoolTalk (by Netscape) and Internet Phone for Windows, VoiceChat/2 and InterCom for OS/2, and Cyberphone and Rat for Unix. The Internet phone calls are free (beyond your service provider's monthly fee to connect to the Internet).

Q: How do I install a new modem on my PC?

A: Tutorial 2.6.1 assumes that your PC has a modem already installed on it. It is seldom that a PC does not have a modem today. So, why should we bother? Well, even if your PC has a modem, you may need to replace it with a faster one. To install a new modem, you need to remove the old one first, if there is one, from your PC system unit, and insert the new one. This is a simple task. The modem is just a board that snaps into a slot inside your PC. Having installed it physically, follow the following sequence to get Windows to recognize the new modem.

Double click the `My Computer` icon.

Double click the `Control Panel` icon.

Double click the `Modems` icon.

Click the `Add` button.

Click the `Next` button.

Click the `Next` button.

Click the `Finish` button.

Q: How can I set my PPP connection to automatically redial my service provider telephone number?

A: This is a useful feature to have in case if the line is busy. After you create a PPP connection, as shown in tutorial 2.6.1, follow the following sequence. (We assume the `Dial-Up Networking` window is open on the desktop).

Click the `Connections` menu of the `Dial-Up Networking` window.

Click the `Settings` menu item of the `Connections` menu.

Enable `Redial`.

Enter the number of times and other information.

Click `OK`.

Q: How can a company determine what servers (hardware) and software products are necessary to start up its own Web site? huge dollars

A: There are three options. The easiest, but not necessarily the least expensive, route is to contract with a service provider who can do all the work for the company. The second option is buy a turnkey system. This is a ready-to-run system that comes with bundled hardware and software from one vendor. This makes it easier for the company to start its Web site quickly. Turnkey vendors offer Web servers with server software ready to run. There are turnkey systems for both Unix and Windows NT operating systems. It is not as sophisticated as it used to be to run a Web server. There many turnkey vendors today, such as Sun Microsystems, Silicon Graphics, Compaq, Dell, Intergraph, etc. Most turnkey systems use the Netscape Communication Server package. The choice of a turnkey Web server depends largely on how functional, reliable, and easy-to-use it is. Some of the criteria that can be used to choose a turnkey vendor are the ease of installation and its customization, the ease of configuring and managing the server software (e.g., use of HTML forms to configure and manage), and the level of security of the Web server. The third option is the do-it-yourself approach. The company buys a Web server from a hardware vendor such as Dell and buys the server software from a software vendor such as Netscape. In this case, the company Web master has to coordinate all efforts, activities, and maintenance between the two vendors. The Web master must also be more knowledgeable than a Web master of a turnkey server.

Q: What is a network computer?

A: Simply put, a network computer (NC), sometimes known as a thin client, is a stripped-down version of a PC. Or it is like the dumb terminals that used to exist before PCs became available. The notion of a thin client has been promoted by companies such as Oracle, IBM, Sun Microsystems, and others. The idea is to use them as an inexpensive computer to connect to the

Internet. NCs do not have much memory or hard disk. The reasoning is that when you connect to the Internet, you do not need much computing power and you can also download (and pay per use for) any software (e.g., a word processor) you need to use during an online session. You do not have to store the software permanently on your NC. Therefore, you need a very simple computer for the connection. A NC uses the client/server model. The NC is the client that can connect to any Web server. For platform independence, it is ideal for both the NC and the Web server to use the Java-based operating systems and applications. The cost of a NC is minimal.

Q: How can I test my PPP connection if I have not yet installed a browser on my PC?

A: Obviously, if you have a PPP connection but no browser, you cannot surf the net to download a free copy of a browser. You have three options. (1) You can buy a browser CD and install it. (2) If you do not want to pay, you can download on a PC that has a browser, and then use a zip drive to download to your PC. (3) Most PCs come with Microsoft Internet Explorer already installed. You can use it to download other browser software if desired.

Q: What is a WebTV?

A: A WebTV is a television set that allows you to connect to the Internet. It is also supposed to enhance TV programs with online content. You can surf the Internet and send and receive e-mail. WebTV would require a box or a receiver (like a cable TV box) that enables you to access the Internet. Thus, a WebTV allows you to use your TV as a PC. As a matter of fact, you can add an optional keyboard and a printer to your TV set. You can do the opposite and use your PC as a TV, by installing a TV card into your PC. With a TV card, you can watch TV in real-time, on your PC, in a window, while you are performing other computer tasks in other windows. In this case you will need an antenna like a conventional TV.

2.8 Summary

Introduction

•Connecting to the Internet requires a service provider.

•Service providers are classified into two groups: online service providers and ISPs.

•Online service providers, such AOL, provide both connection and content.

•ISPs provide connection only.

•The choice of an online service provider versus an ISP depends largely on user needs.

Connection Requirements

•Connecting to the Internet requires both hardware and software. Hardware is computers and networks. Software is TCP/IP (built into OS) and a browser.

•A home connection typically requires a PC and a modem.

•A commercial connection typically requires PCs, workstations, servers, and a dedicated network.

Managing Host Names via DNS

•Each node (computer) on the Internet has an IP address and a URL. They are equivalent. Humans prefer to use URLs; machines prefer to use IP addresses.

•A DNS server is a computer that converts the DNS names (URLs) into numbers (IP addresses).

Types of Connections

•Two methods of connecting to the Internet exist: dedicated (used mainly by companies and corporations), and dial-up (used mainly by households).

•Dedicated connections provide access around the clock, 24 hours a day, via high-speed lines such as T1 and T3 lines.

•Dial-up connections require modems. Types of modems are analog, DSL, cable, digital, satellite, and cellular. Some types offer faster or more convenient connection than others. For example, cellular modems are ideal for laptops.

SLIP/PPP Connection

•A dial-up connection usually uses PPP protocol (thus the name PPP connection).

•A PPP connection requires an account to connect to the service provider server.

•All service providers make the creation of a PPP connection and the setup of an account transparent to the user. *will not quite true!*

•Creating a PPP connection for Windows requires three steps: configuring the modem, configuring the server, and creating a post-dial window.

PROBLEMS

Exercises

2.1   Create your own PPP connection on your computer. Use the following information to create the connection: *(careful)*
            Phone number: (111) 222-3333
            Connection name: EXCONN   *Solution Strategy: Follow tutorial 2.6.1*

2.2   Modify the above connection to use a phone number of (444) 555-6666 instead.

2.3   Change the name of the connection you created in exercise 2 to be "CONN3".

Homework

2.4   Find an article about online service providers. You can use the paper route (e.g., PC magazine) or the Internet route (search engines such as Metacrawler). Summarize the article in a half a page or a page.

2.5   Repeat question 1, but for ISPs.

2.6   Find an article on how to choose an Internet service provider. Do you find any additional guidelines beyond what is covered in section 2.1 of this chapter?

2.7 Surf the Internet, using a search engine, to find the latest on the T1 and T3 lines. There is also what is called fractional T1 line. What is it?

2.8 Surf the Internet, using a search engine, to find the latest on six of the technologies (telephone modems, cable modems, digital modems, B-ISDN lines, satellite, and cellular modems) for dial-up covered in section 2.4.2.

Solution strategy: Type a search engine name (e.g. www.altavista.com) in a browser URL toolbar. Use a search string such as T1, T3 and fractional T1 line. Document your results.

Netscape Communicator

This chapter discusses Internet browsers and the browsing tasks they support. Browsers are considered the backbone of the Web. Without them, surfers cannot surf the Internet. This chapter covers the basic concepts behind browsers, to provide the reader with a sound background about how browsers work and what they can do. To this end, the chapter begins by covering browser definition, the different types of protocols a browser supports, how it finds a URL, the tasks it can perform, and an overview of browsers. This overview is generic and is not related to a particular browser. The overview describes GUI structure of browsers, managing Web pages within a browser, browser cache, helper applications, plug-ins, and customizing a browser. After presenting the basic concepts of browsers, the chapter applies them by covering Netscape Communicator version 4.7. The two main browsers that exist are Netscape Communicator and Microsoft Internet Explorer. Chapter 4 applies these concepts to Microsoft Internet Explorer. For Netscape Communicator, this chapter covers both the downloading and installation procedures, as well as a description of the GUI. The tutorials section at the end of the chapter covers how to use the browser for certain tasks. The tasks covered in the tutorials are e-mail, visiting Web sites, downloading files, checking page encryption and security, running multiple copies of a browser, dealing with Web pages, using a browser to open local files, dealing with bookmarks, and creating and using address books.

3.1 Introduction

To access the Internet, and more specifically the Web, you need an Internet connection and a browser. A Web browser is a program that decodes the hidden tags in Web documents, turning them into richly formatted documents with fonts, graphics, colors, audio, video, and animation. In addition, browsers originate messages that locate and retrieve documents every time you click a hyperlink. The first browser, NCSA Mosaic, was developed at the National Center for Super-computer Applications at the University of Illinois in the late 1980s and early 1990s. It launched the hypertext movement. It was an obscure piece of freeware for viewing academic documents. Mosaic has since spawned many browsers, including the Netscape Communicator and Microsoft Internet Explorer.

A Web browser has a GUI (Graphical User Interface) that allows its users to search the Internet, read their e-mail, participate in discussion groups, display Web pages, run Java applets, and so forth. A browser can, in a broader sense, can be viewed as a platform-independent operating system (OS). This view becomes critical if, in the future, most of the tasks we perform daily become Internet- or Web-based. A Web browser has a complex structure, from a software point of view. A browser is a client/server application. It establishes communication between a remote server and a client user. The browser opens a client connection and requests a specific Web page from a remote server. Figure 3.1 shows the software components of a Web browser.

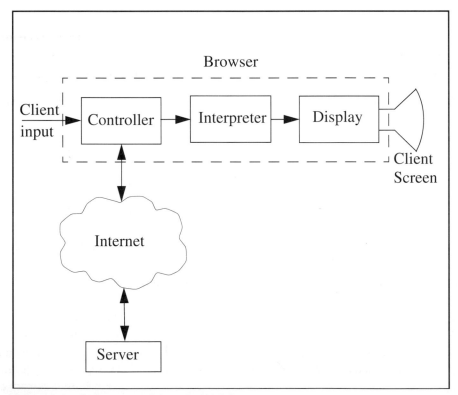

Figure 3.1   Software modules of a Web browser.

In the figure, let us assume that the client is a user of a PC that is connected to the Internet via a dial-up connection. The user input to the browser could be via a mouse or a keyboard.

Once the browser receives input, its controller component determines the type of protocol to use, sends a request to the appropriate server, and waits for a response from the server. Finding the appropriate server is described in section 3.2. Once the controller receives a response, it sends it to the interpreter component. This component uses the same protocol as that of the controller to decode the response. The response is usually a Web page. The display component of the browser displays the contents for the user to view.

There are seven types of protocol used on the Web and supported by browsers:

1. http: hypertext protocol. It is used for Web sites. An example is http://www.nue.edu.

2. mailto: send an e-mail message to a specified address. An example is emailto:zeid@coe.neu.edu.

3. news (NNTP): Usenet news site. An example is news:alt.internet.servics.

4. ftp: file transfer protocol, to access files from remote sites. An example is ftp://ftp.netscape.com.

5. telnet: protocol to access a remote server via terminal emulation. An example is telnet://locis.loc.gov.

6. gopher: protocol to access a gopher site. An example is gopher://gopher.micro.umn.edu.

7. file: display a file on the client local drive without connecting to the Internet. An example is ftp://c://dir1/dir2/filename.txt.

These protocols are used with URLs. The default protocol is HTTP. If a user does not specify a protocol with a URL, the browser uses HTTP to send and receive information from this URL. In addition to protocols, URLs may occasionally use what are known as port numbers. A port is a "logical connection" that allows a client program (such as a browser) to specify a particular server program (such as HTTP). For example, the HTTP server program and the client browser program use (bind to) port 80 to communicate. Port numbers used by the Web are standard and do not have to be specified. A URL containing a port number ends with the number following a colon, such as www.abc.com:80. There are well-known port numbers for the Web types of protocols. They are 80, 25, 110, 119, 21, 23, and 70 for (respectively) HTTP, SMTP (send mail), POP (retrieve mail), news (NNTP), ftp, telnet, and gopher. The TCP/IP protocol, which delivers the specific kinds (HTTP, ftp, etc.) of IP packets across the Internet to a remote server, hands off the packets to the server through the standard port number. This guarantees that the server is able to handle the packets successfully. Some servers may request that packets of a certain type go to a non-standard port number. In this case, this number is used as part of the server URL. One reason port numbers are used in URLs is that a Web site may be experimental, in a development stage, or not ready for public use. In most cases, URLs do not contain port numbers. If you try a URL with a port number and it does not work, try it without the port number.

3.2 Finding a Web Page

This section describes how a browser finds a Web site or a Web page that the user requests. Figure 3.2 shows the process.We can identify four steps in Figure 3.2 that a browser uses to find a Web page.

1. URLs uniquely identify each file on the Web by specifying its name, what server it is on, and where it is in the server's directory structure. Entering a URL directly into your browser or clicking on a hyperlink with an associated URL initiates a communications session that (when successful) ultimately brings that unique file to your PC or workstation. URLs are sent as TCP/IP packets through the Internet, as discussed in Chapter 2. A URL includes the sender's computer (node) IP address as well as the IP address of the server where the document or the Web page resides. Routing information is added to the packets along the way. Once your browser has the IP address of the server containing the document requested, it initiates the communication session with that server.

2. The browser sends a URL to the Domain Name System (DNS) server which replies with the IP address of the server you wish to contact. It does this by checking a lookup table that cross-references server domain names and IP addresses. This is the IP address included in the TCP/IP packets mentioned in step 1. The DNS server may be within a corporate LAN or maintained by a service provider.

3. The TCP/IP packets make their way to the server you want to contact by passing through large numbers of routers, both inside and outside corporate boundaries, before reaching their final destination. Routers can be owned by corporations and Internet providers or be part of the Internet backbone itself. Packets, like post cards, can be read along the path they take. There is no privacy associated with them unless they are sent secure (encrypted).

4. Once the remote Web server receives the TCP/IP packets, it tries to locate the specific file requested. Once found, it sends the file, along with your IP address as outbound TCP/IP packets to your browser. These outbound TCP/IP packets go through various routers to get back to you the fastest possible way.

Security is a major issue in wireless communications, as when we deal with Web pages on the Web. Secure Web pages and connections prevent unauthorized access to the information passed between clients and servers. All e-commerce and online applications that require credit card or social security numbers or other personal sensitive information must be secure to prevent any misuse of the information. Similarly, sensitive online discussions of company secrets between departments must be kept secure.

Encryption and decryption techniques are commonly used over the Internet to create secure connections between Web servers and client computers whenever they are needed. Encryption is defined as the conversion of data into a form (known as a cipher) that is very difficult to understand by hackers if they are ever successful in intercepting the data. Decryption is the opposite process; it converts encrypted data back into its original form that is understandable by humans. The encryption/decryption can start at either the server or the client end, depending on the flow of communication between the two.

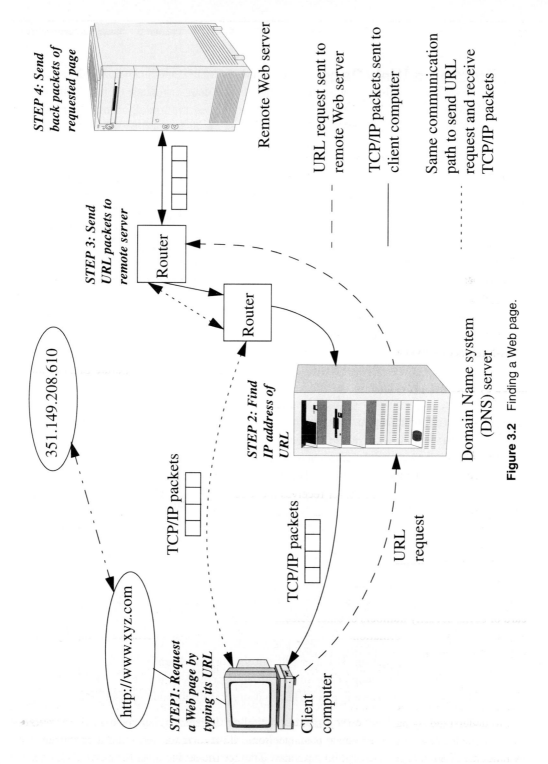

STEP 4: Send back packets of requested page

Remote Web server

STEP 3: Send URL packets to remote server

Router

Router

STEP 2: Find IP address of URL

Domain Name system (DNS) server

351.149.208.610

TCP/IP packets

TCP/IP packets

URL request

http://www.xyz.com

STEP1: Request a Web page by typing its URL

Client computer

- - - URL request sent to remote Web server

——— TCP/IP packets sent to client computer

.... Same communication path to send URL request and receive TCP/IP packets

Figure 3.2 Finding a Web page.

German is good but!

Both encryption and decryption use complex computer and mathematical algorithms. Simple encryption algorithms may rotate the letters of the data, or replace them by numbers, or add frequencies to scramble voice signals. More complex encryption algorithms rearrange the bits of the data in digital signals. Decryption algorithms use decryption keys (complec code) to recover the contents of the encrypted data easily. They undo the work of the encryption algorithms. There are different levels of encryption/decryption. Some algorithms are very complex, producing so-called strong, encryption which is unbreakable without decryption keys. While it is desirable to have strong encryption, it is more expensive to encrypt and decrypt; however, if the encryption algorithm is not complex enough, hackers may decrypt the data via a computer by trying different algorithms of their own.

How is the encryption/decryption technology implemented over the Web? Both Web servers and browsers use a technology that has been developed by Netscape to manage security of data transmission between them. It is known as Secure Sockets Layer (SSL). The communication between Web servers and browsers uses the well-known client/server model. On the basis of this model, they use sockets to connect to each other. There is a server-side socket that "talks" to a client-side socket. SSL creates a layer between the server and the client that implements secure data transmission. Thus, SSL is a program that passes data back and forth, between a Web server and a client browser, securely. SSL is a standard technology used by Web applications. SSL is an integral part of Web browsers. When a user connects to a Web server that requires secure communication, the browser notifies the user. The user does not have to do anything other than feeling better about the security of the data that is about to be communicated between the Web server and the user's browser.

SSL technology uses what is know as the public-and-private key encryption system from RSA Data Security, a subsidiary of Security Dynamics. This system uses two keys: a public key to encrypt data, and a private key to decrypt data. The two keys are a set of two numbers that are generated randomly. The private key is used to decrypt data that has been encrypted by the public key. The keys come in pairs that are not interchangeable. The private key is never sent over the Internet. Only the public key is sent. The private key is known only by its owner. To explain the use of these two keys, we'll consider the filling out of a form with a credit card number for online shopping. When the user downloads the Web page of the form from the Web server of the shopping site, the server generates the two keys, and sends only the public key with the form. When the user's browser receives the Web page, it checks for a key, it finds one, and therefore establishes a secure connection. The user fills out the form and sends it. The browser uses the public key of the page to encrypt the form data and sends it to the server. When the server receives, it uses the corresponding private key to decrypt the data and processes the form.

Another part of encryption is known as digital certificate. Digital certificates are used for digital signature. A digital certificate is an electronic ID similar to, say, a credit card or driver's license. It is issued by a certification authority. The certificate includes the person's name, the expiration date, a public key, and the digital signature of the issuer of the certificate. These certificates are kept in registries, so that their owners can look up their public keys, like a deed of a house.

3.3 Browser Tasks

What should you look for when picking a browser? Part of the answer depends on what you will use the browser for, but any one you consider should include some important core features. The most important is a fast, accurate hypertext markup language (HTML) rendering engine. In picking a browser to use with Intranets, some special considerations apply. While multimedia may not be on the top of your list, programmability (particularly with Java) should be a serious consideration. The common tasks that a good browser should support are the following.

1. Navigation. This task is the bedrock of a browser. Navigation is provided by a logical, attractively designed interface with a full set of well-placed navigation controls. A bookmark system provide a good navigation tool. It provides an easy approach to categorization (organizing sites you have chosen under headings), easily customizable listings, and the ability to import and export bookmarks (as well as editing bookmark names). A browser also provides a caching scheme. The browser maintains a cache of pages you have already visited, so that you can return to a page you have visited without having to reload it from the server, via the "Back" and "Forward" buttons (icons) in the browser interface. The size of the cache and the frequency with which it is updated can be tuned and controlled by the user.

2. Complex viewing. This is a measure of the browser support of HTML standards and common HTML extensions. A browser should support tables and frames and check that they are correctly rendered. It should also support marquee and non-scrolling background, progressive (interlaced) JPEG display, client-side image maps, and secure sockets or secure transmission. Support for *progressive* GIF and JPEG (where a low-resolution version of the image is rendered almost immediately and then progressively sharpened as the remaining information is received) is a good feature for the browser to have. The browser should also support the standard bitmap graphics formats, including .BMP, .GIF, .JPEG (JPG), .PCX and .TIFF.

3. Multimedia and languages. A variety of audio, video, and animation formats, collectively known as MIME (multipurpose Internet mail extension) data types, are now found on a large number of Web sites. There are seven main MIME types. They are text, application, image, audio, video, multipart, and message. All browsers support them and their formats. Image formats are as mentioned in 2. Audio formats include AU, Iwave, RealAudio, and WAV. Video formats include AVI, MPEG, and QuickTime. The languages that browsers support are Java, JavaScript, and VBScript.

4. E-mail, FTP, Telnet, news. These are the tasks that existed before the Web became popular. Browsers support these tasks and make them easier to do. Earlier versions of browsers supported FTP and Telnet tasks, but current versions do not. These tasks are easily achieved via Windows-based shareware as discussed in chapter 4.

5. Downloading files. This is a task that the popularity of the Web made it very easy to achieve. After a user finds a file on the Web, clicking a download hyperlink downloads the file. The browser makes the downloading process fairly simple by guiding the user. Prior to using browsers, the user would have to log in to an FTP site and use FTP commands to download files.

6. Printing. This is a simple but useful task. The user can print a Web page displayed by the browser, via the browser's print function. The user can then include these hard copies in reports or any documents.

3.4 Overview of Browsers

A Web browser is an application that has a GUI that allows Web users to perform the tasks discussed in section 3.3. A browser GUI is based on MOTIF guidelines created by the Open Software Foundation (www.opengroup.org). Many existing GUIs today, including those of browsers, are built using these guidelines. It is therefore not a coincidence that most browsers, including the two popular ones from Netscape Communications (the Communicator) and Microsoft (Internet Explorer), look and feel alike in terms of the placement of their title bars and menus. On this basis, this section provides a generic overview of browsers and covers their related basic concepts. Such coverage and concepts can be mapped very easily to a specific browser that may be of interest to the reader. Sections 3.5 and 3.6 will also map these concepts and coverage to both Netscape Communicator and Microsoft Internet Explorer (MS IE).

3.4.1 Browser GUI Structure

The generic structure of a browser GUI is shown in figure 3.3. The GUI is simple; it consists of several bars on the top of the GUI window and one bar on the bottom. In between is the display area. The title bar is at the very top of the GUI window. It displays the title of the current Web page being viewed. This title is the text that goes between the title HTML tags. (See the HTML part of this book). The menu bar is located directly below the title bar. It contains the pull-down menus that we are familiar with and that are part of the MOTIF standard. These menus, from left to right, are File, Edit, View, Go, xxx, and Help. The xxx is a menu that depends on the specific browser. It is the Favorites menu in MS IE and the Communicator menu in Netscape browser version 4.7. The File, Edit, View and Help menus are similar to those found in word processors' GUIs. For the most part they are self-explanatory and easy to use. The Go menu can be viewed as a navigation menu. It allows the user to go back, forward, to the home Web page, and so forth .

Following the menu bar are several toolbars. These toolbars are used for navigation. Both MS IE and Netscape Communicator have 3 toolbars each. For MS IE, they are Standard Buttons, Address Bar, and Links. For Netscape Communicator, they are Navigation Toolbar, Location Toolbar and Personal Toolbar. The details of these toolbars are covered in Chapter 3 for Netscape Communicator and in Chapter 4 for Microsoft Internet Explorer.

The bar at the bottom of the browser window is the status bar. The browser displays messages to its users in this bar to inform them about the progress of the current task. For example, if the current task is downloading a Web page, the browser displays a text or visual message of how much of the page has been already downloaded and how much is remaining.

The display area of the browser window shows the contents of the current Web page or file. If the Web page is too big to fit within the display area, the browser creates horizontal and/or vertical scrollbars automatically, to enable the user to scroll up/down and/or left/right to view the page.

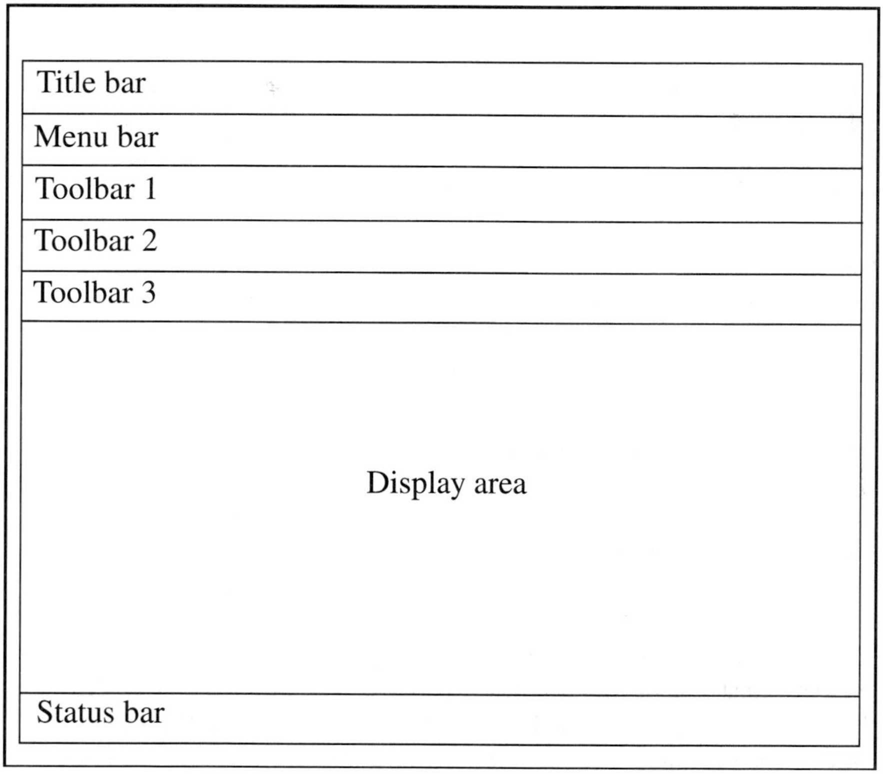

Figure 3.3 Structure of a browser GUI.

3.4.2 Web Pages and Their Management

One can think of the Web as an enormous collection of documents that we refer to as Web pages. We frequently use Web pages, documents, or sites to mean the same thing. A Web page is a file (or an HTML document, as described in chapter 7) that a browser displays on its display area. The file stores the code (HTML tags and JavaScript code) that the browser interprets before displaying the contents of the Web page on its screen. The contents of a Web page include all or some of the MIME types. MIME has had a dramatic impact on Web pages, because it took them far beyond the ASCII text that existed for a long time. MIME is attractive to users because they can easily send and receive e-mail attachments containing pictures, sounds, and other non-ASCII file formats. DDE. (dynamic Data exchange)

Each Web page has three aspects: its URL, its display in the browser, and its HTML file. Managing Web pages deal with these three aspects. A user may be interested in saving the page URL for future downloading; or the user may want to print the page display in the browser; or users who are Web developers may want to look at or save the source including HTML tags and JavaScript code. To save a page URL, the Web surfer uses the browser to create a bookmark (as Netscape calls it) or a favorite (as MS IE calls it). To print a page, the Web surfer uses the print function of the browser. To save the page HTML tags and JavaScript code to the local hard disk, the Web surfer uses the Save As menu item from the browser File menu. This save allows the surfer to view the page code offline at a later, convenient time.

3.4.3 Browser Cache

Browsers, like other applications, use the cache concept to improve document access. You probably have noticed that, when you return to Web pages you have visited during the current session, the browser displays them more quickly than it did the first time. After a Web page is downloaded from the Internet during a session, the browser keeps a copy of it in a cache on the local computer. When the user requests a Web page, the browser checks the cache first before downloading a fresh copy from the Internet. If the requested page is found in the cache, the browser displays it without using the Internet again. Keeping visited Web pages in the browser cache improves performance dramatically, especially at times of heavy Internet traffic.

A cache is a storage location. A browser uses two types of caching schemes: memory and disk. The memory cache is a portion of your computer's RAM that the browser uses to store the most recently downloaded or accessed Web pages or documents during the current session of surfing the Internet. A browser typically has a default size for its cache. The user can change this size if needed. If the total size of the Web pages a user has downloaded during one session exceeds the current size of the browser memory cache, older pages are removed (flushed) from the cache to create space for the new additional pages being downloaded. At the end of a browser session, the memory cache is erased and released back to your computer's available RAM for other applications to use.

The disk cache is a portion of your computer's hard disk that the browser uses to store previously downloaded Web pages. Like memory cache, a browser has a default size for its disk cache that the user can change. The browser disk cache is flushed in a way similar to the memory cache. However, unlike the memory cache, the disk cache retains Web documents between browser sessions.

The browser uses the two types of caches according to the following scenario. Figure 3.4 shows three options that could happen when a user loads a Web page. Let us assume that Web page A is available on the Internet only, Web page B is available in the browser memory cache, and Web page C is available in the browser disk cache. This assumption means that the user has not accessed Web page A prior to the current session of the browser, the user has accessed Web page B during the current session, and that the user accessed Web page C in a previous browser session. Therefore, the browser has three options (as shown in figure 3.4) to retrieve a Web page: from the Internet, from its memory cache, or from its disk cache. The browser retrieves the requested page in the fastest possible way. Thus, it first checks its memory cache, trying to locate the Web page, then its disk cache, and finally the Internet itself. The browser retrieves Web page A from the Internet, Web page B from its memory cache, and Web page C from its disk cache. While it is highly unlikely that Web page B will change during the current session of the browser, Web page C may have changed since the last session the user downloaded. To guard against this possibility, the browser usually contacts the Web server and attempts to verify whether the contents of Web page C have been altered since its last retrieval. If it has, the browser retrieves the latest contents from the server, otherwise it retrieves the page from its disk cache. By contrast with retrieving Web pages from its disk cache, the browser does not contact Web servers when retrieving Web pages from its memory cache. Retrieving Web pages from a browser cache happens when the user uses the Back and Forward buttons of the browser.

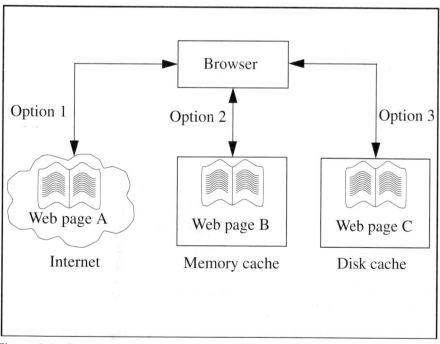

Figure 3.4   Browser caches.

To help users control how a browser handles the cache, most browsers allow their users to change the size of both memory and disk caches. With today's computers, the user should not worry about increasing the sizes of both caches. As the available cache space is filled, old Web pages are replaced with new ones. Decreasing the size of cache will decrease the chances of having Web pages previously retrieved available. A user who does not want to store Web pages between browser sessions should set the disk cache of the browser to zero. Setting the memory cache to zero (see section 3.8 on how to do it for Netscape Communicator using its `Edit` menu) forces the browser to retrieve any Web page from its Web server on the Internet every time during a browser session. Obviously, this affects the speed of accessing Web pages on the Internet.

3.4.4 Helper Applications

Browsers can handle many types of files. For example, browsers in general support JPEG (Photographic Experts Group) and GIF (Graphics Interchange Format) images; however, there may be some files that browsers cannot handle, such as zipped, movies (video), sound, animation, and virtual realty modeling language (VRML). For these types of files, the browser launches a "helper" application that can handle the file or saves the file for you to view later. A helper application is a program that runs independently of the browser. The helper program appears in a new, separate window. A browser starts a helper application when it encounters a type of data or file it cannot handle directly. Users usually do not need to change helper applications, because browsers come preconfigured to handle all common types of files. However, experienced users may want to add a new helper application to handle a new type of a file. This can be accomplished either via the browser or via the operating system.

When a browser encounters a file type that it cannot handle via its existing helper applications or plug-ins, it displays a message letting the user know that it cannot handle the file and requests a helper application or a plug-in. In such a case, the user needs to specify a helper application or install a plug-in. For a plug-in, the user needs to download it, install it, and configure it. This process is almost automatic and easy to follow.

3.4.5 Plug-Ins

Plug-ins offer a more sophisticated alternative. A plug-in is a program that, after installation, runs within the browser window, thus extending its capabilities. Even though it is a separate program, a plug-in appears to be part of the browser. Plug-ins are better to use than helper applications. Plug-ins are, like helper applications, written by third parties, but they are specifically written to an application programming interface (API) exposed by the browser. As such, they can work more transparently with the browser and are able to display MIME contents directly inside the browser window. Experienced users should be able to install plug-ins into their browsers. Disabling a plug-in is equivalent to removing (uninstalling) it from the computer.

3.4.6 Customizing Browsers

Browsers allow their users to customize them to make them look and feel as they want. Users customize browsers by changing their default options. A user can specify the default Web page that the browser uses when it is invoked. A user can also control the fonts and colors that a browser uses, control the toolbars that a browser displays, enable/disable the displaying of images in Web pages, enable/disable Java and/or JavaScript, use style sheets (special sheets that define formats used by browsers to render Web pages), accept cookies (think of cookies as hidden registration forms that are used by some Web sites you visit to collect harmless information about you such as your server name and the date you visit the site), configure mail and newsgroups servers, and change the size of cache. All these activities are part of installing and configuring a browser.

Thus far, the chapter has provided an overview of the basic concepts that any browser utilizes as a foundation. The remainder of the chapter covers the Netscape Communicator version 4.7 (the professional edition); chapter 4 will cover MS IE version 5.0. These are the latest versions of each browser at the time of writing. As the readers go through the mechanics of the two browsers, they should also focus on the concepts behind them. This should enable them to extend the covered material to future versions of both browsers easily.

3.5 Downloading

To obtain the latest version of Netscape Communicator, let us assume that you have an Internet connection, as discussed in chapter 2, and that you have an older version of a browser (either the Communicator or MS IE) running on your PC. With these assumptions, you have two choices to download the latest version. You use the Netscape Web site www.netscape.com or the Netscape anonymous FTP site ftp.netscape.com.

To use the Netscape Web site, type www.netscape.com in your current browser's URL bar. Look for a link that reads "Download" on the Netscape Web page that is loaded into your current browser window. Click the following link sequence separated by =>; Download => Windows 95/98/NT => Download without SmartDownload. After the last click, the browser displays a Save As dialog box that allows you to choose a download directory or folder (Save in:) on your local hard disk and a name for the executable (File name:). It is a good idea to download in the Desktop so that you can easily see the software. While you may specify a directory of your choice, you should accept the default file name (cc32e47). The default name indicates the program name, its type, and its version. In this case, cc32e47 means complete Communicator for 32-bit applications, edition (version) 4.7. Figure 3.5 shows the Save As dialog box. Upon your clicking the Save button of this dialog box, a Saving Location dialog box with a progress meter is displayed, as shown in figure 3.6. The box also displays the directory and the file name you have chosen. If you do not see this dialog box, there may be some delay or some error in connecting with the server that contains the software you want. You may need to try downloading again. When downloading has finished, the dialog box will close.

If you use Netscape FTP to download, type ftp.netscape.com in your current browser's URL bar to connect to Netscape FTP server. Click the following link sequence separated by =>; pub => communicator => english => 4.7 => windows => windows95 or nt => professional edition => cp32e47.exe. This sequence leads to the same two dialog boxes as before. The rest of the downloading process is the same.

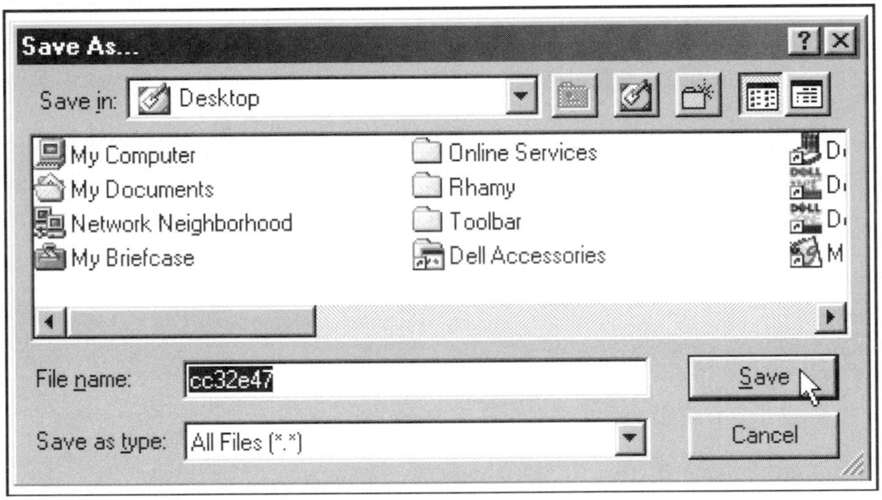

Figure 3.5   Downloading Netscape Communicator: save options.

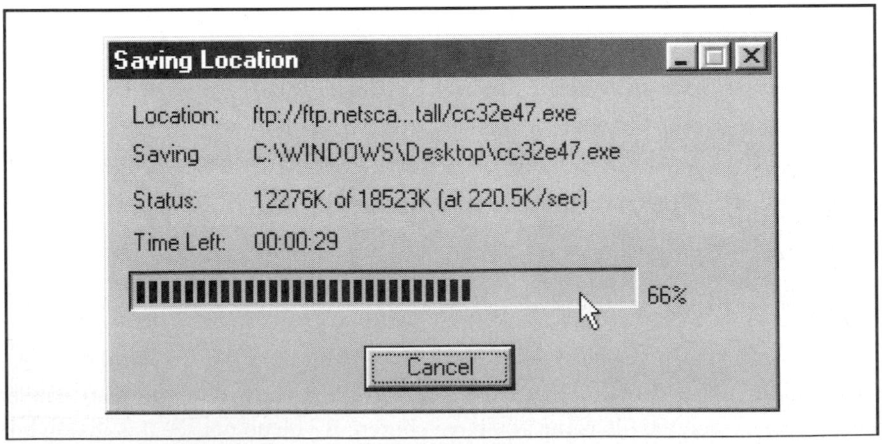

Figure 3.6   Downloading Netscape Communicator: progress meter.

3.6 Installing

Before you can use the software you downloaded, you must install it on your computer. All downloaded software comes compressed (zipped) to save disk space and to speed up the downloading. There are two types of zipped file: self-extracting, and non-self-extracting. The former type unzips and installs itself. The latter type requires an unzip shareware such as WIN-ZIP to unzip. The Netscape executable (cc32e47.exe) is a self-extracting file.

The installation procedure of Netscape Communicator is simple and is almost the same for all operating systems (Windows, Macintosh, Unix, Linux, etc.). We cover the procedure for Windows here. The installation begins by double-clicking the downloaded executable cc32e47.exe. A series of setup dialog windows is displayed. The user reads and responds to them. For successful installation, click the following sequence: Next (to continue with Setup program) => Yes (accept license agreement) => Next (accept defaults for type of setup and destination directory) => Next (accept Netscape Communicator as the Internet default browser) => Next (accept default Program Folder) => Install (accept defaults). Figures 3.7–3.12 show the screen captures of the corresponding displayed dialog boxes to this sequence. At the end of the installation procedure, the setup program notifies you that you must restart your computer for the newly installed browser to work.

If you are replacing an old version of Netscape with a new one, the old version will be overwritten, but the setup program saves your existing bookmarks, preferences, settings, and address book.

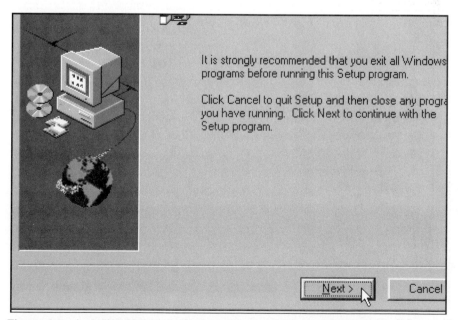

It is strongly recommended that you exit all Windows programs before running this Setup program.

Click Cancel to quit Setup and then close any program you have running. Click Next to continue with the Setup program.

Next >   Cancel

Figure 3.7 Installing Netscape Communicator: continue with setup.

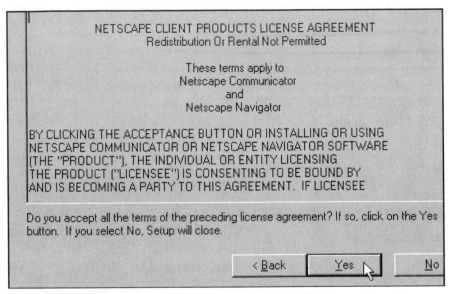

Figure 3.8   Installing Netscape Communicator: accept license agreement.

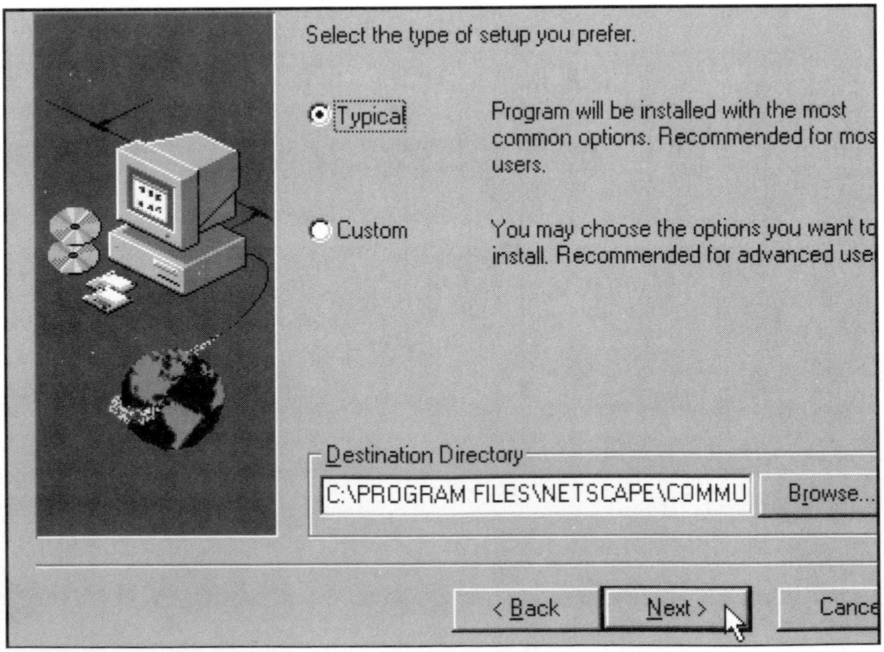

Figure 3.9   Installing Netscape Communicator:accept defaults.

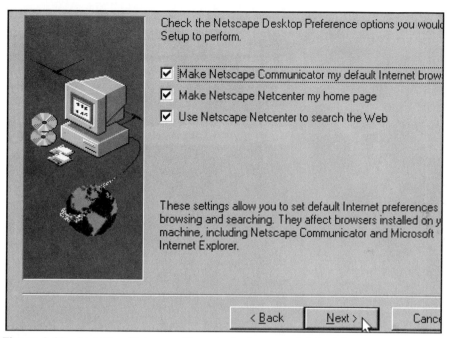

Figure 3.10   Installing Netscape Communicator:accept default browser.

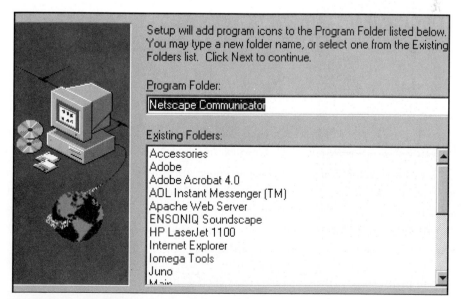

Figure 3.11   Installing Netscape Communicator: accept default program folder.

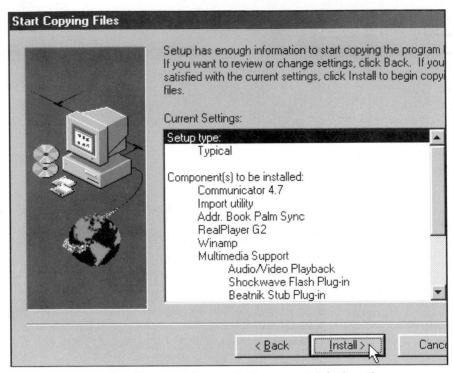

Figure 3.12 Installing Netscape Communicator: accept default settings.

3.7 Graphical User Interface

The Communicator graphical user interface (GUI) is shown in figure 3.13. The figure shows the `Title` bar, the `Menu` bar, the `Navigation Toolbar`, the `Location Toolbar`, the `Personal Toolbar`, and the `Status` bar. The `Title` bar shows the title of the current Web page; that is, Empty page. The browser appends "- Netscape" to the title. The page title is the text that is enclosed between the <TITLE> tags, as we will discuss later in the HTML part of the book.

The Communicator consists of five modules: `Navigator`, `Inbox`, `Newsgroups`, `Address Book`, and `Composer`. Figure 3.13 shows the five modules. The `Navigator` is the essential module, whose GUI is shown in figure 3.13. The `Inbox` and `Newsgroups` modules enable users to deal with their e-mail and newsgroups messages. Users can use the `Address Book` to save e-mail addresses. The `Composer` is the Netscape HTML editor that is used to develop Web pages. This chapter covers the details of the first four modules. The fifth module, the `Composer`, is covered in the HTML part of this book.

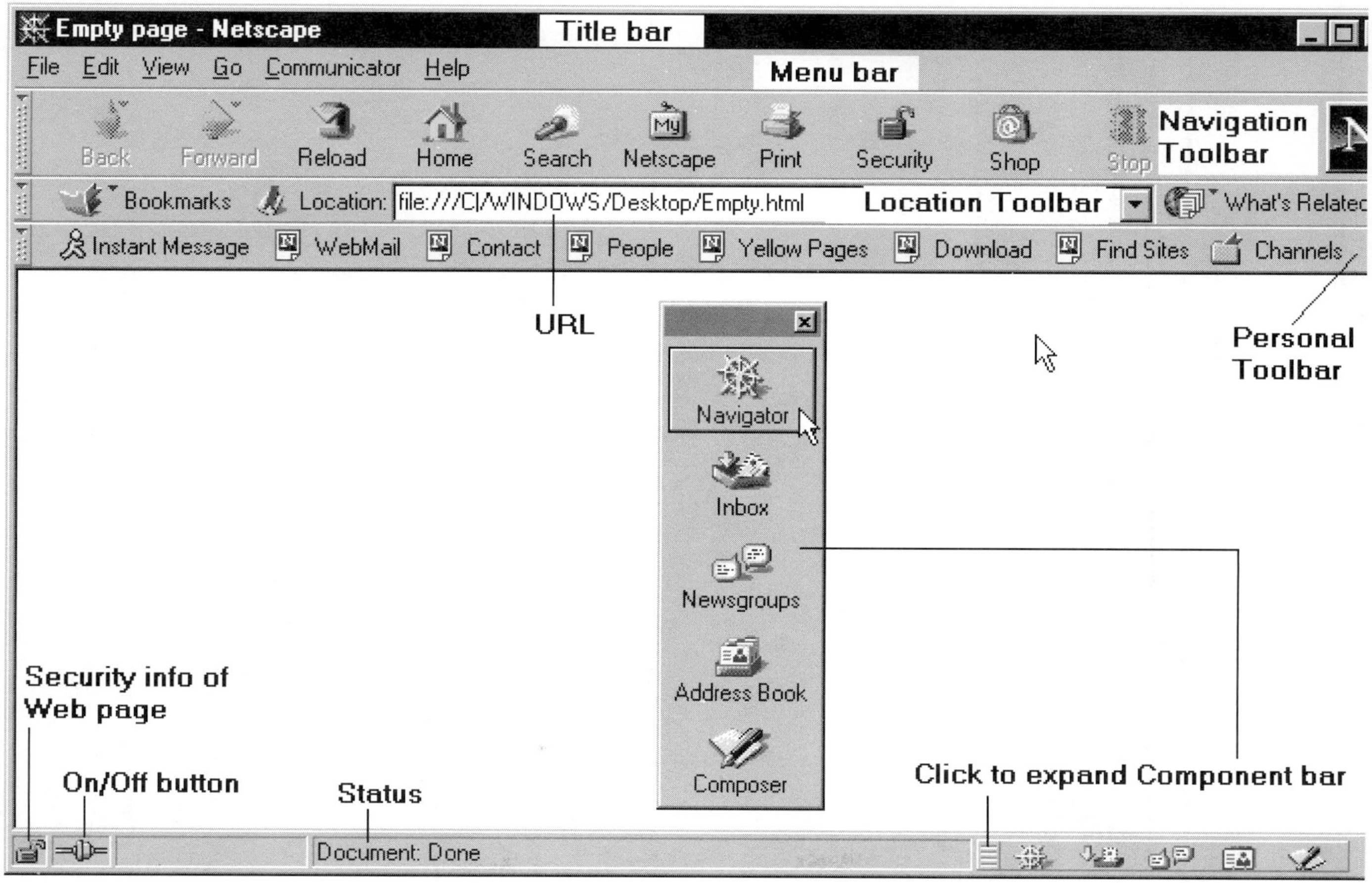

Figure 3.13 The Communicator GUI

3.8 Menu Bar

The Menu bar has six menus: File, Edit, View, Go, Communicator, and Help. The File menu and its submenus are shown in figure 3.14. The File menu is similar to File menus found in word processors. The New submenu allows you to open a new browser (Navigator Window), an e-mail window (Message), or a new Web page (Blank Page, Page From Template, or Page From Wizard) for creation and/or editing. The new Web page could be blank or an existing template. The browser opens the Web page in its HTML editor, as we will discuss later in the HTML part of the book. The Open Page menu item allows the user to open a file or folder in the browser. While this could be any file, we usually open an HTML file (Web page), whether it resides on the local hard disk or on the Internet. The Page Setup, Print Preview, and Print menu items act similarly to the corresponding items one encounters in word processors' GUIs. The Close or Exit menu item closes the current browser window.

The Edit menu and its menu items are shown in figure 3.15. We discuss some of these items here. The Cut, Copy, Paste, and Select All menu items work similarly to the corresponding menu items one encounters on word processors' Edit menu. The Find in Page menu item allows the user to find elements of the currently displayed Web page. The Search Internet invokes Netscape's own search tools to surf the Internet.

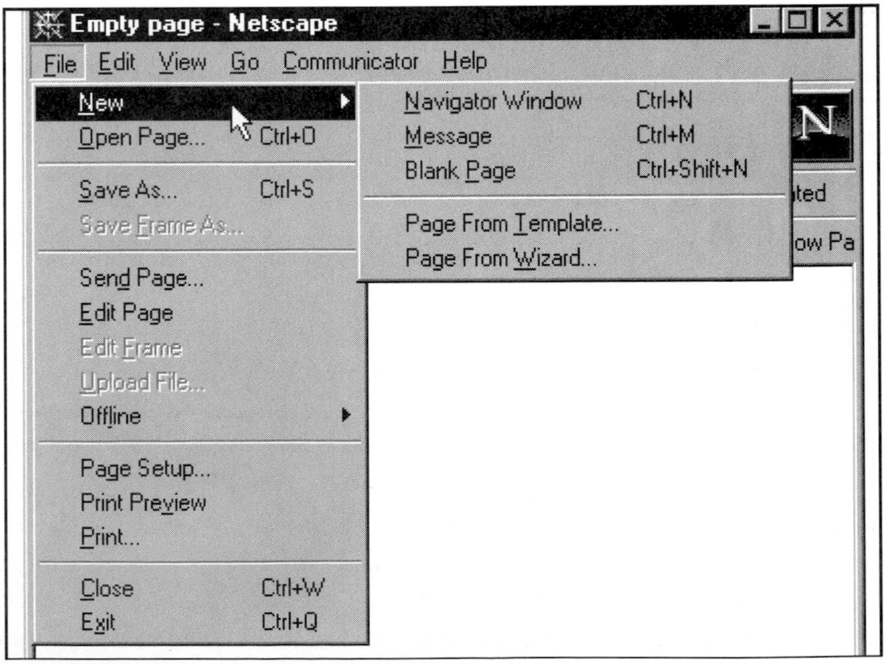

Figure 3.14 The File menu of the Communicator.

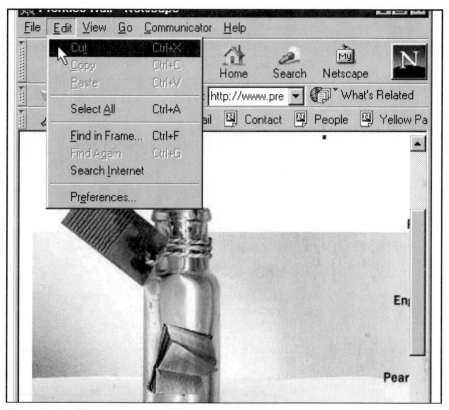

Figure 3.15   The `Edit` menu of the Communicator.

The most important menu item of the `Edit` menu is the last one, `Preferences`. Preferences allow the user to configure and customize the Communicator as needed. Figure 3.16
shows these preferences. There are seven categories of preferences that the user can modify.
These are `Appearance`, `Navigator`, `Mail&Newsgroups`, `Roaming Access`, `Com-
poser`, `Offline`, and `Advanced`. The `Appearance` category allows the user to select the
fonts (type and size) and colors of Web page text, links, and background of choice by overriding
the default values. The `Navigator` category has three choices: `Languages`, `Applica-
tions`, and `Smart Browsing` (covered in chapter 6). Clicking `Languages` shows that the
browser uses English. Clicking `Applications` shows the helper applications for different file
types as shown in figure 3.17. When the user selects a file type (such as GIF Image) shown in
the figure, the `File type details` section shows the file extension of the application, the
file MIME type, and the application that handles the file.

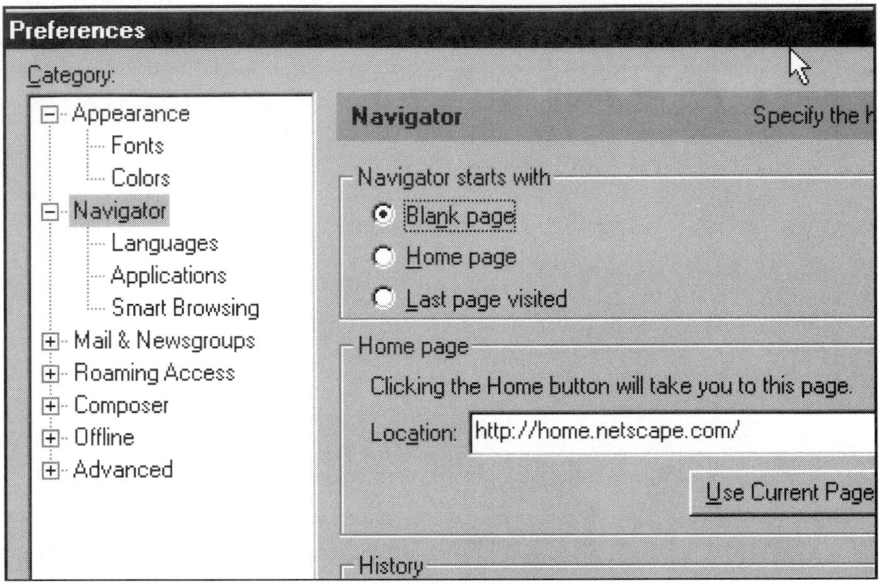

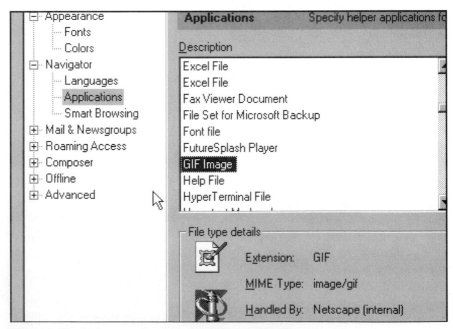

Figure 3.16   Preferences of the Communicator.

Figure 3.17   Helper applications for different file types.

The `Mail&Newsgroups` category, shown in figure 3.18, has many items for the user to configure and customize. Most of these items (`Identity`, `Mail Servers`, `Addressing`, `Messages`, `Window Settings`, `Copies and Folders`, `Formatting`, `Return Receipts`, and `Disk Space`) are for setting and configuring e-mail. Some (`Newsgroup Servers` and `Disk Space`) are for setting and configuring newsgroups. The `Disk Space` item is used for both e-mail and Newsgroups. We cover each of these items in the tutorials section of this chapter.

The `Roaming Access` category lets you connect to the Communicator, with the same preferences, bookmarks, cookies, and other items that you normally use, when you are away from your desk, using a shared computer or working from home. Your network administrator has to set up `Roaming Access` for you before you can use this category. This category is useful if you are a user of the Communicator at work. Your system administrator should set up roaming access for you and tell you which server your roaming profile is on.

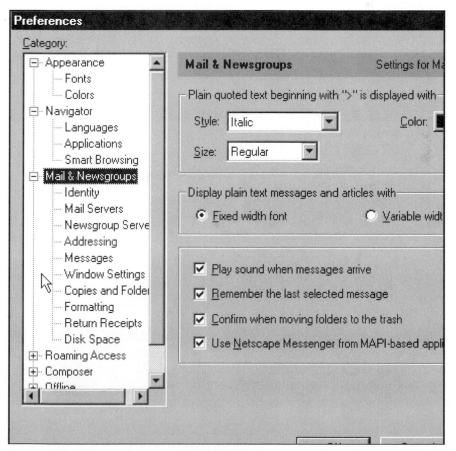

Figure 3.18   Mail and Newsgroups category.

The `Composer` category enables you to set your HTML editor environment and publishing information. This category is useful only if you use the Communicator `Composer` as your HTML editor.

The `Offline` category enables you to work offline using the Communicator and go online only when you need to connect. This category is useful if you are using a modem connection.

The last category in the Preferences is `Advanced`. The user can control an important set of preferences via this category, such as automatic loading of images, Java applets, JavaScript, and style sheets. The user can also control the handling of cookies that may be dropped by Web sites onto the user's computer. The user may accept them without knowledge, disable them, or be warned by the browser before receiving a cookie. The `Advanced` category enables the user to set the size of memory and disk cache (via the `Cache` item under `Advanced`), provide additional security for an Internet connection (via the `Proxies` item under `Advanced`), and set `SmartUpdate` options.

The `View` menu and its items are shown in figure 3.19. The `Show` submenu can turn on and off the Navigation, Location, and Personal toolbars. The other menu items are self-explanatory. The one item that is of particular interest is the `Page Source`. When this item is chosen by the user, the Communicator displays the HTML source (code) of the currently displayed Web page in a different window. Web developers may be interested in learning which HTML tags produce given portions of the Web page.

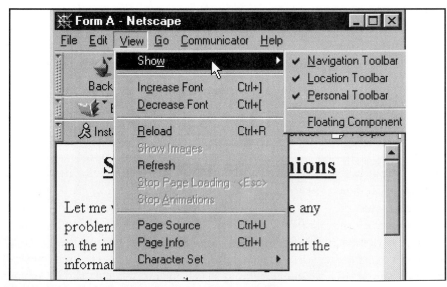

Figure 3.19   The `View` menu of the Communicator.

The Go menu is shown in figure 3.20. Its menu items, Back, Forward, and Home, perform the same functions as the corresponding buttons of the Navigation Toolbar. The last part of the Go menu shows the titles of the Web pages that are currently stored in the memory cache, with a check mark in front of the title of the currently displayed page.

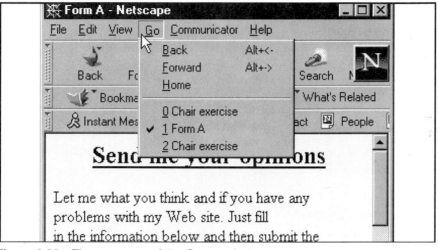

Figure 3.20   The Go menu of the Communicator.

The Communicator menu is shown in figure 3.21. Some of the items of this menu are the Navigator, Messenger, Composer, AOL Instant Messenger Service, Radio, Bookmarks, Newsgroups, and Address Book. The Navigator menu item opens a new browser window. The Messenger menu item opens the mail window. The Composer item opens a Composer window for HTML editing. The AOL menu item opens an AOL Sign On window. The Radio menu item allows users to listen to Netscape online radio. We cover the Bookmarks, Newsgroups, and Address Book menu items in the tutorials section of this chapter. The Tools submenu has, among other things, menu items that enable users to view the history of Web pages previously accessed by the browser (History menu item) and to invoke a Java console (Java Console menu item). The Window menu item shows the currently open browser windows with a check mark in front of the active one.

The last menu on the menu bar of the Communicator is the Help menu. Figure 3.22 shows its menu items. Some of the menu items, such as Software Updates and Register Now, require the user to connect to the Internet to receive help information as the browser downloads it from Netscape Web site. Other items, such as About Plug-ins and About Communicator, work offline. These two items display information about the current plug-ins of the browser and its version. The Help Contents menu item of the Help menu is quite useful; the user can use it as an online help, to search for many details about Communicator operations and use.

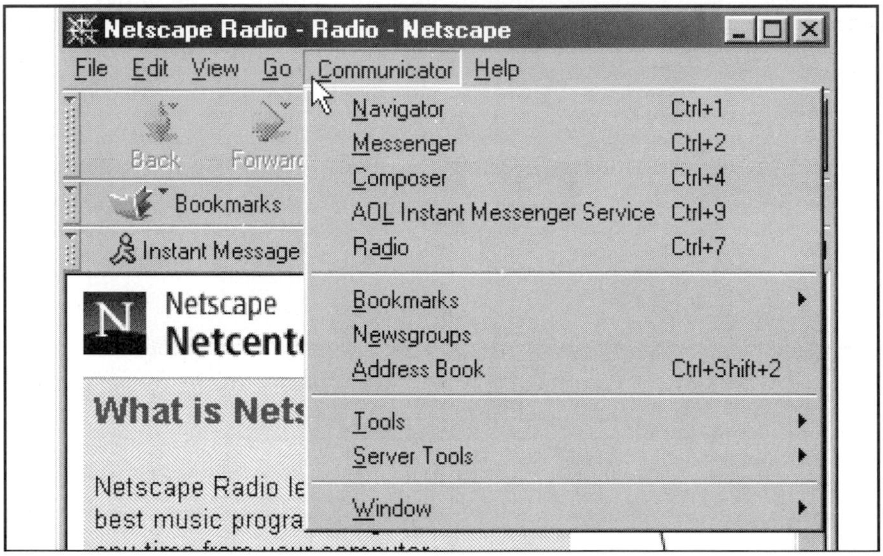

Figure 3.21   The Communicator menu of the Communicator.

Figure 3.22   The Help menu of the Communicator.

3.9 The Communicator Toolbars

The Communicator has three toolbars, as was shown in figure 3.13. The Navigation Toolbar has several useful buttons. Using the Back and Forward buttons, the user can cycle through the history list of the previously visited Web sites and reload any one of them. The browser saves the Web sites the user visits during a session in its memory cache. These Web sites makeup the history list. The Reload button reloads the current Web page. This button is particularly useful for Web developers as they edit the code for their Web pages and must reload these pages to view the latest edited versions. The Home or Netscape button, if clicked, loads the Netscape home Web page, home.netscape.com. The Home button can be set up, via Edit => Preferences, by the user to display a favorite Web page. Using the Search button, the user uses Netscape search tools to navigate the Web. The Print button prints the current Web page or other information as the user sees it on the screen. The Security button (shape of a padlock) shows the security of the current page. If the connection between the client and the server is secure, as in the case of executing an e-commerce transaction, the padlock is shown closed; otherwise, it stays open all the time. The same lock is shown on the left of the Status bar in the bottom of the browser window, as was shown in figure 3.13. The Shop button allows online shopping at Netscape site. The Stop button is used to interrupt the current transfer of information from the server to the client and vice versa. It stops downloading or uploading Web pages, form data, and so forth. It is worth noting that the Back, Forward, and Home buttons of the Navigation Toolbar are also available as menu items in the Go menu, as discussed in section 3.5.3.1. It is a matter of preference where to access them. It is more convenient to access them from the Navigation Toolbar where they are directly visible.

The Location Toolbar begins with a Bookmarks button that may be used to bookmark (file) the current Web site. This button achieves the same function as if the user clicks the Communicator menu on the Menu bar followed by clicking the Bookmarks menu item. Locating the Bookmarks button on the Location Toolbar next to the URL (Netsite) text field makes it more convenient to use and faster to access. The Location text filed is where the user types the URL of a Web site to view its Web page. If it is a Web page, the user does not need to type the protocol. The browser assumes it is http://. The user needs to type only the Web site name, such as www.prenhall.com. The last button on the Location bar is What's Related. Clicking this button shows any information related to the current Web page. For example, you may see other Web sites that might interest you. One can view this button as a marketing button.

The Personal Toolbar includes buttons that provide useful information and services to browser users. Netscape, like other Internet companies, bundles services offered by other online sites to its customers. All these buttons connect the browser user to the Netscape home page, home.netscape.com. Therefore, the user must be online to use them. The Instant Message button invokes the AOL Sign On window. The WebMail button offers users a chance to get free e-mail accounts similar to those offered by, say, Hotmail and Yahoo. The Contact button allows you to join Netscape Netcenter and become a member. As a member, you create your own address book and use it. By clicking the People button, the user can search for addresses, phone numbers, and e-mail addresses of people and friends. The Yellow Pages button enables the user to find the phone number and address of a company within the fifty States of America. International search for a company is also available. Using the Download button, users can download any software product of Netscape, such as the Communicator. The Find Sites button enables users to search the Web using Netscape search engine. Channels is the last button on the Personal Toolbar. This button offers the user an organized content of the Web. The content is grouped into channels such as Autos, Business, Computing and Internet, Education, and so forth.

3.10 The Status and Component Bars

The Status bar, shown in figure 3.13, is divided into five areas. On the left, there is the padlock symbol that indicates the security information of the page. This symbol is the same as the Security button of the Navigation Toolbar. The next area is the online/offline button. The symbol of the button resembles a cable connection. The connection is on by default. The user may click it to go offline. This button forces the browser to go offline, but it does not disconnect the computer connection if there is one at the time of clicking the button.

The next two areas show the status of loading information of Web pages to the browser. The area next to the connection cable shows a progress meter with a percentage. The area next to it shows the same information in a text form.

The last area on the right of the Status bar is the Component bar. This area is known as the docked position of the bar. The bar has five icons: Navigator, Inbox, Newsgroups, Address Book, and Composer as shown in figure 3.13. Moving the mouse over each icon shows its name. Clicking any of these icons opens the corresponding tool. The user can expand the Component bar by clicking the lines at the left edge of the Component bar, shown in figure 3.13. The user can move the expanded bar, shown in figure 3.23, by dragging its title bar to the desired location. To dock the Component bar, the user clicks the close box (x). If the user right clicks on the title bar, a pop-up menu is displayed, as shown in figure 3.23. The user can change the display of the bar by choosing any of the menu items.

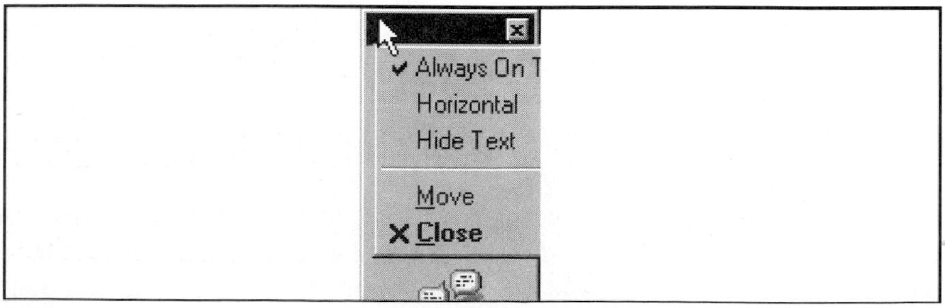

Figure 3.23 The Component bar of the Communicator.

3.11 Tutorials

This section focuses on the hands-on aspects of using the Netscape Communicator. The major uses of the browser are illustrated here.

3.11.1 E-mail

This is the basic tool that most of us begin using once connected. It is simple and intuitive to use. You send e-mail messages to individuals or to groups. You can send an attachment, as well, with the e-mail message. Attachments are usually used if you are sending a file or a long document (e.g., resumes, articles, summaries, etc.) that is already on your computer. You use attachments to avoid typing the document all over again and to make the e-mail message easier to read (especially if you send more than one document with your e-mail message).

Before you can use the Netscape e-mail facility, you need to set up and configure the e-mail environment. To perform this setup, click Edit from the Menu bar, then click Preferences, then double click the Mail&Newsgroups category. You need to set up the Identity and Mail Servers. Click Identity to open the Identity window, shown in figure 3.24. Fill in the text fields with your e-mail information, as shown in the figure.

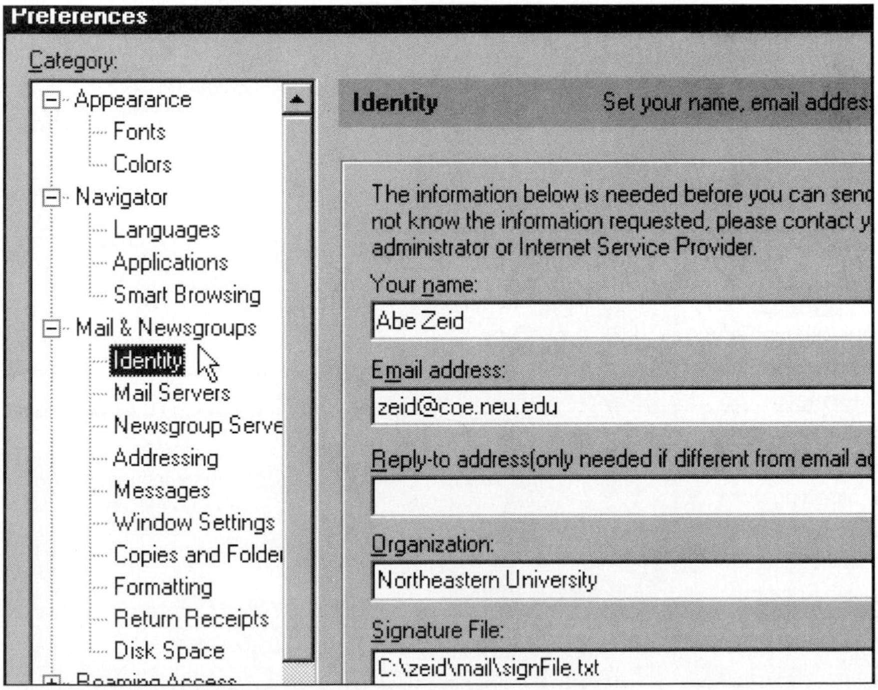

Figure 3.24 Configuring the Identity fields of Netscape e-mail.

Two noticeable fields are `Email address` and `Signature File`. Your e-mail address is assigned to you by your service provider. The signature file is a file that you develop yourself in a word processor such as Word. The file usually contains your affiliation, including your name, your company name and address, your phone and fax numbers, your e-mail address, and your company logo. The browser appends your signature file automatically to every e-mail message you send out. Thus, you save time by not typing that same information over and over. In other words, your signature file acts as a stamp for you.

The vCard checkbox shown in figure 3.24 is another form of e-mail signature that you can use. Instead of showing the full affiliation in every e-mail message you send, the vCard shows as a button. If the receiver of your e-mail message needs the details of your affiliation, he/she clicks the vCard. This is useful to use if you send e-mail messages frequently to friends and colleagues who already know who you are. If you click the vCard checkbox and you have not created the card, Netscape asks you whether you would like to create it. Follow the browser prompts to create it.

The second step in configuring your Netscape e-mail is to set up the mail servers, as shown in figure 3.25. Figure 3.26 shows the communication between a mail server and client

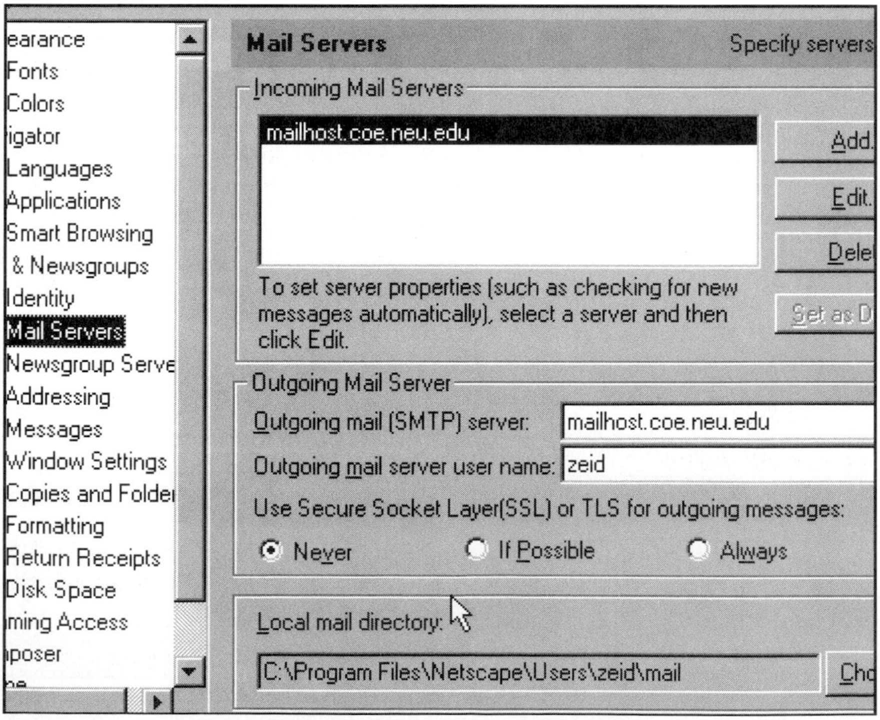

Figure 3.25 Configuring the `Mail Servers` of Netscape e-mail.

computers, to help you better understand figure 3.25. The mail server holds mailboxes for different users, similarly to a traditional post office. Each user can access only his/her mailbox from a client computer on the Internet, to download e-mail messages from the server to the client computer. The client could be the office computer with a dedicated connection or a home computer with a dial-up connection. After downloading the e-mail messages from the server to the client, you have the choice of whether to keep a copy on the server or to delete all messages from the server. Server providers may have two separate mail servers to handle heavy traffic; one for incoming mail, and one for outgoing mail.

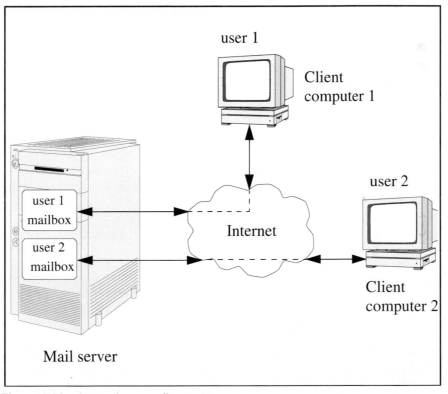

Figure 3.26   Accessing e-mail messages.

Now that you have understood figure 3.26, it is easier to fill the text fields of figure 3.25. Fill in the names of the incoming and outgoing mail servers. If one server handles both, use the same name. Also, type the user name and select the type of security when sending out e-mail messages. Lastly, specify a mail directory on the client in which to store your e-mail messages after the browser downloads them. The names of the incoming and outgoing mail servers and the type of security are provided to you by your server provider.

Three types of mail servers exist. The type of an outgoing mail server is always SMTP (Simple Mail Transfer Protocol). These servers use the SMTP protocol to communicate with the client computer. The SMTP protocol allows the sender to identify him/herself, specify a recipient, and transfer an e-mail message. The type of an incoming mail server could be IMAP (Internet Message Access Protocol) or POP3 (Post Office Protocol). Each of these types has advantages and disadvantages. The IMAP servers provide you with faster e-mail download when using a modem, because, initially, they download message headers only. They also keep your messages, thus saving you the local disk space. The disadvantage of IMAP servers is that not all ISPs support them. The POP3 servers download your e-mail messages to your local computer all at once, thereby making reading them offline easier. You can also specify whether to keep copies of the messages on the server. Most ISPs support POP3 mail servers. There are several disadvantages. If you use more than one client computer, messages might reside on one or the other, but not both. Also, POP3 servers work slowly. In addition, you cannot access all mail folders from multiple locations. Finally, IMAP and POP3 servers do not work together. You can have multiple IMAP servers or one POP3 server, but not both types.

The last step in configuring your Netscape e-mail is to choose the type of the incoming mail server. After typing a name for the incoming mail server, as was shown in figure 3.25, click the `Add` button (if it is new) or the `Edit` button (if it already exists). The `Mail Server Properties` panel shown in figure 3.27 is immediately displayed. Choose the server type (whether IMAP or POP3), type the `User Name`, click the checkbox for `Remember password`, and specify the frequency, in minutes, of checking for mail. If you choose POP3 server type, you need to click the `POP` tab shown in figure 3.27 and click the `Leave messages on server` checkbox, if needed. If this checkbox is checked, the browser will not delete the messages from the server after downloading them to the client computer.

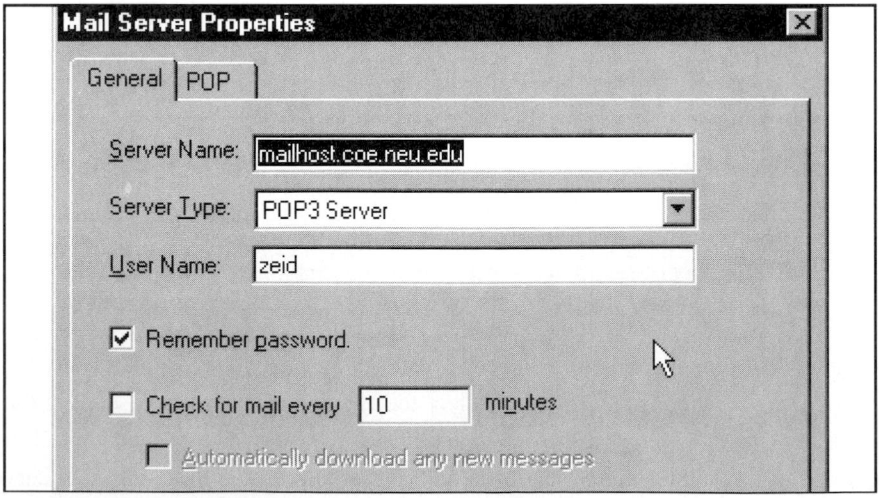

Figure 3.27 Properties of incoming mail servers.

Having finished setting up and configuring the Netscape e-mail facility, let us explore with it. Figure 3.28 shows the mail (messenger) window. The mail window comes in two settings. To choose a setting, click (from the browser Menu bar) Edit followed by Preferences. Double click Mail&Newsgroups, then click Window Settings. In the Window Settings, there are radio buttons for the two settings. Click the desired button, and click OK. Next time you open a mail window, the window is displayed with the selected setting.

The mail window is divided into three frames. The top frame on the right (figure 3.28) holds the headers of the messages that have been downloaded by the browser from the incoming mail server. The bottom frame on the right displays the body of the selected message header in the top frame. The long frame on the left shows the local mail folders that are available on the local computer. The main mail folder (mail) is defined by the path shown in figure 3.25 for the Local mail directory. Several subfolders exist under this folder, as shown in figure 3.28 in the left frame. The Inbox subfolder is where the browser downloads e-mail messages from the mail server. The Uns...ages subfolder is where you may save any unsent messages. You may use the Drafts subfolder to gradually write e-mail messages over a period of time until the message is ready for mailing. This subfolder is good to use if you have to wait for a decision before sending a message. The Templates subfolder stores different e-mail templates that you may use; for example, one template for friendly mail, and one template for business mail. The browser automatically keeps a copy of every message you send in the Sent subfolder. The Trash subfolder keeps all the e-mail messages that the user deletes. When you no longer need to keep a message, say, after reading it, you delete it. Deleting the message for the first time moves it from the, say, Inbox subfolder to the Trash subfolder. To truly delete it from the local hard disk, you must open the Trash subfolder (by simply clicking it), highlight the message header there, and delete it. Similarly, if you need to delete messages from the Sent subfolder, you must delete them twice; once in the Sent subfolder, and a second time in the Trash subfolder.

In addition to its three frames, the mail window has a title bar, a menu bar, and a message toolbar as shown in figure 3.28. You are encouraged to investigate the various menus of the menu bar, and their submenus and menu items.

The message Toolbar has the buttons with all the actions that you need to handle e-mail messages. Here is how you use these buttons. You must be online.

Get mail. To read your e-mail messages, you need to download them from your service provider hard disk (server) to your local disk (your PC disk). Click the Get Msg button to download your e-mail messages. During downloading, the browser displays the messages' headers in the top right frame, as shown in figure 3.28. The browser bolds the newly unread messages' headers and displays a green symbol (diamond shape) next to them, to make it easier for you to identify and read them. The browser arranges all the downloaded messages' headers in alphabetical order by the sender's name.

Read mail. To read an e-mail message, simply click the corresponding message header, or click the Next button on the message Toolbar of the mail window, shown in figure 3.28. The full

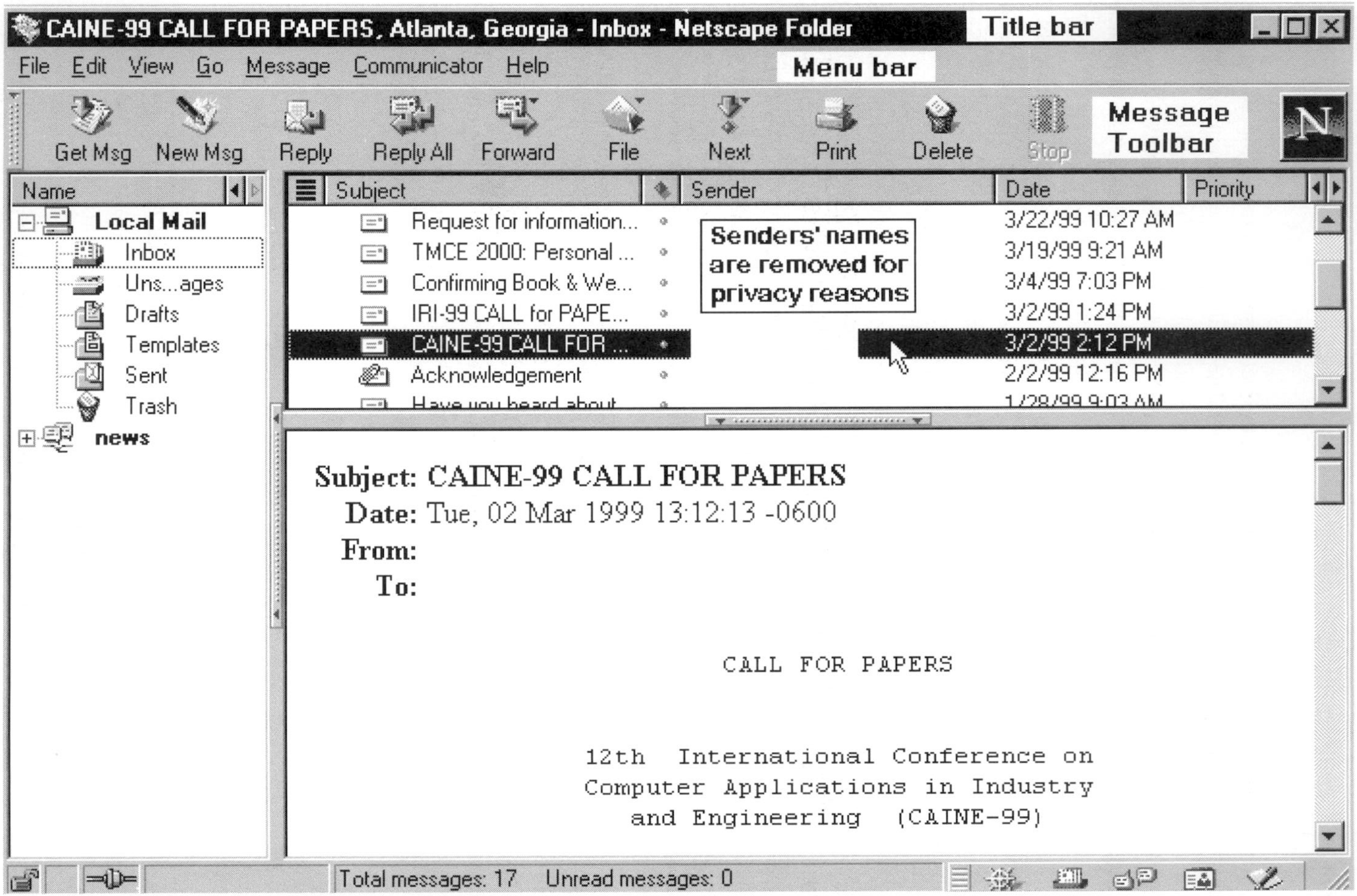

Figure 3.28 Netscape e-mail window.

message is displayed in the bottom right frame, as shown in figure 3.28. You can click all the headers one after the other, or keep clicking the Next button, to read all the messages.

Reply to mail. After reading a message, you have several choices for dealing with it. You may respond to it, forward it, file it, print it, or delete it. To respond to an e-mail message after reading it, click the Reply or Reply All button on the message Toolbar of the mail window, shown in figure 3.28. If the e-mail message you are responding to has the e-mail address of the sender only, you click Reply. The Reply All button is used if you want to send a response to all e-mail addresses listed in the message. Clicking one of these two buttons causes a composition window to pop up, as shown in figure 3.29. You are encouraged to investigate the menus,

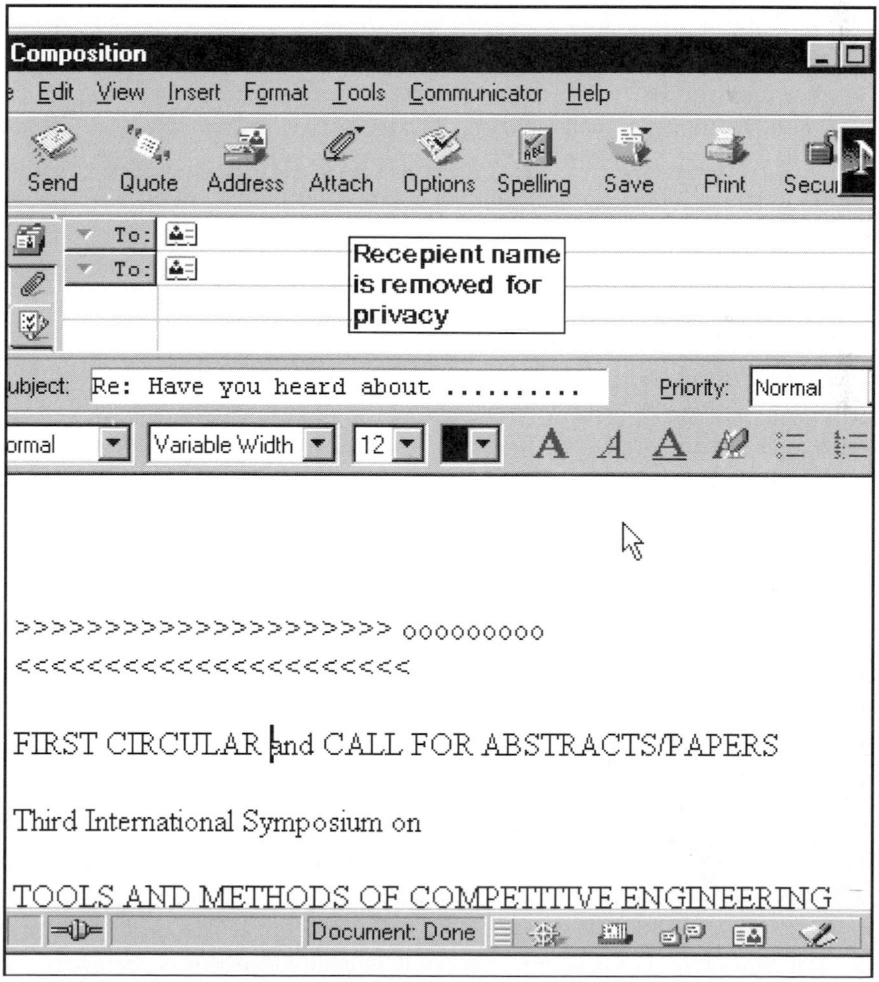

Figure 3.29 Netscape mail composition window.

submenus, and buttons of this window. Fill in the fields of the window, in particular the e-mail addresses the reply message is going to, and the `Subject` field. Write the body of the message, and clicks the `Send` button of the composition window shown in figure 3.29. The browser checks the message text and sends it. To send an attachment with the message, click the `Attach` button of the composition window (figure 3.29) and follow the browser prompts.

Forward mail. To forward an e-mail message, click the `Forward` button of the mail window (figure 3.28). The browser opens its composition window. The window is blank except for the `Subject` field, which shows the title of the message to be forwarded, preceded by `Fwd:`. Type the forwarding e-mail addresses and the body of the message, and click the `Send` button. The browser sends both the message that you type and the forwarded message.

File mail. You may file old already e-mail messages read either by clicking the `File` button of the mail window (figure 3.28) or by dragging the message header from the top left frame and dropping it into the desired folder shown in the long left frame of the mail window. You need to create the desired mail folders. For example, you may create separate folders, such as friends, business, junk mail, and so forth, to save the corresponding messages.

Print mail. To print an e-mail message, click the `Print` button of the mail window (figure 3.28). When you click the button, the browser displays a Print pop-up window allowing you to print all the pages of the message or selected pages. You need to click the `OK` button of the Print window.

Delete mail. To delete an e-mail message, highlight the header of the message and click the `Delete` button of the mail window (figure 3.28).

Send mail. You can send an e-mail message without or with an attachment. To send an e-mail message, click the `New Msg` button of the mail window (figure 3.28). The composition window shown in figure 3.29 pops up. Fill in the e-mail address and the subject. Type the body of the message and then click `Send`. To send a message with an attachment, repeat what you just did. Then click `Attach` in the composition window and follow the prompts. You can send a URL location or a file as an attachment. If you send a URL location as an attachment, the browser gets the corresponding document, say a Web page, and sends it. The receiver can view the document and/or its HTML file by using a browser.

3.11.2 Browsing Activities

We can use browsers to perform a multitude of browsing activities. Here are some example.

Visit some Web sites. Depending on your interest, you can visit many Web sites, Some sites you be may interested in visiting are www.aol.com, www.yahoo.com, www.amazon.com, www.prenhall.com, www.neu.edu, www.fedworld.gov (FedWorld), and marvel.loc.gov (Library of Congress). Go ahead and visit these sites and more.

Download files. You can download audio, video, and image files from sites on the Web into your local hard drive. For example, you can download video games. Be aware that video files are very big and can take a long time downloading. We have discussed downloading files in chapter 1. You can download shareware from www.shareware.com or www.download.com. Go ahead and follow the instructions in chapter 1 to download your favorite files and shareware.

Check encryption and security. You can check whether a Web page or a file is encrypted or not in Netscape. Click the `Security` button (padlock icon) shown in figure 3.13. The browser displays all security information about the page in a window. If the padlock is locked, the page and the Internet connection are encrypted. In addition to encryption, a web page or a message may include a signed digital certificate that verifies the sender. Encrypted files/pages are used for security reasons. For example, financial transactions should all be encrypted, to prevent anybody from intercepting the file (TCP/IP packets) during sending to obtain valuable information, such as credit card numbers.

Run multiple copies of browser. If you are in a rush, you can run multiple copies of the browser in different windows. Every window could be performing a different task. This is useful if you are downloading a file that may take too long, and you want to do something else, such as editing an HTML file, while waiting. To open a new Netscape window, click the following sequence; `File => New => Navigator Window`, or hit CTRL N.

Handle Web pages. Most of the time, you deal with Web pages while using a browser. You can visit, view, print, save, or delete a Web page. Here is how to do them all.

•**Visit a Web page.** Type the URL location in the browser location Toolbar, and press `Enter`.

•**View a Web page source code.** Click `View` from the `Menu` bar of the browser, followed by `Page Source`. The browser displays the HTML code of the currently displayed page. This is useful later, when you start writing your own Web pages as covered later in this book.

•**Print a Web page.** While the page is displayed on the screen, click the `Print` button of your browser. The browser prints the page as you see it displayed on the screen.

•**Save a Web page.** While the page is displayed on the screen, click `File`, then click `Save as`, to save it on your local disk drive. The browser saves the HTML file corresponding to the page.

•**Delete a Web page.** You can delete (only) your own Web pages stored on your local disk drive. This is simply deleting one of your local files. Drag the file into the recycling bin on your desktop, or use a system delete command on your computer.

•**Open a local file.** You can use your browser to open any file, including HTML files. HTML files produce the Web pages as you know them. The browser has an interpreter that interprets HTML tags embedded in these files and displays the results as the Web page. if, however, you open a non-HTML file, the browser displays its contents in its window. You can open an HTML file in the browser or in an HTML editor. When you open the file in the browser, you view the corresponding Web page. When you open the file in an HTML editor, you can change the HTML tags of the file itself. Opening and editing HTML files is useful when you are developing and writing Web pages in HTML.

3.11.3 Bookmarks

As you use your browser to surf the net, you may want to save your experiences for future use. Bookmarks allow you to do just that. You can add, delete, and organize bookmarks. Bookmarks are stored in an HTML file, called `bookmarks`, in your Netscape directory. You can open this file in Netscape. The file has the exact same organization as the Bookmarks you create. Click `Communicator => Bookmarks` as shown in figure 3.30 to access your bookmarks. When you point to any bookmark, Netscape displays the corresponding URL location in the location Toolbar and downloads the Web page. Here is how you use bookmarks in Netscape.

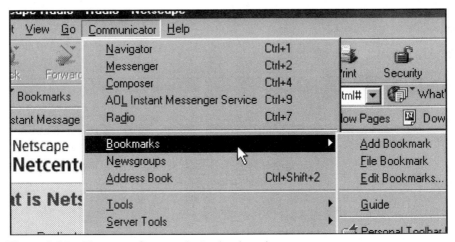

Figure 3.30   Netscape Communicator bookmarks.

Add a bookmark. If you like the Web page that is currently displayed by the browser, click `Communicator => Bookmarks => Add  Bookmark`. The browser adds the new bookmark at the end of the list. If you click `Bookmarks` again, you notice the new bookmark.

Delete a bookmark. Click `Communicator => Bookmarks => Edit  Bookmarks`. The Bookmarks window shown in figure 3.31 is displayed. Highlight the bookmark you want to delete, click `Edit`, and choose `Delete` as shown in figure 3.31.

Organize bookmarks. As you save more and more bookmarks, you will need to organize them in folders. Click `Communicator => Bookmarks => Edit  Bookmarks`, as shown in figure 3.30, to open the Bookmarks window shown in figure 3.31. The `File` menu of the `Bookmarks` window provides you with menu items you need to organize your bookmarks. You can insert a bookmark (click `New  Bookmark` menu item), a folder (click `New  Folder` menu item), or a separator (click `New  Separator` menu item).

When you click the `New Bookmark` menu item, it opens the Bookmark Properties window shown in figure 3.32. This window allows you to insert a bookmark of a Web page that is not currently displayed by the browser. You input the name you would like to use for the bookmark, the URL location, and a description to remind you in the future of what the bookmark is all about. If you want to organize several bookmarks under a separate folder, position the mouse where you want to create the folder in the bookmarks tree (figure 3.31). Then, click the `New Folder` menu item from the `Folder` menu. The browser asks you for a folder's name.

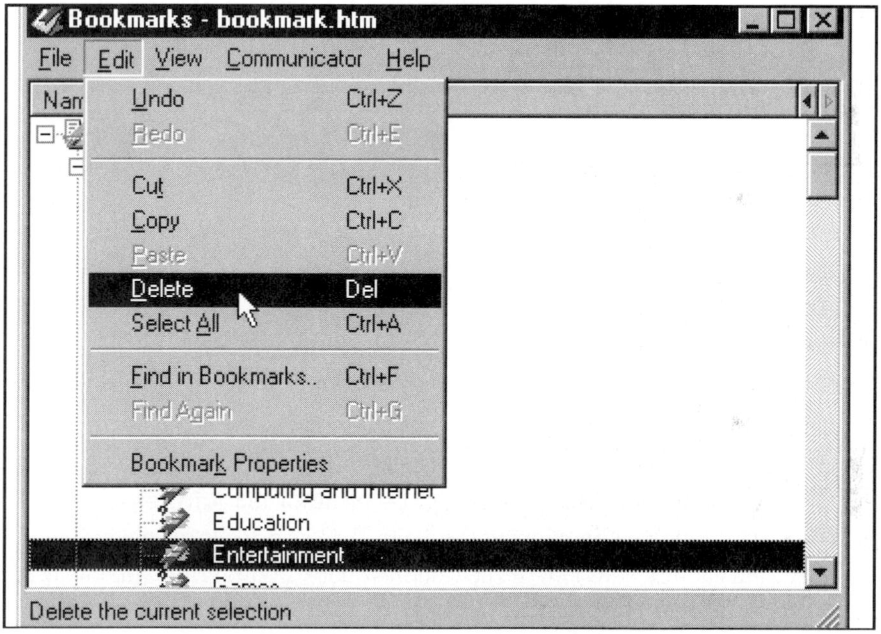

Figure 3.31   Netscape Communicator `bookmarks` window.

Figure 3.32   Netscape Communicator `Bookmark Properties` window.

After creating the folder, you drag the bookmarks one by one, and drop them into the folder. The changes you make to your bookmarks are instantly displayed in the Bookmark Properties window. To view the data of a bookmark or a folder, highlight it, and click the following sequence; `Edit => Bookmark Properties`. (See figure 3.31). To insert a line space between bookmarks, position the mouse where you want to insert the separator in the bookmarks tree Figure 3.31). Then, click the `File` menu of the Bookmarks window followed by `New Separator` menu item. When you insert the separator, you see the <separator> tag in the list of bookmarks. When you view the new organization in the browser, you see the line separators.

3.11.4 Address Book

This facility allows you to store all your e-mail addresses in one location and use them within your browser to send mail to individuals or mailing lists. A mailing list has a name and contains several e-mail addresses, similarly to a conventional paper mailing list. To invoke the address book, click `Communicator => Address Book`, as shown in figure 3.21. The Address Book window is shown in figure 3.33. You can also invoke the Address Book window by clicking the `Address Book` icon of the `Component` bar, shown in figure 3.13. While the window has a menu bar and a set of buttons following it, the buttons are more frequently used than the menus on the menu bar. You are encouraged to investigate the menus of the menu bar on your own. We here show how to use the `Address Book` effectively.

Create a new address book. Click the `File` menu of the `Address Book` window shown in figure 3.33, followed by clicking the `New Address Book` menu item. Type the name (say, Abe Zeid address book), of the new address book in the `Info` window that pops up and click `OK`. The browser creates the book and adds it to the left `Directory` frame shown in figure 3.33. You can also edit the address book that comes with the window (first item in the `Directory` frame) to change its name. Double click the item, and type the name you want to replace the default name (`Personal Address Book`).

Add an address to the address book. Address book entries are known as cards. These cards store names, postal addresses, e-mail addresses, phone numbers, and other information. To add an address to an address book, highlight the address book in the `Directory` frame (figure 3.33), and click the `New Card` button (figure 3.33). Fill in the information in the `New Card` window that pops up and shown in figure 3.34. The window has two additional tabs (`Contact` and `Notes`) that allow you to enter additional information. You can use the `Notes` tab to add any comments or notes about the addressee. Click the `OK` button to finish the creation of the card. The browser shows the card in the right frame of the Address Book window (figure 3.33). To view or edit the card you just created, double click the name in the `Address Book` window.

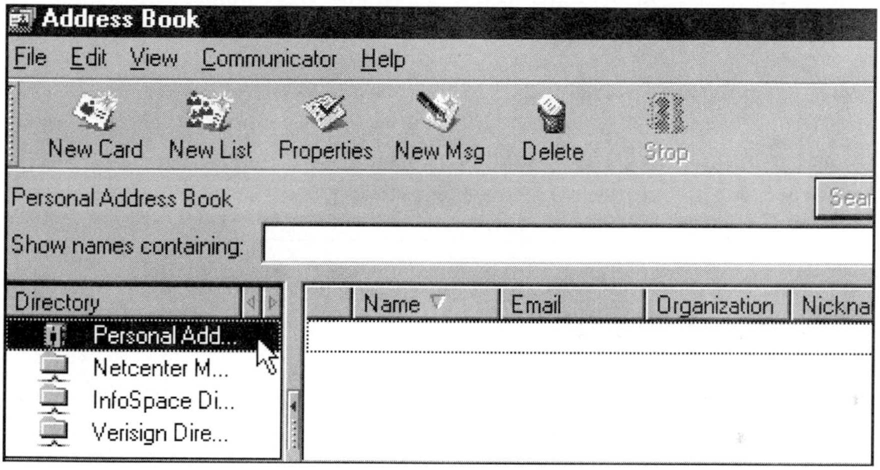

Figure 3.33 Netscape `Address Book` window.

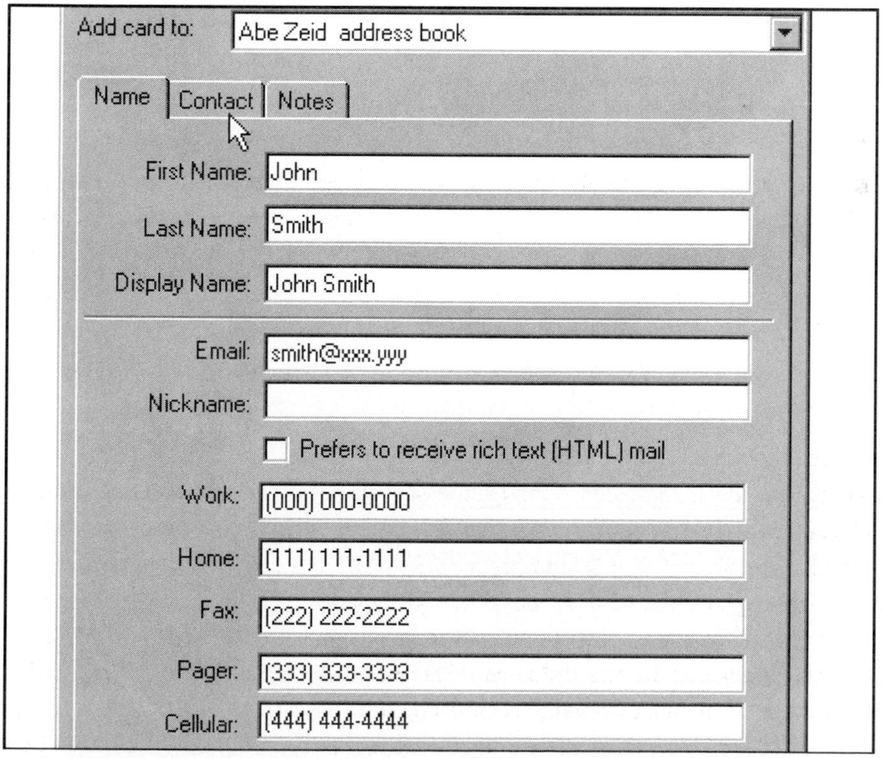

Figure 3.34 Adding an address to Netscape address book.

Create a mailing list. If you regularly send e-mail messages to a group of recipients, you can create a mailing list to send a message to them all at once. To add a mailing list to an address book, highlight the book in the `Directory` frame (figure 3.33), and click the `New List` button (figure 3.33). Fill in the information in the `Mailing List` window that pops up, shown in figure 3.35. Click the `OK` button to finish the creation of the mailing list.

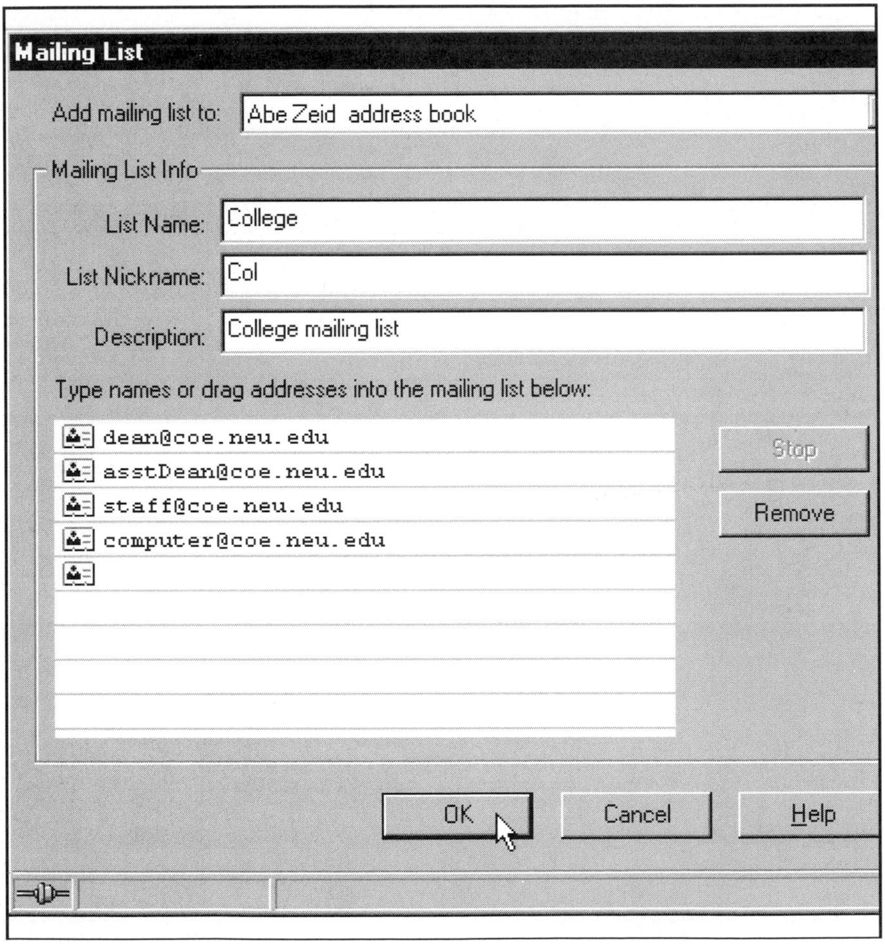

Figure 3.35 Netscape Mailing List window.

As shown in figure 3.35, we create the *College* mailing list with four members: *dean, asstDean, staff,* and *computer.* Repeat the same steps and create another mailing list with the name *Department* and four members: *chair, faculty, staff,* and *students.* The final address book is now shown in figure 3.36. The right frame in the figure shows the non-list members (*John Smith*), the list members (*dean, asstDean, staff, computer; chair, faculty, staff, students*), and the names of the mailing lists (*College, Department*) in alphabetical order. The way you can tell whether a name is a list (in figure 3.36) is simple. The mailing list does not have an e-mail address next to it. Whenever two or more lists use the same name, the browser shows it only once, as in the case of the *staff* name that occurs in both the *College* and the *Department* lists.

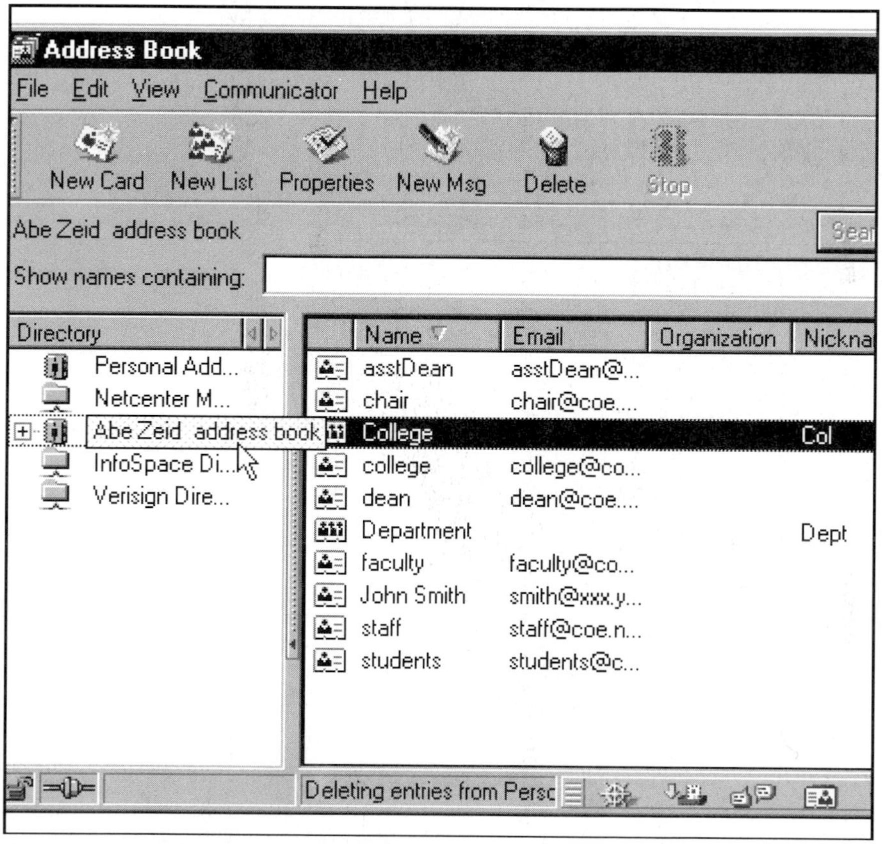

Figure 3.36 Netscape personal address book.

Use an address book. To send an e-mail message to a mailing list or to one person in the address book, highlight the corresponding name in the address book and click the `New Msg` button (figure 3.36) to open the Netscape composition mail window (figure 3.29). Type the message, and click the `Send` button of the composition window to send it. If the address book is not open, you can access it from the browser window by clicking the address book icon (second from the right) on the `Component` bar, shown in figure 3.13.

Remove an e-mail address. Highlight the e-mail address you want to remove in the desired address book (figure 3.36), and click the `Delete` button.

Search an address book. The personal address book gets bigger with time. To search it for names and addresses, type the name of the person you are looking for in the Show names containing field of the Address Book (figure 3.36). If there is a match, the browser scrolls the names in the right frame (figure 3.36) to the top and displays the name you are looking for. Once you find the name, you can double click it to view its card, or click the New MSg button to send an e-mail message.

Import address books. You can import address books: from such other mailers as MS Outlook express or Eudora, or from a previous version of the Communicator. From the File menu (figure 3.36), click Import. Follow the prompts and instructions to import.

Export an address book. From the File menu (figure 3.36), click Export. Follow the prompts and instructions to export.

3.11.5 Help Menu

As you use the above material, you will add your personal experience to it. You will discover other, maybe better, ways to do things. Feel free to explore. Pass any new ideas and tricks you discover to me, please, to include in the FAQs section of future editions of this book. E-mail me at zeid@coe.neu.edu. After you have mastered all the above material, you may want more knowledge. Click Help => Help Contents. There, you find many interesting topics. The browser provides you with search fields where you type the search string. The browser displays the matching information, if it finds any.

3.12 FAQs

This section has FAQs (Frequently Asked Questions) related to the chapter material. Many of these FAQs are also relevant to the Microsoft browser, the Internet Explorer, covered in chapter 4. If you want to contribute to the FAQs in this section and share your experiences with other readers of this book, please e-mail the author at zeid@coe.neu.edu. Credit will be given to you in this section.

Q: What is the general form of a Web page URL?

A: The general form for a Web page URL is as follows:

http://domain_name:port_address/directory_path/object_name#spot.

In this general form,

http:// indicates the protocol or data source;

domain_name:// indicates the domain name of the Web server where the Web page resides;

port_address indicates the default port address for HTTP (usually 80);

directory_path indicates the location of the Web page in the server's file system;

object_name is the actual name of the HTML file of the desired Web page (and has the extension .html or .htm);

#spot is known as an anchor. It is used to drop users of a Web page at a particular location within the page HTML file. This allows the browser to jump right to the specific location identified by #spot.

Q: As I start downloading files and shareware from the Internet on my computer, how can I protect against viruses that might get downloaded as well and infect my hard disk, or other computer components?

A: You should purchase and install anti-virus software, such as Norton utility, on your computer. You should update the installed anti-virus software frequently, because new viruses keep appearing. Simply visit the Web site of the company of your anti-virus software, download the latest patches, and install them.

Q: How can I copy and paste parts of a Web page text?

A: Highlight the text you want to copy. In your browser window, click Edit => copy (or CTRL C for Windows). Then click Edit => Paste (or CTRL V) in the window where you want to paste. This window could be a text editor or a word processor window.

Q: How can I copy an image from a Web page?

A: Right click somewhere on the image. In the pop-up window, click Save Image As.

Q: What are the available graphics formats? Which formats do browsers support?

A: Graphics formats include GIF (Graphics Interchange Format; created by Compuserve), JPG or JPEG (Joint Photographic Experts Group; created by Independent JPEG Group), BMP (bitmap; created by Microsoft), TIFF (Tagged-Image File Format; created by Aldus, Microsoft, and NeXT), and PCX. Browsers support GIF and JPEG formats only.

Q: How can I learn more about DSL?

A: Search the Internet with a search engine. In your favorite browser, type, say, www.metacrawler.com. In the search field of the engine, type DSL as the search string. Browse the resulting hits until you find what you want.

Q: How can I associate a file type (extension) to an application program?

A: This question is equivalent to asking: How can I add a helper application via Netscape? You do not have to do it in Netscape. You can do it at the OS level of your computer, and Netscape recognizes it. Associating a file type to an application program means that the application opens this file type when you double click a file of this type or with this extension. We here explain the procedure of associating the HTML file type to Netscape application for Windows. Let us use the file extension .hml for html files because the .htm and .html extensions already exist. Double click the My Computer icon on your desktop, then click the View menu. Click the Folder Options menu item from the View menu. This opens the Folder Options window shown in figure 3.37. Click the File Types tab as shown in the figure, then click the New Type button. The File Type window shown in figure 3.38 opens up. This window allows you to input the new extension and the application to open it with. Fill in the information, as shown in the figure, and click the New button to choose the application. Type the action (open) and the application (Netscape) in the New Action window that pops up and is shown in figure 3.39. If you do not know where the executable of the application is, use the Browse button, or use the find function of Windows by clicking Start => Find => Files or Folders. Once done, click the Ok button of the New Action window, then click the OK button of the File Type window. The Folder Options window (figure 3.37) should now show the new extension type (hml). You can remove or edit the file type you just created by clicking the Remove or the Edit button of the Folder Options window shown in figure 3.37. Click the Close button of this window to finish. Whenever you double click a file with the extension .hml in the future, Netscape application will open it up and displays the corresponding Web page.

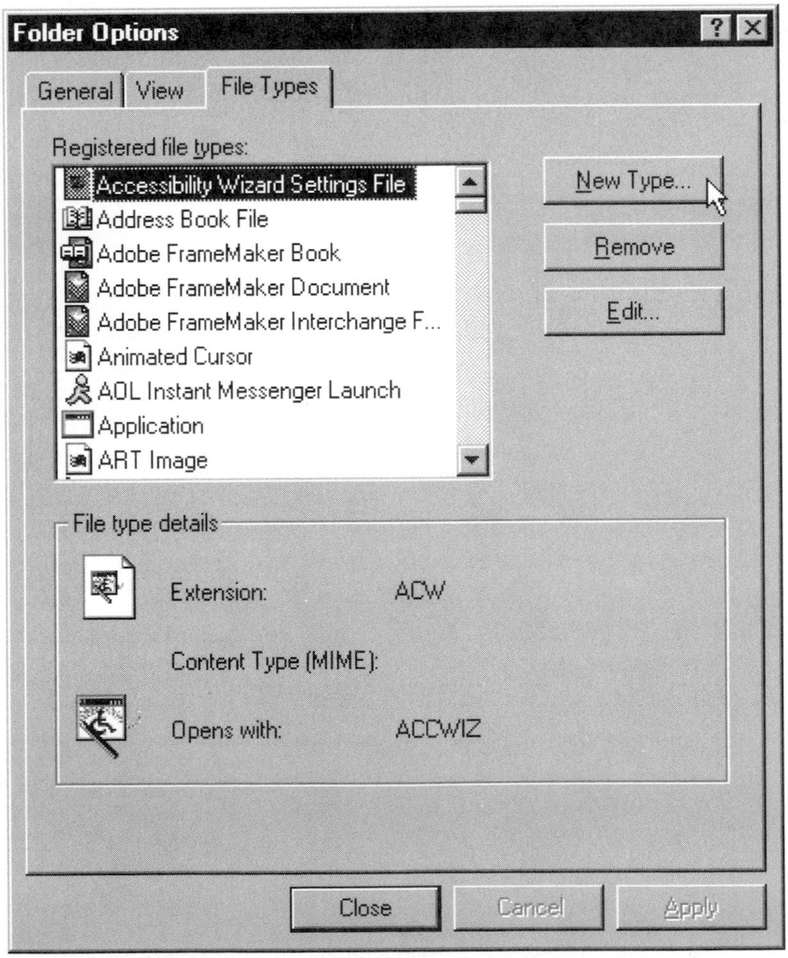

Figure 3.37 The Folder Options window of Windows.

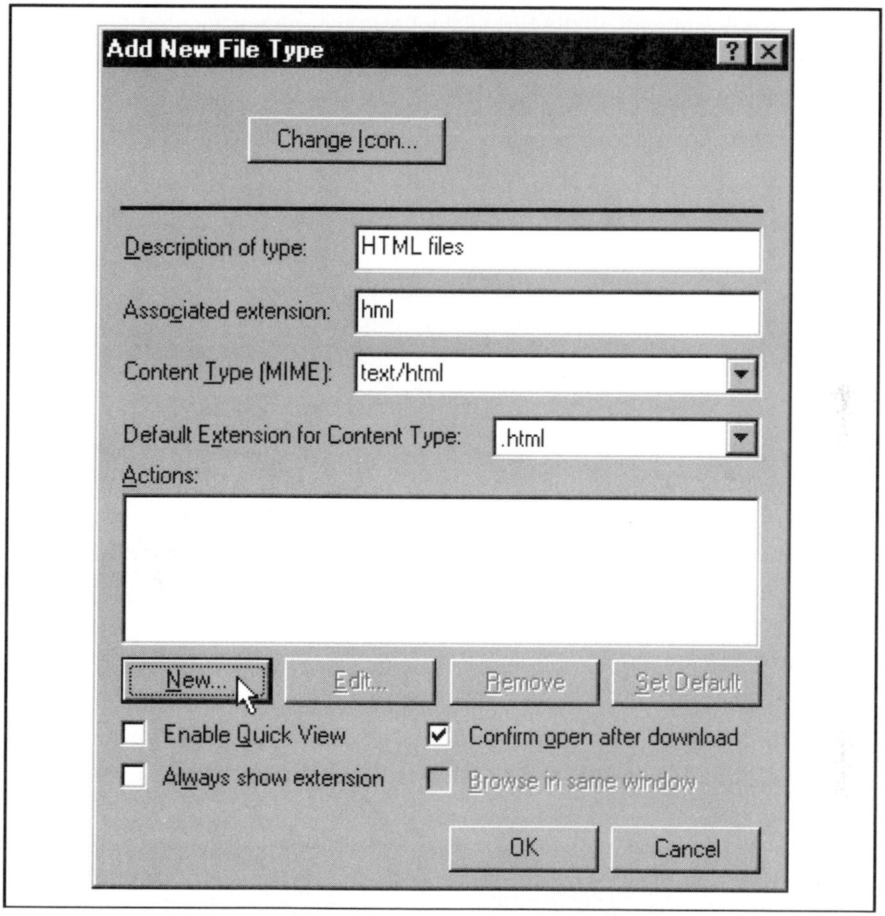

Figure 3.38 The Add New File Type window of Windows.

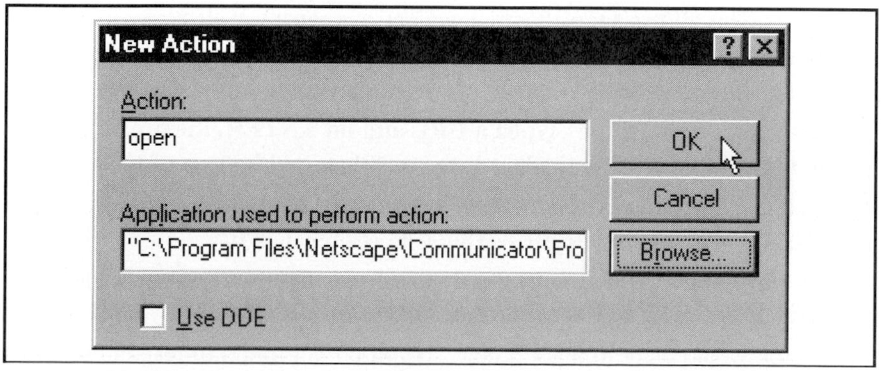

Figure 3.39 The New Action window of Windows.

Another quick answer to this question is to double-click the file that you need to open. Windows opens a window with all the current application programs on your PC and asks you to choose one. When you choose one, it automatically and permanently associates the file type with the application.

Q: How do I know the existing plug-ins in Netscape Communicator?

A: Type `about:plugins` as the URL in the location toolbar. The browser displays useful information. It also provides you with a link to www.netscape.com Web site, to receive additional information.

Q: Where are the Netscape plug-ins stored on my computer?

A: In the folder `C: Program Files` => `Netscape` => `Communicator` => `Program` => `Plugins`.

Q: What is an Adobe Acrobat Reader? When and why do I need it?

A: An Adobe Acrobat Reader is an application written by Adobe that allows you to read and display PDF (Portable Document Format) files as they were originally created. These files require a special viewer, such as the Adobe Acrobat Reader, to display their layouts and rich formats. These readers display the files' formats with greater precision than does HTML. You can download the Acrobat Reader by following links off the main Adobe Web page at www.adobe.com. The downloaded software is a self-extracting file and installs itself as a plug-in in both Netscape Communicator and Microsoft Internet Explorer. Once the Reader is installed, you can associate the PDF file extension to it. Whenever you need to read a PDF file, simply double click it.

Q: What are the advantages of the PDF format?

A: PDF format has two advantages. First, a user can view a PDF file and print it out on any computer: a Windows-based PC, a Mac, or a Unix-based workstation. Second, PDF documents are designed to look and print the same on every combination of computer and printer. That is why government documents are distributed in PDF format. Adobe Acrobat software provides powerful features for creating and managing PDF files. The software can automatically download Web pages from the Internet and use them to create a PDF file, preserving the text, links, and images. This allows a traveller to download a company Web site on a laptop and use it for sales presentation. The software also allows users to create their own digital signatures and use them to "digitally" sign their PDF files.

Q: I just went online. After I typed a URL and hit ENTER, the browser shows a pop-up window telling me I am offline! What is the problem and how can I fix it?

A: Check the `Connection` button on the `Status` bar of your browser. Make sure the connection is on. If the cable (figure 3.13) is shown broken, click it.

Q: How can I mark e-mail messages that I read as new and unread again?

A: This is useful when you read an e-mail message, but you are in too much of a hurry to respond to it. You would want to mark it new, so you do not forget to respond to it later. Click the diamond symbol next to the message.

Q: When I try to set up e-mail on my Netscape Communicator, I get a message saying that the mail server does not have a DNS entry. What is the problem? And how can I solve it?

A: This problem has to do with the configuration of the browser. The problem usually occurs when you try to configure a copy of Netscape that you access over the network (Intranet). Typically, the system administrator disables the ability to configure copies of the browser running on different clients that access the browser off the network server. Check with your system administrator.

Q: How can I keep and run two different versions of Netscape Communicator on my computer?

A: This is not a good practice unless you want to compare the two versions for research purposes. To keep the old version, simply create a new folder for the new version you are about to install. If you install the new version into the Netscape folder that contains your current version, the old version is overwritten. In this case, the installer saves your existing bookmarks, preferences, and settings, so you can use them with the new version.

Q: How can I hide a toolbar of my browser?

A: Click the vertical tab at the left corner of the toolbar you want to hide. This closes the toolbar and shows the tab horizontally. To completely hide the toolbar, including its tab, click this sequence; View (browser menu) => Show => Navigation Toolbar (or another toolbar). Repeat the same sequence to show the toolbar back.

Q: How can I move Netscape toolbars to change the order of their appearance on the screen?

A: Drag the vertical tab of a toolbar and drop it where you want.

Q: How can I add a toolbar button of the currently displayed Web page to the Personal Toolbar of Netscape Communicator?

A: Drag the bookmark icon shown on the Location Toolbar and drop it at the desired position on the Personal Toolbar.

Q: How can I add an existing bookmark to the Personal Toolbar of Netscape Communicator?

A: Open your bookmark folder by clicking Communicator (browser menu) => Bookmarks => Edit Bookmarks. The folder opens in the Notepad window. Drag the bookmark you want to add and drop it at the desired position on the Personal Toolbar. To delete a toolbar button from the Personal Toolbar, drag the corresponding bookmark, in the Bookmarks folder in the Notepad window, from the Personal Toolbar folder to another folder within the Bookmarks folder. Or highlight and click Edit (Notepad window menu) => Delete.

Q: How can I change the Component bar display of Netscape Communicator?

A: Open the Component bar by clicking the lines at the left edge of the bar. Right click on the title bar of the Component bar window. The pop-up menu shows you items that you can try. Go ahead and experiment with them.

3.13 Summary

Introduction

•Web browsers are the main GUIs for communicating with the Internet and the Web.

•Browsers locate Web sites and pages via their unique URLs, and display their content. URLs may occasionally use port numbers such as 80 for http — for example, www.abc.com:80.

•Browsers support the following protocols: http (load Web pages), mailto (send e-mail), nntp (access Usenet newsgroups), ftp (file transfer), telnet (remote access of computers), gopher (access gopher servers), and file (load local files).

Finding a URL

•When a user types or clicks a URL, the browser finds it equivalent IP address via a DNS server. The browser then converts the URL into TCP/IP packets with the IP address and sends them to the remote server identified by the URL. When the remote server sends back the content of the Web page identified by the URL to the browser, the browser displays the page.

•Encryption and decryption techniques are used to create secure connections between Web servers and client computers. Encryption converts data into unreadable form, while decryption converts encrypted data back into its original readable form.

•Both encryption and decryption use complex computer and mathematical algorithms. There are different levels of encryption/decryption. Some algorithms are very complex.

•Both Web servers and browsers use Secure Sockets Layer (SSL) to implement security. SSL is an integral part of Web browsers.

•SSL technology uses two keys: a public key to encrypt data, and a private key to decrypt data. The keys come in pairs that are not interchangeable.

•Another part of encryption is known as digital certificate; it is used for digital signature. A digital certificate is an electronic ID similar to, say, a credit card or driver's license. These certificates are kept in registries so that their owners can look up their public keys, like a deed of a house.

Browser Tasks

•Browsers perform the following tasks: navigation, viewing, multimedia display, e-mail, ftp, telnet, news, downloading files, and printing.

Overview of Browsers

•A browser GUI structure typically consists of, from top of its window to bottom, a title bar, a menu bar, several toolbars, a display area, and a status bar.

•Browsers allow users to manage a Web page via its URL, its display in the browser, and its HTML code. A user can bookmark the page URL, print the display of the Web page, or view and/or print the page's corresponding HTML code.

•Browsers use the cache concept to improve document access. Browsers use both memory and disk cache. Memory cache stores Web pages of the current browser sessions, while disk cache stores Web pages from previous sessions. Browsers allow their users to change the sizes of both memory and disk caches.

•Browsers use "helper" application programs to handle files of types that they do not support internally. A helper program appears in a new window separate from the browser window.

•Plug-ins are application programs that run within the browser window. They, like helper applications, extend the power of the browser.

•Users can customize their browsers to make them look and feel as they want.

Downloading Netscape Communicator

•To download Netscape Communicator for Windows, go to www.netscape.com, and click the following sequence of hyperlinks; Download => Windows 95/98/NT => Download Communicator without SmartDownload. Follow system prompts to choose the name of the file to be downloaded (accept the default name, cc32e47.exe) and the directory to save it in (choose the desktop).

•If you use Netscape FTP to download, type ftp.netscape.com in the browser URL bar to connect to Netscape FTP server. Click the following link sequence; pub => communicator => english => 4.7 => windows => windows95 or nt => professional edition => cp32e47.exe.

Installing Netscape Communicator

•To install Netscape Communicator for Windows, double click the downloaded executable cc32e47.exe. A series of setup dialog windows are displayed. The user reads and responds to them. For successful installation, click the following sequence; Next (to continue with Setup program) => Yes (accept license agreement) => Next (accept defaults for type of setup and destination directory) => Next (accept Netscape Communicator as the Internet default browser) => Next (accept default Program Folder) => Install (accept defaults).

Netscape Communicator GUI

•The Communicator GUI structure consists of the Title bar, Menu bar, three Toolbars (Navigation, Location, and Personal), display area, Status bar, and Component bar.

•The Title bar holds the title of the currently displayed Web page.

•The Menu bar has six menus: File, Edit, View, Go, Communicator, and Help. Each menu has menu items and submenus. The quick reference (below) shows how to use them to achieve certain tasks.

•The Navigation Toolbar holds the most frequently used buttons needed to navigate Web pages in a browser session.

•The Location Toolbar is where the user types the URL of a Web page that the browser should download and display.

•The `Personal` Toolbar has buttons to provide users with useful information. Users may customize this Toolbar.

•The display area is where the browser shows the contents of a Web page.

•The Status bar shows security and downloading information about the currently downloaded or displayed Web page.

•The Component bar has five icons to allow users to access all the Communicator modules. They are the Navigator, e-mail, Newsgroups, address book, and the Composer.

•Quick reference for using Netscape Communicator

1. E-mail. Before you can use the Netscape e-mail facility, you need to set up and configure the e-mail environment (the identity and mail servers).

1.1 Configure e-mail identity; click `Edit` => `Preferences` => `Mail&Newsgroups` => `Identity` => fill info. (See figure 3.24.)

1.2 Configure e-mail servers; click `Edit` => `Preferences` => `Mail&Newsgroups` => `Mail Servers` => fill info. (See figure s3.25 and 3.27.)

1.3 Change mail window setting; click `Edit` => `Preferences` => `Mail&Newsgroups` => `Window Settings` => choose a setting => OK. (Figure 3.28 shows the default setting.)

The following e-mail activities require that Netscape mail window be open. Click the `Inbox` icon on the `Component` bar to open it.

1.4 Get mail; click `Get Msg`.

1.5 Read mail; click the desired message header from the mail window.

1.6 Reply to mail; click `Reply` or `Reply All` => use composition window (figure 3.28) => Sénd.

1.7 Forward mail; click `Forward` => use composition window (figure 3.28) => `Send`.

1.8 File mail; highlight message header => `File`, or drag message header and drop it in desired folder (figure 3.28).

1.9 Print mail; highlight message header => `Print` => OK (figure 3.28).

1.10 Delete mail; highlight message header => `Delete` (figure 3.28).

1.11 Send mail; click `New Msg` (figure 3.28) => use composition window (figure 3.29) => `Send`.

1.12 Send mail with attachment; click `New Msg` (figure 3.28) => use composition window (figure 3.29) => `Attach` => choose file to attach => `Send`.

2. Check page security (encryption). Click the `Security` button (figure 3.13).

3. Run multiple copies of browser. Click `File` => `New` => `Navigator Window`.

4. Managing Web pages.

4.1 Visit a Web page; type the page URL in the browser location Toolbar (figure 3.13).

4.2 View a Web page source code; click `View` => `Page Source` (figure 3.13).

4.3 Print a Web page; while the page is displayed on the screen, click the `Print` button of the browser (figure 3.13).

4.4 Save a Web page; while the page is displayed on the screen, click `File` => `Save as` (figure 3.13).

4.5 Delete a Web page; this is simply deleting one of the local files. Drag the file into the recycling bin on the desktop, or use a system delete command.

5. Open local files in browsers; click `File` => `Open` (figure 3.13).

6. Managing bookmarks.

6.1 Access bookmarks; click `Communicator` => `Bookmarks` (figure 3.13).

6.2 Add a bookmark of currently displayed Web page; click `Communicator` => `Bookmarks` => `Add Bookmark` (figure 3.30).

6.3 Delete a bookmark; click `Communicator` => `Bookmarks` => `Edit Bookmarks`; highlight the bookmark to delete (figure 3.30); click `Edit` => `Delete` (figure 3.30).

6.4 Open Bookmarks window; click `Communicator` => `Bookmarks` => `Edit Bookmarks` (figure 3.30).

6.5 Insert a bookmark of a Web page that is NOT currently displayed; click `File` => `New Bookmark` (figure 3.31).

6.6 Create a bookmark folder; click `File` => `New Folder` (figure 3.31).

6.7 Insert a separator; click `File` => `New Separator` (figure 3.31).

6.8 View data of a bookmark or a folder; click `Edit` => `Bookmark Properties` (figure 3.31).

7. Managing address book.

7.1 Access address book; click the `Address Book` icon of the Component bar (figure 3.13).

7.2 Create a new address book; click `File` => `New Address Book` => type info. => `OK` (figure 3.32).

7.3 Add an address to the address book; highlight the address book in the Directory frame (figure 3.33). Click `New Card` => type info. => `OK` (figure 3.33).

7.4 Create a mailing list; highlight the address book in the Directory frame (figure 3.33). Click `New List` => type info. => `OK` (figures 3.34 and 3.35).

7.5 Use an address book to send an e-mail message to a mailing list or to one person; highlight the corresponding name in the address book => click `New Msg` => type message => `Send` (figures 3.36 and 3.29).

7.6 Remove an e-mail address; highlight the e-mail address => click `Delete` (figure 3.36).

7.7 Search an address book; type the name of the person in the `Show names containing` field of the `Address Book` window (figure 3.36).

7.8 Import address books; click `File` => `Import` => follow prompts (figure 3.36).

7.9 Export an address book; click `File` => `Export` => follow prompts (figure 3.36).

PROBLEMS

Exercises

3.1   Configure the e-mail tool on your computer to read and send e-mail messages.

3.2   Use the e-mail functions provided by your e-mail tool: reply to your e-mail messages, forward them, file them, print them, and delete them.

3.3   Create an e-mail list, with the name *class*, that contains the e-mail addresses of five of your classmates. Use it to send a message to them.

3.4   Choose some of the local files on your computer and try to open them in the browser. What do you see? What is your conclusion?

3.5   Open a PDF file on your computer. If you do not have one, search the Internet for one, and download it. If you do not have the Adobe Acrobat Reader installed on your computer, download it from www.adobe.com, and install it.

Homework

3.6   Find a recent article(s) that compares browsers, covers their latest versions, and reports on the war between them. You can use the paper route (e.g., PC magazine, PC World, etc.) or the Internet way (use a search engine). If you use a search engine, use the proper search string, such as *Netscape Communicator versus MS Internet Explorer.* Summarize the article in a half a page or a page.

3.7   Visit some Web sites. Create bookmarks for them. Organize them by category. Print them out, and submit them with your homework.

3.8   Create an address book of your favorite e-mail addresses. Print and submit them.

3.9   Create your e-mail signature. Print and submit it.

3.10 Associate the HTML file type to MS IE instead of Netscape and vice versa, depending on what is currently available on your computer. Submit screen captures of the series of steps you have followed.

Solution strategy:

3.3. Follow tutorial 3.11.4 which shows how to use an address book. You must have already cofigured Netscape e-mail tool as described in tutorial 3.11.1 in order for you to use the mailing list.

3.9. - Follow tutorial 3.11.1 to create your e-mail signature file, or your vCard. Use any word processor, or editing tool to create your signature file. You can include all text information as well as a logo or image. You can print the file via your word processor.

    - If you need to use the vCard, click the vCard checkbox (figure 3.24). To get to the checkbox, click Edit ⇒ Preferences ⇒ Mail & Newsgroups ⇒ Identity. Netscape Communicator asks you to create it. If you click the Create Card button, the Communicator displays a card window. Fill the info.

Microsoft Internet Explorer

T he two major Internet browsers are Netscape Communicator and Microsoft Internet Explorer. We have covered the details and the use of the former in chapter 3. In this chapter, we cover the details and the use of Microsoft Internet Explorer. We apply all the generic concepts covered in chapter 3 to the Internet Explorer version 5.0, as we did with the Communicator. We cover both the downloading and the installation procedures, as well as a description of the GUI. The tutorials section at the end of the chapter covers how to use the Explorer for various tasks. The tasks covered in the tutorials are e-mail, visiting Web sites, downloading files, checking page encryption and security, running multiple copies of a browser, dealing with Web pages, using a browser to open local files, dealing with bookmarks, and creating and using address books.

4.1 Introduction

There are two major browsers that Internet users utilize to navigate the Web. They are the Netscape Communicator and Microsoft Internet Explorer (MS IE). Both browsers are the same conceptually. They offer similar functionality, and it is a matter of personal preference which one to use. They perform very much the same tasks. The differences between the two browsers are mainly in appearance and performance. The two browsers look different. For example, the customizing and the setup parameters of Netscape Communicator are found in the sequence `Edit => Preferences`. Similar parameters of the MS IE are found in the sequence `Tools => Internet Options`. Netscape bookmarks are found in the sequence `Communicator => Bookmarks`. MS IE calls bookmarks favorites, and they are found in the `Favorites` menu. Netscape has a *smart browsing* feature and its Netcenter that are useful for searching the Internet, as covered in chapter 6. MS IE has channels that perform a similar role, as covered in chapter 6. MS IE is fully integrated with Windows desktop. Microsoft considers it as part of Windows OS. This chapter, together with the previous chapter, should provide users of both browsers with the background they need to install and use their preferred personal browser.

Despite their differences, there similarities in their GUIs. For example, the toolbars are almost the same. The e-mail facility of each browser allows its users to perform the same activities. However, Netscape Communicator has its mail tool integrated into its software and accessible through its GUI, while MS IE has separate software called Outlook Express as its e-mail tool. The mail software comes with MS IE. Installing the browser installs Outlook Express automatically. After the installation, an icon called Outlook Express is displayed on the desktop. The user clicks this icon to perform e-mail tasks.

There have been debates and studies about the performance, the speed, and the ease of using these two browsers. Most of us are aware of what has been dubbed in the literature as the browsers war. Whenever a new version of one browser is released, the other browser's competing version is usually released within a short period of time. It is up to the user's preference to use any browser. Many users have both browsers installed on their computers. Many clients and servers do that, because Web developers may want to test their Web pages under, both browsers, to look for inconsistencies before making their pages public.

4.2 Downloading

We assume here, as we did in chapter 3, that an older version of some browser already exists on your PC. We here download from www.microsoft.com. Depending on which browser you use to download MS IE, you get a different Web page. To stay consistent with the downloading procedure of Netscape Communicator described in section 3.5, we discuss the downloading steps of MS IE using the Netscape browser. Type www.microsoft.com in Netscape URL bar. Look for a link that reads `Internet Explorer Download it free` in Microsoft Web page that is loaded into your current browser window. Click the following link sequence; `Internet Explorer Download it free` => `Download` => `Internet Explorer 5 and Internet Tools` (under `Windows 98 or Windows 95 and Windows NT 4.0`) => `Next` (accept default language; English) => `Next` (accept default download site). After the last click, the browser displays the `Save As` dialog box as discussed in section 3.5 and shown in figure 3.5. The user accepts the default file name (`ie5setup`) and clicks the `Save` button. This sequence of clicks does not download MS IE. Instead, it downloads a setup executable (`ie5setup.exe`). To continue downloading, the user double clicks the `ie5setup` executable and follow the following sequence of clicks. `Next` (to activate this button, the user must click `I accept the agreement` first) => `Next` (accept default set of components) => Next (accept default download site). A progress window is displayed as shown in figure 4.1, and the explorer software begins downloading.

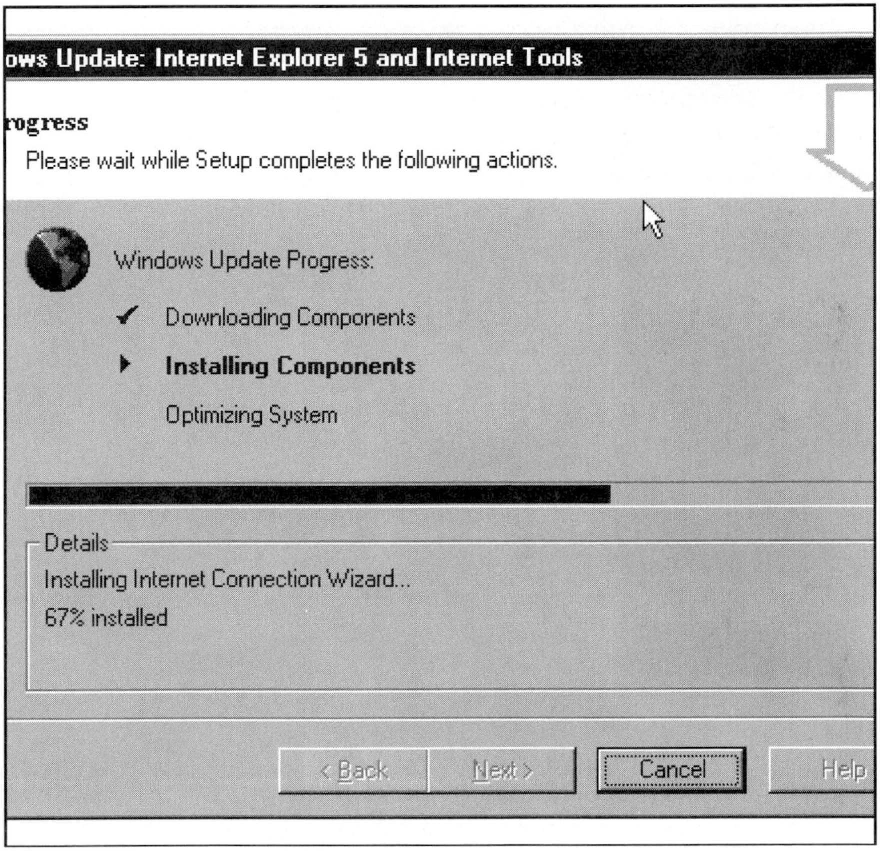

Figure 4.1   Installing Microsoft Internet Explorer: progress window.

4.3 Installing

Microsoft makes downloading and installing its IE browser transparent to the user. The progress window (figure 4.1) shows the three steps required to install MS IE fully. First, the IE components are downloaded. These components are stored in the folder C:\Program Files\Internet Explorer. Second, they are installed. Third, Windows settings are updated to incorporate MS IE. After the third step is complete, a Windows update window, shown in figure 4.2, pops up. After the user saves all work and closes all windows as requested in this window, the user clicks the Finish button. Upon the clicking of this button, Windows re-boots to complete installation and update systems settings. The user should realize that this automatic installation of MS IE changes the system browsing defaults, in particular those set up by Netscape. To get Netscape defaults back, the user can simply and easily reinstall Netscape software.

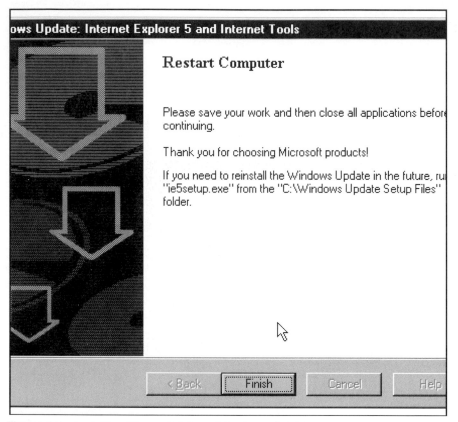

Figure 4.2   Installing Microsoft Internet Explorer: finishing.

4.4 Graphical User Interface

The MS IE GUI is shown in figure 4.3. The figure shows the Title bar, the Menu bar, three toolbars (Standard Buttons, Address Bar, and Links), and the Status bar. The title bar displays the title of the current Web page. The browser appends "- Microsoft Internet Explorer" to the title. The following sections cover the details of the MS IE GUI.

4.5 Menu Bar

The Menu bar has six menus: File, Edit, View, Favorites, Tools, and Help. The File menu and its submenus are shown in figure 4.4. The New submenu allows you to open a

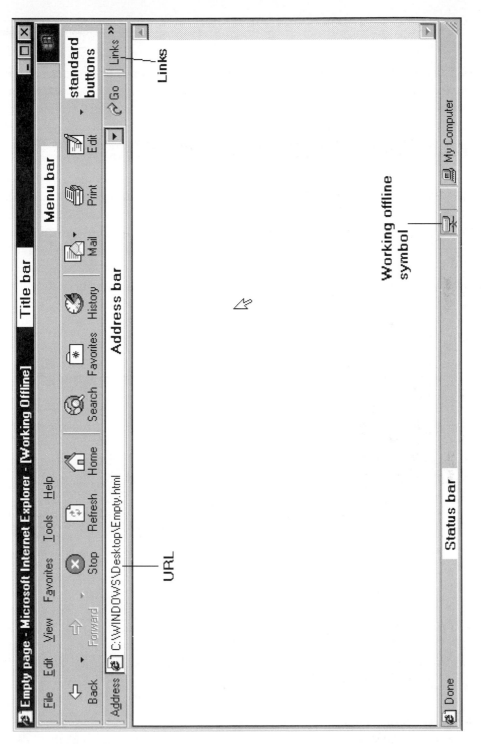

Figure 4.3 The Internet Explorer GUI.

new browser (`Window`), open an e-mail window (`Message`), open an Internet connection to post a the message to a newsgroup (`Post`), open the address book (`Contact`), or use Microsoft NetMeeting software to communicate with others and use video to see them over the Internet (`Internet Call`). The `Internet Call` is similar to video conferencing on the Internet and chat rooms. The `Open` menu item allows the user to open a file in the browser. While this could be any file, we usually open HTML files (Web pages), whether they reside on the local hard disk or on the Internet. The `Page Setup` and `Print` menu items act similarly to the corresponding items one finds in word processors' GUIs. The `Send` submenu allows the user to send a page or a link by e-mail (`Page By Email`, `Link By Email`), or send a shortcut of the Web page currently displayed in the browser to the desktop (`Shortcut To Desktop`). The `Import` and `Export` menu item allows the user to import or export information into or from IE, such as `Favorites` and `Cookies`, from or to other applications or a file on the local disk of the computer on which IE is currently running. The `Properties` menu item lists all the properties of the Web page currently displayed in the browser. The `Work Offline` menu item acts as a checkbox that enables using the browser in an online or offline mode. The `Close` menu item closes the current browser window.

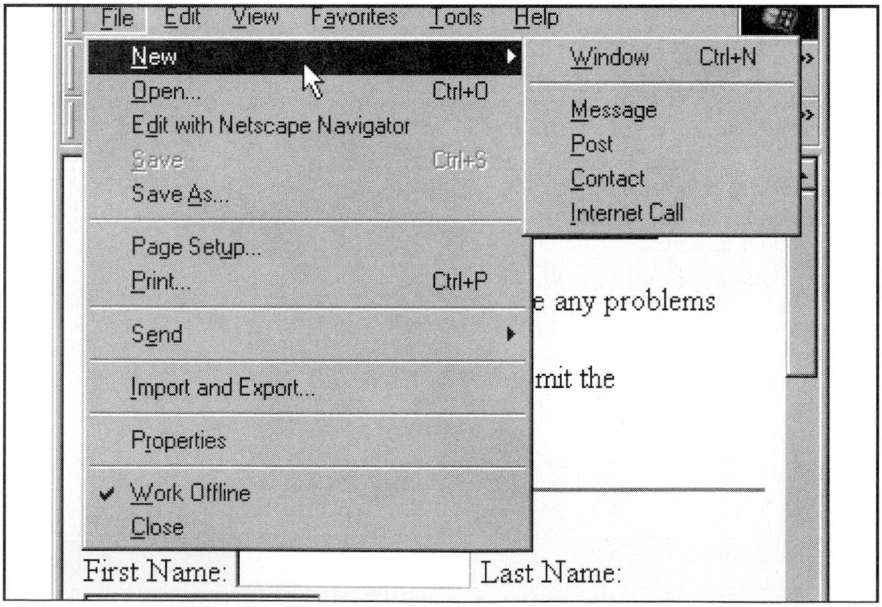

Figure 4.4   The File menu of MS IE.

The `Edit` menu and its menu items are shown in figure 4.5. We discuss some of these items here. The `Cut`, `Copy`, `Paste`, and `Select All` menu items work similarly to the corresponding menu items one encounters on a word processor's Edit menu. The `Find` (on this page) menu item allows the user to find elements of the currently displayed Web page.

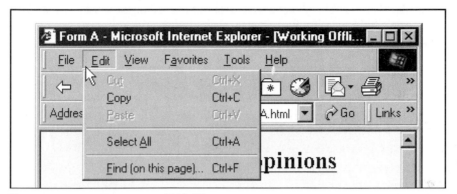

Figure 4.5 The Edit menu of MS IE.

The View menu and its items and submenus are shown in figure 4.6. The Toolbars submenu can turn on and off the Standard Buttons, Address Bar, and Links. The Customize menu item of the Toolbars submenu allows the user to replace the Standard Buttons by other buttons. This is hardly ever done by most users. The Status Bar menu item

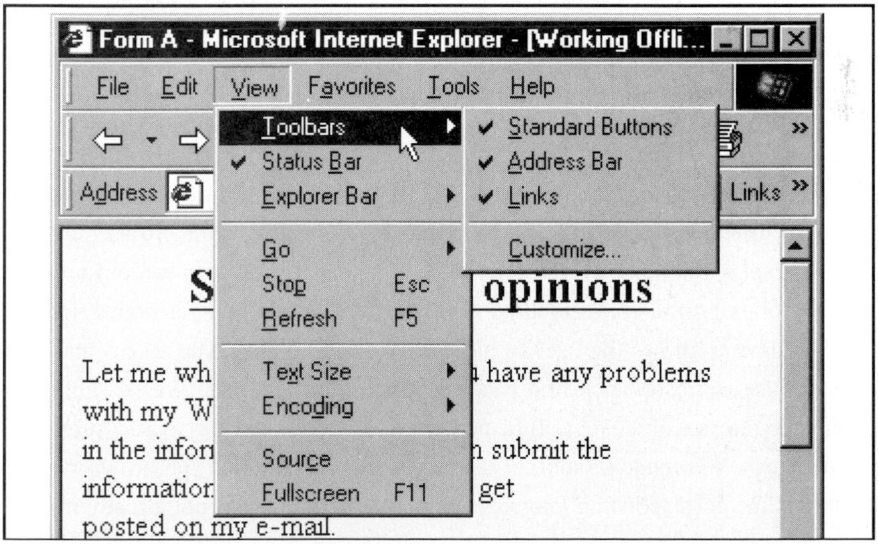

Figure 4.6 The View menu of MS IE.

of the View menu turns on and off the status bar at the bottom of the browser window. The Explorer Bar submenu, shown in figure 4.7, has five menu items: Search, Favorites,

History, Folders, and Tip of the Day. The Search menu item enables the user to search the Internet. The user must be online to use it. The Favorites menu item lists the user's bookmarks. The History menu item lists the history of the current browser window. The Folders menu item lists the folders of the computer the browser is running on. When the

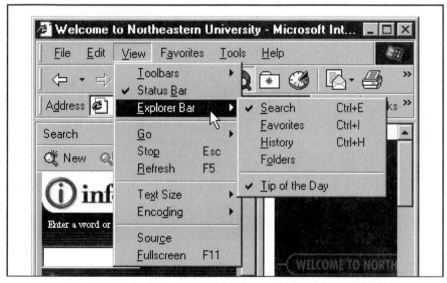

Figure 4.7   Menu items of the Explorer Bar of MS IE.

user clicks any of the first four items, the browser splits its window into two subwindows. The right subwindow holds the current Web page, and the left subwindow holds the results of the submenu item. If the user clicks the fifth item (Tip of the Day), the browser creates a third subwindow, to display the tip, by further dividing its window. The user can close the two new subwindows by clicking the corresponding close button (shown as X at upper right in figure 4.7). The Go submenu allows the user to navigate the history list. The Stop and Refresh menu items stop and refresh the current page respectively. The Text Size submenu allows the user to change the size of the text of the current Web page. The Encoding submenu allows the user to display a Web page in another language, such as Arabic. The browser will ask the user to download the corresponding language support software if it is not already installed. The Source menu item is of particular interest, as it is in Netscape. When the user chooses this item, MS IE displays the HTML source (code) of the currently displayed Web page in a Notepad window. Notepad is the Windows text editor. This is useful for Web developers as they may want to save the source code by clicking File => Save As on the Notepad window. The Fullscreen menu item expands the current window of IE to fill the screen.

The Favorites menu is shown in figure 4.8. Its menu items help the user to deal with bookmarks. The Add to Favorites creates a bookmark of the Web page currently displayed. The Organize Favorites allows the user to manage the bookmarks and move them from one folder to another. The three submenus Channels, Links, and Media of the Favorites menu provide the user with bundled bookmarks that come with MS IE. The My Documents menu item of Favorites allows the user to open the My Documents Windows folder in IE.

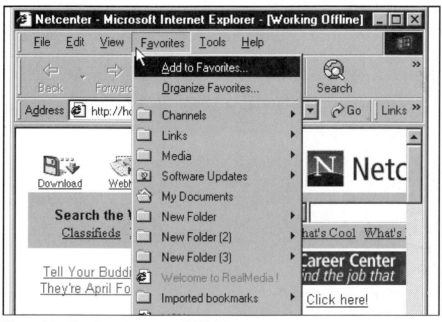

Figure 4.8 The Favorites menu of MS IE.

The Tools menu is shown in figure 4.9. The Mail&News submenu has five menu items that allow the user to read mail (Read Mail), send a message (New Message), send a link (Send a Link), send the current Web page (Send Page), and read newsgroups news

Figure 4.9 The Tools menu of MS IE.

(Read News). When the user clicks the Read News menu item, the browser opens Microsoft Outlook Express software to enable the user to read the news and messages. The Synchronize menu item updates data on the local disk, so the user has access to the latest data. The Windows Update menu item downloads Microsoft Windows Web page for the user to review the latest Windows information. The Internet Options menu item of the Tools menu is a major one, because it allows the user to customize the browser by changing its default settings. When the user clicks this item, a window with six tabs is displayed, as shown in figure 4.10. The window provides the user with many choices, to set up MS IE. The General tab allows the user to change the default home page, the Temporary Internet Files, and the History folder. It also provides the user with four buttons (figure 4.10) to change the colors, fonts, languages, and accessibility of the browser. The Security tab allows the user to change the secu-

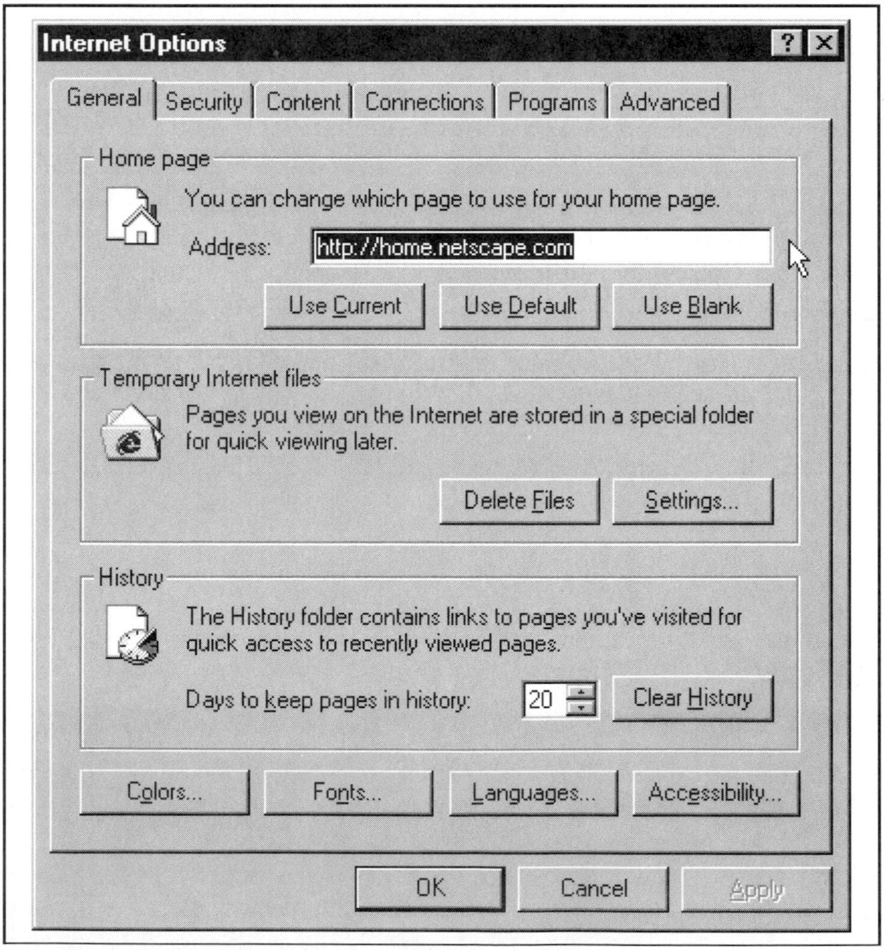

Figure 4.10   The Internet Options window of MS IE.

rity settings of the browser. The Content tab provides the user with control over the information and content of Web pages. The user can set up the browser to prevent bad Web pages from reaching children or to save personal information for later use. The Connections tab helps the user to establish new connections, edit LAN settings, and edit the current dialup connections. The Programs tab allows the user to specify which programs Windows automatically uses for such Internet tasks as HTML editor, e-mail, and so forth. The Advanced tab allows the user to control the settings for accessibility, browsing, multimedia, security, Java VM (virtual machine), printing, searching, toolbar, and HTTP settings.

The last menu on the menu bar of MS IE is the Help menu. Figure 4.11 shows its menu items. Some of the menu items, such as For Netscape Users, Web Tutorial, online Support, and Send Feedback require the user to connect to the Internet to receive help information, because the browser downloads from the Microsoft Web site. The other items of the Help menu (Contents and Index, Tip of the Day, Repair, and About Internet Explorer) work offline. The About Internet Explorer item displays information about the browser and its version. The Contents and Index menu item of the Help menu is quite useful, because the user can use it as an online help to search for many details about MS IE operations and use.

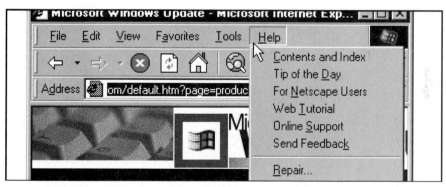

Figure 4.11   The Help menu of MS IE.

4.6 The Internet Explorer Toolbars

MS IE has three toolbars, as shown in figure 4.3. The Standard Buttons toolbar has several useful buttons. Using the Back and Forward buttons, the user can cycle through the history list of the previously visited Web sites and reload anyone of them. The browser saves the Web sites the user visits during a session in its memory cache. These Web sites make the history list. The Stop button is used to interrupt the current transfer of information from the server to the client and vice versa. It stops downloading or uploading Web pages, form data, and so forth. The Refresh button reloads the current Web page. This button is particularly useful for Web developers as they edit the code for their Web pages and must reload these pages to view the latest edited versions. The Home button, if clicked, loads the home Web page defined in the browser settings. Using the Search button, the user uses search tools to navigate the Web. The Favorites button is the same as the Favorites menu on the menu bar, with the exception that it does not allow the user to add or organize bookmarks. The History button gives the same results as clicking the sequence View => Explorer Bar => History, where View is the menu on the Menu bar. Clicking the Mail button produces the same menu items as clicking the following sequence; Tools => Mail&News, where Tools is the menu on the Menu bar. Why do the three buttons (Favorites, History, and Mail) repeat functionality? It is a matter of preference about where to access them. It is more convenient to access them from the Standard Buttons toolbar where they are directly visible. The Print button prints the current Web page or other information as the user sees it on the screen. The Edit button invokes the default HTML editor to edit the currently displayed Web page or another page.

The Address Bar toolbar has the text field where the user types the URL. If the URL is a Web site, the user does not need to type the protocol. The browser assumes it is http://. The user needs to type only the Web site name, such as www.prenhall.com. If the URL is a local file, the user must type the file:// protocol, followed by the file name (including the file full path); for example, file://aaa/bbb/ppp.html. Next to the Address Bar, there is the Go button, as shown in figure 4.3. After the user types the URL in the Address Bar, the user clicks the Go button to download the Web page. Alternatively, the user can simply hit the Enter key on the keyboard.

The Links toolbar is located next to the Go button, as shown in figure 4.3. The user can display it by dragging the bottom edge of the Address bar down. Also, when the user double clicks this toolbar (double click the word Links itself), the Links toolbar expands and displays six buttons that the user can click for useful information. These six buttons are Best of the Web, Channel Guide, Customize Links, Free HotMail, Internet Explorer News, and Internet Start. All the buttons connects the user to the www.microsoft.com Web site. The Links toolbar for MS IE is similar to the Personal toolbar in Netscape Communicator. The Links toolbar covers the Address Bar temporarily. The user can close the Links toolbar by double clicking the word Links.

4.7 The Status Bar

The Status bar shown in figure 4.3 divided into three areas. On the left, there is an area that shows the status of loading information of Web pages to the browser. The second area shows a connection symbol with a red x. The symbol is an indication that the browser is working offline. If the user clicks the sequence File => Work Offline (File is the menu on the browser menu bar), the symbol goes away, allowing the browser to connect to the Internet (assuming that the user is already online). The third area, on the far right (figure 4.3), shows a globe next to the word Internet. If the user double clicks the globe, a security window pops up. This is the same window that pops up when the user clicks the sequence Tools => Internet Options

=>Security, where Tools is a menu on the menu bar and Security is a tab of the Internet Options window, as shown in figure 4.10.

4.8 Tutorials

This section focuses on the hands-on aspects of using the MS IE. The major uses of the browser is illustrated here.

4.8.1 E-mail

This is the basic tool that most of us begin using once connected. It is simple and intuitive to use. You send e-mail messages to individuals or to groups. You can send an attachment, as well, with the e-mail message. Attachments are usually used if you are sending a file or a long document (e.g., resumes, articles, summaries, etc.) that is already on your computer. You use attachments to avoid typing the document all over again, and to make the e-mail message easier to read (especially if you send more than one document with your e-mail message).

Before you can use the MS IE e-mail facility, you need to set up and configure the e-mail environment, as you did with Netscape mail in chapter 3. The MS IE e-mail tool is called Outlook Express. MS IE creates a shortcut with this name on your desktop when installing the browser software. Locate this shortcut on your desktop. To set up your Outlook Express e-mail, double click the Outlook Express shortcut to open the Outlook Express window, shown in figure 4.12. To set up an e-mail account, click the Setup a Mail account hyperlink. Upon your clicking, a panel opens up and asks you to enter your name as you would like it to appear in the From field of the outgoing message. After you type the desired name (say, *Abe Zeid*) click the Next button. Notice that the Next button is not clickable until you type a name. When you click the Next button, an E-mail Address panel opens up. Enter your e-mail address (say, zeid@coe.neu.edu), and click the Next button. Now you need to choose the incoming and outgoing mail servers and enter their names, as shown in figure 4.13. Type the names of your e-mail servers as given to you by your server provider, and click the Next button. Enter your mail login (account name and password), and click the Next button, as shown in figure 4.14. At this point, you are done setting up your mail. Click the Finish button (shown in figure 4.15) to end the setting up. After setting up your mail, notice that the Setup a mail account hyperlink that you clicked (figure 4.12) at the start is now replaced by two new links: Create a new Mail message and Read Mail.

As you have done with Netscape Communicator in chapter 3, you can create and use a signature text or file with your e-mail messages. As with Netscape, you create the signature yourself. To include a signature in your e-mail message, click the Tools menu of the Outlook Express window (figure 4.12). When you click the Options menu item from the Tools menu, the Options window shown in figure 4.16 is displayed. Click the Signatures tab in this window to create the signature as shown in figure 4.17. Click the New button. You now have two ways to create a signature as shown under the Edit Signature heading shown in figure

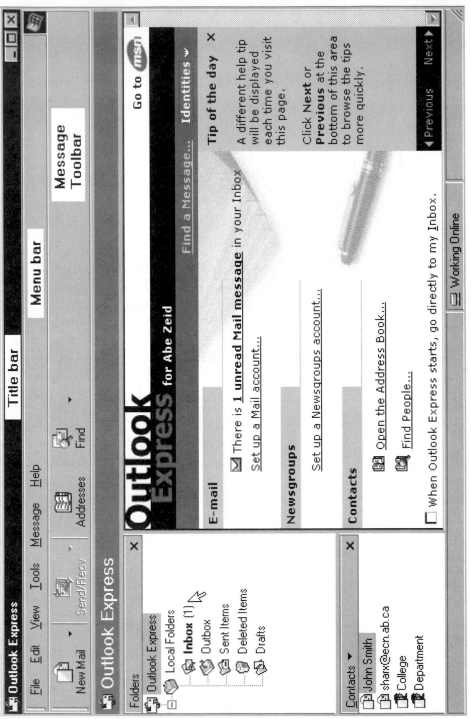

Figure 4.12 MS IE Outlook Express mail window.

4.17. You can either type text (the default choice) or use an existing file. To use an existing signature file, click the `File` button and type the file name, or click the `Browse` button to locate it. To finish off, click the first checkbox (`Add signatures to all outgoing messages`) under the Signature settings heading shown in figure 4.17.

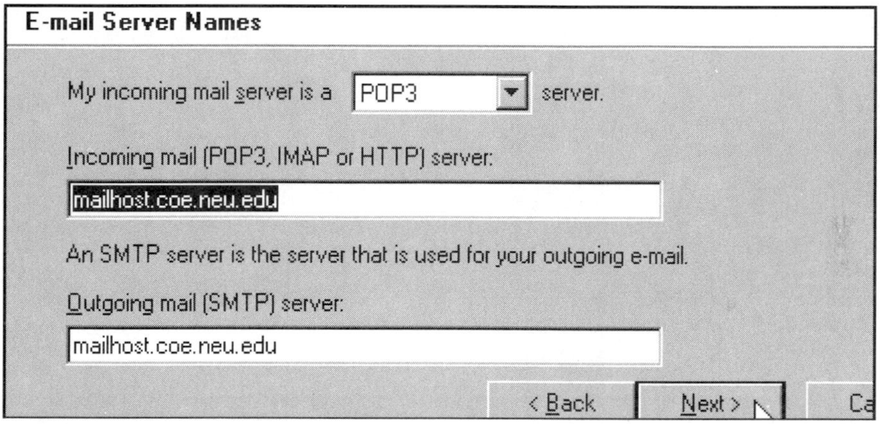

E-mail Server Names

My incoming mail server is a [POP3 ▼] server.

Incoming mail (POP3, IMAP or HTTP) server:

[mailhost.coe.neu.edu]

An SMTP server is the server that is used for your outgoing e-mail.

Outgoing mail (SMTP) server:

[mailhost.coe.neu.edu]

[< Back] [Next >] [Ca]

Figure 4.13   Configuring the identity fields of MS IE e-mail: enter mail servers' names.

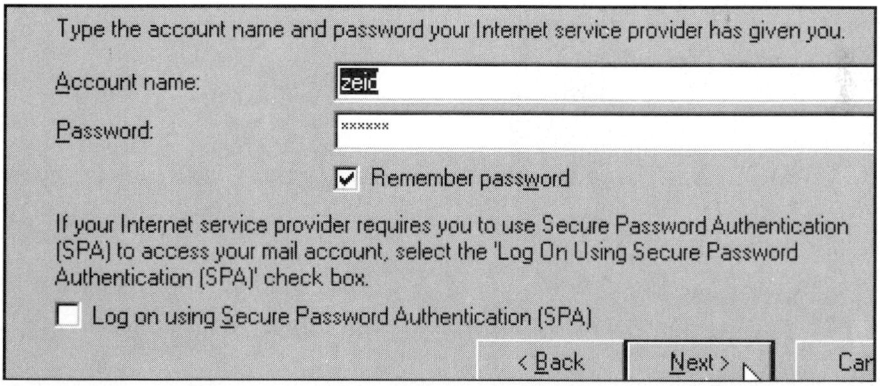

Type the account name and password your Internet service provider has given you.

Account name: [zeid]

Password: [xxxxxx]

[✓] Remember password

If your Internet service provider requires you to use Secure Password Authentication (SPA) to access your mail account, select the 'Log On Using Secure Password Authentication (SPA)' check box.

[ ] Log on using Secure Password Authentication (SPA)

[< Back] [Next >] [Car]

Figure 4.14   Configuring the identity fields of MS IE e-mail: enter mail login.

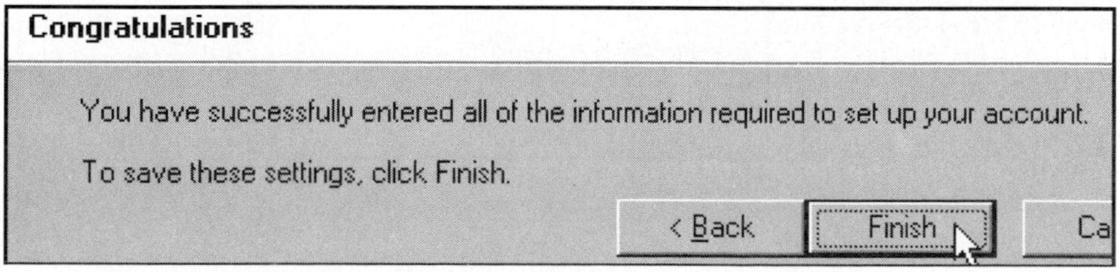

Congratulations

You have successfully entered all of the information required to set up your account.

To save these settings, click Finish.

[< Back] [Finish] [Ca]

Figure 4.15   Configuring the identity fields of MS IE e-mail: finish mail setup.

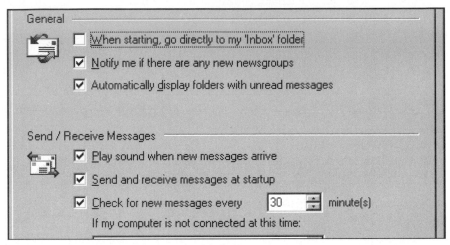

Figure 4.16   The Options window of MS Outlook Express.

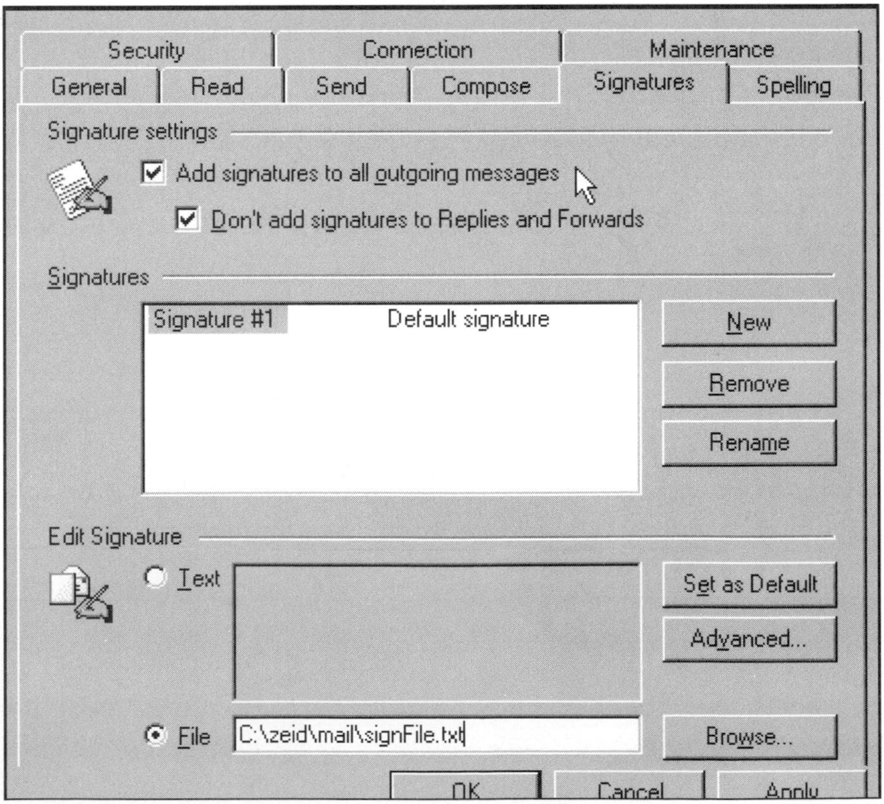

Figure 4.17   Creating a signature in MS Outlook Express.

Instead of using a signature, you may use a vCard. Before you can use a vCard, you need to create it. To start, click the `Tools` menu of Outlook Express, then click the `Address Book` menu item to open the `Address Book - Main Identity` window shown in figure 4.18. Or you can click the `Addresses` button of Outlook Express, shown in figure 4.12. Highlight the name (Abe Zeid, shown in figure 4.18) you want to export a vCard for. Click the following sequence (figure 4.18) to create the vCard; `File => Export => Business Card(vCard)` At the end of this sequence, Outlook Express displays an `Export` window as shown in figure

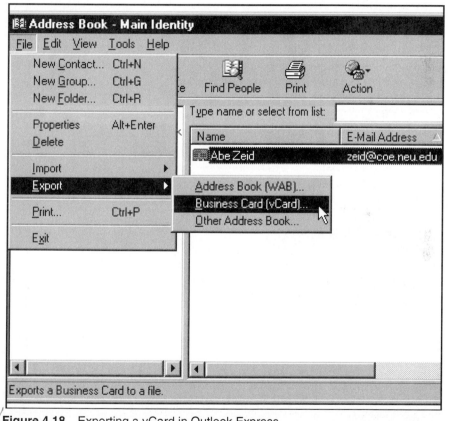

Figure 4.18   Exporting a vCard in Outlook Express.

4.19. Choose a name for the vCard or use the default (Abe Zeid), and select a directory (folder) in which to save it. The vCard files have the extension `*.vcf`. To use the vCard file in e-mail messages, click the `Tools` menu of Outlook Express, then click the `Options` menu item. Click the `Compose` tab of the `Options` window, as shown in figure 4.20. Click the `Mail` checkbox under Business Cards. Click the arrow of the drop list next to the checkbox. Select the business card to include (Abe Zeid). Click the `OK` button to finish.

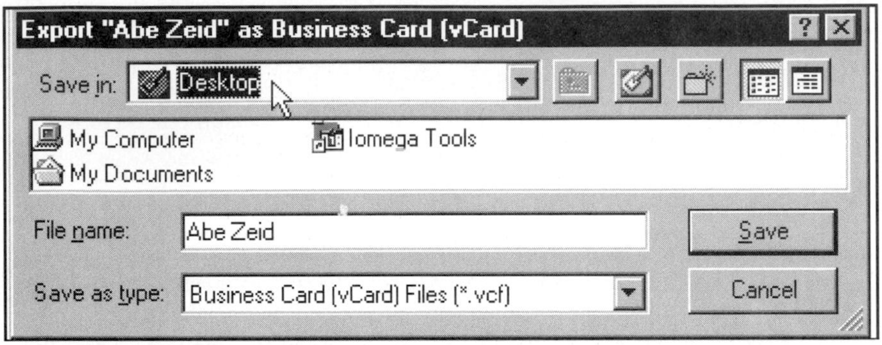

Figure 4.19   Saving vCards using MS Outlook Express.

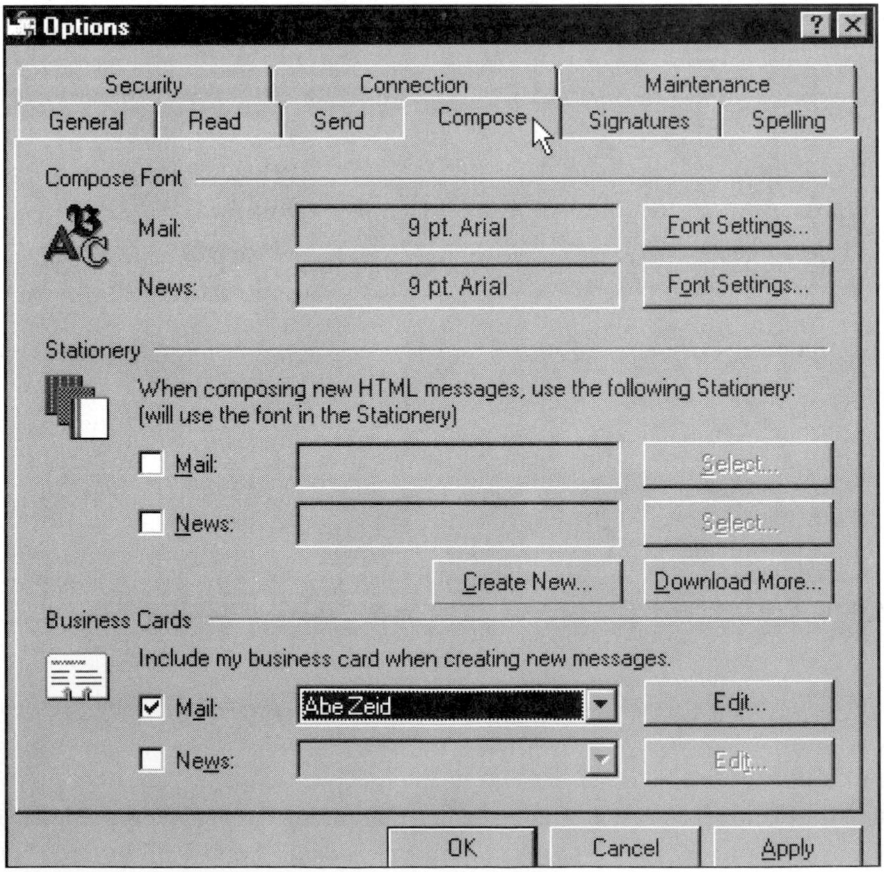

Figure 4.20   Including MS vCards in mail messages.

Having finished setting up and configuring the MS Outlook Express e-mail facility, let us explore with it. Figure 4.12 shows the mail window. The mail window is divided into four frames. The frame on the right displays the `Tip of the day`. The bottom frame on the right displays the body of the selected message header in the top frame. The top frame on the left shows the local mail folders that are available on the local computer. The main mail folder is `Local Folders` as shown in figure 4.12. Several subfolders exist under this folder. The `Inbox` subfolder is where the browser downloads e-mail messages from the mail server. The `Outbox` subfolder is where you may save any unsent messages; it is similar to Netscape's `Uns...ages` subfolder. The `Sent Items`, `Deleted items`, and `Drafts` are similar to Netscape's `Sent`, `Trash`, and `Drafts` subfolders respectively. The `Junk Mail` subfolder is used to store junk e-mail messages. The bottom frame on the left shows the `Contacts` that you have created. You can send an e-mail message to any contact if you double click it. The fourth frame of the Outlook Express mail window is the middle frame (figure 4.12), which has links to enable you to handle e-mail, newsgroups, and contacts.

You can close the right frame and the two frames on the left by clicking their respective closing buttons (x). When you close these frames, the Outlook Express mail window looks as shown in figure 4.21. To open the `Tip of the day` frame, click the `Tips` button (shown next to the hand in figure 4.21). To open the top left frame that shows the local mail folders, click the `Outlook Express` button shown on the top right side of the mail window (figure 4.21). To open the bottom left frame to show the contacts, click (from Outlook Express menu bar) the `View` menu, then click the `Layout` menu item to open the window shown in figure 4.22. You can use this window to customize Outlook Express mail window; you now use it to open the `Contacts` frame. Click the `Contacts` checkbox as shown in figure 4.22, and then click `OK`.

In addition to its four frames, the mail window has a title bar, a menu bar, and a message toolbar, as shown in figure 4.12. You are encouraged to investigate the various menus of the menu bar, and their submenus and menu items. The message toolbar has four buttons to help you to handle e-mail messages. They are `New Mail`, `Reply`, `Reply All`, and `Forward`. If you click the `Inbox` folder, you get a mail window (shown in figure 4.23). Here is how you handle mail in MS Outlook Express. (You must be online.)

Get mail. You need to download your mail first before you can read it. Using the Outlook Express window shown in figure 4.12, click the `Send/Rec` button (or `Tools` (on the menu bar) => `Send and Receive` => `Receive All`) to download your e-mail messages, or, using the `Inbox` window shown in figure 4.23, click the `Send/Rec` button. You may need to resize the top and the bottom left frames of the `Inbox` window by dragging the border between them, as shown in figure 4.23 by the bi-directional vertical arrow. During downloading, the browser displays a progress window. After downloading, the browser displays the messages' headers in the top right frame, as shown in figure 4.23. The browser bolds the newly unread messages' headers, to make it easier for you to identify and read them. The browser arranges all the downloaded messages' headers in ascending order by date. The Outlook Express window

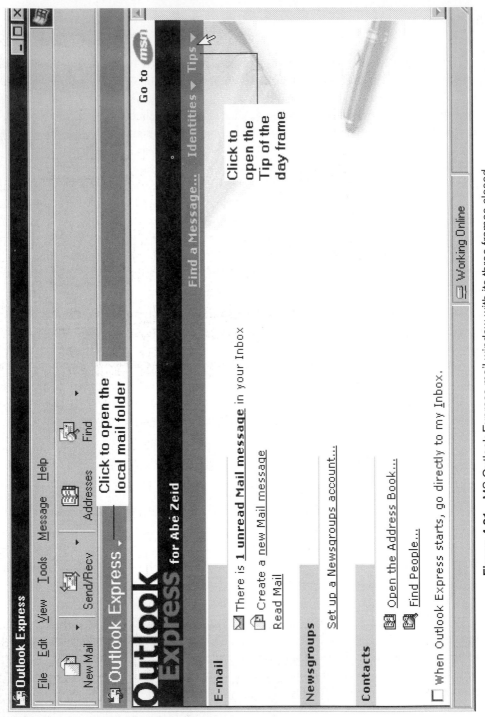

Figure 4.21 MS Outlook Express mail window with its three frames closed.

displays the number of unread mail messages in parentheses next to the Inbox folder, as shown in figure 4.12. A hyperlink is also shown in the middle frame of the window, as shown in figure 4.12.

Read mail. To read your e-mail messages, simply click the Read Mail hyperlink displayed in the Outlook Express window (figure 4.21), or, in the Inbox mail window (figure 4.23), click the desired message header. The full message is displayed in the bottom right frame, as shown in figure 4.23. You can click all the header,s one after the other, to read all the messages.

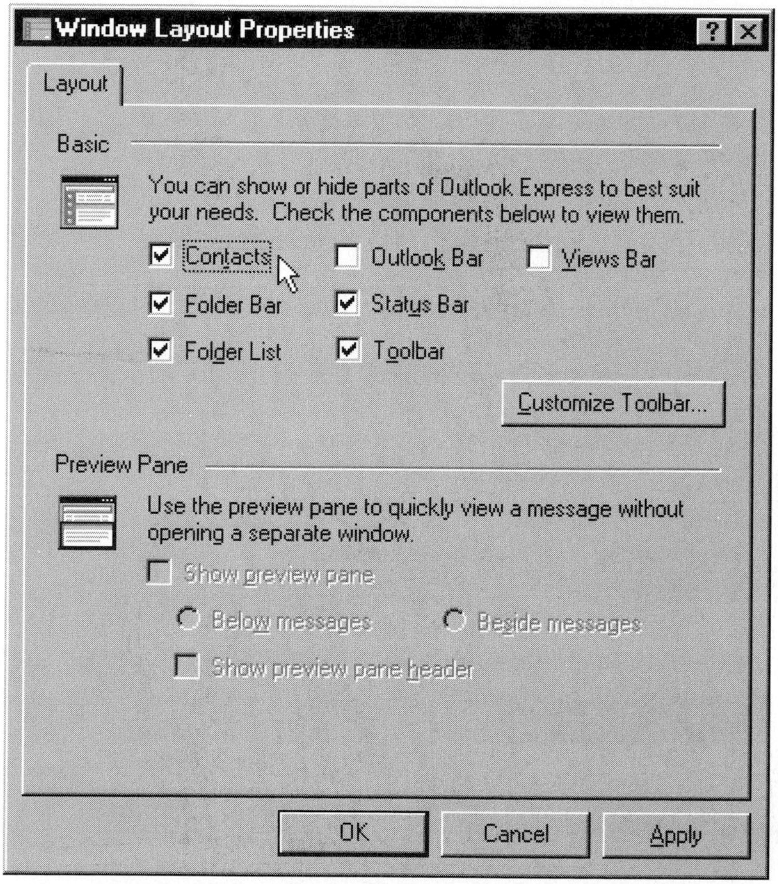

Figure 4.22 Customizing the MS Outlook Express mail window.

Reply to mail. After reading a message, you have several choices of how to deal with it. You may respond to it, forward it, file it, print it, or delete it. To respond to an e-mail message after reading it, click the Reply or Reply All button on the message Toolbar of the Inbox

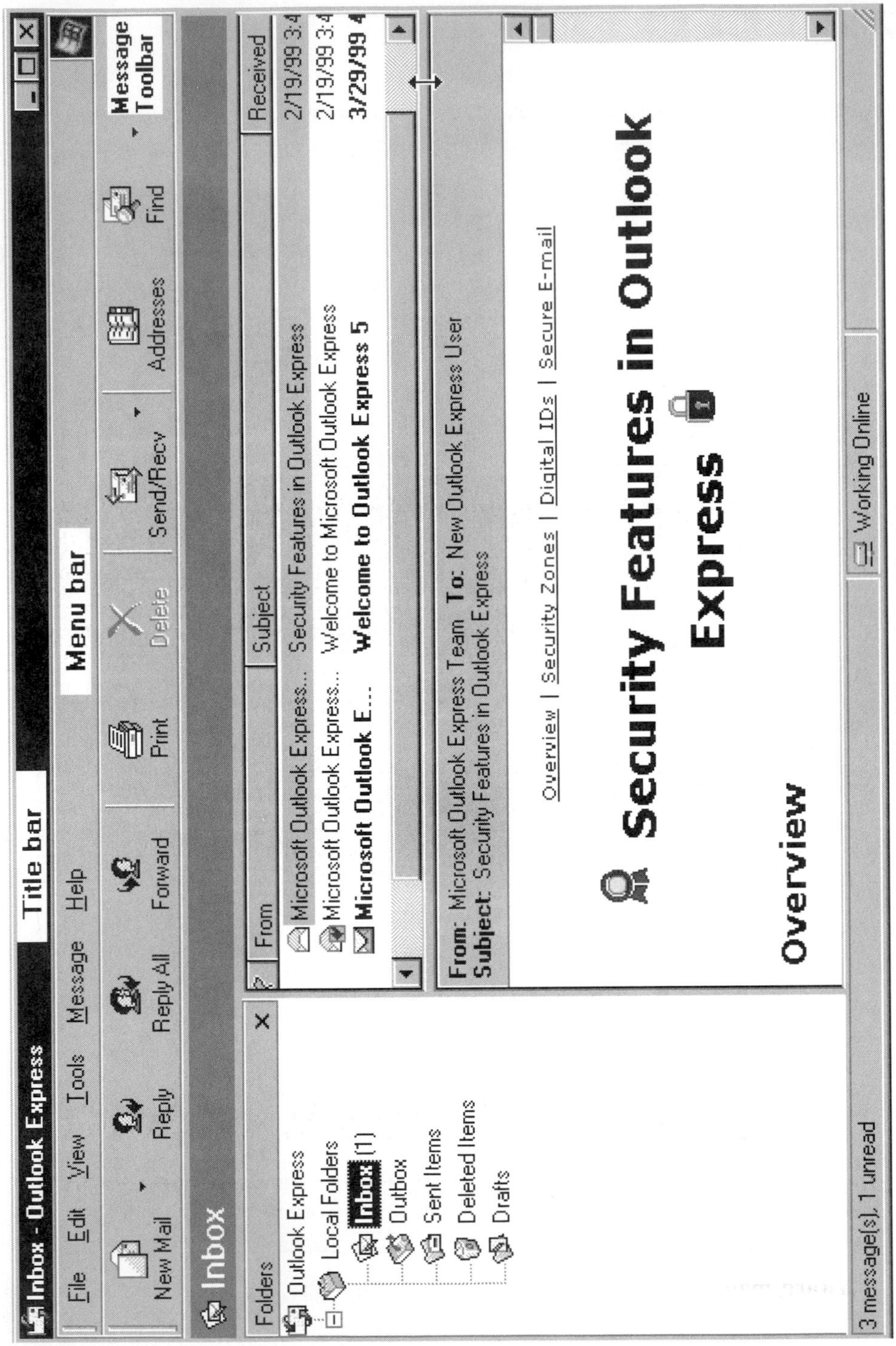

Figure 4.23 MS `Inbox` mail window.

mail window, shown in figure 4.23. If the e-mail message you are responding to has the e-mail address of the sender only, you click Reply. The Reply All button is used if you want to send a response to all e-mail addresses listed in the message. Upon your clicking one of these two buttons, a composition window pops up, as shown in figure 4.24. You are encouraged to investigate the menus, submenus, and buttons of this window. Fill in the fields of the window, in particular the e-mail addresses the reply message is going to, and the Subject field. Write the body of the message, and click the Send button of the composition window shown in figure 4.24. To send an attachment with the message, click the Attach button of the composition window (figure 4.24) and follow the browser prompts.

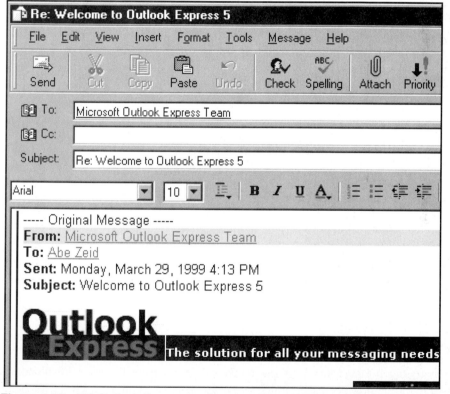

Figure 4.24 MS Outlook Express mail composition window.

Forward mail. To forward an e-mail message, click the Forward button of the Inbox window (figure 4.23). The browser opens its composition window. The Subject field of the window shows the title of the message to be forwarded, preceded by Fwd:. Type the forwarding e-mail addresses and the body of the message, and click the Send button. The browser sends both the message that you type and the forwarded message.

File mail. You may file old e-mail messages already read by dragging the message header from the top left frame and dropping it in the desired folder shown in the left frame of the Inbox window. You need to create the desired mail folders. For example, you can create separate folders, such as friends, business, and so forth to save the corresponding messages.

Print mail. To print an e-mail message, click the `Print` button of the Inbox window (figure 4.23). When you click the button, the browser displays a Print pop-up window allowing you to print all the pages of the message or selected pages. You need to click the `OK` button of the Print window.

Delete mail. To delete an e-mail message, highlight the header of the message, and click the `Delete` button of the Inbox window (figure 4.23). This results in moving the messages to the Deleted Items folder. To truly delete the messages, go to this folder, highlight the messages and click the `Delete` button again. The browser asks you to confirm. Click `Yes`.

Send mail. You can send an e-mail message without or with an attachment. To send an e-mail message, click the `New Mail` button of the Inbox window (figure 4.23). The composition window shown in figure 4.24 pops up. Fill in the e-mail address and the subject. Type the body of the message, and then click `Send`. To send a message with an attachment, repeat what you just did. Then click `Attach` in the composition window and follow the prompts. You can send a URL location or a file as an attachment. If you send a URL location as an attachment, the browser gets the corresponding document (say, a Web page) and sends it. The receiver can view the document and/or its HTML file by using a browser.

4.8.2 Browsing Activities

We can use browsers to perform a multitude of browsing activities. Here are some examples.

Visit Some Web Sites. Depending on your interest, you can visit many Web sites. Some sites you may interested in visiting are www.aol.com, www.yahoo.com, www.amazon.com, www.prenhall.com, www.neu.edu, www.fedworld.gov (FedWorld), and marvel.loc.gov (Library of Congress). Go ahead and visit these sites and more.

Download Files. You can download audio, video, and image files from sites on the Web into your local hard drive. For example, you can download video games. Be aware that video files are very big and can take a long time downloading. We have discussed downloading files in chapter 1. You can download shareware from www.shareware.com or www.download.com. Go ahead and follow the instructions in chapter 1 to download your favorite files and shareware.

Check Encryption and Security. MS IE alerts you (with a `Security Alert` box) that you are about to view pages over a secure connection. The browser requires you to click the `OK` button of the alert box to continue downloading the Web page. When you are done, the browser displays the `Security Alert` box again, notifying you, this time, that you are about to leave a secure Internet connection. Click `OK` to continue. MS IE also offers you the ability to configure security. Click `Tools` from the menu bar, followed by `Internet Options`. In the `Inter-`

net Options window, click the Security and Content tabs. Go ahead and investigate the available options. *favierate !*

Run Multiple Copies of Browser. If you are in a rush, you can run multiple copies of the browser in different windows. Every window could be performing a different task. This is useful *(exercise* if you are downloading a file that may take too long, and you want to do something else, such as editing an HTML file, while waiting. To open a new MS IE window, click the following sequence — File => New => Window — or hit CTRL N.

Handle Web Pages. Most of the time, you deal with Web pages while using a browser. You can visit, view, print, save, or delete a Web page. Here is how to do them all.

•**Visit a Web page.** Type the URL location in the browser location Toolbar.

•**View a Web page source code.** Click View from the menu bar of the browser, followed by Source. The browser displays the HTML code of the currently displayed page in a Notepad window. This is useful later, when you start writing your own Web pages, as covered later in this book.

•**Print a Web page.** While the page is displayed on the screen, click the Print button of your browser. The browser prints the page as you see it displayed on the screen.

•**Save a Web page.** While the page is displayed on the screen, click File then Save as, to save it on your local disk drive. The browser saves the HTML file corresponding to the page.

•**Delete a Web page.** You can delete (only) your own Web pages stored on your local disk drive. This is simply deleting one of your local files. Drag the file into the recycling bin on your desktop, or use a system delete command on your computer.

•**Open a Local File.** You can use your browser to open any, including an HTML file. HTML files produce Web pages as you know them. The browser has an interpreter that interprets HTML tags embedded in these files and displays the results as the Web page; however, if you open a non-HTML file, the browser displays its contents in its window. You can open an HTML file in the browser or in an HTML editor. When you open the file in the browser, you view the corresponding Web page. When you open the file in an HTML editor, you change the HTML tags of the file itself. Opening and editing HTML files is useful when you are developing and writing Web pages in HTML.

4.8.3 Favorites

As you use your browser to surf the net, you may want to save your experiences for future use. Bookmarks allow you to do just that. You can add, delete, and organize bookmarks. MS IE refers to bookmarks as favorites. We continue using the word bookmark(s) here because it is more commonly used. The Favorites menu shown in figure 4.8 allows you to add and organize bookmarks, as shown by the top two menu items. The rest of the menu shows the current bookmarks and/or bookmark folders. When you point to any of these bookmarks, MS IE displays the corresponding URL location in the address bar and downloads the Web page. Here is how you use bookmarks in MS IE.

Add a bookmark. If you like the Web page that is currently displayed by the browser, click `Favorites => Add to Favorites` (figure 4.8) to open the `Add Favorite` window shown in figure 4.25. You can add the new bookmark to any of the existing folders shown in figure 4.25, or you can create a new folder, to save the new bookmark in, by clicking the `New Folder` button (figure 4.25). To save a bookmark in a folder, click the folder, and then click `OK`. If you click the `Favorites` menu again, you notice the new bookmark. If you click the `Make Available Offline` checkbox, as shown in figure 4.25, then click the `Customize` button, you get an `Offline Favorite Wizard` that allows you to customize your bookmark before adding it. Go ahead and practice with the wizard.

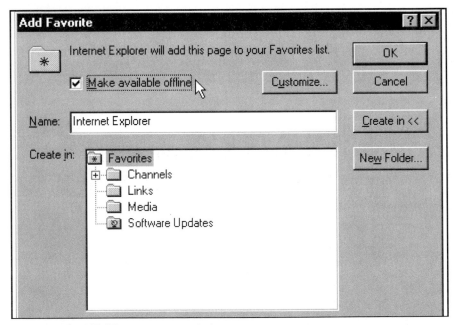

Figure 4.25 MS IE `Favorites` window.

Delete a bookmark. Click `Favorites => Organize Favorites`. The Organize Favorites window shown in figure 4.26 is displayed. Highlight the bookmark you want to delete, and click `Delete` in the window. There are several other useful buttons shown in figure 4.26 that enable you to rename a bookmark, move it to another folder, or change its properties. If you click the `Properties` button, the Properties window shown in figure 4.27 pops up. There are four tabs in the window, as shown in the figure, that you can use to change the properties of a bookmark. Go ahead and try them. Make sure that the `Make available offline` checkbox shown in figure 4.26 is checked to have access to the `Properties` button.

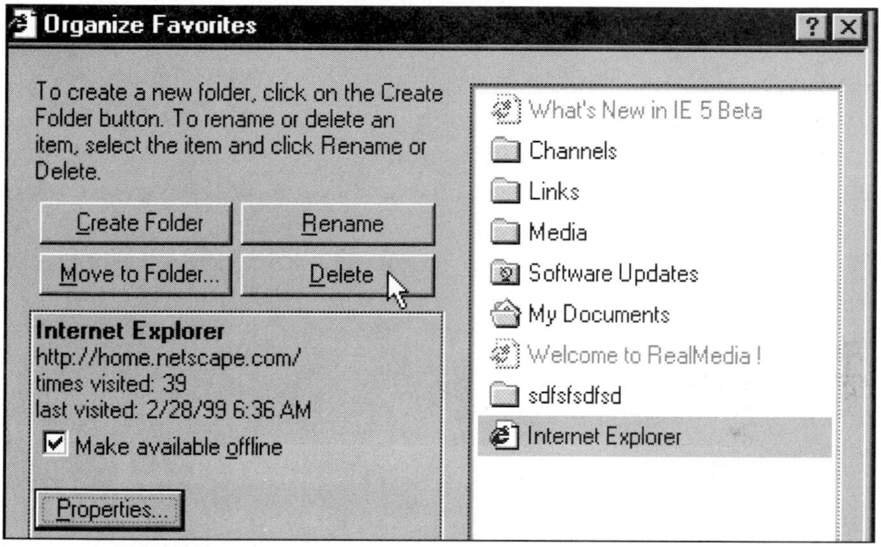

Figure 4.26 MS IE `Organize Favorites` window.

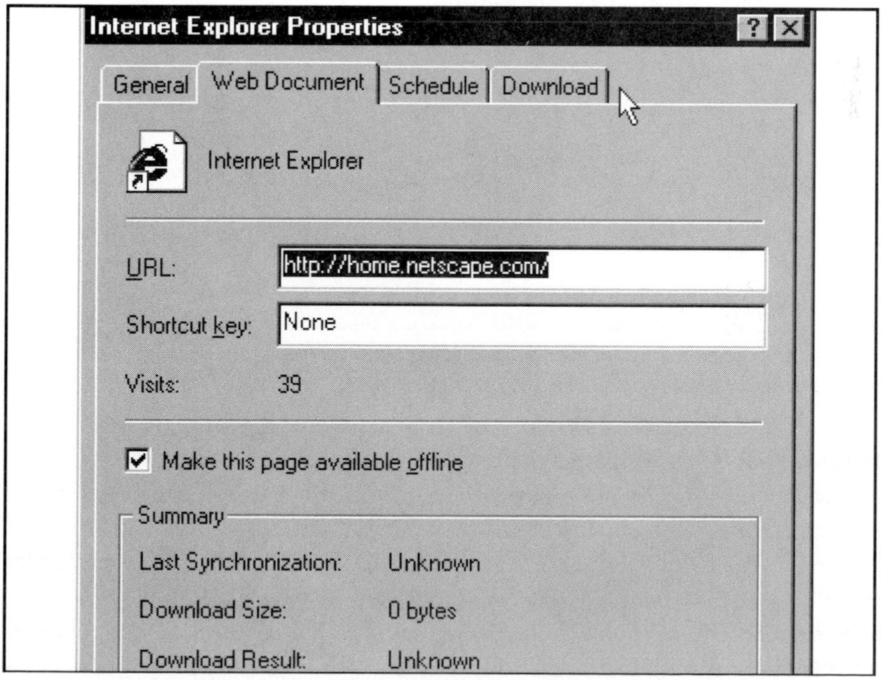

Figure 4.27 MS IE `Properties` window.

Organize bookmarks. As you save more and more bookmarks, you will need to organize them in folders. Click Favorites => Organize Favorites to open the Organize Favorites window shown in figure 4.26. The window provides you with buttons you need to organize your bookmarks. Simply highlight the bookmark you want to move and click the Move to Folder button shown in the figure. Clicking the button opens the Folder window shown in figure 4.28. Click the folder you want to move the bookmark to, and click OK. If you want to organize several bookmarks under a separate folder, click the Create Folder button of the Organize Favorites window (figure 4.26). The browser creates a new folder and waits for you to change its name. After creating the folder, you drag the bookmarks one by one and drop them into the folder. The changes you make to your bookmarks are instantly displayed in the Organize Favorites window. To view the data of a bookmark, highlight it, and click the Properties button shown in figure 4.26. The bookmark properties are shown in figure 4.27. You can change these properties.

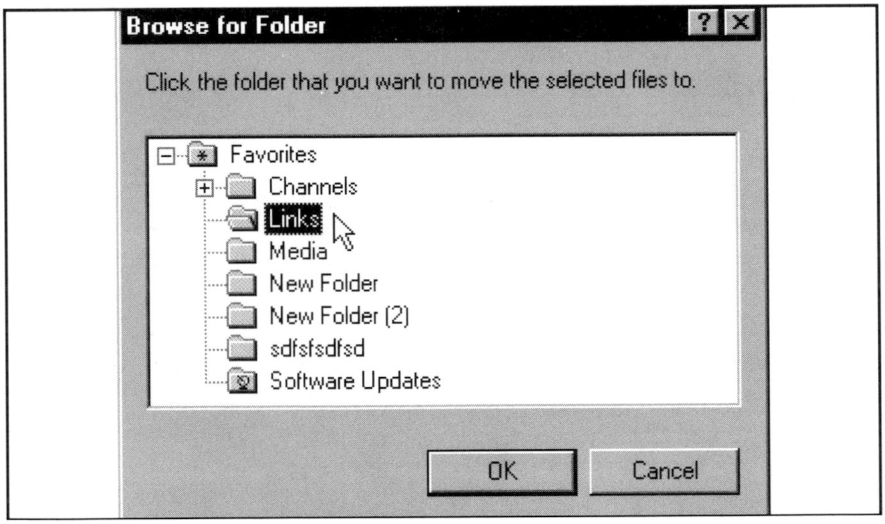

Figure 4.28   MS IE Favorite folder window.

4.8.4 Address Book

This is a great facility to store all your e-mail addresses in one location and use them within your browser to send mail to individuals or mailing lists. A mailing list has a name and contains several e-mail addresses; it is similar to a conventional paper mailing list. To invoke the address book, click the Addresses button shown on the message toolbar of the Outlook Express window, shown in figure 4.12. The Address Book window is shown in figure 4.29. The window has a menu bar and a set of buttons following it; the buttons are more frequently used than the menus on the menu bar. You are encouraged to investigate the menus of the menu bar on your own. Here, we show how to use the Address Book effectively.

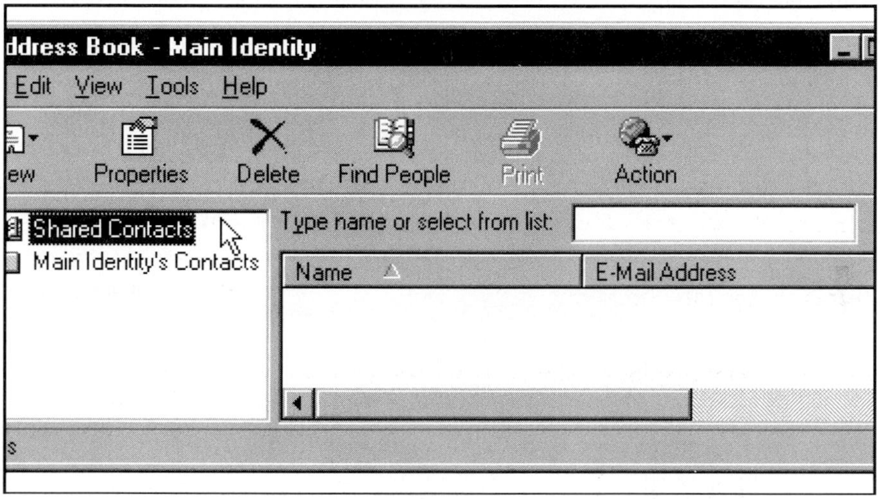

Figure 4.29 MS IE `Address Book` window.

Create a new address book. Click the `New` button of the `Address Book` window shown in figure 4.29, then click the `New Folder` item. Type the name (say, *Abe Zeid address book*) of the new address book in the `Properties` window that pops up, and click `OK`. The browser creates the book and adds it to the left frame shown in figure 4.29.

Add an address to the address book. To add an address to an address book, highlight the address book in the left frame (figure 4.29) to open it. Click the `New` button (figure 4.29), then click the `New Contact` item. Fill in the information in the `Properties` window that pops up, as shown in figure 4.30. The window has five additional tabs (`Home`, `Business`, `Other`, `NetMeeting`, and `DigitalIDs`) that allow you to enter additional information. Click the `Add` button, followed by the `OK` button, to finish the creation of the contact. The browser shows the contact in the right frame of the `Address Book` window (figure 4.29). To view or edit the contact you just created, double click the name in the `Address Book` window. You can also create a contact by clicking the `Contact` frame in the Outlook Express window shown in figure 4.12, then click the `New Contact` item.

Create a mailing list. To add a mailing list to an address book, highlight the address book in the left frame (figure 4.29) to open it. Click the `New` button (figure 4.29), followed by clicking the `New Group` item. Fill in the information in the `Properties` window that pops up, as shown in figure 4.31. Use the bottom two fields (`Name` and `E-Mail`) in figure 4.31 to add the names and e-mail addresses of the members of the mailing list. Click the `Add` button after each duo (name and e-mail entry). Click the `OK` button to finish the creation of the mailing list. As shown in figure 4.31, we create the *College* mailing list with four members: *dean*, *asstDean*, *staff*, and *computer*. Repeat the same steps and create another mailing list with the name *Depart-ment* and four members: *chair*, *faculty*, *staff*, and *students*. The final address book is now shown in figure 4.32. The right frame in the figure shows the individual e-mail addresses (*John Smith*) and the names of the mailing lists (*College*, *Department*) in alphabetical order. The way you can tell whether a name is a list in figure 4.32 is simple. The mailing list does not have an e-mail address next to it. To learn the members of a mailing list, move the mouse over it. The browser shows the members as it shows *John Smith* information in figure 4.32. Alternatively, double click the mailing list name. Notice that the e-mail addresses and the mailing lists you create in the Address Book are shown in the `Contact` frame of the Outlook Express window (figure 4.12).

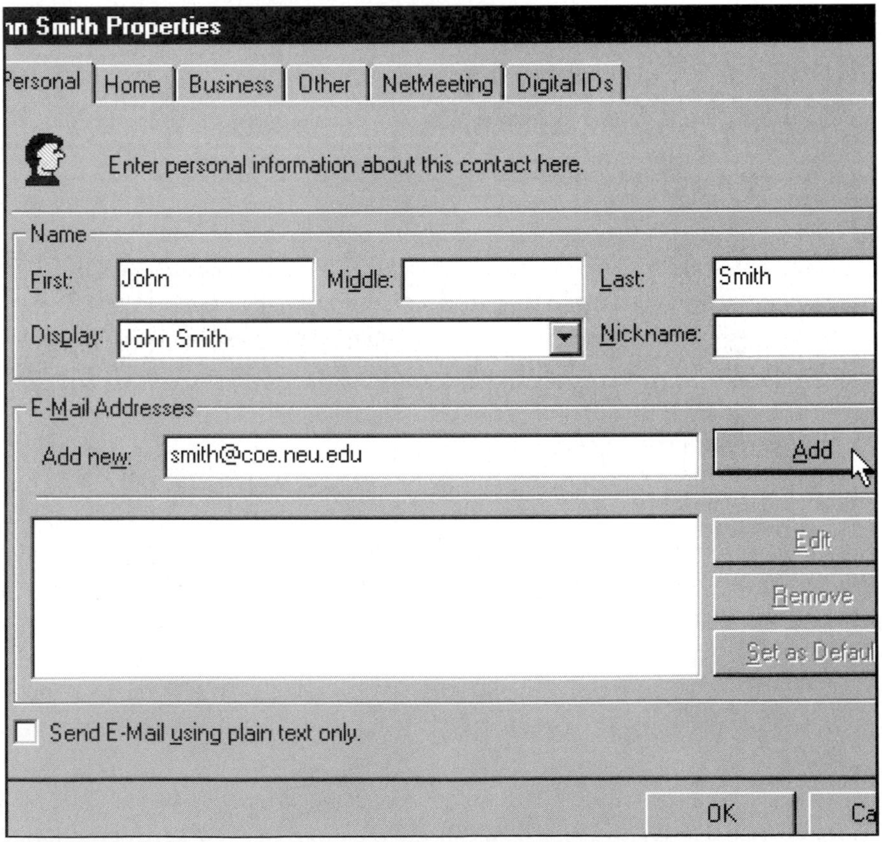

Figure 4.30   Add an address in MS Outlook Express Address Book.

Use an address book. To send an e-mail message to a mailing list or to one person in the address book, highlight the corresponding name in the Address Book. Next, click the `Action` button (figure 4.32), then click the `Send Mail` item to open the MS Outlook Express composition mail window (figure 4.24). Type the message, and click the `Send` button of the Composition window to send it.

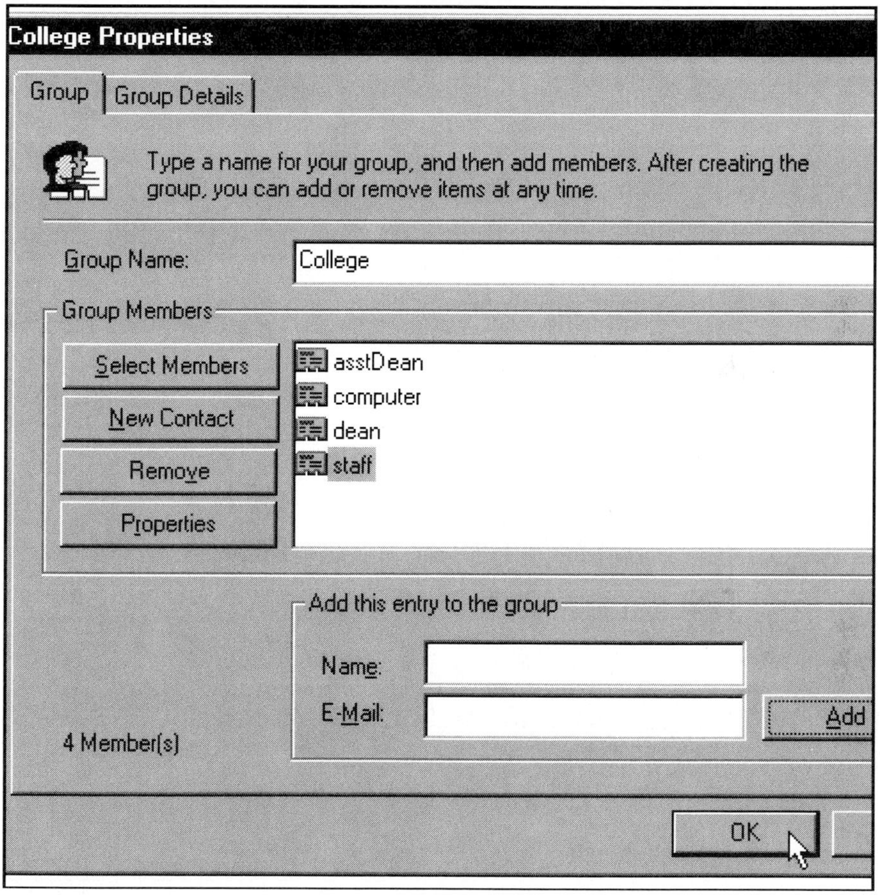

Figure 4.31   MS Outlook Express mailing list window.

Remove an e-mail address. Highlight the e-mail address you want to remove in the desired address book (figure 4.32), and click the `Delete` button. Click `OK` to confirm the deletion.

Search an address book. To search the Address Book for names and addresses, click the `Find People` button (figure 4.32) to open the `Find People` window shown in figure 4.33. Type the name of the person you are looking for. If there is a match, the browser appends it to the bottom of the window (figure 4.33). Once you find the name, you can double click it to view its card, or right click the name, followed by left clicking `Action => Send Mail`, to send an e-mail message.

Import address books. From the `File` menu (figure 4.32), click `Import`, then click the `Address Book`. Follow the prompts and instructions to import.

Export an address book. From the `File` menu (figure 4.32), click `Export`, then click `Other Address Book`. Follow the prompts and instructions to export.

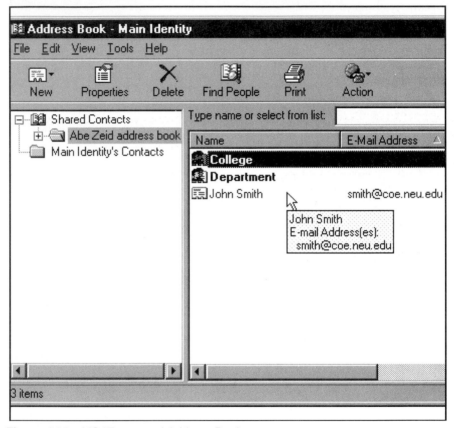

Figure 4.32   MS IE personal Address Book.

4.8.5 Help menu

As you use the above material, you will add your personal experience to it. You will discover other, maybe better, ways to do things. Feel free to explore. Pass on any new ideas and tricks you discover to me, please, to include in the FAQs section of future editions of this book. E-mail me at zeid@coe.neu.edu. After you have mastered all the above material, you may want more knowledge. Click `Help => Contents and Index`. There, you find many interesting topics. The browser provides you with search fields where you can type a search string. The browser displays the matching information, if it finds any.

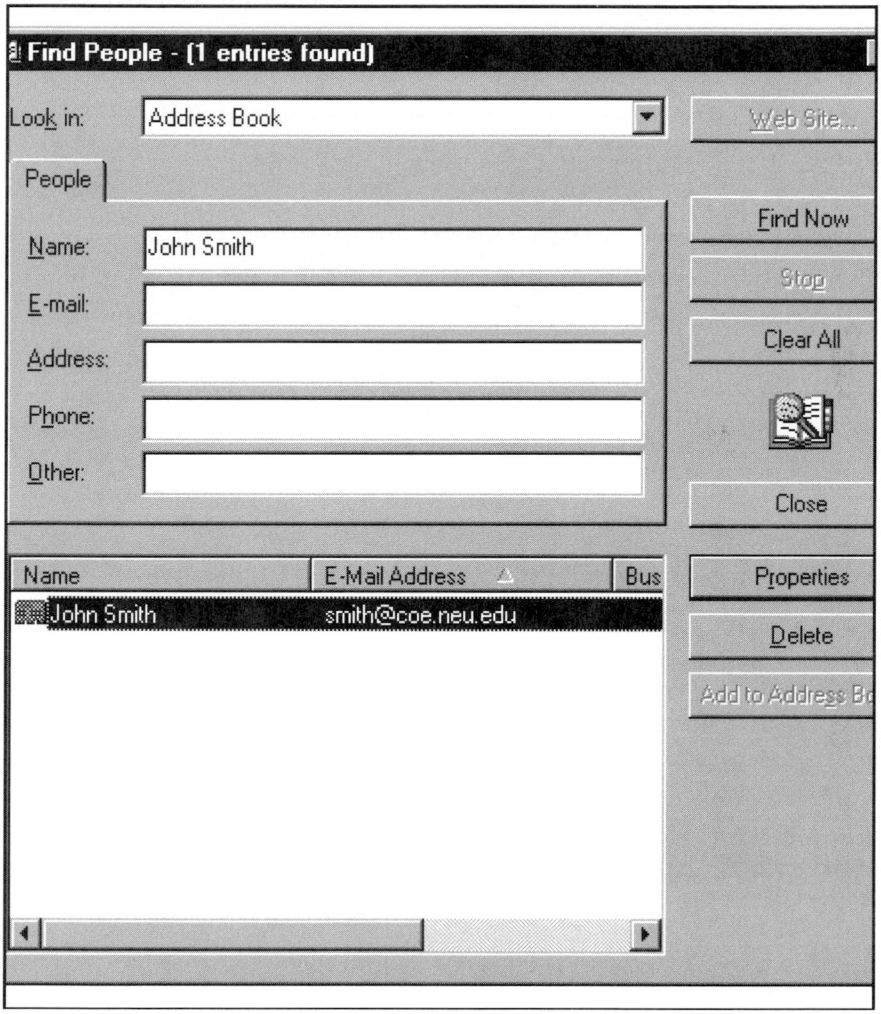

Figure 4.33   MS IE `Find People` window.

4.9 FAQs

This section has FAQs (Frequently Asked Questions) related to the chapter material. If the answer to a question is the same for both Netscape Communicator and MS IE, neither browser is mentioned in the answer. If you would like to contribute to the FAQs in this section and share your experiences with other readers of this book, please e-mail the author at zeid@coe.neu.edu. Credit will be given to you in this section.

Readers should also consult section 3.12, FAQs, in chapter 3, because many of the FAQs there are still very useful and applicable to MS IE. Section 3.12 has several FAQs that are related to Netscape Communicator only, but many others are generic and are useful when you use either browser. This section covers FAQs related only to the Microsoft browser.

Q: How can I copy an image from a Web page?

A: Right click somewhere on the image. In the pop-up window, click **Save Picture As**.

Q: How can I delete a mail server in MS Outlook Express?

A: In Outlook Express, click `Tools => accounts => Mail` (tab). Highlight the mail server you want to delete, and then click `Remove`. Confirm by clicking `Yes`.

Q: How can I mark e-mail messages that I read as new and unread again?

A: This is useful when you read an e-mail message, but you are in too much of a hurry to be able to respond to it right away. You would want to mark it new, so you do not forget to respond to it later. In Outlook Express, right click the message, and click `Mark as Unread` from the pop-up menu.

Q: How can I hide a toolbar of my browser?

A: Click this sequence: `View => Toolbars => Standard  Buttons` (or another toolbar). Repeat the same sequence to show the toolbar once again.

4.10 Summary

Note: the first four sections (Introduction, Finding a URL, Browser Tasks, and Overview of Browsers) of this summary are repeated from chapter 3, for convenience to the book's readers and users. These bullets summarize the generic concepts about browsers. This repetition saves the reader the time and effort of trying to find them in the summary section of chapter 3.

Introduction

•Web browsers are the main GUIs for communicating with the Internet and the Web.

•Browsers locate Web sites and pages via their unique URLs and display their content. URLs may occasionally use port numbers such as 80 for http; for example, www.abc.com:80.

•Browsers support the following protocols: http (load Web pages), mailto (send e-mail), nntp (access Usenet newsgroups), ftp (file transfer), telnet (remote access of computers), gopher (access gopher servers), and file (load local files).

Finding a URL

•When a user types or clicks a URL, the browser finds its equivalent IP address via a DNS server. The browser then converts the URL into TCP/IP packets with the IP address and sends them to the remote server identified by the URL. When the remote server sends back the content of the Web page identified by the URL to the browser, the browser displays the page.

•Encryption and decryption techniques are used to create secure connections between Web servers and client computers. Encryption converts data into unreadable form; decryption converts encrypted data back into its original readable form.

•Both encryption and decryption use complex computer and mathematical algorithms. There are different levels of encryption/decryption. Some algorithms are very complex.

•Both Web servers and browsers use Secure Sockets Layer (SSL) to implement security. SSL is an integral part of Web browsers.

•SSL technology uses two keys: a public key to encrypt data, and a private key to decrypt data. The keys come in pairs that are not interchangeable.

•Another part of encryption is the digital certificates that are used for digital signature. A digital certificate is and electronic ID similar to, say, a credit card or driver's license. These certificates are kept in registries, so that their owners can look up their public keys, like a deed of a house.

Browser Tasks

•Browsers perform the following tasks: navigation, viewing, multimedia display, e-mail, ftp, telnet, news, downloading files, and printing.

Overview of Browsers

•A browser GUI structure typically consists of, from the top of its window to the bottom, a title bar, a menu bar, several toolbars, a display area, and a status bar.

•Browsers allow users to manage a Web page via its URL, its display in the browser, and its HTML code. A user can bookmark the page URL, print the display of the Web page, or view and/or print the page's corresponding HTML code.

•Browsers use the cache concept to improve document access. Browsers use both memory and disk cache. Memory cache stores Web pages of the current browser session; while disk cache stores Web pages from previous sessions. Browsers allow their users to change the sizes of both memory and disk caches.

•Browsers use "helper" application programs to handle files of types that they do not support internally. A helper program appears in a new window separate from the browser window.

•Plug-ins are application programs that run within the browser window. They, like helper applications, extend the power of the browser.

•Users can customize their browsers to make them look and feel the way they want.

Downloading MS IE

•To download MS IE for Windows, go to www.microsoft.com. Look for a link that reads `Internet Explorer Download it free` in the Microsoft Web page that is loaded into your current browser window. Click the following link sequence; `Internet Explorer Download it free => Download => Internet Explorer 5 and Internet`

Tools (under Windows 98 or Windows 95 and Windows NT 4.0) => Next (accept default language; English) => Next (accept default download site).

   •The above sequence of clicks does not download MS IE. Instead, it downloads a setup executable (ie5setup.exe). To continue downloading, the user double clicks the ie5setup executable and uses the following sequence of clicks: Next (to activate this button, the user must click "I accept the agreement" first) => Next (accept default set of components) => Next (accept default download site).

   •Microsoft makes installing its IE browser part of its downloading. It first downloads the software, then installs it, and finally updates Windows.

MS IE GUI

   •The MS IE GUI structure consists of the Title bar, the Menu bar, three Toolbars (Standard Buttons, Address Bar, and Links Bar), the display area, and the Status bar.

   •The Title bar holds the title of the currently displayed Web page.

   •The Menu bar has six menus: File, Edit, View, Favorites, Tools, and Help. Each menu has menu items and submenus. The quick reference (below) shows how to use them to achieve certain tasks.

   •The Standard Buttons Toolbar holds the buttons most frequently needed to navigate Web pages in a browser session.

   •The Address Bar is where the user types the URL of a Web page that the browser should download and display.

   •The Links Toolbar has buttons to provide users with useful information. Users may customize this Toolbar.

   •The display area is where the browser shows the contents of a Web page.

   •The Status bar shows downloading information about the currently downloaded or displayed Web page.

•Quick reference of using Microsoft (MS) Internet Explorer:

   1. E-mail. Before you can use the MS Outlook Express e-mail facility, the user needs to set up and configure the e-mail environment (the identity and mail servers).

> **1.1 Configure e-mail identity;** click the Setup a Mail account link (figure 4.12) => enter name (figure 4.13) => Next => enter e-mail address (figure 4.14) => Next => enter server info. (figure 4.15) => Next => enter login (figure 4.16) => Next => Finish (figure 4.17)
>
> **1.2 Configure e-mail servers;** see item 1.1 above.
>
> *The following e-mail activities require that the Outlook Express mail window be open. Double click the Outlook Express icon to open the window.*
>
> **1.3 Change mail window setting;** click Edit => click the Tips button to open the Tip of the day frame. Click the x mark to close it. See figure 4.21.
>
> Click the Outlook Express button to open the mail folder frame. Click the x mark to close it. See figure 4.21.

To open the Contacts frame, click View => Layout => Contacts (figures 4.21 and 4.22). Click the x mark to close it.

1.4 Get mail; click Send/Rec.

1.5 Read mail; click the desired message header from the mail window.

1.6 Reply to mail; click Reply or Reply All => use the composition window (figures 4.23 and 4.24) => Send.

1.7 Forward mail; click Forward => use the composition window (figure 4.24) => Send.

1.8 File mail; drag the message header and drop it into the desired folder (figure 4.12).

1.9 Print mail; highlight the message header, then click Print => OK.

1.10 Delete mail; highlight the message header, then click Delete => Yes.

1.11 Send mail; click New Mail => use the composition window (figure 4.24) => Send.

1.12 Send mail with attachment; click New Msg => use the composition window (figure 4.24) => Attach => choose file to attach => Send.

2. Check page security (encryption); Outlook Express alerts the user with a Security Alert box.

3. Run multiple copies of browser; click File => New => Window, or use CTRL N.

4. Managing Web pages.

4.1 Visit a Web page; type the page URL in the browser location Toolbar.

4.2 View Web page source code; click View => Source.

4.3 Print a Web page; while the page is displayed on the screen, click the Print button of the browser.

4.4 Save a Web page; while the page is displayed on the screen, click File => Save as.

4.5 Delete a Web page; this is simply deleting one of the local files. Drag the file into the recycling bin on the desktop, or use a system delete command.

5. Open local files in browsers; click **File => Open.**

6. Managing bookmarks.

6.1 Access bookmarks; click Favorites (figure 4.8)

6.2 Add a bookmark of the currently displayed Web page; click Favorites => Add to Favorites (figures 4.8 and 4.25).

6.3 Delete a bookmark; click Favorites => Organize Favorites; highlight the bookmark to delete (figure 4.26); click Delete (figure 4.26).

6.4 Open Bookmarks window; click Favorites => Organize Favorites (figure 4.26).

6.5 Rename a bookmark; highlight bookmark; click Favorites => Organize Favorites => Rename (figure 4.26).

6.6 Create a bookmark folder; click Favorites => Organize Favorites => Create Folder (figure 4.26).

6.7 Move a bookmark; click Favorites => Organize Favorites => Move to Folder (figure 4.26).

6.8 View data of a bookmark or a folder; click Favorites => Organize Favorites (figure 4.26) => highlight bookmark or folder, then click Properties (figure 4.27).

7. Managing address book.

7.1 Access address book; click the Addresses button shown on the message toolbar of the Outlook Express window (figures 4.12 and 4.29).

7.2 Create a new address book; click New => New Folder => type info. => OK (figure 4.29).

7.3 Add an address to the address book; highlight the address book in the left frame (figure 4.29) to open it. Click New => New Contact => type info. => Add => OK; or click the Contact frame in the Outlook Express window (figure 4.12), then click the New Contact item.

7.4 Create a mailing list; highlight the address book in the left frame (figure 4.29) to open it. Click New => New Group => type info. => Add => OK (figures 4.29, 4.31, and 4.32).

7.5 Use an address book to send an e-mail message to a mailing list or to one person; highlight the corresponding name in the address book, then click Action => Send Mail => type message => Send (figures 4.24 and 4.32).

7.6 Remove an e-mail address; highlight the e-mail address, then click Delete => OK (figure 4.32).

7.7 Search an address book; click Find People => type the name of the person in the Look in field of the Find People window (figures 4.32 and 4.33).

7.8 Import an address book; click File => Import => Address Book => follow prompts (figure 4.32).

7.9 Export an address book; click File => Export => Other Address Book => follow the prompts (figure 4.32).

PROBLEMS

Exercises

4.1 Configure the e-mail tool on your computer to read and send e-mail messages.

4.2 Use the e-mail functions provided by your e-mail tool; reply to your e-mail messages, forward them, file them, print them, and delete them.

4.3 Create an e-mail list, with the name *class*, that contains the e-mail addresses of five of your classmates. Use it to send a message to them.

4.4 Choose some of the local files on your computer, and try to open them in the browser. What do you see? What is your conclusion?

4.5 Open a PDF file on your computer. If you do not have one, search the Internet for one and download it. If you do not have the Adobe Acrobat Reader installed on your computer, download it from www.adobe.com, and install it.

Homework

4.6 Find a recent article(s) that compares browsers, their latest versions, and the war between them. You can use the paper route (e.g., PC magazine, PC World, etc.) or the Internet way (use a search engine). If you use a search engine, use the proper search string, such as *Netscape Communicator versus MS Internet Explorer*. Summarize the article in a half a page or a page.

4.7 Visit some Web sites. Create bookmarks for them. Organize them by category. Print them out, and submit them with your homework.

4.8 Create an address book of your favorite e-mail addresses. Print and submit them.

4.9 Create your e-mail signature. Print and submit it.

4.10 Associate the HTML file type to MS IE instead of Netscape and vice versa, depending on what is currently available on your computer. Submit screen captures of the series of steps you have followed.

Internet Resources

This chapter covers the various resources that are available to help you utilize the Internet effectively. These resources include discussion/newsgroups for talking and chatting, FTP for downloading files, and Telnet for remotely connecting to computers. The chapter discusses some of the popular newsgroups including the Big Seven: computer (comp), science (sci), recreation (rec), news, talk, social (soc), and miscellaneous (misc). It presents FTP and shows how to use client FTP software to download and upload files. It also covers Telnet and shows how to use client Telnet software to connect to remote computing resources.

5.1 Introduction

The most popular segment of the Internet is the Web. The Internet and the Web are used almost synonymously today. There are tools, including FTP and Telnet, that are useful to navigate the Web. Those who have been longtime users of networks have used, and still are using, FTP and Telnet. While the majority of activity on the Internet is browsing, sending e-mail, and searching for sites and Web pages, there are other activities that may require talking and chatting with others (Newsgroups), downloading large files (FTP), and connecting to a remote computer on the Internet (Telnet). We cover these basic access tools in this chapter.

5.2 Discussion Groups and Newsgroups

If you have used a forum on CompuServe, chat rooms on AOL, or some other bulletin board system (BBS), you have an idea of what discussion groups and newsgroups are. Practically, discussion groups and newsgroups refer to the same thing. Discussion groups are groups of people who are interested in certain topics or subjects and in sharing opinions and ideas about these topics. Newsgroups are the collections of the messages that the discussion groups post to a news server about a given topic or subject. Newsgroups are also known as Netnews. The trail of messages and replies to a specific question is known as a thread within a newsgroup. There are no newsgroup membership lists or joining fees. The network of computers (news servers) that exchange Netnews is known as Usenet. News servers are maintained by companies, groups, and individuals and can host thousands of newsgroups.

Usenet utilizes software that copies and replies to messages users contribute, so that every participating computer has an exact copy of every message contributed to the network. The Usenet software organizes these messages into newsgroups that you can read. In addition, you can contribute your own messages to these newsgroups. Today, there are many Usenet sites and news groups and millions of regular users. You may want to read newsgroups for a while before you decide to post your own messages.

Usenet started out as a method of sharing information about Unix computer systems between two universities in 1979. Users at those institutions wanted to exchange notes and observations in a fairly loose format and to organize the information by topic. Further, they wanted the information to be available to a group of people, rather than to single recipients (as with e-mail). Hence, Usenet was born. In several years, it spread to many more universities, then it worked its way into corporations and other institutions. During the early 1980s, the software underwent a major revision, to enable it to handle larger volume of messages. This work resulted in the expansion of the Usenet.

The Usenet is intended for technical use, but people use it to discuss social, political, hobby, entertainment, recreation, and controversial issues, such as abortion and the death penalty. The diversion from discussing only technical issues brings with it bad language and out-of-control emotions that ruin the discussion and lead to a "low signal-to-noise ratio" (as Usenet calls it). Even with that, Usenet is still a great resource. Many newsgroups offer intelligent discussion, particularly the moderated ones. In moderated newsgroups, all submissions must pass the approval of a human moderator (editor), who checks whether the message is relevant to the group and its language is acceptable.

The technically oriented newsgroups are of great value. They reflect the spirit of information exchange and resource sharing. One of the best things about Usenet is the FAQs. FAQs attempt to provide answers to questions people are most likely to ask. There are hundreds of these FAQs, and some of them are among the best sources of information on a topic that you can find anywhere.

How do you find anything on Usenet? How is it organized? There are many newsgroups available. You can find newsgroups on practically any subject. The structure of the Usenet newsgroups is hierarchical, similar to a family tree or an organizational chart. At the top level are some very general topics, and under each of these topics are more and more specific topics. Originally the Usenet groups were divided into seven subgroups, which are still called the Big Seven. New hierarchies have come into being since then. Many service providers and Web sites create and maintain their own newsgroups, chat rooms and discussion groups. Every news site usually receives a topic heading of all the Usenet subjects. Listed below are some of the newsgroups that are most likely available, with the Big Seven listed first.

1. comp: topics related to hardware, computer science, programming languages, and games.
2. sci: scientific research and applications topics, such as physics, biology, and psychology.
3. rec: recreational topics, such as sports, music, video making, cooking, and so forth.
4. news: the hierarchy where Usenet talks about itself — it is very useful, especially for new users.
5. talk: loose discussions on unresolved questions — politics and religion are the hottest topics debated in these groups.
6. soc: discussions about social issues relating to countries or regions.
7. misc: other things that do not belong to the above groups, such as job postings, for-sale postings, and so forth.
8. alt: a bizarre mix of topics from alt.chinese.computing to alt.tv.simpsons. It is easier to create a new group in the alt hierarchy than in other hierarchies. Some alt groups are quite useful.
9. k12: discussions and groups relating to education from kindergarten through grade 12, for both teachers and students.
10. fj: discussions of hundreds of different topics in Japanese.
11. de: a hierarchy with the scope and size of alt, but all in German.

Under each hierarchy heading, the name of the group should become more specific. For example, to find a group discussing college basketball, start with the rec hierarchy, then the subtopic sport, then the subtopic basketball.

The newsreader software (could be a browser) helps you deal with newsgroups. You can search for groups and keywords within groups and can respond to articles with articles of your own. You can also e-mail the author of an article. Best of all, your newsreader keeps track of which articles you have already read, so that, the next time you want to read news, it shows you only the articles that are new since the last time you read news. The newsreader software reads and manages articles via using the Net News Transport Protocol (NNTP).

Most newsreaders maintain a list of newsgroups, and you can add or delete groups from the list. This process is called subscribing and unsubscribing. When you subscribe to a newsgroup, the newsreader thereafter displays for you all the postings in that group. If you do not want to see any more postings on that topic, you can unsubscribe. Here are some useful groups, especially for new users;

news.newusers.announce slow
news.newusers.questions
news.answers
alt.answers
alt.internet.services

You may think of Usenet as a big meeting place. Thousands of people use Usenet to keep up with development in their fields and to gather information. These people are busy and do not want to be bothered with trivial questions. So, there are some rules and customs to make the time on Usenet as productive as possible for everyone. These rules and customs are known as Usenet etiquette. It is mostly common sense; for example, select your audience, read before posting, test messages, advertise to small interested groups, and so forth.

Listserv discussion groups combine elements of e-mail and Usenet news. Instead of reading all the messages posted in your newsgroup, you receive e-mail from the moderator of the listserv group. After you formally join a group, the moderator of that group sends each member of the group an e-mail message containing one or more postings of that group. Thus, you do not have to go through a newsreader and request specific articles for review. Some people refer to a listserv discussion group as an automated mailing list system. Listserv groups generally do not accept input from users automatically. The moderator will read submissions, possibly editing the appropriate ones before posting them to the group. Individuals may respond to the contributors whose e-mail adresses are included in their postings. You subscribe and unsubscribe to listserv groups in the same way you do with newsgroups.

5.3 FTP

FTP (File Transfer Protocol) is an important tool of the Internet. FTP is the Internet tool you want to use when you know that the information you seek is stored in a large file in a given location. FTP lets you download a copy of the file from a remote host to your local computer. FTP can transfer two types of files: ASCII files and binary files. ASCII files are text files that you can read after transferring them. Binary files are executables that you cannot read. They are programs that you can install and run on your computer.

FTP is a TCP/IP program. Like all TCP/IP programs, it has two parts: a client part and a server part. The client part runs at your PC or your computer. The server part runs as a daemon program on a remote server or host somewhere. (A daemon is software that responds to user's requests to connect to a computer. It is like a waiter or waitress.) The FTP daemon acknowledges FTP requests and allows valid users (with valid username and password) to send or receive files from the server.

There are three ways to connect to FTP sites or servers: OS, browser, and GUI. Accessing FTP sites at the OS level is popular mainly among Unix users. Unix provides its users with a set of line commands to connect to an FTP site, download the desired file, and log out. For example, the sequence of actions required to access an FTP site may look like this:

ftp xxx.yyy.zz (connect to host or server xxx.yyy.zz)

enter username and password

cd sss (go to subdirectory sss)

ls (list files in sss)

get filename (download or copy filename to your local drive)

put filename (send filename to host or server xxx.yyy.zz)

quit (or **bye**) (end the ftp session)

The bold words listed above indicate FTP commands. There are a lot of FTP commands. You can use *help* or *?* at the ftp> command prompt. (When you ftp to a site or a host, you get the ftp> prompt.) This will show you a list of all the available FTP commands. You can then ask for help on a particular one by typing *help get*. (*get* is the command here). If you are a Unix user, type the Unix command man ftp for online help.   ↓will see!

If these line commands are displeasing, because we are used to windows and to clicking icons and menu items, we can use the other two methods of FTP connection. With a browser, the user is usually able to click a hyperlink that connects to an FTP site and download the desired file. We used this method in chapter 1 of this book when we downloaded shareware. For example, we have used www.shareware.com to search for shareware such as screen capture (SnagIt) or WINZIP. When we click a hyperlink of a certain shareware, the browser presents us with a long list of FTP sites that we can use to download. When we click one of these sites, the browser downloads and saves the software file. We later install the software.

The third method of using FTP is via a GUI. There exists a Windows FTP. FTP is a client/server application. Thus, you can use a Windows FTP client software to avoid using and typing line commands. FTP menu items allow you to do all that you can do with line commands. You connect to the FTP site using the FTP client software. Most Web sites have an FTP site if you replace www by ftp in the site URL — for example, ftp.netscape.com. You need to be aware of the directory structure of the FTP site you connect to, so you can find the software you need to download.

This method is very useful to use because you can move files from your PC disk at home to your account at work or at your ISP, and vice versa. For example, you can upload a Web page, after you fully develop it, to your employer or ISP server.

Most, if not all, the FTP sites we deal with are anonymous sites. Anonymous FTP acts as the underpinning to free exchange of information on the Internet, because it makes files available on the network to anyone who wants them. If you notice, in the line commands above, you need a username and a password to connect to a host. In anonymous FTP, you use the word anonymous for the username. The password could be guest, your e-mail address, any password, or no password. With these multiple password possibilities, how would you know which one to choose to log in to a particular anonymous FTP host? The host will tell you which password to choose. Just follow the instructions after you input anonymous as a username.

Many FTP servers, particularly those for anonymous FTP, store files in compressed formats. This reduces the amount of data that has to be sent across the network, speeding file transfer and conserving precious bandwidth. Compressed files are usually known as zipped files. An important fact about compressed files is that they typically contain multiple files when unpacked. This means it is a good idea to unpack a compressed file in a new subdirectory. Unpacking (unzipping) compressed files requires special programs. Compressed formats for Unix are different from those for PCs, and the programs for uncompressing the two groups of

FTP format !!

formats are also different. For Unix, the programs for compressing and uncompressing are uuencode and uudecode, respectively. Other programs are gzip, gunzip, zip, and unzip. For PC Windows, the program WINZIP does both compressing and uncompressing. For PCs, the file extension for compressed files is .zip.

5.4 Telnet

Like FTP, Telnet is an important tool to access the resources of the Internet. Rather than providing a way to obtain files, it provides a way to obtain computing services from hosts that can be reached on the Internet. Telnet allows you to log in to a remote computer (host) and use it. You must be a valid user and have an account on that computer. When you telnet to a host from a remote location, it asks you for your username and password. Once logged in, you can use your account to run programs or save files. In addition, you can use Telnet to access your workstation at work when you are away from the office and want to check your e-mail. You can also access public Telnet hosts. For example, you can use specialized Telnet applications and databases around the world, such as the Library of Congress (locis.loc.gov), your local library, or the National Weather service (for global and local weather maps and reports).

Telnet, like FTP, is a client-server application. You must run a client program on your local computer to talk to a Telnet daemon that can start a Telnet session on a remote host and then manage communication thereafter. Telnet, like FTP, requires an account on the remote host, but it also comes as anonymous Telnet.

How can you obtain a Telnet connection? In most cases, you need an account on a host to telnet to it. You can telnet to a host using its domain name or its IP address (telnet xxx.yyy.zz, or telnet 167.23.432.180). Once you are connected, you need to type your username and password. Now, you have started a Telnet session. You are actually working on the host computer. All your local computer is doing is displaying the commands and the responses of the host.

Multistage Telnet is sometimes useful to use. Here you telnet from one host to another and then from that host to yet another, to make connections that otherwise would be impossible. For example, you may be able to connect to one host only via another one, or you may have to connect to a host to get access to high-speed modems. In multistage Telnet, you need to pay attention to your links and the time and resources you consume in the intermediate stages.

Multisession Telnet happens when you use multiple copies of the Telnet program to access more than one remote host simultaneously. This is different from multistage Telnet. Multisession Telnet is like doing multiple tasks at the same time — for example, telnet to the Library of Congress and run a search, and, while the search is in progress, start another Telnet session to the National Weather Center in Michigan to get weather information. You can switch back and forth between the library and the weather Telnet sessions.

Anonymous Telnet is available, although it is not as popular as anonymous FTP. Some Internet hosts will let you log in to them to use Telnet without requiring an individual account with a password. In this situation, if you have to deal with large files or run large programs, you may want to consider doing these tasks off-peak hours to keep from slowing and degrading the host performance for other users. The host itself may force you to wait until after hours to execute large, time-consuming tasks.

5.5 Tutorials

This tutorial shows how to use newsgroups, FTP, and Telnet.

5.5.1 Newsgroups Using Netscape Communicator

There are many news servers and newsgroups available on the Internet. There is a newsgroup on just about everything and every subject you can imagine. You need to be aware of the structure of newsgroups and their servers to be able to use them effectively and configure your newsgroups reader, such as Netscape Communicator, MS Outlook Express, or any other. Figure 5.1 shows such a structure conceptually. Any news server supports a number of newsgroups.

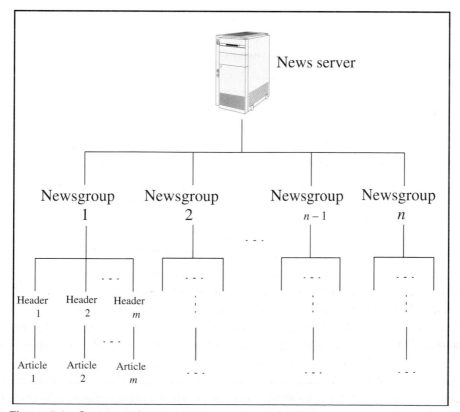

Figure 5.1 Structure of newsgroups.

Each newsgroup consists of a large number of articles that are posted to the group by its members or subscribers. These articles are displayed to the members first as headers, similar to e-mail messages. A member can select (click) a header to access and read the corresponding full article.

You can use Netscape as a Usenet newsreader. All newsreaders, including Netscape, operate at three levels: newsgroup level, headers level, and article level. At the first level, you see a list of newsgroups. When you select a particular newsgroup, you get to the second level, which lists the headers of the current articles in this newsgroup. When you select a particular header, you get to the last level, which shows the text of the actual article. Before you can use Netscape to access Usenet, you must first configure it. You need to supply the domain name of your NNTP (Usenet) server and download the current newsgroup list. Then you choose the ones to which you want to subscribe. Here are the detailed steps.

1. Installing a newsgroup NNTP server. To access Usenet, you need access to an NNTP server, a program that makes Usenet newsgroups accessible to newsreading software. Generally, access to an NNTP server is included with Internet service subscriptions. Check with your service provider and get the NNTP server's domain name. You need to provide Netscape with this name to configure Netscape to read newsgroups. Click the `Newsgroups` icon on the Component bar (or click `Communicator => Newsgroups` from the menu bar) to open the Netscape mail window shown in figure 3.39. Starting with the `Edit` menu of this window, click this sequence; `Edit => Preferences` (Preferences window is shown in figure 3.17) => `Mail&Newsgroups` (double click this item) => `Newsgroups Servers`. This sequence of clicks results in displaying the Preferences window shown in figure 5.2. Click the `Add` button to specify an NNTP server. You can click the button as many times as the number of newsgroups servers you need to specify. To make one of these servers the default, highlight it, and click the `Set as Default` button shown in the window. You can change the number of messages from the default value (500), and/or you can change the default newsgroup directory. When you are finished, click the `OK` button. Netscape Communicator comes with the news server already installed.

2. Downloading newsgroups. If the mail window does not display the current newsgroups under each newsgroup server you have installed, it means that you have not subscribed to any newsgroup yet. To download the newsgroups available on a given server, select the server (news in figure 3.39) in the mail window. Then click `File` (menu of the mail window) => `Subscribe`. This download is done once by the browser. Netscape subscribes you to two newsgroups of the news server: news.software.nntp and comp.software.testing.

3. Subscribe and unsubscribe to Newsgroups. Once you have downloaded the newsgroups of the servers you installed, select the ones you want to subscribe to and read on a regular basis. To subscribe to a newsgroup, click the `Newsgroup` icon on the Component bar to open the Netscape mail window (click news in figure 3.28). From the `File` menu of the mail window, choose `Subscribe` to open the subscription window shown in figure 5.3. Click in the `Subscribe` column next to a newsgroup. The browser adds a checkmark, as shown in figure

5.3, in the column. If you click in the column again, you unsubscribe and the checkmark disappears. To subscribe to more than one newsgroup at the same time, select the newsgroups (hold down the CTRL key for multiple selections) and click the `Subscribe` button as shown in figure 5.3. To select a contiguous set of newsgroups, click the first newsgroup. Then Shift click (hold down the Shift key on the keyboard and click at the same time) to select the last one in the group. Once that is done done, click the `OK` button (figure 5.3) of the subscription window. Your subscription list shows in the left frame of the mail window.

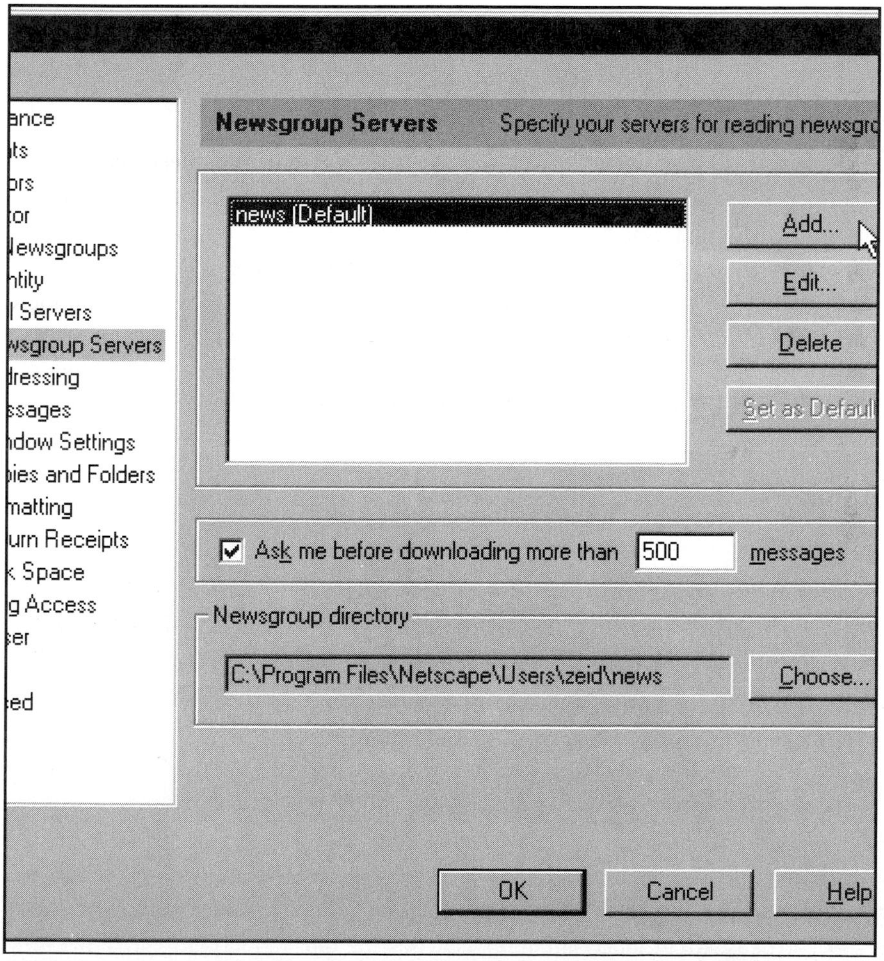

Figure 5.2   Add a newsgroup server name to Netscape Communicator.

To unsubscribe from a newsgroup, select the group name from the left frame of the mail window. Next, click the `Edit` menu of the mail window, then click `Unsubscribe`. Click `OK` in the pop-up window to confirm.

4. Downloading news articles. After subscribing to a newsgroup, you can download its postings or articles. Think of the articles as e-mail messages. Click the `Get Msg` button of the mail window (figure 3.39) to download the latest articles.

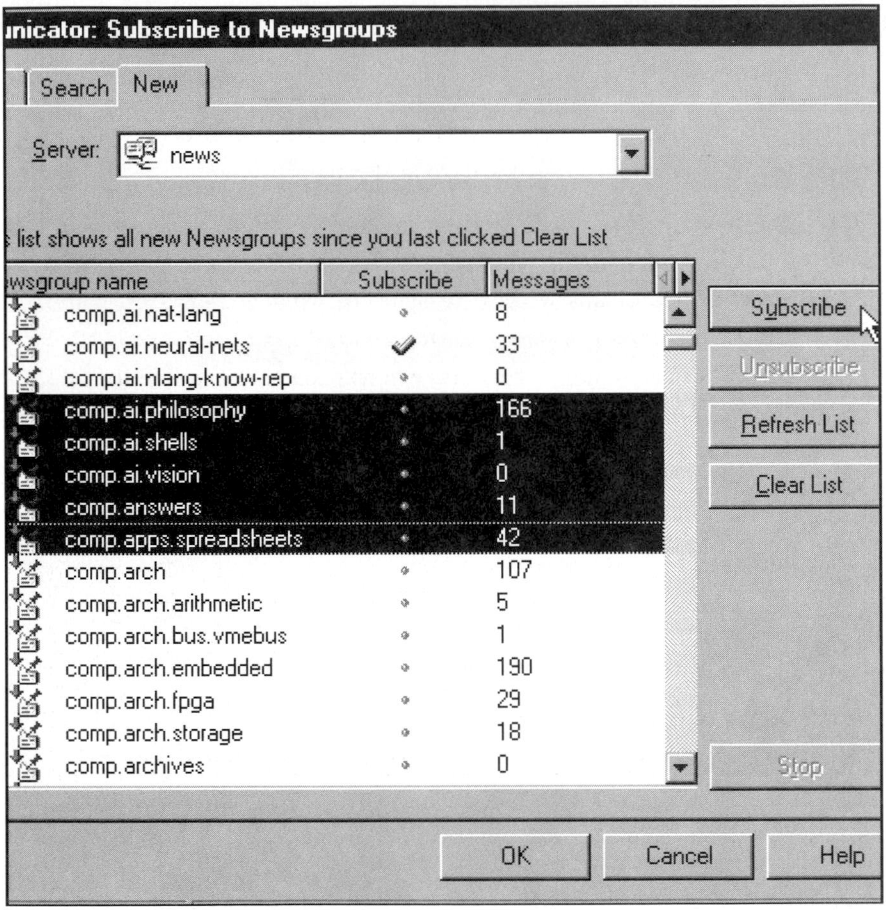

Figure 5.3   Subscribe to newsgroups using Netscape Communicator.

5. Reading the news and articles. To read the articles in a particular newsgroup, click its name in the newsgroup list. Articles' headers appear in the top left frame of the mail window (figure 3.39). Articles are grouped into threads. Click the plus (+) icon to see all the messages in a thread (discussion). The articles' headers are continuously updated; new headers are posted and old ones are deleted. Click an article header to read it. If you like an article, you can print it, respond to it, or deal with it like an e-mail message. For example, to post or start a new thread, click the `New Msg` button of the mail window, compose your message, and click `Send` (in the mail composition window) to post it. You can post a response to contribute to ongoing discussions. Select the header of the message you would like to respond to, and click the `Reply` button of the mail window. To redirect a posting to another newsgroup, select the posting, and click the `Forward` button. Type the name of the newsgroup that should receive the posting as the receiving e-mail address.

6. Posting your own and follow-up messages. Your messages should contribute something of value. You should also be familiar with netiquette, the rules of proper online behavior. Also, create a signature, so people can tell who you are. Use alt.test to post your first message as a test. Once you are comfortable, you can post your own message to Usenet. You can also post a follow-up message to reply to an article you have read in a newsgroup.

7. Searching for a newsgroup. To search for a newsgroup, click the `File` menu of the mail window (figure 3.39) and choose `Subscribe` to open the subscription window (figure 5.3). Click the `Search` tab of this window to open the window shown in figure 5.4. In the `Server` field, choose the server you want to search. In the `Search for` field, type a keyword that represents any part of a newsgroup name, for example .comp. Click the `Search Now` button to begin the search. The results are displayed in the window, as shown in figure 5.4.

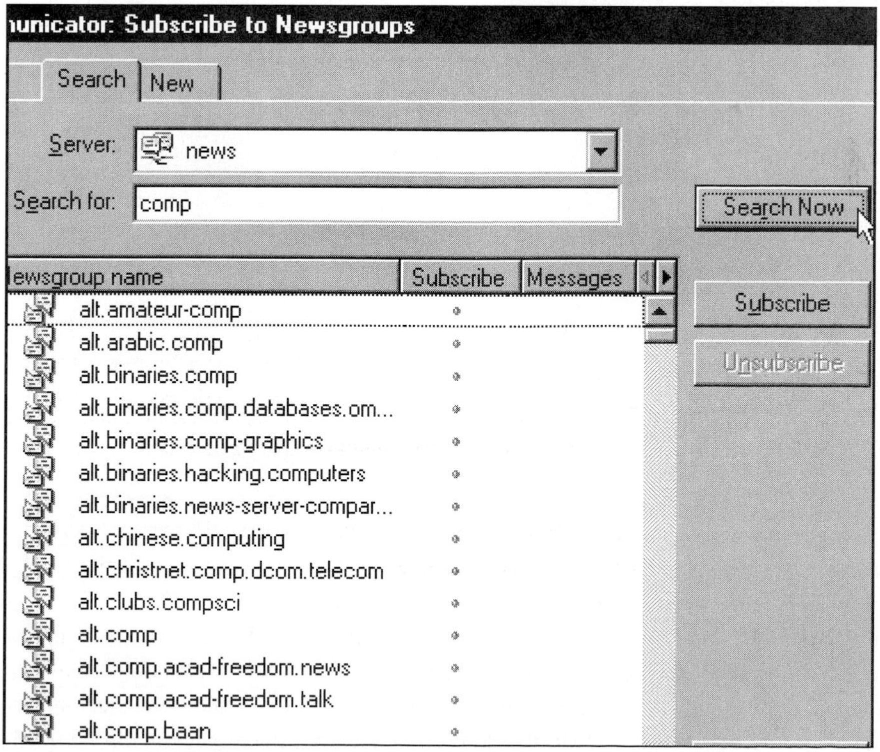

Figure 5.4   Search for a newsgroup name using Netscape Communicator.

5.5.2 Newsgroups Using Microsoft Internet Explorer

You can use MS Outlook Express as a Usenet newsreader. Outlook Express provides you with the tools you need to handle newsgroups. Before you can use Outlook Express to access Usenet, you must configure it first. You need to supply the domain name of your NNTP (Usenet) server and download the current newsgroup list. Then you choose the ones to which you want to subscribe. Here are the detailed steps.

1. Installing a newsgroup NNTP server. You need to provide Outlook Express with the NNTP server's domain name. Starting with the `Tools` menu of the `Outlook Express` window, click this sequence: `Tools => Accounts`, to open the `Accounts` window shown in figure 5.5. Click the `News` tab, then click the `Add` button. When you click `News` from the pop-up menu, the `Connection` window is displayed. You can also open the Connection window by clicking the `Setup a Newsgroups account` hyperlink shown in figure 4.12. Fill in your

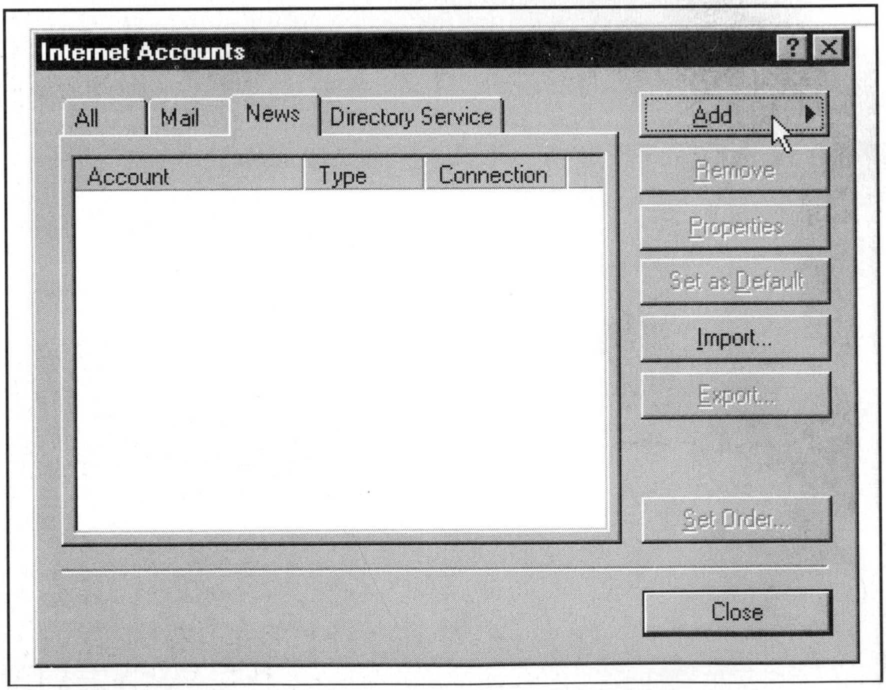

Figure 5.5   Add newsgroup server name to MS Outlook Express.

name and click `Next`. Fill in your e-mail address and click `Next` in the window that pops up. Fill in the name of the NNTP News server, say "news" in the window that pops up, and click `Next`. Click `Finish` in the window that pops up. After you successfully add one or two newsgroup servers, the `Outlook Express` window (figure 4.6) shows them in its Folders frame and provides you with three hyperlinks under its Newsgroups heading. These hyperlinks allow you to subscribe to newsgroups, to read articles, and to post your own.

2. Downloading newsgroups. If the mail window does not display the current newsgroups under a newsgroup server you have installed, it means that you have not yet subscribed to any newsgroup there. To download the newsgroups available on a given server, select the server (news in figure 4.6) in the Outlook Express window. Then click Tools (menu of the Outlook Express window) => Newsgroups. This download is done only once.

3. Subscribe and unsubscribe to Newsgroups. Once you have downloaded the newsgroups of the servers you installed, select the ones you want to subscribe to and read on regular basis. To subscribe to a newsgroup, open the Outlook Express window. From the Tools menu of this window, choose Newsgroups, or click the Subscribe to Newsgroups hyperlink shown in figure 5.6, to open the subscription window shown in figure 5.7. Select the newsgroup, and click the Subscribe button. The browser adds a symbol, as shown in figure 5.7, next to the newsgroup. If you click the Unsubscribe button, you unsubscribe, and the symbol disappears. To subscribe to more than one newsgroup at the same time, select the newsgroups (hold down the CTRL key for multiple selections) and click the Subscribe button as shown in figure 5.7. When you finish subscribing, click the OK button (figure 5.7) of the Newsgroup Subscriptions window. Your list shows, under the news folder, in the Folders frame of the Outlook Express window. The number shown between parentheses next to each newsgroup is the number of the unread messages.

To unsubscribe from a newsgroup, right click the group name from the Folders frame of the Outlook Express window. Then click Unsubscribe from the pop-up menu. Click OK in the pop-up window to confirm.

4. Downloading news articles. After subscribing to a newsgroup, you can download its postings or articles. Click the name of the newsgroup from the Folders frame of the Outlook Express window to download the latest articles. You must be online, and Outlook Express must be in the online mode. To put MS Outlook Express into the online mode, click File (menu of the Outlook Express window) => Work Offline. (This is an on/off menu item, or *toggle*. Make sure it has no checkmark next to it).

5. Reading the news and articles. To read the articles in a particular newsgroup, click its name in the newsgroup list. Articles' headers appear in the top left frame of the Outlook Express window. Articles are grouped into threads. Click the plus (+) icon to see all the messages in a thread (discussion). The articles' headers are continuously updated; new headers are posted, and old ones are deleted. Click an article header to read it. If you like an article, you can print it, respond to it, or deal with it like an e-mail message. For example, to post or start a new thread, click the New Post button of the Outlook Express window, compose your message, and click Send (in the New Message window) to post it. You can post a response to contribute to ongoing discussions. Select the header of the message you want to respond to, and click the Reply button (to send to the author only) or the Reply Group button (to send to the entire newsgroup) of the Outlook Express window. To redirect a posting to another news-

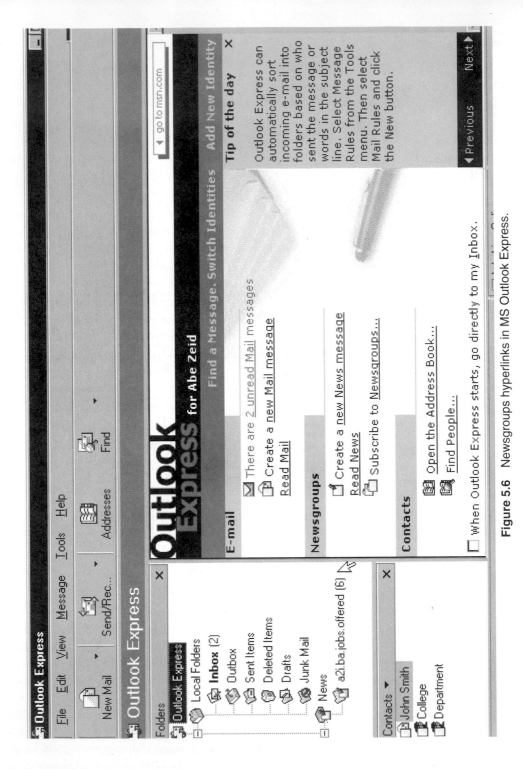

Figure 5.6 Newsgroups hyperlinks in MS Outlook Express.

group, select the posting and click the `Forward` button. Type the name of the newsgroup that should receive the posting as the receiving e-mail address.

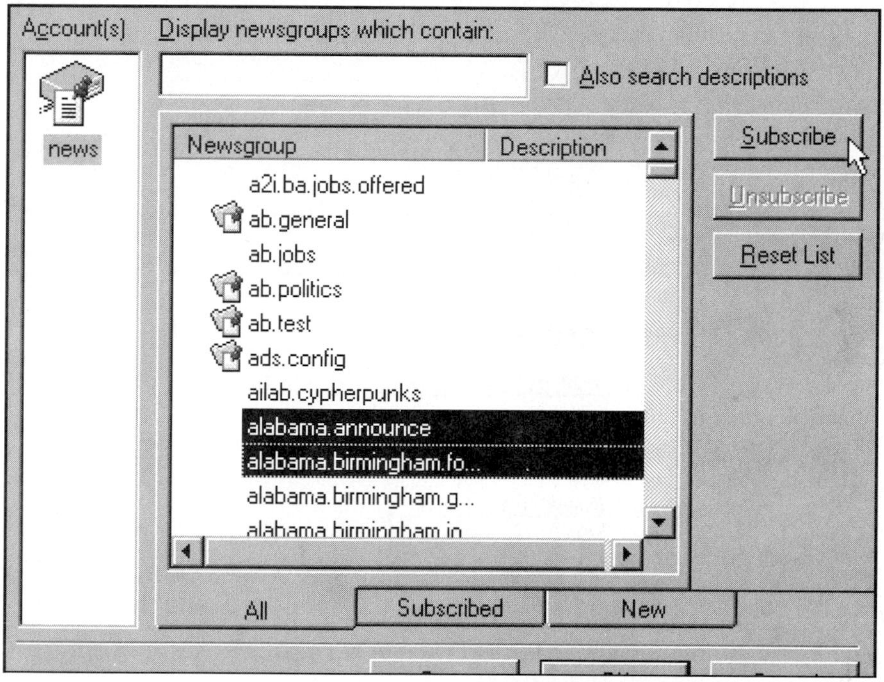

Figure 5.7 `Newsgroup subscriptions` window of MS Outlook Express.

6. Posting your own and follow-up messages. Your messages should contribute something of value. You should also be familiar with netiquette, the rules of proper online behavior. Also, create your signature, so people can tell who you are. Use `alt.test` to post your first message as a test. Once you are comfortable, you can post your own message to Usenet. You can also post a follow-up message to reply to an article you have read in a newsgroup.

7. Searching for a newsgroup article. To search a newsgroup for a message or article, select it first from the `Folders` frame of the `Outlook Express` window. Then, click the `Find` button of the window (figure 5.6). Fill in the information in the `Find Message` window shown in figure 5.8. When you finish, click the `Find Now` button of the window. The results are displayed in the bottom of the window, as shown in figure 5.8.

5.5.3 FTP

The two common methods of accessing FTP sites are via the browser or a GUI, as discussed in section 4.4. We used browser-based FTP when we searched for and downloaded shareware. In this tutorial, we use GUI-based FTP. We need to search for FTP shareware that we can use. Use a search engine. such as www.shareware.com, and type "ftp" as the search string. Choose one of the hits, download the shareware, and install it.

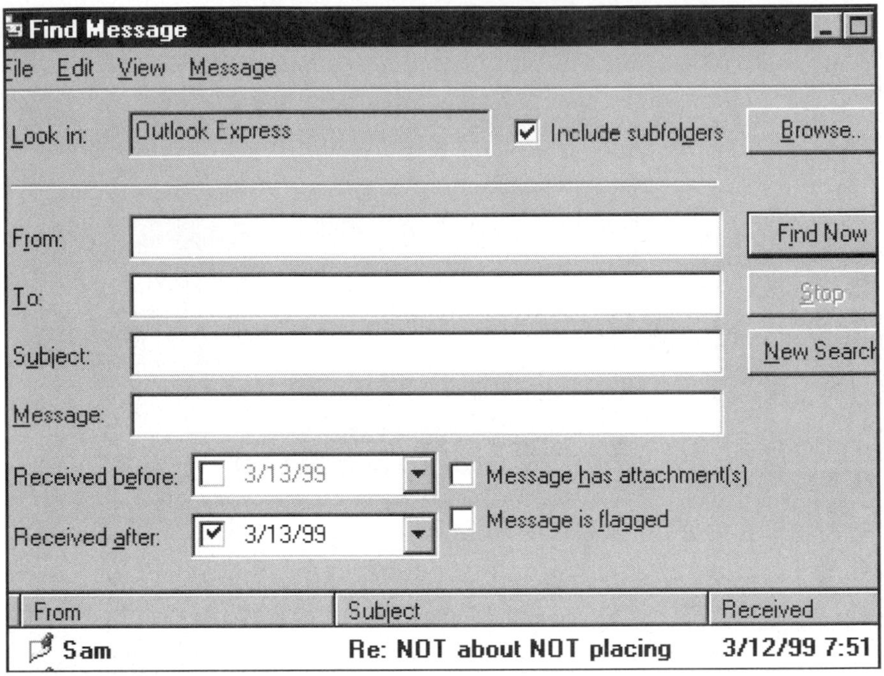

Figure 5.8   Search for a newsgroup message using MS Outlook Express.

Here, we download and install the specific shareware ws_ftp32. Search for this name, download it, and install it. When you double click the shortcut, the FTP GUI shown in figure 5.9 is displayed. The GUI shows two windows. The front window (Session Properties window) is a login window. All you need to do in this window (unless you need to learn more about ws_ftp32) is to type the FTP site you want to connect to. Let us type ftp.netscape.com, to download the Communicator software. Click the OK button to connect to the site. If you are online, the ws_ftp32 program should connect your computer to the Netscape site. The back window displays the ftp site your computer is connected to (in its title bar) and the directory structure of the site (in its Remote System subwindow), as shown in figure 5.10. The other subwindow shown in the figure is for Local System (your computer). This subwindow should show all the drives (A, C, D, etc.) on your computer.

To download the Communicator software, you need to find where the directory resides on the remote system. In the Remote System subwindow, double click this sequence: pub => communicator => english => 4.61 => windows => windows95 or nt => professional edition. You see the executable cp32e461.exe that you want to download. Select it. Before you download, you need to specify the folder on your computer to

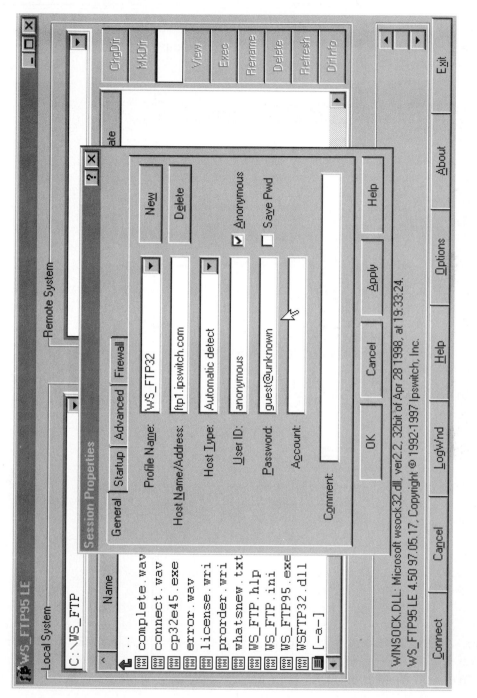

Figure 5.9 Client FTP GUI.

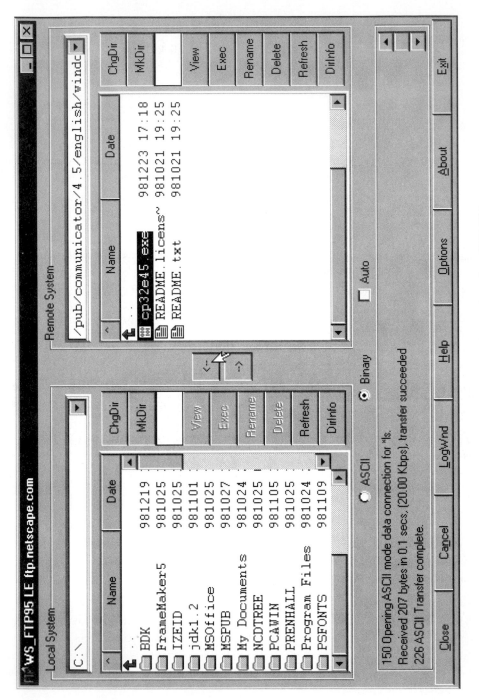

Figure 5.10 Downloading when using client FTP GUI.

download to. In the `Local System` subwindow, double click the arrow at the top, shown in figure 5.10, to go one level up. As shown in figure 5.10, you download the Communicator software to the top level of the C drive.

After choosing the directories on both the remote and local systems, you are ready to download. There are two arrows (one pointing to the left and the other pointing to the right) between the two subwindows. Clicking one of these arrows moves files from one system to the other. In the case of downloading Netscape Communicator, you click the arrow going to the left, (from the Netscape remote site to your local computer). When you click the arrow, the downloading begins. In the case of, say, uploading a Web page file from your computer to your service provider server, you click the arrow going to the right.

When downloading is complete, click the `Close` button to close the connection. After the connection is closed, the `Close` button becomes the `Connect` button. If you need to connect again, click the `Connect` button. As shown in figure 5.10, you can specify ASCII, Binary, or Auto to transfer files from the remote system to your local computer and vice versa. If you do not know the type (ASCII or binary) of file you are transferring, click `Auto`.

5.5.4 Telnet

Telnet is a character-based interface. Users should not expect their Windows screen to show up through Telnet. Telnet is a client/server application. The server computer needs a Telnet server software installed and running for the client to be able to connect to it. The client must also have the Telnet client-side software. To establish Telnet sessions, you need Telnet software that can communicate with the remote site (computer) you need to connect to. You need to download Telnet software and install it. To find it on the Internet, use a search engine, such as www.shareware.com. Here, we download and install `Wintel32` shareware. Once you have downloaded `Wintel32`, unzip it, and install it. Figure 5.11 shown the `Wintel32` GUI. As shown in the figure, you can create a Telnet book to save the Telnet sites you frequently connect to. Click the `New` button (figure 5.11) to open the `Telnet/Rlogin Setting` window shown in figure 5.12. Fill in the `Name` and the `Address` of the Telnet site, and click `OK`. Here we use an address of the *College of Engineering* at *Northeastern University*.

To telnet to this address, click the `Telnetbook` icon on the `Wintel32` window (figure 5.11) to open the `Telnetbook`. Select *engineering*, and click `Connect` as shown in figure 5.13. You must be online already for the connection to work. If the Telnet site is not anonymous, you would need a username and a password to log in, as shown in figure 5.14. Once the Telnet connection is established, you can do your work. Figure 5.15 shows some results (using the *ls* Unix command) of the session.

Once you have finished using the remote site (engineering in this case), click the `Disconnect` icon (figure 5.15) to end the session. To exit `Wintel32`, click `File` (menu of Wintel32 window shown in figure 5.15) => `Exit`.

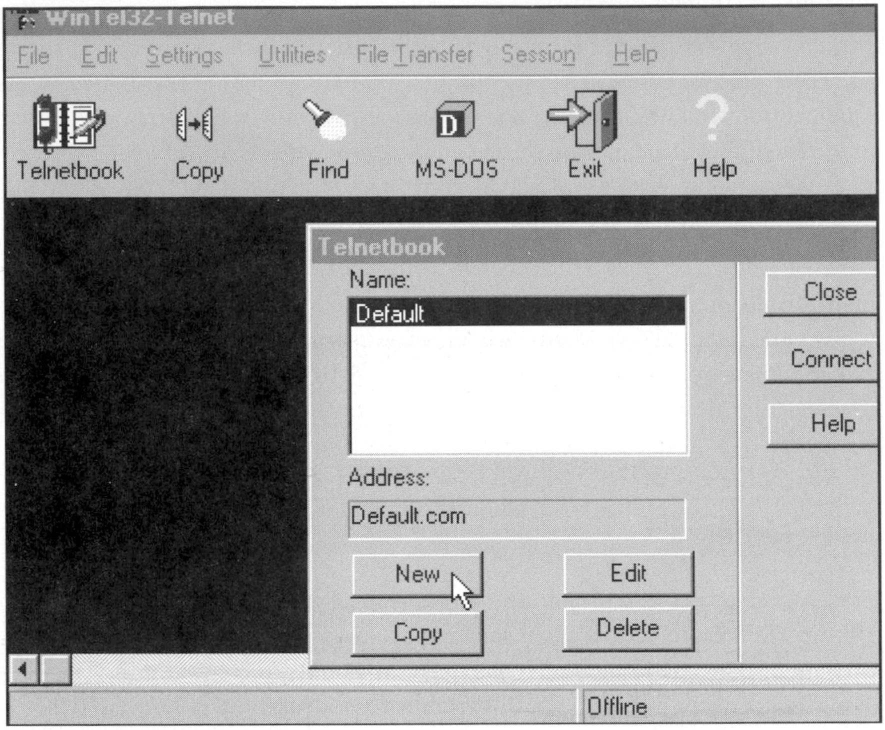

Figure 5.11   Client Telnet GUI.

Figure 5.12   Creating a Telnet notebook.

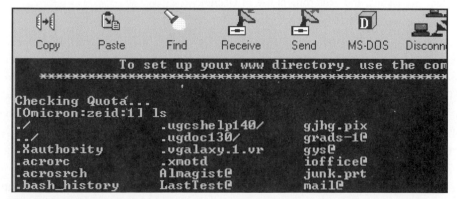

Figure 5.13   Connecting to a Telnet site.

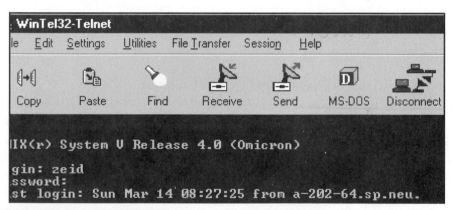

Figure 5.14   Login using Telnet.

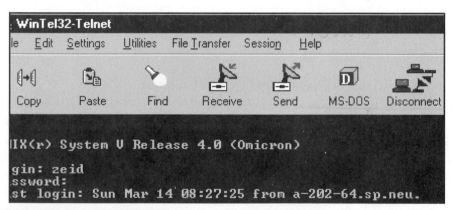

Figure 5.15   Using a Telnet site.

5.5.5 Finger and Ping

These are OS-level commands that are useful for probing computers. They are typically used on Unix systems. The *finger* command allows you to find who is currently logged in to a given host and whether a particular user is logged in. To finger a host, use the command *finger hostname* — for example, *finger neu.edu*. The result of this command is a list of the login name, the name, and the logging time of the users currently logged in on the hostname host (in this example, *neu.edu*). You can then try to chat with one of these users or send an e-mail message that you are on your way. To finger a particular user, use the command *finger user e-mail address* — for example, *finger zeid@coe.neu.edu*. If this user is logged in, you receive back the login name, the name, and the logging time of the user. You need to realize that the finger command may be rejected by some computers, for security reasons.

The *ping* command allows a user on a given system to check on whether another computer system is up and running. The general command syntax is *ping hostname* — for example, *ping neu.edu*. The command returns whether the host is up or down. This command is useful to use before you telnet to the host.

Tracert

5.6 FAQs

Q: How can I find existing newsgroups on the Internet?

A: Using a search engine such as www.metacrawler.com, type newsgroups as a search string. Browse through the hits you receive back, and read what suits your needs. Here is a sample. The Web site www.cis.ohio-state.edu/hypertext/faq/usenet/FAQ-list.html lists newsgroup names in alphabetical order and also provides FAQs about them. The Web site www.faqs.org/faqs/by-newsgroup provides a wealth of FAQs about different topics. The Web site www.dejanews.com allows you to search Usenet news and access newsgroup postings by category or keyword. The Web site www.faqs.org/usenet provides much valuable information about Usenet and newsgroups, such as Usenet definition, resources, moderation, netiquette, software, starting a group, security issues, and government use of Usenet.

Q: How can I find Usenet software?

A: If you use a browser on a client to read newsgroups messages, you do not need to go beyond your browser. If you need separate software that you can install on your computer, use a search engine, such as www.metacrawler.com, and search for Usenet software. The Web site www.faqs.org/usenet provides a wealth of information about, among other things, Usenet software. You need Usenet software if you are in charge of a server that you need to configure to manage newsgroups messages.

Q: How can I find listserv discussion groups?

A: Using a search engine, such as www.metacrawler.com, type Listserv discussion groups as a search string. You will get many good hits. Browse through them, and read what suits your needs. Here is a sample. The Web site ourtown.com/ourtown/journals/listserv.html allows you to subscribe to various mailgroups. The Web site www.lsoft.com/lists/listref.html has a catalog of listserv lists.

Q: Why does my browser not show newsgroups that I can subscribe to?

A: The problem is not your browser. It is your service provider. The service provider must have a link to a news server for you to be able to access it, as shown in figure 5.16. In this figure, the client computer can access *News Server 1* and *News Server 2*, as indicated by the bi-directional arrows. However, it is unable to access *News Server 3*, although that is available on the Internet, because your service provider does not link to it. One of the servers that is always available is news. Both Netscape Communicator and MS Outlook Express recognize it, as is shown in the tutorial. Some service providers limit (or even do not support) newsgroups. For example, if you use your employer as your service provider, do not be surprised if your browser does not show any newsgroups or shows only local ones created by your employer for company business. Many employers consider newsgroups as a drag on employees' time and therefore on their productivity at work.

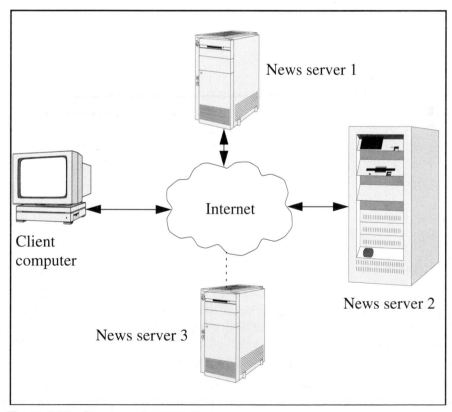

Figure 5.16   Structure of newsgroups.

Q: How can I manage my newsgroups in Netscape Communicator?

A: The Communicator allows you to view or change newsgroup properties. Select the desired newsgroup from the left frame of the mail window (figure 3.28). Click `Newsgroup Properties` of the `Edit` menu of the mail window to display the `Newsgroup Server Properties` window, shown in figure 5.17. Use the three tabs (`General`, `Downloaded Settings`, and `Disk Space`) to change the properties. Click `OK` to finish.

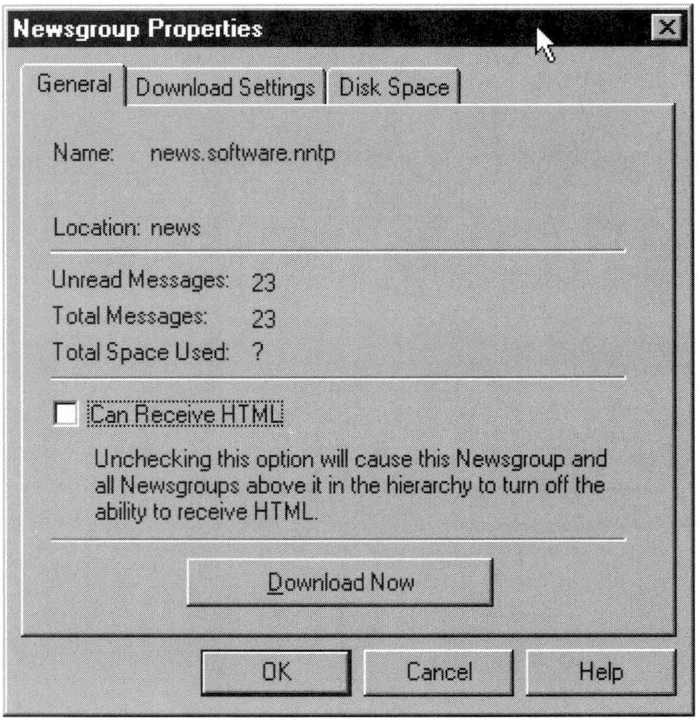

Figure 5.17   Managing newsgroups via Netscape Communicator.

Q: How can I change the properties of a newsgroup server in Netscape Communicator?

A: Select the server from the left frame of the mail window. Click `Newsgroup Server Properties` from the `Edit` menu of the mail window to display the `Newsgroup Server Properties` window, shown in figure 5.18. Change the default by selecting the other button shown. The default is usually used for a secure server connection.

Q: How can I delete a newsgroup server?

A: For Netscape Communicator, click `Edit` (one of Netscape menus) => `Preferences` => `Mail&Newsgroups` (double click to expand, if needed) => `Newsgroups  Servers`.

This sequence opens the `Preferences` window shown in figure 5.2. Select the newsgroup server you want to delete, and click the `Delete` button. Click `OK` to confirm.

For MS IE, open the `Outlook Express` window. Click `Tools` (a menu of the window) => `Accounts`. This sequence opens the `Account` window (figure 5.5). Select the newsgroup server you want to delete, and click the `Remove` button. Click `Yes` to confirm.

Q: Why can I download from an FTP site but cannot upload my files to the site?

A: The ability to download from and upload to FTP sites depends on how the site is set up. Some sites are set up for downloading only (read-only sites). Other sites are set up for both (read/write sites). It is very rare that anonymous FTP sites allow you to upload files to them.

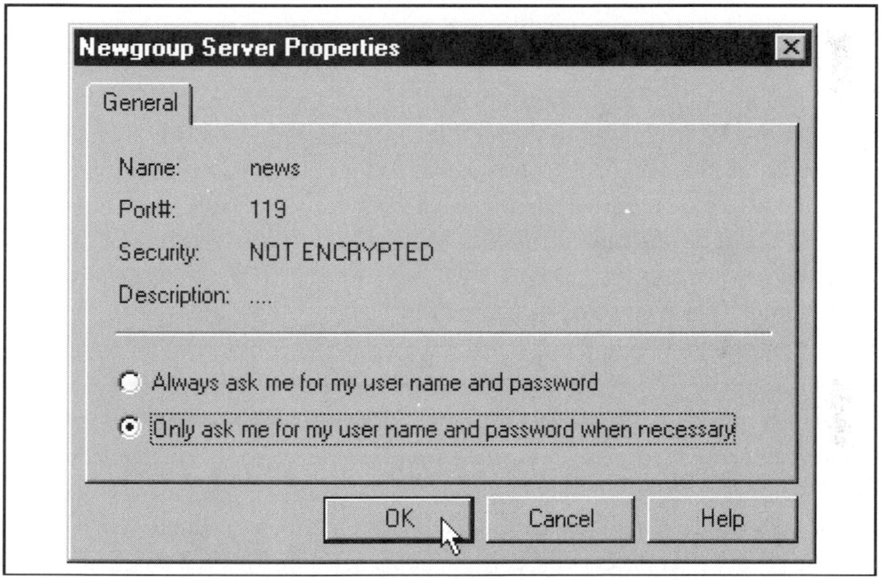

Figure 5.18 Changing newsgroup server properties in Netscape Communicator.

Q: What is the fastest way to send a folder that contains multiple files to someone?

A: To send such a folder, the user can use either e-mail or FTP. The user may e-mail (use *attachment to mail*, as discussed in chapters 3 and 4) or ftp each file in the folder separately. This alternative is not recommended, because the folder loses its hierarchy and structure. The best way to send the folder is to zip it and then e-mail it or ftp it. Zipping the folder converts it into one zip file with the .zip extension. (The user chooses a name for the file.) Zipping the folder achieve two benefits. First, the zipped file maintains the hierarchical structure of the folder. Second, sending the zipped file is much faster, because the user is sending one file, and it is smaller. (Zipped files are compressed.) To zip the folder (assuming Windows OS), right click on the Desktop. Click `New` => `WinzipFile`. This opens a zip file on the desktop. Name the file. Drag the folder that is to be zipped, and drop it onto the zipped file. This step invokes the WINZIP program. Click the I Agree button to finish. Once the zipped file is created, the user can send it via e-mail or FTP.

Q: Does Windows OS have FTP built into it? How can I use it?

A: Yes. Windows OS have FTP built into it. Click the following sequence to start and use a Telnet session; Start (menu on bottom left corner of screen) => Run => type "ftp" in the Open text field that pops up => OK. This sequence opens an ftp window. This window is a DOS window. Thus, you must use FTP line commands as discussed in section 5.3.

Q: Why am I unable to telnet to a site?

A: If the Telnet site is anonymous, it is possible that the site is down, has changed, or is no longer in existence. If the site is not anonymous, it could be down temporarily, or you may be using the wrong username and password.

Q: What can I do to access my files and programs on my computer at home from my computer at work, and vice versa?

A: You can use either FTP or Telnet. If you need to send a copy of a file from home drive to work drive, use FTP. If you want to share a file or a program without copying it, use Telnet. Thinking in terms of FTP and Telnet solves a common problem that many computer users face. That is the difficulty of keeping the computers at home and at work synchronized. The availability of FTP and Telnet all the time requires a dedicated Internet connection on both sides. For example, a cable connection (or a DSL line) at home and a T1 line at work provide full-time Internet availability. However, a dial-up connection at home is not enough.

Q: How can I telnet from home to my account at work by using my browser?

A: Both Netscape Communicator and MS IE will let you telnet to your account at work from home or any other location. Simply type the following in the browser URL bar: telnet://telnet xxx.yyy.zzz, where xxx.yyy.zzz is the site you need to telnet to. For example, to telnet to the *College of Engineering* server (through an elvis workstation or node) at *Northeastern University*, one types telnet://telnet elvis.coe.neu.edu. Once a connection is established, a username and a password are needed to connect to the corresponding account. This is a different, and an easier, way to telnet to a site without having to install client-side Telnet shareware (as discussed in section 5.5.4 of this chapter).

Q: Does Windows OS have Telnet built into it? How can I use it?

A: Yes. Windows OS have Telnet built into it. Click the following sequence to start and use a Telnet session; Start (menu on bottom left corner of screen) => Run => type "telnet" in the Open text field that pops up => OK. This sequence opens a Telnet window. Now, click the following sequence to log in and start a Telnet session; Connect (menu of the Telnet window that is just opened) => Remote System. A Connect window pops up. Use the window to connect and use Telnet, similar to tutorial 5.5.4.

Q: How can I learn more about FTP and Telnet?

A: Use your favorite search engine, and use search strings such as FTP, FTP FAQs, Telnet, and Telnet FAQs. Surf through the hits you get back. For example, the site hoo-hoo.ncsa.uiuc.edu/ftp offers some FAQs about FTP.

5.7 Summary

Introduction

•The most popular segment of the Internet is the Web. There are useful tools, including newsgroups, FTP, and Telnet to navigate the Web.

•The majority of activity on the Internet is browsing, sending e-mails, performing e-commerce, and searching for sites and Web pages

•There are other activities that may require talking and chatting with others (Newsgroups), downloading large files (FTP), and connecting to a remote computer on the Internet (Telnet).

Discussion Groups and Newsgroups

•Discussion groups and newsgroups provide a wealth of useful information about many topics.

•Discussion groups are groups of people who are interested in certain topics and usually share opinions and ideas about these topics.

•Newsgroups are the collections of the messages that the discussion groups post to a news server about a given topic or subject. Messages and replies to a specific question makeup a thread within a newsgroup. *Usenet is made up of the news servers.*

•The network of computers (news servers) that exchange news is known as Usenet.

•Usenet software organizes messages and distributes copies and replies of these messages to users. It uses Net News Transport Protocol (NNTP).

•The Big Seven discussion groups are comp (computer-related topics), sci (scientific topics), rec (recreational topics), news (Usenet topics), talk (loose topics), soc (social topics), and misc (miscellaneous topics). Other discussion groups include alt (mix of topics), k12 (education topics), fj (Japanese topics), and de (German topics).

•Some useful newsgroups for new users are news.newusers.announce, news.newusers.questions, news.answers, alt.answers, and alt.internet.services.

•Usenet etiquette defines the rules and customs of participating in discussion groups. The etiquette is mostly common sense — for example, select your audience, read before posting, test messages, advertise to small interested groups, and so forth. *called working*

•Listserv discussion groups combine elements of e-mail and Usenet news.

•Many listserv groups have a moderator, who filters and edits the submitted messages and responses before distributing and posting them.

FTP   *difference*

•FTP enables users to download files from a remote host to a local computer. It also allows them to upload files from their local computers to remote sites.

•FTP can transfer two types of files: ASCII files, and binary files.

•FTP software uses the client/server model. It has two parts: a client part, and a server part.

•There are three ways to connect to FTP sites or servers: OS, browser, or GUI.

•The OS-level FTP is popular mainly among Unix users. It uses line commands.

•With a browser, the user is usually able to click a hyperlink that connects to an FTP site and download the desired file.

•The GUI-based FTP uses client/server software. Users avoid typing FTP line commands by using a client FTP GUI.

•Most, but not all, the FTP sites are anonymous sites. Anonymous FTP does not require a login. The word *anonymous* may be used for the username, and the password could be *guest*, an e-mail address, any password, or no password.

•Many FTP servers, particularly for anonymous FTP, store files in compressed formats. Compressed files are usually known as zipped files.   *think . of*

•Compressed formats for Unix are different from those for PCs, and the programs for uncompressing the two groups of formats are also different.

•For Unix, the programs for compressing and uncompressing are uuencode and uudecode, respectively.

•For PC Windows, the program WINZIP does both compressing and uncompressing. For PCs, the file extension for compressed files is .zip.

Telnet

•Telnet provides a way to log in to a remote computer (host) and use it.

•Telnet usually requires a username and a password.

•Telnet is a client-server application.

•Multistage Telnet happens when a user telnets from one host to another and then from that host to yet another, to make connections that otherwise would be impossible.

•Multisession Telnet happens when a user accesses more than one remote host simultaneously.

•Anonymous Telnet is available, although it is not as popular as anonymous FTP.

•Quick reference to using Netscape (NS) Communicator as a News reader

NS1. **Install a newsgroup NNTP server;** open the mail window (figure 3.28). Click `Edit => Preferences => Mail&Newsgroups` (double click this item) `=> Newsgroups Servers => Add =>` specify an NNTP server (figures 3.16 and 5.2).

NS2. **Downloading newsgroups;** click `File => Subscribe`.

NS3. **Subscribing and unsubscribing to Newsgroups;** click `File => Sub-scribe =>` highlight desired newsgroups `=> OK` (figure 5.3). To unsubscribe from a newsgroup, select the group name from the left frame of the mail window `=>` click `Edit => Unsubscribe => OK`.

NS4. **Downloading news articles;** click `Get Msg` (figure 3.28).

NS5. Reading the news and articles; to read the articles in a particular newsgroup, click its name in the newsgroup list. Articles' headers appear in the top left frame of the mail window (figure 3.28).

NS6. Posting your own and follow-up messages; same as replying to e-mail and sending e-mail messages. (See chapters 3 and 4.)

NS7. Searching for a newsgroup; click `File => Subscribe` (to open the subscription window, figure 5.3) => click `Search` tab (to open the window shown in figure 5.4) => choose server to search => type a keyword that represents any part of a newsgroup name — for example, *comp* => click `Search Now` (figures 5.3 and 5.4).

•Quick reference to using Microsoft (MS) Outlook Express as a News reader

MS1. Install a newsgroup NNTP server; open the Outlook Express window (figure 4.12). Click `Tools => Accounts =>` click News tab `=> Add => News =>` type name `=> Next =>` type e-mail address `=> Next =>` type NNTP News server `=> Next => finish` (figures 5.5 and 5.6).

MS2. Downloading newsgroups; click `Tools => Newsgroups`.

MS3. Subscribing and unsubscribing to Newsgroups; click `Tools => Newsgroups => Subscribe to Newsgroups =>` select the newsgroup `=> Subscribe` (figures 5.6 and 5.7). To unsubscribe from a newsgroup, right click the group name from the Folders frame of the `Outlook Express` window `=> Unsubscribe => OK`.

MS4. Downloading news articles; click the name of the newsgroup from the `Folders` frame of the `Outlook Express` window to download the latest articles.

MS5. Reading the news and articles; to read the articles in a particular newsgroup, click its name in the newsgroup list. Articles' headers appear in the top left frame of the `Outlook Express` window. Articles appear as threads.

MS6. Posting your own and follow-up messages; same as replying to e-mail and sending e-mail messages (see chapter 4).

MS7. Searching for a newsgroup; click `Find` (figure 5.6) `=>` type info in the `Find Message` window shown in figure 5.8 `=>` click `Find Now`.

PROBLEMS

Exercises

5.1 Configure the browser you have on your computer to read newsgroups. Subscribe to your favorite ones.

5.2 From the list of the newsgroups that your browser has downloaded in Exercise 1, can you identify the Big Seven? List the high-level structure of the newsgroups you have; for example sci, alt, rec, and so forth. How many more do you have beyond the Big Seven?

Follow tutorial 5.5.1 for Netscape or 5.5.2 for MS IE. The tutorial shows how to configure and use a browser as a newsreader.

5.3   If you are a Unix, MAC, or Windows user, what is the best newsgroup available on the Internet for Unix, MAC, or Windows users, respectively?

5.4   Download and install a client FTP shareware. Use it to download your favorite shareware, for example *SnagIt* screen capture software. Use it also to download a local file (from a local non-Internet server) to your computer, and to upload one of your local files to a local non-Internet FTP site.

5.5   Download and install a client Telnet shareware. Use it to telnet to some anonymous sites. On site is the Library of Congress, with address locis.loc.gov.

Homework

5.6   Does your service provider offer its own newsgroups? If yes, what are they? How different are they from the Big Seven? Can you relate them to the Big Seven?

5.7   The Internet is a fast-moving medium and a very dynamic source of information. To stay up-to-date, you need to develop strategies for finding knowledge. FAQs are a great source. Many Web sites provide you with good ones. The concept of FAQs is an outcome of the Internet. Using the FAQs of your favorite Web site, find the information you need about a subject. Summarize your work. Search at least two subjects. Write a paragraph or two about each subject.

5.8   Choose your favorite three newsgroups subjects. Search the Internet, and find the active newsgroups and subgroups that are active in these subjects. Summarize the hot and current topics of discussion within these groups.

5.9   Download and install a client FTP shareware on your PC at home. Use it to download your favorite shareware, for example WINZIP software. Use it, also, to download a local file (from a local non-Internet server) to your computer, and to upload one of your local files to a local non-Internet FTP site.

5.10   Download and install a Telnet client software on your PC at home. Log in to your account at work or at your ISP. List the files in your directories there. Submit screen captures. If you do not have any accounts, use the Library of Congress at locis.loc.gov.

5.11   Use a search engine, such as www.yahoo.com, and find anonymous Telnet sites you can log in to. Use a search string, such as *USA government Telnet sites*. Use some of the sites. Submit screen captures of your results. **Note:** in some cases, the Telnet site name is the same as the Web site name without www; for example csu.edu, newheart.net, and flora.org. Simply remove the www from any Web site and try to telnet to it to find out whether it works. In many cases, you need a username and a password to log in. Some sites let you get an account on the fly.

Follow the tutorial 5.5.3 to download and install an FTP shareware. Use a search engine to find a shareware.

CHAPTER 6

Navigating the Internet

This chapter discusses the search tools available for finding information on the Internet. We are all familiar with search engines and have done some searching, but the chapter formalizes these experiences and focuses them. One can search the Internet and the Web for knowledge and information about topics, consumer e-services, companies, people, domain names, and so forth. Effective and efficient searching of the Internet cuts down on the time that one has to spend to find information. It is also part of the mental model that one needs to develop to deal with the Internet as an information medium. This medium is randomly distributed and organized (hence the word Web in WWW), not cataloged or indexed (like traditional libraries, for example), and fast and dynamically changing. This chapter presents the available navigation tools, when to use them, and how to use them. It also presents search methodologies that can be used to narrow a search to find the correct information.

6.1 Introduction

The Internet is an endless repository of information. It is a global information network that is too big to use like a conventional library source; there are no librarians, several catalogs exist, and you dare not just wander aimlessly through the thousands of Web pages, sites, databases, newsgroups, and mailing lists, looking for what you need. Internet is all about questions. To make the Internet work for any of us requires a different model. We need to know how to harness the power of its computers — learn how to run software engines and how to formulate a search strategy. The Web is the most popular segment of the Internet. Many Web search engines and tools exist; however, it is a mistake to assume that searching only the Web suffices to find what one is looking for. There are other databases and sites that are as valuable. Many users, however, limit their search activities to the Web, as it is sufficient most of the times.

An Internet search can be very time-consuming and frustrating. To perform a successful search, one needs to know what to search for and how to search for it. Without these two search elements, a search will be very difficult to conduct and to bring to a successful conclusion. For example, consider performing a search for an automobile trip. A traveler needs to know the destination. Once the destination is identified, the traveler needs to find ways to get information about it and about the route to get there. The traveler's search tools could be of many forms. The traveler may ask friends and relatives, read articles in newspapers and travel magazines, call the Chamber of Commerce of the destination, call AAA, go to a local library, buy books, and/or read maps. Thus, if we are going to surf the Internet for information, we need to be aware of the Internet-equivalent tools, such as search engines, and how to use them.

6.2 The Web

The Web uses hypertext links to display information. They enable the reader to jump from one item to another within the document or to jump from one document to another. Thus, the reading of a document does not have to be sequential. It then becomes driven by the reader's need for information. With hypertext, there is no single way to read a hypertext document. This is profoundly different from reading textbooks. Hypertext links between documents create an information space without formal pathways. You begin at one entrance and explore. No two paths are precisely the same. The Web connects its users to numerous resources, from Telnet to FTP and more. It also provides Usenet newsgroups, FAQs, mailing lists, graphics images, and sound files. As a browsing environment, the Web offers a great access to network resources with little overhead. Also, a user can become proficient in using the Web within minutes and then spend hours surfing and browsing the net. The price of browsing is time. As you browse, you reveal sites and files. There exist many search engines for the Web, such as Yahoo. Some of these engines are more accurate than others. Some are less comprehensive (and so faster) than others.

Hypertext is based on a simple idea. If one set of ideas is closely related to others, and if we can associate them together within the document and make it possible for the reader or user of information to move between them, then we have expanded the intellectual process by making knowledge more available; and if we can link, in addition to text, other forms of media, such as graphics, sound, and video, then we have a way to make the entire range of digital resources available in an easy-to-use environment. Within this environment, the information hunter does little work to obtain solid results. Therefore, the very nature of the Web makes it easy to navigate and search, via such easy-to-use navigation and search tools as search engines.

6.3 Navigation Tools

Before we discuss search techniques and methodologies, we need to be aware of the available search tools and the potential and the limitation of every tool. In other words, we need to know which tool to use for what search. Because of the rapid evolvement of the Internet, some of the old segments of the Internet and their search tools are no longer useful. The gopher servers (known as the gopher space) and their search tools, such as Veronica and Jughead, are now obsolete. Most, if not all, of these servers are now Web servers — or you may be able to access a gopher server through the Web, but even doing that is not a common practice today. Another example is FTP servers (FTP space) and their Archie search tool. FTP servers are still important, but Archie is no longer used to search them. Instead, a search site, such as www.shareware.com can be used. Ironically, you can use a search engine, such as www.metacrawler.com, to search for gopher, Veronica, Jughead, and Archie. In this book, we focus on searching and navigating the Web space.

There are several primary navigation tools that are available to Internet users to help them find information on the Web. These tools are search engines, directories, hybrid search engines, metasearch engines, Boolean-based searches, smart browsing, channels, and Web portals. With the exception of channels and Web portals, all the other tools are variations of search engines. In essence, the main navigation tools of the Internet and the Web are search engines. All information on the Web is organized in Web pages or sites, so search engines always return Web sites as their search results. That is why listing Web sites with search engines is important to increase traffic to these sites.

While there are technical differences between search engines and directories, Internet users know them both as search engines. A true search engine, such as www.metacrawler.com, creates its own listings automatically by crawling the Web and returning relevant Web pages as hits. A directory (also known as a subject guide), such as www.yahoo.com, searches its own database to create the listings. Each directory builds and maintains its own database. Web sites interested in being listed in a directory submit short descriptions to the directory editors for review. Some search engines maintain associated directories. These engines are known as hybrid search engines, because they can search both their databases and the general Web. We do not distinguish between search engines, directories, and hybrid search engines in this book. We refer to all of them as search engines.

6.4 Search Engines

The Internet has tens of millions of Web sites, and its growth has been exponential. Finding what we want on the Internet is sometimes equated with finding a needle in a haystack or a fly in a web. That search engines are able to find information with amazing accuracy is due to their design. A search engine has three major software parts: the spider (crawler), the index (catalog), and the searching software. The spider crawls the Web and wanders around reading Web pages. It follows the hyperlinks within each page to other pages. The spider returns to Web pages on a regular basis, say every month, to look for changes in these pages. The spider results are stored in the index of the search engine. The index is like a database that has a copy of every Web page that the spider finds. With its index available and updated on regular basis, a search engine is ready to serve its customers and Web surfers. The searching software finishes the search engine job. When a surfer types a search string (keywords) in the engine's search field, the software sifts through the index to find matches to the string. The software ranks the Web pages (hits) in the order it thinks is most relevant and displays them for the surfer to review and use.

How do search engines rank their hits? They use, among other rules, a rule called it the *title/frequency method*. According to this method, search engines first check the *titles* (defined in the HTML part of this book) of the Web pages they have found, to see whether the search keywords appear in them. This is analogous to searching a traditional library for books on a subject — say, golf. Books that have the keyword golf in their titles are excellent candidates for the search. In the next step, search engines check to see whether the keywords appear, and with what frequency, in the meta tag (defined in the HTML part of this book) and/or the first several paragraphs of Web pages. This step is based on the notion that any Web page relevant to the topic being searched should mention the keywords right from the beginning with great frequency. Search engines analyze how often keywords appear relative to other words in the page. Higher frequency quite often indicates higher relevancy. *not necessarily.*

In the context of the foregoing, the reader may ask two questions. How come search engines do not always return good hits? And, why does the same search, using the same search string and keywords, produce different hits on different search engines? For the first question, search engines should not be the only factor to blame for the failure of a search. Other factors include how the authors of Web pages design their pages and (more importantly) how a surfer formulates a search. If the authors do not select/write the titles and the content of their pages carefully, search engines may miss finding them during a search. If the surfer is careless or vague in defining a search string, search engines return irrelevant results. This happens during searches in traditional libraries as well. The big difference is that the human element (working with a librarian) refines the search in traditional libraries until it ends with a successful conclusion. The concept of intelligent agents can be used to address this difference

The answer to the second question stems from the fact that each search engine uses its own secret features to search the Web, while it uses the title/frequency method only to a degree. This is analogous to taking a known recipe and adding secret ingredients to it. As a start, some search engines index more Web pages than others and update them more often. This leads to different search engines having different databases to search through. A search engine may also give preference to more popular and heavily visited Web pages over others that are less popular, or it may prefer Web pages reviewed by its own editors. There are many other features that search engines use to make themselves unique. Interested readers should visit the Web site www.searchenginewatch.com.

visit!

All search engines perform keyword searches against their databases and the Web. Most searching proceeds in a linear fashion, starting with the entering of a request for information or the making of a choice from a menu. The Web, as a hypermedium, allows users to move through information and items by making jumps between the various kinds of data they need. This allows a search to move faster and more intuitively than it would using other search tools. Search engines for the Web have been used as browsing tools.

There is no one correct way to find information on the Web; the nature of its structure (web-like) implies that there will be multiple paths to the same information. This good and bad. It is good, because as users explore, they uncover links to new information they never thought of before. It is bad because it requires working through several layers of linked information, thus slowing the retrieving of it. It is important to remember that searching the Web requires curiosity and patience.

There are many search engines, catalogs, databases, indexes, and lists that exist on the Web. We cannot cover them all, and we do not expect anyone to know or use them all. They are also changing rapidly, and new ones are appearing. What a user needs to know is how to find these search engines and choose from them. One quick way to find some of these search engines is to visit the Web site www.search.com, which itself is a search engine. It lists some of the currently available search engines, as shown in figure 6.1. Some of the search engines that exist are AltaVista (www.altavista.com), BigBook (www.bigbook.com), Deja News (www.dejanews.com), Direct Hit (www.directhit.com), Dogpile (www.dogpile.com), Download (www.download.com), Excite (www.excite.com), GoTo (www.goto.com), HotBot (www.hotbot.com), InferenceFind (www.infind.com), Infoseek (www.infoseek.com), LookSmart (www.looksmart.com), Lycos (www.lycos.com), MetaCrawler (www.metacrawler.com or www.go2net.com), MetaFind (www.metafind.com), MetaSearch (www.metasearch.com), MiningCo.com (www.miningco.com), Northern Light (www.northernlight.com), Planet Search (www.planetsearch.com), ProFusion (www.profusion.com), SavvySearch (www.savvysearch.com), Snap (www.snap.com), Thunderstone (www.thunderstone.com), Webcrawler (www.webcrawler.com), and Yahoo (www.yahoo.com). AltaVista, Excite, Infoseek, Lycos, and Yahoo are popular search engines. In addition, www.download.com and www.shareware.com are useful to search for software to download.

Search engines provide easy-to-use GUIs. The surfer types a search string into a search field and clicks a search button, as shown in figure 6.1. The way search engines work can be described as follows. Each search engine has its own knowledge and information banks such as databases, catalogs, lists, and so forth. The engine utilizes sophisticated search techniques and algorithms to probe its banks of information in an attempt to match the surfer search string against the Web pages, lists, and other documents in its banks. If the engine finds a match, it returns it as a hit. Once the search is finished, the search engine displays a list of the hits in the browser window. The engine usually displays these hits in descending order of closeness of match to the search string. Some engines, such as www.metacrawler.com, use a scale of 1 to 1000. Others, such as www.shareware.com, use the date of publication (latest shareware first) and a five star (square) system (to rank dependability of download FTP sites). The hits are always hyperlinks that can be clicked to access the corresponding full Web pages.

The Web search space is huge, so some of the above search engines give the user the option of searching a smaller subspace of the Web. Search engines implement the idea of a subspace by providing the surfer with a list of choices of subspaces. For example, www.search.com has a pull-down list of options, as shown in figure 6.2; www.northernlight.com offers tabs at the top of the page.

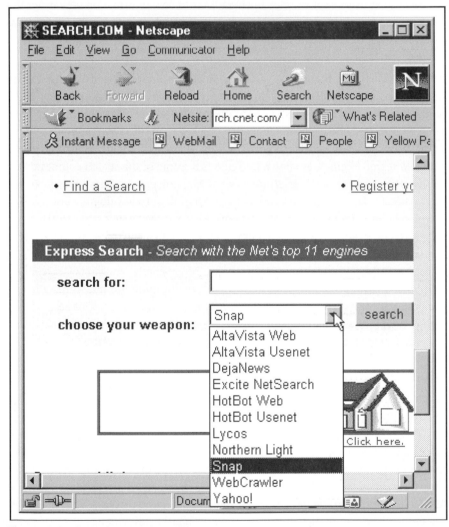

Figure 6.1   Sample search engines.

Most of the above search engines are based on robot-like programs called spiders or worms. These spiders look for new URLs. Most search engines do little more than catalog the words in the URL and the document's title and move on. Some spiders index the first several dozen words in the document itself, and a few index all the words in the entire document. There is a trade off. If the spider indexes only the words in the URL, it can index a lot of documents; the search goes quickly, but this type of search may not yield good results. If the spider indexes the full text of the document, it gives better search results; however, the search takes longer, and the database to search is not usually big.

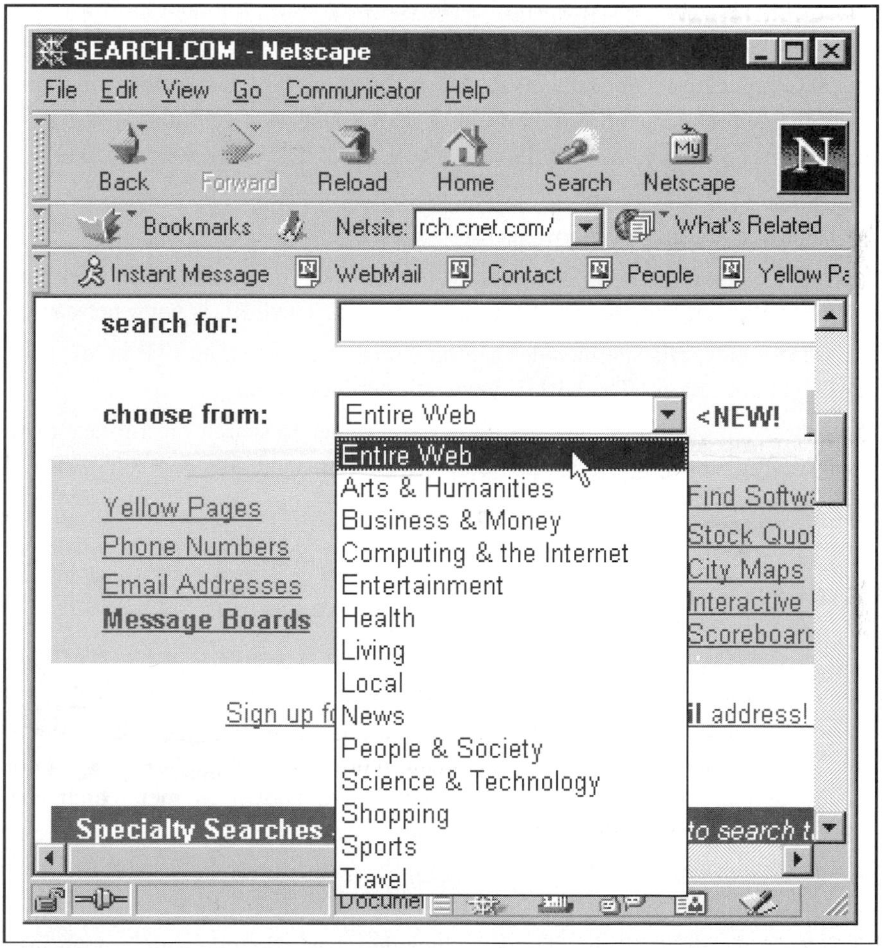

Figure 6.2 Sample Web subspaces.

Other search tools exist on the Internet. While they are not known as search engines, they nevertheless perform in a similar fashion. We can think of them as specialty search engines. Here is a partial list:

•AAUP Journal Catalog; this site is useful for locating scholarly journals and books. It is maintained by the Association of American University Presses. Its URL is aaup.pupress.princeton.edu.

•INFOMINE; it shows what the government makes available online. It covers many U.S. government resources. The URL is lib-www.ucr.edu/govpub.

•Yellow Pages; some sites use the traditional concept of yellow pages to group information by category and form their online databases. Some of these databases are searchable by keyword or category. Sample examples are the Web sites theyellowpages.com and www.yellow.com. The latter site is a world-wide yellow pages guide that allows you to search for a domestic or international business.

•InterNIC Directory; this is the Web site of Network Solutions which assigns domain names to companies. The site allows its users to search Network Solutions' database of registered domain names by using the WHOIS search tool. The URL is www.internic.net.

•Amazon.com; It allows you to search for books, music CDs, videos, and collectable items. The URL is www.amazon.com.

•Netscape; Netscape has its Netcenter which allows you to use either Netscape's own search engine or other engines such as Lycos and Infoseek. The URL is www.netscape.com.

•The OTIS Index; this site includes a commercial sites index, an FTP index, and links to newsgroups and publications. The URL is www.otis.net/index.html.

•The Library of Congress; this site allows you either to search the Library of Congress online card catalog or to telnet to the library (as described in chapter 5). The URL is www.loc.gov or lcweb.loc.gov/catalog. *doll*

6.5 Metasearch Engines

When it comes to building and developing search engines, there are two distinct approaches. The typical, straightforward approach is to develop an engine that searches the Internet. The other, less obvious but interesting, approach is to build an engine that searches many other search engines at once for every search request — that is, performs a multi-engine search. Search engines that use this latter approach are known as metasearch engines. A metasearch engine, therefore, speeds up an Internet search and makes it more convenient than using multiple search engines. If a search engine is down for some reason, the metasearch engine automatically skips searching it. *stupid!*

Examples of metasearch engines include www.dogpile.com, www.infind.com, www.metacrawler.com, www.metafind.com, and www.profusion.com. Most metasearch engines, for example www.dogpile.com, www.infind.com and www.metacrawler.com, do not give the user a choice of which search engines to deploy in the search. Some engines, however, such as www.metacrawler.com, show the engines they are using during the search, as shown in figure 6.3. They also display their search results grouped by search engine they have used in the search or else display the name of each search engine next to the hit it found. Other search engines, such as www.profusion.com, allow the user to choose which search engines to use in a search, as shown in figure 6.4. The user simply clicks the checkbox next to a search engine to include it or exclude it in a search. When the checkbox has a checkmark in it, the corresponding search engine is included in the search.

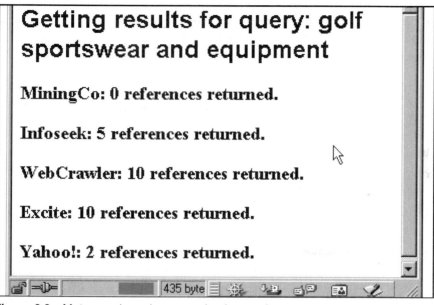

Figure 6.3 Metasearch engines search other engines.

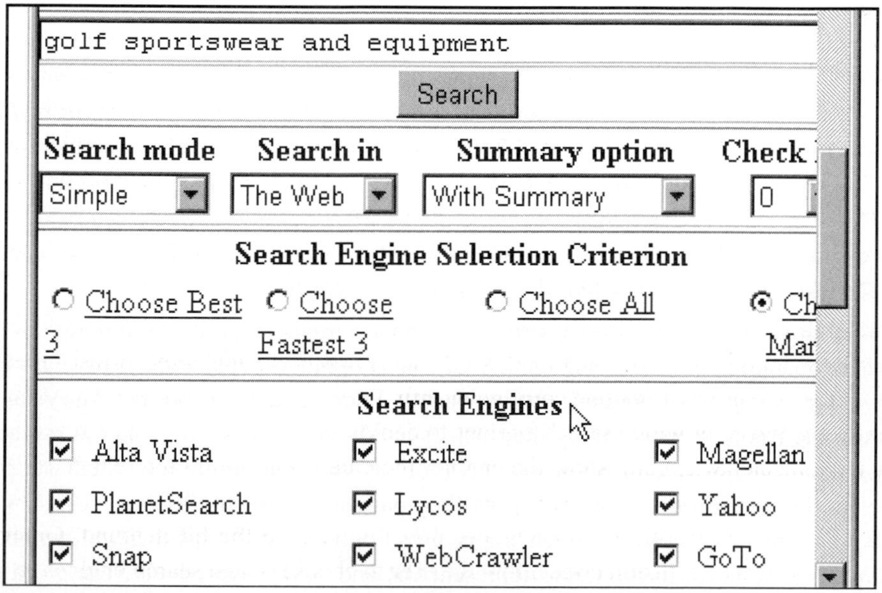

Figure 6.4 Choosing search engines in a metasearch.

There is an interesting side benefit to using metasearch engines. That is learning about the existence of other search engines. As you watch a metasearch engine display the names of the engines it is searching, you add the ones you did not know into your search tools and bookmark them.

It is important to realize that the word *meta* in a search engine name does not mean it uses the metasearch approach. For example, despite its name, www.metasearch.com is not a metasearch engine. However, it is *almost* always true, as in the cases of www.metacrawler.com and www.metafind.com.

6.6 Boolean Search

Some search engines provide their users with such advanced search features as Boolean search. These features help users to focus their search results. Boolean searches are based on the classical Boolean operations found in the mathematics and science fields. Boolean operations are performed via Boolean operators. The most commonly available Boolean operators are union (OR operator), intersection (AND operator) and subtraction (NOT operator). Symbols are sometimes used for the operators. The symbols for AND, OR, and NOT are often &, |, and ! respectively. The union operator provides the widest possible search, thus producing the highest number of hits. However, some of these hits may be irrelevant to what the search is looking for. The intersection operator provide the narrowest possible search, thus producing the smallest number of hits. In some cases, this number could be zero if the search is very restrictive. The subtraction operator excludes certain outcomes from a search results. Thus, it provides a search that produces results between those of the other two operators.

The following example illustrates how to conduct a Boolean search. We need to search for golf sportswear and equipment. If you want to find everything about golf, sportswear or equipment, you use the OR operator. The search string becomes *golf OR sportswear OR equipment*. This search is vague because you get hits about each word (golf, sportswear, equipment) without any relation between them. If you want sportswear and equipment of the golf sport only, you use the AND operator. The search string becomes *golf AND sportswear AND equipment*. If you want to exclude golf balls from the equipment search, you use the NOT operator. The search string becomes *(golf AND sportswear AND equipment) NOT balls*.

Different search engines implement the concept of Boolean search differently. Some use the Boolean operators by their name (AND, OR, NOT). Others replace them by plain English phrases — for example, "all words", "some words". For example, Yahoo and AltaVista search engines use the Boolean operators by their names, as shown in figure 6.5 and 6.6 respectively. AltaVista allows you to enter a Boolean expression, as shown in figure 6.6. AltaVista requires you to click the Advanced hyperlink in its Web page to invoke its Boolean search window, shown in figure 6.6. Metacrawler search engine uses English words, as shown in figure 6.7. The words *any* and *all* shown in the figure represent OR and AND respectively. The word *phrase* means search for the words in the order given in the search string.

6.7 Smart Browsing

Finding information on the Internet by using search and metasearch engines can some-times prove difficult and time-consuming. Using search engines can be a long and involved pro-cess. They frequently return many hits. Users have to study the long lists of links, continually refine their search strategies, check the resulting Web sites, and go back to the search engine if necessary. In some ill-formulated searches, many returned hits are irrelevant. As the Internet grows in complexity and volume, it becomes harder and more time-consuming to navigate to find information and services. At the same time, the number of people using the Internet is growing. And the pool of people using it is becoming more diverse, with many nontechnical users relying on it.

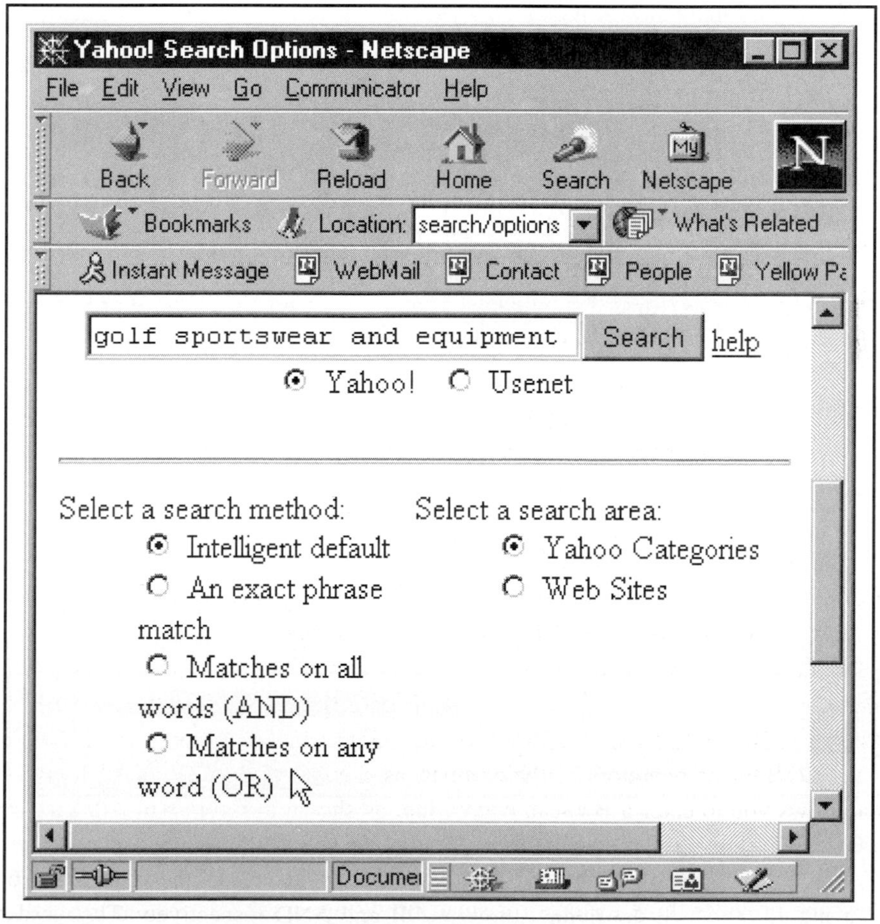

Figure 6.5   Boolean search using names of operators.

To overcome the shortcomings of search engines, a fundamental improvement to the process of navigating the Internet and finding information and services is needed. Netscape introduced the idea of smart browsing. This idea provides intelligent and fast access to information. The idea integrates Netscape Communicator with the contents of the Web through Netscape Netcenter. Netcenter is a Netscape database that stores all kind of Internet information. Thanks to this integration, users are able to type their search strings directly in the Communicator location Toolbar, preceded by the word search — for example, *search golf sportswear and equipment*. Moreover, users can type a company name if they do not remember its exact URL — for example, *Ford motor company*.

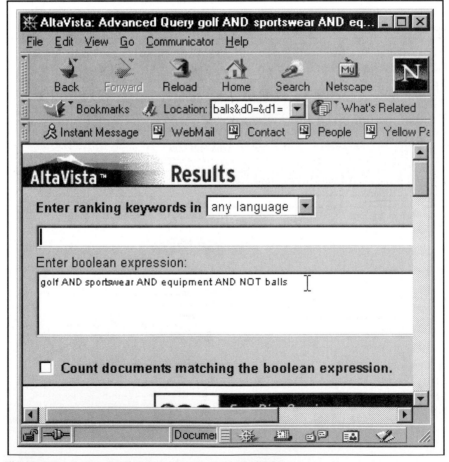

Figure 6.6   Using Boolean expressions in AltaVista.

Netscape provides three features for smart browsing: What's Related, Internet Keywords, and NetWatch. What's Related is list of URLs related to the page a surfer is currently viewing. To view the related sites, the surfer clicks the What's Related button located at the right of the location Toolbar (figure 3.13). For example, a surfer reading news about ancient Egypt and its pyramids may want more in-depth information, or a consumer shopping for a car on the Internet might want comparisons between auto makers from independent resources such as magazines.

Internet Keywords provide a shorthand way of typing addresses into the location Toolbar. Users can enter regular words, rather than the exact URL, and go right to the corresponding Web page that has the information they want. For example, typing *Honda Accord* in the location Toolbar followed by pressing the Enter button takes the user to the Honda Web site. The Communicator forwards the string *Honda Accord* to Netcenter, Netcenter looks up the string in its database of keywords, finds the Honda Web site as a match, and returns it to the user.

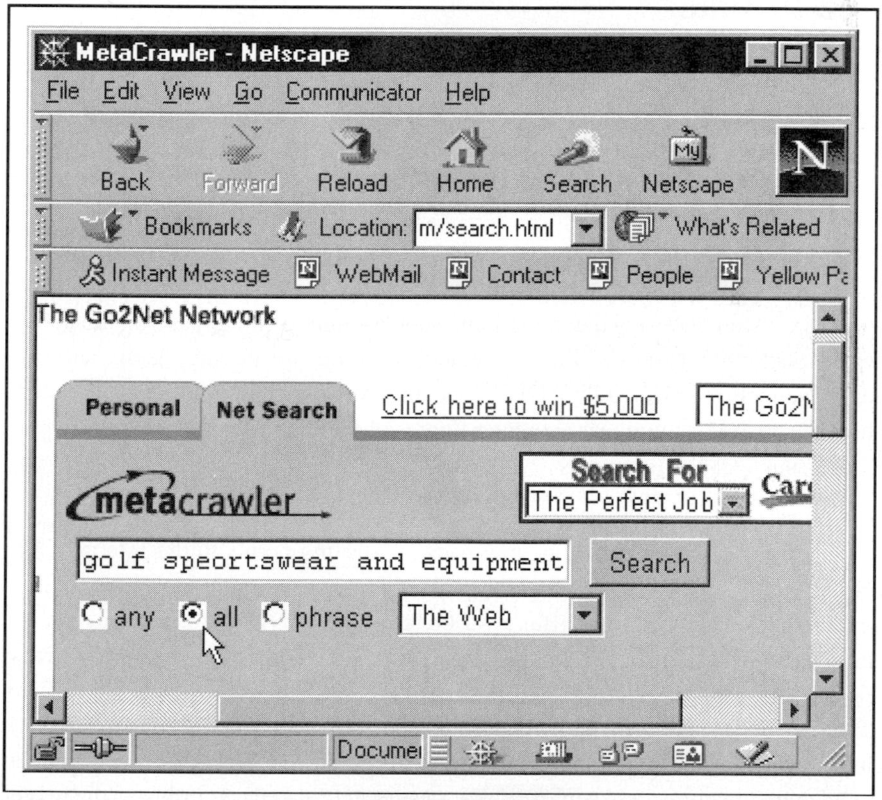

Figure 6.7 Boolean search using English statements.

NetWatch is a protection feature that lets users controls the type of Web pages that can be viewed on their computers. NetWatch filters out inappropriate pages so that users and their families do not view them. The Communicator screens Web pages intelligently, on the basis of users' choices and settings. `NetWatch` is based on the Internet rating standard known as PICS (the Platform for Internet Content Selection).

The idea of smart browsing is based on what one might call intelligent navigation of the Web. It draws upon information about how people habitually navigate the Web; then, it uses sophisticated algorithms to compile lists of related sites. Smart browsing can be implemented only by companies that have their own browsers, such as Netscape and Microsoft. Smart browsing is a dynamic concept. As people's navigation habits change, so do the smart browsing algorithms. They evolve continually over time to include all kind of information and services related to the Web site being viewed. They provide a continuously growing and evolving set of features and benefits that help users find what they need quickly and easily.

6.8 Web Portals

As the Internet and its Web grows and matures, Web content and information have been exploding exponentially. Web companies and services have been working to help users find what they need more easily. Pre-configured bookmarks, personalized pages, channels, and Web portals can help direct users to new information. While we are familiar with bookmarks and pages, channels and Web portals offer a range of services and information in a concentrated way. Channels are one of the key functions of Web portals. Channels are directories of general topics, such as sports, travel, shopping, and so forth. They categorize information, to make it easy for surfers to locate. After choosing a generic topic such as computers, the user is transported to the computer channel, with dozens of links to related resources for buying, using, and researching computers. Channels are offered by AOL (Netscape), Microsoft, and others. Netscape Communicator has a `Channels` button, as shown in figure 3.13, and MS IE has the `Favorites` menu (figure 3.27) which leads to channels.

Web portals (also known as portal sites, or just portals) are metaphors used to describe Web sites that work as gateways, launching pads, or starting points to the Internet. They act as tables of contents (information meccas) to the Web. Web portals aggregate a lot of content in one place for users' convenience. They offer a variety of online services, such as travel, chat rooms, news, forums, e-mail, weather forecasts, stock quotes, sports, shopping, search engines, and so forth. Web portals are Web megasites (or all-in-one Web supersites), with a very high volume of Web traffic (or users) using them and what they offer. Therefore, a portal, by definition, is a popular, heavily visited Web site. Portals continually offer their visitors and customers a barrage of services and content to lure and keep them. Portal sites are ranked according to the percentage of Web users that visit them on a daily, weekly, or monthly basis. The higher the percentage, the more popular the site. Most of the traditional search engines, such as Yahoo, Excite, Infoseek, and Lycos, have transformed themselves into Web portals to attract and keep large audience. The leading portal companies include AOL, Microsoft, and Yahoo. Portal companies buy up content they believe will attract new users to their sites. For example, Microsoft portal includes a partnership with NBC television, and Infoseek portal includes a partnership with the Walt Disney Company.

The main premise behind portals is that they offer entryways to the Internet. They offer one-stop information sites where consumers can launch their Web surfing expeditions. Many portal sites such as Yahoo provide a way to customize the site according to the user's personal interest. They are becoming a lot like television. There may be three to six general-interest portals, just like there are about four big television networks. Users of the Internet, like TV viewers, turn to the top portals for Internet services and content. In turn, portals are able to attract advertisements from smaller, less well known Web sites that want to have exposure to the massive numbers of portal users to sell their products. In essence, portals become brand names of the Internet, just as the big TV networks are the brand names of television.

What do portals have to do with navigating the Web? They have a lot to do with it. We can think of portals as special, well-organized search engines. A portal site provides users with the best known products, services, and content, organized in categories. Each category is loaded with links to the Web sites where users can get to buy what they need by clicking the hyperlinks. In essence, portals serve as entry directories to the maze of the Internet. These directories are organized in channels that should make navigating the Internet quick and easy. Portals represent one-stop shopping on the Internet.

6.9 Ranking Search Hits and Web Sites

When users search for information on the Internet by using a search engine and a search technique, as discussed in this chapter, the search engine ranks its search hits by using a numerical system. Different search engines use different techniques to develop their ranking systems. For example, AltaVista give more prominent display to sites that pay it advertising fees. MiningCo.com has a team of free-lance writers whom it pays to evaluate and rank Web sites, to help searchers find hits relevant to their search topics. Direct Hit ranks sites based on its users' demographic profile. Yahoo and Lycos have an army of paid editors and staff who evaluate Web sites.

All these approaches to creating ranking systems are faced with a monumental challenge. As the number of Web pages increases dramatically on every imaginable subject, search engines should try to do more than just list every available page on a given subject. One logical solution is to turn the ranking system over to users. This is the main idea behind a project that is called "Open Directory Project" and is run by Netscape Communications, a subsidiary of America online. The project started in 1998. The project acknowledges that it is impossible for a search service (engine) to know everything about anything. Thus, the project turns to user themselves. It invites users to evaluate sites within their areas of expertise and help create lists of the most useful sites, within certain subject areas. For example, experts in the area of child education can create lists of links to pages that they believe offer the best information.

The "Open Directory Project" provides a way for search engines and Web portals to get much more content into their services than what editors or free-lance writers could provide alone. Search engines and Web portals that have the most content should get the most traffic and therefore become the leaders. Some Web portals, such as Lycos, have realized the potential of the project and have joined it.

The "Open Directory Project" may be compared to the movement for "free software" that uses the process of peer review to create superior operating systems such as Linux. The project is based on volunteer work by people who love what they do and do it for free. The project should lead to building a superior method to organize the Web contents, especially as they become more difficult to manage by a handful of individuals working for search engines and Web portals.

6.10 Search Methodologies and Strategies

In this chapter, we have introduced various search engines, smart browsing, channels, portals, and various types of searches, such as single-engine search, multi-engine (meta) search, and Boolean search. With this background, one can begin to formulate a search methodology. First, a user needs to decide between using search engines, smart browsing including channels, or portals. If the user decides on using smart browsing or portals, the search is intuitive and easy. If the user needs to use search engines, here are some guidelines. Always check to see what resources the search engine or tool makes use of. Some search engines focus on newsgroups, such as www.dejanews.com, others are general, such as www.yahoo.com. Then, examine how the material is indexed once it gets into the database of the search engine. In that way, you can determine the best strategy to use as you formulate your search terms. Many search engines display the subspaces or the categories you can search.   *This help you search properly.*

The only effective way to construct a search methodology is to use a variety of search engines and tools. As you do more searches using these engines and tools, you will accumulate valuable experience. Do not use only one or two tools and become expert in them. Try, if possible, all tools. Try to run benchmark searches until you understand how search engines and tools work. Run multiple searches for the same problem. Very quickly, you will reach the conclusion that one search rarely gives complete results.

Choose your search-string carefully.
There is no substitute to experience and spending time searching.

6.11 Tutorials

These tutorials investigate further the Web navigation tools covered in the chapter, mainly search engines, metasearch engines, Boolean search, smart browsing, channels, and customizing Web portals. The tutorials also show how to conduct successful Internet searches and how to formulate search strategies.

6.11.1 Web Navigation via Basic Search

Most surfers can find satisfactory search results by conducting basic search using any search engine. A basic search implies that the surfer types a search string in the search field (figure 6.1) of the search engine. However, some search engines also allow users to focus searches by using certain symbols and words. Symbols include + (add), - (subtract), and quotation marks (multiply and order). Here are examples of formulating search strings:

+golf+sportswear+equipment returns Web pages that have references to the three words.

dogs returns Web pages that have references to the word dogs (very vague search)

+dogs+breed returns Web pages with both words in them (focuses the search)

+dogs-breed returns Web pages that reference the word dogs and not the word breeds. The search engine first inds all the Web pages that have the word dogs, and then removes any of them that have the word breed.

+dogs-breed-food returns Web pages about dogs excluding their breed and food

Searches that use the + symbol may return results you are not interested in. With the + symbol, the search engine returns Web pages that have all the words included in the search string, but not necessarily near each other or in the order you want. The quotation marks resolve this ambiguity in the search. A search that uses the quotation marks is known as a "phrase" search. For example the search string *"florida winter vacations"* tells the search engine to return the Web pages that have all the three words in the exact order shown in the quotes.

Users can combine both symbols and quotation marks to make their searches more focused; for example *"two door vehicles" -trucks -"two wheel drive"* should return all four-wheel-drive two-door passenger cars. All major search engines, such as AltaVista, Excite, Hot-Bot, Lycos, Snap, WebCrawler, and Yahoo support the math-based search described above.

There are other ways to conduct searches when using search engines. These include word, title, and site (URL) searching. In word searching, the search engine allows you to match ANY or ALL the words in the search string, or you can match the entire string as a PHRASE. A PHRASE match is equivalent to using quotation marks. Search engines that use word searching have ANY, ALL, and PHRASE radio buttons that users can select from. In title searching, the search engine searches the <TITLE> tag of a Web page. The rationale here is that the page title should an accurate indicator of the page content. A title search uses a *title:* (used by such engines as Altavista, HotBot, Infoseek, Lycos, and Snap) or a *t:* (used by Yahoo) command, followed by the search string — for example, *title: dog food* or *t: dog food*. Site searching allows the user to search the Web pages of a particular Web site or search it for given information. The command to use is *site:* (used by Infoseek), *host:* (used by AltaVista), or *domain:* (used by HotBot and Snap). Examples of site search are:

host: www.neu.edu returns all the Web pages available on this host.

host: www.netscape.com -"Navigator4.0" returns all Web pages excluding those about Navigator 4.0.

"Netscape Communicator" -"host:com" returns all Web pages about Netscape Communicator excluding those from commercial sites.

"soccer games" + "host:uk" returns all Web pages on English Web sites about soccer games.

To investigate all the above types of searches and their results, let us formulate searches about the sport of soccer. We use AltaVista and Yahoo for searching using math symbols, Hot-Bot for word searching, AltaVista and Yahoo for title searching, and AltaVista and HotBot for site searching. Here are some results:

1. Using math symbols; type www.altavista.com in your browser location bar. Type the search string *soccer*. Click the `Search` button. AltaVista returns 2,833,382 hits. If you repeat the same search in Yahoo, it returns 2500 hits. As expected, the search results differ from one search engine to another. This echoes searching traditional libraries, where different libraries give different results due to the different databases that are searched.

Let us try to refine the search by finding information about world cup soccer. If you type *+world+cup+soccer* as the search string, AltaVista returns 100 hits and Yahoo returns 37607 hits. While AltaVista narrowed the search results, Yahoo did the opposite. One explanation is that Yahoo is a directory and may be more popular worldwide than AltaVista. One conclusion here is that you cannot makes searching using search engines a science. A good search strategy is to try different search engines with different search types and strings until you find exactly what you want.

2. Using word search; type www.hotbot.com in your browser location bar. Type the search string *soccer*, and click the `Search` button. HotBot returns 514,500 hits. If you type *world cup soccer*, you can use *all the words*, *any of the words*, or *exact phrase*, as shown in figure 6.8. Searching by using *any of the words* returns 1,326,500 hits — as expected, because it widens the search scope (it makes the search less focused). Searching by using *all the words* returns 78,250 hits. Searching by using *exact phrase* returns 6,920 hits. As expected, the *exact phrase* search is the most focused.

3. Using title search; type www.altavista.com in your browser location bar. Type *title:soccer* as the search string. AltaVista returns 62,182 hits. This is many fewer hits than it returned for the symbol search. It you type *title:world cup soccer*, it returns 4,542,459 hits, as one would expect; however, if you type *title:"world cup soccer"*, it returns 613 hits, because the quotation marks force a PHRASE title search. If you use Yahoo instead, the *t:world cup soccer* search returns 131 hits, and the *t:"world cup soccer"* search returns 3 sites.

4. Using site searching; type www.altavista.com in your browser location bar. Type *soccer +host:com* as the search string. This string searches for all the Web pages about soccer from US company sites. Altavista returns 1,252,707 hits. If you type *"world cup soccer" +host:com*, it returns 8,052. If you use HotBot instead, the *soccer +domain:com* search returns 268,210 hits, and *"world cup soccer" +domain:com* returns 6,990. To perform the *soccer +domain:com* search in HotBot, click the MORE SEARCH OPTIONS button. Then type *soccer* in the search field, select the `Domain` button shown in figure 6.9, type *.com* in the domain field shown in figure 6.9, and click the SEARCH button. Repeat the same steps for the *"world cup soccer" +domain:com* search.

Note: The reader may not be able to generate the exact number of hits reported in this tutorial, because the databases and indexes of the search engines change continually; however, the reader should understand the concepts behind the tutorial and repeat them as they are or with changes.

6.11.2 Web Navigation via Metasearch

Metasearch is not different from the basic search covered in the previous tutorial, except that surfers use metasearch engines to conduct their searches, instead of just search engines. Surfers should find more satisfactory search results by conducting metasearch using any metasearch engine. A metasearch can use all the methods of the basic search: symbols, word, title, and site, and all the combinatorial rules — for example, combine symbols and quotation marks.

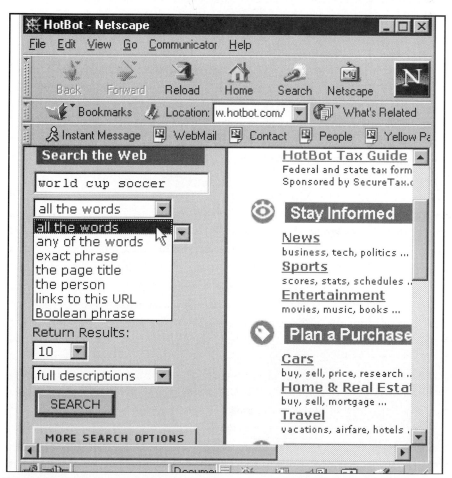

Figure 6.8   Word search using the ANY, ALL, and PHRASE modifiers.

Let us repeat some of the searches about the soccer sport from the previous tutorial, using the following metasearch engines: www.dogpile.com, www.infind.com, www.metacrawler.com, and www.profusion.com. While doing this tutorial on your computer, open four browser windows, one for each of these search engines, to facilitate working. Here are the results:

1. Using symbols; type www.dogpile.com in your browser location bar. Type the search string *soccer*. Click the Fetch button. Dogpile searches three search engines and returns 3071 hits: 240 from GoTo, 2810 from Yahoo, and 21 from Thunderstone. If you repeat the same search in the other search engines, InferenceFind returns 38 hits, MetaCrawler returns 60 hits, and ProFusion returns 178 hits.

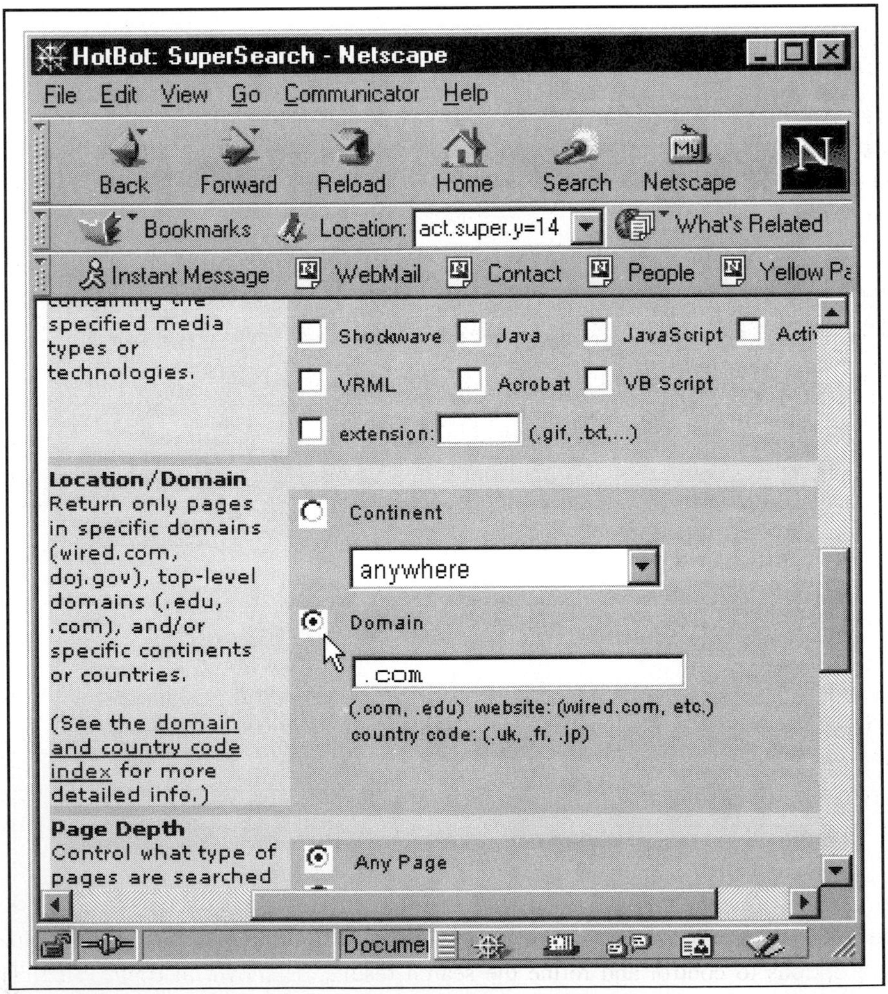

Figure 6.9   Site Searching, using HotBot search engine.

Let us refine the search by finding information about world cup soccer. If you type *+world+cup+soccer* as the search string, Dogpile returns 2676 hits (240 hits from GoTo, 199 hits from Yahoo, and 2237 from Thunderstone), InferenceFind returns 38 hits, MetaCrawler returns 44 hits, and ProFusion returns 173.

2. Using word search; type www.dogpile.com in your browser location bar. Type the search string *world cup soccer*. Dogpile and InferenceFind treat this search as a math search by default and look for *+world+cup+soccer*. MetaCrawler allows you to choose *any, all*, or *phrase*. Searching by using *any* of the words returns 63 hits. Searching by using *all* the words returns 53 hits. Searching by using *phrase* returns 45 hits. ProFusion provides the *any, all*, and *phrase* modifiers, as shown in figure 6.10. The *any* and *all* searches return 173 hits each. The *phrase* search returns 155 hits.

6.11.3 Web Navigation via Boolean Search

Boolean search is offered by some search engines as an advanced search feature. Surfers who desire to use a Boolean search should look for a hyperlink to lead them to it. Sample search engines that offer Boolean search are AltaVista, Dogpile, and Yahoo. Let us use AltaVista and Yahoo in this tutorial to search for *world cup soccer*.

Type www.altavista.com in your browser location Toolbar. Click the Advanced hyperlink shown on the top right side of the Web page to access the Boolean text area shown in figure 6.6. Type the following Boolean search string; *world AND cup AND soccer*, and click the Search button to begin the search. AltaVista returns 78,530 hits. If you search for *world AND cup OR soccer*, AltaVista returns 947,960.

Type www.yahoo.com in your browser location Toolbar. Click the advanced search hyperlink shown next to the Search button to access the Boolean menu shown in figure 6.5. Type the search string *world cup soccer*, click the Matches on all words (AND) button (figure 6.5), and click the Search button to begin the search. Yahoo returns 187 hits.

6.11.4 Web Navigation via Smart Browsing

In this tutorial, we use Netscape to investigate the *smart browsing* concept. Type www.netscape.com in your browser location Toolbar. To activate the smart browsing options (if they are inactive), click the Edit menu (figure 3.13), then click the Preferences menu item. Double click the Navigator category (figure 3.16), then click the Smart Browsing item, as shown in figure 6.11. Click the checkboxes shown to enable them and click OK to finish. Following are the ways to perform smart browsing in Netscape:

1. Using the search keyverb; type the search string *search world cup soccer* in the location Toolbar, and hit Enter on your keyboard. Netscape returns 516,234 hits. Netscape offers you three options to control and refine the search results, as shown in figure 6.12. The first option is that it provides three radio buttons to control the display of the results on the screen.

The three buttons are `Full Descriptions`, `No Descriptions`, and `Web Site Only`. The first button is the default. Try the other buttons to experience their results.

The second option is the `About Your Results` hyperlink shown in figure 6.12. This link explains how to interpret the search results. It is a useful feature, which can guide surfers to conduct more successful searches. The third option is the `Narrow Your Search` hyperlink (shown partially, next to the cursor, in figure 6.12). When you click this link, you get the word search menu as shown in figure 6.13. Set the options as shown in the figure, type the search phrase *world cup soccer*, and click the `Submit` button. Netscape returns 3040 hits instead of the original 516,234 hits. Before you click the `Submit` button, you can choose from the three options to display the search results. Repeat the search to study the effect of these options on displaying the search results.

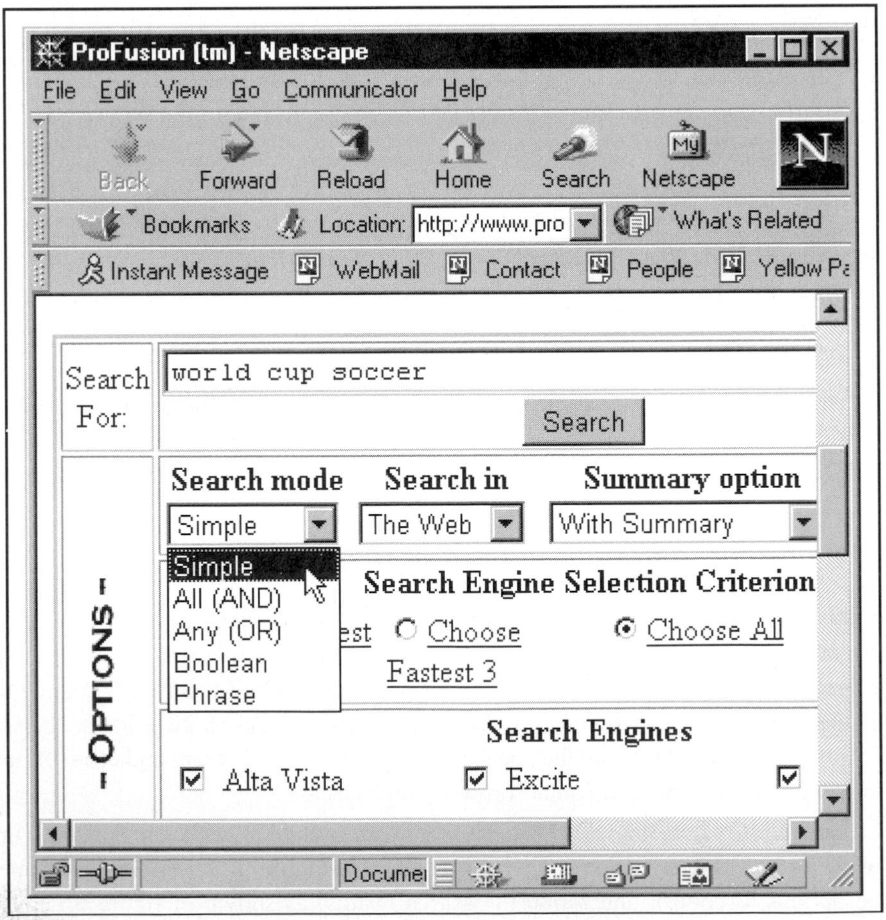

Figure 6.10 Word search using ProFusion search engine.

2. Using the `goto` keyverb; type a company or an organization name, preceded by the keyverb *goto*, and watch Netscape downloading its Web page in its window. Sample companies are Ford Motor company, Honda, and Sun Microsystems. While Netscape can find almost any company by typing its name, it does not work consistently to find other organizations' Web sites that do not end with the top domain .com, such as educational institutions (.edu domain). Try typing your institution name and see what you get back.

3. Using `What's  Related`; This is truly a smart feature. Type a Web site, such as www.neu.edu, click the `What's  Related` button of Netscape, and watch the pop-up list of the related items, as shown in figure 6.14. If you click any item, Netscape downloads the corresponding Web page. Type your favorite Web site, and then click the button to learn more about it.

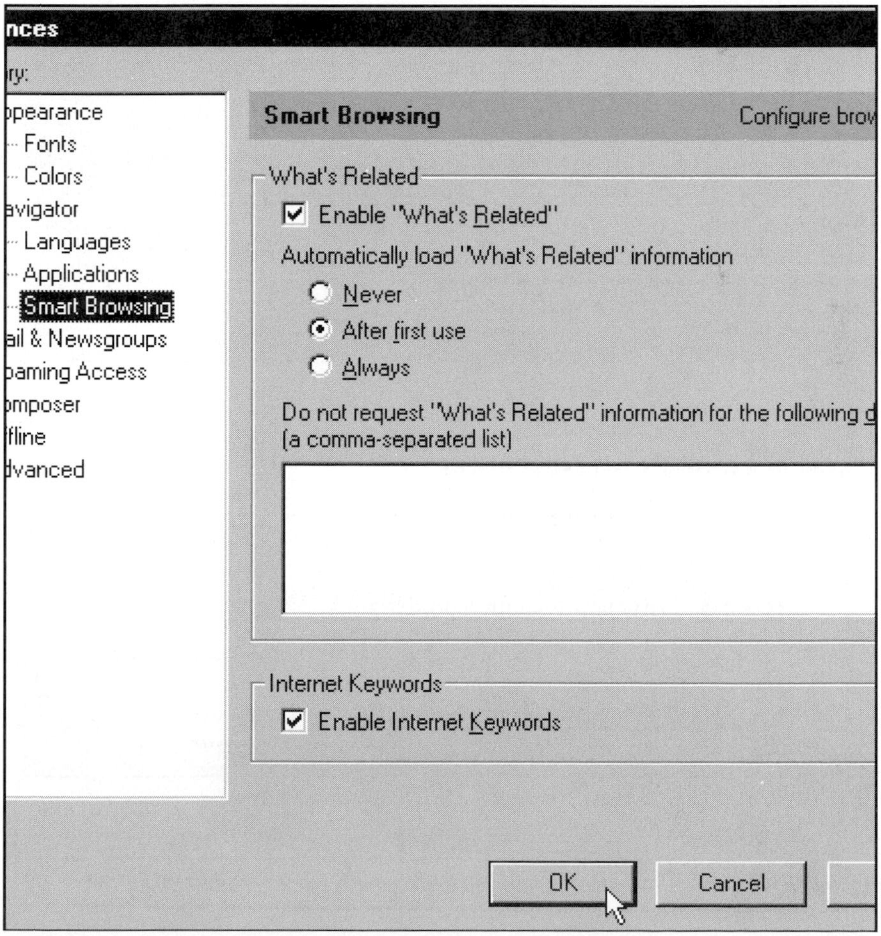

Figure 6.11   Setting smart browsing features in Netscape Communicator.

4. Using `NetWatch`; `NetWatch` is the built-in ratings protection feature of Netscape Communicator. It controls the type of Web page that can be viewed on your computer, according to the PICS rating standard. After you set it up on your computer, it compares the rating of a Web page that is about to be downloaded on this computer with the protection level used in the setup. If the page contains higher levels than the protection levels, `NetWatch` prevents its downloading. You can also set NetWatch to block pages that have not been rated.

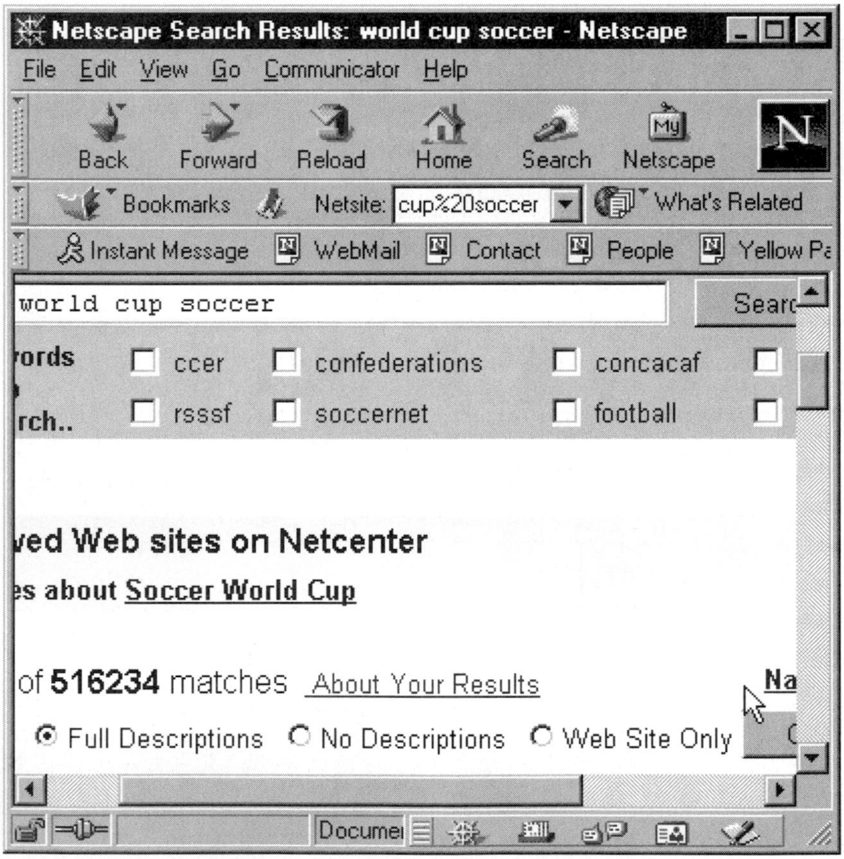

Figure 6.12 Smart browsing using the Netscape `search` keyword.

Your `NetWatch` settings are private and are protected by a password that neither Netscape nor any other Web pages can read or know. To set up `NetWatch` with this password, click the `Help` menu, then click the `NetWatch` menu item, as shown in figure 6.15. Follow the instructions. You must have enabled both the Java and the JavaScript features of Netscape for NetWatch to work. To enable them, choose `Preferences` from the `Edit` menu, then click `Advanced`. Make sure that Java and JavaScript are both enabled. Click `OK` to finish.

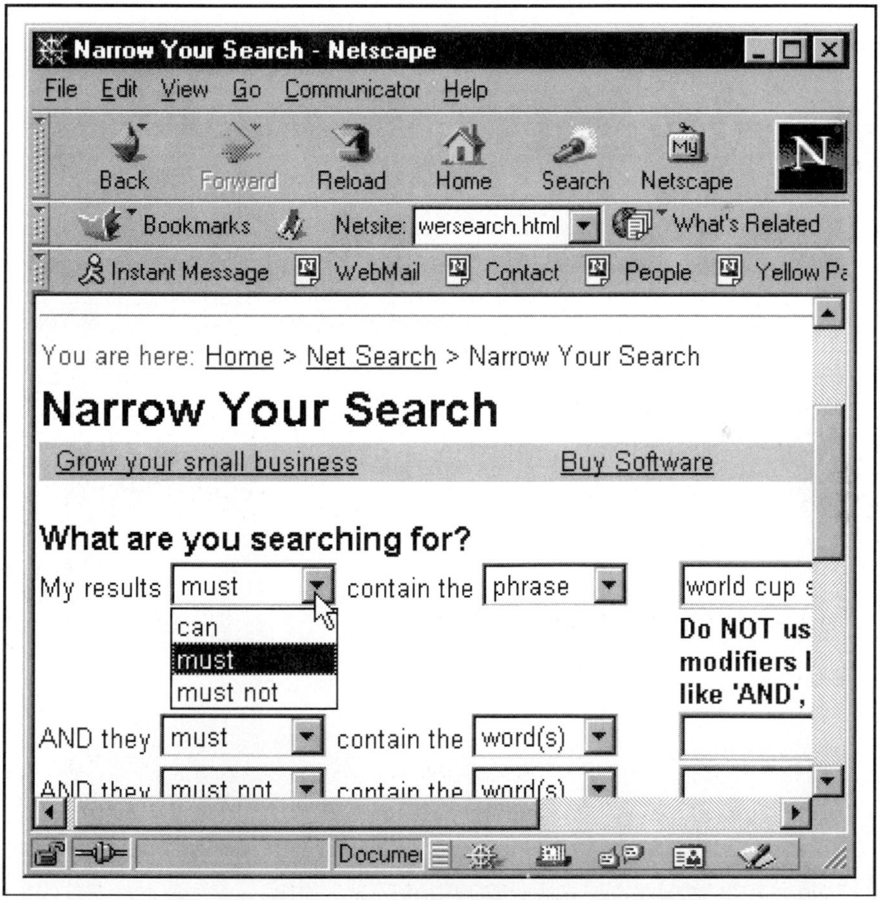

Figure 6.13 Narrowing smart browsing in Netscape Communicator.

6.11.5 Web Navigation via Channels

Channels can be thought of as folders or directories that are used to organize Web content. Channels are considered integral parts of Web portals. Both Netscape Communicator and MS IE provide channels. Netscape has a `Channels` buttons which, if clicked, displays the directories shown in figure 6.16. To access channels in MS IE, click this sequence: `Favorites` (a menu of MS IE) => `Channels` => `Microsoft Channel Guide`. Figure 6.17 shows the channels of MS IE. You must be online for the channels to work. These channels are treated as bookmarks that you can edit in both Netscape Communicator and MS IE, as we have shown in chapter 3. When you click one of the channels, the browser downloads the corresponding Web page. That Web page acts as a directory or a guide that is full of hyperlinks to other Web sites related to the channel subject. For example, clicking the `Autos` channel of Netscape Communicator downloads a Web page with auto-related subjects.

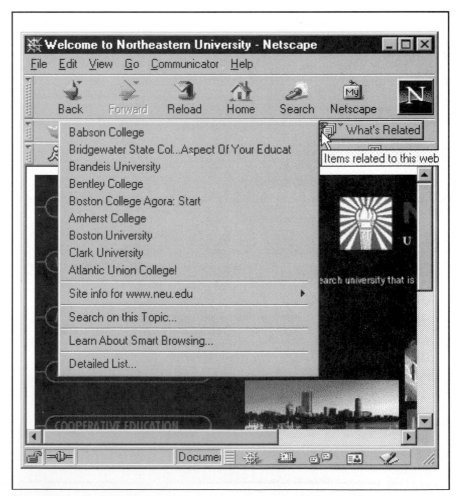

Figure 6.14   Results of `What's Related` feature of Netscape Communicator.

6.11.6 Web Navigation via Web Portals

Both Microsoft and Netscape channels can be viewed as Web portals. Click each channel of both Microsoft and Netscape. Study the offerings of each channel. Microsoft offers a way to make your desktop a custom Web portal. It allows you to add channels to it. Here is the procedure to make your current desktop a portal. Right click on the desktop, and then click `Properties`. On the `Web` tab, click the `View my Active Desktop as a web page` checkbox. Then click `OK`. The custom portal is shown in figure 6.18. It contains MS channels. If you click the arrow at the right of the Address text field, you see the structure of the Desktop, as shown in figure 6.18. You can add new channels if you click the `New` button on the `Web` tab before clicking `OK`.

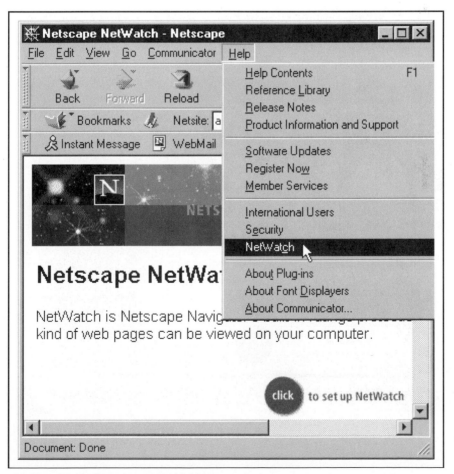

Figure 6.15   Setup of Netscape `NetWatch`.

You can also customize the Yahoo Web page to create your own custom portal. Click the My Yahoo hyperlink (shown as a circle on the top right of the Yahoo Web page). Follow the instructions to finish the procedure.

6.12 FAQs

Q: What is the best way to search the Internet, using search engines?

A: This is a two-part question. First, what is the best search engine to use? There is really no best engine. This chapter presents a wide range of engines, including the metasearch engines,

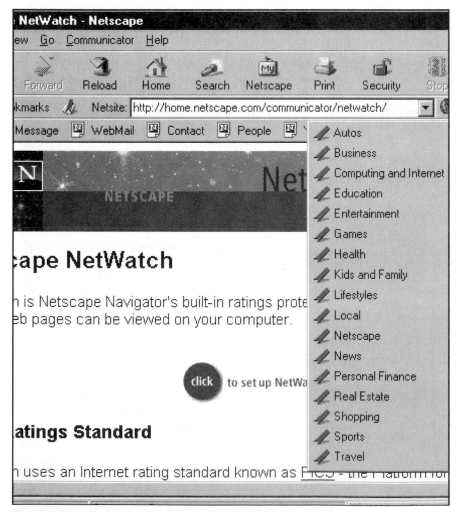

Figure 6.16   Channels of Netscape Communicator.

without making any recommendations. It is left up to the reader to try all of them to find out the engine that is most suitable. Second, what search type (basic, word, Boolean, smart, or portal) to use? Experience has it that complex searches produce better results than simple searches. It is worth spending the time learning, and experimenting with, the search types covered in this chapter, because they provide more rewarding and fulfilling search experiences in the long run; how-

Figure 6.17 Channels of Microsoft Internet Explorer.

ever, most users may want to start their searches by using the PHRASE modifier (supported by many search engines) until they are able to conduct more complex searches.

Q: How can users find individual people's pages and e-mail addresses?

A: There are many resources, including search engines such as HotBot. Users might try www.bigfoot.com and people.yahoo.com.

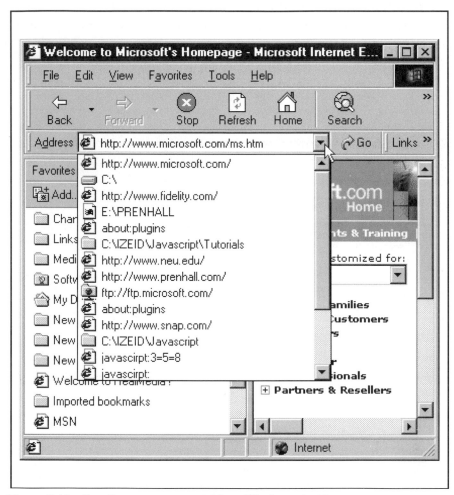

Figure 6.18   Creating a custom portal from Windows desktop.

Q: How does Netscape Smart Browsing using Internet Keywords work?

A: Netscape has created lists of keyword-URL pairs that are saved on a server at www.netscape.com. When the user types a search string, the server compares it against these lists. If a match is found to a keyword-URL pair, the server returns the URL part of the pair and downloads the Web page at this URL site. If no match is found, Netscape downloads its search page, with the search query being the typed string.

Q: What is the difference between Internet Keywords and keyverbs?

A: Keyverbs are a feature of `Internet Keywords` to help conduct smart browsing. The existing keyverbs are `goto` (e.g., *goto dell*), `search` (e.g., *search boston red sox*), `quote` (for stocks — e.g., *quote sunw*, where sunw is the symbol for Sun Microsystems), and `help` (e.g., *help e-mail*). While you do not have to use the keyverbs, using them produces better search results because they help focus the search. Let us search for diet programs using Netscape Communicator. Using the search string *diet programs* does not produce such good results as using *search diet programs*.

Q: Is a Web portal equivalent to simply creating and maintaining a well-chosen array of bookmarks?

A: No. For one thing, most users do not have the time to keep up with the fast pace of changing Internet content. In addition, Web portals have their own databases and directories. Above all, most Web portals are free to users. They generate their revenues from paid advertisements.

Q: How do I make a Web portal load when my browser starts?

A: A Web portal is simply a Web site, so this question is about making a Web portal the default home page. As covered in chapter 3, in Netscape Communicator, click the `Edit` menu (figure 3.13), then click the `Preferences` menu item. In the `Preferences` window shown in figure 3.16, select the `Home page` button, and type the URL of the portal site in the `Location` text field. In MS IE, click the `Tools` menu (figure 4.9), then click the `Internet Options` menu item. In the **Internet Options** window shown in figure 4.10, type the URL of the portal site in the `Address` text field of the `General` tab.

Q: What are custom portals?

A: The concept of a custom portal is introduced to allow a user to tailor the contents of Web portals to specific needs. Web portals offer a variety of content, but some users may be interested in less content and more depth. Custom portals are offered by Netscape, Yahoo (My Yahoo!), Excite (My Excite), and other enterprise software companies such as PeopleSoft. A custom portal is based on a Web portal database and content. For example, a custom portal may use the Netscape Netcenter portal, in which case it uses the specialized content it needs from Netcenter database — for example, e-mail, stock quotes, and so forth.

Both companies and individual users can create their own custom portals. For example, Netscape offer the custom portal service to both groups. A company IT (information technology) manager or an individual user can set up a custom portal by using a Netscape Web site. Companies may use portals in different ways. Some use their custom portals only on their Intranets. Others use them to create what are known as "vertical portals". A vertical portal is a company-specific site that can be accessed both by the company Intranet (its employees) and by its Extranet (its customers and partners). Companies can set up vertical portals for e-commerce and procurement.

6.13 Summary

Introduction

•To perform an effective and successful Internet search, one needs to know what to search for and how to search for it. The "what" question requires a specific and well-defined search string. The "how" question requires the surfer to use existing search engines effectively.

The World Wide Web

•The fact that the Web consists of Web pages linked together makes it easy to search it via search engines.

Navigation Tools

•The existing search tools for the Web are search engines, metasearch engines, Boolean search, smart browsing, Web portals, and channels.

Search Engines

•Search engines are the primary tool to navigate the Web. They are easy to use.

•Search engines do not always return good hits, especially if the search string is ill formed.

•Search engines use, among other rules, the title/frequency method to conduct searches. They match the search string against the titles and the beginning several lines of Web pages to determine page matching (hits).

•Different search engines return different search results for the same search string. All search engines perform keyword searches against their databases.

•There are many search engines. They include www.altavista.com, www.bigbook.com, www.dejanews.com, www.directhit.com, www.download.com, www.excite.com, www.goto.com, www.hotbot.com, www.infoseek.com, www.looksmart.com, www.lycos.com, www.metasearch.com, www.miningco.com, www.northernlight.com, www.planetsearch.com, www.savvysearch.com, www.search.com, www.snap.com, www.thunderstone.com, www.web-crawler.com, and www.yahoo.com. AltaVista, Excite, Infoseek, Lycos, and Yahoo are popular search engines. Additionally, www.download.com and www.shareware.com are useful to search for software to download.

Metasearch Engines

•Metasearch engines perform a multi-engine search for efficiency purposes.

•Metasearch engines include www.dogpile.com, www.infind.com, www.metacrawler.com (also known as www.go2net.com), www.metafind.com, and www.profusion.com.

Boolean Search

•Boolean searches yield more focused results. They use three Boolean operators: union (OR operator), intersection (AND operator) and subtraction (NOT operator).

•The union operator produces the greatest number of hits, and the intersection operator produces the smallest number of hits.

•Different search engines implement the concept of Boolean search differently. Some use the Boolean operators by their name (AND, OR, NOT). Others replace them by plain English phrases — for example, all words, some words.

Smart Browsing

•Smart browsing provides intelligent and fast access to information by integrating Netscape Communicator with the database of Netscape Netcenter.

•Netscape provides three features for smart browsing: What's Related, Internet Keywords, and NetWatch.

Web Portals and Channels

•Web portals offer entryways to the Internet. They act as tables of contents for the Internet.

•Web portals are useful navigation tools of the Web. We can think of them as special, well-organized search engines. *They provide so many resources. Examples include AOL, Yahoo, and MSN.*

•Channels are directories of such general topics as sports, travel, shopping, and so forth. They categorize information to make it easy for surfers to locate.

• Web portals are similar to the traditional malls.

Ranking Search Hits and Web Sites

•The "Open Directory Project" managed by Netscape Communications enables search engine and Web portals to get users involved in evaluating and ranking Web sites to improve their search results.

Search Methodologies and Strategies

•The only effective way to construct a search methodology is to use various search engines, concepts, and tools described in this chapter. There is no substitute for experience.

PROBLEMS

Exercises

6.1 Using symbols, perform an Internet search on physical fitness. Use the search string *physical fitness programs*. Refine the search by excluding aerobics due to bad knees. Submit a report on the various combinations of symbols used, the number of hits each produces, and which search strategy is the most successful. Also, summarize the three most relevant Web pages about the search. Use at least two search engines to conduct the search.

6.2   Using word search, repeat problem 6.1.

6.3   Using title search, repeat problem 6.1.

6.4   Using URL search, repeat problem 6.1.

6.5   Using metasearch, repeat problem 6.1.

6.6   Using Boolean search, repeat problem 6.1.

6.7   Using smart browsing, repeat problem 6.1.

Homework

6.8   Repeat problem 6.1 - 6.7 on the following search strings (choose one):

side effects of diet programs;

importing and exporting regulations;

health problems due to smoking;

current status of the ozone layer;

types and prices of digital cameras;

home loans, mortgages, and refinance;

choosing a college for high-school students;

types of music, bands, and CDs;

goals of the foreign policy of USA;

local and national newspapers;

tips on traveling to the Far East;

various disciplines of engineering;

what do engineers do?

how do human beings learn languages?

how can we protect the environment?

existing religions in the world.

6.9   Use the www.whois.net Web site to find information about your favorite existing domain name or about a new domain name you are considering useing for a new start-up business. Submit screen capture to show your results.

6.10 Many search engines offer help and guidelines on how to conduct searches using them. AltaVista, Excite, Infoseek, MetaCrawler, and Yahoo are a few of them. Users of search engines can access their help and guidelines via hyperlinks with names such as Tips (Infoseek), Help (AltaVista), Search Help (Excite), advanced search (Yahoo), FAQ (MetaCrawler), and so forth. These hyperlinks are usually placed at the top or the bottom of the search engine Web page or next to the Search button of the engine. Using your favorite search engine, locate and study its help contents. Compare these contents with the chapter material on searches and their types. Submit a report citing which types of searches your favorite search engine supports and including any new knowledge, if any, that is not covered in this chapter.

6.11 Use Netscape smart browsing to search for your favorite product, person, subject, and company. If you need, you can narrow the search using the Narrow Your Search feature. Submit a report summarizing the search strings you use, the number of hits returned, and a summary of the results and whether you are satisfied or not.

6.12 Search the Internet for the PICS (Platform for Internet Content Selection) rating system. Submit a one page report describing the system, how it works, and its various levels of protection. Then set up NetWatch on your computer using this system. Test it by downloading some

Web pages and observing whether they get blocked. Document your work and experience.

6.13 Edit the Channels of your favorite browser (Netscape Communicator or MS IE) to customize them to suit your needs. Submit the procedure you followed and screen captures.

6.14 Extend the procedure covered in tutorial 6.10.6 to create new channels to add to your Desktop. Submit the procedure you follow, as well as screen captures.

6.15 Customize your favorite Web portal (use Excite, www.excite.com, if you do not have any) to fit your personal needs. Note: Excite provides the `Personalize Your Page!` hyperlink, shown on the top left corner of its Web page. Submit the procedure you follow and screen captures.

6.1. Follow tutorial 6.11.1. Use a search engine such as www.altavista.com.
Use + physical + fitness + program as the search string

6.9. Use a domain name such as www.sun.com. Watch the results you get.

HTML

T his part of the book covers HTML 4.0. This is the latest version available at the time of writing this book. HTML 4.0 is backward compatible with the previous versions; HTML 3.2 and HTML 2.0. HTML 4.0 supports more multimedia options, scripting languages, style sheets, and better printing facilities. It also tries to make Web documents more accessible to users with disabilities, and more internationalized. In this part, we cover all the possible elements that make up a Web page. Any Web page could have in it text, lists, colors, graphics, images, image maps, sound, video, forms, frames, and tables. **Chapter 7** covers the basic HTML including text, hyperlinks, special characters, and the related tags. **Chapter 8** presents the different types of lists and list tags. **Chapter 9** covers colors and color tags. **Chapter 10** discusses images, their formats, how to create them, and image tags. **Chapter 11** extends images and covers image maps, how to use them, and the tags required to create them. **Chapter 12** presents sound as a multimedia element in Web pages, and the related sound tags. Video and their tags are covered in **Chapter 13**. **Chapter 14** presents forms and their tags. Forms are widely used in e-commerce applications to receive orders from online shoppers. **Chapter 15** covers frames and their tags. **Chapter 16** presents tables, how to use them, and their tags. While tables are conventionally used to tabulate data, HTML uses them to format Web pages very effectively. The last two chapters in this part are related to designing and developing Web pages. **Chapter 17** covers some of the existing HTML editors used to build Web pages. Sample editors are Netscape `Composer` and Microsoft `FrontPage`. **Chapter 18** covers CGI scripting and server-side processing of Web pages. Server-side scripting is needed to process data entered in forms.

Basic HTML

$\mathbf{T}$he coverage of HTML 4.0 begins in this chapter. Some of the major changes between HTML 3.2 and HTML 4.0 come in tags and attributes. The new tags are <ABBR>, <ACRONYM>, <BDO>, <BUTTON>, <COL>, <COLGROUP>, <DEL>, <FIELDSET>, <FRAME>, <FRAMESET>, <IFRAME>, <INS>, <LABEL>, <LEGEND>, <NOFRAMES>, <NOSCRIPT>, <OBJECT>, <OPTGROUP>, <PARAM>, <SPAN>, <TBODY>, <TFOOT>, <THEAD>, and <Q>. The following tags have been deprecated: <APPLET>, <BASEFONT>, <CENTER>, <DIR>, <FONT>, <ISINDEX>, <MENU>, <STRIKE>, and <U>. A deprecated tag is still supported by HTML 4.0, for back-ward-compatibility reasons, but it should not be used to develop new Web pages. Deprecated elements are outdated by newer constructs and may become obsolete in future versions of HTML. The tags <LISTING>, <PLAINTEXT>, and <XMP> are obsolete (no longer available) in HTML 4.0. They should be replaced by the <PRE> tag instead. In addition to these changes in HTML tags, almost all attributes that specify the presentation of an HTML document, such as alignments, fonts, and colors, have been deprecated and replaced by style sheets. The coverage of these new tags and attributes takes place throughout Part II of this book. With HTML 4.0 in mind, this chapter covers basic HTML. It begins by a definition of HTML as a markup script. It then covers the design, building, and developing of HTML documents (Web pages). The chapter presents the general structure of HTML documents, then covers HTML tags and their categories to help the reader build a coherent understanding of HTML. Of these tag categories, this chapter covers the document structure tags, text tags, hyperlink tags, and special characters. The tags in each category are covered with their attributes (if they have any) and with examples to illustrate how to use them. Tutorials show how to use these tags to write full simple Web pages.

7.1 Introduction

When surfers browse the Web, they are accessing and reading home Web pages and pages that are linked to them. These pages are written using a scripting language called HTML (HyperText Markup Language). Here, we begin covering HTML and page layout, organization, and design.

The power of HTML is its simple content. It is a collection of plain characters that can be generated by virtually any text editor or word processor. The two key concepts behind HTML are hypertext and markup. Hypertext is a way to create multimedia documents with links between and within them. This is different from conventional documents in two ways. First, an HTML document can include both video (animation) and audio (sound), in addition to the conventional text and graphics. Second, the reader of an HTML document does not have to follow the conventional sequential way to read the document. The document may contain multiple paths to read it to accommodate different audiences and interests. For example, one reader may follow one sequence of links to read the document, while another reader may follow another sequence to read the same document.

The markup language is a way to embed special tags that describe the structure and the formatting of a document. The markup language allows the non-sequential reading of HTML documents. The simplicity and power of HTML let anyone create Web documents. Making Web documents is easy and straightforward. The markup nature of HTML is what is behind the incredible breadth and reach of the Web.

HTML supports links to completely different documents elsewhere on the Web and within the same document. Both types of links use the same HTML tag (the anchor tag), as we discuss later in this chapter. When readers of a Web page click on a link in the page, they are transported to the new location specified by the link. Links come in two forms: underlined text and images. Browsers provide visual clues (color change) for underlined-text links. Also, the screen cursor changes from an arrow to a hand when it moves over a hyperlink. For images links, surfers see no direct visual clues until they move the screen cursor to the image. If it is a link, the screen arrow changes to a hand. Thus, surfers may want to explore a displayed page on the screen for links by moving the screen cursor around and watching for visual clues.

The MIME (Multipurpose Internet Mail Extensions) format allows the inclusion of nontext content, such as sounds, images, and video, in Web pages. The MIME format makes it possible for a Web server to deliver multiple forms of data to a browser in a single transfer. Here is how this works. After requesting a Web page from a Web server, the browser begins downloading immediately. The text portion of the page arrives first, and the browser displays it immediately. Because the text arrives first, surfers may see place holders or icons for images when they first see the Web page. The images or other forms of data replace these place holders after their related content arrives. While the surfer views the Web page, the browser receives contents in the background and then displays them. Some of the common file types used on the Web are the following:

1. **Sound formats.** RA (RealAudio), SBI (Sound Blaster Instrument), SND, AU, and WAV (Microsoft Waveform).

2. **Still-Video (image) formats.** GIF (Graphics Interchange Format), JPEG (Joint Photographic Experts Group), JPG, PDF (Portable Document Format), PS (PostScript), and XBM (X-Window Bitmap).

3. Motion-Video formats. AVI (Audio Video Interactive), FLI (Flick), MOV (QuickTime), up).

ge sound like a great idea; however, they may be quite download and display, especially via a modem connec- witch off the graphics display of their browsers to speed view the graphics of the Web page. To turn off graphics cator, click Edit (menu on main browser window) => tomatically load images (this is a checkbox). ls (menu on main browser window) => Internet) => Show pictures (this is a checkbox). When it pages, Web developers and designers need to follow the mbnail size) to reduce their file sizes; use GIF or JPEG r the same image); and keep the number of graphics ele-

is all in the layout of the page. The layout involves the ey are arranged, and how much space is around them. the task is as challenging as the task of an advertising or ner needs to know what the message of the page is and goal is to question something, the issues at question are is to sell, attractive visuals are needed. If the goal is to too many eye-catching displays.

lesigner should overcome the linear, sequential way of thinking that we are used to when writing or reading books. Hypertext can do very creative things with linking and hypermedia. The designer needs to exploit the hypertext capabilities and hyperlinks in appealing and useful ways. HTML hyperlinks can link pages together serially (the old fashion way), create hierarchies between pages, create multiple tracks for multiple audiences, and/or create a "hotlist." The hotlist is a page that has hyperlinks to other documents. The hotlist is important for search engines because they usually index pages with hotlists before others.

7.3 Markup Language

Assuming that a Web page design has been completed, one now needs to know the elements of HTML to write the HTML code that converts the design into a Web page (HTML document) that can be viewed within a browser. All the HTML elements are covered in this book. HTML is a way of converting ordinary text into hypertext by adding special code, known as tags, that instructs Web browsers how to display the text contents. HTML is a descriptive markup language that describes in a simple way, using tags, the formatting of a document. This allows authors of Web pages to concentrate more on content and structure, and less on formatting and presentation.

HTML syntax describes how a Web browser can recognize and interpret the instructions contained in the markup tags. The browser parser reads and executes the tags to allow the browser to take the appropriate action. The special control characters that separate HTML markup from ordinary text are < (left bracket) and > (right bracket). These brackets enclose the HTML tags. The generic form of a tag is <tag_name>text</tag_name>. The first or starting tag identifies the beginning of the instruction, and the second or ending tag indicates the end of the instruction. Note the / in the ending tag. For example, the sentence:

```
<B>This is bold</B>
```

displays the text "This is bold" in bold. A browser would display it as **This is bold**.

The HTML specifications published by the W3 consortium distinguish between elements and tags. Each element has a tag. For example the head element of an HTML document can be created using its <HEAD> tag. The head element of the document is always there, regardless of whether the <HEAD> tag is used. This book, however, does not make this distinction, for simplicity and ease of presentation. When we use a tag, we mean both the tag and its corresponding element.

Tags may have properties, called attributes, associated with them. Each attribute may be assigned a value by Web authors. The attribute/value pairs appear before the final ">" of the tag. For example, a Web author may use this <A> tag: <A HREF = "http://www.neu.edu">. The attribute here is HREF, and its value is http://www.neu.edu. The author can use double quotation marks, single quotation marks, or no marks at all to specify values of attributes. W3 consortium recommends using quotation marks. In this book, we use double quotation marks.

HTML is a scripting language; it is not a programming language. Thus, an HTML document is not a program. It is simply a document that provides structuring and layout control to manage the appearance and the linkage mechanisms of the corresponding Web page. HTML is a subset of Standard Generalized Markup Language (SGML). HTML is defined by Document Type Definition (DTD) within SGML. SGML was developed in the 1960s, by IBM, to solve the problems of exchanging documents across multiple hardware platforms. Thus, HTML is platform independent.

7.4 Developing HTML Documents

Using HTML is very simple. All Web authors need is an editor to write HTML files and a browser to view them. The editor could be a text editor or an HTML editor, depending on the approach taken to generate HTML code. We identify two approaches in this book: the bottom-up approach and the top-down approach. These two approaches work the opposite of each other. There are two outcomes to each approach. These are the HTML file and the corresponding Web page. In the bottom-up approach, the HTML file is generated first and the Web page is viewed later. Therefore, the Web page is considered a result of the HTML file. In the top-down approach, the Web page is developed first and the HTML file is generated in the background. Therefore, the HTML file is a result of the Web page development.

In the bottom-up approach, the Web author writes the HTML file (code), using HTML tags, in a text editor such as the Notepad for Windows, Simpletext for Mac, or vi for Unix. After saving the file, the author can review the results of the code by running the HTML file in a browser. The Web author obviously needs to know HTML syntax to write the file. The development environment to create HTML files under this approach uses the following steps:

1. Open a file in a text editor of choice.
2. Enter text and tags.
3. Save the file as text only and add the extension .htm or .html. Close the file.
4. Open the file in a Web browser and review it.
5. Edit the HTML file by repeating steps 1 through 4, as many times as necessary, until the Web page takes its final desired form.

To facilitate this approach, the Web author should have a browser window and a text editor window open at the same time on the screen. The author edits the file, saves it, and opens it in the browser window — by using the `Reload` (for Netscape) or `Refresh` (for MS IE) button, or by dragging and dropping the HTML file icon into the browser window.

In the top-down approach, the Web author designs and develops the Web page using an HTML editor such as Netscape Composer, MS Front Page, HotDog, HotMetal, and so forth. These editors provide the author with icons that corresponds to HTML tags. Thus, the author does not have to use the HTML tags directly and fully know their syntax. After developing the Web page, the author can review the resulting HTML code, if needed, by opening the corresponding HTML file in a text editor. The development environment to develop Web pages under this approach uses the following steps:

1. Open an HTML editor of choice.
2. Add elements of the Web page by using the desired HTML icons.
3. Save the automatically generated HTML code of the page.
4. Exit the HTML editor to review the Web page in a a Web browser.
5. Edit the Web page by repeating steps 1 through 4, as many times as necessary, until the Web page takes its final desired form.

To facilitate this approach, the Web author has a browser window and an HTML editor window open at the same time on the screen. The author edits the Web page, saves its corresponding HTML file, and opens it in the browser window by using the `Reload` (for Netscape) or `Refresh` (for MS IE) button, or by dragging and dropping the HTML file icon into the browser window.

Which of these two approaches should Web authors use? Our belief is that the black-box (trial-and-error) philosophy is not productive in the long run. If Web authors do not fully understand HTML syntax and scripting, their productivity using HTML editors will be very poor. The trial-and-error idea defeats the purpose of using these editors, although it might work to develop simple Web pages. The best strategy should be to use the bottom-up approach during the learning of HTML scripting, followed by using the top-down approach. Following this strategy guarantees increasing the productivity of Web authors by leaps and bound when they begin using HTML editors. This book follows this strategy. It covers all the basics of HTML scripting and uses the bottom-up approach in the tutorials. It then covers some available HTML editors and shows how to use them.

7.5 HTML Document Structure

A well-structured HTML document should have three parts: header, body and footer. The header identifies the document as HTML, establishes its title, and includes its <META> tag. An entire HTML document should be enclosed between the tags <HTML> to open it and </HTML> to close it. These tags enable the browser to interpret the document's contents properly. A document title is flagged by the HTML tags <TITLE> to open the title section and </TITLE> to close it. A browser uses this title as the name of the title bar of its window that displays the document.

The entire content for any HTML document occurs in the body section, which is enclosed between the <BODY> and </BODY> tags. The body is where the Web author describes the document's layout and structure by using a variety of tags for text headings, embedded images, text paragraphs, lists, and other elements. For example, the <IMG> tag allows the author to link to an image file. The body also holds all the hyperlinks that appear on the page. The author can link to other points within the same document or to outside documents, by using the anchor tags (<A>, </A>) with the appropriate attributes.

While HTML does not provide tags for a footer, it is good practice that each Web page include a footer part. A footer should include information to describe the document, its authors, the document's vintage and content, and the date and version of the HTML document. Author information allows the page readers to send feedback. The date and version of the document show how old the document is. This should trigger the authors to update the HTML file.

The basic structure of an HTML file looks like this:

```
<HTML>
<HEAD>
<META>
<TITLE> Web page title goes here</TITLE>
</HEAD>
```

```
<BODY>
Web page contents go here
</BODY>
</HTML>
```

HTML tags do not have to appear in capitals, as shown above. For example, <HEAD> could be written as <Head> or <head>. They are not case-sensitive; however, we present all tags in uppercase for readability and for ease of identifying and following.

7.6 HTML Tags and Categories

HTML tags follow two general format rules. First, they usually come in pairs (an opening tag and a closing tag), for example <HTML>... </HTML>. (Some tags, such as <HR>, do not come in pairs.) Second, tags may have attributes that allow more control over their results. Some attributes take on values, while others do not. In the latter case, if the attribute is present, its value is true (turned on); if not, its value is false (turned off). The use of the attributes of a tag is optional. None, one, several, or all attributes can be used at the same time. The attributes are specified inside the tag brackets and separated by spaces.

We can divide HTML tags into several categories. The first category is related to the document structure. Aside from the document structure category, the best division of HTML tags can be based on the possible elements of a Web page. These elements include headings, text, hyperlinks, lists, colors, graphics, images, image maps, sounds, videos, forms, frames, and tables. Instead of listing the tags in each related category now, we defer them until the details of each element are covered in its own chapter. At that time, all the tags, and their attributes for each element, are covered in details with examples. Also at that time, the summary of each chapter will have a summary of the tags and their attributes to serve as a quick reference for the reader. In this chapter, we cover the tags for document structure, headings, text, and hyperlinks.

One tag that is used throughout the HTML code of a Web page is the comment tag (statement). It has the form <!...> or <!-- ... -->. In this book, we use the former form. In HTML, the comment statement can spread over one or more lines. As in other programming languages, the Web author can insert this tag ahead of groups or sections of tags, as a reminder of what each group or section of tags accomplishes.

7.7 Document Structure Tags

As per section 7.5, the tags that control the structure of an HTML document are the following:

<HTML>...</HTML> enclose the entire HTML document;

<HEAD>...</HEAD> is the document head;

<META> specifies page information for use by servers and search engines;

<TITLE>...</TITLE> is the document title;

<BODY>...</BODY> is the document body;

<ADDRESS>...</ADDRESS> serves as part of a page footer.

7.7.1 <HTML> Tag

The <HTML> tag encloses all the other tags that define an HTML document. This tag is used by the browser SGML interpreter to parse the other tags correctly and generate the corresponding Web page. Browsers can still interpret the HTML code correctly without this tag, but it is a good habit to use it all the time. This tag does not have any attributes.

7.7.2 <HEAD> Tag

The <HEAD> tag provides information about the HTML document, including the title. The <HEAD> tag can encompass other tags that provide useful information about the document to browsers and search engines. These tags are as follows:

<BASE> specifies a base address of the HTML document;

<LINK> provides relationships between documents;

<META> allows Web authors to specify to search engines how they wnat their documents to be indexed;

<STYLE> specifies style sheets used within the document;

<TITLE> specifies the document title.

Tutorials at the end of the chapter show how to use some of these tags. The <HEAD> tag has one attribute, PROFILE, which specifies a URL for the meta data used in the <META> tag.

7.7.3 <TITLE> Tag

Each HTML document should have a title. The document title is crucial to its accessing and indexing by search engines. The browser displays the page title in its title bar when users view the page. An example of using the <TITLE> tag is as follows:

```
<TITLE>My first Web page</TITLE>
```

The <TITLE> tag does not have any attributes.

7.7.4 <BODY> Tag

The <BODY> tag encloses all the other tags that create the contents of the Web page including the footer part of the page. The <BODY> tag has several attributes that are related to colors. They are covered in chapter 9 of this book.

7.7.5 <ADDRESS> Tag

This tag allows the Web author to create a footer for the Web page. Information that is used within the <ADDRESS> tag includes author name, e-mail address, copyright symbol, and last date of page revision. Browsers typically display the address information in italic typeface. Here is an example:

```
<ADDRESS>
Copyright &#169; 2000<BR>
John Smith, Web master<BR>
please e-mail us at webmaster@xyz.com<BR>
Revised - January 2000<BR>
</ADDRESS>
```

The <BR> tag forces a line break or a carriage return; otherwise the entire address will display on one continuous line. The <ADDRESS> tag does not have any attributes.

Example 7.1 Develop a Web page that illustrates the use of the document structure tags.

Solution This example creates an empty Web page. The page may serve as a template that a Web author can save and use as a basis to write future Web pages. This template eliminates the repetition associated with typing the same document structure tags. Follow the following steps to write and view the template Web page. (These steps are used throughout the book.)

• Using a text editor such as the Notepad, type the following code:

```
<HTML>
<HEAD>
<TITLE>My Web page Template</TITLE>
</HEAD>
<BODY>
Page contents go here
<ADDRESS>
Copyright &#169; 2000<BR>
Abe Zeid<BR>
please e-mail me at zeid@coe.neu.edu<BR>
Revised - January 2000<BR>
</ADDRESS>
</BODY>
</HTML>
```

• Save the file as *example7.1.html*.
• View the page in a browser by typing its URL in the browser URL bar, or by dragging its file and dropping it in the browser window, or by duoble clicking the file. Alternatively, click this sequence for Netscape: File => Open Page => Choose File => browse and click *example7.1.html* file => Open => Open, or click this sequence for MS IE:

File => open => Browse => browse and click *example7.1.html* file => Open => OK.
The URL of the page in this example is simply the file name with the full path, preceded
by the file protocol. For example, if the file is in the temp directory in drive C, the URL of
the Web page becomes *file://c:/temp/example7.1.html*.

Figure 7.1 shows the resulting Web page.

7.8 Text and Text Tags

One of the main elements of a Web page is text. As in traditional documents, the text of a
Web page is structured and organized into basic units of headings, sections, and paragraphs.
Each paragraph consists of statements and words. HTML provides tags to format each of these
units. There are heading tags, paragraph tags, and word/character tags. These tags, their
attributes, and their use are covered in this section.

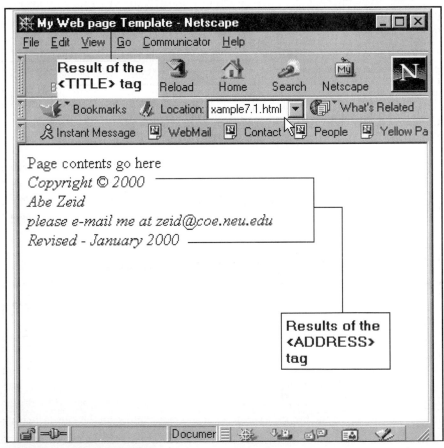

Figure 7.1   HTML template.

7.8.1 Headings and Heading Tags

HTML provides six different sizes of headings. These sizes are defined by six tags: <H1>, <H2>, <H3>, <H4>, <H5>, and <H6>. The <H1> tag provides the largest size heading while <H6> provides the smallest size heading. Each of these tags has an ALIGN attribute. The possible values of this attribute are left (default), center, and right.

Example 7.2 Develop a Web page that illustrates the use of the heading tags.

Solution This example creates a Web page with some text written using the six heading tags <H1> – <H6>, to show the effect of these tags. Each one of these tags must be closed to terminate its effect on the text. For example, open the <H1> tag by using <H1> and close it by using </H1>. The <BR> tag used in the code of this example is to force each line of text onto a separate line in the Web page. Using a text editor, type the code shown below and save it as *example7.2.html*. View the page in a browser. Figure 7.2 show the resulting Web page.

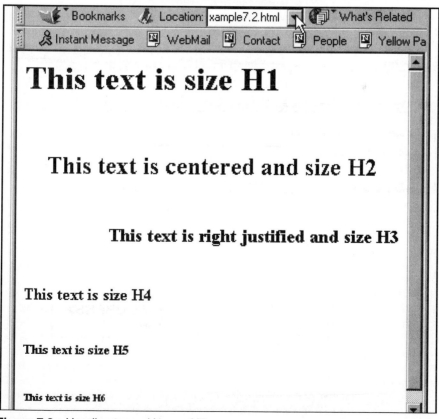

Figure 7.2   Heading tags <H1> – <H6>.

```
<HTML>
<HEAD>
<TITLE>Heading tags Web page</TITLE>
</HEAD>
<BODY>
<H1>This text is size H1</H1><BR>
<H2 ALIGN = "center">This text is centered and size H2</H2><BR>
<H3 ALIGN="right">This text is right justified and size H3</H3><BR>
<H4>This text is size H4</H4><BR>
<H5>This text is size H5</H5><BR>
<H6>This text is size H6</H6>
</BODY>
</HTML>
```

7.8.2 Paragraphs and Paragraph Tags

Paragraphs are created in Web pages using the <P> tag. The <P> tag may or may not be closed by using </P>. The effect of the <P> tag is to create a line space ahead of the text that defines the paragraph. The <P> tag has one attribute: the ALIGN. The values of the attribute are right, center, and left (the default). The attribute aligns the entire paragraph text. This attribute is used mostly when a Web author wants to align a paragraph that is one line of text only.

Example 7.3 Develop a Web page that illustrates the use of the paragraph tag.

Solution This example creates a Web page with some text organized into two paragraphs by the use of the <P> tag. The example code shows each <P> tag starting at a new line (only for convenience). Using a text editor, type the code that follows, and save it as *example7.3.html*. View the page in a browser. Figure 7.3 show the resulting Web page.

```
<HTML>
<HEAD>
<TITLE>Paragraph tag Web page</TITLE>
</HEAD>
<BODY>
This page illustrates how to use the paragraph tag to create para-
graphs.
<P>When surfers browse the Web, they are accessing and reading home
Web pages and pages that are linked to them. These pages are writ-
ten using a scripting language called HTML (HyperText Mark up Lan-
guage). We here begin covering HTML and page layout, organization
and design.
<P>The markup language is a method to embed special tags that
describe the structure as well as the formatting of a document. The
markup language allows the non-sequential way of reading HTML docu-
ments. The simplicity and power of HTML let anyone create Web docu-
ments. Making Web documents is easy and straight forward. The
```

markup nature of HTML is what is behind the incredible breadth and
reach of the Web.
`</BODY>`
`</HTML>`

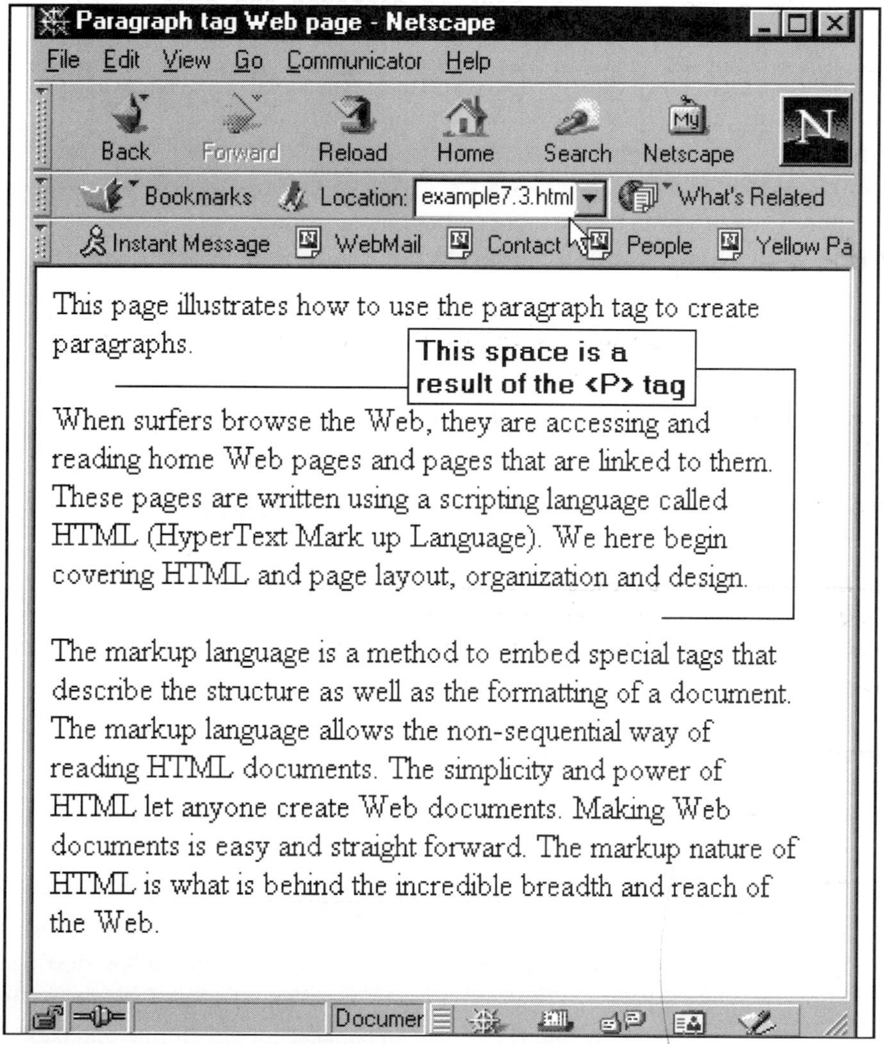

Figure 7.3 Paragraph tag <P>.

7.8.3 Words and Word Tags

HTML provides a wealth of tags to format words and characters. Many of these tags produce results similar to traditional formatting. Here is a list of some tags and what they do:

<B> bolds text. It has no attributes.

<BASEFONT> specifies a base font. It has the SIZE = *value* attribute, where *value* is an integer between 1 and 7, inclusive. (Default value is 3.) For example <BASEFONT SIZE = 5>.

<BIG> provides big text. It has no attributes.

<BLOCKQUOTE> formats text quoted from a specific source. It has no attributes.

 forces a line break. It has no attributes.

<CENTER> centers text. It has no attributes.

<CITE> specifies a citation reference. It has no attributes.

<CODE> specifies any code, such as computer code, equations, and so forth. It has no attributes.

<EM> provides a typographic emphasis. It has no attributes.

<FONT> specifies text size and color. It has two attributes: SIZE, and COLOR. For example, <FONT SIZE = 5 COLOR = "green">. SIZE could be any integer between 1 and 7 inclusive.

<HR> creates a horizontal line. This tag has several attributes: ALIGN, COLOR, NOSHADE, SIZE, and WIDTH. The values of the ALIGN attribute are left (default), center, and right — for example, ALIGN = "center". The value of the COLOR attribute is any color name or hex code (chapter 9) — for example, COLOR = "green". The COLOR attribute is browser dependent; MS IE supports it, but not Netscape Navigator. The SIZE attribute specifies the line thickness in pixels — for example, SIZE = 20. The WIDTH attribute specifies the length of the line; the default is the width of the Web page. The value of the WIDTH attribute is a number of pixels (for example, WIDTH=60) or a percentage of the page width (for example, WIDTH=50%).

<I> italizes text. It has no attributes.

<KBD> specifies keyboard font. It has no attributes.

<SMALL> displays text with a small font. It has no attributes.

<STRIKE> displays a horizontal line through the text. It has no attributes.

<STRONG> provides a typographic emphasis. It has no attributes.

<U> underlines text. It has no attributes.

In some cases, the Web author may nest some of the formatting tags. For example, some text may be bold, italic, and underlined. Thus, the <B>, <I>, and <U> tags must enclose the text. The nesting rule of tags to get the desired result is "first open, last closed" or "last open, first closed" — for example, <B><I><U>This is bold, italic, and underlined text</U></I></B>. This is a general rule that is used throughout HTML for all its tags, not only formatting tags.

Example 7.4 Develop a Web page that illustrates the use of the word/character tags.

Solution This example creates a Web page with some text formatted by the use of the formatting tags described in this section. Using a text editor, type the code that follows and save it as *example7.4.html*. View the page in a browser. Figure 7.4 show the resulting Web page.

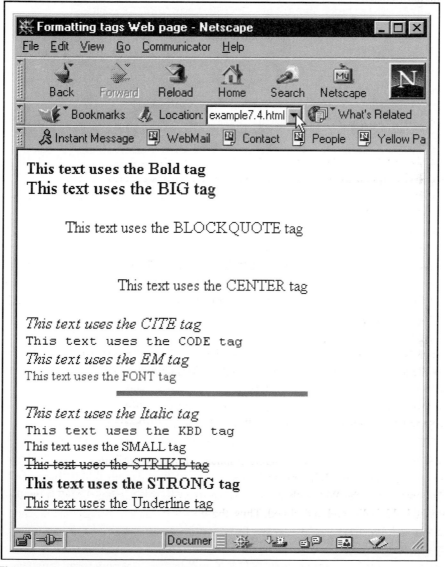

Figure 7.4 Word/character formatting tags.

```
<HTML>
<HEAD>
<TITLE>Formatting tags Web page</TITLE>
</HEAD>
<BODY>
```

```
<B>This text uses the Bold tag</B><BR>
<BIG>This text uses the BIG tag</BIG><BR>
<BLOCKQUOTE>This text uses the BLOCKQUOTE tag</BLOCKQUOTE><BR>
<CENTER>This text uses the CENTER tag</CENTER><BR>
<CITE>This text uses the CITE tag</CITE><BR>
<CODE>This text uses the CODE tag</CODE><BR>
<EM>This text uses the EM tag</EM><BR>
<FONT SIZE=2 COLOR="green">This text uses the FONT tag</FONT><BR>
<HR SIZE= 5 WIDTH=50% ALIGN="center" NOSHADE>
<I>This text uses the Italic tag</I><BR>
<KBD>This text uses the KBD tag</KBD><BR>
<SMALL>This text uses the SMALL tag</SMALL><BR>
<STRIKE>This text uses the STRIKE tag</STRIKE><BR>
<STRONG>This text uses the STRONG tag</STRONG><BR>
<U>This text uses the Underline tag</U><BR>
</BODY>
</HTML>
```

Figue 7.4 shows that the <CITE>, <EM>, and <I> tags produce the same result. Similarly, the results of the <CODE> and <KBD> tags look the same. This means that the browser implementation of these tags is the same, producing the same result.

7.9 Links and Link Tags

Hyperlinks, or links for short, are one of the two key concepts behind HTML (the other being markup). Hyperlinks create hypertext. Hyperlinks produce two effects when Web authors include them in Web pages. First, they link other Web pages and files to the current Web page. This makes it easier for readers of the page to find related information and content. Second, the reader of an HTML document can click any link in the page, at any time, at random. A link is a connection from one Web source to another. Despite its simplicity, the link has been one of the driving forces behind the Web's success.

HTML provides three tags to help Web author create and control hyperlinks. They are the anchor tag <A>, the link tag <LINK>, and the base tag <BASE>. The <A> tag is the primary tag for creating links. The other two tags provide control for it.

7.9.1 <A> Tag

A link is the basic hypertext construct. A link has two ends or parts, known as anchors, and a direction, as shown in figure 7.5. The link starts at the "source" anchor or "visible" part and points to the "destination" anchor or "invisible" part. The source anchor may be a text, an image, or a list item. The destination anchor may be an HTML document (Web page), a file, a program, an image, a video clip, a sound bite, an FTP download, a Telnet connection, or an e-mail address. The general structure of the <A> tag is: <A "invisible part">"visible" part</A>, as shown in figure 7.5. The visible part of the <A> tag is what the user sees displayed on the Web page. The invisible part is the destination that the user goes to upon clicking (activating) the visible part. The default, common, and implicit behavior of a link is the retrieval of a Web source upon selecting it by clicking it with a mouse.

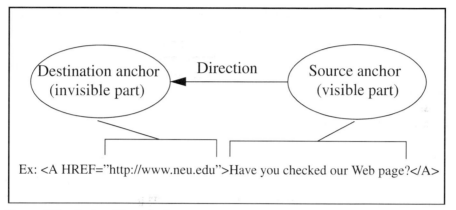

Figure 7.5 Parts of the <A> tag.

The <A> tag has several attributes. They are HREF, TITLE, NAME, CHARSET, TYPE, HREFLANG, REL, REV, ACCESSKEY, SHAPE, COORDS, and TABINDEX. These attributes are described in what follows:

•The HREF attribute specifies the destination anchor or the invisible part. This attribute accepts any Web protocol, such as http:// (see figure 7.5 for an example), file://, ftp://, telnet://, or mailto:. Here is an example: <A HREF = "mailto: zeid@coe.neu.edu">Please send us your feedback</A>.

•The TITLE attribute specifies a title for the link, which shows when the user moves the mouse over the link.

•The NAME attribute names the current link so that it can be used as the destination of another link. This attribute is typically used to create intradocument links, as discussed in section 4.9.2. The HREF creates interdocument links.

•The CHARSET attribute specifies the character encoding of the destination document (Web page). If a link points to, say, a Web page written in a language that uses characters different from those of the English alphabet (such as the Arabic language), this attribute should be used by the Web author. The browser needs it to render the destination Web page correctly.

•The TYPE attribute specifies the MIME type of the destination document. The most common type is text/html.

•The HREFLANG attribute specifies the language of the destination document, if it is not English. This attribute and the CHARSET may be used together. For these two attributes to work, the browser version rendering the document must have the proper interpreter. Consider two documents, one in French and the other in Arabic. The <A> tag that uses the French document as a destination Web page must use the HREFLANG attribute.

<A HREFLANG = "fr" HREF = "french.html">Read a French paper</A>.

The <A> tag that uses the Arabic document as a destination Web page must use both the HREFLANG and the CHARSET attributes.

<A HREFLANG = "ar" CHARSET = "ISO 8859-6" HREF = "http://www.xxx.com/arabic.html>Read an Arabic paper</A>.

•The REL (specify forward link), REV (specify reverse link), ACCESSKEY (accessibility key character), SHAPE (used with client-side image maps), COORDS (used with client-side image maps), and TABINDEX (used for tabbing) attributes are not covered here, because they are seldom used with the <A> tag.

A link (its source anchor or visible part) in a Web page may have one of three states: link, active link (alink), or visited link (vlink). If a user has not clicked the link, it is known as just a link. During the time that the user is pressing the mouse button and holding it down on the link, but before releasing it, the link is said to be active. (Thus, the name active link.) After the releasing of the mouse button, the link becomes a visited link. When the user returns to the Web page holding the link, it is a visited link. Browsers use three colors to display the three states of links. The default colors are blue for a link, red for an alink, and purple for a vlink. The Web author can override these default colors by using the proper attributes of the <BODY> tag, as shown in chapter 9. Browsers remember link states in the same page for a period of time that can be set by configuring the browser, as discussed in chapters 3 and 4.

The URLs used in conjunction with the HREF attribute of the <A> tag may be specified on an absolute or a relative basis. The reference base is the location of the HTML document using the <A> tag. This location could be a Web server on the Internet, a local directory, or a folder. Web authors need to think of an HTML document as a file name and of its URL as a path to the file. From this point of view, all conventional rules of using path names relative to each other apply here to HTML documents and their URLs. Three cases exist. The first case is that the location (directory) of the destination HTML file is the same as that of the HTML file using the tag. (Call it the current HTML file.) In the second case, the destination file is in a directory one level above that of the current HTML file. The last case occurs when the destination HTML file is in a directory below that of the current HTML file.

Consider the following example to show how to specify the file path in each of the three cases. Let us assume that an HTML document with the name *source.html* resides in the directory http://www.xxx.com/dir1 and uses an <A> tag that links to an HTML file called *destination.html*. If both files reside in the same directory, the Web author uses <A HREF = "destination.html">. The path to this file resolves to *http://www.xxx.com/dir1/destination.html*. Figure 7.6, case A, shows the directory structure for this case. If *destination.html* resides in a directory (say, *dir2*) at the same level as that of *source.html*, the Web author specifies the path as <A HREF = "../dir2/destination.html". The two periods (..) indicate the directory above the current one. This relative path resolves to *http://www.xxx.com/dir2/destination.html*. Figure 7.6, case B,

shows the directory tree structure. If *destination.html* resides in a directory, *dir3*, one level beneath that of *source.html*, the Web author specifies the path as <A HREF = "dir3/destination.html">. This relative path resolves to *http://www.xxx.com/dir1/dir3/destination.html*. Figure 7.6, case C, shows the directory structure. These three cases are by no means the only possible ones.

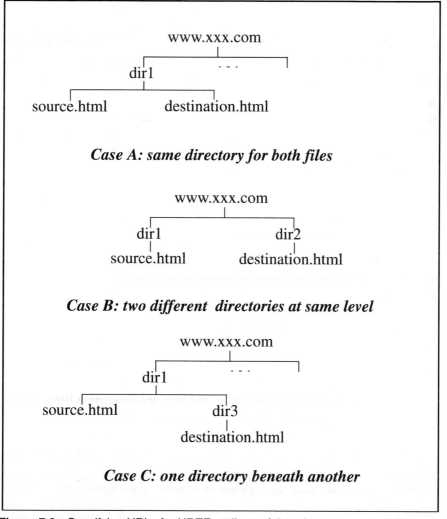

Figure 7.6   Specifying URLs for HREF attribute of the <A> tag.

If Web authors use the absolute path, they should specify the full path. For the above three cases, they would use respectively, the following path names: *http://www.xxx.com/dir1/destination.html*, *http://www.xxx.com/dir2/destination.html*, and *http://www.xxx.com/dir1/dir3/destina-*

tion.html. These are the same as the resolved path names shown above. It is recommended that one use absolute path names because html documents are constantly being moved from one directory to another on Web servers.

Example 7.5 Develop a Web page that illustrates the use of the link tag.

Solution This example creates a Web page with links created using the <A> tag and its attributes described in this section. The HREF attribute uses both local files and Web sites as destination locations. Both relative and absolute file names are also illustrated. When clicking a link in the page of this example, the reader should remember to press and hold the mouse button to observe the change of color of the link. Using a text editor, type the code that follows, and save it as *example7.5.html*. View the page in a browser. Figure 7.7 show the resulting Web page.

```
<HTML>
<HEAD>
<TITLE>Hyperlink tag Web page</TITLE>
</HEAD>
<BODY>
<H2>This Web page uses the &#60;A&#62; tag with some of its
attributes</H2>

<! Link to a Web page on the Web>
<A HREF = "http://www.neu.edu">This link uses a Web server</A><BR>

<! Use different protocols with HREF attribute>
<A HREF = "mailto:zeid@coe.neu.edu">This link uses the mailto: pro-
tocol</A><BR>
<A HREF = "ftp://ftp.netscape.com">This link uses the ftp: protocol
</A><BR>
<A HREF="telnet://elvis.coe.neu.edu">This link uses the telnet:
protocol</A><BR>

<! Usethe TITLE and CHARSET attributes of the link tag>
<A HREF = "http://www.neu.edu" TITLE = "Northeastern Univ. Web
site">This link has a title to illutrate using the TITLE
attribute</A><BR>
<A HREF = "http://www.w3.org" CHARSET="ISO-8859-1">This link uses
the CHARSET attribute</A><BR>
<! Link to the local file example7.4.html by using the file: proto-
col>
<A HREF = "example7.4.html">This link uses the relative path of a
local file</A><BR>
<A HREF = "file://c:/windows/desktop/example7.4.html">This link
uses the absolute path of a local file</A><BR>
</BODY>
</HTML>
```

Here are several comments about this example HTML code:

•<H2> tag gives the page a heading.

•We use special characters inside the <H2> tag to display <A> in the Web page. Special characters are covered in section 7.10 in this chapter.

•The code is divided into blocks separated by blank lines and started with comment statements, to facilitate following and understanding each block.

•Each <A> tag is ended with a <BR> tag, to force line breaks for better design of the Web page.

•When the mouse is positioned over the link whose tag uses the TITLE attribute, the browser displays the link title as shown in figure 7.7.

•Netscape Communicator 4.7 does not display the title of the link whose <A> tag uses the TITLE attribute. MS IE 5.0 does.

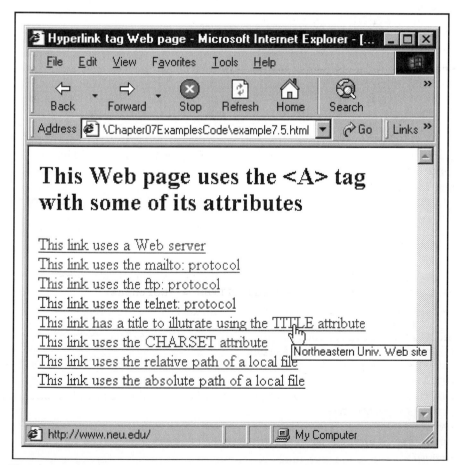

Figure 7.7 Link tag <A>.

7.9.2 Anchors

While the <A> tag most often is used to link Web pages together, it can also be used to create links within the same page. Links that connect external Web pages to a particular Web page are known as Interdocument links, whereas links that connect different sections within the same page are known as intradocument links or anchors. Thus, the destination anchor for an intradocument link is a tag within the same document creating the anchor.

There are two useful cases for anchors. First, a Web author might create a table of contents, whose headings link to the corresponding sections in the page. At the end of each section, there should be an anchor that takes the page viewer back to the table of contents. Using a table of contents allows Web authors to develop long Web pages (one to three screens long) to maintain continuity of ideas. Tables of contents with intradocument links have the effect of splitting Web pages, but yet maintaining continuity of ideas. This concept is sometimes known as chunking an HTML document. The rule is to chunk the document at the concept level. Large chunks are slow to scroll and render, while small chunks make the concept fuzzy. The design issue here is content stream versus control stream.

The other case of using anchors is to specify a given location in a Web page that is used as the destination document in an interdocument link. That location is usually important in the Web page and deserves the user attention immediately after the user downloads the page — for example, a menu of products. In this case, the anchor positions the location at the top of the browser screen.

The creation of an anchor requires two <A> tags and the NAME attribute. This attribute gives a name to an <A> tag by using NAME = "label", thus making it available as destination tag. Another <A> tag in the same HTML document can reference this named tag by using HREF = "#label", thus serving as the source tag. The name *label* is case-sensitive, and must be the same, including spaces, in both <A> tags to be recognized correctly by the browser that renders the HTML document. Also, the name must be preceded by the # sign when it is used with the HREF attribute.

Example 7.6 Develop a Web page that illustrates the creation of intradocument anchors.

Solution This example creates a Web page with anchors created using the <A> tag and its NAME attribute. Using a text editor, type the code that follows, and save it as *example7.6.html*. View the page in a browser. Figure 7.8 shows the resulting Web page.

```
<HTML>
<HEAD>
<TITLE>Anchors Web page</TITLE>
</HEAD>
<BODY>
<H2>This Web page creates intradocument anchors using the
&#60;A&#62; and its NAME attribute</H2>
```

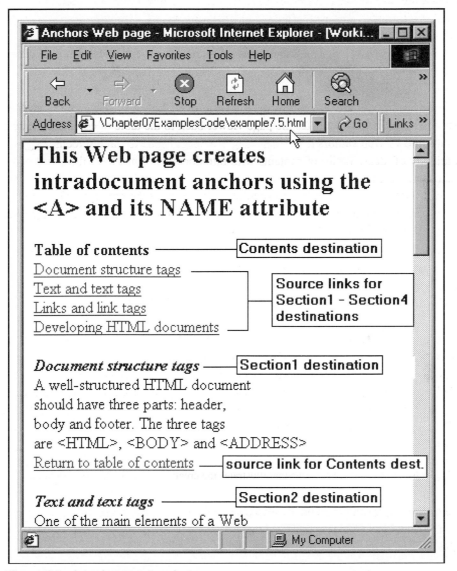

Figure 7.8   Intradocument anchors.

```
<! Define a destination tag>
<A NAME = "Contents"><B>Table of contents</B></A><BR>

<! Define source tags>
<A HREF = "#Section1">Document structure tags</A><BR>
```

```
<A HREF = "#Section2">Text and text tags</A><BR>
<A HREF = "#Section3">Links and link tags</A><BR>
<A HREF = "#Section4">Developing HTML documents</A><BR>

<! Define destination tag for Section1 source tag>
<P><A NAME = "Section1"><B><I>Document structure tags</I></B><BR>
A well-structured HTML document<BR>
should have three parts: header,<BR>
body and footer. The three tags<BR>
are &#60;HTML&#62;, &#60BODY&#62 and &#60ADDRESS&#62;<BR>

<! Define a source tag for the first destination tag on the top>
<A HREF = "#Contents">Return to table of contents</A>

<! Define destination tag for Section2 source tag>
<P><A NAME = "Section2"><B><I>Text and text tags</I></B><BR>
One of the main elements of a Web<BR>
page is text. Similar to traditional<BR>
documents, the text of a Web page is<BR>
structured and organized into basic<BR>
units of headings, sections, and<BR>
paragraphs. Each paragraph consists<BR>
of statements and words. HTML provides<BR>
tags to format each of these units.<BR>
There are heading tags, paragraph tags,<BR>
and word/character tags. These tags,<BR>
their attributes, and their use are<BR>
covered in this book.<BR>

<! Define a source tag for the first destination tag on the top>
<A HREF = "#Contents">Return to table of contents</A>

<! Define destination tag for Section3 source tag>
<P><A NAME = "Section3"><B><I>Links and link tags</I></B><BR>
Hyperlinks, or links for short, is<BR>
one of the two key concepts behind<BR>
HTML, the other being markup.<BR>
Hyperlinks create hypertext.<BR>
Hyperlinks produce two effects<BR>
when Web authors include them in<BR>
Web pages. First, they link other<BR>
Web pages and files to the current Web page.<BR>
This makes it easier for readers of the page<BR>
to find related information and content.<BR>
Second, the reader of an HTML document<BR>
can click any link in the page at any<BR>
time at random. A link is a connection<BR>
from one Web source to another. Despite<BR>
```

```
its simplicity, the link has been one<BR>
of the driving forces behind the Web success.<BR>

<! Define a source tag for the first destination tag on the top>
<A HREF = "#Contents">Return to table of contents</A>

<! Define destination tag for Section4 source tag>
<P><A NAME = "Section4"><B><I>Developing HTML documents</I></B><BR>
Using HTML is very simple. All Web<BR>
authors need is an editor to write<BR>
HTML files and a browser to view them.<BR>
The editor could be a text editor or an<BR>
HTML editor, depending on the approach<BR>
taken to generate HTML code. We identify<BR>
two approaches in this book: the bottom-up<BR>
approach and the top-down approach. These<BR>
two approaches work opposite to each other.<BR>
There are two outcomes to each approach.<BR>
These are the HTML file and the corresponding<BR>
Web page. In the bottom-up approach, the<BR>
HTML file is generated first and the Web<BR>
page is viewed later. Therefore, the Web<BR>
page is considered a result of the HTML file.<BR>
In the top-down approach, the Web page<BR>
is developed first and the HTML file is<BR>
generated in the background. Therefore,<BR>
the HTML file is a result of the Web page development.<BR>

<! Define a source tag for the first destination tag on the top>
<A HREF = "#Contents">Return to table of contents</A>
</BODY>
</HTML>
```

Here are several comments about this example HTML code:

•<H2> tag gives the page a heading.

•Many <BR> tags are used purposely to force the Web page to be long, to demonstrate the benefits of intradocument anchors.

•There is an intradocument anchor that takes the Web page user back to the table of contents at the top of the page if needed. This is a good design of the Web page.

•When the user clicks an anchor, the name of the anchor is appended to the URL. For example, if the user clicks the *Text and text tags* link, its name, *#Section2*, shows in the URL. This provides a good idea for loading pages initially. If the Web author wants to drop the user to an important location in a Web page, the HREF attribute would include an anchor name. For example, the Web author uses <A HREF="example7.6.html#Section2"> to drop the user to

Section2 of the Web page directly. Netscape Communicator 4.7 recognizes the anchor in the URL, but MS IE 5.0 does not.

7.9.3 <LINK> Tag

The <LINK> tag usually appears in the <HEAD> section of an HTML document. The <LINK> tag does not have an end (closing) tag; i.e. </LINK> is forbidden. The attributes of the <LINK> tag are HREF, CHARSET, HREFLANG, TYPE, REL, REV, TITLE, LANG, and MEDIA. The first six are the same as the attributes of the <A> tag. The TITLE attribute specifies the title of a document alternative to the current one. The LANG attribute specifies the language of the alternate document. The MEDIA attribute specifies the rendering medium of the alternate document.

The <LINK> tag can be used in an HTML document in two contexts.

1. Refer to external documents. In this context, the tag provides relationship information between the document and other documents. For example, if an HTML document uses style sheets that are defined in a different document, the HTML document can reference the style sheets in its <LINK> tag. The following example of the <LINK> tag specifies, to the browser, that the current HTML document points to the file *myStyleSheets.css*, whose MIME type is text/css, and whose relationship to the current document is *stylesheet*. It also specifies to the browser that the title of the style sheet document is *Cascade style sheets definitions* and that the document is found in the Web site www.xxx.com;

```
<HEAD>
<TITLE>Using style sheets defined in another document</TITLE>
<LINK REL = "stylesheet" TYPE = "text/css" HREF = "http://
www.xxx.com/myStyleSheets.css" TITLE = "Cascade style sheets defi-
nitions">
</HEAD>
```

2. Help search engines access and index Web sites. In this context, Web authors may use the <LINK> tag to provide a variety of information to search engines. Here are sample examples.

•Specify different language versions of a document to an indexing engine, to provide search results to users in their native languages. For example, here is how to specify a French version of an HTML document, which is written in German, to a search engine.

```
<HEAD>
<TITLE>Search engine returns a French Version of this document for
French users</TITLE>
<LINK REL = "alternate" TYPE = "text/html" HREFLANG = "de" HREF =
"www.xxx.com/tourist.html" LANG = "fr" TITLE = "Les attractions
touristes dans Paris">
```

```
</HEAD>
```

The French title means "the tourist attractions in Paris".

•Indicate the beginning of a collection of documents. It is useful for a search engine to return a particular page, requested by a user, in the collection, as well as the beginning of it, in case if the user may be interested — for example,

```
<HEAD>
<TITLE>Specify the start of a collection of documents to search
engines</TITLE>
<LINK REL = "start" TYPE = "text/html" HREF = "http://www.xxx.com/
document1.html" TITLE = "First Web page in the collection">
</HEAD>
```

•Specify different media versions of a document to search engines. For example, a post-script version of a document is more suitable for printing than is its HTML version; in the following HTML code, the Web author tells search engines where to find the printed version of a manual:

```
<HEAD>
<TITLE>Tell search engines where to find postscript version of a
manual</TITLE>
<LINK REL = "alternate" MEDIA = "print" TYPE = "application/post-
script" HREF= "www.xxx.com/manual.ps" TITLE = "The manual in post-
script">
</HEAD>
```

7.9.4 <BASE> Tag

The <BASE> tag allows Web authors to specify a reference URL (path) from which all relative URLs in an HTML document are measured. For example, URLs used in the <A> tag may be measured relative to the <BASE> URL. This eliminates repetition in the specifying of the URLs. The <BASE> tag must be used in the <HEAD> section. It does not have an end tag. Its only attribute is HREF. The HREF attribute can accept the http or file protocol. The following HTML code shows how to use the <BASE> code:

```
<HTML>
<HEAD>
<TITLE>The BASE tag Web page</TITLE>
<! Specify the folder (path) where the HTML files of the <A> tags
shown below reside>
<BASE HREF = "file://c:/windows/desktop/">
</HEAD>
<BODY>
```

```
<A HREF = "myFileOne.html">Check our first product</A>
<A HREF = "myFileTwo.html">Check our second product</A>
<A HREF = "myFileThree.html">Check our thirdproduct</A>
</BODY>
</HTML>
```

When the browser runs the foregoing HTML code, it resolves the URLs of the three <A> tags to *c:/windows/desktop/myFileOne.html*, *c:/windows/desktop/myFileTwo.html*, and *c:/windows/desktop/myFileThree.html*. While using the <BASE> tag eliminates repeating the typing of the path, it may not be a good idea to use, because the files may change locations in the future.

7.10 Meta Data and the Meta Tag

Web authors have two goals in mind when they design and develop their Web pages: design for surfers and design for search engines. While authors strive to increase the traffic to their Web sites and increase the number of hits of their pages, they must keep in mind that search engines must find these pages first to index them. One of the effective design tools that increases the chances of page indexing is the use of the <META> tag.

The <META> tag allows authors to specify meta data of Web pages. Meta data refers to data about an HTML document rather than the document content. Browsers do not render meta data. Such data is used by search engines for indexing and ranking page hits in a given search. Web authors can define meta data in a variety of ways. For example, data could include a brief description of the Web page, some keywords, and the name of the author.

The <META> tag has the following attributes:

•The NAME attribute defines a property and its value in the HTML document. One <META> tag defines only one property/value pair. Web authors use multiple <META> tags to define multiple property/value pairs such as author, copyright, date, keywords, description, and so forth.

•The CONTENT attribute defines the value of a property defined by the NAME attribute. Thus, these two attributes come in pairs.

•The HTTP-EQUIV attribute is used by HTTP servers to gather information needed to display the Web page, such as an ISO character set.

•The SCHEME attribute defines a way to interpret the property value. The scheme is usually found in the URL (meta data profile) defined by the PROFILE attribute of the <HEAD> tag.

The specification of meta data in a Web page requires two steps. First, the Web author specify the URL of the profile that defines the property/value pairs, by using the PROFILE attribute of the <HEAD> tag. Second, the Web author uses the <META> tag as many times as needed to define property/value pairs.

The following examples illustrate some uses of the <META> tag:

1) Specify as many properties as needed for document indexing by search engines.
```
<HTML>
```

```
<HEAD PROFILE = "http://www.xxx.com/myProfile">
<META NAME = "description" CONTENT = "Everything you would want to
know about using HTML.">
<META NAME = "keywords" CONTENTS = "HTML 4.0, tags, attributes,
editors">
<META NAME = "keywords" LANG = "fr" CONTENT = "voyage, Europe, Les
Alpes, Les gens">
<TITLE>Using the META tag</TITLE>
</HEAD>
```

The last <META> tag specifies the French language to the search engine. The words in the CONTENT attribute mean respectively travel, Europe, the Alps, and people.

2) Replace the use of <LINK> tag.

<LINK REL = "myDocument" TYPE = "text/plain" HREF = "ftp://ftp.xxx.com/ myFile.txt">

may be rewritten as

<META NAME = "myDocument" CONTENT = "ftp://ftp.xxx.com/myFile.txt">

3) Specify some action using the HTTP header.

•<META HTTP-EQUIV = "Expires"

CONTENT = "Sunday, December31, 2000 16:32:45 GMT">. This declaration results in the HTTP header Expires: Sunday, December 31, 2000 16:32:45 GMT.

•<META HTTP-EQUIV = "refresh" CONTENT = "5, http://www.xxx.com/ news.html">. This declaration should load news.html Web page after 5 seconds from loading the other Web page that contains this <META> tag. This action may not be supported by all browsers.

•<META HTTP-EQUIV = "PICS-Label" CONTENT = '(PICS-1.1 "http:// www.gcf.org/v2.5" labels on "1994.11.05T08:15-0500" until "1995.12.31T3:59-0000" for"http://w3.org/PICS/overview.html" ratings (studs 0.5 density 0 color/hue 1))'>. This declaration uses the PICS (Platform for Internet Content Selection) rating system to help parents and teachers control what children can access on the Internet. This declaration includes a PICS 1.1 label with the Web page. The PICS system facilitates other uses for labels, such as code signing, privacy, and intellectual property protection.

•<META HTTP-EQUIV = "Content-Type" CONTENT = "text/html" CHARSET = "ISO-8859-5">. This declaration specifies that the default character encoding document is ISO 8859-5.

4) Specify some action using the SCHEME attribute.

```
<HTML>
<HEAD PROFILE = "http://www.xxx.com/myProfile">
<META SCHEME = "ISBN" NAME = "identifier" CONTENT = "007-072857-7">
<TITLE>Using the META tag</TITLE>
</HEAD>
```

The values for the SCHEME attribute are defined by the name/value pairs whose context is stored in the profile file.

7.11 Special Characters

There are several special characters, such as Latin characters and Greek symbols. These special characters and symbols are represented by certain HTML code. A need for special characters also arises when a Web page must use some of the characters reserved by HTML, such as < or >, as part of its text. If the Web author uses < or >, the browser attempts to render it as part of a tag, and therefore renders the HTML code incorrectly. In such a case, the author uses a special character that represents < or >.

Special characters in HTML are represented by a character entity or a numeric code. The character entity begins with & and ends with ;. The numeric code beings with &# and ends with ;. For example, the copyright symbol is represented by the character entity © or by the numeric code ©. Character entities use words, numeric code uses numbers. Common practice uses numeric codes. When a Web page uses special characters, the browser looks up these symbols and replaces them with equivalent characters while rendering the document.

There are three distinct character sets in HTML. The ISO 8859-1 (Latin-1) character set contains the Latin characters, including the already commonly used   (blank space), © (copyright symbol), and ® (registered mark symbol). The first numeric code in this set is 32, and the last code is 255. Thus, the first special character in this set is   and the last one is ÿ. The codes in between are incremented by 1. Figure 7.9 shows a sample of the ISO Latin-1 characters. Each code in the figure must be preceded by &# and ended by ;. The reader can find the other characters in many ways. The reader can write a Web page with all the other codes to discover the corresponding characters, or the reader can use a search engine and search for ISO Latin-1 characters as a search string, or the reader can check the Web site http://WWW.ifm.liu.se/Computers/WWW/latin1.html.

The second character set is the symbols, mathematical symbols, and Greek letters. These characters are available in the Adobe font "Symbols". This set contains all the modern Greek letters. It is not intended for producing Greek text. Figure 7.10 shows a sample of this character set. Each code in the figure must be preceded by &# and ended by ;. The small rectangles shown in the figure columns indicate that the browser does not support the corresponding codes. This set has subsets as follows:

1) Latin extended-B; the code for this character is ƒ

2) Greek characters; the first code in this set is Α and the last code is ϖ. The codes in between are incremented by 1. However, the following codes are not present in the sequence: 930, 938 - 944 inclusive, 970 - 976 inclusive, and 979 - 981 inclusive. If a Web page uses any of these codes (say, Ϊ), the browser displays the code as it is, because it cannot render it.

3) General punctuation; the codes for this subset are • (bullet = small black circle), … (horizontal ellipsis = three dot leader), ′ (prime for feet, minutes, etc.), ″ (double prime for inches, seconds, etc.), ‾ (spacing overscore or overline), and ⁄ (fraction slash).

4) Letterlike symbols; the codes for this subset are ℑ (blackletter capital I), &#8472 (script capital P), ℜ (blackletter capital R), ᴺ (trade mark sign), and ℵ (aleph symbol).

5) Arrows; the codes for this subset are ← (leftwards arrow), ↑ (upwards arrow), → (rightwards arrow), ↓ (downwards arrow), ↔ (left – right

Code	Char	Code	Char	Code	Char	Code	Char	Code	Char
32		48	0	64	@	80	P	96	`
33	!	49	1	65	A	81	Q	97	a
34	"	50	2	66	B	82	R	98	b
35	#	51	3	67	C	83	S	99	c
36	$	52	4	68	D	84	T	100	d
37	%	53	5	69	E	85	U	101	e
38	&	54	6	70	F	86	V	102	f
39	'	55	7	71	G	87	W	103	g
40	(	56	8	72	H	88	X	104	h
41	)	57	9	73	I	89	Y	105	i
42	*	58	:	74	J	90	Z	106	j
43	+	59	;	75	K	91	[	107	k
44	,	60	<	76	L	92	\	108	l
45	-	61	=	77	M	93	]	109	m
46	.	62	>	78	N	94	^	110	n
47	/	63	?	79	O	95	_	111	o

Figure 7.9   Sample ISO 8859-1 (Latin-1) characters.

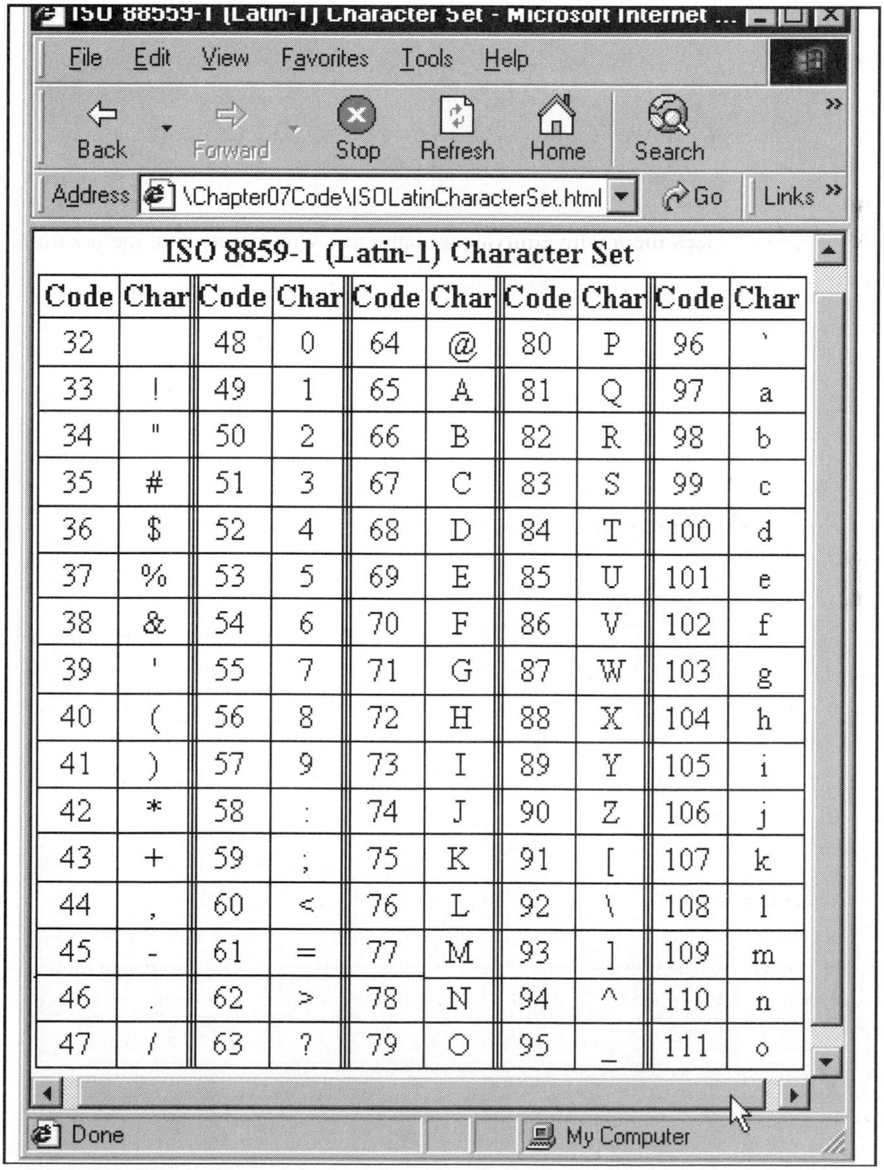

arrow), `&#8629;` (downwards arrow with corner leftwards = carriage return), `&#8656;` (leftwards double arrow), `&#8657;` (upwards double arrow), `&#8658;` (rightwards double arrow), `&#8659;` (downwards double arrow), and `&#8660;` (left – right double arrow),

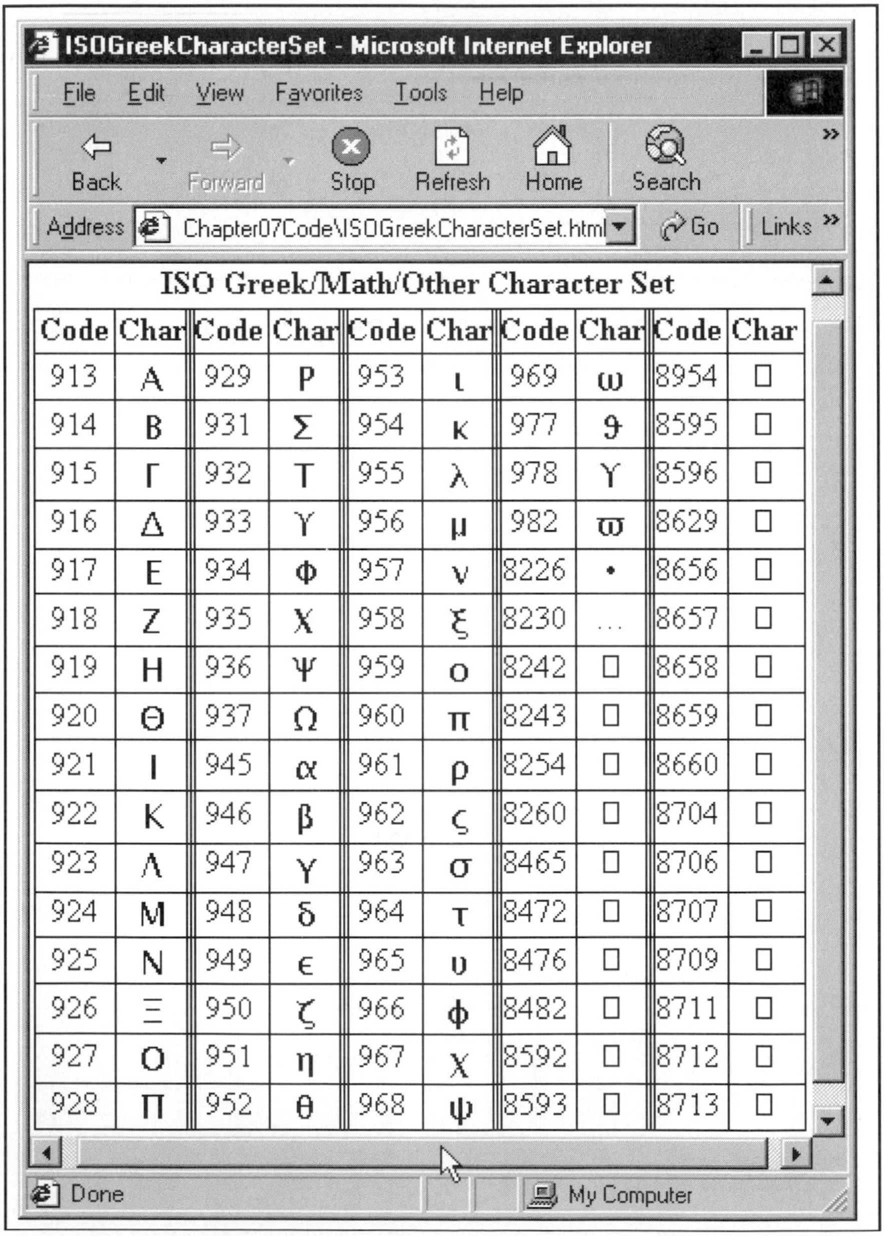

ISOGreekCharacterSet - Microsoft Internet Explorer

File Edit View Favorites Tools Help

Back   Forward   Stop   Refresh   Home   Search

Address Chapter07Code\ISOGreekCharacterSet.html   Go   Links

ISO Greek/Math/Other Character Set

Code	Char	Code	Char	Code	Char	Code	Char	Code	Char
913	A	929	P	953	ι	969	ω	8954	☐
914	B	931	Σ	954	κ	977	ϑ	8595	☐
915	Γ	932	T	955	λ	978	Υ	8596	☐
916	Δ	933	Υ	956	μ	982	ϖ	8629	☐
917	E	934	Φ	957	ν	8226	•	8656	☐
918	Z	935	X	958	ξ	8230	…	8657	☐
919	H	936	Ψ	959	ο	8242	☐	8658	☐
920	Θ	937	Ω	960	π	8243	☐	8659	☐
921	I	945	α	961	ρ	8254	☐	8660	☐
922	K	946	β	962	ς	8260	☐	8704	☐
923	Λ	947	γ	963	σ	8465	☐	8706	☐
924	M	948	δ	964	τ	8472	☐	8707	☐
925	N	949	ε	965	υ	8476	☐	8709	☐
926	Ξ	950	ζ	966	ϕ	8482	☐	8711	☐
927	O	951	η	967	χ	8592	☐	8712	☐
928	Π	952	θ	968	ψ	8593	☐	8713	☐

Done   My Computer

Figure 7.10 Sample ISO Greek characters and math and other symbols.

6) Mathematical operators; the first code in this subset is `∀`, and the last code is `⋅`, with several codes missing in between. Interested readers should consult the www.w3c.org Web site for these codes and their meanings.

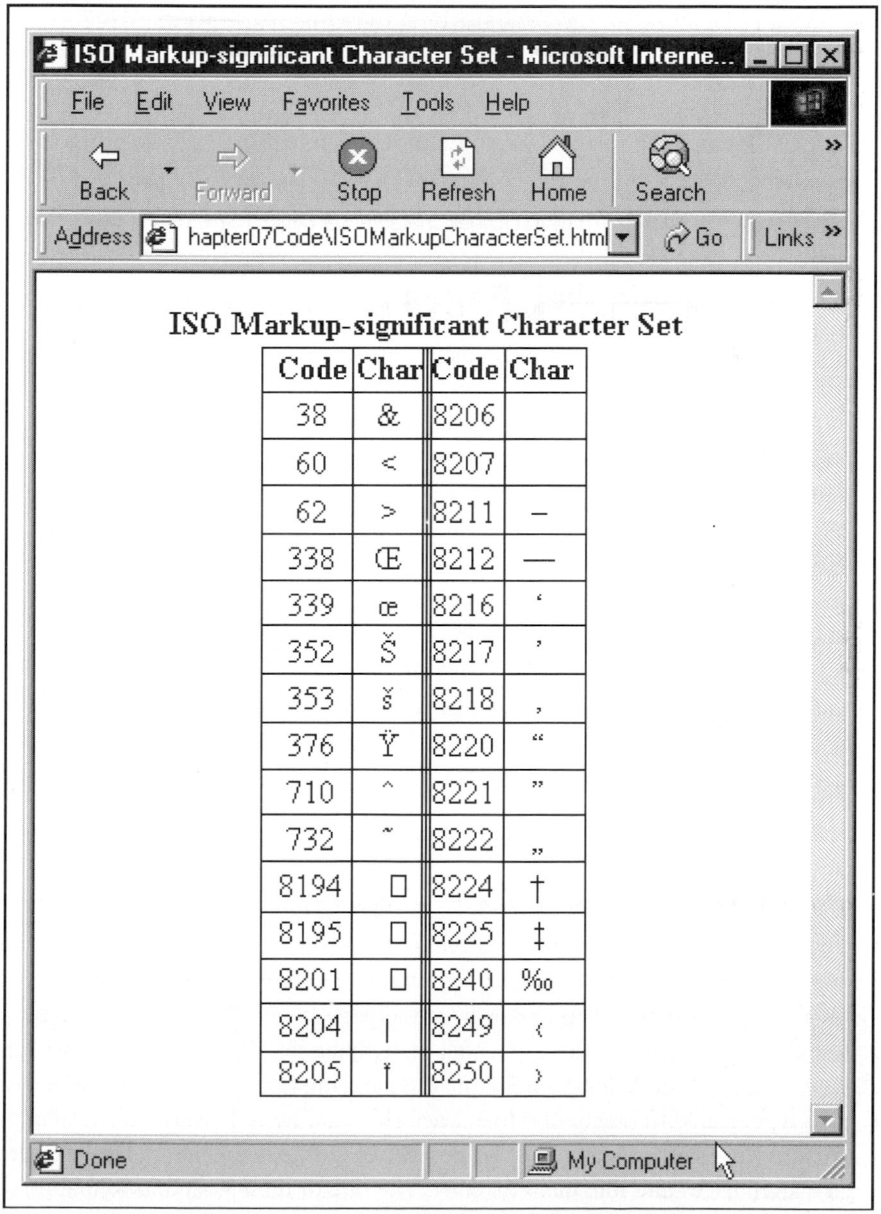

ISO Markup-significant Character Set

Code	Char	Code	Char
38	&	8206	
60	<	8207	
62	>	8211	–
338	Œ	8212	—
339	œ	8216	‘
352	Š	8217	’
353	š	8218	‚
376	Ÿ	8220	“
710	ˆ	8221	”
732	˜	8222	„
8194	□	8224	†
8195	□	8225	‡
8201	□	8240	‰
8204	|	8249	‹
8205	ǂ	8250	›

Figure 7.11 ISO markup-significant and Internationalization character set.

7) Geometric shapes; the only code for this subset is ◊ (lozenge).

8) Miscellaneous technical; the codes for this subset are ⌈ (left ceiling), ⌉ (right ceiling), ⌊ (left floor), ⌋ (right floor), 〈 (left-pointing angle bracket), and 〉 (right-pointing angle bracket).

9) Miscellaneous symbols; the codes for this subset are ♠ (black spade suit), ♣ (black club suit), ♥ (black heart suit), and ♦ (black diamond suit).

The third and last character set is the markup-significant and internationalization characters. These are escaping characters for denoting spaces and dashes. The subsets of characters that make up this set are Controls and Basic Latin, Latin Extended-A, Spacing modifiers, Letters, and General Punctuation. Figure 7.11 shows all these characters and their codes. As shown in the figure, the codes 8194, 8195, 8201, 8206, and 8207 are rendered correctly by the browser.

7.12 Building Basic Web Pages

With all the HTML coverage in this chapter, it is time to begin building Web pages and writing their corresponding HTML documents. Building good Web pages is very important to survival on the World Wide Web. Web authors should always remember that first impression is very important. Web authors should think of themselves as marketing, advertising, and/or PR (public relations) directors. They have about 45 seconds or a minute to keep the attention of first-time visitors to their Web pages. Unless hooked up to their pages with excellent look and content, visitors will move on very quickly to other Web sites, especially if these visitors have to go through tens of page hits returned by search engines. The best rule to follow in Web page design is to keep it simple. Web authors should also keep in mind that Web page design, like any design, evolves with time. Changing Web page design is easy to do. The basics to Web page design are content, first impression, and simplicity. The basics to Web page building are layout, title and headings, content, paragraphs, and lists. Readers who require more depth and knowledge of Web page design should consult the Web site http://info.med.yale.edu/caim/manual/contents.html.

7.12.1 Page Layout

Page layout is crucial to the ultimate success of a Web page. The page layout is like a master plan for a house to be built or an outline for a book or an article to be written. It is all in the layout. It is a good idea that a Web author have the page layout drawn by hand on a piece of paper, to test all design ideas. It is also essential to organize the Web page logically so that surfers can follow it easily. Web authors should put the most important information at the top of the page, in large type, and with plenty of white space surrounding it, because the span of attention of Web surfers is very short. Finally, there is no need to stuff too much into the page. It is quite easy to make more pages and link them together. The rule of thumb, similar to that for slides or overhead transparencies, is that a single home page should not try to convey more than four to six pieces of related information.

7.12.2 Page Title and Headings

A Web page title is used for indexing by Web spiders or robots. Also, browsers use the title to create a bookmark for the page. Web authors should make titles as descriptive as possible if they want people to find and read their pages. A page title should fit on a single line. The best way to find a title is to think first of keywords that describe the page content, then of sentences, and finally of titles. Here is an example:

words: stamps, rare stamp collection, stamp history.

sentence: This is a rare stamp collection with its history.

Title: History of a rare stamp collection.

A Web page may have headings throughout the document, as well as <META> tags that describe the document. These headings and tags are used by the Web indexing spiders, together with the title, to index the Web page. When a surfer runs a search using a search engine, the engine returns the title, the heading, and the URL of the page, or a combination.

7.12.3 Page Content

The content of a Web page is its heart. The page <BODY> tag holds its content. The content is the information that Web authors want to put online. Such content should be developed carefully, to appeal to the targeted audience. There are two general categories of Web pages: personal, and commercial. Personal Web pages are generally quite different from business, academic, and government ones in their content and form, although the layout for each category may be very similar.

The content of personal Web pages tends to contain textual introduction, followed by some images, and then links to local/remote pages. For example, a typical personal Web page may include the following elements: an introductory text with an image, followed by links to a resume, personal history, favorite hobbies and activities (such as travel, ice fishing, boating, gardening, cooking, etc.), favorite sports, and favorite Web site.

The content of a commercial Web page might contain text and images to describe, say, the company, followed by links to the company product line, job opportunities, human resources, worldwide office locations, distribution channels, orders online, and so forth. The contents of many government agency documents contain large amounts of text.

Web authors should be conscious about how much text to include in the body of Web pages. As a general rule, too much scrolling while viewing Web pages almost always signals too much text. The text of a Web page should be kept at a balance, not too little or too much. Web authors should have the text organized into, say, three to five short, well-written paragraphs. These paragraphs should also be interspersed with moderately sized headings, enough white space, and small graphics to add visual interest. Finally, Web page length should be kept between one and three screens long. Web authors, who may be forced to use multiple-screen Web pages to maintain continuity of ideas, should consider using intradocument links and creating tables of contents, as discussed in section 1.9.2.

Here are some rules to follow during Web page design.

•Web authors whose Web sites have multiple Web pages should keep the layout of the pages consistent, to provide continuity for visitors to these sites.

•Write short paragraphs, and intermix them with graphics and links to provide more visual contrast on the page.

•Use meaningful graphics, and keep them to minimum.

•Provide enough white space and headings for easy visual scanning.

•Use links to additional pages, instead of making Web page readers scroll up and down to read page content.

•When creating links, avoid using wording such as "Click here" — instead, choose meaningful hyperlink words. For example, instead of saying "<u>Click this link</u>", say "<u>Check our new exotic ice cream flavors</u>".

7.12.4 Page Paragraphs

Writing paragraphs for HTML documents is no different from writing them for conventional documents. Web authors should write strong and concise paragraphs, avoid repetition or unnecessary sentences and words, and write short, direct sentences. Here are some rules for Web authors to develop good paragraphs:

•Develop an outline, and then convert each heading or main point in the outline into a paragraph.

•Edit the text carefully to eliminate repetition.

•Use spell checkers and proofread the text.

•Solicit feedback from volunteers before publishing online.

•Revise the text and the paragraphs according to the feedback.

7.12.5 Page Lists

Some Web pages might be better written if they include lists. Lists are usually used to provide some form of indentation to distinguish lines of text from paragraphs. They can be necessary to display specific information optimally in Web pages. There are three kinds of lists. Chapter 8 covers HTML lists in more details.

7.13 Hierarchy of Web Pages

More often than not, Web sites have many Web pages linked together. Multiple Web pages are an outcome of keeping individual Web pages short and avoiding clutter in their contents. How can a Web author organize the structure and hierarchy of Web pages? Web authors can devise elegant, sophisticated, well-planned structures, but the most natural one is the web structure. A web structure suggests that a Web author begins with a home page that includes hyperlinks to other Web pages, which in turn may include other hyperlinks. Some of the hyperlinks may even point back to the home page, if needed. Thus, all the Web pages form a web that begins at the home page. The web structure is not at all restrictive. Web authors can, in the future, add new hyperlinks to their existing Web pages as the need grows, thus increasing the size of their webs.

In designing web structures, Web authors may draw the design on a piece of paper as shown in figure 7.12. Each arrow connecting two Web pages represents a hyperlink. The Web page that is at the arrow tail has the hyperlink in it, while the arrow head points to the page that is loaded if the hyperlink is clicked by a Web surfer. The home page is the first Web page that is loaded when a surfer visits the corresponding Web site.

As figure 7.12 suggests, it is quite natural and easy to edit and change the web structure. If a web page becomes obsolete, the corresponding links to it are deleted from all other Web pages that point to it. If a new Web page is added to the web, links are added in the same way. Web authors can add (or delete) hyperlinks in Web pages by editing the corresponding HTML files, using a text editor. Once the HTML file is open in the text editor, the Web author deletes the <A> tags that correspond to the obsolete hyperlinks.

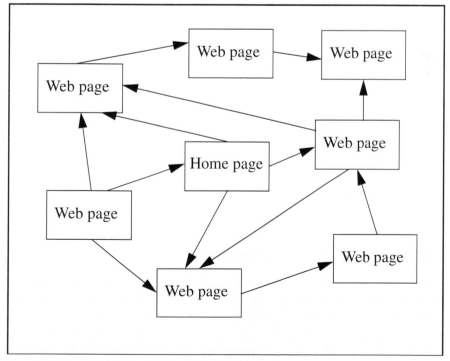

Figure 7.12   Creating a web structure of Web pages.

7.14 Tutorials

This section focuses on the hands-on aspects of using the HTML tags covered in this chapter to build and develop HTML documents. Any Web browser can be used to display the corresponding Web pages. It is a good idea to create a directory structure to save HTML files. This helps Web authors to organize HTML files and makes it easy to find them.

7.14.1 Creating a Personal Web Page Using Hyperlinks

This tutorial shows how to create a personal Web page. Figure 7.13 shows a possible design of the page. The design has nine Web pages. The home page is the master or the main that links to the other eight Web pages. It should be displayed first by the Web site. The *Professional* Web page links to the *Resume* Web page, and the *Personal* Web page links to the *Family tree* Web page. In this tutorial, we develop the page partially. Mainly, we develop the home page with three links: *Resume*, *Professional*, and *Personal*. The full development of the page is completed in the first exercise of this chapter. Using a text editor, type the code that follows, and save it as *tutorial7.14.1.html*. View the page in a browser. Figure 7.14 show the resulting home page.

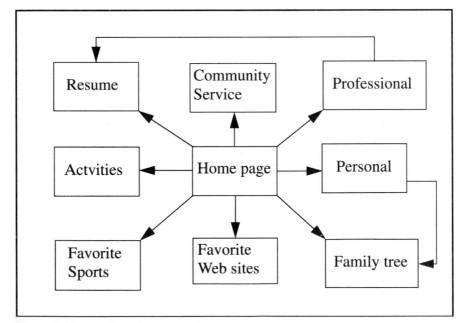

Figure 7.13   Design of a personal Web page.

```
<HTML>
<HEAD>
```

```
<TITLE>My personal Web page</TITLE>
</HEAD>
<BODY>
<H2><B><CENTER><FONT COLOR = "red">Welcome to my Web page</FONT></
CENTER></B></H2>
<B><CENTER><FONT COLOR = "red">Name goes here</FONT></CENTER></B>
<B><CENTER><FONT COLOR = "red">Address goes here</FONT></CENTER></
B>
<B><CENTER><FONT COLOR = "red">phone number goes here</FONT></CEN-
TER></B>
<P>Let me introduce myself. I have mastered HTML.<BR>
I have been working with many people. This is my personal<BR>
Web page, in case you want to know more about me.
<P>
<A HREF = "resume.html">Resume</A><BR>
<A HREF = "professional.html">Professional</A><BR>
<A HREF = "personal.html">Personal</A><BR>
<P>
<ADDRESS>
Copyright &#169; 2000<BR>
Abe Zeid<BR>
<A HREF = "mailto:zeid@coe.neu.edu">Please e-mail me</A><BR>
Revised - January 2000<BR>
</ADDRESS>
</BODY>
</HTML>
```

The three html files for the three links shown in the above code need to be written. Here is a skeleton for each one:

resume.html

```
<HTML>
<HEAD>
<TITLE>My resume</TITLE>
</HEAD>
<BODY>
<H2>Education</H2>
Education credentials go here
<H2>Experience</H2>
Current and previous employment go here
<H2>Skills</H2>
computer, software, and other skills go here
<! link back to home page>
<A HREF = "tutorial7.14.1.html">Back to my home page</A>
</BODY>
</HTML>
```

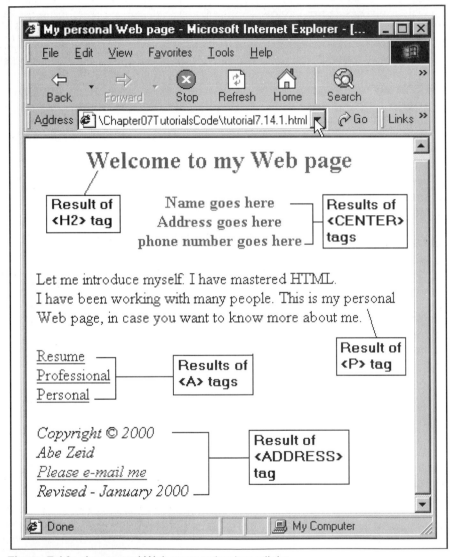

Figure 7.14   A personal Web page using hyperlinks.

professional.html

```
<HTML>
<HEAD>
<TITLE>My professional career and development</TITLE>
```

```
</HEAD>
<BODY>
<H2>Goals</H2>
future goals go here
<H2>Current employment</H2>
Current job duties go here
<H2>Development</H2>
courses and certificate programs go here
<H2>Leadership</H2>
leadership skills go here
<! link back to home page>
<A HREF = "tutorial7.14.1.html">Back to my home page</A>
</BODY>
</HTML>
```

personal.html

```
<HTML>
<HEAD>
<TITLE>My personal profile</TITLE>
</HEAD>
<BODY>
<H2>Family</H2>
immediate family members go here
<H2>Pets</H2>
pets' descriptions go here
<H2>Hobbies</H2>
hobbies go here
<! link back to home page>
<A HREF = "tutorial7.14.1.html">Back to my home page</A>
</BODY>
</HTML>
```

7.14.2 Creating a Personal Web Page Using Anchors

This tutorial shows how to create a personal Web page using anchors or intradocument links. We convert all the hyperlinks developed in the above tutorial, 7.14.1, into anchors. This approach to developing the personal Web page results in one HTML file instead of separate ones. The resulting personal Web page becomes multiple screens long. We have modified the HTML code of tutorial 7.14.1 by using some of the ideas from example 7.6. The two major changes made to the HTML code of tutorial 7.14.1 are the following. First, we replaced each html file in the three <A> tags by a name. Second, we added a blue heading to each of the anchor sections to facilitate the following of the page structure. Using a text editor, type the code that follows, and save it as *tutorial7.14.2.html*. View the page in a browser. Figure 7.15 shows the resulting home page.

```
<HTML>
<HEAD>
<TITLE>My personal Web page</TITLE>
</HEAD>
<BODY>
<H2><B><CENTER><FONT COLOR = "red">Welcome to my Web page</FONT>
</CENTER></B></H2>
<B><CENTER><FONT COLOR = "red">Name goes here</FONT></CENTER></B>
<B><CENTER><FONT COLOR = "red">Address goes here</FONT></CENTER>
</B>
<B><CENTER><FONT COLOR = "red">phone number goes here</FONT>
</CENTER></B>
<P>Let me introduce myself. I have mastered HTML.<BR>
I have been working with many people. This is my personal<BR>
Web page, in case you want to know more about me.
<P>

<! Define a destination tag>
<A NAME = "Contents"><B>Table of contents</B></A><BR>
<! Define source tags>
<A HREF = "#resume">Resume</A><BR>
<A HREF = "#professional">Professional</A><BR>
<A HREF = "#personal">Personal</A><BR>
<P>

<! Define destination tag for resume source tag>
<P><A NAME = "resume">
<B><FONT COLOR = "blue">RESUME</FONT></B><BR>
<B><I>Education:</I></B><BR>
Education credentials go here<BR>
<B><I>Experience:</I></B><BR>
Current and previous employment go here<BR>
<B><I>Skills:</I></B><BR>
computer, software, and other skills go here<BR>

<! Define a source tag for the first destination tag on the top>
<A HREF = "#Contents">Return to table of contents</A>

<! Define destination tag for professional source tag>
<P><A NAME = "professional">
<B><FONT COLOR = "blue">PROFESSIONAL</FONT></B><BR>
<B><I>Goals:</I></B><BR>
future goals go here<BR>
<B><I>Development:</I></B><BR>
courses and certificate programs go here<BR>
<B><I>Leadership:</I></B><BR>
leadership skills go here<BR>
```

```
<! Define a source tag for the first destination tag on the top>
<A HREF = "#Contents">Return to table of contents</A>
<! Define destination tag for personal source tag>
<P><A NAME = "personal">
<B><FONTCOLOR = "blue">PERSONAL</FONT></B><BR>
<B><I>Family:</I></B><BR>
immediate family members go here<BR>
<B><I>Pets:</I></B><BR>
pets' descriptions go here<BR>
<B><I>Hobbies:</I></B><BR>
hobbies go here<BR>

<! Define a source tag for the first destination tag on the top>
<A HREF = "#Contents">Return to table of contents</A>

<P><ADDRESS>
Copyright &#169; 2000<BR>
Abe Zeid<BR>
<A HREF = "mailto:zeid@coe.neu.edu">Please e-mail me</A><BR>
Revised - January 2000<BR>
</ADDRESS>
</BODY>
</HTML>
```

7.14.3 Using HTML Character Sets

This tutorial demonstrates using the ISO 8859-1 (Latin-1) and Greek character sets. We use some of the symbols in both sets. Using a text editor, type the code that follows, and save it as *tutorial7.14.3.html*. View the page in a browser. Figure 7.16 show the resulting home page.

```
<HTML>
<HEAD>
<TITLE>Using HTML character sets</TITLE>
</HEAD>
<BODY>
<H2><B><CENTER><FONT COLOR = "red">Using ISO 8859-1 (Latin-1) and
Greek character sets</FONT></CENTER></B></H2>
54&#62;30
<P>25&#60;10
<P>You may want to consider joining the &#960;&#964;&#931; (Pi Tau
Sigma) and &#964;&#946;&#960; (Tau Beta Pi) honor societies.
<P><ADDRESS>
Copyright &#169; 2000<BR>
Abe Zeid<BR>
<A HREF = "mailto:zeid@coe.neu.edu">Please e-mail me</A><BR>
Revised - January 2000<BR>
</ADDRESS>
```

```
</BODY>
</HTML>
```

Figure 7.15   A personal Web page using anchors.

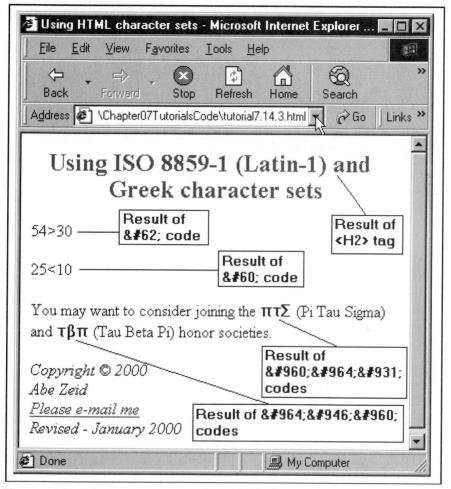

Figure 7.16   Using some characters from ISO Latin-1 and Greek character sets.

7.14.4 Using Hyperlinks as a Page Footer

We have been using the <ADDRESS> tag as a footer for Web pages. Here, we cover another idea. In some cases, as in tutorial 7.14.1, a Web site may have a master Web page that links to other Web pages via hyperlinks. In these cases, it is useful to use hyperlinks as the page footer, so that users can go to any page in the group from any other page in the group. If this type of footer is not available in a Web page, users are forced to use the browser Back button to navigate between pages in the group. Using hyperlinks as page footers is similar to using a link to the table of contents in pages with anchors. (See tutorial 7.14.2.)

Let us add a hyperlink footer to tutorial 7.14.1. Using a text editor, type the code that follows, and save it as *tutorial7.14.4.html*. The code shows two styles for the footer: one that uses a bracket ([ ]) separator, and another that uses a bar (| |) separator. View the page in a browser. Figure 7.17 shows the resulting home page.

```
<HTML>
<HEAD>
<TITLE>My personal Web page with hyperlink footer</TITLE>
</HEAD>
<BODY>
<H2><B><CENTER><FONT COLOR = "red">My Web page with hyperlink
footer</FONT></CENTER></B></H2>
<B><CENTER><FONT COLOR = "red">Name goes here</FONT></CENTER></B>
<B><CENTER><FONT COLOR = "red">Address goes here</FONT>
</CENTER></B>
<B><CENTER><FONT COLOR = "red">phone number goes here</FONT>
</CENTER></B>
<P>Let me introduce myself. I have mastered HTML.<BR>
I have been working with many people. This is my personal<BR>
Web page, in case you want to know more about me.
<P>
<A HREF = "resume.html">Resume</A><BR>
<A HREF = "professional.html">Professional</A><BR>
<A HREF = "personal.html">Personal</A><BR>
<P>
<! Add hyperlink footer>
<! Use this style>
<P><CENTER>[<A HREF = "tutorial7.14.4.html">Master Web Page</A>]
[<A HREF = "resume.html">Resume</A>]
[<A HREF = "professional.html">Professional</A>]
[<A HREF = "personal.html">Personal</A>]
</CENTER>
<! Or use this style>
<P><CENTER>|<A HREF = "tutorial7.14.4.html">Master Web Page</A>|
<A HREF = "resume.html">Resume</A>|
<A HREF = "professional.html">Professional</A>|
<A HREF = "personal.html">Personal</A>|
</CENTER>
<! Add address>
<ADDRESS>
<CENTER>
<A HREF = "mailto:zeid@coe.neu.edu">Send an e-mail</A>
&#169; 2000 Revised - January 2000
</CENTER>
</ADDRESS>
</BODY>
</HTML>
```

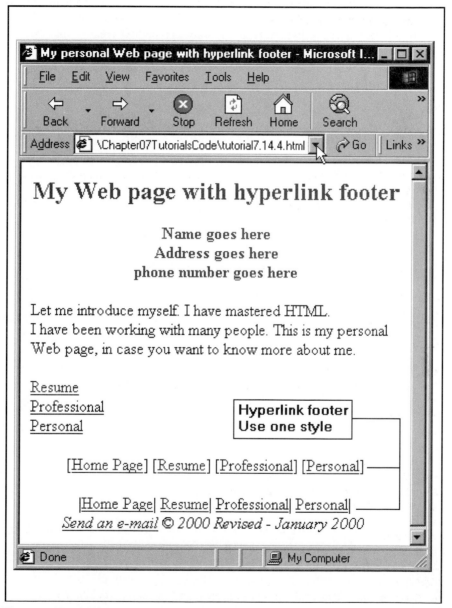

Figure 7.17 A Web page with a hyperlink footer.

7.15 FAQs

Q: What is HTML?

A: HTML is a simple and easy-to-use script to format and create Web pages. Its power stems from two basic concepts: hypertext and markup. Hypertext creates links between Web pages. Markup utilizes tags to format page content.

Q: How has HTML been evolving?

A: HTML was originally developed by Tim Berners-Lee while at CERN, and popularized by the Mosaic browser developed at NCSA in 1993. HTML 2.0 was developed in late 1994, to codify common practice. HTML 3.0 became available in 1995 and proposed much richer versions of HTML. HTML 3.2 was developed in late 1996, to codify common practice, and was released in 1997. HTML 4.0 was developed in 1997 and released in 1998. HTML 4.0 extends HTML with tools for style sheets, scripting, frames, and embodying objects, improved support for text (right-to-left and mixed direction), richer tables and forms, better internationalization of documents (by adopting the ISO/IEC:10646 standard as the document character set for HTML), better accessibility of documents, and easier printing of a Web page and its linked pages (by using the <LINK> tag).

Q: How can one know what version of HTML is used in a Web page?

A: The HTML document of the Web page should declare its version of HTML. A comment statement should be placed before the <HTML> tag, at the top of the HTML document, to declare its HTML version. This *document type declaration* shows the document type definition (DTD) in use by the document. An HTML document should use one of the following three DTDs that HTML 4.0 specifies:

1) The HTML 4.0 strict DTD; this HTML document uses all HTML 4.0 tags except frame tags and deprecated tags. The Web author uses this statement:

```
<!DOCTYPE HTML PUBLIC "-//W3C/DTD HTML 4.0//EN" "http://
www.w3.org/TR/REC-html40/strict.dtd">.
```

2) The HTML 4.0 Transitional DTD; this HTML document uses all HTML 4.0 tags in the strict type, in addition to the deprecated tags, but not the frame tags. the Web author uses this statement:

```
<!DOCTYPE HTML PUBLIC "-//W3C/DTD HTML 4.0 Transitional//EN"
"http://www.w3.org/TR/REC-html40/loose.dtd">.
```

3) The HTML 4.0 frameset DTD; this HTML document uses all HTML 4.0 tags, even the deprecated ones, and the frame tags. The Web author uses this statement:

```
<!DOCTYPE HTML PUBLIC "-//W3C/DTD HTML 4.0 Frameset//EN"
"http://www.w3.org/TR/REC-html40/frameset.dtd">
```

The last two letters, EN, of the declaration shown in the above three types indicate the language of DTD, which is always English for HTML.

Q: Who are the users of HTML?

A: Two distinct groups use HTML: Web authors, and Web implementors. Web authors are those who write Web pages and develop Web sites. Web implementors are those who write rendering engines that read, interpret, and display Web pages. These engines are primarily browsers. Both groups should realize that HTML has its roots in SGML. They should both try to separate the structure of a document from its presentational aspects, to reduce the inconsistency of the document presentation on different platforms and to facilitate future document revisions. One mechanism that achieves such separation elegantly is style sheets. More and more, HTML presentational tags and attributes are being replaced by style sheets.

Q: How could the Web be made more accessible to everyone, especially those with disabilities?

A: Web authors should consider rendering their Web pages on a variety of platforms, such as speech-based browsers and braille readers.

Q: What is incremental rendering of Web pages?

A: This is a way of displaying a Web page in stages, to keep the attention of users as they surf the Internet. HTML 4.0 provides new table features that help browsers render HTML documents more quickly.

Q: How could one keep up with the latest developments of HTML?

A: HTML has been, and still is, going through many changes and revisions. The group that manages the HTML standards is the World Wide Web Consortium or W3C. To find out what is current for HTML, visit their Web site at www.w3.org. You can also search the Web itself, with the aid of search engines. You should be able to find the current specifications, in the form of the HTML DTD, along with online documentation on HTML markup and usage, as well as current information on SGML.

Q: Why is the browser not showing a Web page as it should?

A: In many cases, this happens because of incorrect use of HTML tags, intentionally or unintentionally. A Web author may forget to close a tag, or the author may make a typo mistake. The author should check the HTML code of the page carefully, until all the mistakes are found and corrected. Sometimes, browsers may help the author find the mistakes. For example, Netscape browser sometimes flashes the HTML tags around the area where a mistake is. This happens only if the author views the HTML code of the page by clicking `View => Page Source` on the browser window.

Q: Should the browser provide error messages if HTML code in a Web page is wrong?

A: No, because HTML is not a compiled programming language. The browser has an SGML interpreter that interprets the HTML tags of the Web page. If there are mistakes in using the tags, the browser ignores the tag all together. Thus, the only feedback a Web author receives from the browser is visual. That is, if the author does not get the Web page display as expected from the browser, it means some of the tags are wrong. The author should inspect the HTML code, fix it, and reload the page. This cycle of checking, correcting the HTML code, and reloading the page is repeated as many times as needed, until the page is displayed correctly and as expected.

Q: Why does the browser show the HTML source code of a Web page in its window instead of showing the actual Web page itself?

A: This means that the HTML file is inadvertently saved with the extension *.txt* instead of *.html.* In this case, the browser treats the file as a text file and displays its contents literally. The Web author should resave the file with the *.html* extension or change the existing file extension from *.txt* to *.html.*

Q: Does a browser recognize any formatting, such as indenting and spaces, that a Web author uses in Web page HTML code?

A: No. The browser understands only HTML tags, and it interprets only them. It ignores any other formatting the Web author may use in writing the HTML code of the page. Such manual formatting is a convenience to the readers of the HTML code of the page, especially if the code is too long.

Q: Can I leave spaces inside the brackets of an HTML tag?

A: No. For example, if you write the <B> tag as < B > (one space before B and one after it) or as < B> (one space before it), the browser ignores the tag all together.

Q: Why is the Notepad unable to recognize the .html as a file extension when one is saving an HTML file?

A: By design, the Notepad recognizes the extension *.txt* only. If one tries to save the file as, say, *example4.html*, the Notepad saves it as *example4.html.txt*. There are two solutions to this problem. The first is to rename the file manually from *example4.html.txt* to *example4.html*. The second solution is to associate the file extension *.html* with the Notepad. This has already been done in the FAQs section of chapter 3.

Q: Is it a good idea to use the <BLINK> tag in a Web page?

A: No, because it is a browser dependent. Netscape browser supports it, but not MS IE.

Q: Is it a good idea to use the color attribute of the <HR> tag in a Web page?

A: No, because it is a browser dependent. MS IE supports it, but not Netscape browser. In practice, lines are created as images and then inserted in Web pages.

Q: Is www.xxx.com/tcpip/spec/telnet.html an acceptable URL?

A: Yes. Here is the breakdown of it. *www.xxx.com* is the Web site; *tcpip* is a directory in this Web site; *spec* is a subdirectory of *tcpip*; and *telnet.html* is an HTML file in the *spec* subdirectory.

Q: What is the best way to verify that HTML documents conform to HTML 4.0 DTD?

A: While many Web authors rely on browsers to check that the documents they produce are valid, this method is not very effective, because browsers are forgiving and they have to be backward compatible. For better validation, authors should use an SGML parser, such as `nsg-mls`, to check their documents.

Q: Can a Web author nest links using the <A> or <LINK> tag?

A: No. It is illegal to nest tags in HTML. Links and anchors defined by the <A> or <LINK> tag must not be nested. An <A> tag must not contain another <A> tag.

Q: How can some Web pages display non-English words or statements without using the HREFLANG or CHARSET attributes in the <A> or <LINK> tag?

A: In many such cases, these words or statements are displayed as an image. Web authors scan pre-typed words or statements, store them as .gif or .jpg files, and use them in their Web pages as image files.

Q: Why is the browser unable to display all the links created in an HTML file?

A: The most common reason for this misdisplay is missing the opening or closing quote of the HREF attributes. For example, <A HREF="http://www.xxx.com> causes the browser to ignore displaying this link. For Netscape, if the user clicks the sequence `View => Page Source`, the browser shows the page source with blue flashing text around where the quote is missing. If the Web author closes the quotes and reloads the HTML file, the problem goes away. When it comes to using quotes, the author may use them or not. However, once used, they must be closed. The author may use double quote (") or single quote (').

Q: Why is the browser unable to display the link title when the mouse is placed over the link, despite the use of the TITLE attribute of the <A> tag?

A: This is an implementation issue of HTML specifications. It is browser specific. The TITLE attribute is part of HTML 4.0 specifications. Netscape 4.7 does not render the link title, but MS IE 5.0 does.

Q: What is the <NEXTID> tag and how can I use it?

A: <NEXTID> tag is used to indicate the next document that follows the current one in a logical series of documents. This tag must be used within the <HEAD> tag. It is usually created by HTML editors, although Web authors can insert them manually. The <NEXTID> tag tells search robots used by search engines what the next document is in a series. The only attribute of this tag is N, to specify the URL for the next document in the series — for example,

<NEXTID N = "http://www.xxx.com/myNextDocument.html">. This tag does not have and end (closing) tag.

Q: How could Web authors enhance their Web pages for better indexing and ranking by search engines?

A: Web authors need to realize two facts about search engines and their software that use spiders. First, search engines and their spiders read only text. They cannot see. A picture is worth nothing to a spider. Second, spiders read the contents of the <TITLE> tag and the first several lines or paragraphs of an HTML document. These two facts suggests that the Web author should make the HTML document text-heavy at the top, and only later include images and other MIME types. Here are some specific recommendations.

•Choose a good title.

•Use the <META> tag to provide a description and keywords. Here is an example:

```
<HEAD>
<TITLE>Sports World</TITLE>
<META NAME = "description" CONTENT = "All that you want to know
about the world of sports, from rules to equipment.">
<META NAME = "keywords" CONTENT = "sports, football, basketball,
```

```
hockey, sport memorabilia, trading cards">
</HEAD>
```

A spider reading this HTML document compares the surfer search string with the title or description. If the surfer uses a word search, the spider compares the surfer's words against the keywords of the document. However, the spiders of some search engines (such as Excite) do not honor meta tags.

•When you have JavaScript code as part of the HTML document, add it after the first paragraph or two of text so that the spider can read the text right away.

•Use the header tag <H1> at the top of the HTML document to describe the main topic of the Web page. Use the header tags <H2> and <H3> throughout the document, because spiders use them as an indication of the Web page structure.

•The first paragraph of the Web page should be concise, crisp, and full of keywords. Keep it brief: no more than two or three lines.

•Submit and register the Web page URL with the major search engines. There are automatic submission tools, but tracking the submission and following up is a good idea.

•Promote your Web page by using other traditional marketing tools, such as mailing lists, advertisements, word of mouth, and so forth.

•Link your Web page to other hot links, such as Web sites of professional organizations, user groups, newsgroups, clubs, and so forth.

•If you have many Web pages in your Web site, register the key ones with search engines (although spiders are supposed to index all pages in your site).

•Resubmit your Web pages to search engines any time you make significant changes.

•Consider negotiating reciprocal links with sites that make the top ten hits all the time.

Q: How can one prevent spiders or indexing robots from visiting a sensitive part of a Web site and indexing its pages?

A: There are two levels at which to achieve this prevention: the Web site level, and the Web page level. At the Web site level, there is a file called *robots.txt*. One file is allowed per site. The Web master or administrator places this file at the top director. For example, the Web site http://www.xxx.com has the file path as *http://www.xxx.com/robots.txt*. If spiders find the file, they analyze it to see whether they are allowed to search and index the site Web pages. Web masters may customize the file to allow specific robots or spiders and to disallow access to specific files or directories. Here is a sample *robots.txt* file that prevents all robots from visiting the entire site.

User-agent: *

Disallow: /

The first line applies to all robots, and the second line disallows indexing of all pages. To disallow searching a given directory (say, *myDirectory*), the second line becomes the following:

Disallow: /myDirectory

To disallow indexing the *index.html* in the above directory, we write the following:

Disallow: /myDirectory/

An empty value in the disallow line (i.e. *Disallow:*) indicates that search robots can index the entire Web site. Each *robots.txt* file must have at least one *Disallow* field.

At the Web page level, a Web author can prevent robots from indexing the page by using the <META> tag as follows.

`<META NAME = "robots" CONTENT = "noindex, nofollow">`

The `nofollow` prevents robots from following and analyzing the links in the page. Other values for the CONTENT attribute are `all` and `index`.

Q: What is the significance of the *index.html* (or *index.htm*) file, and how can one use it?

A: This is the default file a browser displays if none is specified during the downloading of a Web site. For example, if a user types www.xxx.com as the URL in the browser URL bar, the browser looks for the file *index.html* or *index.htm* and displays it. If this file does not exist, the browser displays some other default file or the directory structure of www.xxx.com. The *index.html* file can be put to good use. For example, an instructor can create a Web site for a course, say, *MIM1560,* by creating a subdirectory for the course with the name *MIM1560.* In this subdirectory, the instructor creates a file with the name *index.html.* The students taking the course can access the course Web site by typing, say, *www.coe.neu.edu/~zeid/MIM1560* in the browser URL bar. The browser, in turn, downloads the *index.html* Web page that has the course information.

7.16 Summary

Introduction

•Web pages are written using HTML. The two key concepts behind HTML are hypertext and markup. Hypertext links Web pages, and markup embeds special tags in Web pages to structure and format them.

•The MIME (Multipurpose Internet Mail Extensions) format allows the inclusion in Web pages of such non-text content as sounds, images, and video. Common sound formats are RA , SBI, SND, AU, and WAV. Common image formats are GIF, JPEG, and JPG. Common video formats are AVI, MOV, and MPEG (MPG).

Design of Web Pages

•Web page design is crucial to the popularity of the corresponding Web site.

•Web page design should use the power of hypertext to link related information in different documents together.

Markup Language

•HTML code converts a Web page design into an actual Web page that can be viewed within a browser.

•HTML code consists of tags surrounding the Web page content, to format it. The generic form of a tag is <tag_name>...</tag_name>.

•Many HTML tags have attributes to provide more and finer control of the tag formatting results.

Developing HTML Documents

•Web authors may use a text editor or an HTML editor to develop HTML code.

•There are two approaches to developing HTML code: bottom-up and top-down. In the bottom-up approach, the HTML file is generated first, and the Web page is viewed later. In the top-down approach, the Web page is developed first, and the HTML file is generated in the background.

•In the bottom-up approach, the Web author follows these steps:

1. Open a file in a text editor.
2. Enter text and tags.
3. Save the file as text-only, and add the extension .htm or .html.
4. Open the file in a Web browser and review it.
5. Repeat steps 1 through 4 until the Web page takes its final desired form.

•In the top-down approach, the Web author follows these steps:

1. Open an HTML editor.
2. Add elements of the Web page by using the desired HTML icons.
3. Save the automatically generated HTML code of the page.
4. Exit the HTML editor to review the Web page in a a Web browser.
5. Repeat steps 1 through 4 until the Web page takes its final desired form.

•To view a page in a browser, the Web author types its URL in the browser URL bar or drags its file and drops it in the browser window. The Web author can also view a Web page in the Netscape browser by clicking this sequence: File => Open Page => Choose File => browse and click the desired HTML file => Open => Open. The Web author can also view a Web page in MS IE by clicking this sequence: File => open => Browse => browse and click the desired HTML file => Open => OK.

HTML Document Structure

•A well-structured HTML document should have three parts: header, body and footer. The header of an HTML document includes the <HTML>, <HEAD>, and <TITLE> tags. The body includes the <BODY> tag. The footer includes the <ADDRESS> tag.

HTML Tags and Categories

•HTML elements may have a matching start and end tags, for example <HTML> ... </HTML>. Other tags may not close, such as <HR>. Tags may have attributes to allow more control over the tag results.

•The broad categories of HTML tags are structure, text, hyperlinks, lists, colors, images, image maps, sound, video, forms, frames, and tables. These categories are covered throughout the book.

Document Structure Tags

•Document structure tags are <HTML>, <HEAD>, <TITLE>, <BODY>, and <ADDRESS>. With the exception of the <BODY> tag, none of these tags has attributes.

Text and Text Tags

•The text of a Web page is organized into headings (sections), paragraphs, and words.

•Heading tags, in a descending order of text size, are <H1>, <H2>, <H3>, <H4>, <H5>, and <H6>. These tags have the ALIGN attribute, whose values are left (default), center, and right.

•The <P> tag creates paragraphs in a Web page. The <P> tags may or may not be closed using </P>. The <P> tag creates a line space before the text that defines the paragraph. The <P> tag has one attribute: the ALIGN attribute, whose values are left (default), center, and right.

•HTML provides many tags to format characters and words. The tags are <B>, <BASEFONT>, <BIG>, <BLOCKQUOTE>, <BR>, <CENTER>, <CITE>, <CODE>, <EM>, <FONT>, <HR>, <I>, <KBD>, <SMALL>, <STRIKE>, <STRONG>, and <U>. All these tags must be closed (except <HR> and <BR>), and they do not have attributes (with the exception of <BASEFONT>, <FONT>, and <HR>).

•The attribute of the <BASEFONT> tag is SIZE. It takes a value of 1 – 7.

•The attributes of the <FONT> tag are SIZE (takes a value of 1 – 7) and COLOR (takes the name or hex code of any color).

•The attributes of the <HR> tag are ALIGN (takes values of left, center, or right), COLOR, NOSHADE, SIZE (takes a number of pixels), and WIDTH (takes a number of pixels or a percentage of the Web page width).

Links and Link Tags

•The <A> tag creates hyperlinks in documents. It must be closed with </A>.

•The common attributes of the <A> tag are HREF, TITLE, and NAME. The HREF attribute specifies the URL the user goes to when clicking the link. The TITLE and NAME attributes give the link a title and a name respectively.

•Anchors created within documents are used to create tables of contents or to position the displays of Web pages on the screen.

•The <LINK> tag is used to reference external HTML documents in a Web page and to help search engines to access and index the Web page.

•The <LINK> tag is used in the <HEAD> section and does not have an end (closing tag).

•The attributes of the <LINK> tag are HREF, CHARSET, HREFLANG, TYPE, REL, REV, TITLE, LANG, and MEDIA.

•The <BASE> tag allows Web authors to specify a reference URL (path) from which all relative URLs in an HTML document are measured.

•The <BASE> tag must be used in the <HEAD> section. It does not have an end tag. Its only attribute is HREF.

Meta Data and Meta Tag

•The <META> tag allows Web authors to specify the meta data of Web pages. Meta data refers to data about an HTML document rather than the document content. Browsers do not render meta data.

•Meta data is used by search engines for indexing and ranking page hits in a given search.

•The <META> tag must be used in the <HEAD> section. It does not have an end tag.

•The <META> tag attributes are NAME, CONTENT, HTTP-EQUIV, and SCHEME.

Special Characters

•Special characters such as Latin characters and Greek symbols, are represented by certain HTML codes. Special characters are also needed when a Web page must use some of the characters reserved by HTML, such as < or >, as part of its text.

•Special characters in HTML are represented by numeric code. The numeric code begins with &#, followed by numbers, and ends with ;.

•There are three distinct character sets in HTML. The ISO 8859-1 (Latin-1) character set contains the Latin characters. The second character set is the symbols, mathematical symbols, and Greek letters. The third character set is the markup-significant and internationalization characters. These are escaping characters for denoting spaces and dashes.

Building Basic Web Pages

•The best rule to follow in Web page design is to keep it simple.

•The basics to Web page building are content, title and headings, layout, paragraphs, and lists. Organize Web page content logically, so that surfers can follow it easily. Put the most important information at the top of the page, and keep the page length short. Use concise titles and headings for Web pages because they are used by search engines to index Web pages.

•Use the <META> tag to add description keywords to Web pages.

•Break page content into paragraphs of text intermixed with images and hyperlinks. Have plenty of white space throughout the page, to make it easier for visitors to follow its contents.

•The following Web site provides more information about designing and building Web pages; http://info.med.yale.edu/caim/manual/contents.html.

Hierarchy of Web Pages

•The most natural way to organize Web pages in a Web site is to use the web structure. The start of the web is the home page.

•The Web pages are linked together via hyperlinks.

•Adding (deleting) Web pages to (from) a web structure is as simple as adding (deleting) hyperlinks.

•Quick reference of the HTML tags covered in this chapter

Table 7.1 Summary of HTML document structure, text, link, anchor, and meta tags.

Tag	Close	Attribute	Value	Example	Chpt. page
<HTML>	Yes	None	N/A[a]	<HTML>...</HTML>	236
<!....>	No	None	N/A	<! This is a comment>	235
<HEAD>	Yes	PROFILE	url	<HEAD PROFILE = "http:// www.xxx.com/myProfile"> ...</HEAD>	236
<TITLE>	Yes	None	N/A	<TITLE> Page one</TITLE>	236
<BODY>	Yes	See chpt 9	See Chpt. 9	<BODY> Page content and tags go here </BODY>	236
<ADDRESS>	Yes	None	N/A	<ADDRESS> ... </ADDRESS>	237
<H1> - <H6>	Yes	ALIGN	left(def), center, right	<H1 ALIGH = "center"> ...</H1> <H2 ALIGN="right">.</H2>	239
<P>	Yes/ No	ALIGN	left center right	<P> Left is the default <P ALIGN = "center"> ... <P ALIGN = "right"> ...	240
<B>	Yes	None	N/A	<B> Tag bolds text </B>	242
<BASEFONT>	No	SIZE	1 - 7	<BASEFONT SIZE = 4>	242

a.   Not applicable

Tag	Close	Attribute	Value	Example	Chpt. page
<BIG>	Yes	None	N/A	<BIG>Big text here</BIG>	242
<BLOCKQU OTE>	Yes	None	N/A	<BLOCKQUOTE> Quote goes here </BLOCKQUOTE>	242
 	NO	None	N/A	Force a line break 	242
<CENTER>	Yes	None	N/A	<CENTER> Text </CENTER>	242
<CITE>	Yes	None	N/A	<CITE> Cite text </CITE>	242
<CODE>	Yes	None	N/A	<CODE>Comp. code</CODE>	242
<EM>	Yes	None	N/A	<EM>Important text</EM>	242
<FONT>	Yes	SIZE	1 - 7	<FONT SIZE=5>...</FONT>	242
		COLOR	name or hex code	<FONT COLOR="green"> Text goes here </FONT>	
<HR>	No	ALIGN	center, right	<HR ALIGN = "center">	242
		COLOR	name or hex code	<HR COLOR = "green">	
		NOSHADE	None	<HR NOSHADE>	
		SIZE	pixels	<HR SIZE = 15>	
		WIDTH	pixels or %	<HR WIDTH = 70>	
<I>	Yes	None	N/A	<I> Text goes here </I>	242

Tag	Close	Attribute	Value	Example	Chpt. page
<KBD>	Yes	None	N/A	<KBD> Text goes here </KBD>	242
<SMALL>	Yes	None	N/A	<SMALL>Text here</SMALL>	242
<STRIKE>	Yes	None	N/A	<STRIKE> Text </STRIKE>	242
<STRONG>	Yes	None	N/A	<STRIKE> Text </STRIKE>	242
<U>	Yes	None	N/A	<U> Text goes here </U>	242
<A>	Yes	HREF	url	<A HREF="f.html">...</A>	244, 245
		TITLE	text	<A ...TITLE="tt">...</A>	
		NAME	text	<A ... NAME="nn">...</A>	
		CHARSET	set name	<A...CHARSET="..">..</A>	
		TYPE	mime	<A TYPE=text/html>..</A>	
		HRE-FLANG	lang.	<A HREFLANG="fr">...</A>	
		REL	file	<A .. REL="doc.">...</A>	
<LINK>	No	HREF	url	<LINK HREF = "f.html">	254
		TITLE	text	<LINK TITLE="Food page">	
		CHARSET	set name	<LINK CHAARSET="ISO...">	
		TYPE	MIME	<LINK TYPE="text/css">	

Tag	Close	Attribute	Value	Example	Chpt. page
		HRE-FLANG	lang.	`<LINK HREFLANG="fr">`	
		LANG	lang.	`<LINK LANG="fr">`	
		REL	file	`<LINK REL="alternate">`	
		REV	file	`<LINK REV="f.html>`	
		MEDIA	type	`<LINK MEDIA="print">`	
<BASE>	No	HREF	url	`<BASE HREF="www.xx.com">`	255
<META>	No	NAME	text	<META NAME = "keywords">	256
		CON-TENT	text	<META CONTENT="text/html">	
		HTTP-EQUIV	keyword	<META http-equiv="content-type">	
		SCHEME	keyword	<META SCHEME="ISBN">	

PROBLEMS

Exercises

7.1 Extend the home page of tutorial 7.14.1 to include hyperlinks to the remaining pages shown in figure 7.13. They are Family Tree, Community Service, Activities, Favorite Sports, and Favorite Web Sites. Design and write the skeleton Web page for each hyperlink (similar to tutorial 7.14.1).

7.2 Design and write each skeleton Web page in exercise 7.1 fully.

7.3 Add the TITLE attribute to all the link tags of exercises 7.1 and 7.2.

7.4 Add a hyperlink footer to each Web page shown in figure 7.13 and used in exercise 7.1.

7.5 Following tutorial 7.14.2, convert the home Web page of exercise 7.1 from using hyperlinks to using anchors.

7.6 Use the ISO Latin-1 character set to write this statement in a Web page: Borrowing $5000 @ 10% annual rate costs $500 a year.

7.7 Use the ISO Greek character set to write this statement in a Web page: "Here are some Greek fraternities: Phi Kappa Epsilon, Tau Beta Pi, and Gamma Alpha Delta".

Homework

In problems 7.8 – 7.17, write an HTML document and save it in an HTML file.

7.8 Create a template Web page with your own footer by using the <ADDRESS> tag.

7.9 Create your resume Web page. Hint: if you have your resume as an MS WORD document, you can save it as HTML document. While in WORD, click the sequence `File => Save as HTML`.

7.10 Create your personal Web page, using the structure shown in figure 7.13. Use hyperlinks. Use the TITLE attribute in all the <A> tags you use. Also, use a hyperlink footer.

7.11 Convert your personal Web page of problem 7.10 from using hyperlinks to using anchors.

7.12 Create a Web page that uses as many of the ISO Latin-1 characters as possible.

7.13 Create a Web page that uses as many of the ISO Greek characters as possible.

7.14 Write the HTML code that corresponds to the Web page shown in figure 7.18.

7.15 Create a Web page that describes a house. Use the <A> tag with its TITLE attribute, the <HR> tag with its attributes, and as many of the text tags as necessary.

7.16 Repeat problem 1.15, but for a car.

7.17 Use the <BASEFONT> tag in problem 7.9 above. Change fonts in the Web page relative to it. Hint: use <FONT SIZE =+1> or <FONT SIZE =- 2> to increment or decrement the base font size, respectively.

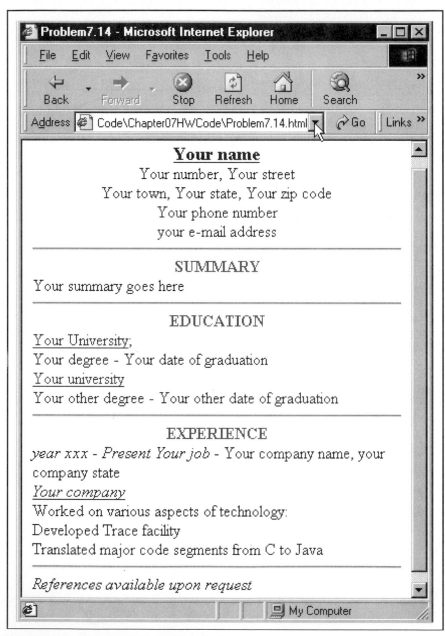

Figure 7.18   Web page for problem 7.14.

Lists and List Tags

T his chapter covers lists, their use in Web pages, their different types, and their tags. HTML offers Web authors three types of lists: unordered list (UL), ordered list (OL), and definition list (DL). The three HTML tags corresponding to these types of lists are <UL>, <OL>, and <DL>, respectively. This chapter covers each tag and its attributes. HTML supports nested lists, a concept that provides Web authors with great flexibility in enhancing Web page design. HTML also allows non-text list items such as hyperlinks.

8.1 Introduction

Lists are an essential element of Web page design. They allow Web authors to specify lines of text in a different way than other text in a page, such as paragraph text. The lines of text, known as list items, are displayed indented in a Web page. Browsers perform the indentation when they execute list tags. Thus, the main purpose of using lists in a Web page is to distinguish certain lines of text from other text, such as paragraphs, via indenting.

The concept of lists is simple, yet powerful. Much text information lends itself to list style naturally. For example, lists could be used to describe the following:

•**Components of a product.** Considering the configuration of a PC, the items of a list would include the CPU (RAM), the hard disk, the monitor, the keyboard, the modem, the printer, and so forth.

•**Steps of a procedure.** The items of a list could be the steps of, say, installing computer hardware and software components.

•**Assembly instructions.** A list could be an instruction set, such as for assembling the components of a product in a do-it-yourself catalog.

•**Tasks of a plan.** The leader of a group may list the tasks and the subtasks needed to achieve, say, certain productivity gains or financial goals.

•**Organizational structure.** The organizational structure of an entity, such as a company or department, can be presented in a Web page via a list.

•**Hierarchical structure.** Lists can display hierarchical structures of, say, a family tree, animal tree, plant tree, directory structure, and so forth.

8.2 Types of Lists

HTML supports three types of lists. They are the unordered list, the ordered list, and the definition list. The unordered list is used to itemize information whose order is insignificant or which has no order. An example is listing the ingredients of a recipe or the components of a car. The ordered list is used to itemize information whose order is important and should be emphasized. An example is listing the steps of a recipe or the steps to tune up a car engine. The definition list is used when one would like to define certain terms. The definition list usually consists of term/definition pairs.

A definition list does not have to be used literally for definitions. It may have other applications for formatting purposes. For one, it can be used to organize advertising information. For example, a sports club may list the benefits of membership in the club in a term/definition format. The term could be "low monthly fee", and the definition could be "for as low as $50 a month, you get access to all the club facilities 7 days a week"; or the term could be "Make new friends", and the definition could be "With over 500 members of the club, and with our weekend group events and parties, you are certain to meet new people and make new friends."

A definition list can also be used for marking up dialogs, with each term naming a person, and each definition containing that person's speech.

HTML provides three tags that implement the three types of lists. They are <UL>, <OL>, and <DL> for unordered list, ordered list, and definition list, respectively. While these tags do not have attributes themselves, the tags of their items have attributes that allow Web authors to control display: namely, symbols of list items. Lists are distinguished from other text in the Web page in two ways: indentation, and list symbol. Web authors have no control over the amount of indentation. This is controlled by the browser displaying the Web page. The authors can, however, control the symbols of list items they create by using the attributes of the lists' tags. HTML provides certain symbols that the authors can choose from, as described here.

8.2.1 <UL> Tag

The <UL> tag creates an unordered list. The tag must be closed. Thus, an unordered list begins with the <UL> tag and ends with the </UL> tag. The <UL> tag has no attributes. The elements or items of a list are created via the <LI> (list item) tag. The <LI> tag may or may not be closed. The attributes of the <LI> tag vary with whether the type of list is <UL> or <OL>. For <UL> lists, the <LI> tag has two attributes: TYPE, and COMPACT. The TYPE attribute specifies the symbol to be displayed for the list item. The three possible values of the TYPE attribute are disc (solid or filled-in circle), square (solid or filled-in square), and circle (hollow or outline circle). The default value depends on the browser and on the level of nesting. (See section 8.3 on list nesting.)

The COMPACT attribute is a Boolean attribute that tells the browser to render the list in a more compact way. The interpretation of this attribute depends on the browser. In many cases, this attribute does not make a difference in rendering lists, and it is not used often.

Example 8.1 Develop a Web page that illustrates the use of unordered lists.

Solution This example creates a Web page with two unordered lists. The first list does not use any attribute to replace the default symbol the browser uses to render lists in a Web page. The second list uses the TYPE attribute of the <LI> tag to control the symbol. The third list uses the COMPACT attribute of the <LI> tag, to show its effect. When using the <LI> tag, we do not need to use the <BR> tag to force a new line; the <LI> tag does it automatically. Using a text editor, type the code that follows, and save it as *example8.1.html*. View the page in a browser. Figures 8.1 and 8.2 show the resulting Web page.

```
<HTML>
<HEAD>
<TITLE>A Web page with unordered lists</TITLE>
</HEAD>
<BODY>
<H2><B><CENTER><FONT COLOR = "blue">Web page with three unordered
lists</FONT></CENTER></B></H2>

<! List uses default list symbols>
Here is my first unordered list
<UL>
    <LI>First list item
    <LI>Second list item
    <LI>Third list item
    <LI>Fourth list item
</UL>

<! List controls list symbols>
Here is my second unordered list
<UL>
    <LI TYPE = "disc">List item using the disc symbol
    <LI TYPE = "circle">List item using the circle symbol
    <LI TYPE = "square">List item using the square symbol
    <LI>List item using no TYPE attribute
</UL>
</BODY>
</HTML>
```

In the preceding code, we show the <LI> tag indented for ease of following and debugging the HTML code. The browser ignores any formatting shown in HTML files unless it is specified by tags. Figures 8.1 and 8.2 show the resulting Web page as rendered by Netscape Communicator 4.7 and by MS IE 5.0. Both browsers use the disc symbol as the default, as shown in the items of the first list. However, they differ in which symbol they use after the Web author uses the TYPE attribute of the <LI> tag. If a Web author does not specify a TYPE attribute for a list item, Netscape Communicator uses the last symbol (square) specified by the attribute, but MS IE uses the default symbol (the disc).

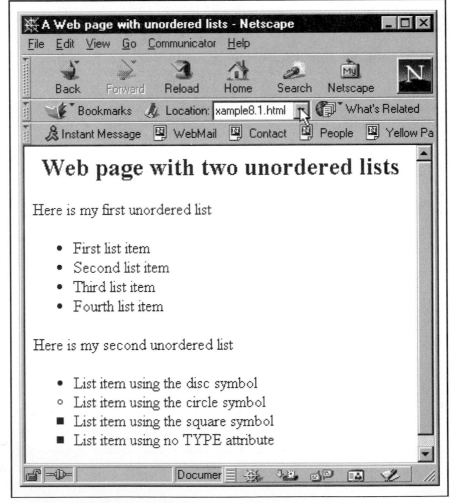

Figure 8.1   Rendering unordered lists in Netscape Communicator.

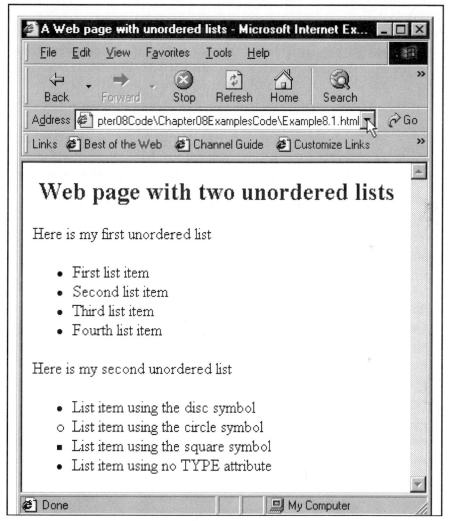

Figure 8.2   Rendering unordered lists in MS IE.

8.2.2   <OL> Tag

The <OL> tag creates an ordered list. The tag is very similar to the <UL> tag. It must be closed. Thus, an ordered list begins with the <OL> tag and ends with the </OL> tag. The <OL> tag has no attributes. The elements or items of a list are created via the <LI> (list item) tag. The <LI> tag may or may not be closed. The <LI> tag has four attributes: TYPE, START, VALUE, and COMPACT. The TYPE attribute specifies the order (numbering) style of the list to be displayed for the list item. The possible values of the TYPE attribute are Arabic numbers (1, 2, 3, etc.), uppercase/lowercase Latin letters (A, B, C, ..., a, b, c, etc.), and uppercase/lowercase Roman numerals (I, II, III, ..., i, ii, iii, etc.). The default value is the Arabic numbers.

The START attribute allows the Web author to control the start number of list items. For example, the Web author may want to assign the first item on a list the Arabic number 6. The START attribute is not supported by current browsers. The VALUE attribute overrides the numbering sequence. For example, the Web author may want to assign a list item a number out of sequence, such as 5 following number 3. The VALUE attribute is not supported by current browsers.

The COMPACT attribute is the same as that of the <UL> tag. It is a Boolean attribute that tells the browser to render the list in a more compact way. The interpretation of this attribute depends on the browser. In many cases, this attribute does not make a difference in rendering lists, and it is not used often.

Example 8.2 Develop a Web page that illustrates the use of ordered lists.

Solution This example creates a Web page with three ordered lists. The first list does not use any attribute, to show that browsers use the Arabic numbers as the default. The second list uses the TYPE attribute of the <LI> tag to impose the Latin letters. The third list uses the same attribute to impose the Roman numerals. Using a text editor, type the code that follows, and save it as *example8.2.html*. View the page in a browser. Figures 8.3 and 8.4 show the resulting Web page.

```
<HTML>
<HEAD>
<TITLE>A Web page with ordered lists</TITLE>
</HEAD>
<BODY>
<H2><B><CENTER><FONT COLOR = "blue">Web page with three ordered
lists</FONT></CENTER></B></H2>

<! List uses default list numbers>
This ordered list uses Arabic (default) numbers
<OL>
    <LI>First list item
    <LI>Second list item
    <LI>Third list item
    <LI>Fourth list item
</OL>

<! List uses uppercase Latin letters>
This ordered list uses uppercase Latin letters
<OL>
    <LI TYPE = "A">List item using uppercase Latin letter
    <LI>List item using uppercase Latin letter
```

```
    <LI>List item using uppercase Latin letter
    <LI>List item using uppercase Latin letter
</OL>
```

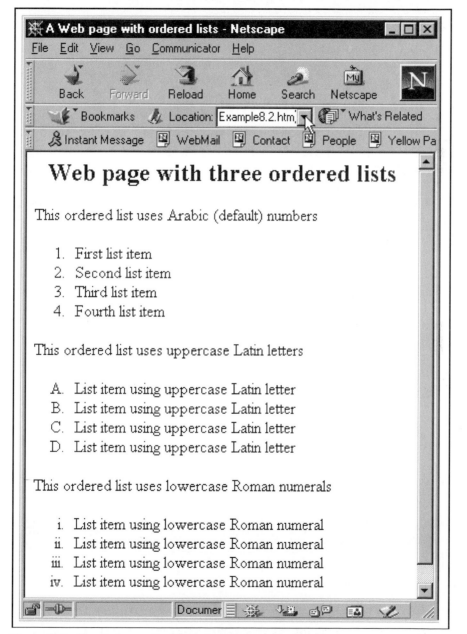

Figure 8.3 Rendering ordered lists in Netscape Communicator.

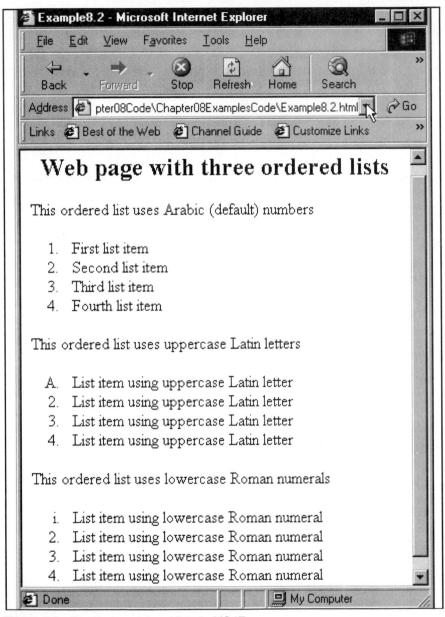

Figure 8.4   Rendering ordered lists in MS IE.

```
<! List uses lowercase Roman numerals>
This ordered list uses lowercase Roman numerals
<OL>
    <LI TYPE = "i">List item using lowercase Roman numeral
```

```
    <LI>List item using lowercase Roman numeral
    <LI>List item using lowercase Roman numeral
    <LI>List item using lowercase Roman numeral
  </OL>
  </BODY>
  </HTML>
```

NOTE: After experimenting with all the attributes of the <LI> tag and their values, we realize that neither Netscape Communicator of MS IE supports the START and the VALUE attributes. For the TYPE attribute, only the first <LI> tag in the list should use it. The VALUE for it should be A, a, I, or i. Any other values do not work. In addition, MS IE does not render the lists correctly as shown in figure 8.4.

8.2.3 <DL> Tag

The <DL> tag creates a definition list. The tag must be closed. Thus, a definition list begins with the <DL> tag and ends with the </DL> tag. The <DL> tag has no attributes. The definition list differ from the other two types of lists. It consists of term/definition (or term/ description) pairs. Thus, two tags are required to build the list. They are the <DT> (definition term) tag that specifies the term to be defined, and the <DD> (definition description) tag that describes the term. Both tags may be closed. Web authors use as many <DT>/<DD> pairs as the number of terms they need to define in a definition list.

Example 8.3 Develop a Web page that illustrates the use of definition lists.

Solution This example creates a Web page with two defintion lists displayed in two styles. The first list uses the <DT> and <DD> tags in pairs; a <DT> tag is followed by a <DD> tag. The second list uses a number of <DT> tags followed by the same number of <DD> tags. Using a text editor, type the code that follows and save it as *example8.3.html*. View the page in a browser. Figures 8.5 shows the resulting Web page. Netscape Communicator and MS IE render the definition list identically to each other.

As shown in the HTML code below, there are two ways to use the <DT>/<DD> pairs. One way is to use a <DT> tag followed by its corresponding <DD> tag. The top list shown in figure 8.5 is the result of this approach. The other way is to use a sequence of <DT> tags, followed by a sequence of the corresponding <DD> tags. The bottom list shown in figure 8.5 is the result of this approach. The browser renders the page from the top to the bottom, so the results of the two ways are different. The first list shown in the top of the Web page shown in figure 8.5 is what we would expect as a definition list. Each term is followed by its definition. This makes it easier to follow and understand the list. The second list shows all the terms to be defined first, followed by their definitions. This organization is more difficult to follow and does not adhere to the conventional wisdom on defining terms. Obviously, while mixing the two ways is possible in theory to build definition lists, it is not recommended to use in Web page design as it is very confusing.

```
<HTML>
<HEAD>
<TITLE>A Web page with definition lists</TITLE>
</HEAD>
<BODY>
<H2><B><CENTER><FONT COLOR = "blue">Web page with two definition
lists</FONT></CENTER></B></H2>

<! List uses DT/DD pairs>
This definition list uses DT/DD pairs.

<DL>
    <DT>Term1
    <DD>Here is the definition of the first term
    <DT>Term2
    <DD>Here is the definition of the second term
    <DT>Term3
    <DD>Here is the definition of the third term
</DL>

<! List uses DT, DT, DT followed by DD, DD, DD>
This definition list uses DT, DT, DT followed by DD, DD, DD.

<DL>
    <DT>Term1
    <DT>Term2
    <DT>Term3
    <DD>Here is the definition of the first term
    <DD>Here is the definition of the second term
    <DD>Here is the definition of the third term
</DL>

</BODY>
</HTML>
```

8.3 Nested Lists

Web authors may need to nest lists to represent multiple levels of hierarchies. The authors may nest lists of the same type or of various types. The three types of lists (unordered, ordered, and definition) may be nested together. The only rule of nesting is dictated by the Web page design. HTML allows multiple levels of nesting, but we seldom use more than two or three levels of nesting. When we nest lists, we make one item or more in a list an entire new list. Thus, we can think of the first list as the main list. The second list which makes an item of the main list, is viewed as a sublist. The main list and the sublist form two levels of nesting. If we make one item or more of the sublist another entire new list, we create a third level of nesting. The main list has a sublist, and the sublist has a sublist in itself.

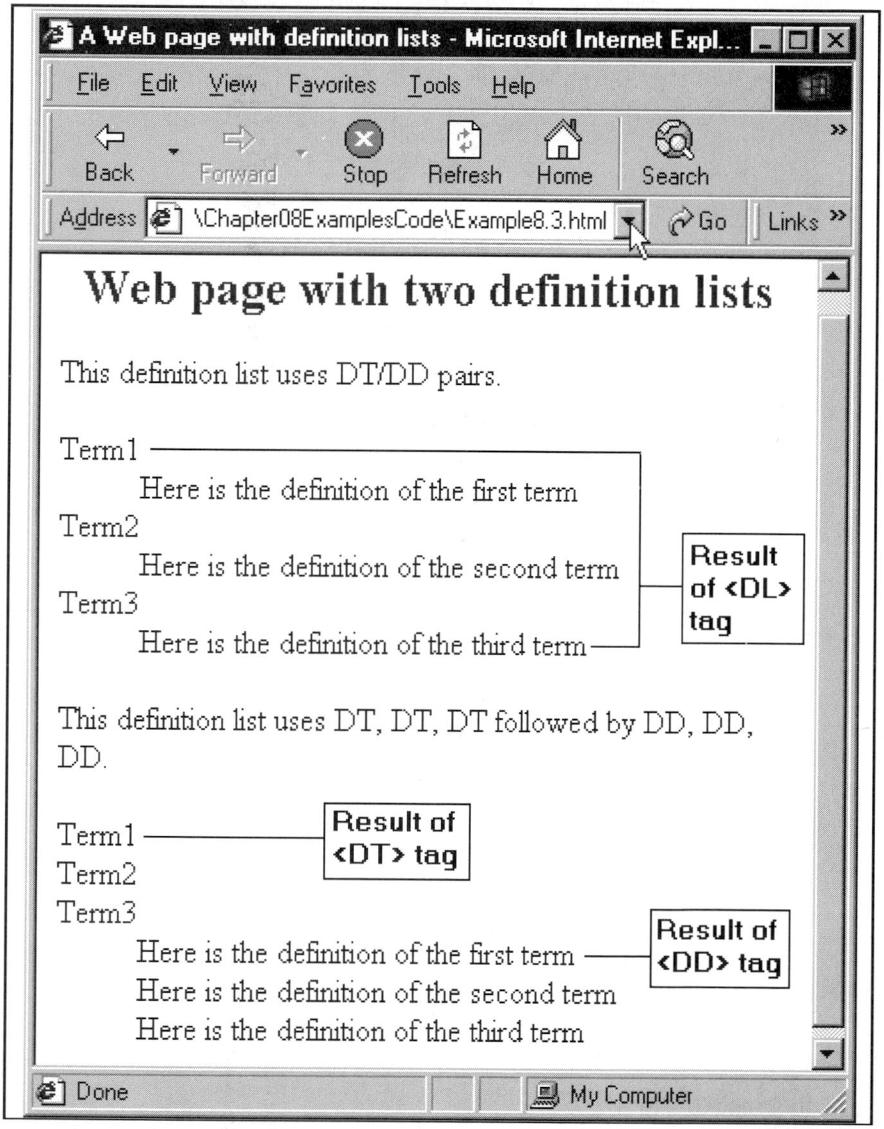

Figure 8.5 Definition list tags.

Example 8.4 Develop a Web page that illustrates the use of nested lists.

Solution This example creates a Web page with three nested lists (i.e. three levels of nesting). The first-level list is an unordered list and has four items. The second-level list is an ordered list and has four items. The third-level list is an unordered list and has three items. None of the lists uses any attributes. Using a text editor, type the code that follows, and save it as *example8.4.html*. It is advisable to indent the list tags when typing the code, to make it easier to follow the beginning and end of these tags. View the page in a browser. Figure 8.6 shows the resulting Web page. As shown in the figure, the browser alternates the symbols of the unordered lists automatically, without using the TYPE attribute, for better visualization of the lists and the items that belong to them.

```
<HTML>
<HEAD>
<TITLE>A Web page with nested lists</TITLE>
</HEAD>
<BODY>
<H2><B><CENTER><FONT COLOR = "blue">Web page with three nested
lists</FONT></CENTER></B></H2>

<! List uses default list symbols>
Here is my three-level nested list

<UL>
    <LI>First-level list item 1
    <LI>First-level list item 2

        <OL>
         <LI>Second-level list item 1
         <LI>Second-level list item 2
         <LI>Second-level list item 3

         <UL>
             <LI>Third-level list item 1
             <LI>Third-level list item 2
             <LI>Third-level list item3
         </UL>

         <LI>Second-level list item 4
        </OL>

    <LI>First-level list item 3

        <DL>
         <DT>Term1
         <DD>Definition Term 1
         <DT>Term2
         <DD>Definition of Term 2
         <DT>Term3
         <DD>Definition of Term 3
```

```
        </DL>

    <LI>First-level list item 4
</UL>

</BODY>
</HTML>
```

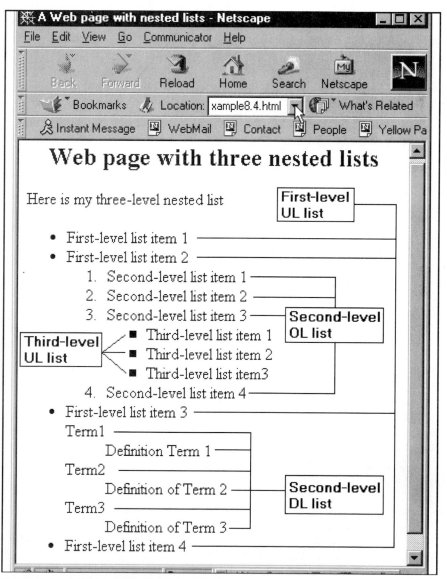

Figure 8.6   A Web page with nested lists.

8.4 Formatting via List Tags

Web authors may use list tags for formatting Web pages. List tags are used primarily to indent a Web page element, such as text. Many list tags result in indentations that are equivalent to tabs. Thus, one can think of using a list tag as using the tab key on the keyboard. The tags that produce indentation effect are <UL>, <OL>, and <DD>. Nesting or combining these tags produce the effect of multiple indentations of the text that they enclose.

While using list tags for formatting Web pages may seem a good idea, it is not recommended in practice. If Web authors need to format Web pages and control their layout, they should use tables instead. Tables provide more formatting control. Using tables for formatting is covered in detail at the end of this part of the book.

Example 8.5 Develop a Web page that illustrates the use of list tags for formatting.

Solution This example is based on the observation that list tags produce indentation effect. The tags that can be used for formatting are <UL>, <OL>, <DL>, <DT> and <DD>. The <LI> tag is not normally used, because it does not indent. It only produces the list symbol. The <DT> tag does not indent either, as shown in the example. Readers are encouraged to use these tags individually, to experience their individual effects.

The example creates a Web page that uses the <UL>, <DT>, and <DD> tags for formatting. These tags are used individually or are nested within each other. Each level of indentation corresponds to one indentation (tab). For example, nesting a <DD> tag inside a <UL> tag produce the effect of two indentations, one by each tag. Nesting a tag, say <UL>, within itself also produces multiple indentations. Using a text editor, type the code that follows, and save it as *example8.5.html*. It is advisable to indent the list tags when typing the code, to make it easier to follow the beginning and end of these tags. View the page in a browser. Figure 8.7 shows the resulting Web page.

```
<HTML>
<HEAD>
<TITLE>Indenting via list tags</TITLE>
</HEAD>
<BODY>
<H2><B><CENTER><FONT COLOR = "blue">Text indentation via list tags
</FONT></CENTER></B></H2>
Here is my formatted text

<! Using the DT tag does not indent text>
<P>
<FONT COLOR = "red">Using the DT tag does not indent text</FONT>
<DT>This text is indented by a DT tag
<DT>This text is indented by a DT tag
```

```
<! Using the DD tag indents text once>
<P>
<FONT COLOR = "red">Using the DD tag indents text once</FONT>
<DD>This text is indented by a DD tag
<DD>This text is indented by a DD tag


<! Nesting the UL and the DD tags indents text twice>
<P>
<FONT COLOR = "red">Nesting the UL and the DD tags indents text
twice</FONT>
<UL>
<DD>This text is indented by
<DD>a UL tag and a DD tag.
<DD>This text is indented by
<DD>a UL tag and a DD tag.
</UL>


<! Nesting the UL tag 5 times indents text 5 times>
<P>
<FONT COLOR = "red">Nesting the UL tag 5 times indents text 5
times</FONT>
<UL>
    <UL>
        <UL>
            <UL>
          <UL>
          This text is indented by<BR>
          nesting five UL tags.
            </UL>
                </UL>
            </UL>
        </UL
</UL>


</BODY>
</HTML>
```

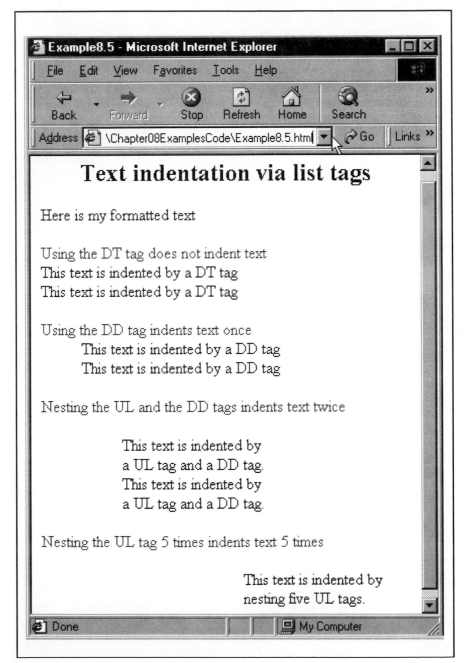

Figure 8.7   Text indenting via list tags.

8.5 Nontext List Items

Items of a list are traditionally text. HTML allows Web authors to use any Web page element as a list item. This is a powerful concept. A list item could, therefore, be a hyperlink, an image, an audio, a video, and so forth. Web authors are not limited to text only. In developing a list with nontext items, Web authors simply use the tag that create the nontext element. For example, we use the <A> tag following an <LI> tag to create a hyperlink for the list item.

Example 8.6 Develop a Web page that illustrates the use of list tags for formatting.

Solution This example creates lists with hyperlinks as list items. The Web page of the example has three lists. The first list has the traditional text items. The second list has all hyperlink items. The third list uses a mix of both types of items. Using a text editor, type the code that follows, and save it as *example8.6.html*. It is advisable to indent the list tags when typing the code, to make it easier to follow the beginning and end of these tags. View the page in a browser. Figure 8.8 shows the resulting Web page.

```
<HTML>
<HEAD>
<TITLE>Nontext list items</TITLE>
</HEAD>
<BODY>
<H2><B><CENTER><FONT COLOR = "blue">Creating nontext list items
</FONT></CENTER></B></H2>
Here are my nontext list items

<! Create a traditional list>
<P>
<FONT COLOR = "red">This is a traditional list</FONT>

<UL>
        <LI>Traditional list item
        <LI>Traditional list item
        <LI>Traditional list item
</UL>

<! Create a list with hyperlink items>
<P>
<FONT COLOR = "red">List with hyperlinks</FONT>

<OL>
        <LI><A HREF = "http://www.neu.edu">Northeastern Univer-
sity</A>
        <LI><A HREF = "http://www.prenhall.com">Prentice Hall pub-
lishing</A>
```

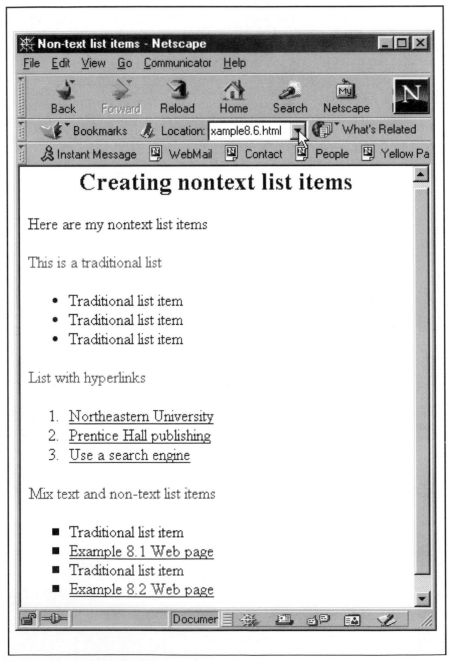

Figure 8.8   Creating hyperlink list items.

```
        <LI><A HREF = "http://www.altavista.com">Use a search
engine</A>
</OL>

<! Mix text and nontext list items>
<P>
<FONT COLOR = "red">Mix text and nontext list items</FONT>

<UL>
        <LI TYPE = "square">Traditional list item
        <LI><A HREF = "Example8.1.html">Example 8.1 Web page</A>
        <LI>Traditional list item
        <LI><A HREF = "Example8.2.html">Example 8.2 Web page</A>
</UL>

</BODY>
</HTML>
```

8.6 Tutorials

This section focuses on using the list tags covered in this chapter. Any Web browser can be used to display the corresponding Web pages. However, users should be aware of the differences, already discussed in this chapter, in how Netscape Communicator and MS IE render lists in Web pages. It is a good idea to create a directory structure to save HTML files. This helps Web authors to organize HTML files and makes it easy to find them.

8.6.1   Using a Definition List for Marketing

An interesting and non-traditional use of a definition list is to use it for marketing and advertising on the Web. A Web author could use the <DT> tag to display key marketing ideas, and use the <DD> tag to elaborate each of these ideas. Using a text editor, type the code that follows, and save it as *tutorial8.6.1.html*. View the page in a browser. Figure 8.9 shows the resulting Web page.

```
<HTML>
<HEAD>
<TITLE>Using definition List for marketing</TITLE>
</HEAD>
<BODY>
<H2><B><CENTER><FONT COLOR = "blue">Welcome to Virtual Sports Club
</FONT></CENTER></B></H2>

<P>Summer is fast approaching. Our team has been<BR>
working hard designing and developing an exciting<BR>
membership program. Here are the program highlights.
```

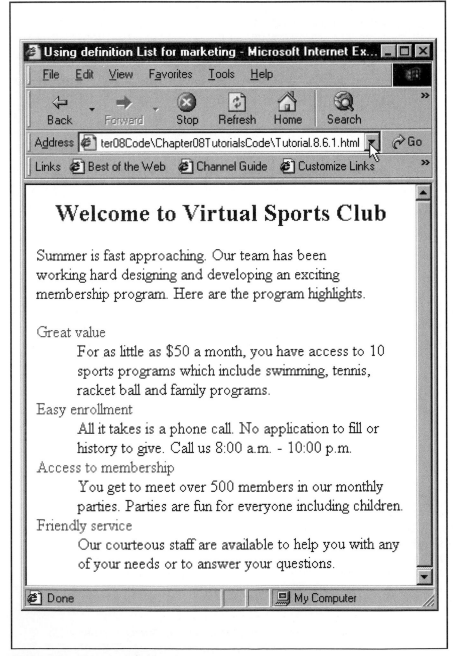

Figure 8.9   Using a definition list for marketing.

```
<! Use a DL list>

<DL>
        <DT><FONT COLOR = "red">Great value</FONT>
        <DD>For as little as $50 a month, you have access to 10
sports programs which include swimming, tennis, racket ball and
family programs.
        <DT><FONT COLOR = "red">Easy enrollment</FONT>
        <DD>All it takes is a phone call. No application to fill or
history to give. Call us 8:00 a.m. - 10:00 p.m.
        <DT><FONT COLOR = "red">Access to membership</FONT>
        <DD>You get to meet over 500 members in our monthly par-
ties. Parties are fun for everyone including children.
        <DT><FONT COLOR = "red">Friendly service</FONT>
        <DD>Our courteous staff are available to help you with any
of your needs or to answer your questions.
</DL>

</BODY>
</HTML>
```

8.6.2 Using a Definition List for Marking Up Dialogs

This tutorial shows another nontraditional use of a definition list. A list is used to record a conversation between an instructor and a student. Using a text editor, type the code that follows, and save it as *tutorial8.6.2.html*. View the page in a browser. Figure 8.10 shows the resulting Web page.

```
<HTML>
<HEAD>
<TITLE>Using definition List for marking up dialogs</TITLE>
</HEAD>
<BODY>
<H2><B><CENTER><FONT COLOR="blue">Recording Instructor/student chat
</FONT></CENTER></B></H2>
<P>A conversation takes place in a classroom<BR>
between an instructor and a student.<BR>
The conversation is recorded in this Web page.
<! Use a DL list>
<DL>
        <DT><FONT COLOR = "red">Student</FONT>
        <DD>Execuse me Professor; I have a question.
        <DT><FONT COLOR = "red">Professor</FONT>
        <DD>Certainly; what is the question?
        <DT><FONT COLOR = "red">Student</FONT>
        <DD>How can you change text color in HTML?
        <DT><FONT COLOR = "red">Instructor</FONT>
```

```
            <DD>You can use the FONT tag or style sheets.
            <DT><FONT COLOR = "red">Student</FONT>
            <DD>Thank you Professor.
            <DT><FONT COLOR = "red">Professor</FONT>
            <DD>You are welcome.
    </DL>
    </BODY>
    </HTML>
```

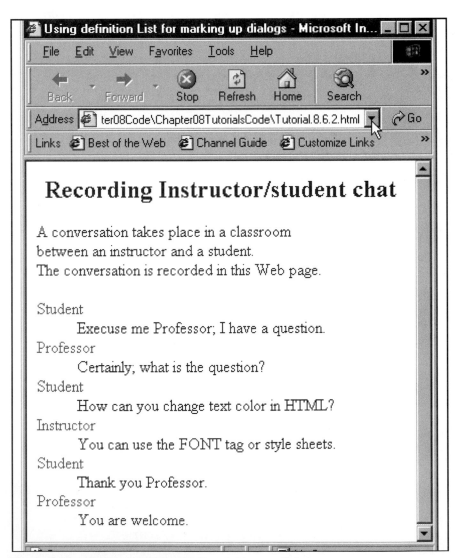

Figure 8.10   Using a definition list for marking up dialogs.

8.6.3 Organization Hierarchical Structure

This tutorial uses nested lists to create the structure of a typical university college. We use a mix of UL and OL lists. Using a text editor, type the code that follows, and save it as *tutorial8.6.3.html*. View the page in a browser. Figure 8.11 shows the resulting Web page.

```
<HTML>
<HEAD>
<TITLE>Organization structure</TITLE>
</HEAD>
<BODY>
<H2><B><CENTER><FONT COLOR = "blue">Organization structure of
a college</FONT></CENTER></B></H2>
<P>Here is the structure of a college in a university

<! First-level UL list>
<UL>
        <LI>Dean's office

<!Second-level UL list>
        <UL>
            <LI TYPE = "square">Dean
            <LI>Associate dean
            <LI>Assistant dean
            <LI>Staff

<! Third-level OL list>
          <OL>
            <LI>Staff 1
            <LI>Staff 2
            <LI>Staff 3
          </OL>
        </UL>
        <LI>Department

<! Second-level OL list>
        <OL>
            <LI>Chairman
            <LI>Associate chairman
            <LI>Faculty

<! Third-level UL list>
        <UL>
            <LI>Group 1
            <LI>Group 2
            <LI>Group 3
        </UL>
```

```
        <LI>Staff
        <LI>Graduate students
        <LI>Undergraduate students
     </OL>

</UL>
</BODY>
</HTML>
```

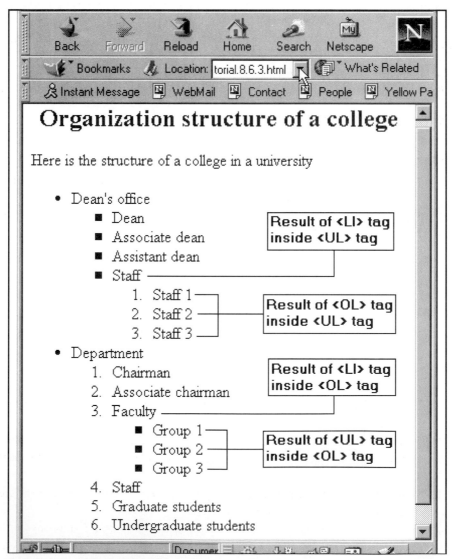

Figure 8.11   Creating an organization structure via list tags.

8.7 FAQs

Q: Why does my browser not display the lists as I expect?

A: This is usually due to the improper closing of the list tags, especially for nested lists. Check all the list tags, and make sure they are closed at the right locations.

Q: What is the difference between ordered and unordered lists?

A: Both types are rendered in an identical manne,r except that browsers use numbers for items of ordered lists and symbols for items of unordered lists.

Q: Can an ordered list continue list numbering automatically from a previous list?

A: No. Ordered lists cannot hide numbering of some list items, either.

Q: How can I get better control of list formatting, for example numbering, indenting, and so forth.?

A: Style sheets allow better control of list formatting.

8.8 Summary

Introduction

•Lists allow Web authors to organize and indent text in Web pages. Browsers perform the indentation when they execute list tags.

•Lists could be used to describe components of a product, steps of a procedure, tasks of a plan, organizational structure of an entity, and hierarchical structures.

Types of Lists

•HTML supports three types of lists: ordered, unordered, and definition.

•Ordered lists are used to itemize information whose order is important. Items of an ordered list are sequenced with Arabic numerals, alphabetical characters, or Roman numerals.

•Unordered lists are used to itemize information whose order is insignificant or useless. Items of an unordered list are designated by one of three symbols: disc, square, or circle.

•Definition lists are used to define certain terms. The definition list usually consists of term/definition pairs. It can be used for non-traditional cases, such as marketing and dialogs.

•The three HTML list tags are <UL>, <OL>, and <DL>.

•The <LI> (list item) tag is used with both <UL> and <OL> tags. Its attributes are TYPE and COMPACT when it is used with the <UL> tag, TYPE, START, VALUE, and COMPACT when it is used with the <OL> tag.

•The values of the TYPE attribute are disc, square, and circle for <UL>, Arabic numerals, alphabetical characters, and Roman numerals for <OL>.

•The values of the START and VALUE attributes of the <LI> tag are numbers.

•The two tags used with the <DL> tag are <DT> (definition term) and <DD> (definition description).

Nested Lists

•The three types of lists may be nested together. HTML allows multiple levels of nesting, but we seldom use more than two or three levels of nesting.

Formatting via List Tags

•Web authors may use list tags to indent a Web page element, such as text. Many list tags result in indentations that are equivalent to tabs. Nesting or combining these tags produces the effect of multiple indentations of the text that they enclose.

Nontext List Items

•Nontext list items are supported by HTML. A list item could be a hyperlink, an image, an audio, a video, and so forth.

•Quick reference of the HTML tags covered in this chapter

Table 8.1   Summary of HTML list tags.

Tag	Close	Attribute	Value	Example	Chpt. page
<UL>	Yes	None	N/A[a]	<UL> . . . </UL>	292
<OL>	Yes	None	N/A	<OL> . . . </OL>	295
<DL>	Yes	None	N/A	<DL> ...</DL>	299
<LI>	No	TYPE(for UL)	disk	<LI TYPE = "disc">	292 293
			square	<LI TYPE = "square">	
			circle	<LI TYPE = "circle">	
		TYPE(for OL)	letter	<LI TYPE = "A">	295 296
			roman	<LI TYPE = "I">	
		COM-PACT	boolean	<LI COMPACT= true>	
		START (for OL)	number	<LI START= 4>	
		VALUE (for OL)	number	<LI VALUE = 7>	
<DT>	No	None	N/A	<DT>Term 1	299
<DD>	No	None	N/A	<DD>Definition 1	299

a.   Not applicable

PROBLEMS

Exercises

8.1   Create an unordered list of the names of 10 people.

8.2   Create an ordered list of the top 10 winners of your favorite competition.

8.3   Create a definition list of the following terms: Internet, Intranet, Extranet, POP, IP address, TCP/IP, browser, search engine, and metasearch engine.

8.4   Create a nested list of two levels. The first level is an unordered list of 3 items, and the second level has three ordered lists; one list for each item of the unordered list. The unordered list items are winning categories — for example, best design, best effort, and best attitude. Each nested ordered list has 3 names of winners, for first, second, and third places.

Homework

In problems 8.5 – 8.15, write an HTML document and save it in an HTML file.

8.5   Redesign your personal Web page you developed in chapter 7 to include the three types of lists: unordered, ordered, and definition. Use hyperlink list items in your new design.

8.6   Find an innovative application for a definition list similar to that in tutorial 8.6.1. Use hyperlinks in the definition.

8.7   Use a definition list for marking up dialogs between three people.

8.8   Use nested lists to create your family tree. Use hyperlinks as list items.

8.9   Write the HTML code to generate the list shown in figure 8.12.

8.10 Write the HTML code to generate the list shown in figure 8.13.

8.11 Write the HTML code to generate the list shown in figure 8.14.

8.12 Write the HTML code to generate the list shown in figure 8.15.

8.13 Write the HTML code to generate the list shown in figure 8.16.

8.14 Write the HTML code to generate the list shown in figure 8.17.

8.15 Write the HTML code to generate the list shown in figure 8.18.

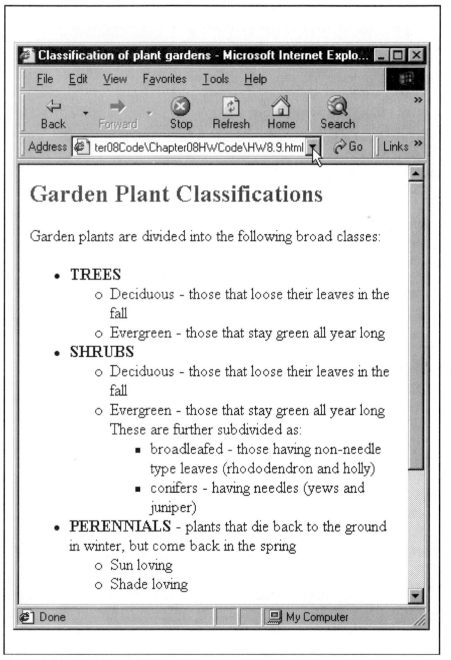

Figure 8.12   Problem 8.9.

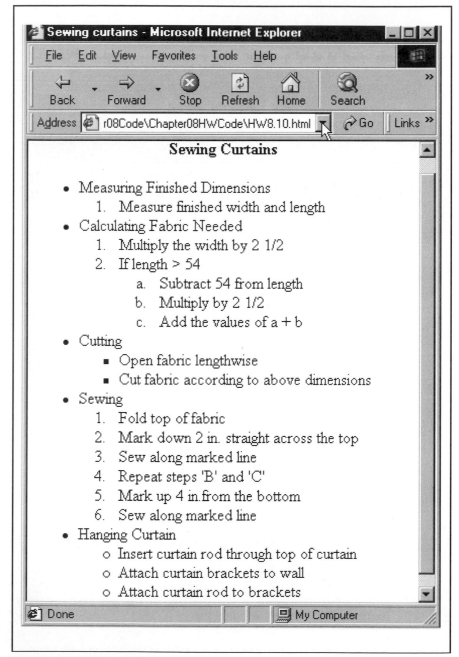

Figure 8.13 Problem 8.10.

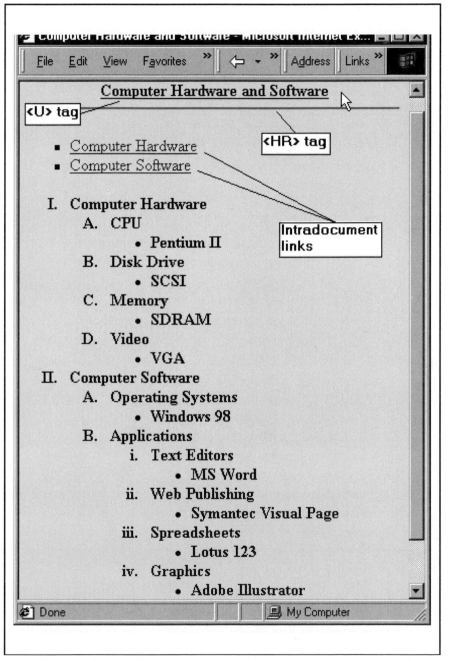

Figure 8.14 Problem 8.11.

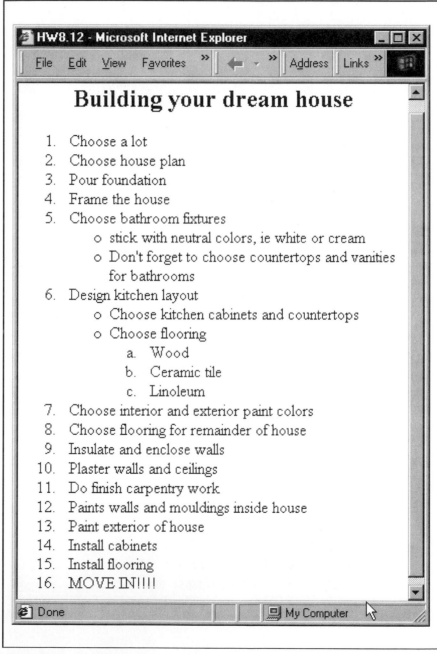

Figure 8.15   Problem 8.12.

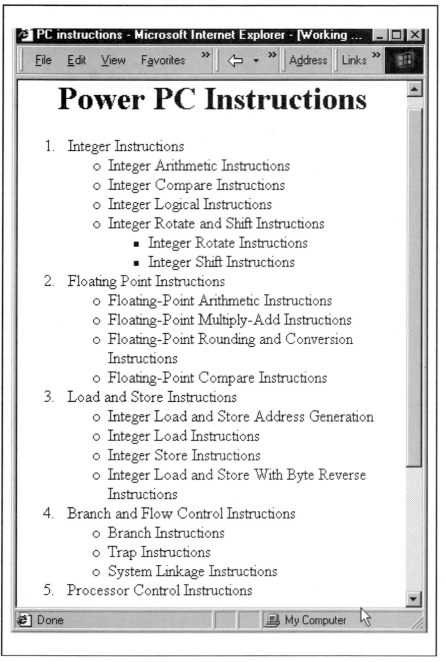

Figure 8.16 Problem 8.13.

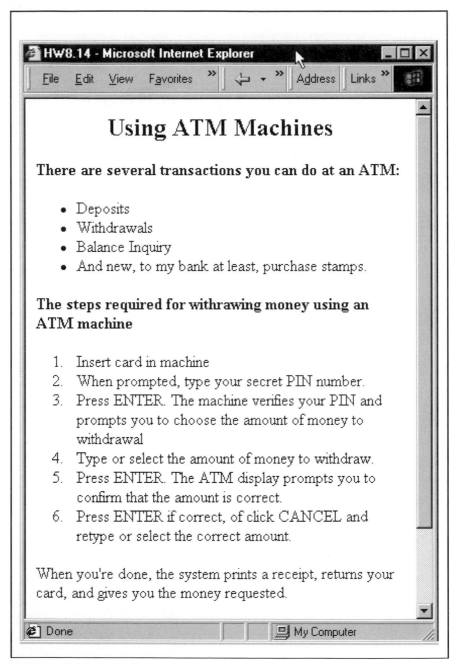

Figure 8.17   Problem 8.14.

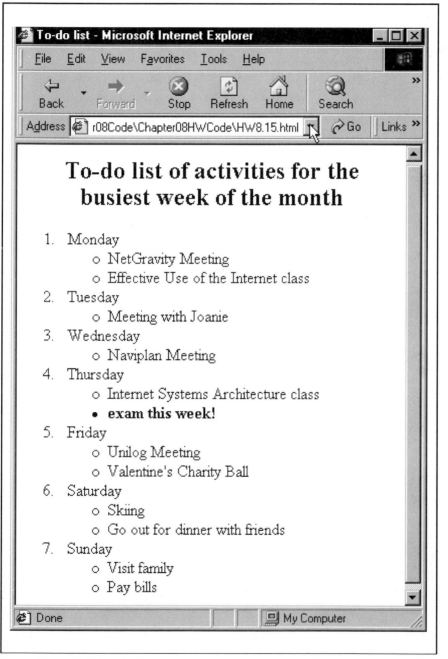

Figure 8.18 Problem 8.15.

Colors and Color Tags

T his chapter covers colors and their use in Web pages. It introduces basic background material about colors, such as existing color models (section 9.2), particularly the RGB mode, color palettes and lookup tables (section 9.3), color hex codes (section 9.4), and color dithering (section 9.5). It also covers using colors in Web pages (section 9.6), plus the HTML color-related attributes (section 9.7) and how browsers execute them (section 9.8).

9.1 Introduction

Color is one of the essential elements of a Web page. The design, visualization, and readability of Web pages all are greatly enhanced by the appropriate use of color combinations and contrast. Choosing colors for page background and text that work together enhances the page look. For example, light-color text displays well against dark-color background. Web authors should be sensitive to improper use of colors in their Web pages because this may produce negative effects. Some color combinations of text and background may even be harmful to the eyes if surfers stare at the Web page for long time. In addition, some color combinations may cause problems to some people.

One of the benefits of HTML is that it makes using colors in a Web page very easy. Web authors can specify their color choices by setting values of the attributes of some tags, as covered in section 9.7 in this chapter. It should be noted here that these attributes are deprecated (not recommended for future use in future Web pages) in HTML 4.0, in favor of using style sheets: however, many Web authors still use these attributes to add colors to their Web pages.

Using colors in Web page design seems attractive at first glance, but Web authors should be aware of several tips. Excessive use of colors may distract viewers from the value and content of a Web page. In addition, the use of unusual colors in the page, say in an image, may cause browsers to render the page differently on different platforms — for example, PC, Mac, or Unix.

9.2 RGB Color Model

Colors used in HTML are based on traditional color concepts. At the heart of these concepts are existing color models that are used to generate colors by mixing primary colors. A color model is a three-dimensional space with three coordinate axes. Each axis represents a set of colors. The color model is represented by a unit cube. Each color is represented by a point inside or on the cube. There are several color models available. The most popular and most commonly used one is the RGB (red, green, and blue) model shown in figure 9.1. Any point (color) in the space is obtained by mixing the three RGB primaries. Thus, the space is additive. This is analogous to how painters create colors by adding the three primary colors: red, green, and blue. This color model is used in computer monitors, mainly CRTs (cathode ray tubes), as well as television sets, scanners, and digital cameras.

The main diagonal of the RGB cube, as shown in figure 9.1 is the locus of equal amounts of each primary color. Thus, this diagonal represents the shades or levels of gray. One end point of the diagonal, the origin of the RGB model (cube), represents the black color, while the other end point represents the white color.

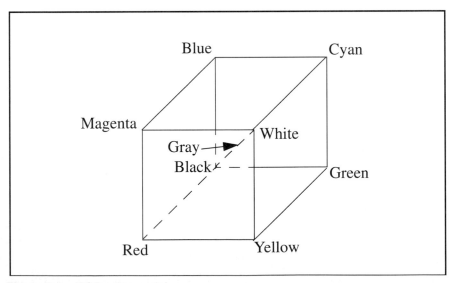

Figure 9.1 RGB color model.

Other existing color models include the CMY (cyan, magenta, and yellow model). This model is the complement to the RGB model, just as cyan, magenta, and yellow are the complements of red, green, and blue respectively. The CMY model is a subtractive model, because the primary colors are subtracted from white to form different colors in the model. This model is used by color printers. Another color model is the HSB (hue, saturation, and brightness) model. Colors in this model are formed by mixing three values, one for each primary signal. The values for each signal is between 0 and 1 (or any other two limits — for example, 0 and 255).

The RGB model is the one HTML uses. To understand how HTML uses this color model, we present an overview of how computer color monitors work. These monitors are similar to TV sets. They are raster displays. The display (computer) screen of a raster monitor is divided horizontally and vertically into pixels (picture elements). The pixels in both directions make the monitor resolution. For example, a monitor with a resolution of 800×600 has 800 and 600 pixels in the horizontal and vertical, directions respectively.

The value of each pixel is controlled by a certain number of bits in the computer memory (known in practice as graphics RAM, adapter, or card). A pixel can hold any one of many values, depending on the number of bits representing it. For example, if the pixel is represented by 8 bits, the pixel can hold 256 values, ranging from 0 to 255. This is because the value of a bit can be 0 or 1 in the computer binary system. Thus, all the possible values the pixel can have are $2^8 = 256$.

9.3 Color Palettes and Lookup Tables

How are pixel values converted into colors? Pixel values are converted into colors via the display (computer) monitor itself. The hardware design of the monitor performs this conversion. More specifically, the graphics adapter or card of the monitor saves all the possible pixel values and their corresponding colors. For example, if the display monitor has 8 bits, there are 256 pixel values, and therefore 256 available colors. The available colors are usually known as the color palette, and the mappings from pixel values to colors are stored in the monitor color lookup table.

The number of colors in a lookup table does not have to be exactly equal to the number of pixel values. As a matter of fact, many display monitors of computers today have a color palette size of $2^{24} = 16,777,216$ colors, usually referred to as a palette of 16.7 million colors. Thus, their color lookup tables have that many colors available for applications, such as a browser rendering a Web page, to choose from. However, the number of colors that can be displayed simultaneously by an application on the display monitor can be no more than the number of distinct values of one pixel, which is controlled by the number of bits/pixel. Thus applications running on a monitor with 8 bits/pixel can display only 256 simultaneous colors which they choose from among the 16.7 million available colors. Applications use the monitor lookup color table to choose these colors.

While color palettes and lookup tables are part of monitor hardware, the applications must use them. Applications first determine the number of bits/pixel of the monitor, to determine the number of simultaneous colors they can choose, and display, from the lookup table. Applications are usually written for different monitors with different number of bits/pixel. If an application is written to run on a monitor with 4 bits/pixel, it should use only $2^4 = 16$ colors to display at run time. All Internet applications, programming languages such as Java, and scripts such as JavaScript and HTML support the 24-bit RGB (red, green, and blue) color model. In this model, 3 primary colors or signals (red, green, and blue) are mixed together to produce any color. Each primary color or signal has values from 0 to 255. Thus, these applications and languages support 16.7 million colors. However, in many cases, the applications are written for 256-color display monitors.

Browsers, considered as applications, have predefined color tables that they use to display the colored text and images of Web pages. These tables typically have 256 colors. While displaying colored text is straightforward, displaying images is quite different. Colored text usually has one color, unless the Web author uses different colors for different words or characters. By contrast, each image has multiple colors. Thus, each image has its own color table that browsers use to display it correctly with the original colors. Displaying an image involves the use and mapping between three color tables: that of the image, that of the browser, and that of the monitor. The browser reads the image file and its associated color table. It then maps the colors in the image color table to its own colors, defined in its own color table. Finally, the browser maps its colors to those defined in the color table of the monitor. If at some time during the mapping between these three color tables a color is not found, the browser dithers it, as is explained in section 9.5.

9.4 Hexadecimal Codes

According to the RGB color model, each color is unique and is represented by a point in the color cube shown in figure 9.1. The point is defined by three coordinates measured along the three axes of the cube. These coordinates are the values of the primary colors that are mixed to create the color. The values of the primary colors could be specified as decimals or as hexadecimals (hex for short). Hex values are preceded by a pound (#) sign. For example, the color red has the decimal values [255, 0, 0] or the hex value of #FF0000 in the 24-bit RGB color model. The hex values 00 and FF correspond to the decimal values 0 and 255, respectively. Thus, the hex value of a color consists of three hex numbers. Each hex number represents a value of a primary color and is between 00 and FF. A maroon color has the decimal values [176, 48, 96] and the hex value #B03060. Here the hex numbers B0, 30, and 60 represent the values of the red, green, and blue primary colors respectively.

Colors are specified in HTML by using names or hex codes. It is strongly advised that one use hex codes because they uniquely specify colors. Names are not unique. For example, the color red could mean any one of many shades. The color #FF0000 is red and the color #FF4500 is orange red. Thus, the name *red* could mean different shades on different computers. There are many Web sites that provide tables that list both the decimal and the hex values of many colors. One such site is www.lynda.com. Table 9.1 shows sample colors with their hex codes.

9.5 Dithering

Dithering can be thought of as a method of interpolation to resolve missing colors. The method is used by browsers during the rendering of Web pages. Some of these pages may have images that use colors that are not available in the browser color table. When faced with this situation, the browser can ignore the colors missing from its table altogether, or it can try to find the closest colors to them by dithering or mixing colors from its table. Browsers, by default, dither missing colors. Browsers perform dithering by combining color codes. Browsers analyze

Table 9.1 Color names and their hex codes

Color name	Hex code	Color name	Hex code	Color name	Hex code
Aqua	#00FFFF	Godzilla	#145F0A	Purple	#800080
Black	#000000	Green	#008000	Red	#FF0000
Blue	#0000FF	Hard Hat	#F6EF31	Scarlet	#8C1717
Blue Violet	#9F5F9F	Hedgehog	#A78424	Silver	#C0C0C0
Braindead	#4566C9	Hunter Green	#215E21	Spicy pink	#FF1CAE
Brass	#B5A642	Indian Red	#4E2F2F	Spring Green	#00FF7F
Brown	#A62A2A	Khaki	#9F9F5F	Steel Blue	#236B8E
Copper	#B87333	Lime	#00FF00	Succotash	#94BD44
Coral	#FF7F00	Maroon	#800000	Summer Sky	38B0DE
Corn Dog	#F0C373	Navy	#000080	Tan	#DB9370
Dark Brown	#5C4033	Neon Blue	#4D4DFF	Teal	#008080
Dusty Rose	#856363	Neon Pink	#FF6FC7	The Family Rat	#827964
Fledspar	#D19275	Old Gold	#CFB53B	Thistle	#D8BFD8
Firebrick	#8E2323	Olive	#808000	Turquoise	#ADEAEA

Table 9.1   Color names and their hex codes

Color name	Hex code	Color name	Hex code	Color name	Hex code
Fuchsia	#FF00FF	Orange	#FF7F00	Wheat	#D8D8BF
Full Bladder	#FFC136	Pink	#BC8F8F	White	#FFFFFF
Gray	#808080	Plum	#EAADEA	Yellow	#FFFF00

the trio of RGB values of a missing color and try to match them with any existing trio. For example, if the missing color is a shade of purple, a browser may change the color values to have more red and/or more blue.

Dithering colors is not a good practice. The look of a Web page becomes unpredictable from one platform to another. The same Web page looks different when it is displayed on a PC, a Mac, or a Unix workstation. The main drawback of dithering is that colors do not stand out distinctively, especially when one is viewing high-resolution images. This drawback is less noticeable for low-resolution images.

The perfect solution to eliminate dithering is for the browser to have a large color lookup table or palette — 16.7 million colors. While this solution seems simple, it fails on account of hardware limitations. Many PCs have color tables of size 256. Moreover, the OS, for example Windows OS, may reserve some of these colors for its own display management. Thus, browsers have to play it safe when it comes to displaying colors. They have to assume the worst-case scenario. They use what is known as a browser-safe or Web-safe color palette as a minimum palette. This palette is based on the 256 colors all PCs and Macs support. However, PCs and Macs share only 216 of these 256 colors. Thus, the browser-safe color palette has a size of 216 colors. The remaining 40 colors are platform-dependent, or proprietary. As a result, browsers use an RGB color cube of size 6X6X6 = 216. This cube ensures that images and their Web pages look the same on both PC and Mac monitors. The colors defined by the cube consist of all the hex trio combinations of 00, 33, 66, 99, CC, and FF. The Web site www.lynda.com lists the 216 safe colors with their decimal values and hex codes.

Web authors can have control over the color palette for the images they create. Many image-creation and editing tools such Adobe Photoshop allow authors to define an image color palette. Authors can even read predefined color palettes, save them, and apply them to images. Thus, author can use the browser-safe color palette to ensure consistency of rendering and displaying images. Images created by scanning real photographs should be saved as JPEG files because this format minimizes the dithering effect on them.

9.6 Using Colors in Web Pages

Web authors set and control the colors of the text, the background, and the images on Web pages. Text could be simple plain text or hyperlinks. The default text color is black. Text colors can be set globally (known as the *foreground* color) and/or locally (known as *spot* colors). Spot colors are assigned to individual characters or words. Spot colors override the foreground color. Depending on design needs, a Web author may set the foreground color to blue. In this case, all the page text is displayed in blue. Whenever the author needs to sprinkle different colors into the page for some words in the text, to attract surfer's attention to them, spot colors are used.

Hyperlink colors can be set depending on their state whether they are links, alinks, or vlinks, as discussed in chapter 7. Each state can be assigned a color. Browsers use default colors for these states. They are blue, red, and purple for links, alinks, and vlinks, respectively. Web authors can override these default colors.

Background color is the color of the background of the Web page. The default background color is white. Web authors can override this color for design considerations. It is always important to choose the background color to contrast well with the foreground color. The background of a Web page could be an image instead of a color. We cover this topic in more detail in chapter 10. Web authors should be aware that they can only use one or the other, not both at the same time. If a Web author tries to use both at the same time, the image always prevails as the page background. As a matter of fact, the browser displays the background color first, and then it covers it with the image.

Colors of images are usually set during image creation. Once images are created, their files are used in Web pages, as will be covered in chapter 10. An image file can be used to display the image in the Web page, or it can be used as a page background, as described earlier.

9.7 Color Tags

Web authors need HTML tags or attributes to change and set colors in their Web pages. HTML does not have separate tags for colors. It has only color attributes. The two tags that have color attributes are the <BODY> and <FONT> tags. The one color attribute of the <FONT> tag specifies spot (local) characters, while those of the <BODY> tag specifies the other colors. The <FONT> tag is still used to specify colors by many Web authors and HTML editors, although it has now been largely replaced by style sheets.

9.7.1 <BODY> Tag

The <BODY> tag has the following attributes.

•TEXT; this attribute sets the foreground color of the Web page (i.e., the default color of the page text). It overrides the default (black) color.

•LINK; this attribute sets the color of the normal, unfollowed links in a Web page. It overrides the default (blue) color.

•ALINK; this attribute sets the color of an active link (has mouse button pressed on it, but not released yet) in a Web page. It overrides the default (red) color.

•VLINK; this attribute sets the color of the visited (already followed) links in a Web page. It overrides the default (purple) color.

•BGCOLOR; this attribute sets the background color of the Web page. It overrides the default (white) color.

•BACKGROUND; this attribute uses an image as a background for a page. In this case, the image is tiled, i.e. repeated in rows and columns to fill the browser window. This tiling effect is created by the browser.

9.7.2 <FONT> Tag

The <FONT> tag has the COLOR attribute which can be used to specify a color for certain characters or words. The <FONT> tag encloses these characters or words. The COLOR attribute of the <FONT> tag overrides the TEXT attribute of the <BODY> tag.

9.8 Tutorials

This section focuses on using the color attributes covered in this chapter. The section tutorials are not new. They extend tutorials created in previous chapters by adding colors to them. It is a good idea to create a directory structure to save HTML files. This helps Web authors to organize HTML files and makes it easy to find them.

9.8.1 Text Color

This tutorial utilizes the TEXT attribute of the <BODY> tag. We change the text color from black to blue in the Web page created in example 7.3 and shown in figure 7.3. Retrieve the file *example7.3.html*. Using a text editor, edit the file to replace the <BODY> tag as follows, and save it as *tutorial9.8.1.html*.

<BODY TEXT = "#0000FF">

View the page in a browser.

9.8.2 Link Colors

This tutorial utilizes the LINK, ALINK, and VLINK attributes of the <BODY> tag. We change the default colors of links, an active link, and visited links to green, aqua, and brown respectively, in the Web page created in example 7.5 and shown in figure 7.7. Retrieve the file *example6.5.html*. Using a text editor, edit the file to replace the <BODY> tag as follows, and save it as *tutorial9.8.2.html*.

<BODY LINK = "#008000" ALINK = "#00FFFF" VLINK = "#A62A2A">

View the page in a browser.

9.8.3 Background Color

This tutorial utilizes the BGCOLOR attribute of the <BODY> tag. We change the page background color from white to yellow in the Web page created in tutorial 9.8.1. Thus, the resulting page has blue text and yellow background color. Retrieve the file *tutorial9.8.1.html*. Using a text editor, edit the file to replace the <BODY> tag as follows, and save it as *tutorial9.8.3.html*.

<BODY TEXT = "#0000FF" BGCOLOR = "#808080">

View the page in a browser.

9.8.4 All Colors

This tutorial utilizes all the color attributes of the <BODY> tag except BACKGROUND. It combines the attributes of the <BODY> tag of tutorials 9.8.1, 9.8.2 and 9.8.3 and uses them in example 8.6 (shown in figure 8.8). Retrieve the file *example8.6.html*. Using a text editor, edit the file to replace the <BODY> tag as follows, and save it as *tutorial9.8.4.html*.

<BODY TEXT = "#0000FF" BGCOLOR = "#808080" LINK = "#008000" ALINK = "#00FFFF" VLINK = "#A62A2A">

View the page in a browser.

9.8.5 Spot Colors

This tutorial utilizes the COLOR attribute of the <FONT> tag. We create a line of text with characters and words of different colors. Using a text editor, type the following code, and save it as *tutorial9.8.5.html*.

```
<HTML>
<HEAD>
<TITLE>Spot colors</TITLE>
</HEAD>
<BODY TEXT = "#0000FF" BGCOLOR = "#808080">
<H2><B><CENTER><FONT COLOR = "blue">Using spot colors</FONT></CEN-
TER></B></H2>
Here are my spot colors. Run the code in a browser to see col-
ors.<BR>

<! Show "Hello" in Blue and "World" in a different color (yellow)>
<H2><B>Hello <FONT COLOR = "#FFFF00">World!</FONT></B></H2><BR>

<! Give me a T in one color>
<H1><FONT COLOR = "#FF7F00">T</FONT>

<! Give me an h in one color>
<FONT COLOR = "#EAADEA">h</FONT>
```

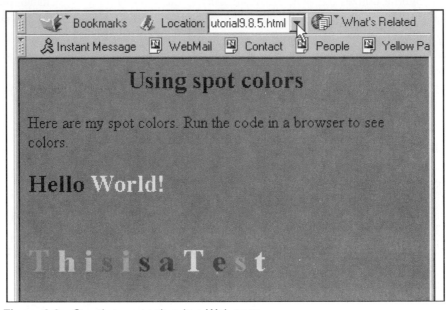

Figure 9.2   Creating spot colors in a Web page.

```
<! Give me an i in one color>
<FONT COLOR = "#00FFFF">i</FONT>

<! Give me an s in one color>
<FONT COLOR = "#4566C9">s</FONT>

<! Give me an i in one color>
<FONT COLOR = "#B5A642">i</FONT>

<! Give me an s in one color>
<FONT COLOR = "#145F0A">s</FONT>

<! Give me an a in one color>
<FONT COLOR = "#008000">a</FONT>

<! Give me a T in one color>
<FONT COLOR = "#F6EF31">T</FONT>
<! Give me an e in one color>
<FONT COLOR = "#215E21">e</FONT>

<! Give me an s in one color>
<FONT COLOR = "#9F9F5F">s</FONT>
```

```
<! Give me a t in one color>
<FONT COLOR = "#ADEAEA">t</FONT></H1>
</BODY>
</HTML>
```

View the page in a browser. Figure 9.2 show the resulting Web page.

Note: We could have created all the characters, with their colors, as an image, in an image application such as Photoshop and used the image file in the Web page to reduce the amount of HTML code writing. (See chapter 10.)

9.9 FAQs

Q: Why should a Web author not specify colors by names?

A: While many browsers allow the use of color names in HTML code, there is no list of color names that work the same in all browsers. Specifying colors via hex codes is safer and works consistently in all browsers.

Q: Why does the display on a computer monitor appear with funky colors while it is using Netscape Communicator?

A: This is a common problem with all application programs that change the color palette of the monitor. Before Netscape starts, the existing colors in the monitor color palette are mapped to the Netscape palette, and they cause other applications to show confusing colors. How to restore the original color palette of the monitor depends on the OS. For Windows, restore and then minimize the program manager. For Unix, the palette is restored once you exit Netscape.

Q: What is the difference between color matching and dithering?

A: Color matching means that the browser finds the nearest color, in its color table, to the requested color and uses it. Color dithering means that the browser mixes some pixels of one color with some pixels of another color. It is not clear when a browser matches or dithers colors. It is also hard to notice the effect of either.

Q: Why do scanned photographs and great graphics used in Web pages not look as good as the originals?

A: The original colors may be degraded because of too much dithering on the browser's part. Dithering can also create a lot of little spots (dither pattern) in a background color of a Web page.

Q: How does a browser display images that are created using the 24-bit RGB color model on a client monitor that supports 256 (8-bit RGB model) colors?

A: The color table accompanying the image is run through a color-matching algorithm, and the resulting color table is used to display the image. The resulting image gets dithered into the closest possible colors available in the color palette of the client monitor. Thus, colors of the original image may be lost twice; once during the matching process, and once during the dithering process.

9.10 Summary

Introduction

•Color is important to the appearance of Web pages.

•Excessive use of colors, or the use of the wrong mix of colors, in Web pages can create an adverse effect during the viewing of these pages.

•HTML makes using colors in Web pages very easy.

RGB Color Model

•HTML uses the RGB (red, green, and blue) color model to specify colors.

•The RGB color model is a cube whose sides are the primary colors. The three primary colors in the RGB model are red, green, and blue.

•Colors in the RGB model are created by mixing the three primary colors: red, green, and blue

•Each primary color may use 8 bits. Thus, it has 256 (2^8) decimal values, from 0 to 255.

Color Palettes and Lookup Tables

•Browsers and client monitors have color palettes whose values are stored in color lookup tables.

•The size of a color palette depends on the number of bits per color. In the 24-bit RGB color model, the palette size is 2^{24} = 16.7 million colors. In the 8-bit RGB color model, the palette size is 2^8 = 256.

•Many client monitors use the 256-color palette.

•There are 216 colors out of the 256 that are identical between the PC and the Mac platforms. These are known as browser-safe or Web-safe color palettes (safe colors).

•The browser-safe color palette uses a 6 X 6 X 6 (216) RGB color cube.

•The colors defined by the cube consist of all the combinations of 00, 33, 66, 99, CC, and FF.

Hexadecimal Codes

•Each color has a unique hex value. Hex values are preceded by a pound (#) sign.

•Hex values 00 to FF correspond to decimal values 0 to 255.

•Colors should be specified by their hex codes, instead of their names, to ensure consistency of display of Web pages on different clients by different browsers.

•The Web site www.lynda.com lists the 216 safe colors with their decimal values and hex codes.

Dithering

•Dithering is a method used by browsers to resolve colors missing from their color tables.

•Browsers perform dithering by changing the color code. For example, if the missing color is a shade of purple, a browser may change the color values to have more red and/or more blue.

Using Colors in Web Pages

•Using colors in a Web page entails specifying colors for its text, hyperlinks, background, and images.

•Spot colors are used for specific characters or words.

•A hyperlink is assigned a color depending on its state: whether it is unfollowed (link), active (alink), or visited/followed (vlink).

•The default colors for links, alinks, and vlinks are, respectively, blue, red, and purple.

•The background of a Web page could be a color or an image. When an image is used as a background for a page, it is tiled (i.e. repeated in rows and columns to fill the browser window). This tiling effect is created by the browser.

•Quick reference of the HTML tags covered in this chapter

Table 9.2 Summary of HTML color tags.

Tag	Close	Attribute	Value	Example	Chpt. page
<BODY>	Yes	TEXT	hex code	<BODY TEXT = "#FF0000">	333 334
		LINK	hex code	<BODY LINK= "#00FF00">	
		ALINK	hex code	<BODY ALINK = "#0000FF">	
		VLINK	hex code	<BODY VLINK = "#FFFF00">	
		BGCOLOR	hex code	<BODY BGCOLOR= "#FF0000">	
		BACK-GROUND	image file	See chapter 10	
<FONT>	YES	COLOR	hex code	<FONT COLOR = "#ADEAEA">	334

PROBLEMS

Exercises

9.1 Write a Web page that displays the first 9 colors in table 9.1. Create the following text in the page with H1 bold heading: **This is color 1**. Replace 1 by 2, 3, ..., 9.

9.2 Repeat exercise 9.1 for the next 9 colors in table 9.1. Continue repeating until you finish the 54 colors listed in the table. Each 9 colors is a separate exercise.

9.3 Add text and background colors to the Web page created in exercise 8.1.

9.4 Repeat exercise 9.3 for exercises 8.2 through 8.4. Each exercise is a separate assignment.

Homework

9.5 Add text, link, alink, vlink, and background colors to the Web page created in problem 8.5.

9.6 Repeat problem 9.5 for problems 8.6 through 8.15. Each problem is a separate assignment.

CHAPTER 10

Images and Image Tags

This chapter covers images, their use in Web pages, and image tags. Images are an important multimedia element that spices Web pages and makes them look more attractive than just having all text. After an introduction, the chapter covers image file formats. It then covers image software that is available to create images. It also presents the image tag and all its attributes in details. In addition, it covers ideas on how to use images in Web pages. This includes creating image hyperlinks, multiple use of the same image in a page, and using images as list items. The chapter concludes with tutorials and summary.

10.1 Introduction

There is much more to building Web pages than just good layout design and text. Multimedia features of HTML, such as images and video clips, make pages more powerful and more attractive. Web authors can add icons, logos, and high-impact images to their pages. When working with images, authors need to focus on page content and to use images only to enhance the content and the idea behind it. Images in themselves do not add much value to a Web page. Web authors should choose the image size carefully to fit the layout and the purpose of each Web page.

The use of images in Web pages bring up two important issues. First, the image size and complexity usually affects the first impression of a Web page. If the size and complexity of the image is not overwhelming relative to the page other contents, the image is the right one. On the hand, if it detracts surfers from the page focus, the image size and complexity must be reconsidered.

The second issue has to do with the size of the image file and the length of time required to download it. The larger the size of the image file, the longer it takes to download. Thus, the Web page becomes slow to display. The downloading time of a Web page is a function of the Internet connection used, whether it is a dedicated connection, for example cable connection, or a modem connection. The slower the connection, the larger the downloading time.

When it comes to using images in Web pages, Web authors need to realize that surfers can configure their browsers to turn off image display in the Web pages they download and view. Surfers do that to speed up their surfing activities. As a result, authors should know their audience. They need to focus on page design and adding excellent content to the page.

Web authors have two choices to use images. They can create their own images, store them locally, and add them to their Web pages; or, they can refer to images available on the Internet via a hyperlink. When a surfer clicks the hyperlink, the particular image is downloaded from its server to the client monitor. In some cases, linking to Internet images is a necessity. Examples include weather images. Linking to Internet images has two drawbacks. First, it takes more time to download an image from the Internet than from the local disk. Second, if the image server is down, the image cannot be loaded.

There are some common-sense rules that Web authors should follow when it comes to including images in a Web page:

•Images should enhance the text, the page layout, and the content.

•Keep images small and simple.

•Use thumbnail versions of the images to reduce the downloading time of the Web page.

•Use icons and logos of organizations as images to distinguish the Web page. In many cases, traditional icons, logos, and trademarks are scanned and used as images in Web pages.

10.2 Image Formats

Two important variables of images are resolution and format. Images can be created with high, medium, or low resolution. The higher the resolution, the larger the size of the image file. For many Web pages, medium resolution images are satisfactory.

Many image formats exist. These formats are related to the image resolution and file size. Three existing formats are bitmap (BMP), Joint Photographic Experts Group (JPEG), and Graphics Interchange Format (GIF). If the same image is saved using these formats, the BMP format produces the largest file size (therefore best colors), while the GIF format produces the smallest file size (least colors). In some cases, the size of a GIF image is smaller than that of JPEG, and in other cases the opposite is true. This depends on the size of the color palette saved with the image. A BMP file size is larger than that of a JPEG file for the same image, and a JPEG file size is larger than that of a GIF file for the same image with the same color palette. In practice, both the GIF and JPEG formats are widely used.

A list of the most common image formats follows:

•BMP; BitMaP; created by Microsoft (MS);

•JPEG or JPG; Joint Photographic Experts Group; created by the Independent JPEG group;

•GIF; Graphics Interchange Format; created by CompuServe;

•PNG; Portable Network Graphics;

•PCX; PC Paintbrush file; created by Zsoft Corp;

•TIFF; Tagged-Image File Format; created by Aldus, MS, and NeXT.

The JPEG, GIF, and PNG formats are the only three formats supported widely by the major Internet tools, browsers, application programs, and programming languages, such as Java, JavaScript, and HTML. Any other format is not supported and should not be used. If an image is available in one of the other formats and it must be used in a Web page, the Web author must convert it to either JPEG or GIF. The Web author uses an image program, such as Photoshop, or a screen capture program, such as SnagIt or Lview, reads the image with the current format, and then saves it under, say, the JPEG format.

Of these three formats, GIF and JPEG are the most popular. The GIF format supports a palette that can consist of 256 (8 bits) colors, each of which is represented in true color. The JPEG format supports the 16.7 million (24-bit) colors. These two format are significantly different from each other in how they compress and store graphics. GIF keeps the original colors of the image, while JPEG may remove some colors. This is why GIF is referred to as a lossless format and JPEG as a lossy format. For Web authors, we offer the following general guidelines. The GIF format is usually used for simple drawings of paint programs and screenshot images, images with several distinct colors, and sharp images with borders or text. These images usually have fewer colors than the maximum (256 colors) the GIF format supports. The JPEG format is usually used for high-quality images, as well as for photographic images or scanned photographs. These images have many more than 256 colors. Image software usually allows its users to save JPEG images in low (small size file) or high (large size file) resolution.

Images take a long time to load, so the JPEG and GIF formats allow the progressive loading of images. In progressive JPEG or GIF, the image is loaded with gradually increasing resolution. The image is first loaded quickly with low resolution, just to keep the attention of the Web page viewer. The image resolution gets better, and the image becomes clearer progressively with time. Progressive images are also known as interlaced images. Noninterlaced images are loaded by browsers all at once. If the loading is slow, viewers look at a white area (the image space) until the image is displayed. The size of an interlaced image is slightly larger than that of its noninterlaced version. It is the job of the browser to load the image progressively. Some browsers may not support image interlace.

There are two GIF formats: 87a and 89a. The 87a format is the original GIF format, designed by CompuServe in 1987. This format was enhanced in 1989, thus the name 89a. The new enhancement features in 89a format are image interlace (discussed earlier), transparency, and animated GIF. Transparency allows the viewer to see the background of a Web page through the part of the image that is transparent. Transparency is used effectively to blend an image with page background. For animation, a GIF89a file can contain several images stored in it. When viewed in a browser, these images are displayed one after another, producing the effect of animation or motion.

10.3 Image Software

Images can be created in a variety of ways — for example, creation, scanning, and digital cameras. Web authors can create images using graphics and image software. Some existing software packages include Adobe Photoshop, Adobe Illustrator, Mapedit, Paint Shop Pro, ThumbsPlus, WebEdit PRO, WebImage, Windows Paint, and WS FTP LE. Prices range from fifty to several hundred dollars. Some of these packages, such as Adobe products, provide advanced tools to add true realism to images. Windows Paint is free — it comes with MS Windows. The Paint program creates images in BMP format, by default, because this format does not cause loss of colors after saving the images. This format is good for creating and editing images, but Web authors have to convert the resulting files into JPEG or GIF, as discussed in section 10.2.

All graphics and image software are two-dimensional pixel-based programs. All the coordinates are measured in pixels, and not in inches or other units. Vector-based programs allow non-pixel coordinates. These programs utilize a universal coordinate system, shown in figure 10.1. The system has its origin, (0, 0), in the top left corner of the drawing window of the software, with the +X going to the right and the +Y going down, as shown in the figure.

Great images can be generated by scanning real photographs and saving them as JPEG images. After the scanning, scanning software allows its users to edit or crop the resulting image, if needed. Editing an image implies adding some visual effects or adding some text. Cropping is a process by which a user can cut out part of an image and save it as a separate image. Scanning products that relate to Web sites is a common practice. Web authors scan cars, houses, pets, and so forth and add the images to the related Web pages.

Images of real objects and people can be generated directly, by using digital cameras to circumvent the scanning process. Digital cameras generate frames and save them as JPEG images on a floppy disk. Users can, in turn, copy the image files from the floppy into a client hard disk, making them ready for editing or for use in Web pages.

In addition to image creation and editing software, there is another group that is just as important. It is image viewing software, or simply image viewers. Web authors who work with images on regular basis should use image viewers; they simplify viewing, maintaining, and cataloging images. Also, image viewers load and open image files faster than image editors. Image viewers are usually used when Web authors want to just look at images; image editors are used to edit and change images and their content.

Good image viewers offer cataloging features, such as thumbnails and contact sheets. With thumbnails, an image viewer displays an entire folder of images on the screen side by side, to aid the sorting and choosing of images for full-size viewing. Contact sheets are pages of thumbnails, either in printed hard copy or as graphics files. Image viewers should allow their users to specify the width and height of thumbnails and their arrangement on a page. Also, some image viewers generate the thumbnails on the fly, so they take longer to display. Others generate the thumbnails and store them in files, for faster display.

Other features of image viewers include the image formats they support, the customizing of sizes of thumbnails, the adding of keywords, the launching of an external image editor, the viewing of fonts, search tools, and the generation of slide shows. Sample image viewing software include CompuPic (Windows and MAc), LView Pro, ThumbsPlus (Windows and Mac), ViewSafe (Windows), and SnapShot (Windows). Readers looking for more may use www.shareware.com and run a search using "image viewing" or "image viewers" as a search string.

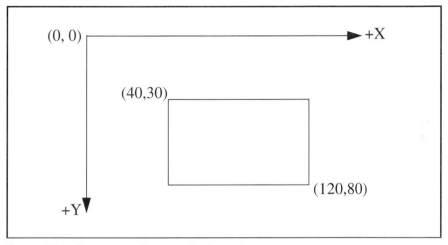

Figure 10.1   Image creation coordinate system.

10.4 Image Tags

HTML provides Web authors with one tag to handle images in Web pages. It is the <IMG> tag.

10.4.1 <IMG> Tag

The <IMG> tag has enough attributes to provide good control of image insertion in Web pages. These attributes are as follows:

•SRC: This attribute specifies the image file name. This file must have the *jpeg* (or *jpg*), the *gif*, or the *png* extension only. Image files can be specified using the absolute or relative path, as discussed in chapter 7.

•ALT: This attribute specifies alternate text that is rendered in case a browser cannot display the image or does not support the image type (such as BMP). Browsers usually show this text while loading the image and before the loading is complete. Specifying alternate text helps users without graphics display terminals, visually impaired users, and users who have configured their browsers not to display images. Web authors should exercise care when using the ALT attribute. As a general rule, they should not specify irrelevant or meaningless alternate text. For example, do not use the ALT attribute for an image of a blue ball that is used as a bullet symbol.

In this case, it is irrelevant to use ALT = "blue ball". Meaningless text may be something like ALT = "dummy text".

•LONGDESC: While the ALT attribute provides a short description of the image, the LONGDESC specifies a link to a longer and richer description of the image. The value of this attribute is an HTML file that has the long description of the image. This attribute is not recognized by current browsers.

•BORDER: This attribute specifies a border in pixels that surrounds an image. When an image is used as a hyperlink, the browser surround it with a border automatically.

•WIDTH and HEIGHT: These two attributes specify a new width and height that the browser uses to render the image. These two attributes override the original size of the image. In effect, they scale the original image. Browsers usually do their best to scale the image, without distortion, to match the width and height specified by these two attributes. It is recommended that one scale images down, not up because their resolutions degrade when they are enlarged. The width and height provide the browser with an idea of the size of an image, so that the browser can reserve a space for it and continue to render the HTML document while waiting for the image data.

•ALIGN: An image is seldom the only element of a Web page. With other elements such as text making up the page, the need arises to place images relative to the page elements. The ALIGN attribute specifies the position of an image with respect to its context. There are five values of this attribute. They are top, middle, bottom (the default), left, and right. The first three values align the image with respect to the surrounding text. The top, middle, and bottom values align the image vertically (top, middle, bottom, respectively) with the current text baseline. The left and right values justify (default) the image to the left or right of the page text respectively.

•HSPACE and VSPACE: These two attributes provide horizontal and vertical white space around an image respectively. This space makes the Web page look less crowded; the page text surrounding the image is not very close to it. The values of these two attributes are specified in pixels.

•USEMAP: This attribute specifies that the image is used as a client-side image map. Its value is an anchor. This attribute is discussed in more detail in chapter 11.

•ISMAP: This attribute specifies that the image is used as a server-side image map. Its value is an anchor. This attribute is discussed in more detail in chapter 11.

10.5 Dealing with Images

There are various ways to deal with images. Web authors may create new images, edit existing ones, copy existing images, use an image as a hyperlink, use an image more than once in a Web page, use an image as a list item, or create GIF animation. We discuss some of these ideas here.

10.5.1 Image Creation

Web authors have two options ingenerating images for their Web pages. They can create them, or they can buy them. There are many artists and small businesses that can create images for a fee. Many of them advertise on the Web. They have many samples, clip-arts, and thumbnails to choose from, and they create custom images to meet certain layout and design requirements of Web pages.

In this section, we focus on creating images. Web authors can create images in three ways. They can use an image program, use a digital camera, or scan existing photos. Here, we use the MS Windows Paint program to create simple images. To access this program, click the following sequence (assuming Windows OS); Start => Programs => Accessories => Paint. The Paint program is simple and intuitive to use. Figure 10.2 shows the program GUI. The program is pixel-based and uses the coordinate system shown in figure 10.1.

The GUI, as shown in figure 10.2, consists of the menu bar, the Tool Box, the Color Box, the Status Bar, and the drawing area. The menu bar has the File, Edit, View, Image, Colors, and Help menus. Two interesting menu items of the File menu allow users to set an image as a Wallpaper (tiled or centered) for the desktop background. A user opens an image in Paint and chooses one of these two items. Paint displays the image on the desktop background. To change the background back to no tiling, double click the sequence My Computer => Control Panel => Display => None (under the Background tab) => OK.

The Edit menu has two important items: Undo and Repeat. The Undo can delete several steps back. This item is sometimes better to use than the eraser to erase existing graphics, because of the pixel nature of the graphics. For example, erasing a circle intersecting a line may be tricky because the user may erase part of the line inadvertently. Using the Undo does the erasing quite easily. The Repeat menu item allows the user to repeat the last construction step. It performs the function opposite to Undo.

The View menu enables the user to turn on/off the display of the Tool Box, the Color Box, the Status Bar, and the Text Toolbar. It also has a Zoom submenu which is useful during construction.

The Image menu enables the user to manipulate the image by flipping it, rotating it, and/or stretching it. The Attributes item of the Image menu enables the user to set the size of the image by specifying its width and height before or after creating it. The user should set the image size before creating an image. If the size is changed after the image is created, the image may be clipped. Once it is clipped, the user cannot recover the clipped part of the image, because of its pixel nature.

The Color menu may be used to change the colors of the Paint program. The Help menu provides general help about the program.

The Tool box has a few buttons. If the user moves the mouse over each button, the button name is displayed. The shape buttons allow drawing a line, a curve, a rectangle, a polygon, an ellipse, or a rounded rectangle. The Pencil and the Brush buttons are for drawing shapes. The Pencil draws shapes with thin boundaries; the Brush draws thick boundaries. The Fill

With Colors button fills shapes with colors. The A button is the text button. When selected, a Text Toolbar is displayed, which allows users to control the text size, font, and style.

The Color box has many buttons of different colors. The user chooses a color for drawing or filling by clicking the corresponding button. The user should be careful not to choose the background color for foreground construction, otherwise entities will be invisible.

The Status Bar displays the (x, y) pixel coordinates of the current mouse location. If the user clicks the Pencil button, moves the mouse in the graphics window of Paint, and watches the Status Bar, the pixel coordinates change continuously. These pixel coordinates are sometimes needed by HTML tags, as in the case of creating shapes for an image map, as discussed in chapter 11.

After this quick coverage of the Paint program, we can draw the image shown in figure 10.2. Before drawing the image, we set the image size to 200×250 pixels. We draw a simple crude image of a boy. We select the pencil mode by clicking the Pencil button. We then select the Circle button and draw the head and the eyes. We select the Rectangle button and draw the neck, the body, and the legs. We select the Line button and draw the nose and the arms. We then fill each part of the body with a different color by clicking the Fill With Color button, clicking the desired color from the Color Box, and clicking in the body part. When we are done, we save the image as *myImage*. The image format is BMP by default; thus, the image file name is *myImage.bmp*. Paint supports other formats, mainly 16-Color Bitmap, 256-Color Bitmap, 24-bit Bitmap, JPEG, and GIF. To save in one of these formats, we use the Save As menu item of the File menu and then choose the desired format. Figure 10.2 shows the image. In addition, the figure shows the features of the Paint GUI itself such as the Tool Box, the Color Box, and the Status Bar. The Status bar shows pixel coordinates of (165, 60) for the current position of the pencil.

Example 10.1 Develop a Web page that illustrates the use of images.

Solution This example creates a Web page with one image. The example uses the image shown in figure 10.2. Before we can use this image in the Web page, we have to convert it to either GIF or JPEG format. We convert it to GIF because it does not have many colors. We use a graphics program, such as SnagIt to convert. We read the image file as a BMP file and resave it as a GIF file. We show this step here, because some old versions of Paint support the BMP format only. The <IMG> tag in this example uses a few of its attributes as shown below. Using a text editor, type the code that follows, and save it as *example10.1.html*. (Figure 10.3 shows the resulting Web page.)

```
<HTML>
<HEAD>
<TITLE>A Web page with images</TITLE>
</HEAD>
<BODY>
<H2><B><CENTER><FONT COLOR = "blue">Web page with a simple image
```

```
</FONT></CENTER></B></H2>
<! Include the image>
<IMG SRC = "myImage.gif" ALT = "A GIF image drawn in Paint"
BORDER = 5 ALIGN = "middle" HSPACE = 10 VSPACE = 15>Text aligned
middle<BR>This text is placed 15 pixels<BR>below the image<BR>
</BODY>
</HTML>
```

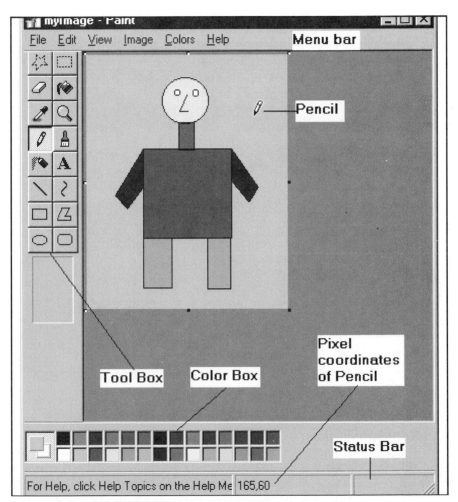

Figure 10.2   Microsoft Windows Paint program.

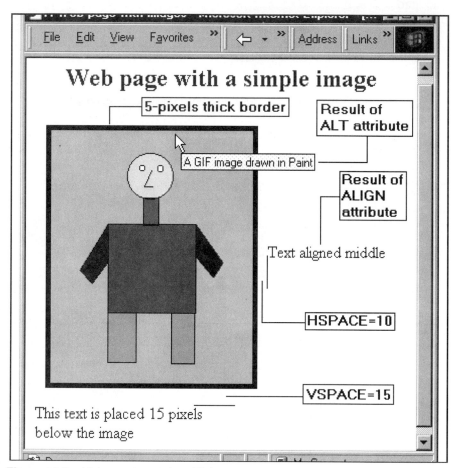

Figure 10.3   Using an image in a Web page.

10.5.2 Image Editing

Image editing implies one of two changes. First, a Web author can change the image contents: by cropping (removing parts of) the image, and by adding graphics, color, and/or text. Image software such as Paint Shop Pro provides many image-editing tools, such as zooming in or out of the image (to enlarge it or reduce it respectively), moving it, selecting an area in the image to edit, adding new colors, changing the image color palette, free-hand drawing, copying parts of the image, replacing colors, filling parts of the image with colors, and adding text.

Second, a Web author may compress (encode) and decompress (decode) the image to change its size. An important advantage of GIF is that the original image is reproduced exactly as it was before after compression, and then decompression. On the contrary, the JPEG compression scheme reduces the number of colors of the image, to minimize the space required to save the image color table. Thus, colors are permanently eliminated from the image, on the assumption that the human eye cannot distinguish very small color variations. Thus, it is not recommended to compress and decompress a JPEG image more than once. Smaller image size means faster downloading of the image over the Internet.

Due to the JPEG compression schemes, Web authors should edit the original JPEG images and then export them, because exporting compresses them and causes color loss. If a compressed JPEG image suffers too much from compressions, Web authors can scale the image down a little and use anti-aliasing to enhance its look. Other visual enhancements may be provided by image software. Many image editors provide such filters as blur or unsharpen, despeckle, noise reduction, and dust/scratch removal.

10.5.3 Image Capture

On many occasions, surfers of the Internet may have a need to capture and save images they find in Web pages for their own use. This is legitimate, as long as it does not violate the copyright laws. Surfers may need to get permissions from authors of these Web pages. Assuming the legalities of this issue are resolved, a surfer right-clicks on the image. Netscape Communicator and MS IE display the pop-up menus shown in figures 10.12 and 10.13 respectively. The surfer then clicks the `Save Image As` item in Netscape, or `Save Picture As` item in MS IE. The surfer inputs the desired image name and folder in the `Save As` window. The image is now stored on the local hard disk and the surfer can use it offline.

10.5.4 Image Scaling

The WIDTH and HEIGHT attributes of the <IMG> tag can be used to scale images. The browser scales the image up or down, using the values of these attributes in such a way to prevent image distortion. It is not recommended to scale an image up as its resolution usually worsens. What is known as the staircase effect (jaggedness of the image boundaries) becomes very visible, especially for non-horizontal or non-vertical shapes. For example, a horizontal or a vertical line is not affected by scaling up, but a line oriented at 45 degrees or a circle shows bad jaggedness. This is attributed to the fact that pixels are horizontal and vertical squares. Thus entities that cut through them lose their edge smoothenness if the original scale changes.

Example 10.2 Develop a Web page that illustrates scaling of images.

Solution This example creates a Web page with one image. The example uses the image created in example 10.1. It scales it by half. The WIDTH and the HEIGHT attributes take pixel values. Thus, we need to remember the size of the image. This image has a size of 200×250 pixels. If one forgets the size, simply open the image in an image program such as Paint, and view its attributes. Half of this size is 100×125. Thus, the scaled image has a width of 100 pixels and a height of 125 pixels. All the attributes of the <IMG> tag used in example 10.1 are left untouched in this example for comparison purposes. Using a text editor, type the code as follows, and save it as *example10.2.html*. Figures 10.4 shows the resulting Web page.

```
<HTML>
<HEAD>
<TITLE>A Web page with scaled images</TITLE>
</HEAD>
<BODY>
<H2><B><CENTER><FONT COLOR = "blue">Web page with a scaled image
</FONT></CENTER></B></H2>
<! Include the image>
<IMG SRC = "myImage.gif" ALT = "A GIF image drawn in Paint"
BORDER = 5 ALIGN = "middle" HSPACE = 10 VSPACE = 15
WIDTH = 100 HEIGHT = 125>Text aligned middle<BR>
This text is placed 15 pixels<BR> below the image<BR>
</BODY>
</HTML>
```

Figures 10.4 shows the resulting Web page.

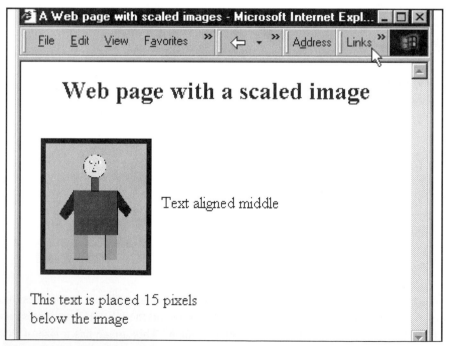

Figure 10.4   Scaling an image in a Web page.

10.5.5 Images Hyperlinks

Images can be used as hyperlinks. Instead of using text as the link, an image is used. As with text hyperlinks, the mouse cursor changes to a hand when a surfer moves the mouse over the image hyperlink. All the attributes of the <A> tag are still valid; however, unlike text links, image links do not change colors to reflect whether they are links, active links, or visited links.

To create an image link, a Web author replaces the text used in the visible part of the <A> tag by the <IMG> tag as follows: <A destination anchor> <IMG> tag </A>. A specific example is <A HREF = "www.neu.edu"> <IMG SRC = "myImage.GIF"> </A>. If we replace the <IMG> by text, the link becomes <A HREF = "www.neu.edu"> Check our new offerings </A>. The browser adds a border of its own to the image link. All the attributes of the <IMG> tag can be used when the tag creates an image link.

Example 10.3 Develop a Web page that illustrates using images as hyperlinks.

Solution This example creates a Web page with an image hyperlink. The example uses the image created in example 10.1. We scale the original image down by 80%, to 40×50 pixels. Using a text editor, type code as follows, and save it as *example10.3.html.*

```
<HTML>
<HEAD>
<TITLE>A Web page with image hyperlink</TITLE>
</HEAD>
<BODY>
<H2><B><CENTER><FONT COLOR = "blue">Web page with an image hyper-
link</FONT></CENTER></B></H2>
<! Include the image>
<A HREF = "myIMage.gif"><IMG SRC = "myImage.gif" ALT = "A GIF image
drawn in Paint" ALIGN = "middle" HSPACE = 10 VSPACE = 15 WIDTH = 40
HEIGHT = 50></A>Text aligned middle<BR>
This text is placed 15 pixels<BR>
below the image<BR>
</BODY>
</HTML>
```

Figure 10.5 shows the resulting Web page.

The image hyperlink in this example points back to the original image file, myImage.gif, as the destination anchor. When the surfer clicks the image hyperlink, the full original image is displayed in the browser. This destination anchor could be any anchor the Web author may desire, depending on the page design.

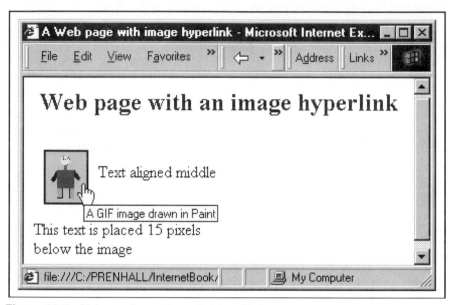

Figure 10.5   Using an image hyperlink in a Web page.

10.5.6 Multiple Use of Images

The same image could be used more than once in the same Web page. In each use, an <IMG> tag is needed. Thus, the uses could have the same attributes or different ones. For example, one <IMG> tag could use the original size of the image, while another tag could scale it down; yet the same image could be used as a hyperlink.

The browser creates multiple instances (copies) of the original image file and uses them according to the attributes of the image tag. This obviously slows down the Web page downloading. Thus, using multiple instances of the same image has the same effect on downloading the page as using different images. It is typical to see a company logo or an icon used twice in a Web page: once at the top and once at the bottom. A full-size version is used at the top, a thumbnail version at the bottom.

Example 10.4 Develop a Web page that illustrates multiple use of images.

Solution This example creates a Web page that uses an image three times; the original image, a 50% scaled version of it, and an 80% scaled hyperlink version. The example uses the image created in example 10.1. Using a text editor, type the code as follows, and save it as *example10.4.html*. (Figure 10.6 shows the resulting Web page.)

```
<HTML>
<HEAD>
<TITLE>A Web page with image multiple use</TITLE>
</HEAD>
<BODY>
<H2><B><CENTER><FONT COLOR = "blue">Web page with image multiple
use</FONT></CENTER></B></H2>

<! Include the image>
<IMG SRC = "myImage.gif">
<IMG SRC = "myImage.gif" WIDTH = 100 HEIGHT = 125>
<A HREF = "myIMage.gif"><IMG SRC = "myImage.gif" ALT = "A GIF image
drawn in Paint" ALIGN = "middle" HSPACE = 10 VSPACE = 15  WIDTH = 40
HEIGHT = 50></A>Text aligned middle<BR>
This text is placed 15 pixels<BR> below the image<BR>
</BODY>
</HTML>
```

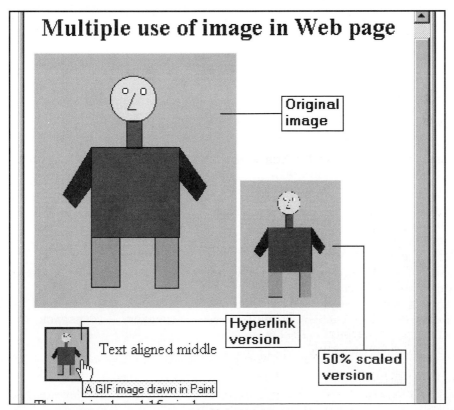

Figure 10.6   Multiple use of an image in a Web page.

10.5.7 Image List Items

Images can be used as list items in unordered, ordered, or definition lists. They can also be used as hyperlink list items. In essence, they can replace text in lists. Why would Web authors use images as list items? It is entirely up to Web authors to use any innovative ideas to distinguish their page design from others. We offer some examples. A definition list of medical tissues, flowers, seeds, or chemistry atoms may use an image for each as a <DT>, followed by the definition. Authors may use images as hyperlink list items in, say, a product summary. When a surfer clicks a given item, a full image with product description is displayed.

Web authors are advised to use thumbnail versions of images when using them as list items, otherwise the Web page becomes excessively long. In addition, one can mix text with images as list items.

Example 10.5 Develop a Web page that illustrates the use of images as list items.

Solution This example creates a Web page that uses an image in a definition list. The example uses the image created in example 10.1. The image is used twice: once as a <DT>, and once as a hyperlink <DT>. The hyperlink <DT> could be used to provide a brief description of the image, with a detailed followup if the user clicks the hyperlink. Using a text editor, type the code as follows, and save it as *example10.5.html*.

```
<HTML>
<HEAD>
<TITLE>A Web page with image list items</TITLE>
</HEAD>
<BODY>
<H2><B><CENTER><FONT COLOR = "blue"> Web page with image list items
</FONT></CENTER></B></H2>
<! Include the image>
<DL>
<DT><IMG SRC = "myImage.gif">
<DD>This is the original image
<FONT COLOR = "red"><DT>Image list item</FONT>
<DD>An image may be used as a list item in unordered, ordered, or
definition lists.
<DT><A HREF = "myIMage.gif"><IMG SRC = "myImage.gif" ALT = "A GIF
image drawn in Paint" ALIGN = "middle" HSPACE = 10 VSPACE = 15
WIDTH = 40 HEIGHT = 50></A>
<DD>This is an image hyperlink as a list item.
</BODY>
</HTML>
```

Figures 10.7 shows the resulting Web page.

As figure 10.7 shows, an image acts as an item in a list. Unless images are used carefully as list items, they could be confusing to surfers and may detract from the Web page design.

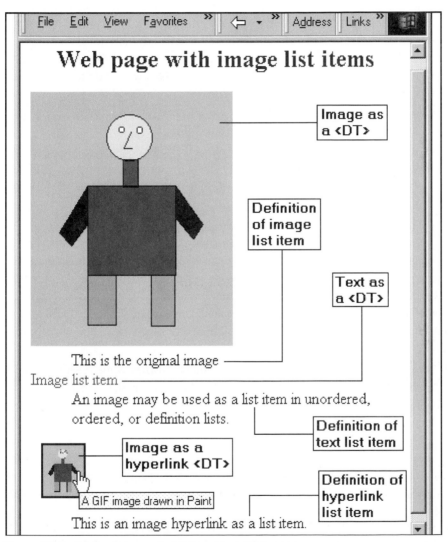

Figure 10.7 Using images as list items in a Web page.

10.5.8 GIF89a Image Animation

There are many ways to include animation in Web pages. Web authors may use Java, JavaScript, or GIF. Java allows authors to write Java applets and include them in Web pages via the <APPLET> or the <OBJECT> tag. JavaScript provides functions or methods that can be used to display a sequence of images (frames) consecutives, with time delays, thus creating an illusion of animation. GIF89a creates animation by including the image sequence in one file. When a browser displays the files, it produces the effect of animation. Java is the most difficult way to create animation, followed by JavaScript. GIF89a is the easiest way to create animation. Java requires knowledge of OOP (object oriented programming) concepts. JavaScript requires knowledge of the script itself. GIF89a does not require any additional knowledge beyond HTML, other than how to use a GIF software to create an animated GIF file, and that is fairly simple. Thus, GIF89a is a valuable tool for non-programmers who want to create animation in their Web pages.

GIF89a animation allows a Web author to create a set of image frames in the desired sequence and save them in one GIF file. The file also saves a script that has a set of instructions about how the browser is to display the file such as the time delay to display each frame and whether to cycle through the frames repeatedly. Thus, including an animated GIF89a file in a Web page is no different from including a GIF file. The Web author uses the <IMG> tag with all its attributes.

Creating an animated GIF file requires three steps: creating individual frames, using the frames to create the animated GIF file, and making an animated GIF loop. The first step involves creating the sequence of animation. Let us assume that we want to animate a bouncing ball by using five frames. Using an image software, we create the five frames as shown, in figure 10.8. The top left part of the figure shows the animation sequence. After creating the five frames, the animation software creates the sequence and makes the loop. Once it is done, we save the sequence as a GIF89a file. We use the file in an <IMG> tag in a Web page to view the animation.

It is highly recommended to optimize GIF animation files while creating them, to minimize their sizes. Here are some tips. The fewer the colors, the smaller the file size. If the animation software permits it, reduce the number of bits per pixels (the pixel depth). Also, save a local color palette with each frame, instead of saving a global palette at the beginning of the file. Finally, use incremental frames, by specifying (x, y) coordinates for each frame. For example, we create the background frame (the box) for the animation shown in figure 10.8. Each ball becomes an incremental frame whose (x, y) coordinates are specified relative to the background frame. This saves drawing the background with each ball frame and thus reduces the size of the final GIF file.

10.5.9 Tiling a Web Page

An image can be used as a background for a Web page. In this case, the browser uses the image and repeats it horizontally and vertically across the page to create a pattern. This pattern is known as tile, or a tiling effect. If an image is used as a page background, it overrides the color of the background, as discussed in chapter 9.

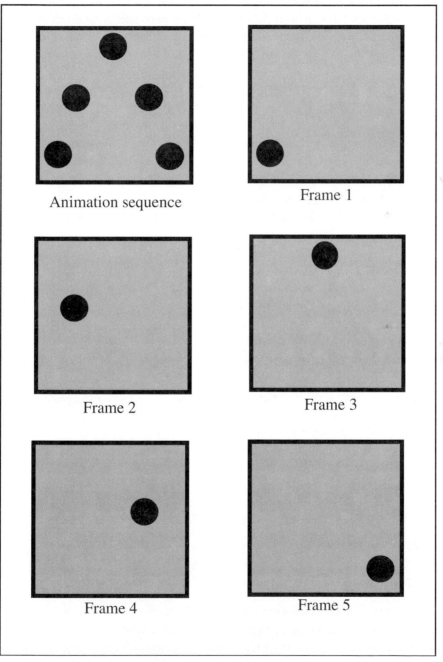

Figure 10.8 Animation sequence of a ball.

Images that are used for tiling a Web page are usually light in color and design, so that they do not overshadow the essential page content. For example, if the background has tiling with loud colors, the page text may become difficult to read. There is always a fine line between page aesthetics and legibility. A well-chosen tiling for a page background can greatly enhance the page appearance. The downside is that tiled Web pages take longer for the browser to download.

Web authors use the BACKGROUND attribute of the <BODY> tag to use an image file for tiling as follows; <BODY BACKGROUND = "myImage.gif">. The browser takes care of generating the pattern for the background.

Example 10.6 Develop a Web page that illustrates the use of images for tiling.

Solution This example creates a Web page that uses an image for tiling a Web page. The example uses the image created in example 10.1. The example is identical to example 10.5, except for the addition of the tiling effect. Using a text editor, type the code as follows, and save it as *example10.6.html*.

```
<HTML>
<HEAD>
<TITLE>A Web page with tiling</TITLE>
</HEAD>
<BODY BACKGROUND = "myBox.gif">
<H2><B><CENTER><FONT COLOR = "blue">Web page with tiling</FONT></
CENTER></B></H2>
<! Include the image>
<DL>
<DT><IMG SRC = "myImage.gif">
<DD>This is the original image
<FONT COLOR = "blue"><DT>Image list item</FONT>
<DD>An image may be used as a list item in unordered, ordered, or
definition lists.
<DT><A HREF = "myIMage.gif"><IMG SRC = "myImage.gif" ALT = "A GIF
image drawn in Paint" ALIGN = "middle" HSPACE = 10 VSPACE = 15
WIDTH = 40 HEIGHT = 50></A>
<DD>This is an image hyperlink as a list item.
</BODY>
</HTML>
```

Figure 10.9 shows the resulting Web page. As shown in figure 10.9, this tiling is bad; it makes the Web page impossible to read. Nevertheless, the tiling effect is obvious: The pattern of the background image is repeated in the page background.

10.6 Tutorials

This section focuses on using the image tag covered in this chapter. Any Web browser can be used to display the corresponding Web pages. It is a good idea to create a directory structure to save HTML files. This helps Web authors to organize HTML files and makes it easy to find them.

Figure 10.9   Using an image for tiling a Web page.

10.6.1 Right-justify an Image in a Web Page

The <IMG> tag, like many other HTML tags, left justifies images in Web pages. Wrapping the <CENTER> tag around the <IMG> tag centers the image. In this tutorial we use the <IMG> tag with the ALIGN attribute to right-justify an image relative to the text in a Web page. Using a text editor, type codethat follows, and save it as *tutorial10.6.1.html*.

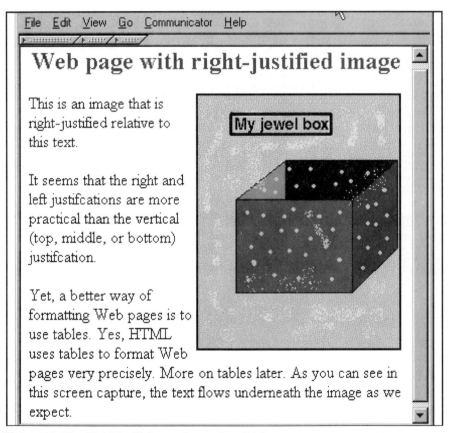

Figure 10.10   Right-justifying an image in a Web page.

```
<HTML>
<HEAD>
<TITLE>A Web page with right-justified image</TITLE>
</HEAD>
<BODY>
<H2><B><CENTER><FONT COLOR = "green">Web page with right-justified
image</FONT></CENTER></B></H2>
```

```
<! Include the image>
<IMG SRC = "myBox.gif" BORDER = 2 ALIGN = "right">This is an image
that is right-justified relative to this text.
<P>It seems that the right and left justifications are more practi-
cal than the vertical (top, middle, or bottom) justification.
<P>Yet, a better way of formatting Web pages is to use tables. Yes,
HTML uses tables to format Web pages very precisely.
More on tables later. As you can see in this screen capture, the
text flows underneath the image as we expect.
</BODY>
</HTML>
```

View the page in a browser. Figure 10.10 shows the resulting Web page.

10.6.2 Left-justify an Image in a Web Page

This tutorial uses the value of the ALIGN attribute opposite to the one used in tutorial 10.1. It left-justifies an image relative to the page text. It should be realized that left justification is not the default for the <IMG> tag. The bottom alignment is the default value. Using a text editor, modify the code of tutorial 10.6.1 by changing the ALIGN attribute of the <IMG> tag to read ALIGN = "left". Also, change the text "right-justified" to "left-justified". Save the new code as *tutorial10.6.2.html*. View the page in a browser. Figure 10.11 show the resulting Web page.

10.7 FAQs

Q: Why is the browser not displaying the image in my Web page?

A: The reason is usually unintentional misuse of the <IMG> tag. Quite often a Web author forgets to close the quotes in the <IMG> tag; for example, <IMG SRC = "xxx.jpg">. Check the <IMG> tag carefully and ensure that its syntax is correct.

Q: Why is the browser showing a "broken image" icon instead of displaying the actual image?

A: This usually happens for one of three reasons; the image file name, the image file format, or the path to the image file. If the image file name is wrong, the browser would not find it. If the image file format is not JPEG, GIF, or PNG, the browser does not know what to do and displays the *broken* icon, as shown in figure 10.12 for Netscape Communicator and in figure 10.13 for MS IE. If the path or directory to the image file is wrong, the browser would not find the file. The rule for specifying image file names is the same as that discussed in chapter 7 for relative path names. The relative path name is measured with respect to the directory of the HTML file of the Web page using the image file. To get a clue about why the browser does not display the image, right click the broken-image icon, and then click the pop-up item, shown in figure 10.12 for Netscape and figure 10.13 for MS IE, to display the dialog window shown in figure 10.14 for Netscape and in figure 10.15 for MS IE. These windows show the full image path as the browser sees it as well as the file name with its extension. Examine the file name, its path, and its extension carefully to isolate the problem and fix it.

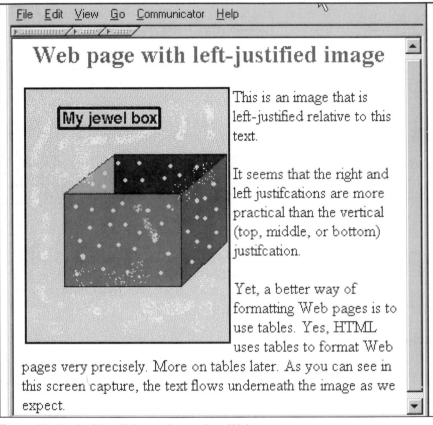

Figure 10.11   Left-justifying an image in a Web page.

Q: Why am I unable to open an image file that I created by scanning a photograph?

A: In some cases, an image file created by scanning is corrupt from to a bad scan or because of lack of experience in the use of the scanner and its software. Delete the file and scan the photograph again.

Q: An image in a Web page does not display in the browser. I get a broken image icon instead. I checked the <IMG> tag. Everything seems to be correct. The image displays by itself fine. What is the problem, and how to fix it?

A: The problem is that the image is somehow corrupt. Recreate the image and try again.

Q: How can I control the positioning of text around an image in my Web page?

A: Positioning of text around images in Web pages cannot be controlled without using tables to format the page, as discussed in chapter 16 of this book. Without tables, Web authors can use the ALIGN attribute which aligns text as shown in figures 10.4 and 10.5.

Q: How can I control the color of an image border when I use the BORDER attribute of the <IMG> tag?

A: Surround the <IMG> tag with the <FONT> tag as follows;

<FONT COLOR = "red"><IMG SRC = "myImage.jpg" BORDER = 5></FONT>

It should be mentioned here that Netscape communicator recognizes the above <FONT> tag, while MS IE ignores it altogether and uses a black border instead.

Q: A follow up to the above question; how can I control the color of the border that a browser puts around an image hyperlink?

A: Surround the <IMG> tag used for the link with the <FONT> tag as follow;

<A HREF = "myImage.jpg"> <FONT COLOR = "red"> <IMG SRC = "myImage.jpg"> </FONT></A>

It should also be mentioned here that Netscape communicator recognizes the above <FONT> tag, while MS IE ignores it altogether and uses a blue border instead.

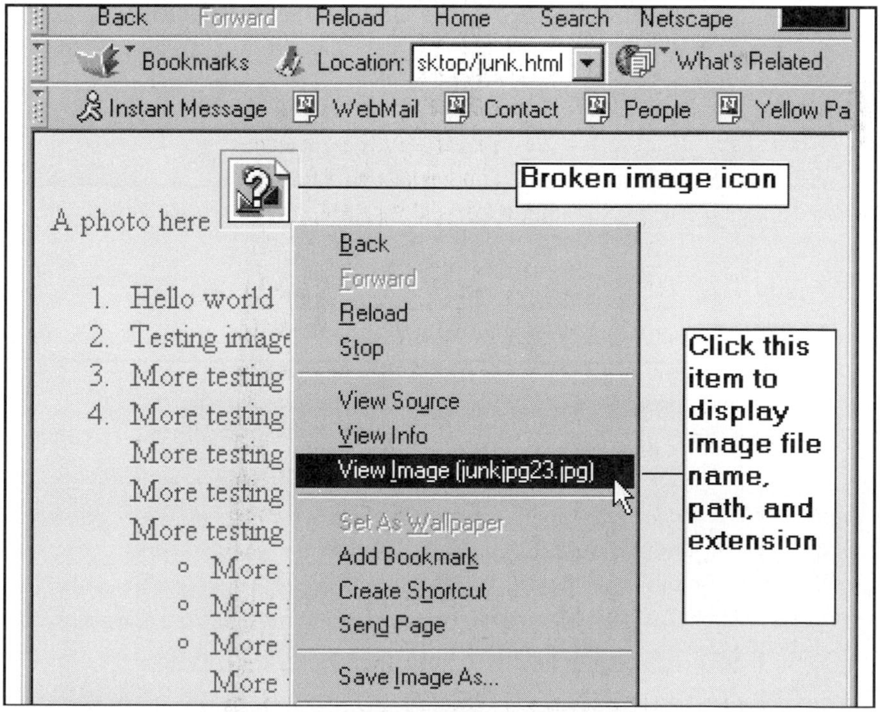

Figure 10.12 Netscape Communicator broken-image icon.

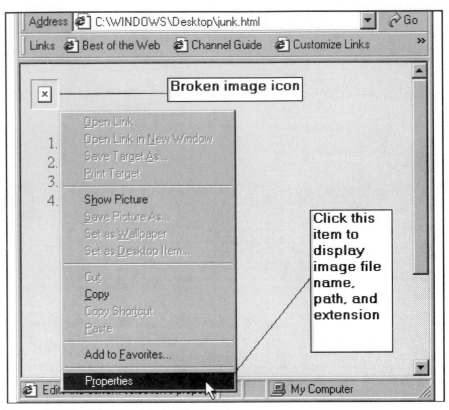

Figure 10.13   MS IE broken-image icon.

Figure 10.14   Image file name, path, and extension in Netscape Communicator.

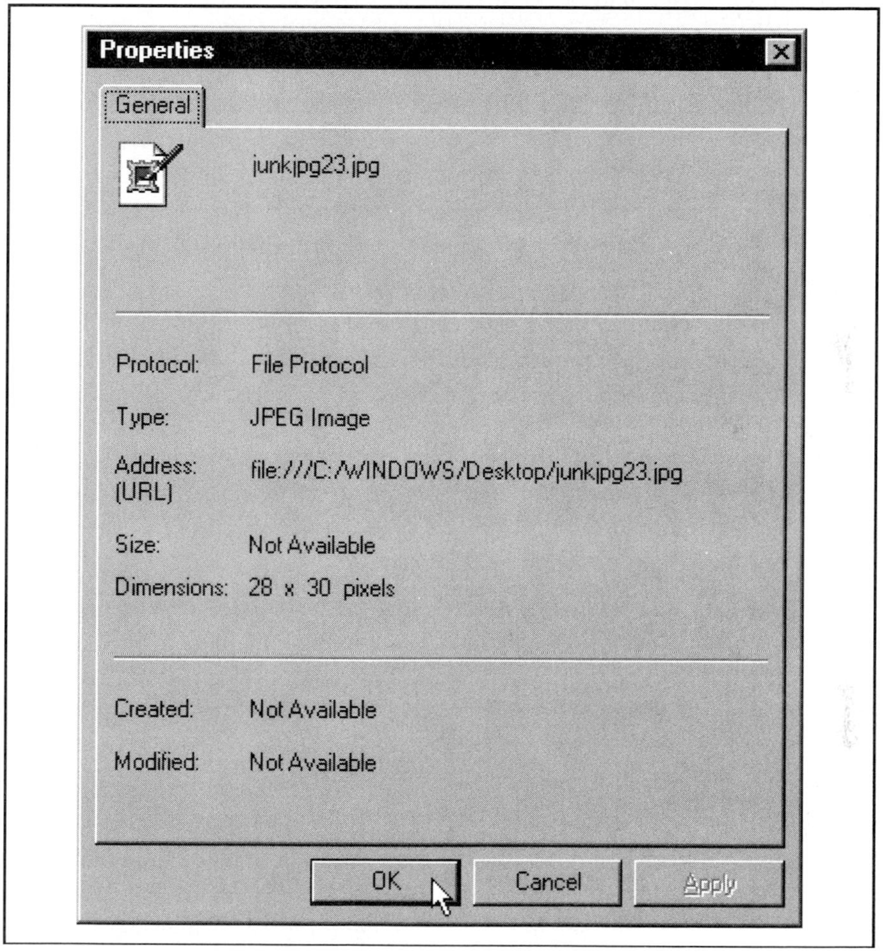

Figure 10.15 Image file name, path, and extension in MS IE.

Q: How can I center an image in a Web page?

A: There is no attribute of the <IMG> tag for centering an image, but Web authors can use the <CENTER> tag to achieve the desired effect as follows;

<CENTER> <IMG SRC = "myImage.jpg"> </CENTER>

Q: How can I turn off image display in a browser to speed up page loading?

A: If you are using Netscape Communicator, click this sequence, starting from the Edit menu: Edit => Preferences => Advanced => click on the checkbox marked Automatically load images => OK. To see the effect of this sequence, you must close the current browser window and open a new one. The browser shows the page with broken-image icons (figure 10.12). To turn images back on, click the checkbox again, so that the check mark is displayed. You do not have to close the browser window after you click the checkbox. Simply reload the page into the existing window. If you want to keep images off in the browser setting, but want to see images in a page already loaded, click the `Show Imgaes` menu item from the `View` menu of the browser. If you are using MS IE, click this sequence, starting from the Tools menu; `Tools => Internet Options =>` `Advanced` (this is a tab) `=>` click on the checkbox marked `Show pictures` under the Multimedia heading `=>` `OK`. To see the effect of this sequence, reload the current page by clicking the `Refresh` button of the browser. The browser shows the page with broken-image icons (figure 10.13). To turn images back on, click the checkbox again, so that the check mark is displayed.

Q: What are the benefits of the PNG image format?

A: The PNG (Portable Network Graphics) format is an image format that combines the best of both the GIF and JPEG formats. More specifically, it combines the 24-bit encoding of JPEG with the lossless compression and transparency of GIF. The PNG format also supports image progression (interlacing). The PNG format should enable Web authors to compress and decompress real-life scanned photographs as many times as needed without any loss of image quality.

Q: How can I get around the lossy nature of the JPEG format?

A: Use a non-JPEG format, say BMP, for the original image. Whenever you need a JPEG file of the same image, save it under a different name. If you need to make revisions to the image, you retrieve the original image, edit it, and save it under the same JPEG name.

Q: What is the difference between paint and drawing programs?

A: Many commercial products exist for creating images. Painting and drawing programs differ in the way they create images. Paint programs create images as a collection of pixels bounded by the image boundaries. An example is the Windows Paint program. Drawing programs create images as a collection of primitive shapes, such as lines, rectangles, arcs, ellipses, polygons, and splines. These primitives are considered by the drawing program to be distinct objects, instead of just a set of unrelated pixels. An example is Adobe Illustrator. In general, paint programs are easier to learn and use; drawing programs produce higher-quality results.

Q: What are some good tips of using images in Web pages?

A: Images typically slow down Web pages' downloading. That is not to say that Web authors should not use images in their Web pages. On the contrary, images are an important MIME element of many web sites. Here are some of the facts Web authors need to keep in mind when using images.

•Text loads much faster than graphics.

•The bigger the image, the slower it downloads.

•JPEG images are, in general, smaller than GIF images.

•Animated GIF images are costly during the downloading and even the running of Web pages. A page with an animated GIF tends to slow down the user communication and interactivity with the page.

•Change an image's format and its color depth (number of bits per pixel) to reduce its size.

•GIF images support transparency.

Q: How do I create an interlaced image?

A: First, use an image program to create the image. Invoke interlacing only when you save the image. There is a save option that allows you to choose the number of passes. When an image is saved by using one pass, it is not interlaced. When it is saved with, say, four passes, it becomes interlaced. On each pass, certain scan lines (a scan line is a horizontal row of pixels on the computer screen) of the image are saved to the image file. A browser decodes the image file in the same way it is encoded by the save option of the image program. For a four-pass image, the browser starts at scan line 0 and displays every eighth line in the first pass. In the second pass, it starts at scan line 4 and displays every eighth line. In the third pass, the browser starts at scan line 2 and displays every fourth line. In the fourth and final pass, it starts at scan line 1 and displays every other line.

10.8 Summary

Introduction

•Images enhance Web page design and presentation. Icons and logos are considered images.

•The sizes of an image influences the downloading speed of a Web page that usees it. Web surfers can configure their browsers to turn off image display in the Web pages they download and view.

•Web authors can create their own images, or they can link to images that reside on Internet servers, such as weather maps and images.

•Rules for using images in Web pages include keeping images small and simple, using thumbnail versions, and using icons and logos if they exist.

Image Formats

•Images have both resolution and format. Both affect the image file size. The higher the image resolution is, the larger is its file size.

•Among the many image formats, three are supported by browsers by default. They are Graphics Interchange Format (GIF), Joint Photographic Experts Group (JPEG or JPG), and Portable Network Graphics (PNG).

•The GIF and JPEG formats are the most popular. GIF is referred to as a lossless format, JPEG as a lossy format.

•The GIF format supports the most commonly used 256 (8-bit) colors; the JPEG format supports the 16.7 million (24-bit) colors.

•The GIF format is usually used for simple drawings of paint programs and screenshot images, images with several distinct colors, and sharp images with borders or text. There are two GIF formats: 87a and 89a. GIF89a supports interlacing, transparency, and animation.

•The JPEG format is usually used for high-quality images, as well as for photographic images or scanned photographs.

•The JPEG and GIF formats allow the progressive loading of images. Progressive (interlaced) images support progressive loading.

Image Software

•Images can be created via drawing, via scanning, and via digital cameras. Image creation software includes Adobe Photoshop, Adobe Illustrator, Mapedit, Paint Shop Pro, ThumbsPlus, WebEdit PRO, WebImage, Windows Paint, and WS FTP LE.

•Image software is two-dimensional pixel-based programs. The coordinate system of an image software has its origin, (0, 0), in the top left corner of the drawing window of the software, with the +X going to the right and the +Y going down.

•In addition to image-creation and image-editing software, there is image-viewing software. This software aids Web authors in viewing, maintaining, and cataloging images.

•Image-viewing software include CompuPic (Windows and MAc), LView Pro, ThumbsPlus (Windows and Mac), ViewSafe (Windows), and SnapShot (Windows).

Image Tags

•The HTML <IMG> tag with its attributes provides Web authors with the control they need to deal with images effectively.

•The attributes of the <IMG> tag are SRC, ALT, LONGDESC, BORDER, WIDTH, HEIGHT, ALIGN, HSPACE, VSPACE, USEMAP, and ISMAP.

Dealing with Images

•There are various ways to deal with images. Web authors may create new images, edit existing ones, copy existing images, use an image as a hyperlink, use an image more than once in a Web page, use an image as a list item, or create GIF animation.

•The MS Windows Paint program can be used to create images. Click this sequence to use it: Start => Programs => Accessories => Paint. The Paint program has a menu bar with a few menus, a Tool Box for drawing and filling, a Color Box to change colors of construction, and a Status Box that displays the current pixel coordinates of the drawing pencil.

•Image editing may mean changing the image contents: cropping, and adding graphics, color, and/or text; or it may mean compressing (encoding) and decompressing (decoding) the image to change its size.

•The GIF compression maintains the image original colors. The JPEG compression scheme reduces the number of colors of the image, to minimize the space required to save the image color table. Web authors should not compress and then decompress a JPEG image more than once.

•Internet surfers may capture and save images they find in Web pages for their own use. Right-click on the image. Click the `Save Image As` item in Netscape, or `Save Picture As` item in MS.

•The WIDTH and HEIGHT attributes of the <IMG> tag can be used to scale images.

•To create an image link, a Web author replaces the text used in the visible part of the <A> tag by the <IMG> tag as follows: <A destination anchor> <IMG> tag </A>.

•The same image could be used more than once in the same Web page, by specifying its file in multiple <IMG> tags.

•Images can be used as list items or as hyperlink list items, in unordered, ordered, or definition lists.

•Surround the <IMG> tag with the <FONT> tag (as follows) to control the color of the border of an image:

<FONT COLOR = "red"><IMG SRC = "myImage.jpg" BORDER = 5></FONT>

Netscape Communicator recognizes the above <FONT> tag, while MS IE ignores it altogether and uses a black border instead.

•Surround the <IMG> tag used for a hyperlink with the <FONT> tag (as follows), to control the color of the border that a browser puts around an image hyperlink:

<A HREF = "myImage.jpg"> <FONT COLOR = "red"> <IMG SRC = "myImage.jpg"> </FONT></A>

Netscape Communicator recognizes the above <FONT> tag, while MS IE ignores it altogether and uses a blue border instead.

•Surround the <IMG> tag with the <CENTER> tag (as follows), to center an image in a Web page:

<CENTER> <IMG SRC = "myImage.jpg"> </CENTER>

•Quick reference of the HTML tags covered in this chapter

Table 10.1   Summary of HTML Image tags.

Tag	Close	Attribute	Value	Example	Chpt. page
<IMG>	No	SRC	img. file	`<IMG SRC="myImage.gif">`	345 346
		ALT	text	`<IMG ALT="image text">`	
		LONG-DESC	url	`<IMG longdesc="xx.html">`	
		BORDER	pixels	`<IMG BORDER=5>`	
		WIDTH	pixels	`<IMG WIDTH=100>`	
		HEIGHT	pixels	`<IMG HEIGHT=150>`	
		ALIGN	top	`<IMG ALIGN="top">`	
			middle	`<IMG ALIGN="middle">`	
			bottom	`<IMG ALIGN="bottom">`	
			left	`<IMG ALIGN="left">`	
			right	`<IMG ALIGN="right">`	
		HSPACE	pixels	`<IMG HSPACE=10>`	
		VSPACE	pixels	`<IMG VSPACE=15>`	
		USEMAP	anchor	See chapter 11	
		ISMAP	anchor	See chapter 11.	

PROBLEMS

Exercises

10.1 Use MS Windows Paint and create the image shown in figure 10.2.

10.2 Use MS Windows Paint and create your favorite image that is 400 pixels wide and 200 pixels high.

10.3 Use the above two images in a Web page.Use the first image as is, and scale the second one down by 50%. Use the ALT, BORDER, WIDTH, HEIGHT, ALIGN, HSPACE, and VSPACE attributes of the <IMG> tag.

10.4 Browse the Internet for Web pages with images. Capture and save two images from those pages to the local hard disk of your client computer.

10.5 Create a Web page that uses the image of exercise 10.1 as a hyperlink, which in turn uses the image of exercise 10.2 as the destination anchor. Scale the image of exercise 10.1 down by 50%.

10.6 Use the image of exercise 10.2 three times in a Web page, with the following sizes: original size, 50% of original size, and 30% of original size.

10.7 Convert the images of exercises 10.1 and 10.2 from BMP format to GIF and JPEG formats. Use image software, such as SnagIt, Lview, or something else. Compare file sizes. Document your findings.

10.8 Create a Web page that uses the image of exercise 10.2 for a tiling effect.

Homework

In problems 10.9 - 10.15, write an HTML document and save it in an HTML file.

10.9 Use a search engine, and find four images: one GIF, one interlaced GIF, one JPEG, and one progressive JPEG. Find their file sizes. Write a paragraph on the size comparisons and display of these image formats.

10.10 Redesign the personal Web page you developed in chapter 7 to include three of your favorite images, such as yourself, your pets, your family, your house, and so forth. Scan your photographs.

10.11 Use your photograph twice in our personal Web page: once at the top, and once at the bottom. Make the one on the bottom a hyperlink.

10.12 Develop a Web page that makes good use of images. Use some of the images more than once with and without scaling, and use some as hyperlinks.

10.13 Search the Web for a GIF89a animation shareware. Use www.shareware.com as your search engine and "GIF animation" as a search string. Download the shareware and create a file that animates a bouncing ball by using seven frames. Display the animation in a Web page.

10.14 Create your favorite GIF89a animation.

10.15 Create a Web page that uses an image for a tiling effect. Choose your favorite image for tiling. You could draw it or download it.

CHAPTER 11

Image Maps and Map Tags

Thing chapter covers image (clickable) maps, their use in Web pages, and the associated map tags. Image maps are considered useful navigation tools in Web pages. They have a double effect. As images, they add to the design and attractiveness of Web pages, and surfers can click on them to access particular information. After an introduction, the chapter covers the types of image maps. It then covers image map software that is available to create maps. It also presents the image map tags and their attributes in detail. In addition, it covers ideas on how to build image maps and use them in Web pages. The tutorials section puts all the chapter material into practice.

11.1 Introduction

Images are a valuable addition to a Web page for their visual appeal, but their use as navigation tools is limited: We can use only an entire image as a hyperlink. It could be more useful to subdivide the image into multiple regions and use each region as a hyperlink. In some applications, an image may have valuable information associated with it in such a way that various regions of the image have different information. Consider the case of an image of a weather map of the United States (shown in figure 11.1). Different states or cities have different weather and climates. If we link each, say, state (a region) to a weather report, a Web surfer would receive weather information of a particular state by clicking its region on the weather map.

The HTML concept that allows us to create multiple hyperlinks from a map is known as an image map or clickable map. An image map is defined as a single image that links to multiple URLs or HTML documents. The image is divided into regions, sometimes known as "hot spots" or as "hotlinked" regions. By clicking on a hot spot or a hotlinked region, the Web surfer goes to the corresponding URL. Thus, instead of referencing the same URL no matter where the surfer clicks, image maps associate different HTML documents with different regions within the image, as shown in figure 11.1; thus, the name map. Early image maps were server-side maps — that is, they were supported by Web servers only. Today, browsers support both client-side and server-side image maps.

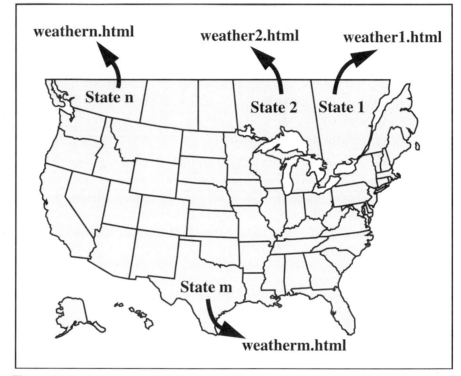

Figure 11.1   Image map definition.

Can Web authors substitute for an image map a bunch of individual hyperlink images? This impractical for several reasons. First, formatting individual images would require using a table to line them up properly. Second, the collection of the individual images may not convey the desired visual context as a map can. Consider the example of the weather map shown in figure 11.1. It is not practical to stack the regions that represent the states next to each other to make the entire map. Third, an image map would not only load at once, as one image, it would load faster than the collection of image files. This speed issue is more apparent for server-side image maps. A browser running on a client would send one request to the server, asking for the image map, and receive one response back, as opposed to sending multiple requests, one per hyperlink image, and receiving multiple responses. Fourth, links for image maps can be maintained in a center file known as the map file. Fifth, image maps are easy to create and use, and provide effective and easy-to-understand communication and interactivity for Web surfers.

Image maps ban be used innovatively and cleverly in many applications. For example, they can be used as a GUI menu, a geographic menu, and a data query interface. To use an image map as a GUI menu, a Web author uses an image software to create an image with shapes that have the look and feel of GUI buttons. These shapes form the regions of the image map that can be linked to different URLs. When a surfer clicks a "button" on the map, the corresponding HTML document is displayed; this simulates the effect of a button. During the construction of the image of the image map, related buttons can be grouped together to facilitate using the map.

Physical maps can be used as a basis for image maps to provide geographic menus. Examples include road maps, layouts (of homes, plants, and other facilities), libraries, campuses, and so forth. Here, the physical map is divided into clearly labeled regions. The collection of these regions makes up the geographic menu. Physical maps are usually scanned to create an image. Regions or hot spots are overlaid on the image. Care must be exercised here because the physical map may overshadow the hot spots. Web authors need to provide clear instructions on how to use the map. In addition, they may want to edit the scanned image, to add boundaries and labels for the hot spots for easier identification by the users.

Using image maps as a query interface is quite interesting. In this context, we use them to request data and/or information. We offer two distinct ideas. The first is to use an image map in place of a form. A Web user may click on a region in a map to request the balance of a bank account, a product ID or a price, or the deadline for purchasing tickets. In this case, the image is created by using an image software. The second idea is to use an image map for learning purposes in such subjects as anatomy, chemistry, and so forth. Here, the images are generated by scanning existing photographs. In anatomy, we divide a human body or skeleton image into its individual parts, such as head, neck, body, arms, legs, and so forth. Each part links to an HTML file that holds all the information students need to learn about the part. In chemistry, we divide, say, a tissue into cells.

There are advantages and disadvantages to using image maps. Here are some advantages: They give Web authors more design flexibility than single-image hyperlinks. They spice up Web pages and the way they look. They work very well as navigation bars or GUI buttons. For server-side image maps, they involve fewer request transactions between the client and the server. They provide easier maintenance of the related links and the files. On the other hand, they are slow to load. They may require substantial development time to design and draw the image, unless a photograph is scanned. Web surfers who are still using old versions of browsers do not see the map, because these versions do not support image maps.

11.2 Types of Image Maps

There are two types of image map we can create: server-side and client-side. The core difference between these two types is in the processing of a Web surfer mouse click. To understand this difference, let us review the steps in processing the click. First, a Web surfer, using a client computer, clicks on a hot spot of the image map. The client browser converts the click into (x, y) coordinates. These coordinates are mapped to a region of the image map by looking them up in the map file of the image. Once they are mapped, the corresponding URL to the region is loaded into and displayed in the client browser.

In the server-side image map, the processing of the coordinates of the mouse click takes place on the Web server. The browser sends the coordinates across the Internet to a script that resides on the server. The script, in turn, uses a configuration or a map file (this file has the coordinates of all the map regions) to associate the coordinates with a region, and consequently with a URL. The URL is sent back to the client browser, which displays the corresponding Web page.

In the client-side image map, the processing of the coordinates of the mouse click is done locally, on the client, by the browser itself, without interaction with the server. The configuration or the map information (coordinates) is part of the HTML code of the Web page that contains the image map. The browser compares the coordinates with the coordinates of the map regions. Once the browser finds the region within which the coordinates fall, it requests the corresponding URL and/or displays the HTML file. The browser also displays the URL associated with the region in its status bar, so that the Web surfer may review it before clicking on the region.

If both types (server-side and client-side) of image maps solve the same problem, why do both exist, and which one should a Web author use? The reason for the existence of both types is mainly historical and evolutionary. Server-side image map were developed first. As Web browsers and HTML were evolving, neither supported client-side image maps. Thus, server-side maps were used to overcome this deficiency. The use of server-side maps reveal some serious problems. First, they are slow, because the client browser has to send the coordinates of mouse clicks to the server and wait to receive the URL back. Second, these maps overload the server and its traffic. Third, their maintenance is a problem, because the Web master has to communicate with the Web author regarding the versions and the locations of the map HTML file and the script that performs the processing. Fourth, the implementation of server-side image maps depends on the type of the HTTP server used. There are two main types: NCSA and CERN. The NCSA type is popular in the United States, the CERN type in Europe. Fifth, debugging and testing server-side image maps during their development phase is cumbersome, because the Web author has to deal with a Web server and its master.

Client-side image maps overcome all of the above problems that server-side maps suffer from, primarily because all the processing is confined to the client side. Thus, the Web author has full control over the HTML code. The Webmaster needs to deal with only one file, which is the Web page that Web surfers download. When a surfer using a client computer downloads the page with its image map, the client browser contacts the server only to request the URL that corresponds to the hot spot (region) that the surfer clicks. The only drawback that may exist is that not all client browsers may support client-side image maps; however, this drawback may no longer exist as you read these words becuase browsers' latest versions are free and available worldwide, very convenient to download, and very easy to install.

In the context of the foregoing, Web authors should use the client-side type of image maps, only, in their Web pages. In this book, we cover only this type. Readers may refer to other Internet resources if they are still interested in server-side image maps. It is worth mentioning that Web authors may use both types simultaneously to implement one image map. Yes, we can create a map that is both server-side and client-side at the same time. This is achieved by using both the ISMAP and USEMAP attributes of the <IMG> tag simultaneously; however, this is not recommended because it doubles the development effort, and it brings back all the headaches associated with server-side maps.

11.3 Developing Image Maps

The development of an image map centers around creating the image and the regions and linking the two along with the HTML documents. More specifically, we identify four steps needed to develop an image map completely. The first step is to create the image that the map uses. This image is no different from any of the images covered in chapter 10. The Web author developing the map can draw the image, scan it, or use a digital camera. If an image is drawn, the author would need image software. Once the image is created, the Web author saves it in a file with the GIF or JPEG extension.

The second step is to define the regions (areas) that make up the hot spots of the map. These regions are not drawn or shown physically on the image of the map. One can think of them as invisible imaginary (virtual) shapes that overlap with certain areas of the image. Figure 11.2 shows the relationship between the shapes and the image and between the shapes and the HTML files. A valid virtual shape must satisfy two constraints. First, the coordinates of its corner points must be located within the image. Second, the boundaries of the shape must overlap with the desired region of the image. The virtual shape does not have to overlap perfectly with the desired region of the image. For example, the rectangle, circle, and polygon shown in figure 11.2 are within their corresponding regions of the image; however, if the user of the map clicks outside the virtual shapes, nothing would happen (i.e., the browser would not load the corresponding HTML file). If needed, the Web author could use the polygon shape with small sides to follow the boundaries of a complex region accurately.

HTML provides three virtual shapes: a rectangle, a circle, and a polygon. Figure 11.3 shows how these shapes are defined. A rectangle is defined by the two endpoints of one of its diagonals. A circle is defined by its center and radius. And a polygon is defined by its vertices (corner points). A polygon definition does not require the first and the last vertices to be the same to close the polygon. Pixel values are allowed only to define these shapes.

The exact coordinates of the virtual shapes must be determined before using them. The Web author reads the image file into an image map software or an image software. The author then uses the software tools to measure the coordinates by recording the (x, y) positions of the mouse in the desired locations on the image. The examples and tutorials in this chapter show, for specific software, how to measure these coordinates.

The third step is to link the virtual shapes to the image and to the corresponding HTML files, as shown in figure 11.2. This step is known as configuring the image map. Section 11.6 shows more details about this step.

The fourth and last step in creating an image map is to write the HTML files that correspond to the virtual shapes. These files are the destination anchors (URLs), as in the case of the <A> tag covered in chapter 7. The virtual shapes serve as the source anchors. The Web author developing the image map should pay close attention to the paths of the HTML files to ensure their correct resolutions. The virtual shapes could be thought of as individual hyperlink images, as discussed in chapter 10. The shapes do not necessarily have to point to distinct HTML files. Several shapes may point to the same HTML file. This is strictly a map design issue.

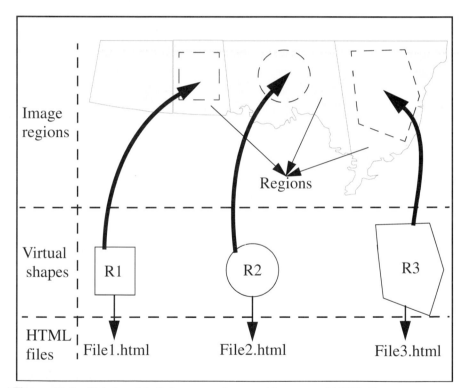

Figure 11.2   Relationship between regions and image and HTML files.

11.4 Image Map Software

We can use the image software discussed in chapter 10 to create image maps, but special map software exists. This software permits Web authors to find the coordinates of the virtual shapes easily. Example software is Mapedit (for PC Windows and Unix) and WebMap (for the

Mac). Some HTML editors have built-in image-map editors. To use such software, the user reads in the image file, defines a shape, and specifies a file or URL that the shape should link to. The user repeats the shape definition and the URL specification as many times as there are regions in the image map. The map software provides its users with a menu of the virtual shapes. For, say, a rectangle, the user locates the mouse at the desired location on the image and clicks the left mouse button, moves the mouse until the rectangle covers the desired region of the image, and clicks the left mouse button again. The software records the coordinates of the two mouse positions and uses them as the two diagonal points that define the rectangle.

Once all the hot spots of the image map are created, the map software enables its users to test the resulting map before posting the Web page or using it on the Web. There is usually a test button or menu. The user makes any adjustments and changes and/or corrects any mistakes. Once testing is complete, the map software generates an HTML file that has all the necessary HTML code to run the map. The user can run it in a browser as a further test.

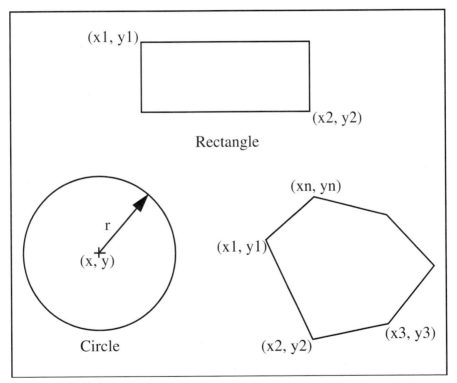

Figure 11.3 Definitions of HTML shapes.

The user could do, by hand, all that the map software does, using an image software such as Windows Paint. Image software usually displays the (x, y) coordinates of a mouse location within the currently displayed image. The user can also use the software to draw an image from scratch. In this case, the virtual shapes could be real parts of the image being drawn. The user would need to write down the coordinates needed to define the shapes. These coordinates are used in the HTML files defining the image map, as will be discussed in sections 11.5 and 11.6.

Map software is fairly intuitive and easy to use. We mentioned Mapedit and Webmap software, but Web authors can find other shareware by running a search, using www.shareware.com.

11.5 Image Map Tags

As shown in figure 11.2, we need to define the map image, the virtual shapes, and the HTML files or URLs to create an image map. The map image is defined by the <IMG> tag. The virtual shapes are defined by using the <AREA> tag. We also need something else that is less obvious. That is, we need to somehow associate the virtual shapes to the image of the map. The need for this association can be explained as follows. The image has its own origin and XY coordinate system. The virtual shapes have (x, y) coordinates of their points. When a browser displays a Web page using the image map, it must be told the context within which these coordinates must be interpreted. In other words, the browser must be told to use the coordinate system of the image to interpret these coordinates. It is the map or configuration file that defines this context, with the <MAP> tag.

11.5.1 <IMG> Tag

The use of the <IMG> tag in an image map application is no different from its use to define an image as described in chapter 10. All the attributes are still valid; however, the attribute USEMAP or ISMAP must be used if the image is to be used for a map. The former attribute is used for client-side maps, the latter for server-side maps. We use only the USEMAP attribute in this chapter, because we create client-side maps only, as follows:

<IMG SRC = "myMapImage.gif" ALT = "My image map" USENAME = "#myMap">

The value of the USEMAP attribute is a map name that must always be preceded by a pound sign (#). This pound sign acts essentially as an intradocument link, as discussed in chapter 7. The map name is the choice of the Web author. This name is used in the <MAP> tag, as shown in section 11.5.3.

11.5.2 <MAP> Tag

The <MAP> tag provides the configuration or the mapping required to define the map. It uses the name of the map image and it encompasses all the <AREA> tags of the map. Thus, the <MAP> tag acts as a container for other tags. The <MAP> tag must be closed. The only attribute of the <MAP> tag is NAME. The value of this attribute must be the same name that is used in the USEMAP attribute of the <IMG> tag. The <MAP> tag is used as follows:

```
<IMG SRC = "myMapImage.gif" USEMAP = "#myMap">
```

```
<MAP NAME = "myMap">
<AREA ...>
<AREA ...>
    .
    .
    .
</MAP>
```

11.5.3 <AREA> Tag

This is the tag that is used to define virtual shapes. This tag does not close. The tag can be used as many times as are needed to define all the hot spots of an image map. The <AREA> tag has several attributes. They are HREF, SHAPE, COORDS, ALT, NOHREF, TABINDEX, and ACCESSKEY. The first four attributes are described below, the others are hardly used.

•The HREF attribute specifies the destination anchor that is associated with the virtual shape defined by the <AREA> tag. Its value is an HTML file or a URL.

•The SHAPE attribute defines the virtual shape. The possible values of this attribute are *default, rect, circle,* and *poly.* The *default* value specifies the entire image as one shape. Obviously, this value has little use. The other three values specify the three virtual shapes shown in figure 11.3.

•The COORDS attribute is the companion to the SHAPE attribute. Once a virtual shape is specified by the latter, the former defines the shape by specifying the coordinates of its points as according to figure 11.3. The coordinates of the points can be separated by spaces or commas. For example, we can use a generic form — either COORDS = "x1, y1 x2, y2" or COORDS = "x1, y1, x2, y2" — to define a rectangular shape. Double, single, or no quotes can surround the coordinate values. For a circle, the generic form is COORDS = "x, y r", and for a polygon, the generic form is COORDS = "x1, y1 x2, y2 x3, y3, ..., xn, yn". In all these generic forms, the x, y and r variables are replaced by pixel values.

•The ALT attribute specifies alternate text for the virtual shape. It is similar in function to the ALT attribute the <IMG> tag.

11.6 Building Image Maps

On the basis of figure 11.2, we have, in section 11.3, identified four steps for developing an image map completely. Using the tags covered in section 11.5, we describe these steps as follows.

1. Create the map image and use it. After creating the image, use the <IMG> tag with the USEMAP attribute.

2. Define the hot spots (virtual shapes) of the map. The <AREA> tag is used to define the HTML virtual shapes that best describe the regions of the image that serve as the map hot spots.

3. Create the configuration file. This file is also known as the map file. It is an HTML file that links the virtual shapes to the image of the map and to their corresponding HTML files or URLs that are invoked when these shapes are clicked. This map file uses the <IMG> and <AREA> tags defined in the two previous steps, as well as the <MAP> tag.

4. Create the HTML file or the URL for each hot spot. Each hot spot links to either an HTML file or a URL. If the HTML files are local, they are stored on the hard disk drive of the client computer; otherwise, they are stored remotely on the hard disk of a server. It is beneficial during the development and testing of an image map, to use local HTML files to expedite the development and the testing process. Once this process is complete, the local files are replaced by the final remote URLs.

The above four steps generate a set of files that corresponds to the number of hot spots in the image map. Step 1 generates the image file. Step 2 does not generate any files. Step 3 generates one HTML file. It is the configuration or the map file. Step 4 generates a number of HTML files. Assuming that each hot spot has its own HTML file, the total number of files needed to create an image map with n hot spots is n + 2. The two additional files account for the image and the map files.

Example 11.1 Develop a Web page that illustrates the use of client-side image maps.

Solution This example creates a clickable map with three hot spots. We need a total of five files to create the map. We use a rectangle, a circle, and a triangle as the shapes for the spots. Each shape is filled with a color and has a descriptive text in the middle of it. Each hot spot links to a simple HTML file. The three HTML files are saved in a sub-directory, under the directory of the image and map files, called map. We use Windows Paint as the image software to create the image and the virtual shapes. The image is actually the three virtual shapes. Using a text editor and your Windows GUI, create the code in steps 1, 3, and 4, and save it as *example11.1.html*. View the page in a browser. Figures 11.4 and 11.5 show the results. Following, section 11.6, here are the four steps to build the Web page.

1. Create the three shapes. Open the Paint program by clicking the sequence `Start` (located at the bottom left corner of screen) => `Programs` => `Accessories` => `Paint`. Before we start drawing, we set the image size to 300 pixels wide and 100 pixels high. Starting with the `Image` menu of Paint, click `Image` => `Attributes` => replace width by 300 and height by 100. Click on the `Rectangle` icon. Drag the mouse to the image box, press the left mouse button, and drag the mouse to draw the rectangle. Release the mouse button when satisfied. Repeat for the circle (click the `Circle` icon) and the triangle (click the closed polygon icon). Figure 11.4 shows the map image. We need to measure the coordinates of these shapes. Simply move the mouse over a corner point and write down the corresponding pixel coordinates shown in the `Status Bar` of Paint. In figure 11.3, the coordinates of the three shapes are respectively, from left to right, [(17, 15), (115, 80)], [(175, 45), 40], and [(215, 75), (255, 20), (295, 75)]. To find the radius of the circle, measure the coordinates of a point on the circumference that forms a horizontal or vertical line with the center. Find the difference between the X

(Y) coordinates of the point and of the center if the line is horizontal (vertical). During these measurements, we do not have to be perfect, because the pixels are very small in physical size. (We have about 100 pixels per inch.)

We now add colors to the image. Click the Fill With Color icon (shown as a pouring gallon of paint). Click the red color from the Color Box in the bottom of the computer screen, and then click the rectangle. Repeat for the circle, the triangle, and the background to change their colors to yellow, green, and light blue, respectively. We add text to each shape. Click the Text icon (shown as the letter A). Open a text box over each shape, and write the desired text, as shown in figure 11.4. Save the resulting image under the name *myMapImage*, with the *gif* extension. Thus, the file name becomes *myMapImage.gif*. We save the file at the desktop directory.

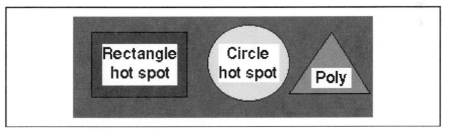

Figure 11.4   The virtual shapes of an image map.

2. Define the three hot spots of the map. Using the coordinates from the above step, plus the <AREA> tag, we create the three virtual shapes, as shown in the next step.

3. Create the map file. Using the results from the above two steps, type this map file:

```
<HTML>
<HEAD>
<TITLE>A Web page with a client-side image map</TITLE>
</HEAD>
<BODY>
<H2><B><CENTER><FONT COLOR = "blue">Web page with a client-side
image map</FONT></CENTER></B></H2>
<H2><B><FONT COLOR = "red">Select a shape</FONT></CENTER></B></H2>

<! Specify the map image>
<IMG SRC = "myMapImage.gif" ALT = "My image map" USEMAP = "#myMap">

<! Create the hot spots>
<MAP NAME = "myMap">
<AREA SHAPE = "rect" COORDS = "17,15 115,80" ALT = "My rect spot"
HREF = "map/rectSpot.html">
<AREA SHAPE = "circle" COORDS = "175,45 40" ALT = "My circle spot"
HREF = "map/circleSpot.html">
```

```
<AREA SHAPE = "poly" COORDS = "215,75 255,20 295,75" ALT = "My poly
spot" HREF = "map/polySpot.html">
</MAP>
</BODY>
</HTML>
```

4. Create the spots' HTML files. We need three HTML files, one each for the rectangle, the circle, and the poly hot spots. The files are simple and almost identical. Here is the file for the rectangle hot spot:

```
<HTML>
<HEAD>
<TITLE>Rectangle hot spot</TITLE>
</HEAD>
<BODY>
<H2><B><CENTER><FONT COLOR = "blue">Rectangle of a client-side
image map</FONT></CENTER></B></H2>
<H2><B><FONT COLOR = "red">Welcome to the world of red rectangles</
FONT></CENTER></B></H2>
</BODY>
</HTML>
```

Save the preceding file as *redSpot.html* in the map subdirectory. Replace the word "rectangle" by the word "circle" and the word "red" by the word "yellow", and save the resulting file as circleSpot.ht,ml. Replace the word "rectangle" by the word "poly" and the word "red' by the word "green" and save the resulting file as *polySpot.html*.

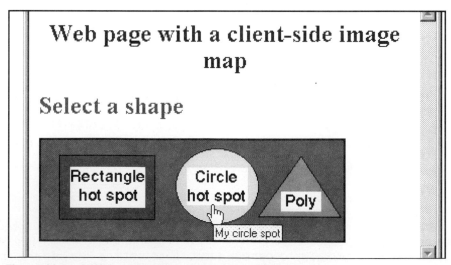

Figure 11.5 A Web page with a client-side image map.

We have finished creating the five HTML files for this example. Which file should we start with to display the image map? The map file is always the driver or the home page for the image map that is loaded first into a browser. Figure 11.5 shows the Web page with the map.

11.7 Tutorials

11.7.1 Using the "default" Value of the SHAPE Attribute

In some cases, it might be advisable to let the image map respond to a user's click outside any of the map's hot spots. This would require the use of the "default" of the SHAPE attribute. This value defines a shape the size of the entire image of the map. Thus, this shape overlaps with the hot spots. Therefore, according to HTML rules (first defined in the map file, first used), this value must be used in the map file as shown in this example. We extend the example 11.1 code in this tutorial. Using a text editor, add the following <AREA> tag right above the closing <MAP> tag of example 11.1, and save it as *tutorial11.7.1.html*.

<AREA SHAPE = "default" ALT = "My default shape" HREF = "index.html">

View the page in a browser.

Observe that the mouse cursor changes to a hand when the mouse is anywhere over the map image. If you click anywhere outside all three of the hot spots shown in figure 11.5, the index.html file is displayed in the browser window, as shown in figure 11.6. Netscape Communicator recognizes the "default" value of the <AREA> tag, but MS IE does not. The contents of index.html are listed below.

```
<HTML>
<HEAD>
<TITLE>Default shape</TITLE>
</HEAD>
<BODY>
<H2><B><CENTER><FONT COLOR = "blue">Welcome to the world of a cli-
ent-side image map</FONT></CENTER></B></H2>
<H2><B><FONT COLOR = "red">You have clicked outside the hot spots
of the image map.<BR>
Please click inside the rectangle, circle, or the poly.
<BR>Thank you, and enjoy using the image map.</FONT></B></H2>
</BODY>
</HTML>
```

11.7.2 Overlapping Hot Spots

In some image maps, it is unavoidable for a Web author to have overlapping shapes. In these cases, the Web author must be aware that the order of the <AREA> tags inside the <MAP> tag is critical. The virtual shape that appears first in the HTML document takes precedence. In this tutorial, we create a dart board. We use three concentric circles to represent three circular hot spots. For these hot spots to work properly, the <AREA> tag of the smallest circle should come first, and be followed by the tag for the middle circle. The last tag is for the largest circle. Any other order does not work properly. Create the map image (300×300) using Paint, and save it as "overlap.gif." We save the HTML files that correspond to the three hot spots in a subdirectory called "board." Using a text editor, type the code that follows figure 11.6, and save it as *tutorial11.7.2.html*. View the page in a browser. Figures 11.7 – 11.10 show the resulting Web page.

Figure 11.6   The Web page corresponding to the default shape of the image map.

```
<HTML>
<HEAD>
<TITLE>A Web page with a client-side image map</TITLE>
</HEAD>
<BODY>
<H2><B><CENTER><FONT COLOR = "blue">A page with overlapping hot
spots</FONT></CENTER></B></H2>
<H2><B><FONT COLOR = "red">Select a color</FONT></CENTER></B></H2>

<! Specify the map image>
```

```
<CENTER><IMG SRC = "overlap.gif" ALT = "My image map" USEMAP =
"#dartBoard"> </CENTER>
```

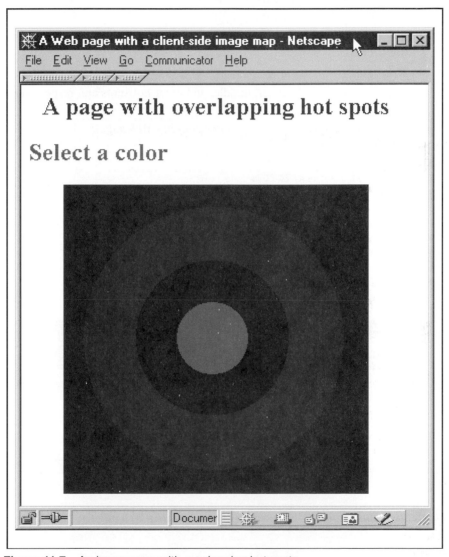

Figure 11.7 An image map with overlapping hot spots.

```
<! Create the hot spots>
<MAP NAME = "dartBoard">
<AREA SHAPE = "circle" COORDS = "145,145 35" ALT = "Inner zone"
HREF = "board/innerZone.html">
```

```
<AREA SHAPE = "circle" COORDS = "145,145 75" ALT = "Middle zone"
HREF = "board/middleZone.html">
<AREA SHAPE = "circle" COORDS = "145,145 130" ALT = "Outer Zone"
HREF = "board/outerZone.html">
<AREA SHAPE = "default" ALT = "My default shape" HREF =
"index.html">
</MAP>
</BODY>
</HTML>
```

The three HTML files for the inner, middle, and outer hot spots are, respectively, as follows:

innerZone.html (figure 11.8 shows the corresponding Web page):

```
<HEAD>
<TITLE>Highest score</TITLE>
</HEAD>
<BODY>
<H2><B><CENTER><FONT COLOR = "blue">Inner score zone</FONT></CEN-
TER></B></H2>
<H2><B><FONT COLOR = "red">You scored 500 points</FONT></B></H2>
</BODY>
</HTML>
```

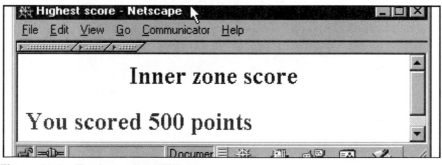

Figure 11.8   The inner zone Web page.

middleZone.html (figure 11.9 shows the corresponding Web page):

```
<HTML>
<HEAD>
<TITLE>Highest score</TITLE>
</HEAD>
<BODY>
<H2><B><CENTER><FONT COLOR = "blue">Middle score zone</FONT></CEN-
TER></B></H2>
```

```
<H2><B><FONT COLOR = "red">You scored 300 points</FONT></B></H2>
</BODY>
</HTML>
```

OuterZone.html (figure 11.10 shows the corresponding Web page):

```
<HTML>
<HEAD>
<TITLE>Highest score</TITLE>
</HEAD>
<BODY>
<H2><B><CENTER><FONT COLOR = "blue">Outer score zone</FONT></CEN-
TER></B></H2>
<H2><B><FONT COLOR = "red">You scored 100 points</FONT></B></H2>
</BODY>
</HTML>
```

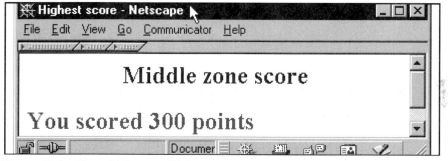

Figure 11.9   The middle zone Web page.

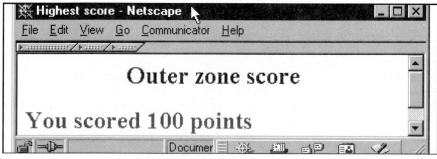

Figure 11.10   The outer zone Web page.

11.7.3 Creating a Vertical Image Map

Example 11.1 and figures 11.4 and 11.5 show the use of what we call it a "horizontal" image map. This tutorial creates a "vertical" image map. There is really no technical difference between the two types of maps, other than the orientation of the map image. In one map, the image is horizontal, going across the page, as shown in figures 11.5 and 11.6. In the other map, the map image is vertical, going down. In this tutorial, we modify tutorial 11.7.1 to convert its horizontal image map into a vertical one. One quick and dirty way of converting the horizontal image shown in figure 11.4 into a vertical image is to rotate it by using the Paint Image menu, as follows: Image => Flip/Rotate => **Rotate by angle** => click the 270 degrees radio button. Paint rotates the image in a clockwise direction. If rotated this way, the text of each hot spot is shown in an awkward way. Instead, we create the image again.

Here, we set the image size to 100 pixels wide by 300 pixels high (opposite to the sizes used in example 11.1). We create the image and save it as "verticalMapImage.gif". As in figure 11.3, the coordinates of the rectangle, the circle, and the polygon are respectively [(3, 10), (95, 75)], [(50, 150), 40], and [(10, 285), (90, 285), (50, 225)].

We use the same files we created in example 11.1. All we do is modify the map file to include the new coordinates of the hot spots and the name of the new image. Using a text editor, type the code that follows, and save it as *tutorial11.7.3.htm*l. View the page in a browser. Figure 11.11 shows the resulting Web page.

```
<HTML>
<HEAD>
<TITLE>A Web page with a client-side vertical image map</TITLE>
</HEAD>
<BODY>
<H2><B><CENTER><FONT COLOR = "blue">Web page with a client-side
vertical image map</FONT></CENTER></B></H2>
<H2><B><FONT COLOR = "red">Select a shape</FONT></CENTER></B></H2>

<! Specify the map image>
<IMG SRC = "verticalMapImage.gif" ALT = "My vertical image map"
USEMAP = "#myVerticalMap">

<! Create the hot spots>
<FONT COLOR ="black"><MAP NAME = "myVerticalMap"></FONT>
<AREA SHAPE = "rect" COORDS = "3, 10 95, 75" ALT = "My rect spot"
HREF = "map/rectSpot.html">
<AREA SHAPE = "circle" COORDS = "50, 150 40" ALT = "My circle spot"
HREF = "map/circleSpot.html">
<AREA SHAPE = "poly" COORDS = "10, 285 90, 285 50, 225" ALT = "My
poly spot" HREF = "map/polySpot.html">
</MAP>
</BODY>
</HTML>
```

11.8 FAQs

Q: How can I turn off the border color that the browser adds around an image map?

A: Use the BORDER attribute of the <IMG> tag with a value of zero (i.e., BORDER = 0).

Q: How many image maps can a Web author use in one Web page?

A: As many as needed. However, practice has it that there is usually at most one image map per page.

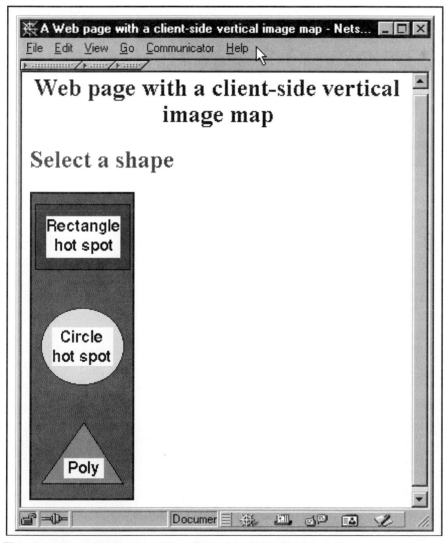

Figure 11.11   A Web page with a client-side vertical image map.

Q: How can I define a triangular shape in an image mapW

A: HTML allows three shapes (rectangle, circle, and polygon). we can think of a triangle as a special case of a polygon (i.e., a three-sided polygon). Thus, create a polygon with three sides. This polygon requires three points (vertices). As with any polygon, whether the order of these vertices is clockwise or counterclockwise is not important.

Q: Are the three HTML shapes enough to define any complex region in an image for a map?

A: Yes, if we understand why a region is used in the first place in image maps. The purpose of a region in an image map is not to trace the boundaries of a physical image area precisely. Rather, its purpose is to define an area that the map user can click on to invoke the corresponding HTML file. With this in mind, the region could be simple. Figure 11.2 shows the HTML shapes used within the boundaries of three states. While the physical boundaries of the states look complex, the boundaries of the shapes are not following them precisely. If the Web author insists that the boundaries of the shape and the image part be almost identical, the HTML polygon can be used with enough small sides.

Q: A follow-up to the above question: What happens if a surfer clicks on the image area, but outside the virtual HTML shape? For example, what happens if a surfer clicks within the state boundaries shown in figure 11.2, but outside the virtual HTML circle?

A: Nothing would happen. The surfer would not be able to invoke the corresponding HTML file.

Q: Another follow-up question: How does the surfer know whether the click is within the virtual HTML shape?

A: When the mouse enters the shape, the mouse arrow changes to a hand, in a behavior similar to that for text-based hyperlinks. The virtual HTML shape defines, in essence, a hyperlink image.

Q: A final follow-up question: Where should a Web author place a virtual HTML shape inside an image area, if the former is smaller than the latter?

A: In the center or the middle of the area. Study of human psychology shows that if we are asked to click within an area, we click right in the center of it subconsciously.

Q: How does a surfer know whether a Web page has an image map or not?

A: It is the job of the page designer to indicate to the surfer visually that there is a map and to provide explicit instructions on how to use it. Such a visual indication and instructions are usually in the form of several lines of text in the Web page using the image map.

Q: My image map is not working properly. When I click on one region, it invokes the HTML file of another region. I checked all the tags and the files. Everything seems in order. What is the problem?

A: In many cases, this problem occurs due to the use of the wrong coordinates in defining HTML virtual shapes. The wrong coordinates may result in one HTML shape enclosing a neighboring one. Thus, when you click the map, the browser does not know which shape to use and may invoke the wrong HTML file. This usually happens if the Web author is not using an image map software such as Mapedit, but rather using an image software such as Paint and measuring the coordinates of the shapes there manually. Double check the coordinates and correct the wrong ones.

Q: When I move the mouse over a hot spot in my map, I get no links. All the tags and files seem correct. What is the problem, and how do I fix it?

The pixel coordinates used to define the hot spot are most likely wrong. For example, using the coordinates [(20, 50) (25, 57)] for a rectangle defines a 5×7 rectangle. This is a very small rectangle, and the mouse may not detect it. Check and correct the pixel coordinates.

Q: What happens if two or more virtual shapes overlap in an image map?

A: The browser still invokes one of the associated HTML files or URLs, according to the following rule. The virtual shape that appears earlier in the HTML document takes precedence; its associated URL is the one displayed as a response to the user click.

Q: All the hot spots in my image map are not working. When I move the mouse over any spot, the mouse cursor does not change into a hand. What is the problem? How can I troubleshoot it?

A: This is an indication that there is something wrong related to the image of the map. Perform the following troubleshooting. Double check the image name and its path used in the <IMG> tag. Make sure that the image name used in the <IMG> and the <MAP> tags is the same. Make sure that the pound sign (#) precedes the image name in the USEMAP attribute. Make sure that the quotes (double or single) surrounding the image name in both the <IMG> and the <MAP> tag are closed. The browser allows you to use quotes or not. If you use them, you must close them. Finally, make sure that the <MAP> tag is closed properly and correctly.

Q: Sometimes I do not see the ALT text used in the <AREA> tag for the virtual shapes of an image map. Why is that, and how do I fix it?

A: This is a problem of consistency on the part of the browser. There is nothing you can do about it.

11.9 Summary

Introduction

•Image maps (also known as clickable maps) add multiple hyperlinks to a Web page, via only one image. An image map is defined as a single image that links to multiple URLs.

•.The image is divided into regions, sometimes known as "hot spots" or "hotlinked" regions, which act as source anchors.

•Image maps can be used innovatively and cleverly in many applications, such as a GUI menu, a geographic menu, or a data query interface.

•Image maps have many advantages. They are more flexible than individual images. They also spice up Web page design and look. Image maps may, however, be slow to load. They may also require substantial development time to design and draw the image, unless a photograph is scanned.

Types of Image Maps

•Two types of image maps exist: client-side and server-side. Browsers support both client-side and server-side image maps. The core difference between these two types is in the processing of a Web surfer mouse click.

•In the server-side image map, the processing of the coordinates of the mouse click takes place on the Web server. Server-side image maps increase traffic to Web servers, and they are hard to implement, test, and maintain.

•In the client-side image map, the processing of the coordinates of the mouse click is done locally, on the client, by the browser itself, without interaction with the server. Client-side image maps overcome all of the problems of server-side maps. Web authors should use only client-side maps in their Web pages.

Developing Image Maps

•The development of an image map centers around creating the image and the regions and around linking the two with the HTML documents.

•Four steps are required to develop a client-side image map: 1) create or scan the map image, 2) create the virtual shapes of the hot spots, 3) create the configuration or map file, and 4) write the HTML files that the virtual shapes link to.

•HTML provides three virtual shapes: a rectangle, a circle, and a polygon. A rectangle is defined by the two endpoints of one of its diagonals. A circle is defined by its center and radius. A polygon is defined by its vertices (corner points). A polygon definition does not require the first and the last vertices to be the same to close the polygon. Pixel values only are allowed to define the virtual shapes.

•The virtual shapes do not necessarily have to point to distinct HTML files. Several shapes may point to the same HTML file. This is strictly a map design issue.

Image Map Software

•Web authors may use image software (such as Windows Paint, Photoshop, PaintShop Pro, etc.) or special map software (such as Mapedit for PCs and Unix, Webmap for Mac, etc.) to create image maps.

•Some HTML editors have built-in map editors as well.

•Map software enables Web authors to define virtual shapes easily and to develop the map file automatically. The map software also enables its users to test the resulting map before posting the Web page or using it on the Web.

Image Map Tags

•The tags that are needed to create image maps are <IMG>, <AREA>, and <MAP>. The <IMG> tag defines the image of the map. The <MAP> tag defines the configuration of the map. The <AREA> tag defines the virtual shapes of the map.

•The attribute of the <IMG> tag that defines a client-side image map is USEMAP.

•The value of the USEMAP attribute is a name preceded by the pound (#) sign.

•The attributes of the <AREA> tag are SHAPE, COORDS, ALT, and HREF.

•The values of the SHAPE attribute are *default, rect, circle,* and *poly.*

•The only attribute of the <MAP> tag is NAME. Its value is the same value as the USEMAP attribute, but without the pound sign.

Building Image Maps

•The four steps, using the map tags, needed to create image maps are the following.

1. Create the map image, and use the <IMG> tag with the USEMAP attribute.

2. Define the hot spots (virtual shapes) of the map by using the <AREA> tag.

3. Create the configuration (or map) file using the <MAP> tag. This file also includes the <IMG> and the <AREA> tags.

4. Create the HTML file or the URL for each hot spot.

•The above four steps generate a set of files that reflects the number of hot spots of the image map. Step 1 generates the image file. Step 2 does not generate any files. Step 3 generates one HTML file. It is the configuration (or map) file. Step 4 generates a number of HTML files.

•Assuming that each hot spot has its own HTML file, the total number of files needed to create an image map with n hot spots is $n + 2$. The two additional files account for the image and the map files.

•Web authors can create horizontal or vertical image maps.

Quick reference of the HTML tags covered in this chapter

Table 11.1 Summary of HTML image map tags.

Tag	Close	Attribute	Value	Example	Chpt. page
<IMG>	No	USEMAP	#name	`<IMG ... USEMAP = "#myIm-age">`	382
<MAP>	Yes	NAME	name	`<MAP NAME = "myImage"> ...</MAP>`	382

Table 11.1   Summary of HTML image map tags.

Tag	Close	Attribute	Value	Example	Chpt. page
<AREA>	No	SHAPE	default	`<AREA ... SHAPE = "default>`	384
			rect	`<AREA ... SHAPE = "rect">`	
			circle	`<AREA .. SHAPE = "circle">`	
			poly	`<AREA ... SHAPE = "poly">`	
		COORDS	pixels	`<AREA ... COORDS="5,8 20,25">`	
		ALT	text	`<AREA ... ALT = "my hot spot">`	
		HREF	html file	`<AREA ... HREF = "myFile.html">`	

PROBLEMS

Exercises

11.1 Create an image map for the image shown in figure 11.12. Each shape should link to a Web page with an unordered list. The list items for the Sports hot spot are Baseball, Bas-

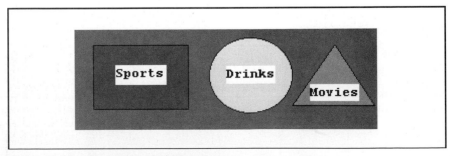

Figure 11.12   Entertainment image map.

ketball, and Tennis. The list items for the Drinks hot spot are Soda, Beer, and Wine. The list items for the Movies hot spot are Titanic, The Sixth Sense, and Air Force 1. If you need to, use the same coordinates as in example 11.1 for the virtual shapes.

11.2 Repeat exercise 11.1, but for a vertical map. If you need to, use the same coordinates as in example 11.3 for the virtual shapes.

11.3 Create an image map for the image shown in figure 11.13. The APPETIZERS button links to an ordered list with these items: Fish Calimari, Steamers, and Oysters Rockefeller. The DINNERS button links to the definition list shown in figure 11.14. The DESSERTS button links to an unordered list with these items: Cheesecake, Chocolate Layer Cake, and Key Lime Pie. If you need to, use the following pixel coordinates to create the image. Image size is 490 × 147 pixels. APPETIZERS rect: [(22, 25), (150, 115)]. DINNERS rect: [(176, 25) (304, 115)]. DESSERTS rect: [(332, 25) (450, 115)]. Use the following colors for the image: light blue for the image background, red for the APPETIZERS rect, yellow for the DINNERS rect, and green for the DESSERTS rect. The background color of each list page should be the same as the corresponding button.

11.4 Repeat exercise 11.3, but for a vertical map.

Homework

11.5 Create an elaborate image map with horizontal buttons.

11.6 Change the above map so that it has buttons in a vertical layout instead of a horizontal layout.

11.7 Create an elaborate image map of your favorite application.

11.8 Find a geographic map, scan it, and create an image map that uses it.

11.9 Find an image that relates to your favorite topic (such as anatomy or chemistry), scan it, and create an image map by using it.

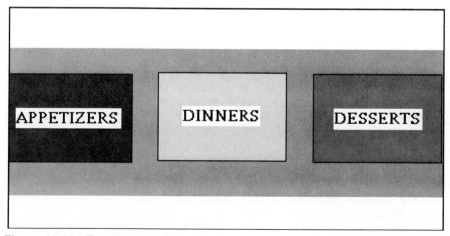

Figure 11.13 Entertainment image map.

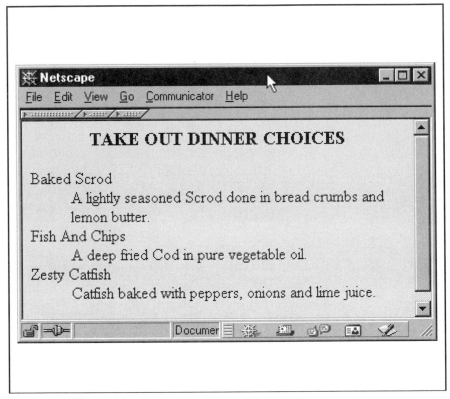

Figure 11.14   Definition list for entertainment image map.

11.10 Find, or scan, an image of your favorite car, and create an image map using it.

11.11 Find, or scan, an image of the United States, and use it to create an image map listing statistics about its states. Choose your four favorite states.

11.12 Find, or scan, an image of your favorite campus, and create an image map by using it.

11.13 Find, or scan, an image of your favorite road map, and create an image map by using it.

11.14 Find, or scan, an image of your family, and create an image map by using it. Use the face of each family member as the hot spot to access that member's biography or short resume.

11.15 Create an image map for birdwatching lovers. The image consists of images of five birds next to each other. Each bird in the map should link to a Web page that shows a larger image of the bird, followed by its description, habitat, and nesting habits.

In problems 11.16 – 11.20, create the image maps and their related HTML files.

11.16 The diet image map shown in figure 11.15. Figures 11.16 – 11.18 show the Web pages for the first three buttons.

11.17 The flowers image map shown in figure 11.19. Make each flower button in the map link to a bigger image of the same flower.

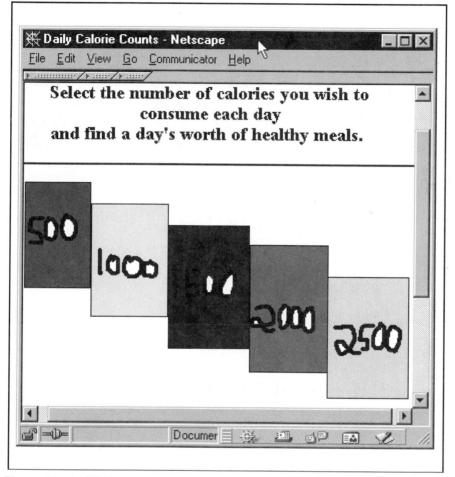

Figure 11.15 Diet image map.

11.18 The counting game image map shown in figure 11.20. Figures 11.21 – 11.25 show the Web pages for the five buttons.

11.19 The college structure image map shown in figure 11.26. Each shape should link to a Web page with ordered/unordered list. Use example 7.6.3 and its figure 7.11 for the buttons' Web pages. You need to create a list of your own for the College Departments button. Use your favorite college — for example, arts and sciences, business, law, medicine, engineering, computer science, and so forth.

11.20 The office supplies image map shown in figure 11.27. Each shape should link to a page similar to the one shown in figure 11.28, with different text on the top. The text for the paper clip shape is "Paper clips are in the holder (on your desk!)". The text for the folder shape is "See Julie for file folders."

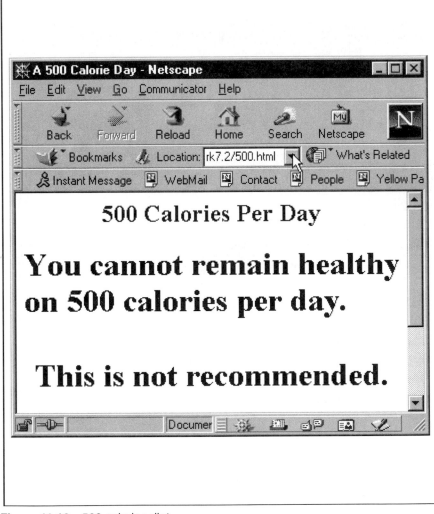

Figure 11.16   500 calories diet.

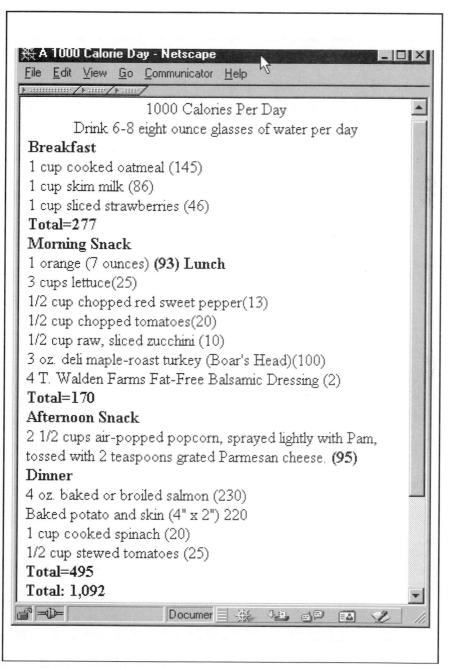

Figure 11.17 1000 calories diet.

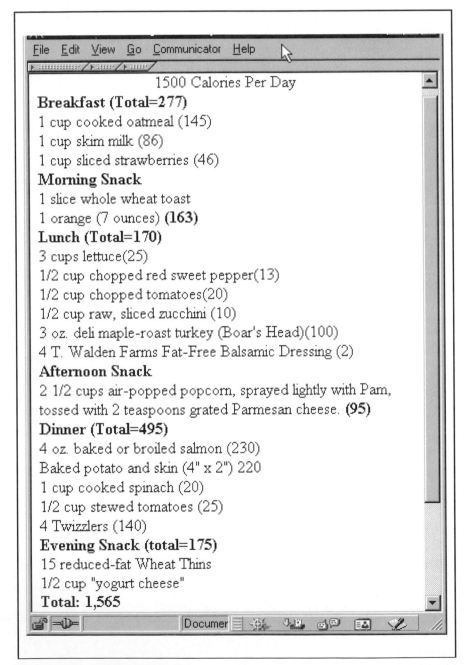

Figure 11.18   1500 calories diet.

Figure 11.19 Flowers image map.

:

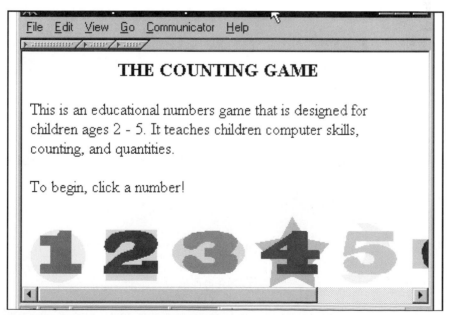

Figure 11.20 Counting game image map.

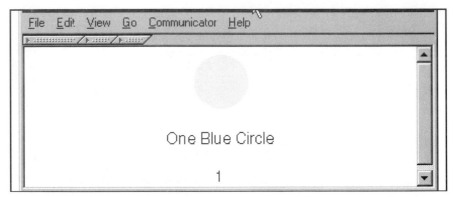

Figure 11.21   Counting to 1.

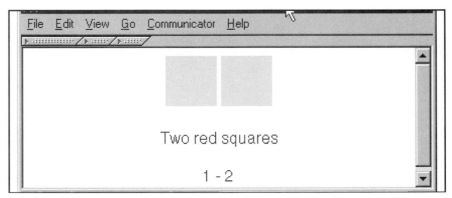

Figure 11.22   Counting to 2.

Figure 11.23   Counting to 3.

Figure 11.24   Counting to 4.

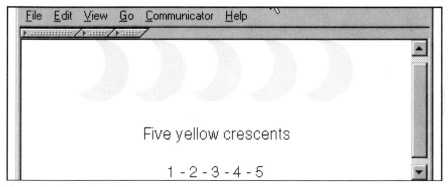

Figure 11.25   Counting to 5.

Figure 11.26   College structure image map.

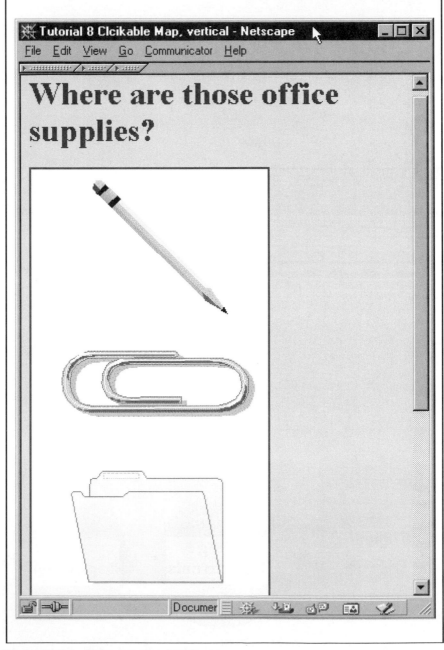

Figure 11.27   Office supplies image map.

Figure 11.28   Pencils Web page.

CHAPTER 12

Sound and Sound Tags

T his chapter provides an in-depth coverage of sound, of its use in Web pages, and of the sound tags. Sound is a multimedia element that can be used in Web pages. Sound is not as widely used in Web pages as images are. The use of sound in Web pages requires that a sound card be installed on the client computer running these Web pages. After an introduction, the chapter covers sound file formats. It then covers sound software. It also presents the sound tags and all their attributes, in detail. In addition, the chapter concludes with tutorials and summary.

12.1 Introduction

Sound is one of the MIME types that can be used in Web pages. Including images and sound in Web pages make them more exciting than the traditional text-based documents. More-over, the ease of including them makes them very attractive to use. Web authors simply use the appropriate tags. Sound is used in Web pages for various reasons. It can be used to attract atten-tion once the page is loaded. Web authors can use it to demonstrate how certain products sound in real life. Sound, together with images, is a valuable tool in child education. A Web page could have hyperlinked images of, say, animals or other characters. When a child clicks an image link, the corresponding sound is played.

What is sound, and how do our ears hear it? There is a sound source that generates sound waves. Examples of sound sources are our speech, drums, radios, musical instruments, moving objects, and so forth. These sound waves travel, or are transmitted, in the air until they reach our ear drums. Think of sound waves as wave fronts you see in water when someone throws a rock into the water. Waves are generated from the source (the rock) as small circles and start traveling in the water until they disappear.

Sound waves travel through the air via vibration of air particles. Wave fronts compress the particles ahead of them and expands the particles behind them, creating the vibration effect. Sound waves have a sinusoidal shape, because of the way the air particles move in space. Figure 12.1 shows a sine wave that represents a sound wave. The characteristics of sound waves are derived from those of a sine wave. A sound wave has a basic shape that repeats itself with time, as shown in the figure. This shape is known as a wave or a cycle. Each cycle has a time duration, known as the wave length, and a magnitude, known as the amplitude.

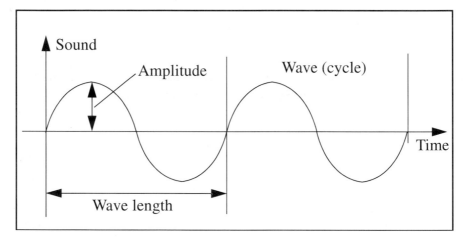

Figure 12.1   A sound wave.

In addition to its wave length and amplitude, a sound wave travels in space with a certain speed. It turns out that sound speed is constant. The speed of sound is 340 meters/second; however, the number of cycles per second changes. This number is known as the frequency of sound. The higher the sound frequency, the higher the number of cycles that travel through the air per second. Sound frequency is measured by the number of cycles per second. One cycle per second is known as one Hertz (Hz). The audible frequency spectrum that a human ear can hear ranges from 20 Hz to 20 kiloHertz (kHz). One kHz is equal to 1000 Hz. A human ear cannot hear any sound with a frequency outside this range.

The speed of sound is constant and its frequency changes, so it follows that its wave length changes inversely with the frequency. For example, a sound that travels at 100 Hz has 100 cycles moving per second, while a sound that travels at 50 Hz has 50 cycles per second. Thus, the first sound has double the waves and half the wave length of the second sound.

How are the sound amplitude, wave length, and frequency related to the physical characteristics of sound as we hear it? Because wave length and frequency are related as discussed above, sound characteristics depend on its frequency and amplitude. The sound frequency affects its pitch. A sound with high frequency has a high pitch. The human ear hears it as a thin, high, and sharp sound. A sound with low frequency has a low pitch. The human ear hears it as a thick, low, and deep sound. Some of us have a high-pitched voice, others a low-pitched voice — it depends on the strength of our vocal cords, and the frequency they generate.

Sound amplitude controls how loud the sound is. The larger the amplitude, the louder the sound. The volume dials of sound equipment, such as radios, control the sound amplitude, hence how loud the sound is. The amplitude, shown in figure 12.1, is an indication of how much energy the sound wave carries with it. High energy pushes more air particles and so causes air to vibrate more strongly. The result is a louder sound.

Now that we understand sound and its characteristics, how do computers and other digital equipments generate sound? Sound as we have described it above is known as natural or analog sound. The waves are continuous. Sound as generated by computers and used over the Internet is known as digital sound. We are all aware of the many digital music instruments, such as pianos, and of synthesized voices we hear on answering machines and recorded messages. Digital sound can be generated directly from analog sound, or it can be created from scratch. In the former way, we use a digital-to-analog (D/A) converter. Such a converter converts the continuous natural sound waves into digital sound waves. Recording equipment can do that. In some other cases, sounds are simulated and created digitally, without the need for a natural sound to convert.

How is digital sound created? It is created in the same way the natural sound is created, but with one difference. The natural sound is created in a continuous way, but the digital sound is created discretely, in increments. If a natural sound wave is replaced by increments that resemble its sinusoidal shape, playing these increments back should produce almost the same sound effect. The smaller the size of the increments is and the larger their number is, the closer the digital sound is to the natural sound. This process of converting a natural sound to a digital one is known as *sampling* a sound wave. Figure 12.2 shows the sampling of a sound wave.

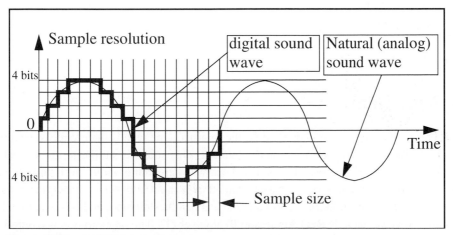

Figure 12.2   A digital sound wave.

As figure 12.2 shows, a digital sound must capture the two important characteristics of a sound wave — the wave length and the amplitude. To capture the wave length, we break it up into increments or samples. This produces the sample size (figure 12.2) and the sampling rate of the sound wave. The sample size is related to the wave length. It is equal to the result of dividing the wave length by the number of samples for one cycle. The sampling rate is defined as the number of increments or samples per second. The higher the sampling rate is, the better is the quality of the digital sound. Typical sampling rates are between 8000 and 44,100 samples/second.

The variable heights of the samples represent the amplitude of the sine wave. The values of these heights must be stored. We store these values in bits. We typically store the amplitude in 8 or 16 bits, the way we do colors, as covered in chapter 9. The number of bits per sample is known as the sampling resolution. Figure 12.2 shows an 8-bit resolution. Notice that there are 4 bits per sample on each side of the time axis.

There is one more issue related to sound. It is the number of channels that the sound is coming from. A mono sound uses one channel, a stereo sound uses two channels, and so forth. Each channel has its own digital sound. Thus, all the sound characteristics and sampling discussed so far apply to one channel. The sampling rate and resolution are always measured per channel.

Digital sounds are stored in files by using certain formats, similar to those for images and text. Sound formats are covered in section 12.2 in this chapter. The size of a sound file depends on the duration of the sound clip, its sampling rate, its sampling resolution, and its number of channels. For the remainder of this chapter, we focus on digital sound clips, their creation, and their use in Web pages.

What does all the foregoing background have to do with Web pages and sound tags? It has everything to do with them. This background is useful and important for being able to use sound software to create sound clips with varying quality to include in Web pages. It also has to do with the sizes of sound files. Typically, sound files, like image files, are large. To reduce their size, Web authors may use smaller sampling rates or smaller resolution, as long as the quality of the resulting sound clip is acceptable.

12.2 Sound Formats

There are two types of sounds used on the Internet. One type is the broadcast sound coming from broadcast stations operating on the Internet. This sound is similar to that of real audio and conventional radio stations. This type is known as streaming audio. Web surfers can use streaming audio to listen to live broadcasts from all over the world. Sound cards that come with PCs can play streaming audio if the software that can handle streaming audio is installed. Examples of such software include Real Audio and Realplayer G2. The latter comes as a plug-in with Netscape Communicator. Netscape also has a plug-in for Real Audio. The Microsoft Internet

Explorer also comes configured to play sound. It uses audio software called Indeo, developed by Intel.

Web listeners need the proper connection speed to listen to streaming audio on their computers over the Internet. Streaming audio is encoded before it is sent to computers over the Internet. The encoding process uses the available connection speeds. For example, one streaming audio may require a 28.8K connection speed, while another may require a 56K connection. The source of the streaming audio should tell listeners the required connection speed. Some Web pages post the required connection speed (required bandwidth of the stream), in parentheses, next to the audio clips they provide. It is important to realize that 56K connections (modems) never achieve 56K speed (bandwidth). Thus, a 56K streaming audio is not heard correctly using a 56K modem. If the connection speed does not match the speed required by streaming audio, listeners cannot hear the sound correctly. For example, a 56K modem causes pauses in a 56K audio stream, because it does not transmit data at 56K. Thus, listeners end up with pauses, or interruptions, in the stream that force the sound to lose its quality.

The other type is the sound stored in files and included in Web pages as sound clips. This type is known as static audio. The sound clip is created, and it is stored in a file using a particular sound format. We cover the available sound formats in this section. The sound file is embedded in a Web page via the sound tags, in a way similar to the embedding of image files. When the Web page is loaded, the sound is played. The Web surfer does not hear the sound until the entire sound file in the Web page is downloaded to the client computer requesting the page. Sound files are usually long, and they may take a considerable amount of time to download. This is why many Web pages use short sound clips that last from 30 seconds to one minute, to keep the size of the sound file small and, consequently, its download time short.

There are many sound formats available to produce static audio. Any of these formats is used to store sound clips in files. As we expect, these formats depend on the type of the client computer and its operating system. There are formats for PCs, Macs, Sun workstations, and so forth. Some of these formats use certain compression schemes to keep file sizes small. Compression schemes, however, may result in loss of sound quality. Here is a list of some available formats.

1. **AU format.** This format (AUdio) is developed by Sun Microsystems. It supports 8 bits or 16 bits, mono or stereo, any number of channels; and may use the μ –law compression scheme. These files use the extension `.au`. The AU format is widely supported over the Internet by all browsers; it is also supported by the Java programming language. the sound quality using this format is, however, not very good.

2. **WAV format.** This format (WAVeform) was invented by Microsoft for its Windows OS. It supports all common sampling rates, bit resolutions, number of channels, as well as mono and stereo. The format does not support any compression. Sound files using this format have the extension `.wav`.

3. **MIDI format.** This format (Musical Instrument Digital Interface) produces extremely small file sizes, because these files are text files. The files instruct a sound card what note to play on what instrument and for how long. A one-minute MIDI sound file is about 20 KB. Sound files using this format have the extension `.mid`.

4. **AIFF format.** This format (Audio Interchange File Format) is developed by Apple for Mac computers. The Mac OS allows its users to create and play AIFF files. The format is flexible; it supports all common sampling rates, bit resolutions, number of channels, as well as mono and stereo. It does not support compression. Sound files using this format has the extension `.aif`.

The first three formats are the ones most widely used. The AU format is supported by PCs, Macs, and Unix workstations. Browsers support all three formats. Including sound clips in any of these formats in a Web page should be safe.

12.3 MIDI Sound Format

The MIDI sound format is an entirely different concept from the digitized audio that normally uses the other sound formats discussed in section 12.2. In digitized audio, analog sound is digitized and converted into digital signals and formats as, covered in section 12.1. The audio file stores the digitized audio, with all its characteristics and contents. When the file is embedded in a Web page and played by a browser, or when it is played using audio software, the browser or the software passes the digitized signals to the computer sound card that, in turn, plays the sound back.

The MIDI format does not use digitized sound, nor does it store any sound signals. Instead, it stores a series of commands or instructions (known as MIDI messages) that tell a sound synthesizer, such as a computer sound card, how to play an audio clip. The MIDI format stores only information about which notes make up the sound. An example of a MIDI command is "play F sharp for 1 second". The synthesizer receiving the MIDI commands or data generates the actual sound. The synthesizer could be a musical instrument, such as a piano, or a sound card. The MIDI format is very popular among musicians and composers. It is also used by computer applications that use sound, such as computer games, educational software, and multimedia presentations.

The General MIDI (GM) system is an integral part of the MIDI format. It specifies the standardization of synthesizer functions and capabilities. Before the GM system became available, synthesizers were not compatible. Different synthesizers would produce different sounds for the same MIDI sequence (MIDI data). The GM specifications include the definition of a sound set (assigning numbers to different sounds), a percussion map (relating percussion sounds to sound numbers), and a set of performance capabilities (number of sounds, types of recognized MIDI commands, etc.). The GM system ensures that a MIDI sequence of commands produces the same sound on any synthesizer.

There are advantages to generating sound with a MIDI synthesizer rather than from digitized audio stored on a disk or a CD. First, the MIDI file is much smaller than the corresponding digitized audio file for the same audio clip. The MIDI file does not contain any audio data. It only contains instructions (the MIDI messages) to the synthesizer on how to play the sound. Second, users are able to edit the audio files. These files are text files. Users are able to change the sound speed and pitch to alter the audio.

Many sound cards that come with computers support the MIDI format. The sound card has two main parts: the MIDI interface, and the MIDI synthesizer module. An audio application software reads a MIDI file, and sends the MIDI data (commands) to the MIDI interface. The MIDI interface converts this data to the format (known as serial MIDI data) required by the MIDI sound module. Finally, the MIDI sound module plays the sound correctly. The details of the communication and the configuration of both the MIDI interface and the synthesizer on the sound card depend on the manufacturer of the card. These details are beyond the scope of this book.

MIDI files can be edited using sequencers. A sequencer may be thought of as a sound editor. The sequencer provides, in addition to editing, "time-stamping" for the MIDI data and commands. This stamping is important if different applications share the same MIDI file. In addition to time-stamping, MIDI sequencers can manage multiple MIDI data streams (tracks). The MIDI format defines three file types to allow the handling of data streams. Type 0 stores all of the MIDI data in a single track, in one file. Type 1 stores the MIDI data in multiple tracks, in one file. Type 2 stores several independent MIDI data in one file. Types 0 and 1 are the most widely used. Type 1 is generally preferred, because Type 1 files are can be viewed and edited easily and more directly.

12.4 Sound Hardware and Software

In order for sound software to work properly on a computer, the computer must have a sound card, sound drivers, and external speakers installed. This card and speakers are different from the computer internal sound that is generated in the form of beeps as responses to OS activities. Users also need to install the proper sound (audio) drivers for the sound card to work. These drivers are software programs that come as part of the computer OS. Drivers' updates can be obtained from sound card manufacturers, normally via downloads from their Web sites. If users would like to record different sounds, they must have microphones installed on their computers.

Sound software is available for both types of sounds; the static audio and streaming audio. We focus on static audio software in this section. Sound software should support sound operations such as playing, recording, editing (cut and paste), and adding sound effects to an application. The software should also support conversion between the different sound formats discussed in section 12.2 without noticeable loss in sound quality.

The various operations supported by sound software are simple and intuitive to use. Sound recording requires a user to open a new file, select the recording source (microphone, a CD ROM, and so forth), specify the recording length, adjust the volume, and specify the sound attributes (sampling rate, sample resolution, mono or stereo, and the number of channels). For CD quality recording, users should use stereo and 44,100 Hz sampling rate.

Sound playing allows Web authors to test the sound clips they have recorded before using them in Web pages. During playing, users may need to adjust the playing volume.

Sound editing is an interesting activity to perform by using sound software. Users, however, should realize that they cannot edit MIDI sound files because these files do not contain any digital audio. They contain only text instructions on how to play music and not the music itself. Editing sound is like editing text. Users can cut and paste blocks of audio data. Users must be aware that if they cut large amounts of data using Windows OS, the system may freeze because there may not be enough RAM for the clipboard to store the data. One editing function users may perform is noise reduction, such as of hiss or hum. Sound software usually guides the user on how to perform noise reduction.

Many sound software programs exist. Sample names include GoldWave, CoolEdit, Macromedia SoundEdit Pro II, Sound catcher, Sox, Kamboo! Factory, Synchrome's Maestro V, Acoustica, Sound Forge, and many others. Users can always search for the latest and greatest shareware by using the Web site www.shareware.com; type *audio* or *sound* as the key search word.

12.5 Sound Tags

Sound tags allow the audio plug-ins of such browsers as Netscape Communicator and MS IE to play common sound formats such as AU, WAV, MIDI, and AIFF. Unfortunately, there are no standard sound tags that can be used in Web pages. The Web (W3) consortium does not have standards for sound tags. The existing sound tags have evolved from the browsers that introduced them. For example, the <EMBED> and the <BGSOUND> tags were introduced by Netscape Communicator and MS IE, respectively. Three sound tags exist in the literature. They are <EMBED>, <BGSOUND>, and <SOUND>. Testing the three tags in different Web pages with different browsers showed that the <EMBED> tag is the only tag that is supported by both Netscape Communicator and MS IE. Therefore, we cover only this tag here.

12.5.1 <EMBED> Tag

This tag is used to embed sound clips in Web pages. This tag must close. The tag can be used as many times as needed to play audio clips in a Web page; however, it is recommended not to use more than one clip in one page, unless the page is written exclusively to test different sound clips. The <EMBED> tag can create a control console (panel), as shown in figure 12.3. The tag is the same, but each browser creates a slightly different-looking console. The control console allows users to play, stop, or pause the sound. The user clicks the desired button shown in figure 12.3 to achieve the desired control. Simply put, the use of the control console is identical to using an audio cassette player or a CD player. As shown in the figure, Netscape Communicator has a volume level that can be adjusted by dragging it with the mouse. This acts as an override to the VOLUME attribute of the <EMBED> tag. MS IE does not have a volume level. Instead, it has a progress meter that moves to the right while the sound clip is playing. When the browser finishes playing the sound clip, it positions the meter back to the start position shown in figure 12.3.

The <EMBED> tag has several attributes. Some attributes are supported only by Netscape Communicator, while others are supported only by MS IE. We cover only the attributes that are supported by both browsers. They are SRC, WIDTH, HEIGHT, VOLUME, AUTOSTART, HIDDEN, and LOOP. These attributes are described below.

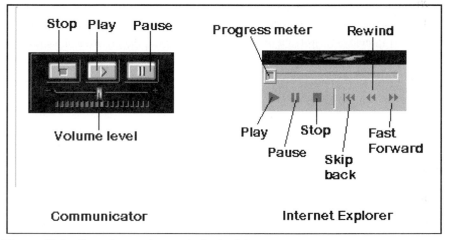

Figure 12.3   Sound control console for both browsers.

•The SRC attribute specifies the file of the sound clip to be included in the Web page. The file could be in any of the sound formats discussed, for example .au, .wav, .aif, or .mid. The sound file and the HTML file that uses it are usually in the same directory. If they are not, the rules of specifying relative and absolute paths that are discussed in chapter 7 must be followed.

•The WIDTH and HEIGHT attributes specify the size of the control console, shown in figure 12.3, in pixels. The typical values that guarantee the display of the full console are 145 pixels for the width and 60 pixels for the height. The Web author can use different values, if needed, according to the Web page design; however, using values less than these could result in the cutting off of a portion of the control console.

•The VOLUME attribute determines the volume level (how loud) of the sound when the browser plays the sound clip. It can take a value between 1 and 100. The default value is 50, the middle of the range. Users of Web pages must also remember to check the volume setting of the external sound speakers. If the volume level of either the speakers or the sound control console (figure 12.3) is not set properly, users would not hear the sound embedded in the Web page.

•The AUTOSTART attribute takes a value of *true* or *false*. If the Web author wants the sound clip to play automatically when the Web page is loaded, the AUTOSTART = "true" is used. The default value is *false*. If Web authors do not want to start sound automatically, they simply leave this attribute out or set it to false. Web authors must think hard if they like to set this attribute value to true, as this may annoy Web surfers.

•The HIDDEN attribute takes a value of *true* or *false* (the default). If the Web author uses HIDDEN = "true", the control console is not displayed in the Web page. The surfer does not have a way to control the sound. In such a case, the Web author must set the value of AUTOSTART attribute to true. This is possible to do, but it is not recommended, because it could be annoying to Web surfers.

•The LOOP attribute allows the browser to play the same sound clip more than once. Its value could be *true* or *false*. The default value is *false*, in which case the browser plays the sound clip only once. If the value of the LOOP attribute is set to *true*, the browser plays the sound clip repeatedly until the Web surfer stops the sound (by clicking the Stop button of the control console shown in figure 12.3).

12.6 Dealing with Sound

Dealing with sound implies creating sound clips and then using them in Web pages. We discuss both ideas in this section.

12.6.1 Sound Creation

Creating sound clips requires the use of sound software to record and edit sound. Section 12.3 discusses sound software in general. We here cover an audio program that comes with Windows. The program name is Sound Recorder. To access this program, click this sequence: Start (Windows menu on bottom left corner) => Programs => Accessories => Entertainment => Sound Recorder. The program window is shown in figure 12.4. The program is intuitive, simple, and easy to use. There are five buttons at the bottom of the window as shown in the figure. They control the recording and playing activities. The Record button is used to record a new sound clip. The Play button plays already-recorded existing sound clips. The other two buttons position the slider to the start (rewind) or the end (fast forward) of a sound clip.

The slider shown above the five buttons moves left to right during the recording or the playing of a sound clip. If the user clicks the Stop button to stop recording or playing, the slider stops in its current position. The user can click the Record or the Play button to continue from the current position of the slider, or the user can click the Seek to Start (Seek to End) button to position the slider at the start (end) of the sound clip.

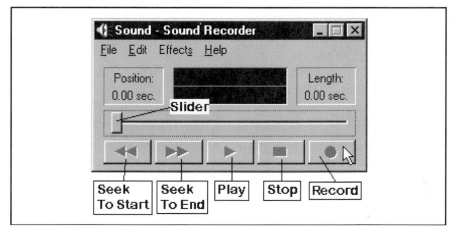

Figure 12.4   Windows Sound Recorder.

There are three areas above the slider as shown in figure 12.4. The Length area shows the length, in seconds, of the sound clip being recorded or played. The default length during recording is one minute, or 60 seconds. Stopping the recording at any point allows the user to record a sound clip with any length less than 60 seconds. The Position area shows, in seconds, the current position of the slider. The area in the middle shows the sound waves as the sound clip is recorder or played. If there are no waves displayed during recording, it means there is no sound recorded. In such a case, the user is recording silence.

The Sound Recorder program has its menu bar on the top of its window as shown in figure 12.4. The File menu allows the user to save a sound clip, after recording it, by clicking the Save or Save as menu items. To play an existing sound clip, the user clicks File => Open. The Edit menu allows the user to mix sound clips and to cut and paste. The Effects menu allows the user to increase or decrease the sound volume; it also allows the user to control how fast to record or play a sound clip.

The use of the Sound Recorder program is simple. Let us record a sound clip. When the program window comes up for the first time, the circle in the middle of the Record button is shown in red., and the slider position is in the far left side. Once the source (a person, a radio, a product, etc.) of the sound to be recorded is ready, the user clicks the Record button. The red circle disappears, the slider starts moving to the right, and the length of the clip is displayed and incremented. When the recording is finished, the user clicks the Stop button and saves the clip in a file by clicking File => Save As (or Save). The program saves the file in the WAV format. Thus the file extension is .wav. The user can use another sound program, such as Sox, to convert the WAV format to any other sound format, such as AU.

To play a sound clip, the user must first open the file of the sound clip by clicking `File` => `Open`. Now the sound clip is ready to play. The user clicks the `Play` button to hear it. The user can also edit the clip.

12.6.2 Sound Use

Once sound is recorded, we can play it in Web pages. Most PCs come with sound cards installed. Depending on the quality of the sound card, sound coming off the PC could be of low or high quality. Higher-level sound cards can produce sounds of high quality.

Embedding sound in Web pages can be achieved via two alternatives. First, the sound clip can be used in a hyperlink. In this case, the sound file is used as the destination anchor. Thus, when the Web surfer clicks the link on the Web page, a pop-up window with the control console (figure 12.3) is displayed on the screen, and the sound clip begins playing. The Web surfer can use the control console to deal with the sound clip. Figures 12.5 and 12.6 show the windows for the two browsers. As shown in the figures, Netscape Communicator uses the control console shown in figure 12.3; MS IE uses a slightly different window. Also, depending on the PC soft-

Figure 12.5   Netscape sound pop-up window.

ware and setup, the window of the Media Player shown in figure 12.6 may be different. Actually, some PCs may have two players; one is called Windows Media Player, the other is called Media Player. Both of them can play audio and video clips. We cover the Media Player program in chapter 13. In addition, the user can run the Media Player application independent of a browser, by clicking this sequence; `Start` (Windows menu on bottom left corner) => `Programs` => `Accessories` => `Entertainment` => `Windows Media Player`. The last item in this sequence may show as `Media Player` instead of `Windows Media Player`. The Media Player program is stored in the Windows folder. Thus, alternatively one can run the program by double clicking this sequence; `My Computer` => `Drive C` => `Windows` => `Mplayer`. If the player cannot be located as described here, the reader is encouraged to search for it, using the Windows search tool, by typing the following sequence: `Start` => `Find` => `Files or Folders` => type the search string `media player` in the window that pops up. If the program is installed on the computer, the search will find it.

The second alternative for embedding sound in Web pages is by using the <EMBED> tag. This tag provides Web authors with more control of the sound clip, via the attributes of the tag. For example, Web authors can set the LOOP attribute to true; or they can set the AUTOSTART attribute to false and let Web surfers click the `Play` button on the control console when they want to hear the sound clip.

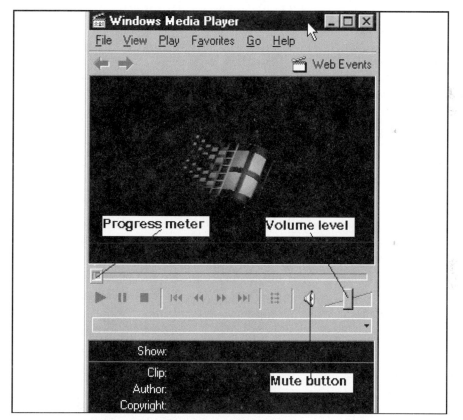

Figure 12.6 Microsoft Windows `Media Player`.

12.6.3 MP3 Digital Music

If sound files can be embedded in Web pages and transmitted over the Internet, can we transmit music over the Internet too? As with sound in general, music and songs are recorded in analog signals. The successful use of digital music over the Internet has three requirements. First, we must convert the analog signals to digital signals. This conversion uses the same ideas and techniques discussed in sections 12.1 and 12.2. Second, the sound quality of the digital music must be the same as the quality of the original analog CD sound. Third, the size of the files of the digital music must be small enough for fast transmission and distribution over the Internet, to allow downloading the digital music to hear it. Listening to music over the Internet is known as *listening to online radio*. The downloading of digital music requires large bandwidth or much time, so Web surfers cannot listen to MP3 music over the Internet when using dial-up modem connections. They need high speed access via, say, cable or DSL modems; however, dial-up surfers can download the MP3 files and listen to them offline.

The MP3 format is designed to meet the above three requirements. MP3 makes digital music a realty. MP3 is short for MPEG Audio Layer 3. MP3 is defined as a file format which stores digital music and songs in computer files. Thus, in a way similar to storing text in a file using, say, ASCII format, we can store music in a file using the MP3 format. This allows computer users to play, buy, and manage CD-quality songs and music on their PCs. It also allows musicians to distribute their own songs from their Web sites directly to their listeners and fans, thus possibly eliminating the need for record companies.

The MP3 format uses an audio-compression algorithm that is part of the MPEG standard. This standard has MPEG-1, MPEG-2, and MPEG-3 specifications. These specifications are known as layer 1, layer 2, and layer 3 respectively. MP3 uses layer 3. The three layers define the compression schemes used to convert analog audio signals to digital signals. Layer 3 uses special audio encoding and acoustic compression to remove all the redundant and irrelevant parts of a sound signal that the human ear cannot hear anyway. It also increases the frequency resolution of the digital sound, by adding a filter known as Modified Discrete Cosine Transform (MDCT). As a result, layer 3, and thus MP3, compresses the original analog sound at a near-CD quality by a factor of 12, without sacrificing the original sound quality and fidelity.

MP3 creators and users need a variety of software tools. MP3 players allow users to play MP3 files on their PCs. CD rippers are software programs that allow users to extract songs from an audio CD, covert them into MP3 format, and save them in MP3 files. These files have the extension .mp3. These ripper programs are used to create and distribute MP3 music. MP3 encoders and decoders allow users to convert any WAV file into a corresponding MP3 file, and vice versa. There are other programming utilities that help users to integrate MP3 files into programming environments.

Most Web surfers use MP3 players. A Web surfer must have the same sound hardware that we described in section 12.3 to hear MP3 music. In addition, the surfer needs to download and install an MP3 player on the PC. One common player for Windows is WINAMP, offered by www.winamp.com. WINAMP provides a comprehensive GUI interface with a wide variety of functions and options, as shown in figure 12.7.

Converting a CD into an MP3 file takes two steps. First, we create a WAV file from the CD using a CD ripper. Second, we use an MP3 encoder to convert the resulting WAV file into an MP3 file. We can hear the resulting music with an MP3 player. We reverse these two steps to make a CD from an MP3 file. First, we convert the MP3 file into a WAV file by using an MP3 decoder. Second, we write the WAV file to a CD by using a CD-writer. Some CD-writer software goes straight from MP3 to CD, bypassing the WAV step.

Figure 12.7   WINAMP GUI.

12.7 Tutorials

This section focuses on using the sound tag covered in this chapter. Any Web browser can be used to display the corresponding Web pages. It is a good idea to create a directory structure to save HTML files. This helps Web authors to organize HTML files and makes it easy to find them.

12.7.1 Creating a Sound Hyperlink in a Web Page

In this tutorial, we use the <A> tag to create a sound hyperlink. The destination anchor is the file that stores the sound clip. We use the Windows Sound Recorder program, discussed in section 12.5.1, to record a simple sound clip that is 10 seconds long. We use the computer microphone to record the message "just testing; one, two, three; one, two, three; one, two, three." If you have other sound clips on your computer, you can use them instead of recording your own clip. Check your computer for audio clips already existing. There are two ways to check. You can use the search tool of Windows by clicking this sequence: Start => Find => Files or Folders => type the search string *.wav or *.mid in the window that pops up. The "*" represents the wild card typically used in computer searching. If there are any audio clips installed on the computer, the search will find them. The other way of looking for pre-installed audio clips is to check the Media folder. This folder is a subfolder under the Windows folder. You can open this folder by double clicking this sequence; `My Computer` => `Drive C` => `Windows` => `Media`. The Media folder stores both audio and video files that come with Windows on your computer.

Using a text editor, type the code following figure 12.8, and save it as *tutorial12.6.1.html*. View the page in a browser. Figure 12.8 shows the resulting Web page. When you click the hyperlink, the browser plays the sound clip and displays its pop-up window, as discussed in section 12.5.2.

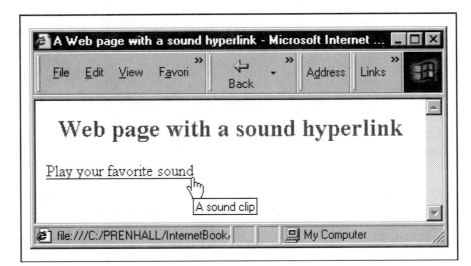

Figure 12.8   A sound hyperlink in a Web page.

```
<HTML>
<HEAD>
<TITLE>A Web page with a sound hyperlink</TITLE>
</HEAD>
<BODY>
<H2><B><CENTER><FONT COLOR = "green">Web page with a sound hyper-
link</FONT></CENTER></B></H2>
<A HREF = "mySound.wav" TITLE = "A sound clip">Play your favorite
sound</A>
</BODY>
</HTML>
```

12.7.2 Using the <EMBED> Tag in a Web Page

This tutorial illustrates the use of the <EMBED> tag with its attributes discussed in section 12.4. We use only four attributes that should not annoy the Web surfer. The reader is encouraged to try the other attributes. Using a text editor, type the code that follows, and save it as *tutorial12.6.2.html*. View the page in a browser. Figures 12.9 and 12.10 show the resulting Web page.

```
<HTML>
<HEAD>
<TITLE>A Web page with the EMBED sound tag</TITLE>
</HEAD>
<BODY>
<H2><B><CENTER><FONT COLOR = "green">A Web page with the EMBED
sound tag</FONT></CENTER></B></H2>
Click the desired button on the control console shown below.
<P><CENTER><EMBED SRC = "mySound.wav" WIDTH = 145 HEIGHT = 60 VOL-
UME = 70>
</EMBED></CENTER>
</BODY>
</HTML>
```

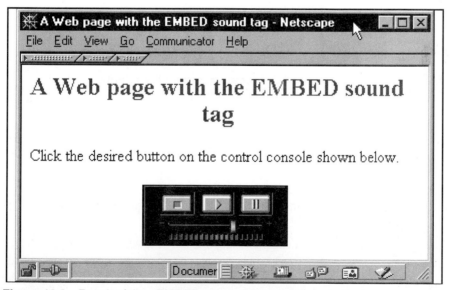

Figure 12.9 Result of the <EMBED> tag in Netscape Communicator.

In the HTML code for this tutorial, we use the <CENTER> tag to center the sound control console in the Web page. We also use the <P> tag to push the console further down away from the text above it, for better visualization of the page.

Figure 12.10   Result of the <EMBED> tag in MS IE.

12.8 FAQs

Q: What are some of the useful Internet resources for sound?

A: There are many Web sites, newsgroups, and FAQs dedicated to issues about sound and its use in Web pages. Here is a brief list.

Newsgroups: com.dsp, comp.music, rec.audio.tec, alt.binaries.sounds, comp.answers, comp.news.answers, and comp.sys.ibm.pc.soundcard (devoted to sound cards, and has its own FAQs).

Mailing list: csound-list-request@maths.exeter.ac.uk

Q: I cannot hear the sound from an applet in my Web page. What is the problem and how can I fix it?

A: Java, which is used to write applets, supports only the AU sound format. Make sure the sound file the applet is using is stored in this format. The file extension should be .au. If it is not, you must convert it from its current format to the au format with μ–law mono attribute. You can do that conversion by using a program such as Sox. For example, use the following command at the OS level to convert a file named myFile from the wav format to the au format: sox myFile.wav myFile.au. In addition, make sure that the sound file and the HTML file that runs the applet are in the same directory.

Q: How can I learn more about streaming audio?

A: You can search the Internet with a search engine. For a quick start, check these two Web sites; www.realaudio.com (Real Audio software), and www.real.com (Realplayer G2 software).

Q: I am using the <EMBED> tag in a Web page. The sound control console shows fine in MS IE, but it does not show at all when I display the page in Netscape Communicator. I checked the syntax. It is correct. What is the problem, and how can I fix it?

A: The problem is that the sound file you are using in the <EMBED> tag does not exist, or it is not in the right directory. If Netscape Communicator cannot find the sound file, it does not display the control console. MS IE is more forgiving than the Communicator. It displays the control console regardless of the existence of the sound file.

Q: Is it a good idea to use background sound in my Web page?

A: It is not a good idea to use background sound, for two reasons. First, Netscape Communicator does not support the <BGSOUND> tag. Only MS IE does support it. Second, a background sound could be very annoying to the surfers of your Web page, because it plays automatically. This could be embarrassing to some surfers who may be surfing the Internet privately at work or at home.

Q: How do I record sound from my TV, VCR, or stereo system to create sound clips? Should I use the computer microphone?

A: You should not use the computer microphone to record audio signals. This method produces poor results. You can use the microphone to record someone's voice, but to record an audio signal, you need to take the signal directly from the TV, the VCR, or the stereo into the sound card of your computer. On the back of each of these devices, there is an output socket labeled Audio Out. On the back of your computer, there are probably three mini sockets. They are most likely labelled Audio Out, Line In, and Mic. The Audio Out socket is where the external sound speakers should be plugged to. You need to connect an audio cord from the Audio Out socket on the sound device (TV, VCR, or stereo) to the Line In socket on your computer. If you turn the device on, you should hear the sound over the computer speakers. One last thing you need is a sound software to record the audio signal. A program such as GoldWave can be used. Once the sound is recorded, you edit by using the program's editing functions.

12.9 Summary

Introduction

•Sound is one of the MIME types that can be used in Web pages. Sound is used in Web pages to attract attention, to demonstrate how certain products sound in real life, or to teach children.

•Sound travels in space as waves. Sound waves have a sinusoidal shape. Each sound wave (cycle) has a wave length, an amplitude, and a frequency. The length is the time duration of a wave. The amplitude is the magnitude of the wave. The frequency is the number of waves (cycles) per second.

•Sound frequency is measured in Hertz (Hz, the number of cycles per second). The audible frequency spectrum for a human ear is 20 Hz to 20 kiloHertz (kHZ).

•The sound frequency affects its pitch. A sound with high frequency has a high pitch. The human ear hears it as a thin, high, and sharp sound. A sound with low frequency has a low pitch. The human ears hears it as a thick, low, and deep sound.

•Sound amplitude controls how loud the sound is. The larger the amplitude is, the louder the sound is.

•The volume dials of sound equipment, such as radios, control the sound amplitude, hence how loud the sound is.

•Natural sound is known as analog sound. Sound generated by computers and used over the Internet is known as digital sound.

•Digital sound can be generated directly from analog sound (by discretizing the analog sound waves), or it can be created digitally from scratch.

•The process of converting a natural sound to a digital one is known as sampling a sound wave.

•A digital sound is characterized by its sampling rate and resolution. The sampling rate represents the sound wave length, and the sampling resolution represents the wave amplitude.

•The sampling rate is defined as the number of increments or samples per second. The higher the sampling rate, the better the quality of the digital sound. Typical sampling rates are between 8,000 and 44,100 samples/second.

•The sampling resolution is the number of bits used to store an amplitude. We typically store the amplitude in 8 or 16 bits.

•A sound can be mono or stereo, depending on the number of channels that it comes from.

•A mono sound uses one channel, a stereo sound uses two channels, and so forth. Each channel has its own digital sound signal.

Sound Formats

•There are two types of sound used on the Internet: streaming, and static.

•Streaming sound is the broadcast sound coming from broadcast stations operating on the Internet. This sound is similar to that of real audio and conventional radio stations.

•Web listeners need the proper connection speed to listen to streaming audio on their computers over the Internet. Streaming audio is encoded at 28.8K, 56K, or higher bandwidth.

•Sound cards that come with PCs can play streaming audio, if the software that can handle streaming audio is installed. Examples of such software include Real Audio and Realplayer G2.

•Static sound is the sound stored in files and included in Web pages as sound clips.

•Sound files are usually large, and may take a considerable amount of time to download.

•Web pages use short sound clips that last between 30 seconds and one minute to keep the size of the sound file small and (consequently) its download time short.

•The available sound formats are AU (Sun), WAV (Microsoft), MIDI, and AIFF. The file extensions (types) for these formats are .au, .wav, .mid, and .aif, respectively.

MIDI Sound Format

•The MIDI format does not use digitized sound.

•it stores sound as a series of commands or instructions (known as MIDI messages) that tell a sound synthesizer how to play an audio clip.

•The General MIDI (GM) system specifies the standardization of synthesizer functions and capabilities.

•MIDI sound files are much smaller than those that store digitized audio.

•MIDI files can be edited using sequencers (sound editors).

•The MIDI format defines three file types to allow handling data streams. Type 0 stores all the MIDI data in a single track. Type 1 stores the MIDI data in multiple tracks. Type 2 stores several independent MIDI data. Types 0 and 1 are the most widely used. Type 1 is generally preferred, because it is easy to view and edit the sound file.

Sound Hardware and Software

•Sound software for static sound should support such operations as playing, recording, editing (cut and paste), and adding sound effects to an application. The software should also support conversion between the different sound formats.

•In order for sound software to work properly on a computer, the computer must have a sound card, sound drivers, and external speakers installed. This card and speakers are different from the computer internal sound generator that produces beeps as responses to OS activities.

•If users would like to record different sounds, they must have microphones installed on their computers.

•Some sound programs are GoldWave, CoolEdit, Macromedia SoundEdit Pro II, Sound catcher, Sox, Kamboo! Factory, Synchrome's Maestro V, Acoustica, and Sound Forge; there are many others.

•Users can always search for the latest and greatest shareware by using the Web site www.shareware.com; type *audio* or *sound* as key search word.

•There are no standard sound tags that can be used in Web pages. The Web (W3) consortium does not have standards for sound tags. The existing sound tags have evolved from the browsers that introduced them.

Sound Tags

•Three sound tags exist in the literature. They are <EMBED>, <BGSOUND>, and <SOUND>.

•From testing the three tags in different Web pages using different browsers, we found that the <EMBED> tag is the only tag that is supported by both Netscape Communicator and MS IE. Therefore, we cover only this tag here.

•The <EMBED> tag can create a control console (panel) to allow Web surfers to control the sound clip embedded in a Web page.

•The attributes of the <EMBED> tag are SRC, WIDTH, HEIGHT, VOLUME, AUTOSTART, HIDDEN, and LOOP.

•The SRC attribute specifies the sound file.

•The WIDTH and HEIGHT attributes specify the size of the control console. Their usual values are 145 and 60 pixels, respectively.

•The VOLUME attribute has values that range from 1 to 100. The default value is 50.

•AUTOSTART, HIDDEN, and LOOP can be set to `true` or `false`. Their default values are `false`. It is not recommended to use them , because they may annoy Web surfers.

Dealing with Sound

•Dealing with sound implies creating sound clips and using them in Web pages.

•Creating sound clips requires the use of sound software to record and edit sound.

•MP3 format allows playing near CD-quality digital music and songs over the Internet and on PCs.

•An audio program that comes with Windows is `Sound Recorder`.

•To access this program, click this sequence: `Start` (Windows menu on bottom left corner) => `Programs` => `Accessories` => `Entertainment` => `Sound Recorder`.

•Another audio program that comes with Windows is `Media Player`.

•To access this program, click this sequence: `Start` (Windows menu on bottom left corner) => `Programs` => `Accessories` => `Entertainment` => `Media Player`.

•If you have a PC running Windows, check the Media folder for audio and video clips that may have come pre-installed. To access this folder, double click this sequence; `My Computer` => `Drive C` => `Windows` => `Media`.

•Embedding sound in Web pages can be achieved via two alternatives: the <A> tag, or the <EMBED> tag. In either case, the browser displays the control console for the convenience of the Web surfer.

•Quick reference of the HTML tags covered in this chapter

Table 12.1 Summary of HTMLsound tags.

Tag	Close	Attribute	Value	Example	Chpt. page
<EMBED>	Yes	SRC	name	<EMBED SRC="mySound.au">	418 419
		WIDTH	pixels	<EMBED WIDTH = 145>	
		HEIGHT	pixels	<EMBED HEIGHT = 60>	
		VOLUME	number	<EMBED VOLUME = 70>	
		AUTOSTART	boolean	<EMBED AUTOSTART = "true">	
		HIDDEN	boolean	<EMBED HIDDEN = "true">	
		LOOP	boolean	<EMBED LOOP = "true">	

PROBLEMS

Exercises

12.1 Create a Web page that uses your favorite sound clip as a hyperlink.

12.2 Create a Web page that uses your favorite sound clip in the <EMBED> tag. Try all the attributes of the tag.

Homework

12.3 Create a Web page that uses both sound and images. Make each image a hyperlink that links to a sound file. Choose your favorite application.

12.4 Repeat problem 12.3 for sounds and images of birds.

12.5 Repeat problem 12.3 for sounds and images of animals

12.6 Repeat problem 12.3 for sounds and images of TV characters — for example, Simpsons characters (Homer, Bart, etc.), Batman, and others.

12.7 Repeat problem 12.3 for sounds and images of movie characters — for example, Austin Powers, Pochahontas, the Little Mermaid, Winnie the Pooh, and others.

12.8 Repeat problem 12.3 for child education.

12.9 Repeat problem 12.3 for your family members and friends.

12.10 Repeat problem 12.3 for your own pets.

CHAPTER 13

Video and Video Tags

$\mathbf{T}$he multimedia aspects of the Web are the driving force behind its popularity. This chapter provides an in-depth coverage of video, its use in Web pages, and the video tags. Video is a multimedia element that can be used in Web pages. Video, like sound, is not as widely used in Web pages as images are. After an introduction, the chapter covers video file formats. It then covers video software. It also presents the video tags and all their attributes in detail. In addition, the chapter concludes with tutorials and summary.

13.1 Introduction

We can argue that real time multimedia on the Web is the ultimate goal of using the Web. We all hope that the Web will become the ultimate tool for interactive communication. Without achieving this goal, the Web remains, in one extreme view, just another form of publishing medium. The bandwidth is what is holding this hope back. Once the bandwidth increases enough, the Web will realize its potential. Examples of Web real-time applications are shopping for a car or sharing someone's birthday party. In the car example, it would be great to view videos of the exterior and the interior of a car in full color on the Web before making a decision to buy. In the birthday example, it would be great to view video clips of the party on the Web within minutes after it's over. This is the promise of real-time multimedia on the Web.

Video represents a major component of multimedia on the Web. Web video is different from TV video and video games, in the sense that it does not have the same picture quality, because of the bandwidth limitations. Delivering video via the Web requires some compromises. Web-based video uses a quarter or a sixteenth of a TV screen. TV sets refresh the screen at a rate of 30 Hz, to prevent the screen from flickering. Web video uses a refresh rate of 15, 10, or even fewer Hz. TV video does not use a lot of compression (see end of this section for a definition of compression) of the pictures. Web video uses a lot of compression. Web video is compressed to as little as 1/200th of its original size, so that it can be transmitted at standard 28.8 modem speed. If high-speed connections, such as 56K, ISDN, or T1 lines are used, video can be compressed less to increase its clarity. Another difference between Web video and TV video is that Web video does not use noise reduction and color fidelity as good as TV video does, because of limited bandwidth.

As with audio, there are analog and digital video. Analog video is video as we know it and watch it on TV and video tapes (VHS and 8 mm formats). Analog video is transmitted in continuous *composed* (combining both color and brightness) signals that use a standard transmission code, such as the National Television System Committee (NTSC), phase alteration line (PAL), and Systeme Electronic Pour Coleur Avec Memoire (SECAM). NTSC is used mostly in North America and Japan. PAL is used mostly in Western Europe, England, and the Middle East. SECAM is used in France and Russia. Analog video is a continuous stream of both sound and images. There are usually sound tracks that accompany the video images. When the sound and images are played in a synchronous way, we see and hear video as we know it.

Analog video has two characteristics: frame rate and frame size. Frame rate is defined as the number of frames displayed per second. It is also known as the refresh rate. Frame size is defined as the pixel size of the video image. In TV video, the frame rate is 30 frames per second, and the frame size is the size of the TV screen itself. In some TV sets that support "picture in picture" (PIP) technology, the user can adjust the frame size by splitting the TV screen into, say, four or nine subscreens, each possibly displaying a different video (i.e., channel).

Before a video signal can travel over the Web, it has to be converted from analog to digital format and compressed to allow viewing in real time. For example, a VHS video tape can be converted to AVI or QuickTime digital video format and written to a digital videotape or to a CD-ROM. This conversion process is sometimes known as digitizing a video tape. Digital video is usually small clips. It is not the same quality as TV images or movies. Web video is usually tiny and jerky, but, as the broadband width technology improves, the Web will achieve near-TV-quality video. It would be very exciting to surf video Web pages.

Digital video has many applications and advantages over analog video. It is easy to use and more portable. Depending on its length, digital video can be stored on a CD-ROM or a floppy disk. Thus, digital video becomes more convenient to use on the road for such applications as trade shows, presentations, and training. These applications could be included in Web pages and viewed on the Web from anywhere at anytime.

The several existing video formats are covered in section 13.2. While they have a lot in common, they have some differences between them. Some of them are dedicated to playback on the Web, while others are suitable for CD ROMs. Many of them work best on a specific computer. Video software (section 13.3) creates and plays video. Such software is usually installed as a plug-in for the browser that renders a Web page with a video clip in it.

Digital video must capture the same characteristics of analog video in order to represent it. Thus, digital video has a frame rate and a frame size. The frame rate of digital video is similar to the sampling rate of digital sound. A video board in a computer supports a certain frame rate and size. The board captures the analog video at certain time intervals to create the corresponding digital video. The higher the frame rate is, the better is the quality of the resulting digital video, and the closer it is to the original analog video.

That the frame rate and size of digital video are much smaller than their counterparts for analog video is due to the limitations of computer speed and of the bandwidth transmitting the frames. To display already-existing digital frames (video), they must first be read from the Web site server, then transmitted over the Internet, and then displayed on the client computer screen. This process requires fast servers, fast transmission lines, and fast graphics display systems on the client computers. The combination of these three stringent requirements is not available for many Web surfers.

Digital video is also compressed, in addition to having its frame rate and size kept small. Video compression reduces the size of digital video further. The size of uncompressed video is very large. About 27 MB of space is needed for one second of video. This large size makes it impossible to transmit and download inline video on the Web practically. In order to make desktop video feasible, video compression schemes are used. These schemes remove redundant audio and video data to reduce the size of the video signal and in turn compress the signal. Some compression schemes may remove less important data from the video signal to reduce its size dramatically. However, this may result in some audio and image degradation.

Video compression schemes use codec (**co**mpression/**dec**ompression) algorithms. These algorithms compress the video to store and transmit it and decompress it to play it. Each video format has a codec algorithm built in it. Each codec has its strengths and weaknesses. Some codecs are good for the Web, some for CD-ROM. Some codecs are symmetric, some are asymmetric. A symmetric codec compresses and decompresses the video signal at the same rate. In other words, the symmetric codec takes an equal amount of time to compress and to decompress the video signal. An asymmetric codec compresses the signal very slow, but it decompresses it very fast. Thus, the asymmetric codec takes a longer time to compress the video signal and less time to decompress it. The rationale here is that compression is usually done offline, where speed is not critical, while decompression is done online. Figure 13.1 shows a visual representation of codecs. The T_c and T_u variables represent the compression and decompression times respectively. As the figure shows, considering the horizontal time axis, T_c and T_u are equal for symmetric codecs, while T_c is greater than T_u for asymmetric codecs.

Some of the Web codecs include Sorenson Video, RealVideo, H261, H263, MPEG-4, and Photo-JPEG. The Sorenson and MPEG-4 codecs produce high-quality Web video that can be played back on a desktop computer (PC or Mac). The RealVideo codec is most suitable for video data rates below 3 kiloBytes per second (KBps). The H261 and H263 codecs are used for videoconferencing. H261 and H263 are suitable for low-quality and medium-quality videoconferencing respectively. The Photo-JPEG codec is used to store *still* (photographic) images.

Digital videos are stored in files in certain formats, as sound is. The size of a video file depends on the duration of the video clip, its frame rate, its frame size, and its compression level. For the remainder of this chapter, we will focus on digital video clips, their creation, and their use in Web pages.

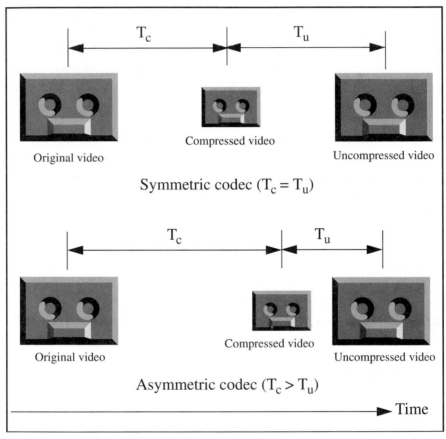

Figure 13.1   Video codecs.

13.2 Video Formats

As with audio, there are two types of video used on the Internet: streaming and playback. Streaming video is the real-time video. It is the ultimate goal of the Web. Video streaming is much more demanding than audio streaming. For example, streaming an MPEG video at full-motion quality (30 frames per second) consumes more than 10 times the bandwidth that RealAudio sound does. Streaming video allows Web surfers to view video as it is downloaded. Thus, surfers do not have to wait for the entire video clip to download before watching it. Streaming video, therefore, allows Web surfers to watch video in real time. Web surfers can use streaming video to watch live events from all over the world. Video cards that come with PCs can play streaming video if the software that can handle streaming video is installed.

The other type of video is the video stored in files and included in Web pages as video clips. We call this type playback video. The video clip is created and stored in a file using a particular video format. We cover the available video formats in this section. The video file is embedded in a Web page via the video tags, similar to those embedding audio files. When the Web page is loaded, the video is played in a little window, assuming that there is a video player application installed on the client computer. The Web surfer does not hear the video until the entire video file in the Web page is downloaded to the client computer requesting the page. Video files are usually long (longer than audio files), and may take a considerable amount of time to download. This is why many Web pages use short video clips that last between 30 seconds and one minute: to keep the size of the video file small, and (consequently) its download time short.

There are many video formats available to produce playback video. Any of these formats can be used to store video clips in files. As we expect, these formats depend on the type of the client computer and its operating system. There are formats for PCs, Macs, Sun workstations, and so forth. Some of these formats use certain codecs to keep file sizes small. Here is a list of the available common formats:

1. **AVI format.** This format (Audio Video Interleave) is developed by Microsoft. It is a de facto standard for PCs. It is built into Windows OS. It supports both 16-bit and 32-bit video. It also supports 320×240 resolution and 30 frames per second. One of the applications that can create and play AVI files is Windows Media Player which comes installed with Microsoft Windows. To play AVI files on the Mac, Apple's QuickTime format (see below) has a plug-in for its users. The AVI format is widely supported over the Internet by all browsers. AVI files use the extension `.avi`.

2. **QuickTime format.** This format is developed by Apple Computer. It is built into the Mac OS. PCs can run QuickTime files with the help of special plug-ins. The QuickTime format is supported over the Internet by all browsers. The ISO standard uses it as the basis to define its MPEG-4 video standard. This format supports video streaming. Files using this format have the extension `.mov` or `.qt`.

3. **MPEG format.** This format (Moving Picture Experts Group) stores and compresses video. It generally produces better-quality video than the AVI or the QuickTime format. This format produces small-size video files, because it achieves a high compression rate by storing only the changes in the image from one frame to another, instead of each entire frame. This is known as frame differencing. (See FAQs section for more details.) The latest version of MPEG is MPEG-4. It is an ISO standard and is based on the QuickTime format. Check the Web site www.mpeg.org for more details. Files using this format have the extension `.mpg`.

4. **MJPEG format.** This format (motion-JPEG) stores and compresses video. The MJPEG

format extends the JPEG format for images, covered in chapter 10. Each frame in the MJPEG format is stored as a JPEG image. Files using this format have the extension `.mjpg`.

The QuickTime and MPEG formats are the most widely used. Browsers support both of them. Including video clips in any of these two formats in a Web page should be safe. If a Web author uses another format, such as the AVI format, the browser shows one frame as an image and ignores the rest of the video clip.

13.3 Video Hardware and Software

Video software is available for both types of video: playback video, and streaming video. We focus on playback software in this section, although some of the same software supports streaming video. Video software should support such video operations as playing, capturing, compressing, editing (cut and paste), and adding sound effects to an application. The software should also support conversion between the different video formats discussed in section 13.2, without noticeable loss in video quality. Most video software is easy to use. It provides GUIs with predefined settings to make it easier for users.

In order for video software to work properly on a computer, the computer must have a video capture card, video drivers, and external speakers installed (to play the sound associated with video). Users also need to install the proper video drivers for the video capture card to work. These drivers are software programs that come with the cards. Drivers' updates can be obtained from video card manufacturers, normally via downloads from their Web sites.

The various operations supported by video software are simple and intuitive to use. To capture video, a user may use a digital camcorder connected to a computer. The user can control the operations of the camcorder from the computer keyboard. During the shooting of a video, users may record their voices to narrate the video. Video playing allows Web authors to test the video clips they have recorded before using them in Web pages. Video editing is an interesting activity to perform with video software and includes editing the video colors, the sound, the images, the frame rate, and the codecs. For example, The Microsoft VidEdit program allows its users to change the video frame rate. If the video is captured at 30 frames per second (fps), users can change them to, say, 10 or 15 fps, to reduce the size of the video file. Users can also crop a video file, to use a smaller rectangular region of the original video. During the editing of a video file, users may change the codecs used to compress the video.

Many video software programs exist. Some For Windows are Intel Indeo video, Microsoft Active Movie, Maplay 32, Winamp, and VMPEG. The first two programs support the AVI, QuickTime, and MPEG formats. The last three support the MPEG format only. For the Mac, sample programs are MpegCD and Macamp. They both support the MPEG format only. For Unix and OS/2, there is Maplay, which supports MPEG format only. For Linux, there is Xaudio which also supports MPEG format only. Some of the products that allow users of digital camcorders to capture and edit video are EditDV, MotoDV, PhotoDV, and FilmTextures. They are available for both PC and Mac platforms. Some of these products, such as MotoDV, use Adobe Premiere nonlinear video editor.

Users can always search for the latest and greatest shareware using the Web site www.shareware.com, and type *video* as key search word.

13.4 High-Definition Television

Television (TV) is one of the common household video appliances. A TV set receives and displays transmitted video and audio signals from broadcasting TV stations. These signals could be analog or digital. If TV sets can receive digital video and audio signals, TV can support streaming video and audio. Such TV sets can therefore be used, like computers, in the endless Internet and Web applications. Web surfers can use their TV sets both for entertainment and for surfing the Internet. They can, for example, check their e-mail while they are watching their favorite show or sport event.

The high-definition TV (HDTV) makes it possible to receive both digital broadcast programs and Internet data. HDTV is a digital TV. It receives and displays digital video and audio signals, as well as data. Broadcasting TV stations must send their signals in digital format over the air. HDTV is a better television system than the analog NTSC-based system. HDTV improves the quality of the production and the reception of TV broadcasting. It provides high-quality video and audio, both in digital streaming formats. One of the distinguishing features of HDTV is its 16:9 aspect ratio. The aspect ratio is the ratio of the picture width to its height. The analog NTSC-based TV set supports a 4:3 aspect ratio. The HDTV aspect ratio provides a display quality similar to what movie theaters provide. Thus, HDTV can create a home theater atmosphere. Using such a home theater to surf the Web provides a pleasant experience similar to that of watching a wide-screen movie in a movie theater.

The idea for HDTV began in Japan in the 1960s. Two Japanese companies (Sony and the Japanese broadcasting company NHK) developed an HDTV system in the early 1980s and demonstrated it to movie producers. After the introduction of HDTV to the film industry, interest began to build to develop an HDTV system for commercial broadcasting. Since then, development of HDTV systems has taken off in Europe, Japan, and the United States. In 1987, the United States started searching for an advanced TV technology to replace its NTSC-based analog television system, which was designed in the late 1930s and early 1940s as a black-and-white system, with color added a decade later.

The United States focused its development efforts on finding an advanced TV technology that was not just an extension of or improvement over the existing NTCS technology. The new technology should support a more challenging terrestrial broadcasting system, and should support digital transmission to replace the NTSC analog transmission. Moreover, the digital transmission should be based on the TCP/IP protocol, which allows transmitting any combination of video, audio, and data. Thus, an HDTV system is capable of transmitting both broadcasting TV programs and Internet content. An HDTV transmission system is capable of sending 19.3 mega-bits (Mbits) of data per second. This bandwidth allows TV stations, Internet service providers, and Web sites to send content to TV viewers during broadcasting of HDTV programs. For example, while you are watching a soccer game, a soccer Web site or store could broadcast information about the latest soccer equipment.

HDTV systems support both dynamic allocability and scalability. Dynamic allocability is the ability to send data and content during HDTV programs, as described in the above soccer example. Dynamic scalability is the ability of an HDTV set to support both high-resolution and low-resolution TV programs. Low-resolution programs utilize the standard, NTSC-quality TV programs. This scalability is particularly important because it accelerates the transition from an NTSC-based television system to an HDTV-based one. Examples of high-resolution programs are the broadcasting of sports, movies, and prime-time programming. TV talk show programs are examples of low-resolution TV programs. Low-resolution programs do not require high-quality pictures. An HDTV system can broadcast several low-resolution programs simulta-neously.

The HDTV broadcast signal has three channels. They are the video, the audio, and the data channels. The video channel carries the foreground pictures of TV scenes, while the audio chan-nel carries the accompanying sound. The data channel carries the background scenes of the main video. This data channel is capable of transmitting data at the speed of 19.3 Mbits per second. Scenes with limited motion, where the background does not change too much, do not use the full transmission capacity of the data channel. Thus, more data, such as Internet content, could be transmitted during these static backgrounds of the main video. The weather map is an example of a TV scene where the background does not change. In this case, raw digital data (Internet content) could be sent over the unused portion of the data channel. Another example is the use of commercial time to send more data. A software company could send out an interactive game while its commercial is running on TV. Users who like the game and want to try could do so immediately.

The video of an HDTV signal is based on the MPEG video format covered in section 13.2. The audio of the signal is compressed and is based on the Dolby AC-3 system. The audio sam-pling rate is 48 kHz. These video and audio specifications are compatible with the Web multi-media data and content. Thus, an HDTV set could be used to surf the Internet.

While the HDTV concept offers one form of digital TV technology that is usable with the Internet and the Web, PCs offer another form of digital TV. A PC can be used to receive TV pro-grams. A PC can come with a TV card installed that allows users to watch TV programs on it. The walls between PCs and TVs are crumbling. The concept of using a PC as a TV is sometimes known as a PC/TV, PC theater, or interactive TV. The concept of PC/TV is more than just installing a TV board in a computer. As a matter of fact, a PC could use an HDTV set as its dis-play monitor. The opposite view is to use the HDTV set as the computer itself and add a key-board and a mouse to it. Before the ultimate merge between HDTV and PC technologies can be achieved, their differences [such as the number of scan lines of the display — whether it is 480 lines (PCs) or 1080 (HDTV) — and the scan format — whether it is progressive (PC) or inter-laced (HDTV)] have to be resolved first. The WebTV that is discussed in the FAQs section of chapter 2 is an example of using a TV as a computer to surf the Internet. A WebTV uses a set-top box.

13.5 Video Tags

Video tags allow the video plug-ins of browsers such as Netscape Communicator and MS IE to play common video formats such as AVI, QuickTime, MPEG, and MJPEG. Video tags allow Web authors to control, to loop, and to start video. As in the case with sound, there are no standard video tags that can be used in Web pages. The Web (W3) consortium does not have standards for video tags. The <EMBED> tag that we used to embed sound clips in Web pages can also be used to embed video clips in Web pages.

13.5.1 <EMBED> Tag

This is the same tag, with the same attributes, that was used to embed audio clips in Web pages, and covered in chapter 12. This tag can also be used to embed video clips in Web pages. This tag must close. The tag can be used as many times as needed to play video clips in a Web page. However, it is recommended not to use more than one clip in one page, unless the page is written exclusively to test different video clips. The <EMBED> tag invokes the browser's video player plug-in, which in turn creates a control bar as shown in figure 13.2. .The bar is attached to

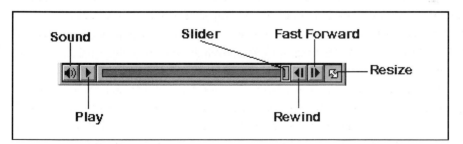

Figure 13.2   Video control bar.

the bottom of the video image (movie). The control bar allows the users to play, to stop, or to pause the video. The user clicks the desired button shown in figure 13.2 to achieve the desired control. The Sound button indicates the loudness level of the sound associated with the video clip. The user can click it to adjust the loudness level. The Play button is used to play, to pause, or to stop the video clip. If the clip is playing and the user clicks it, the clip pauses. If the user clicks it again, the video clip starts playing again starting from where it has left off. As the video clip is playing the slider moves from left to right. The user can also drag it with the mouse and place it as desired. The Rewind and Fast Forward buttons are similar to those found on VCRs. The Resize button allows the user to change the size of the window displaying the movie or the video clip. It is not recommended to resize the video window as the resizing usually distorts the image of the video and worsens the look of its resolution. The original size of the video clip should always be maintained.

The <EMBED> tag is used to embed both audio and video clips in Web pages. Its attributes are SRC, WIDTH, HEIGHT, VOLUME, AUTOSTART, HIDDEN, and LOOP. These are the same attributes covered in chapter 12; however, some of the attributes take on a slightly different meaning when they are used with video clips, as described below.

•The SRC attribute specifies the file of the video clip to be included in the Web page. The file could be in any of the sound formats discussed, for example .avi, .mov, .mpg, or .mjpg. The video file and the HTML file that uses it are usually both in the same directory. If they are not, the rules for specifying relative and absolute paths that are discussed in chapter 7 must be followed.

•The WIDTH and HEIGHT attributes specify the size, in pixels, of the window that contains the video clip. The browser uses these values as a guide to best display the video without distorting it.

•The VOLUME attribute determines the volume level (how loud) of the sound when the browser plays the video clip. It can take a value between 1 and 100. The default value is 50, the middle of the range. Users of Web pages must also remember to check the volume setting of the external sound speakers. If the volume level of the speakers is not set properly, users would not hear the sound of the video clip.

•The AUTOSTART attribute takes a value of *true* or *false*. If the Web author wants the video clip to play automatically when the Web page is loaded, the AUTOSTART = "true" is used. The default value is *false*. If Web authors do not want to start video automatically, they simply leave out this attribute or set it to false. Web authors must think hard if they like to set this attribute value to true, because doing so may annoy Web surfers.

•The HIDDEN attribute takes a value of *true* or *false* (the default). If the Web author uses HIDDEN = "true", the video clip is not displayed in the Web page. The video clip becomes entirely hidden, and the Web surfer cannot see it. The HIDDEN attribute should not be used.

•The LOOP attribute allows the browser to play the same video clip more than once. Its value could be *true* or *false*. The default value is *false*, in which case the browser plays the video clip only once. If the value of the LOOP attribute is set to *true*, the browser plays the sound clip repeatedly until the Web surfer stops the video by clicking the Play button of the control toolbar shown in figure 13.2.

13.6 Dealing with Video

Dealing with video implies creating video clips and then using them in Web pages. We discuss both ideas in this section.

13.6.1 Making a Video

Making video clips requires a video device, such as a camcorder or screen capture software, and the use of video software to edit the resulting video. The use of a camcorder allows Web authors to make video clips of real-life events. The use of screen capture software allows Web authors to make video clips of events happening on the computer screen, such as the opening of a window or the moving of the mouse. These events are not exciting, but they get the point across about how to make a video clip. We here cover the use of the SnagIt screen capture program to make a video. The program generates AVI video files. We have introduced and used this program in chapter 1 of the book. We assume that readers have downloaded and installed this program as explained in chapter 1. There is no pre-installed software that comes with Windows that can be used to make video clips. For the Mac, QuickTime comes pre-installed with the Mac OS.

To start the SnagIt program, double click its shortcut on the desktop. The program window opens up and is shown in figure 13.3. The figure shows that SnagIt can capture images,

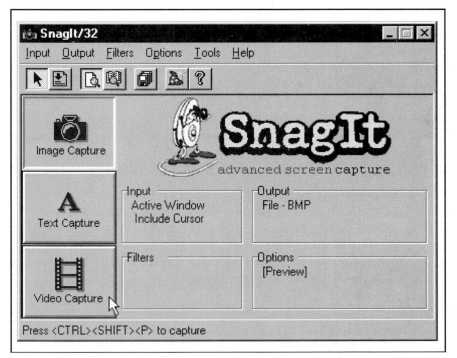

Figure 13.3 SnagIt GUI.

text, and video. The user clicks the Video Capture button shown in figure 13.3, the <CTRL>, <SHIFT>, and <P> buttons simultaneously, as shown at the bottom of figure 13.3, to begin making a video clip. The combination of these three buttons is known as the hot-key of the program. The user needs to choose the input source of the video before pressing the hot-key. The `Input` menu allows the user to capture the screen, a window, the active window, a region, or a fixed region. Let us assume that the user selects the `Active Window` option. The user then clicks a window on the screen, to make it active, and presses the hot-key. `SnagIt` puts a border around the active window that is about to be captured to make the video, as shown in figure 13.4. It also displays a `Video Capture` window, as shown in the figure. The window shows the frame rate and size and other statistics that are used to make the video.

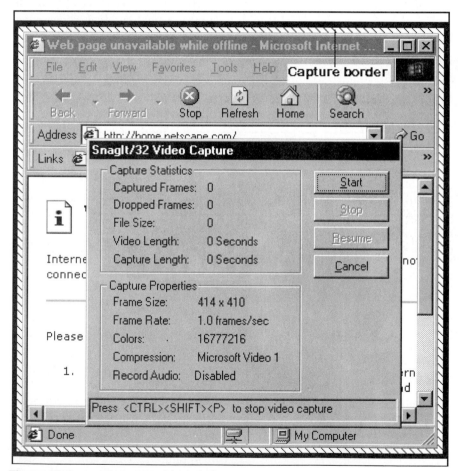

Figure 13.4   `SnagIt` start-video window.

To begin making the video clip, the user clicks the `Start` button (shown in figure 13.4). `SnagIt` records the activities that happen in the designated active window until the user stops the recording by pressing the hot-key (as advised at the bottom of the window shown in figure

13.4). Upon that action, SnagIt stops recording and displays its Video Capture window with the statistics of the resulting video clip, as shown in figure 13.5. The window shows a Resume button that the user can click to begin recording again. The figure shows a video clip that is 17 seconds long, with 17 frames. The resulting AVI file size is 175 KB. Here the user has recorded the downloading of the search engine www.altavista.com.

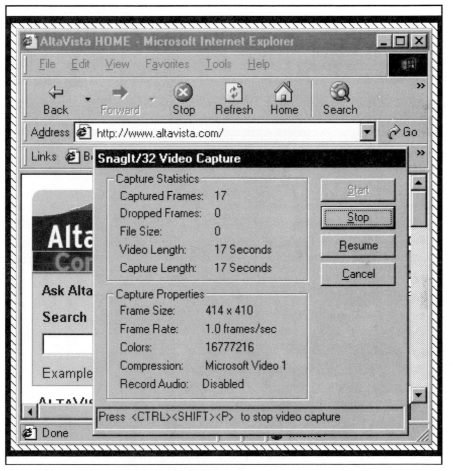

Figure 13.5 SnagIt end-video window.

The user needs to click the Stop button shown in figure 13.5 to continue. Upon the clicking of this button, SnagIt opens its Capture Preview window, shown in figure 13.6. The user can click the Play button shown to play the video clip just recorded. The other buttons next to it can be used to fast forward, rewind, and/or go to the beginning or end of the clip. Clicking the Play button the starts playing of the video clip. Depending on the computer video capture card and its software, SnagIt itself may play the clip, or it may invoke the Windows

Media Player, shown in figure 12.6, to play it. In either case, the clip file is an AVI file with AVI format. Thus, the user needs an AVI player or an editor to convert to other formats such as QuickTime or MPEG.

If satisfied with the recorded video clip, the user must save it in a file. The user clicks the following sequence: File (menu on the Capture Preview window shown in figure 13.6) => Finish Output => input file name and choose directory to save in. If SnagIt invokes Windows Media Player during the preview, the user must save the clip using the File menu of the player, by clicking File => Save As => input file name and choosing the directory to save in. Figure 13.7 shows Windows Media Player playing the video clip.

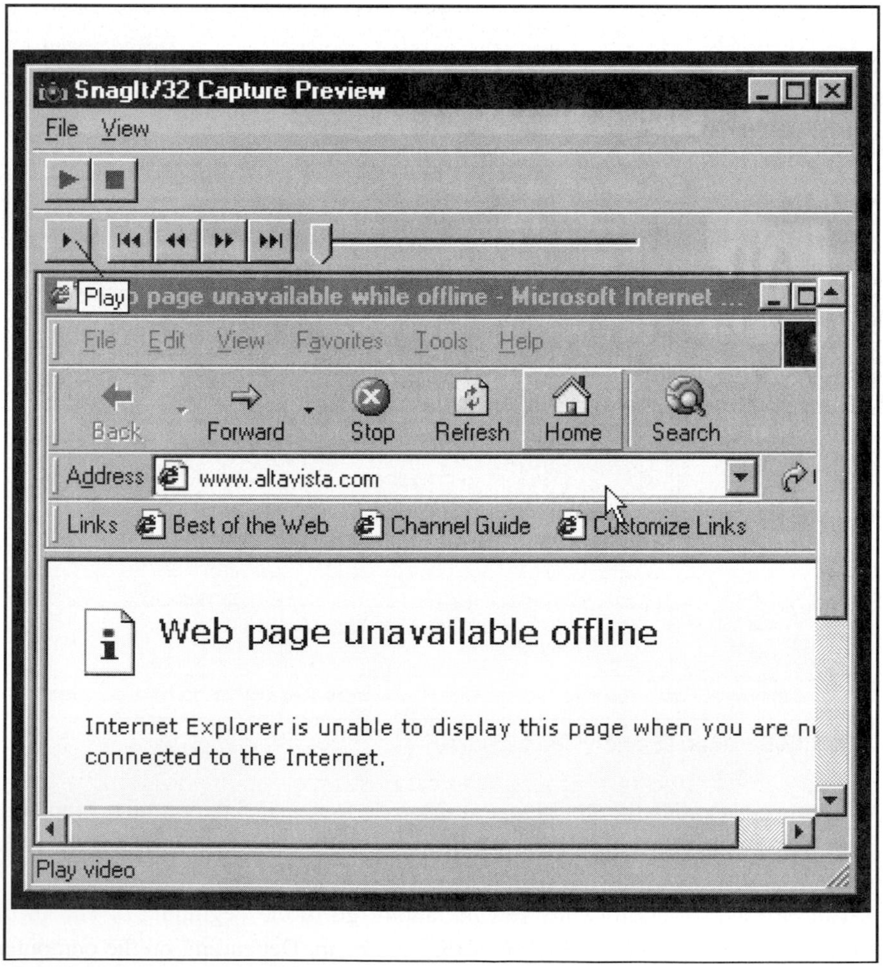

Figure 13.6 SnagIt Capture Preview window.

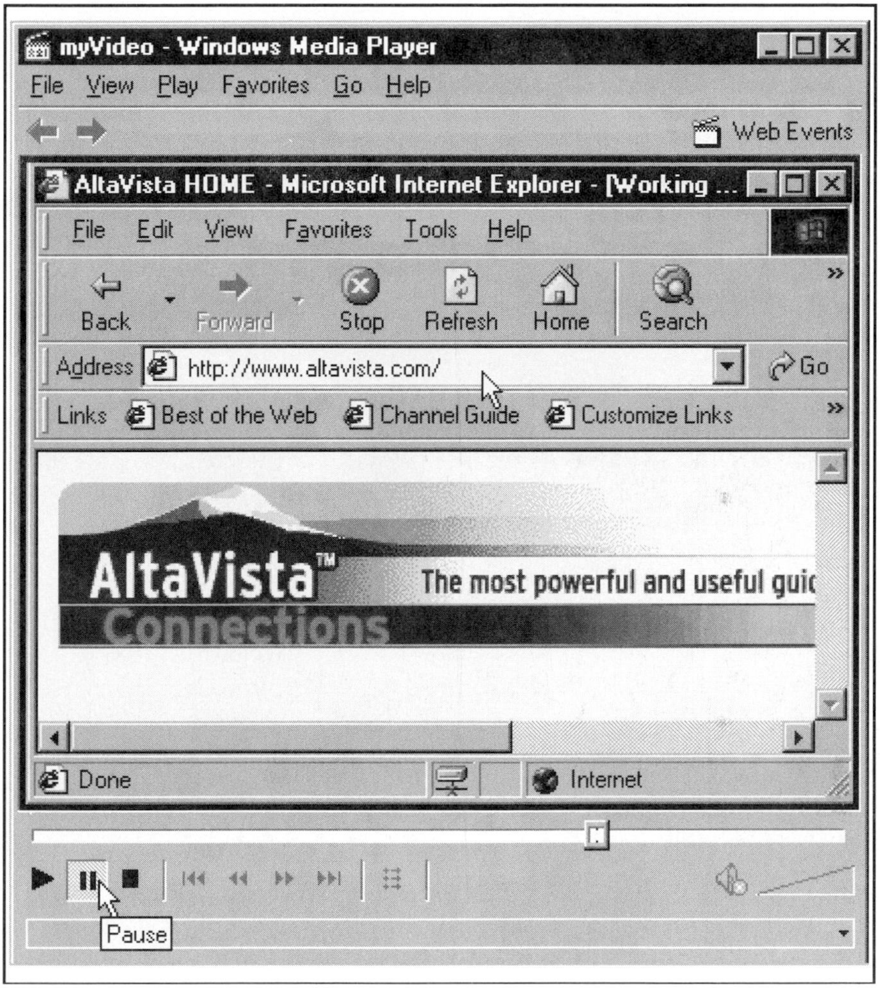

Figure 13.7 Windows Media Player.

13.6.2 Using Video

Once video is recorded, we can play it in Web pages. Most PCs come with video cards installed. Depending on the type of the video card, different video players may be available. There are two video players that come with Windows. One is the Media PLayer covered in chapters 12 and 13 and shown in figure 13.7. This player plays both sound and video clips. Video clips must be in AVI format. The other player is the Movie Player. This player plays video clips only (no sound clips) that are in QuickTime or MPEG format. It does not play AVI files. Figure 13.8 shows the window of Windows Movie Player.

Figure 13.8   Windows Movie Player.

Figure 13.8 shows a video clip that came with Windows. To find it, use the Windows search tool by clicking Start (located at the bottom left corner of screen) => Find => Files or Folders => type *.mov or *.mpg. Web authors can use this video clip and others that are available, to write Web pages or to test video players on PCs. This saves them the headache of having to buy a camcorder or create their own video clips (until they are serious) to get into Web video. As shown in the figure, the Movie Player uses the same control bar shown in figure 13.2. Viewers can use the control bar exclusively, to manipulate the currently playing movie, and they can use the menus shown at the top of the player window to manipulate video files. The

File, Edit, Movie, Window, and Help menus shown in figure 13.8 have very interesting menu items. Readers who are interested are encouraged to experiment with them. The Help menu is very useful and easy to use.

Embedding video in Web pages can be achieved via two alternatives. First, the video clip can be used in a hyperlink. In this case, the video file is used as the destination anchor. Thus, when the Web surfer clicks the link on the Web page, the browser invokes its video plug-in and displays the video clip with the control bar shown in figure 13.2 in a new Web page. The surfer may click the Back button of the browser to go back to the Web page that has the original link.

The second alternative for embedding video in Web pages is using the <EMBED> tag. This tag provides Web authors with more control of the video clip, via the use of the necessary attributes of the tag. For example, Web authors can set the LOOP attribute to true; or they can set the AUTOSTART attribute to false and let Web surfers click the Play button on the control bar when they want to watch the video clip.

13.7 Tutorials

This section focuses on using the video tag covered in this chapter. Any Web browser can be used to display the corresponding Web pages. It is a good idea to create a directory structure to save HTML files. This helps Web authors to organize HTML files and makes it easy to find them.

13.7.1 Creating a Video Hyperlink in a Web Page

In this tutorial, we use the <A> tag to create a video hyperlink. The destination anchor is the file that stores the video clip. We use an existing video file called sample.mov. If you have other video clips on your computer, you can use them. Check your computer for already-existing video clips. There are two ways to check. You can use the search tool of Windows by clicking this sequence: Start => Find => Files or Folders => type the search string *.mov or *.mpg in the window that pops up. The "*" represents the wild card typically used in computer searching. If there are any video clips installed on the computer, the search will find them. The other way of looking for pre-installed video clips is to check the Windows or Media folder. The Media folder is a subfolder under the Windows folder. You can open this folder by double clicking this sequence; My Computer => Drive C => Windows => Media. The Media folder stores both audio and video files that come with Windows on your computer.

Using a text editor, type the code just before figure 13.9, and save it as *tutorial13.6.1.html*. View the page in a browser. Figure 13.9 shows the resulting Web page. When you click the hyperlink, the browser displays the video clip in an new Web page, as shown in figure 13.10. You can use the control bar to manipulate the clip.

Figure 13.10 shows four frames that are captured during the playing of the video clip to convey the essence of the movie. We should say that only the first frame is displayed by the browser in the middle of the Web page. Figure 13.10 has been edited for illustrative purposes.

The first frame (top left) shows how the browser displays the movie first. When you click the Play button of the control bar, the movie starts to play. There is an accompanying noise that sounds like a swish followed by a clock sound. The square shown in the right top frame starts to appear as a rotating object. Toward the end of the movie, the square starts to transform, as shown in the bottom right frame. Finally, the QuickTime frame (bottom left) appears as the final frame in the movie. You can replay this movie over and over by clicking the Play button of the control bar. When you click the button, the browser begins playing the movie by displaying its first frame (top left). If you need to go back to the Web page that has the hyperlink, click the Back button of the browser.

```
<HTML>
<HEAD>
<TITLE>A Web page with a video hyperlink</TITLE>
</HEAD>
<BODY>
<H2><B><CENTER><FONT COLOR = "green">Web page with a video hyper-
link</FONT></CENTER></B></H2>
<A HREF = "sample.mov" TITLE = "A video clip">Want to watch a
movie</A>
</BODY>
</HTML>
```

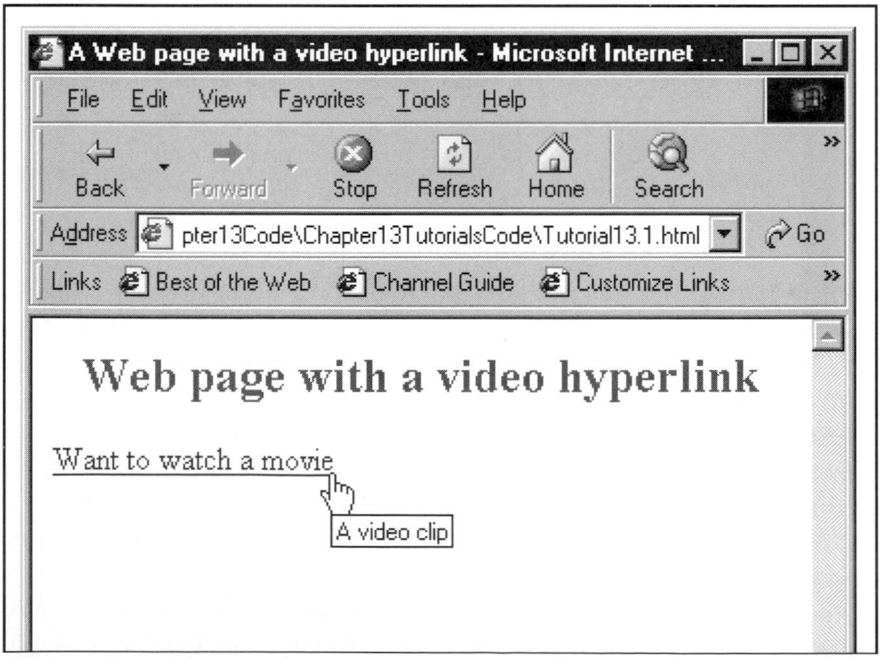

Figure 13.9   A video hyperlink in a Web page.

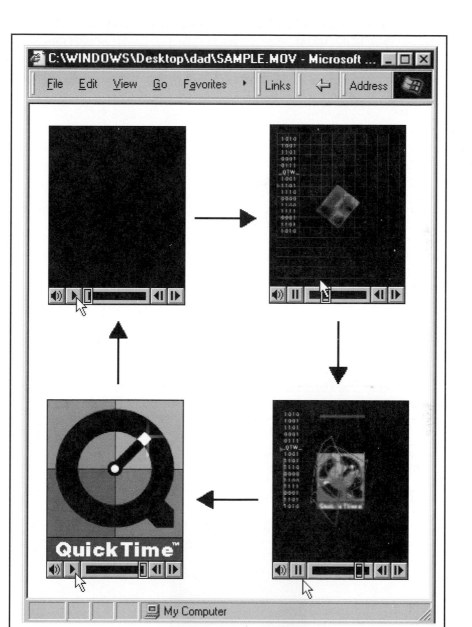

Figure 13.10 Playing the video clip.

13.7.2 Using the <EMBED> Tag in a Web Page

This tutorial illustrates the use of the <EMBED> tag with its attributes discussed in section 13.4. We use only the four attributes that should not annoy the Web surfer. The reader is encouraged to try the other attributes. Using a text editor, type the code that follows and save it as *tutorial13.6.2.html*. In the HTML code for this tutorial, we use the <CENTER> tag to center the video clip in the Web page. View the page in a browser. Figure 13.11 shows the resulting Web page. The first frame of the movie clip is displayed in the Web page with the control bar. When you click the `Play` button, the movie begins playing in the page.

```
<HTML>
<HEAD>
<TITLE>A Web page with the EMBED video tag</TITLE>
</HEAD>
<BODY>
<H2><B><CENTER><FONT COLOR = "green">A Web page with the EMBED vid-
eotag</FONT></CENTER></B></H2>
Click the Play button to start the movie.
<CENTER><EMBED SRC = "sample.mov" WIDTH = 400 HEIGHT = 300 VOLUME
=70></EMBED></CENTER>
</BODY>
</HTML>
```

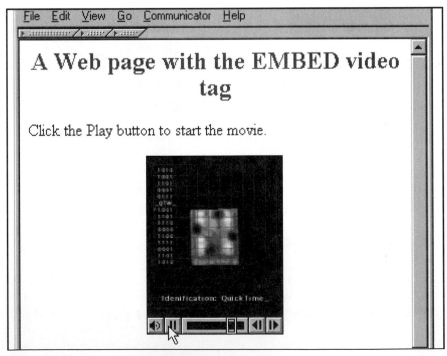

Figure 13.11   Result of the <EMBED> tag.

13.8 FAQs

Q: What is a good source on MPEG format?

A: The Web site www.mpeg.org provides useful information. Another important Web site is drogo.cselt.stet.it/mpeg. This is the site of a working group of the International Standards Organization/International Electrotechnical Commission (ISO/IEC) in charge of developing MPEG international standards for compression, decompression, processing, and so forth.

Q: What is video on demand, and how is it different from Web video?

A: *Video on demand* is the type of video we experience in hotel rooms when we order a movie to watch for the night. Streaming Web video is the closet the Web can come to video on demand. Currently, the Web technology supports video on demand. It is not yet popular. Some companies offer video on demand on their Intranets. These companies can transmit live performances, such as executive meetings, across the Intranet. Video on demand has not made it to the typical home. Bringing movies to homes on demand could be the catalyst to achieve this goal. Movies on demand must be affordable and simple to use before they can be widely used at homes.

Q: What are Web cameras? Can you name some Web sites that use Web cameras?

A: Web cameras are known as webcams. A webcam is a video camera used by a Web site. The webcam takes a picture (image) of a scene every some minutes or seconds, depending on the required update rate. The image is then automatically placed on the Web site for viewing over the Internet. All you need to view Web sites that use webcams is your browser. You do not need a video viewer or plug-in. The reason you do not need a viewer is that you are really viewing images that change constantly with time, every certain number of minutes or seconds. This constant change gives almost the same effect as the watching of a real video. Some webcam Web sites are listed in the Web page www.mediachannel.com/guides/webcams.htm. The Web site itself, www.mediachannel.com, is dedicated to video that can be viewed on the Internet.

Q: Are video clips considered animation?

A: Technically, video in a Web page is not considered animation in the page, although some users refer to it as such. Including animation in a Web page can be achieved in two ways: GIF or Java. We have covered GIF animation in chapter 10. Java animation is included in a Web page by using the <APPLET> tag in the Web page HTML code. Writing applets require full knowledge of the Java programming language; however, there are small companies that sell applets.

Q: What is frame differencing? How does it help digital video?

A: It is a method used by many codecs to compress video. It helps reduce the video file size and the decompression time and speed up the display of frames on client computers. Frame differencing stores, in each frame, the difference in image content between two consecutive frames. During the display of the frames on a computer screen, each frame content builds on the contents of the previous frames. Consider, for example, the display of a video of a runner. The difference between two subsequent frames could be in the position of the runner, while the scenery around the runner could be the same, or only slightly different. In this case, the first frame stores the image of both the scenery and the runner. The second frame stores the image of the runner only. When it is time to display the full video of the running race, the first frame is displayed, then the second frame is imposed on top of it. This produces the desired continuous effect of the digital video in the fastest possible way. Frame differencing has one limitation: It works best for videos that have large static backgrounds with small changing areas of the frames. When the image changes drastically from one frame to another, frame differencing loses its advantage.

Q: What are the existing videotape formats? How are they related to Web video formats?

A: There are two types of videotapes: analog and digital. Analog videotapes have been in existence for a while. Digital videotapes were introduced later, in 1995 – 1996. There exist two sets of formats; one for analog videotapes, one for digital videotapes. The primary difference between the two sets is in the way the data is stored on the tape. The analog formats store the video data (color and brightness) in an analog form. The digital formats encode the data into binary values and store them as sets of ones and zeros. This difference in the storing of data enables the digital videotape formats to produce video with superior quality, in comparison to what the analog videotape formats produce. The binary nature of the digital videotape formats produces a very large amount of data to represent a video. Thus, compression must be used. Most digital formats use a 5:1 compression ratio.

Some of the existing analog videotape formats are Video Home System (VHS), Super VHS (S-VHS), Compact VHS and S-VHS (VHS-C and S-VHS-C), 8 mm, Hi8, Betacam, and Betacam SP. We all know the VHS format and tapes used by tabletop VCRs and camcorders. VHS format is still important in taping and distribution, but it should not be used to produce video clips for Web use, because the quality of the original image on the VHS tape is not very good. That is why S-VHS was introduced. The S-VHS format splits the video signal into color and brightness before storing it on the tape. This splitting results in better quality image during playback of the tape. The VHS and S-VHS formats are not compatible. S-VHS format is used by commercial and industrial applications. A good S-VHS camcorder costs about $10,000. The VHS-C and S-VHS-C formats were created to allow for smaller camcorders. Typically, a VHS-C or a S-VHS-C cassette holds about 30 to 40 minutes of tape in regular play. VHS-C tapes can be played in regular VHS VCRs by using an adapter. 8 mm is a format that was introduced in 1983 by Sony to use a much smaller tape size than VHS. The quality of the 8 mm format is roughly the same as that of the VHS format. The Hi8 format does for 8 mm what S-VHS does for VHS. Betacam was introduced by Sony in 1982 for broadcast use. Betacam produces video with much better quality than all of the above mentioned formats, especially in the color and the 3D effect of the video. The Betacam SP, introduced in 1986, differs from the Betacam format in that it uses a metal tape, which produces better video. Betacam equipment is expensive and can cost from $6,000 to $40,000, depending on the quality, the number of lenses, and the size of the camcorders purchased.

Some of the existing digital videotape formats are Digital Videocassette (DV or DVC), DVCPRO, and DVCAM. The DV format is the first consumer digital videotape format and was introduced in 1996. This format uses the 5:1 compression ratio before storing data on the cassette. The quality of the video produced by this format is close to the quality produced by broadcast systems. The price range for DV camcorders is from under $2,000 to $11,000. For under $2,000, one can buy a simple one-piece camcorder that is sufficient to produce video clips for use on the Web. The DVCPRO format is similar to DV, except that the cassette speed is twice the speed of DV. Panasonic introduced it in 1995. While DVCPRO players can read and play back DV cassettes, the opposite is not true. DVCPRO camcorders can cost from $9,000 to $22,000. The DVCAM format was introduced by Sony in 1996, to compete with DVCPRO from Panasonic. The two formats are not compatible.

Which format should you use to produce video clips for the Web? The digital videotape formats are better than the analog videotape formats. If you plan to produce your own video, DV seems to be the most affordable format, because you can buy a DV camcorder for under $2000. Remember that you still have to convert the DV format to one of the Web formats discussed in section 13.2.

Q: What is "slide-ware"? Why does it happen?

A: Slide-ware is a term associated with the viewing of streaming video on the Web. Slide-ware occurs when a Web surfer attempts to download a Web page with video content via a slow Internet connection, such as 28.8K modem. The slow connection cannot handle the continuous flow of frames, so the video display on the client computer screen looks choppy, and the screen freezes. At 28.8K speed, the connection can transmit two frames per second, at best. With powerful compression methods, the connection may handle 8 – 12 frames per second. Narrowband connections, such as 28.8K or 56K modems, are not fast enough to handle streaming video. Broadband connections, such as cable and T1 lines, display very smooth full-motion video with no problem. Web surfers need higher bandwidth to be able to enjoy viewing Web pages with audio and video content. The higher bandwidth Internet is our dream that should be realized in the near future, as the technology becomes affordable and available to many of us.

Q: What are some of the existing authoring tools to create AVI files?

A: Authoring tools that can create AVI files directly include 2D and 3D animation and multimedia applications. Samples of these applications include `LightWave 3D` (www.newtek.com), `Caligari Truespace` (www.caligari.com), `Fractal Design Ray Dream Studio` (www.fractal.com), and `Macromedia Director` (www.macromedia.com).

Q: How can I create video files from analog video?

A: The video capture board on your PC can convert analog video signals (coming from videotapes, video cameras, or camcorders) to video files by a process known as digitizing the analog video. This process is similar to the sampling of sound discussed in chapter 12. Most likely, the board on your PC is a 32-bit PCI bus card that plugs into the 32-bit PCI slot in the motherboard. In addition to the video board or card, you should also have the video software installed on your PC. It is an application program. The preceding answer lists some programs.

Most video capture cards provide either composite video (for VHS analog format) or S-Video (for S-VHS analog format) connectors. Most cards also perform hardware-based (firmware) video compression before sending the compressed video to the hard drive of the PC via the PCI bus. With both the hardware and software installed, you plug the analog video device, be it a camera or a camcorder, into the back of the PC and start creating the video files using the software.

Q: How can I create video files from TV shows and programs?

A: You have two options. You can follow the approach covered in the answer to the preceding question. That is, you tape your favorite show on a VCR tape as you have been doing. Then you plug your VCR or camcorder into the PC to create the video file. The VCR or camcorder outputs the composite analog video signal to the PC video capture board. The other option is that you can install a PC/TV tuner card on your PC. The reason you need a PC/TV tuner is that TV signals are transmitted over the air (or through coaxial cables for Cable TV (CATV)) as radio frequency (RF) waves. The video analog signals (NTSC, PAL, or SECAM format) are modulated onto RF waves to create the known TV channels. After their reception, these waves are demodulated, inside the TV box or inside the set-top box for CATV, back to the original analog video signal. Thus, the PC/TV tuner demodulates the TV signal into a composite video analog signal that can be fed to the PC video capture card, which, in turn, converts it into an AVI file. You connect the antenna or cable of your TV set to the back of your PC. The PC/TV tuner card and its related software, together with the PC video capture card and its related software, convert your favorite TV programs to video files. If you are interested in PC/TV tuners, run a search by using your favorite search engine with a search string such as *PC/TV tuners*, *PC/TV cards*, or *PC/TV boards* — or check this Web site: www.ati.com.

Q: How can I output a video file to a videotape?

A: You need yet another piece of hardware, known as a scan converter. A scan converter takes the Video Graphics Adapter (VGA) signal going to the computer monitor and converts it into a composite video or S-video signal (NTSC, PAL, or SECAM). This signal can then be recorded by using a typical VCR or camcorder. The scan converter could be internal (integrated into the video board) or external (a small box sitting between the PC system and its monitor). The Web site www.ati.com offers some scan converters.

Q: Is it possible to capture video through the PC parallel port?

A: Yes. This is a more convenient way than opening the computer case to install the video capture board. There are some systems that connect to the parallel port of a PC to enable video capture. A system is usually simple, consisting of a camera and an adapter that plugs into the port, a Windows driver, and software. Example systems include `Alaris QuickVideo Transport` (www.alaris.com), and `Connectix QuickCam` (www.connectix.com).

Q: What is good advice about the effective use of video in a Web page?

A: Keep the video clips small, because some of the surfers of your Web page may not have broadband Internet connections. More importantly, make sure that the video clip tells a story — otherwise, it becomes boring. In today's age of using multimedia, pretty pictures are no longer enough to attract anybody's attention. For example, characters and human personalities sell. Make sure the video clip has an attractive sound track. Post the size of the video clip in the Web page, so that the surfers of your page can estimate how long their Internet connection will need to download the clip. A clip size of 320×240 or larger should be used. Finally, do not compress the video too much, to avoid losing the image details.

13.9 Summary

Introduction

•Video represents a major component of multimedia on the Web.

•As with audio, there is analog and digital video. Analog video is video as we know it and watch it on TV and video tapes (VHS and 8 mm formats).

•Analog video is transmitted in continuous composed (combining both color and brightness) signals that use a standard transmission code, such as NTSC, PAL, and SECAM. Analog video has two characteristics: frame rate and frame size.

•Frame rate (also known as refresh rate) is defined as the number of frames displayed per second. In TV video, the frame rate is 30 frames per second.

•Frame size is defined as the pixel size of the video image. In TV video, the frame size is the size of the TV screen itself, unless the screen is split between multiple channels.

•Analog video can be converted to digital video via a conversion process known as digitizing the analog video. Digital video is usually small clips.

•Digital video, like analog video, has a frame rate and a frame size. The values for both are usually smaller than those for analog video, because of Web bandwidth limitations.

•Digital video is also compressed, in addition to having its frame rate and size kept small. Video compression reduces the size of digital video further. The size of uncompressed video is very large. About 27 MB of space is needed for one second of video.

•Video compression schemes remove redundant audio and video data, thus reducing the size of the video signal, to in turn compress the signal.

•Video compression schemes use codec (**co**mpression/**dec**ompression) algorithms. These algorithms compress the video to store and transmit it, and decompress it to play it.

•Each video format has a codec algorithm built in it. Some codecs are symmetric, some are asymmetric.

•A symmetric codec compresses and decompresses the video signal at the same rate. In other words, the symmetric codec takes equal amounts of time to compress the video signal and to decompress it.

•An asymmetric codec compresses the signal very slowly, but it decompresses it very fast. Thus, the asymmetric codec takes longer time to compress the video signal, and less time to decompress it.

•Some of the Web codecs include Sorenson Video, RealVideo, H261, H263, MPEG-4, and Photo-JPEG. Sorenson and MPEG-4 codecs produce high-quality Web video. RealVideo codec is most suitable for video data rates below 3 kiloBytes per second (KBps). H261 and H263 are suitable for low-quality and medium-quality videoconferencing, respectively. Photo-JPEG codec is used to store still (photographic) images.

Video Formats

•Digital videos, like sound, are stored in files using certain formats. The size of a video file depends on the length of the video clip, its frame rate, its frame size, and its compression level.

•As with audio, there are two types of video used on the Internet: streaming and playback.

•Streaming video is the real-time video. Streaming video allows Web surfers to view video as it is downloaded. Web surfers can use streaming video to watch live events from all over the world. Video cards that come with PCs can play streaming video if the software that can handle streaming video is installed.

•Playback video is the video created in advance, stored in files, and included in Web pages as video clips. When the Web page is downloaded, the video is played in a small window after it's fully downloaded, assuming that there is a video player application installed on the client computer.

•There are many video formats available to produce playback video. The available common formats are AVI (Audio Video Interleave), QuickTime, MPEG (Moving Picture Experts Group), and MJPEG (Motion JPEG). The file extensions (types) for these formats are `.avi`, `.mov`, `.mpg`, and `.mjpg`, respectively.

•The QuickTime and MPEG formats are the most widely used. Browsers support both of them. Web authors should use either one in their Web pages.

Video Hardware and Software

•A computer must have the following hardware components installed to play video: video capture card, video drivers (software), and external speakers (to play the sound associated with video).

•Video software is available for both types of video: the playback video, and streaming video. We focus on playback software in this chapter.

•Video software should support such video operations as playing, capturing, compressing, editing (cut and paste), and adding sound effects to an application. The software should also support conversion between the different video formats.

•Most video software is easy to use. It provides GUIs having predefined settings, to make it easier for users.

•Many video software programs exist — Some for Windows include Intel Indeo video, Microsoft Active Movie, Maplay 32, Winamp, and VMPEG. They all support the MPEG format.

•For Mac, sample programs are MpegCD and Macamp. They both support the MPEG format only.

•For Unix and OS/2, there is Maplay, which supports MPEG format only.

•For Linux, there is Xaudio, which also supports MPEG format only.

•Some of the products that allow users of digital camcorders to capture and edit video are EditDV, MotoDV, PhotoDV, and FilmTextures.

•Users can always search for the latest and greatest shareware by using the Web site www.shareware.com, with *video* as the key search word.

High-Definition Television

•High-definition TV (HDTV) is a digital TV that can receive both digital broadcast programs as well as Internet data.

•HDTV provides high-quality video and audio, both in digital streaming formats. One of the most distinguishing features of HDTV is its 16:9 aspect ratio.

•HDTV transmission is based on the TCP/IP protocol, and allows an HDTV system to transmit both broadcast TV programs and Internet content at the rate of 19.3 Mbits per second.

•HDTV systems support both dynamic allocability and scalability. Dynamic allocability is the ability to send data and content during HDTV programs. Dynamic scalability is the ability of an HDTV set to support both high-resolution and low-resolution TV programs.

•The HDTV broadcast signal has three channels: video, audio, and data. The video channel carries the main video of TV scenes. The audio channel carries the accompanying sound. The data channel carries the background video of TV scenes, as well as other data.

•HDTV video is based on the MPEG format. The audio of HDTV is based on the Dolby AC-3 system, with a sampling rate of 48 kHz.

•PCs offer another form of digital TV. The concept of using a PC as a TV is sometimes known as PC/TV, PC theater, or interactive TV.

Video Tags

•The <EMBED> tag allows Web surfers to embed video clips in Web pages.

•The attributes of the <EMBED> tag are SRC, WIDTH, HEIGHT, VOLUME, AUTOSTART, HIDDEN, and LOOP.

•The SRC attributes specifies the video file.

•The WIDTH and HEIGHT attributes specify the size of the video clip frame in pixels.

•The VOLUME attribute has values that range from 1 to 100. The default value is 50.

•The AUTOSTART, HIDDEN, and LOOP can be set to `true` or `false`. Their default values are `false`. It is not recommended to use them, because they can annoy Web surfers.

Dealing with Video

•Creating video clips requires the use of video software and of a video recording device such as a camcorder, to record and edit video.

•Embedding video in Web pages can be achieved via two alternatives: the <A> tag, or the <EMBED> tag.

•Depending on the type of the video card, different video players may be available on a computer.

•There are two video players that come with Windows. One is the Media PLayer. This player plays both sound and video clips. Video clips must be in AVI format. The other player is the Movie Player. This player plays video clips only (no sound clips) that are in QuickTime or MPEG format. It does not play AVI files.

•To find pre-installed video clips on a PC, use the Windows search tool by clicking Start (located at bottom left corner of screen) => Find => Files or Folders => type *.mov or *.mpg.

•The other way of looking for pre-installed video clips is to check the Windows or Media folder.

•The Media folder is a subfolder under the Windows folder. You can open this folder by double clicking this sequence; My Computer => Drive C => Windows => Media. The Media folder stores both audio and video files that come with Windows on your computer.

•Quick reference of the HTML tags covered in this chapter

Table 13.1   Summary of HTML video tags.

Tag	Close	Attribute	Value	Example	Chpt. page
<EMBED>	Yes	SRC	name	<EMBED SRC="mySound.mov">	443 444
		WIDTH	pixels	<EMBED WIDTH = 400>	
		HEIGHT	pixels	<EMBED HEIGHT = 300>	
		VOLUME	number	<EMBED VOLUME = 70>	
		AUTOSTART	boolean	<EMBED AUTOSTART = "true">	
		HIDDEN	boolean	<EMBED HIDDEN = "true">	
		LOOP	boolean	<EMBED LOOP = "true">	

PROBLEMS

Exercises

13.1 Create a Web page that uses your favorite video clip as a hyperlink.

13.2 Create a Web page that uses your favorite video clip in the <EMBED> tag. Try all the attributes of the tag.

Homework

13.3 Create a Web page that uses both movies and images. Make each image a hyperlink that links to a movie file. Choose your favorite application.

13.4 Repeat problem 13.3 for videos and images of birds.

13.5 Repeat problem 13.3 for videos and images of animals

13.6 Repeat problem 13.3 for videos and images of TV characters — for example Simpsons characters (Homer, Bart, etc.), Batman, and so forth.

13.7 Repeat problem 13.3 for videos and images of movie characters — for example Austin Powers, Pochahontas, the Little Mermaid, Winnie the Pooh, and so forth.

13.8 Repeat problem 13.3 for child education.

13.9 Repeat problem 13.3 for your family members and friends.

13.10 Repeat problem 13.3 for your own pets.

13.11 Create a Web page that can be used for training that uses video clips, if you can use a camcorder.

13.12 Repeat problem 13.11 for entertainment.

13.13 Repeat problem 13.11 for news.

13.14 Repeat problem 13.11 for presentations.

13.15 Repeat problem 13.11 for education.

13.16 Repeat problem 13.11 for a product demonstration.

13.17 Repeat problem 13.11 for a birthday party.

13.18 Repeat problem 13.11 for cooking a recipe.

13.19 Repeat problem 13.11 for capturing a computer session.

CHAPTER 14

Forms and Form Tags

$\mathbf{T}$his chapter covers HTML forms that are widely used over the Internet as an interactive way of communication between Web users and Web sites. HTML Forms are used to collect information from Web users in a logical way. Web users can use forms for a wide range of activities, including performing e-commerce, filling order forms, requesting information, providing customer feedback to companies conducting business over the Web, responding to marketing surveys, signing guest books, reporting problems, and accessing databases. After introducing forms and their importance, the chapter covers their structure. It then covers all the possible elements that can be used to create a form, such as text fields, radio buttons, checkboxes, and so forth. The chapter covers form design and its related issues. It also covers the form tags and their attributes. At the end, the chapter presents some tutorials that illustrate the use of forms in Web pages. It also provides a summary of the important topics covered in the chapter and then some problems.

14.1 Introduction

The HTML background and concepts we have covered in this book thus far allow Web authors to create what we may call "static" or "passive" Web pages. By "static," we mean that users of a Web page cannot communicate with the Web site or the author that publishes the Web page. All that the Web surfers can do is view the page and use its information. At best, these pages can provide surfers with several hyperlinks that they can click if they so choose.

There are several concepts that Web authors can utilize to add interactivity to their Web pages, beyond just clicking hyperlinks. These concepts include using Java with its animation and GUI techniques, JavaScript with its event handling model, and HTML with its forms. We focus on HTML forms in this chapter. HTML forms (we refer to them as forms from now on) are a simple, but powerful concept that allows Web surfers to communicate with Web sites and servers. Forms make Web pages interactive. Forms are utilized pervasively throughout the Web. Many Web pages use forms.

Several factors contribute to the popularity of using forms on the Web. First, they are easy to create. Web authors use HTML tags and attributes to create them. No additional programming background is required unless the form deals with databases. In many applications, including personal Web pages, a Lotus or an e-mail tool is all what Web authors need to process input collected from Web users through forms.

Another reason that adds to the popularity of forms is that they are easy to use. They resemble, in many aspects, the traditional paper forms we use all the time in everyday life. Web forms look like traditional paper forms. There are labeled fields and buttons that need to be filled in or checked. When we finish filling out a paper form, we submit it or send it to the proper organization. Similarly, when we finish filling in a Web form, we submit it or send it to the appropriate Web server, by clicking a *submit* button on the form. The submission process is transparent to the user. If we do not like a paper form after filling it out, we destroy it and start over. Similarly, after filling in a Web form, the Web user can click a reset button to erase the contents of all the form fields and buttons.

Sending the collected information via a form to a Web server is easy and automatic. This is another factor for the popularity of using forms on the Web. The collected information is bundled (encoded) by the browser into what are known as name/value pairs, according to a Common Gateway Interface (CGI) protocol (format). These pairs are sent for processing to the Web server hosting the form. The CGI protocol and concepts are covered in detail at the end of the HTML part of the book, in chapter 18. The CGI method is not the only method available to process form input. Other methods exist. Java servlets, JavaScript, and Active Server Pages (ASPs) are three of these methods.

A last factor that contributes to the popularity of forms is the ease of processing their collected information. When the browser sends the bundled name/value pairs to the Web server, there is an installed program, called a CGI script, on the server. This script decodes the name/value pairs and extracts the values of the form fields and buttons that the user has input during filling the form. These values are used to process the user order. CGI scripts can be written in any programming or scripting language. They can even be generated automatically via HTML editors. CGI scripts are covered in more detail in chapter 18.

HTML provides Web authors with form tags that they can use to add forms to their Web pages. The <FORM> and the <INPUT> tags are the primary tags used to create forms. The <INPUT> tag has many attributes, as covered in section 14.5 of this chapter. These attributes create the elements of the form. These elements can range from text fields, to buttons, to checkboxes, and so forth. Section 14.3 cover all the possible elements of a form.

Information collected from a form can be processed in different ways. It can be written to a file or to a database; this is the case when the form is used for surveying or feedback purposes. Such information becomes a great source to generate statistics that can be used by Web sites to analyze habits of Web surfers or to define emerging trends. For example, a Web site may conduct a survey to find out what is the most popular type of music among teenagers or what is the best way to market a new product.

Another way to process collected information from forms is to submit it to a database; this is the case when the form is used by Web surfers to order products. Consider the case of ordering a book or a music CD over the Internet. When the order form is submitted, the CGI script extracts the book name from the name/value pairs, compares it against the database of books, and informs the surfer about the book's ISBN number, its price, its availability, and its delivery schedule. If the surfer is satisfied with the book, it is shipped immediately.

A third way of processing form information is e-mailing it to someone. E-mailing the information is sometimes awkward if it is e-mailed in its encoded state as name/value pairs. Unless the recipient of the e-mail is aware of the CGI formats and the form itself, it becomes impossible to interpret the e-mail. In essence, the recipient must decode the form information to understand it. If the information is e-mailed so that the recipient can feed it to a CGI script, then the recipient does not have to worry about decoding it. Why would someone want to e-mail form information to someone else? One reason could be security. Some Web sites have contractors who deal with customers. Customers submit forms to the contractors. Contractors, in turn, e-mail the collected information from the forms to their clients for processing by clients' CGI scripts.

How many forms can Web authors have in one Web page? There is no hard and fast rule. Web authors can include as many forms as they need; however, practically, only one form is included. It is very rare to find a Web page with more than one form. For one reason, it may be confusing and boring for Web surfers to deal with more than one form in the same Web page. For another reason, including more than one form makes the Web page multiple screens long, not a good idea from Web page design point of view.

14.2 Form Structure and Communication Cycle

A form has two main distinct parts. One part is included in a Web page; this is the visible part. It is the part that resembles a traditional paper form. A Web surfer sees this part on a Web page on the client computer, fills in its fields, and interacts with it. We refer to this part as the front end of the form. We can think of it as a GUI. The second part is not visible to Web surfers, and they do not interact with it at all. This part is the CGI script that is responsible for processing form information and data received from a filled form, once it is submitted by a Web surfers. It is the CGI script that decodes the name/value pairs that are sent to it by the surfer's browser. We refer to this part of a form as the back end of the form.

Web authors must develop both the front and back ends of a form for it to work successfully. If a Web author develops only the front end of a form, the browser would not know what to do with the name/value pairs that it generates from the form input. It therefore neglects to do anything with them, and the pairs get lost. Thus, information that a Web surfer inputs by filling in the form never gets processed. The Web surfer never receives any warnings from the browser or HTML, because HTML is an interpretive language, not a programming language.

All forms available on the Web obviously have both ends; however, during early stages of developing or learning forms and their tags, Web authors may develop only the front end of a form. It is much simpler to develop the GUI of a form than developing its back end. A form front end requires only HTML tags; its back end requires a knowledge of programming. A CGI script must be written in a language more advanced than HTML, such as JavaScript, Perl, C, C++, or Java. HTML does not provide programming tools, such as control statements, to decode the name/value pairs to extract surfer's input.

What does the back end of a form do, exactly? A form CGI script has two main functions. First, it extracts form input. Second, it processes the input. Consider the case of ordering a book over the Internet that we have already discussed above. First, the CGI script extracts the book name from the name/value pairs and locates the book in the database of the Web server handling the order. Second, it sends a response to the Web surfer who has submitted the order by filling in the form. The response is typically a Web page that the CGI script develops on the fly by using HTML code and sends over the Internet to the client computer. The client browser displays the response Web page to inform the surfer of the status of the order.

What is the communication cycle of a form, from the time a form is filled in by a Web surfer until a response is sent back to the surfer? Figure 14.1 shows the cycle. The two client computers shown in the figure represent the same user and the same client computer. The client computer is shown twice for ease of illustration. As the figure shows, the cycle begins as the Web user (surfer) fills in a form in a Web page. After filling in the form, the user clicks the submit button on the form. The client browser encodes the name/value pairs according to the CGI formats and sends them, across the Internet, to the Web server that has sent the Web page and its form to the user. The server has a CGI script that is already installed. The script reads the name/value pairs and extracts the input of the user. The input is then used by the CGI script to make decisions. The decisions result in the generation of a response, in the form of a Web page that is sent to the user across the Internet. If there is a follow-up that needs to be done, such as sending merchandise, the server administrator takes care of it.

How do the front end and back end of a form recognize each other? The link between a form and its CGI script arises in the <FORM> tag. The tag has an ACTION attribute that specifies the name of the CGI script and its directory on the server that is supposed to handle the form input. Section 14.5 covers the details of the <FORM> tag.

The remainder of this chapter focuses on covering the front end (GUI) of forms and how to build forms. It covers all the possible elements of a form, form layout and design, and the form tags. Chapter 18 discusses in details of CGI scripting and server-side HTML.

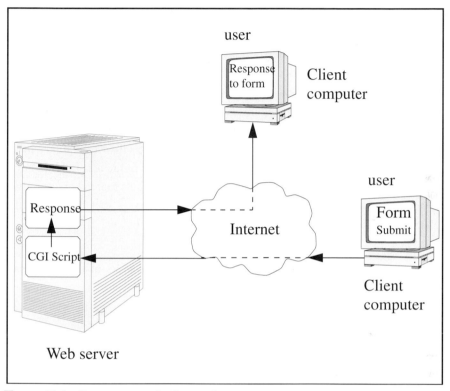

Figure 14.1   Form communication cycle.

14.3 Form Elements

If we examine traditional paper forms carefully, we can easily recognize that there are common elements that are repeatedly used in these forms. Take, for example, multiple choice exams. Any exam form consists of oval shapes that the exam takers fill with their answers. These oval shapes represent the basic element of the exam form. Consider another, more general form, such as a college or a job application form. We can identify several distinct elements in such a form. For example, there may be text fields for the applicant to print name, address, phone numbers, and so forth. There may also be shapes, such as circles or squares, that the applicant can fill in to indicate choices.

HTML forms extend the idea of developing forms by using generic and basic building elements. Web authors can use these elements freely and innovatively to embed forms in the Web pages. HTML provides a comprehensive set of form elements that are guaranteed to meet any design needs of HTML forms. These elements are text fields, radio buttons, checkboxes, menus, text areas, submit buttons, and reset buttons. Figure 14.2 shows the icon (shape) of each element as it appears on a Web page that has a form. As the figure shows, some of these elements, such as text fields and text areas, have certain parameters.

The text field element is typically used when one line of text is needed as input from the Web user who may fill in the form. For example, text fields are used to collect names, addresses, ID numbers (such as social security numbers), phone numbers, and so forth. According to HTML, each text field is displayed as a rectangle, as shown in figure 14.2, and has two parameters to define it: size, and maximum length. Each parameter is specified as a number of characters. The maximum length defines the maximum number of characters, m, that the text field can hold. Out of this number, only the number of characters, n, specified by the size parameter is displayed in the text field. If a form user types more characters in the text field than n, the text scrolls to display only the last n characters typed. If the user inputs more characters than m, the extra characters are ignored by the browser. Figure 14.2 shows a text field with fifteen and twelve characters for the maximum length and the size of the text field respectively; thus $m = 15$ and $n = 12$.

Whenever Web authors have a need to present potential users of their Web pages with nonexclusive multiple choices, they use checkboxes. Users can select them with a click of a mouse. Checkboxes are displayed in a Web page as squares, as shown in figure 14.2. Checkboxes that have already been selected (checked) by a Web user are shown with a checkmark inside them. The first two checkboxes shown in figure 14.2 are checked, while the third one is not. Checkboxes act as on/off or toggle switches. When a user clicks inside a checkbox, its state reverses itself from checked (true) to unchecked (off), or vice versa. Checkboxes are mutually inclusive: A user can check more than one checkbox at the same time. Examples include presenting a user with choices of favorite food, sports, books, and so forth. The user may like pizza, salad, and hamburgers. Or, the user may like football, soccer, and tennis. Or, the user may like fiction, history, and fantasy books.

Whenever Web authors have a need to present potential users of their Web pages with multiple choices of which only one must be selected, they use radio buttons. Radio buttons are displayed in a Web page as circles, as shown in figure 14.2. Radio buttons that have already been selected by a Web user are shown with a filled circle inside them. The middle radio button shown in figure 14.2 is selected, while the other two are not. Like checkboxes, radio buttons act as on/off or toggle switches. When a user clicks inside a radio button, its state reverses itself from selected to unselected, or vice versa. Radio buttons are mutually exclusive; this means that a user can select only one radio button at any one time. Examples include presenting a user with choices of gender, college year, answer to a question, and so forth. The user is only a male or female; or, the user is only a freshman, sophomore, junior, or senior; or, the user's answer to a question is either yes or no.

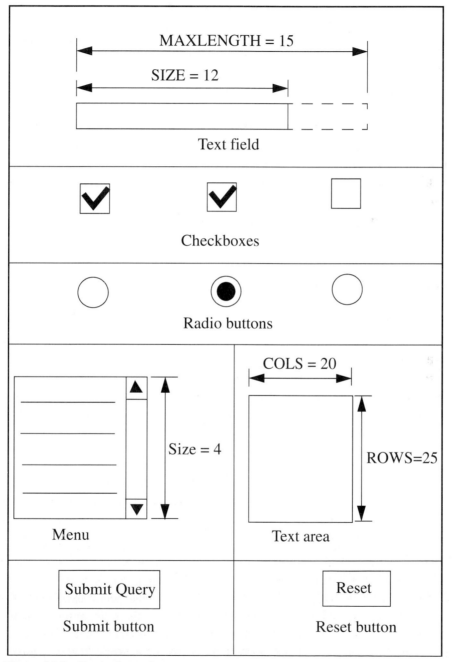

Figure 14.2 Form elements.

A menu is a useful form element. Web authors present users of their forms with menus of choices. A menu may be defined to allow its users to choose either at most one menu item or multiple items at the same time. Checkboxes or radio buttons perform the same function as menus, but menus are usually used whenever there are many choices whose descriptions are verbose. In such cases, the use of checkboxes or radio buttons becomes very cumbersome and inefficient. A menu may be displayed with only one of its items or multiple items as, shown in figure 14.2. HTML provides a size parameter for a menu to control its display. This parameter defines the number of menu items that can be displayed on the screen. Thus, the size parameter controls the size of the menu box. If the menu has a larger number of menu items than that specified by the size parameter, scrollbars are added automatically (by the browser), to the menu display. Figure 14.2 shows a menu with a size of 4. If no size is specified, only one item is displayed, and the menu acts as drop-down menu. A menu is also known as a list. Other names that are frequently used for an HTML menu are option list or menu, select list or menu, and drop-down list or menu.

Unlike the text field element, a text area element provides form users with *multiple* lines of text. Text areas are useful if Web authors need to display many lines of text to users of their forms. For example, Web authors can use text areas to display recipes or instructions on how to fill in forms. Users who fill in the forms can use text areas to send their feedback to Web authors. HTML defines two parameters for a text area: width, and height, as shown in figure 14.2. Both parameters are specified as numbers of characters. Furthermore, the width and the height are referred to as the number of columns and rows respectively. Each column is a character, and each row is a line of text. The text area shown in figure 14.2 is 20 characters wide by 25 characters deep; thus, this text area can hold 500 characters.

Two more form elements are special buttons. They are the submit and the reset buttons shown in figure 14.2 These buttons act globally, at the form level. A user clicks the submit button of a form, after filling it in, to submit its contents to the CGI script installed on the designated Web server. Clicking the submit button triggers the browser to collect the form input, encodes the input as name/value pairs according to the CGI formats, and sends the pairs to the Web server. The label of the submit button is known as its value. The default value is `Submit Query`. Web authors can use different values, such as `Send it`, `Send this form`, `Send Entry`, and so forth.

The reset button is the complement to the submit button. It performs an opposite function. It erases or clears the form input. If the user is not satisfied after filling in a form or decides not to submit it, the user clicks the reset button. All the user input is erased and replaced by the default values of the form. These default values are defined in the form HTML code, as we will discuss in sections 14.4 and 14.5 in this chapter. The label of the reset button is known as its value. The default value is `Reset`. Web authors can use different values, such as `Erase`, `Clear Form and Start Over`, `Reset all Values and Start Over`, and so forth.

There are other form elements that are provided by HTML but are less frequently used. They are the hidden and password elements. The hidden element is never displayed on the screen as a form element. Thus, form users never see it. Hidden elements are used by Web authors to track information between clients and servers. To find out whether a Web page uses hidden elements, simply view the page source and look for them. The password element allows Web authors to request passwords from users before allowing them to access secure Web pages or documents. Examples include accessing a stock market account or reading a magazine online. Hidden and password elements are typically used in Web pages that use JavaScript code in addition to HTML code.

14.4 Form Layout and Design

When Web authors need to create forms, they think in terms of the form elements covered in section 14.3. The design and layout of a form are what distinguish it from other forms. However, there is a common theme for form layout and design. First, each form must have a submit button and a reset button. Second, each form must have an ACTION attribute, to tell the browser how to process the name/value pairs. Third, each form must have a METHOD attribute, to tell the browser how to send the name/value pairs to the Web server that hosts the form CGI script. Beyond this common theme, each form has a different body that contains the proper form elements. Figure 14.3 shows the generic layout of a form. As shown in the figure, the form body represents the top part of the form. The submit and reset buttons represent the bottom part of the form, and are usually placed at the end of the form.

There are many useful tips and rules that Web authors usually follow to design HTML forms. They are mostly simple and logical and follow common sense. Here is a partial list of these tips (readers can augment it as they need):

1. **Keep the form short.** A form should not be more than one computer screen long. A half-screen-long form is ideal. We learn from tradition. Long traditional paper forms tend to discourage us from filling them out. HTML forms are no exception.

2. **Keep the form simple.** Simple form goes hand in hand with short form. Web authors should ask for only the information they need, in order to keep forms short and simple. Web authors generally receive many more responses from a short, simple form than from a long, complicated one.

3. **Keep the form organized.** Web authors should group related fields together. The form body should be divided into logical sections or groups. Let us consider designing a form for ordering books online. We can divide the form body into three sections. The first section could be for collecting shipping information, such as a person's name, a shipping address, and a phone number. The second section could be a list of books to choose from. The third section could be for choosing a method of shipping. It is also beneficial to add

headings that stand out at the beginning of each section, to alert the form user to the type
of information needed in the section.

4. **Surf the Web for existing design ideas.** Imitating is a great way of learning. Web authors
   may opt to go online and surf the Web looking for Web pages with forms, so that they can
   learn from them. They can also search traditional paper forms. As a matter of fact, many
   Web sites translate their paper forms into HTML forms. Consider the application form of a
   University — almost all universities have put their application forms online.

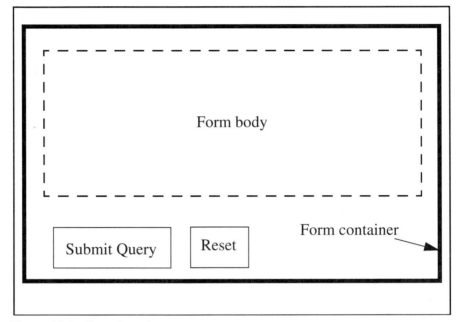

Figure 14.3   Form layout.

14.5 Form Tags

HTML provides the necessary tags to create forms. More specifically, HTML form tags
allow Web authors to create the front ends, or the GUIs, of forms that Web surfers see on the
screen and interact with. These tags allow Web authors to specify the name and the location of
the CGI script that is responsible for processing form input — that is, name/value pairs. HTML
cannot be used to write the CGI script itself.

HTML form tags must meet three requirements to successfully create forms. First, they
must provide a way to allow Web authors to create the form layout they design. HTML provides
the <FORM> tag to meet this requirement. This tag acts as a container of the form elements. The
form elements are displayed on the computer screen in the order of their use inside the <FORM>
tag. The <FORM> tag also has two important attributes. One is the ACTION attribute, which

specifies the name and the location of the CGI script that should parse the name/value pairs in order to make use of them. The other attribute is the METHOD attribute, which specifies the way the name/value pairs are sent to the Web server.

The second requirement is that HTML must provide tags to create all the form elements discussed in section 14.3. These tags are <INPUT>, <SELECT>, and <TEXTAREA>. The <INPUT> tag has attributes to create the other form elements; namely text fields, checkboxes, radio buttons, submit button, and reset button. Each of these tags has attributes to allow Web authors more control over their outcomes.

The third requirement is that HTML must provide a way to initialize form elements as needed; that is the ability to specify initial values. For example, we may want to display text fields or text areas with initial text, or, we may want to display a set or group of radio buttons or checkboxes with one of them already selected or checked. Each tag that creates a form element has the ability to specify an initial value. These initial values appear in the form when it is displayed initially in the Web page. Web surfers may replace these initial values with their specific values. These values become the current values. However, the initial values of form elements do not change. Therefore, when a form is reset via the reset button, each element's current value is reset to its initial value. If an element does not have an initial value, resetting it shows it blank (text fields and text areas), unselected (radio buttons), or unchecked (checkboxes).

The remainder of this section discusses in detail all the form tags and their attributes.

14.5.1 <FORM> Tag

This is the tag that act as a container to define the form layout. it is sometimes known as the form header. It also specifies how to process the form name/value pairs and the method of sending them from the client computer to the Web server. This tag must close. A Web page may use this tag as many times as needed to create forms; however, it is not recommended to create more than one form per Web page. The <FORM> tag has several attributes. They are NAME, ACTION, METHOD, ENCTYPE, ACCEPT-CHARSET, and ACCEPT. These attributes are described in the following list.

•The NAME attribute specifies the name of the form. This attribute is useful if the Web page uses JavaScript in addition to HTML. JavaScript is a programming language.

•The ACTION attribute specifies a way to process the form data. When a Web surfer clicks the form submit button, the browser encodes the form data into name/value pairs and sends it according the ACTION attribute. This attribute can specify some options. It can specify a CGI script, an e-mail address to send the form data to, or any other protocol, such as opening a file.

•The METHOD attribute specifies the method that the browser uses to send the form data to the Web server. This attribute has two values: GET and POST. The former is the default. The difference between the two values comes in how form data is sent to a Web server. If a form uses the GET method, the browser extracts all the name/value pairs of the form, appends them to the URL specified by the ACTION attribute, and sends the resulting string to the Web server. The

URL is separated from all the name/value pairs by a question mark (?) that the browser adds as required by the CGI protocol and formats. Thus, the form's contents are parsed all at once. The CGI script reads the string and parses it by extracting the input values. During parsing, the CGI script uses the question-mark separator to remove the URL from the string.

If a form uses the POST method, the browser sends the form data set to the Web server, instead of appending it to the URL as a string, as in the GET method. Once the Web server has received a request from a form using POST, it knows to continue "listening" for the rest of the information. POST is the preferred method that should always be used by Web authors.

The GET method is typically used when a form does not cause any changes or side effects, such as the searching of databases. If the form is expected to cause side effects, such as modifying a database or subscribing to a service, the POST method should be used. The GET method may run the risk of losing form data if the string of name/value pairs is too long. Some Operating Systems, such as Unix, have a limit on how long a single string can be. The Unix limit is 255 characters.

•The ENCTYPE attribute specifies the content type used to submit the form data to the Web server. This attribute is used only with the POST method. Its default value is `application/x-www-form-urlencoded`. If a Web author uses the value FILE for the TYPE attribute of the <INPUT> tag, the value of the ENCTYPE should be `multipart/form-data`.

•The ACCEPT-CHARSET attribute specifies the list of character encoding for the input data that the Web server processing the form data should accept. We seldom use this attribute, and we let the browser use its default value.

•The ACCEPT attribute specifies the content types that the Web server processing the form can handle correctly. Again, we seldom use this attribute, and we let the browser use its default value.

The NAME, ACTION, and METHOD are the most widely used attributes of the <FORM> tag. Here are some examples to show their use:

1. <FORM NAME = "myForm" ACTION ="http://www.abc.com/cgi-bin/cgiScript" METHOD = "post"> ... form body goes here ... </FORM>. In this example, the form data is processed by the CGI script `cgiScript` that resides on the Web server www.abc.com in the directory `cgi-bin`. Two types of CGI scripts exist: server side, and client side. Server-side scripts run at the server. Client-side scripts run at the client. It should be noted here that some organizations and webmasters do not allow users to get to cgi-bin directories.

2. <FORM NAME = "myForm" ACTION = "mailto:zeid@coe.neu.edu" METHOD = "post"> ... form body goes here ... </FORM>. In this example, the form data is submitted to the e-mail address zeid@coe.neu.edu.

14.5.2 <INPUT> Tag

This is the tag that creates many of the form elements. More specifically, this tag allows Web authors to create text fields, checkboxes, radio buttons, password fields, submit buttons, reset buttons, and hidden fields. This tag must not close. A form may use this tag as many times as needed to create the needed form elements. The <INPUT> tag has several attributes. These attributes can be divided into two groups: independent, and dependent. The independent group has the attributes that stand alone. They are TYPE, VALUE, and NAME. The dependent group has attributes that depend on other attributes. For example, the SIZE attribute can be used only if a text field is used. The CHECKED attribute can be used only if a checkbox or a radio button is used. These attributes are described next.

•The TYPE attribute specifies the type of the form element to create. The values for this attribute are text, checkbox, radio, password, submit, reset, hidden, image, button, and file. The default value is `text`. This value creates text fields. The examples at the end of this section show how to use the various values of this attribute to create form elements in different layouts. It should be mentioned that the password element acts in a normal way, hiding the actual characters and replacing them by an echo character (such as an asterisk); however, it provides only minimal security protection. Applications that require higher security should use additional (encryption) techniques.

•The VALUE attribute specifies the initial value of the form element. This value serves as the default value for the element. The value of this attribute takes on different meanings, depending on the form element that it is used with. It is the initial (default) text string when it is used with a text field. It is the name of a checkbox when it is used with checkboxes. It is the name of the group of a set of radio buttons when it is used with radio buttons. (Radio buttons do not work properly (mutually exclusive) unless the same group name is used for all of them.) It is the password if it is used with a password field. It is the label of the submit or reset button (that Web surfers read on a Web page) if it is used with either one.

•The NAME attribute assigns a name to a form element. This name is used by the browser to create the name/value pairs before submitting the form to the Web server. The creator of the CGI script also uses these names during the writing of the script code that parses the pairs.

•The SIZE and MAXLENGTH attributes are dependent attributes. They are used only with the text field or password element. The SIZE attribute specifies the visible width of the text field as shown in figure 14.2. Its value is given as the number of characters. The MAXLENGTH attribute specifies the maximum number of characters that the user can enter. The default value of the MAXLENGTH attribute is infinity.

•The CHECKED attribute is used only with checkboxes and radio buttons. It is a boolean attribute whose default value is ON. When it is used in a form, the checkbox(es) and/or the radio button using it are displayed with checkmark. It can be used more than once with checkboxes, but only once with radio buttons.

•The SRC attribute is used only with the image element. As in the <IMG> tag, it specifies the image file name. This attribute can be used to create a decorated graphical submit button only. It cannot be used to create a decorated reset button. It is seldom used in practice.

Example 14.1 Develop a Web page that illustrates the use of text fields in a form.

Solution This example creates a Web page with a form that has several text fields. The form has eight <INPUT> tags, to create six text fields, one submit button, and on reset button. Using a text editor, type the code that follows, and save it as *example14.1.htm*l. Figures 14.4 and 14.5 show the resulting Web page. Figure 14.4 shows the initial (default) values. while figure 14.5 shows current user-input values.

```
<HTML>
<HEAD>
<TITLE>A Web page with a form using text fields</TITLE>
</HEAD>
<BODY>
<CENTER><FONT COLOR = "blue"><H2>A form using text fields</H2></
FONT> </CENTER>

<FORM NAME = "myForm" ACTION = "mailto:zeid@coe.neu.edu" METHOD =
"post">

<FONT COLOR = "red">Enter your name:</FONT><BR>
First Name:<INPUT NAME = "firstName" VALUE = "Abe" SIZE = 10>
MI:<INPUT TYPE = "text" NAME = "middleInitial" SIZE = 1>
Last Name:<INPUT TYPE = "text" NAME = "lastName" VALUE = "Zeid"
SIZE = 10 MAXLENGTH = 15><BR>

<FONT COLOR = "red">Enter your address:</FONT><BR>
Address:<INPUT TYPE = "text" NAME = "address" VALUE = "number and
street go here" SIZE = 22 MAXLENGTH = 30><BR>
City:<INPUT TYPE = "text" NAME = "city" SIZE = 10 MAXLENGTH =
15><BR>
State:<INPUT TYPE = "text" NAME = "state" SIZE = 10 MAXLENGTH = 15>
Zip code:<INPUT TYPE = "text" NAME = "zipCode" SIZE = 5 MAXLENGTH =
10><BR>
Country:<INPUT TYPE = "text" NAME = "country" SIZE = 10 MAXLENGTH =
15><BR>

<FONT COLOR = "green">Thank you. Come again!</FONT><BR>
<INPUT TYPE = "submit"  NAME = "submitButton">
<INPUT TYPE = "reset"   NAME = "resetButton">
</FORM>
</BODY>
</HTML>
```

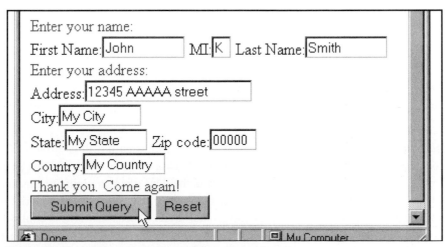

Figure 14.4 A form using text fields: initial values.

Figure 14.5 A form using text fields: current values.

Here are several comments about this example HTML code:

•The form tag uses the e-mail protocol as its ACTION attribute.

•The layout of the form elements is such that they flow in the Web page from top to bottom and from left to right, except when we use the <BR> tag to force them to start on a new line when we need to.

•We have randomly used all the attributes of the <INPUT> tag that are associated with a text field element, to show their effect.

•We have not used the TYPE attribute in the first <INPUT> tag purposely, because we know that the default type is text.

•All the text fields that use the VALUE attribute are displayed with the default or initial values specified by the attribute. A form user can replace these initial values by clicking the mouse inside the desired text field to bring the focus there, deleting the existing text, and then typing new text.

•The user clicks the reset button whenever needed, to re-initialize the form elements again.

•The labels that precede the form elements are not part of the <INPUT> tags. The Web author creates them as text to clarify, to the form user, the intent of each form element. Such text can be added before or after the form elements. It is a matter of personal preference and design convention.

•We have purposely not used values for the submit and reset buttons, so HTML uses the Submit Query and Reset values, respectively, for the two buttons.

•After filling in the form, as shown in figure 14.5, the user can either click the reset button to start over, or click the submit button to submit the form data. If the user clicks the submit button, the browser sends the name/value pairs to the designated e-mail address in the ACTION attribute of the form tag. These pairs are sent as an attachment to the e-mail message. We will cover this topic in more details in chapter 18; here is how the name/value pairs for the form data shown in figure 14.5 look, for now:

```
firstName=John&middleInitial=K&lastName=Smith&address=12345+AAAAA+
street&city=My+City&state=My+State&zipCode=00000&country=My+Coun-
try&submitButton=Submit+Query
```

Example 14.2 Develop a Web page that illustrates the use of checkboxes in a form.

Solution This example creates a Web page with a form that has three groups of checkboxes: food, sports, and books. Each group has three checkboxes. The first checkbox in the first group, the second in the second group, and the third in the third group are initially checked. Two types of layouts of the checkboxes are used: horizontal and vertical. The vertical layout is more commonly used in form design than is the horizontal layout, because it is less confusing and easy to follow. A Web surfer checks the desired checkboxes by clicking them. Clicking a checkbox once reverses its current state. The boxes currently checked show a checkmark inside them, as shown in figure 14.2. Using a text editor, type the code that follows, and save it as *example14.2.htm*l. Figure 14.6 shows the resulting Web page with the initial (default) values.

```
<HTML>
<HEAD>
<TITLE>A Web page with a form using checkboxes</TITLE>
</HEAD>
<BODY>
<CENTER><FONT COLOR = "blue"><H2>A form using checkboxes</H2></
FONT> </CENTER>
<FORM NAME = "myForm" ACTION = "mailto:zeid@coe.neu.edu" METHOD =
"post">

<FONT COLOR = "red">Select your favirote food:</FONT><BR>
<INPUT TYPE = "checkbox" NAME = "food" VALUE = "pizza"
CHECKED>Pizza
<INPUT TYPE = "checkbox" NAME = "food" VALUE = "salad">Salad
<INPUT TYPE = "checkbox" NAME = "food" VALUE = "burgers">Burg-
ers<BR>

<FONT COLOR = "red">Select your favirote sports:</FONT><BR>
<INPUT TYPE = "checkbox" NAME = "soprts" VALUE = "football">Foot-
ball
<INPUT TYPE = "checkbox" NAME = "sports" VALUE = "soccer"
CHECKED>Soccer
<INPUT TYPE = "checkbox" NAME = "soprts" VALUE = "tennis">Ten-
nis<BR>

<FONT COLOR = "red">Select your favirote books:</FONT><BR>
<INPUT TYPE = "checkbox" NAME = "books" VALUE = "fiction">Fic-
tion<BR>
<INPUT TYPE = "checkbox" NAME = "books" VALUE = "history">His-
tory<BR>
<INPUT TYPE = "checkbox" NAME = "books" VALUE = "fantasy"
CHECKED>Fantasy<BR>
<FONT COLOR = "green">Thank you. Come again!</FONT><BR>
<INPUT TYPE = "submit" NAME = "submitButton"  VALUE = "Send it">
<INPUT TYPE = "reset" NAME = "resetButton"  VALUE = "Clear it">

</FORM>
</BODY>
</HTML>
```

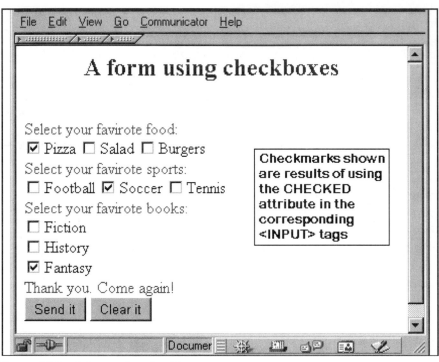

Figure 14.6   A form using checkboxes.

Example 14.3 Develop a Web page that illustrates the use of radio buttons in a form.

Solution In this example, we create a Web page with a form that has three groups of radio buttons: gender, college year, and an answer to a question. The value of the NAME attribute must be the same for all the buttons that belong to the same group. This is how the browser can tell which radio buttons belong to which group, so that it can make them mutually exclusive. The first group (NAME = "sex") has two buttons (male or female). The second group (NAME = "year") has four buttons (freshman, sophomore, junior, and senior). The third group (NAME = "gradSchool") has two buttons (yes or no). No default button is set for the first group. The first button in the second group is checked. The Yes button in the third group is set as the default. As with checkboxes, radio buttons may be organized in a horizontal or vertical layout. The vertical layout is more commonly used in form design than the horizontal layout. Radio buttons act similarly to checkboxes. A Web surfer selects the desired radio button by clicking it. Clicking a radio button once reverses its current state. The currently selected radio buttons show a black circle inside them, as shown in figure 14.2. Using a text editor, type the code that follows, and save it as *example14.3.html*. Figure 14.7 shows the resulting Web page with the initial (default) values.

```
<HTML>
<HEAD>
<TITLE>A Web page with a form using radio buttons</TITLE>
</HEAD>
<BODY>
<CENTER><FONT COLOR = "blue"><H2>A form using radio buttons</H2></
FONT> </CENTER>

<FORM NAME = "myForm" ACTION = "mailto:zeid@coe.neu.edu" METHOD =
"post">

<FONT COLOR = "red">Check your gender:</FONT><BR>
<INPUT TYPE = "radio" NAME = "sex" VALUE = "male">Male
<INPUT TYPE = "radio" NAME = "sex" VALUE = "female">Female<BR>
<FONT COLOR = "red">Check your current college year:</FONT><BR>
<INPUT TYPE = "radio" NAME = "year" VALUE= "first" CHECKED>Freshman
<INPUT TYPE = "radio" NAME = "year" VALUE = "second">Sophomore
<INPUT TYPE = "radio" NAME = "year" VALUE = "third">Junior
<INPUT TYPE = "radio" NAME = "year" VALUE = "fourth">Senior<BR>
<FONT COLOR = "red">Do you plan to go to graduate school after
graduation?</FONT><BR>
<INPUT TYPE = "radio" NAME = "gradSchool" VALUE = "go"
CHECKED>Yes<BR>
<INPUT TYPE = "radio" NAME = "gradSchool" VALUE = "noGo">No<BR>
<FONT COLOR = "green">Thank you. Come again!</FONT><BR>
<INPUT TYPE = "submit" NAME = "submitButton"  VALUE = "Send">
<INPUT TYPE = "reset" NAME = "resetButton"  VALUE = "Erase">

</FORM>
</BODY>
</HTML>
```

Example 14.4 Develop a Web page that illustrates the use of images, a password, and hidden fields in a form.

Solution In this example, we create a form that uses an image as a submit button. However, an image cannot be used as a reset button. If you try to use two different images for the two buttons, the browser treats both of them as submit buttons. All attributes of the <IMG> tag can be used with the image. There are minor differences in the rendering of the image between the two common browsers. Netscape Communicator adds a border around the image, and does not render the image ALT attribute. MS IE does not add a border, treats the image as a hyperlink, and renders the ALT attribute. It is uncommon to use an image as a button. Actually, it may be confusing to the form users, unless the form is targeted specifically for children. This example also uses a password field and a hidden field. When a Web surfer types the password in the field, the browser displays an asterisk as the echo character. The hidden field is never displayed on the computer screen as part of the form. A hidden element could be the e-mail address that the form should be sent to. In this case, the VALUE of the field is the e-mail address. The use of the password and hidden fields requires the use of a programming language, such as JavaScript, in order to process them. Using a text editor, type the code that follows figure 14.7, and save it as *example14.4.html*. Figure 14.8 shows the resulting Web page with the initial (default) values.

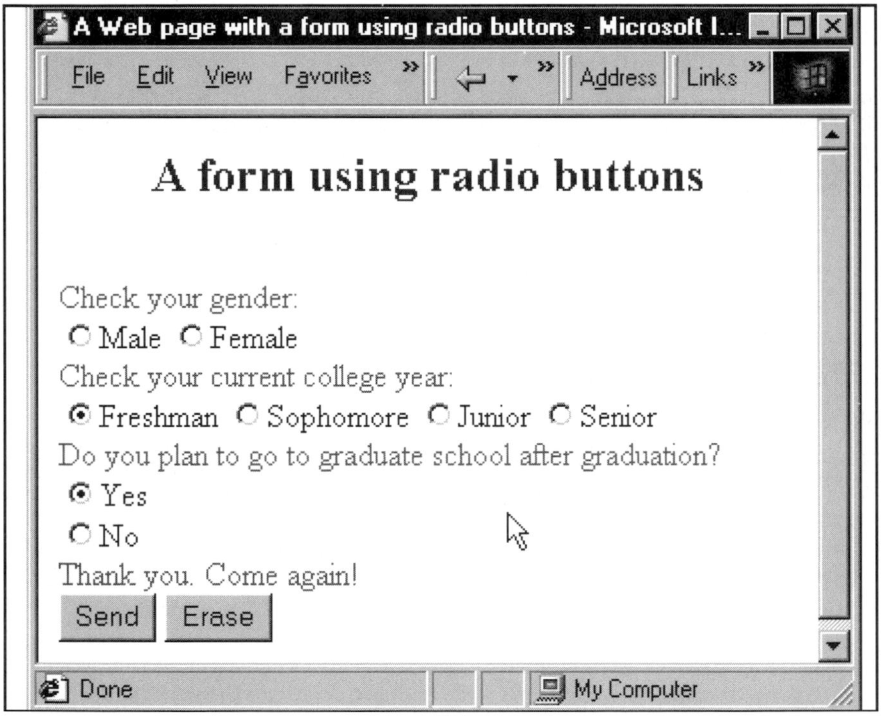

Figure 14.7   A form using radio buttons.

```
<HTML>
<HEAD>
<TITLE>A Web page with a form using images, and password and hidden
fileds</TITLE>
</HEAD>
<BODY>
<CENTER><FONT COLOR = "blue"><H2>A form using images, and password
and hidden fields</H2></FONT></CENTER>
<FORM NAME = "myForm" ACTION = "mailto:zeid@coe.neu.edu" METHOD =
"post">
```

```
<INPUT TYPE = "hidden" NAME = "trackmyForm" VALUE = "EMailMarket-
ing">
<FONT COLOR = "red">Enter your password:</FONT><BR>
<INPUT TYPE = "password" NAME = "pass" SIZE = 12><BR>
<FONT COLOR = "green">Thank you. Come again!</FONT><BR>
<INPUT TYPE = "image" VALUE = "submit" SRC = "submitButton.jpg" ALT
= "Send it">
<INPUT TYPE = "reset" VALUE = "Clear it">

</FORM>
</BODY>
</HTML>
```

In this example, we use the hidden field to track the effectiveness of the e-mail marketing technique. Let us assume that we advertise the Web page of this example via direct e-mail, ads in search engines, and ads in portal sites. Using a hidden field with a different value for each marketing technique allows us to find which of these three marketing technique is the most effective. The HTML code of this example looks at direct e-mail. Anytime a Web surfer submits the form of this Web page, the name/value pair that corresponds to the hidden field is submitted to the CGI script on the Web server for processing. In this case, the name/value pair reads *trackmyForm=EMailMarketing*. The CGI script has a counter that is incremented for every hit.

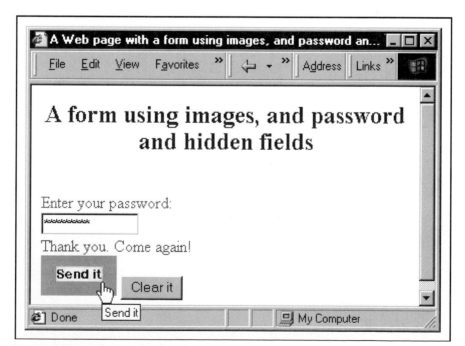

Figure 14.8 A form using an image, a password, and hidden fields.

Example 14.5 Develop a Web page that illustrates the use of files in a form.

Solution This example creates a form that uses a file. The FILE attribute of the <INPUT> tag allows a Web surfer to submit a file name with a form, to send its contents. This may be a useful attribute in sending files over Intranets and Extranets. A <P> tag is used to space out the form elements. Using a text editor, type the following code and save it as *example14.5.htm*l. Figure 14.9 shows the resulting Web page.

```
<HTML>
<HEAD>
<TITLE>A Web page with a form using files</TITLE>
</HEAD>
<BODY>
<CENTER><FONT COLOR = "blue"><H2>A form using files</H2></FONT> </
CENTER>
<FORM NAME = "myForm" ACTION = "mailto:zeid@coe.neu.edu" METHOD =
"post" ENCTYPE = "multipart/form-data">
<FONT COLOR = "red">Select the file name you like to send with this
form</FONT><BR>
<INPUT TYPE = "file" NAME = "myFile" SIZE = 32><BR>
<P>
<FONT COLOR = "green">Thank you. Come again!</FONT><BR>
<INPUT TYPE = "submit" VALUE = "Send it">
<INPUT TYPE = "reset" VALUE = "Clear it">
</FORM>
</BODY>
</HTML>
```

Figure 14.9   A form using a file.

As shown in the figure, the browser renders the TYPE = "file" attribute of the <INPUT> tag as a text field followed by a browsing button. The button allows a Web surfer to browse the local directories on the surfer's computer for a particular file. When the file element is used in a Web page form, the browser sends both the file name, with its full path as it is on the client computer sending the form, and its contents. The Web author must use the ENCTYPE="multipart/form-data" attribute in order for the browser to send the file contents. If this attribute is not used, the browser uses the ENCTYPE default value which is application/x-www-form-urlencoded. In such a case, the browser does not send the file contents. It instead sends the file name as a name/value pair. The file name for this example is C:\WINDOWS\Desktop\FormTest.html. The encoded name/value pair for this element follows below (where the browser uses the element name as myFile).

```
myFile=C%3A%5CWINDOWS%5CDesktop%5CFormTest.html
```

Example 14.6 Develop a Web page that illustrates the use of buttons in a form.

Solution This example creates a Web page that uses buttons. The FILE attribute of the <INPUT> tag allows a Web surfer to submit a file with a form. The <P> tag is used to space out the form elements. Using a text editor, type the code that follows, and save it as *example14.6.html*. Figure 14.10 shows the resulting Web page.

```
<HTML>
<HEAD>
<TITLE>A Web page with a form using buttons</TITLE>
</HEAD>
<BODY>
<CENTER><FONT COLOR = "blue"><H2>A form using buttons</H2></FONT>
</CENTER>
<FORM NAME = "myForm" ACTION = "mailto:zeid@coe.neu.edu" METHOD =
"post">
<FONT COLOR = "red">Select your favorite season</FONT><BR>
<INPUT TYPE = "button" NAME = "button1" VALUE = "Fall">
<INPUT TYPE = "button" NAME = "button2" VALUE = "Winter">
<INPUT TYPE = "button" NAME = "button3" VALUE = "Spring">
<INPUT TYPE = "button" NAME = "button4" VALUE = "Summer"><P>
<FONT COLOR = "red">Select the furniture you need for your office
</FONT><BR>
<INPUT TYPE = "button" NAME = "button5" VALUE = "Desks"><BR>
<INPUT TYPE = "button" NAME = "button6" VALUE = "Chairs"><BR>
<INPUT TYPE = "button" NAME = "button7" VALUE = "Book Cases"><P>
<FONT COLOR = "green">Thank you. Come again!</FONT><BR>
<INPUT TYPE = "submit" VALUE = "Send it">
<INPUT TYPE = "reset" VALUE = "Clear it">
</FORM> </BODY>
</HTML>
```

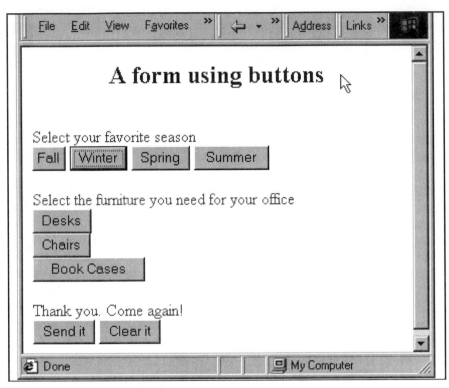

Figure 14.10   A form using buttons.

Figure 14.10 shows two groups of buttons; one group for the four seasons, and one group for office furniture. Two types of layouts of the buttons are used: horizontal, and vertical. The horizontal layout is more commonly used in form design than the vertical layout, because it looks more appealing and better organized. This is opposite to the preferred layout (vertical) of checkboxes and radio buttons. A Web surfer selects the desired buttons by clicking them. These buttons are useless or dysfunctional as such, in the Web page, because they do not generate name/value pairs. They generate events that the browser cannot process for lack of a program, such as a JavaScript, that can handle them. Without event handling, Web surfers cannot use the buttons. Covering event handling of these buttons' events is beyond the scope of this book. Nevertheless, it is useful for the reader to know that these form elements exist.

14.5.3 <SELECT> Tag

This tag creates a special form element. This element is known as a select list, an option list, or a drop-down menu. All these different names reflect the three characteristics of the element created by the <SELECT> tag. The element is a select list with items that Web surfers choose from. It is sometimes known as an option list, because there is an <OPTION> tag that is used inside the <SELECT> tag to create the list items or options. It is also known as a drop-down menu, because a menu shows up when a user clicks the list. A select list is more versatile than checkboxes or radio buttons. Whenever the choices become too many, the use of check-boxes or radio buttons becomes impractical. The Select list is the perfect alternative. This tag must close. A Web page may use this tag as many times as needed. The <SELECT> tag has three attributes. They are NAME, SIZE, and MULTIPLE, and are described in the following list:

•The NAME attribute specifies the name of the select list. This attribute is useful if the Web page uses JavaScript in addition to HTML.

•The SIZE attribute specifies the number of visible rows of the list on the computer screen. The default value of this attribute is one.

•The MULTIPLE attribute allows multiple selections from the select list. The default is a single selection. The Web surfer must hold down the CTRL or SHIFT key on the keyboard, and click the desired rows to achieve multiple selections.

The use of the <SELECT> tag by itself is useless; it does not create any list items. The <OPTION> tag, discussed in the next section, is always used inside the <SELECT> tag to create the list items. If the <SELECT> tag is used without the <OPTION> tag, the browser creates a menu with no items. Curious readers can create a Web page that opens and closes the <SELECT> tag, i.e. <SELECT></SELECT>.

14.5.4 <OPTION> Tag

This tag allows Web authors to create menu elements. The tag is usually enclosed inside the <SELECT> tag. A <SELECT> tag must contain at least one <OPTION> tag. It is optional to close the <OPTION> tag. This tag has three attributes. They are SELECTED, VALUE, and LABEL. These attributes are described in the following list:

•The SELECTED attribute specifies the pre-selected option of the menu. It is a boolean attribute. If it is not specified, the default is the first option in the <SELECT> tag.

•The VALUE attribute specifies the initial value of the menu item.

•The LABEL attribute allows Web authors to specify a shorter label for an item than its actual content.

The last two attributes are not recognized by today's browsers when they render the <OPTION> tags. Both Netscape Communicator and MS IE ignore them. Thus, Web authors should not use them.

Example 14.7 Develop a Web page that illustrates the use of menus in a form.

Solution This example creates a Web page that uses a menu. The menu has six menu items. The <P> tag is used to space out the form elements. Using a text editor, type the code that follows, and save it as *example14.7.html*. Figure 14.11 shows the resulting Web page.

```
<HTML>
<HEAD>
<TITLE>A Web page with a form using menus</TITLE>
</HEAD>
<BODY>
<CENTER><FONT COLOR = "blue"><H2>A form using menus</H2></FONT> </
CENTER>
<FORM NAME = "myForm" ACTION = "mailto:zeid@coe.neu.edu" METHOD =
"post">
<FONT COLOR = "red">Select your computer harddware needs:</
FONT><BR>
<SELECT NAME = "compHardware">
<OPTION>Disk drive
<OPTION>More RAM
<OPTION SELECTED>External zip drive
<OPTION>New monitor
<OPTION>Faster printer
<OPTION>New mouse
</SELECT>
<P>
<FONT COLOR = "green">Thank you. Come again!</FONT><BR>
<INPUT TYPE = "submit" NAME = "submitButton"  VALUE = "Send it">
<INPUT TYPE = "reset" NAME = "resetButton"  VALUE = "Clear it">
</FORM>
</BODY>
</HTML>
```

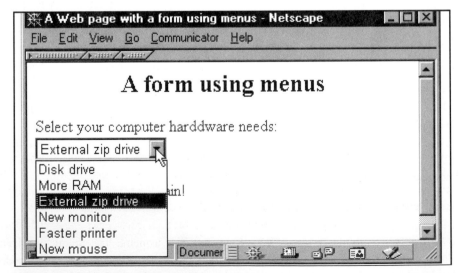

Figure 14.11   A form using a menu.

Figure 14.11 shows all the menu resulting from the clicking of the arrow icon in the menu box. Clicking this arrow generates the drop-down menu effect. Before clicking the icon, the menu box shows only one row with the SELECTED item in it. The figure shows the menu box as per the used attributes of both the <SELECT> and the <OPTION> tags. The former tag does not use the MULTIPLE attribute, and the latter tag uses the SELECTED attribute with the item displayed on the screen. If we use other attributes of the <SELECT> tag, the menu display changes. For example, if we use the MULTIPLE attribute of the <SELECT> tag, the menu is rendered in full on the screen as shown in figure 14.12 for MS IE. Netscape Communicator and MS IE render the menu box slightly differently (the former does not use a scrollbar, the latter does); however, both browsers highlight the SELECTED item as shown in the figure. We can still change the look of the menu by using the SIZE attribute of the <SELECT> tag, say SIZE =3.

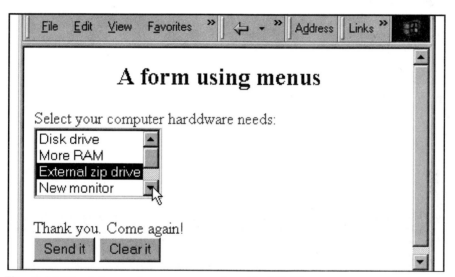

Figure 14.12   A form using a menu rendered by MS IE.

14.5.5 <TEXTAREA> Tag

Text fields allow the input of one line of text only. This form element is suitable for input such as names, code numbers, and so forth. In some cases, such as user's feedback, multi-line text input is usually needed, in a "free form". HTML defines the textarea element to serve this purpose. Textareas can be created with initial text or blank. If initial text was used, users who fill the text area simply delete the initial text and replace it by their text input. The <TEXTAREA> tag allows Web authors to create textarea elements. The tag must close. This tag has four attributes. They are NAME, ROWS, COLS, and WRAP. These attributes are described in the following list:

•The NAME attribute specifies the name of the text area. This attribute is useful if the Web page uses JavaScript in addition to HTML.

•The ROWS attribute specifies the height of the text area as a number of lines of text, as shown in figure 14.2. This attribute does not stop users of a text area from typing more lines of text than the value of ROWS.

•The COLS attribute specifies the width of the text area as a number of characters per line, as shown in figure 14.2. Thus, the maximum number of characters a text area can hold is equal to $ROWS \times COLS$.

•The WRAP attribute specifies to the browser how to wrap the text typed in a text area. If this attribute is not used by Web authors, text input continues on one line, scrolling to the right, until the user presses the Enter key on the keyboard to start a new line. The values of this attribute are SOFT and HARD. The HARD wrap forces a carriage return at the end of each line of text in the text area. The length of each line of text is equal to the value of the COLS attribute of the text area. The SOFT wrap forces a new line of text without physically placing a carriage return at the end of each line of text. The choice of either value depends on the CGI script written to process the name/value pairs of the form. if the HARD value is used, the CGI script must strip the carriage returns at the ends of the lines of text.

Example 14.8 Develop a Web page that illustrates the use of textareas in a form.

Solution This example creates a Web page that uses a textarea that is defined to be 10 rows, with each being 25 characters wide. The textarea is initialized with the text shown. The WRAP attribute is used with a SOFT value. The <P> tag is used to space out the form elements. Using a text editor, type the code that follows, and save it as *example14.8.html*. Figure 14.13 shows the resulting Web page.

```
<HTML>
<HEAD>
<TITLE>A Web page with a form using text areas</TITLE>
</HEAD>
<BODY>
<CENTER><FONT COLOR = "blue"><H2>A form using text areas</H2></
FONT> </CENTER>

<FORM NAME = "myForm" ACTION = "mailto:zeid@coe.neu.edu" METHOD =
"post">
<FONT COLOR = "red">We love to hear from you:</FONT><BR>
<TEXTAREA NAME = "myTextArea" ROWS = 10 COLS = 25 WRAP ="soft">
Please input up to 10 lines of text as your feedback and comments.
Any additional lines beyond the first ten are ignored by our data-
base. Thank you for your cooperation!
</TEXTAREA>
<P>
```

```
<FONT COLOR = "green">Thank you. Come again!</FONT><BR>

<INPUT TYPE = "submit" NAME = "submitButton"  VALUE = "Send Form">

<INPUT TYPE = "reset" NAME = "resetButton"  VALUE = "Clear Form">

</FORM>

</BODY>

</HTML>
```

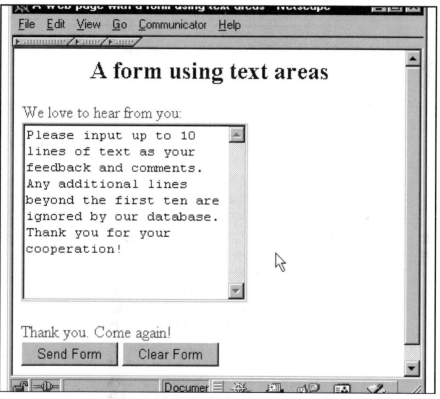

Figure 14.13 A form using a textarea.

Figure 14.13 shows the textarea with its initial text. As shown in the figure, the browser displays the text area in the Web page with the defined size of 10×25. If you count the number of characters, including spaces, in the fifth and in the sixth line, of the textarea, each has exactly 25 characters. Also, the number of rows displayed is 10. (The last two rows are shown blank.) A web surfer can delete the initial text and replace it by a new one. The Web surfer needs to bring the focus to the textarea before typing, by simply clicking the mouse anywhere within the area box.

14.6 Tutorials

This section focuses on using the form tags covered in this chapter. Any Web browser can be used to display the corresponding Web pages. It is a good idea to create a directory structure to save HTML files. This helps Web authors to organize HTML files and makes it easy to find them.

14.6.1 Performing E-commerce

The most popular use of a form is to order products online. Web surfers find order forms in almost every Web site they visit. In this tutorial, we create an order form for buying bikes. The form uses many of the form elements. Using a text editor, type the code that follows, and save it as *tutorial14.6.1.html*. View the page in a browser. Figure 14.14 shows the resulting Web page.

```
<HTML>
<HEAD>
<TITLE>A Web page with an order form</TITLE>
</HEAD>
<BODY>
<CENTER><FONT COLOR = "blue"><H2>A bike order form</H2></FONT> </
CENTER><BR>
<FORM NAME = "myForm" METHOD = "post" ACTION = "http://www.xxx.com/
cgi-bin/bikecgi/bikeOrder">
<FONT COLOR = "red">What type of bike do you want to purchase? </
FONT><BR>
<INPUT TYPE = "radio" NAME = "bikes" VALUE = "stree" CHECKED>Street
bike
<INPUT TYPE = "radio" NAME = "bikes" VALUE = "mountain">Mountain
bike
<INPUT TYPE = "radio" NAME = "bikes" VALUE = "dirt">dirt bike
<P>
<FONT COLOR = "red">What accessories do you need?</FONT><BR>
<INPUT TYPE = "checkbox" NAME = "accessories" VALUE =
"gloves">Gloves
<INPUT TYPE = "checkbox" NAME = "accessories" VALUE = "helmet"
CHECKED>Helmet
<INPUT TYPE = "checkbox" NAME = "accessories" VALUE = "bag">Camel
water bag
<P>
<FONT COLOR = "red">Where do you go biking?</FONT><BR>
<SELECT NAME = "mountBiking" SIZE = 2 MULTIPLE>
<OPTION>Parks
<OPTION SELECTED>Bike routes
<OPTION>Mountains
<OPTION>Races
```

```
<OPTION>Streets
</SELECT>
<P>
<FONT COLOR = "red">Shipping information</FONT><BR>
First Name<INPUT TYPE = "text" NAME = "firstName" SIZE = 10 MAX-
LENGTH = 13>
Last Name<INPUT TYPE = "text" NAME = "lastName" SIZE = 10 MAXLENGTH
= 15><BR>
Address<INPUT TYPE = "text" NAME = "address" SIZE = 20>
City<INPUT TYPE = "text" NAME = "city" SIZE = 10><BR>
State<INPUT TYPE = "text" NAME = "state" SIZE = 10>
Zip code<INPUT TYPE = "text" NAME = "zipCode" SIZE = 5>
<P>
<FONT COLOR = "red">Special delivery instructions</FONT><BR>
<TEXTAREA NAME = "myTextArea" ROWS = 2 COLS = 25 WRAP ="soft">
</TEXTAREA>
<P>
<FONT COLOR = "red">Payment information</FONT><BR>
Credit card number<INPUT TYPE = "text" NAME = "cardNumber" SIZE =
16>
Expires<INPUT TYPE = "text" NAME = "expires" VALUE = "12/05" SIZE =
5>
<P>
<INPUT TYPE = "submit"  NAME = "submitButton" VALUE = "Send Order">
<INPUT TYPE = "reset"  NAME = "resetButton" VALUE = "Start Over">
</FORM>
</BODY>
</HTML>
```

Here are several comments about this example HTML code:

•The form tag uses the HTTP protocol in its ACTION attribute. When the Web surfer submits the form, the encoded name/value pairs are sent to the server, www.xxx.com, where the CGI script bikeOrder processes them. The server has a directory called cgi-bin. It is quite common to find a directory with this name on Web servers. The directory is usually used for security reasons. All filled forms submitted by customers go to this area of the server only. The directory may be subdivided further into subdirectories if the Web site sells more than one product. In this example, we use the bikecgi subdirectory.

•Some of the form elements, such as radio buttons and checkboxes, are laid out horizontally to keep the form short.

•The Web surfer can fill in the text fields by clicking the mouse in each one to bring the focus there. Figure 14.14 shows the focus during the typing of the first name.

•The select list shows two items, because we use the SIZE = 2 attribute for the <SELECT> tag. The default selected item is shown highlighted. The Web surfer can scroll the list up and down to read its items.

•The Web server of this form must establish a secure connection with the client computer using this form, to ensure that the credit card information of the customer is protected.

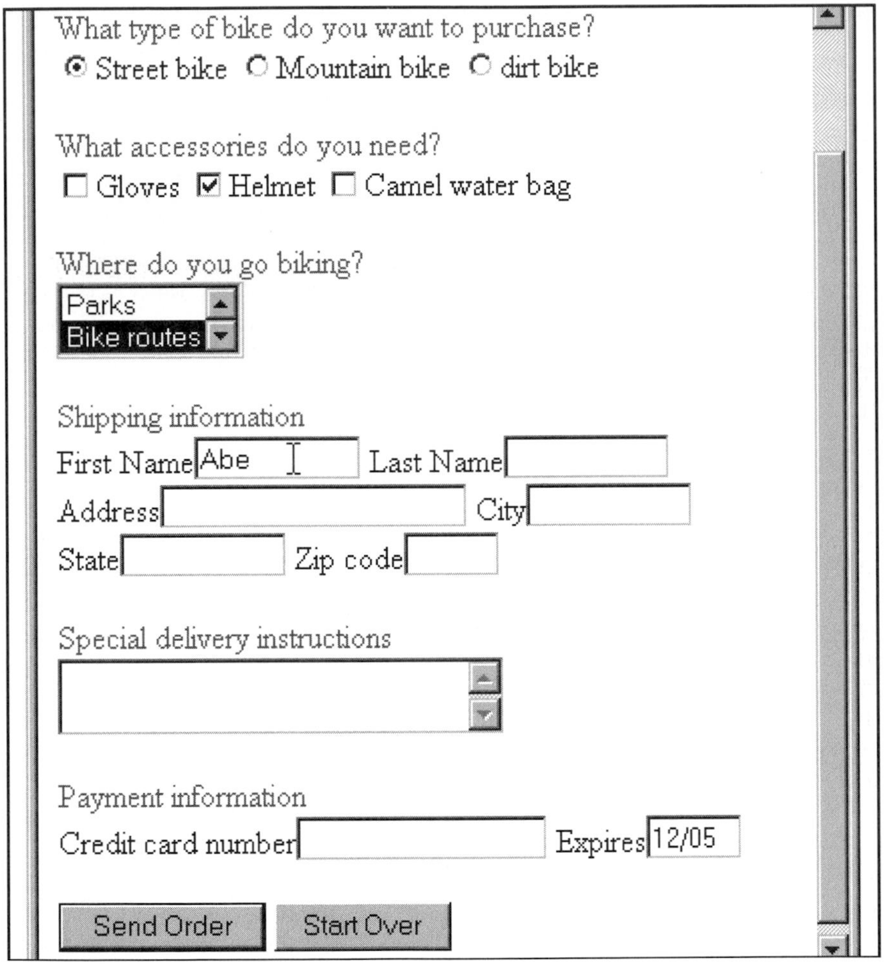

Figure 14.14   A bike order form.

14.6.2 Guest and Alumni Books

Some Web sites use forms to create what is known as guest and alumni books. For example, a university may create a form to collect information about its alumni to keep up with them. The form uses a CGI script that creates a database of the alumni from form entries. The university can use the database for mailing event letters, newsletters, and so forth. This is very convenient for both the university and its alumni, especially for those who move and change addresses frequently. Using a text editor, type the code that follows, and save it as *tutorial14.6.2.html*. View the page in a browser. Figure 14.15 shows the resulting Web page.

```
<HTML>
<HEAD>
<TITLE>A Web page to create a guest/alumni book</TITLE>
</HEAD>
<BODY>
<CENTER><FONT COLOR = "blue"><H2>A Guest/alumni book form</H2></
FONT> </CENTER><BR>

<FORM NAME = "myForm" METHOD = "post" ACTION = "http://www.xxx.edu/
cgi-bin/guestbook">
First Name<INPUT TYPE = "text" NAME = "firstName" SIZE = 10 MAX-
LENGTH = 13>
Last Name<INPUT TYPE = "text" NAME = "lastName" SIZE = 10><BR>
E-mail<INPUT TYPE = "text" NAME = "address" SIZE = 20>
Year of graduation<INPUT TYPE = "text" NAME = "year" SIZE = 4><BR>
College<INPUT TYPE = "text" NAME = "college" SIZE = 10>
Major<INPUT TYPE = "text" NAME = "major" SIZE = 10>
<P>
<FONT COLOR = "red">Comments</FONT><BR>
<TEXTAREA NAME = "myTextArea" ROWS = 2 COLS = 25 WRAP ="soft">
</TEXTAREA>
<P>
<FONT COLOR = "red">Would you like to share your comments with oth-
ers?</FONT><BR>
<INPUT TYPE = "radio" NAME = "share" VALUE = "yes" CHECKED>Yes
<INPUT TYPE = "radio" NAME = "share" VALUE = "no">No
<P>
<INPUT TYPE = "submit"  NAME = "submitButton" VALUE = "Send Entry">
<INPUT TYPE = "reset"  NAME = "resetButton" VALUE = "Clear Form">
</FORM>
</BODY>
</HTML>
```

14.6.3 Customer Survey

This tutorial shows how we can use a form for an online customer survey. It is advisable to keep such survey forms short, to encourage Web surfers to fill them out. Using a text editor, type the code that follows, and save it as *tutorial14.6.3.html*. View the page in a browser. Figure 14.16 shows the resulting Web page.

```
<HTML>
<HEAD>
<TITLE>A Web page for customer online shopping survey</TITLE>
```

```
</HEAD>
<BODY>
<CENTER><FONT COLOR = "blue"><H2>Customer online shopping survey</
H2></FONT></CENTER><BR>
```

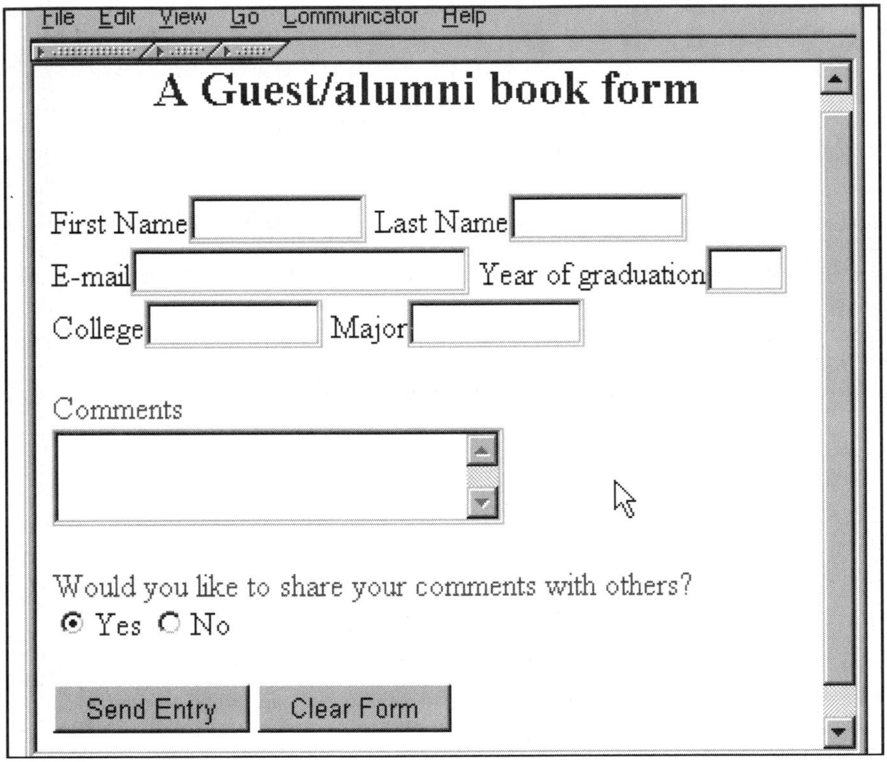

Figure 14.15   A guest/alumni book form.

```
<FORM NAME = "myForm" METHOD = "post" ACTION = "http://www.xxx.com/
cgi-bin/survey">
<FONT COLOR = "red">What type of Internet connection do you have?
</FONT><BR>
<INPUT TYPE = "radio" NAME = "connect" VALUE = "one" CHECKED>modem
<INPUT TYPE = "radio" NAME = "connect" VALUE = "two">Cable
<INPUT TYPE = "radio" NAME = "connect" VALUE = "three">DSL
<INPUT TYPE = "radio" NAME = "connect" VALUE = "two">Others
<P>
<FONT COLOR = "red">How much time do you spend online per day? </
FONT><BR>
<INPUT TYPE = "radio" NAME = "time" VALUE = "first" CHECKED>1 hour
<INPUT TYPE = "radio" NAME = "time" VALUE = "second">1-2 hours
```

```
<INPUT TYPE = "radio" NAME = "time" VALUE = "third">2-3 hours
<INPUT TYPE = "radio" NAME = "time" VALUE = "fourth">Over 3 hours
<P>
<FONT COLOR = "red">What do you buy the most online?</FONT><BR>
```

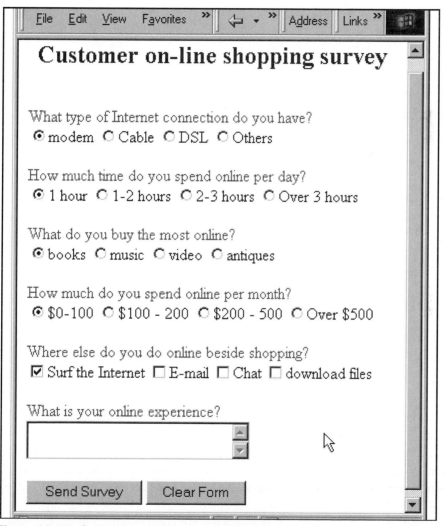

Figure 14.16 Customer online shopping survey form.

```
<INPUT TYPE = "radio" NAME = "items" VALUE = "first" CHECKED>books
<INPUT TYPE = "radio" NAME = "items" VALUE = "second">music
<INPUT TYPE = "radio" NAME = "items" VALUE = "third">video
<INPUT TYPE = "radio" NAME = "items" VALUE = "fourth">antiques
```

```
<P>
<FONT COLOR = "red">How much do you spend online per month? </
FONT><BR>
<INPUT TYPE = "radio" NAME = "spending" VALUE = "first" CHECKED>$0-
100
<INPUT TYPE = "radio" NAME = "spending" VALUE = "second">$100 - 200
<INPUT TYPE = "radio" NAME = "spending" VALUE = "third">$200 - 500
<INPUT TYPE = "radio" NAME = "spending" VALUE = "fourth">Over $500
<P>
<FONT COLOR = "red">Where else do you do online beside shopping? </
FONT><BR>
<INPUT TYPE = "checkbox" NAME = "activity" VALUE = "first" CHECKED>
Surf the Internet
<INPUT TYPE = "checkbox" NAME = "activity" VALUE = "second">E-mail
<INPUT TYPE = "checkbox" NAME = "activity" VALUE = "third">Chat
<INPUT TYPE = "checkbox" NAME = "activity" VALUE = "fourth">down-
load files
<P>
<FONT COLOR = "red">What is your online experience?</FONT><BR>
<TEXTAREA NAME = "myTextArea" ROWS = 2 COLS = 25 WRAP ="soft">
</TEXTAREA>
<P>
<INPUT TYPE = "submit"  NAME = "submitButton" VALUE = "Send Sur-
vey">
<INPUT TYPE = "reset"  NAME = "resetButton" VALUE = "Clear Form">
</FORM>
</BODY>
</HTML>
```

14.7 FAQs

Q: What is an HTML form?

A: A form is simply a Web page element with special HTML tags that instruct Web browsers about how to display the various elements, such as text fields, radio buttons, checkboxes, and so forth.

Q: In the ACTION attribute of a form, I use the mailto protocol to send the form's name/value pairs to myself. When I click the submit button on the form, the browser opens an e-mail composition window instead of mailing the pairs. What is the problem? How can I fix it?

A: The problem is that you forgot to use the METHOD attribute of the <FORM> tag. In such a case, the browser does not know how to send the information, and it instead opens the e-mail composition window. When you add the METHOD attribute, the form submission works fine. Thus, the syntax should look like this:

<FORM ACTION = "mailto: zeid@coe.neu.edu" METHOD = "post">

Q: Can I use more than one submit button in my form?

A: Yes, you can. However, it is not advisable to do so as you may confuse the users of your Web page.

Q: What is the best language that one can use to write CGI scripts to process form input?

A: There is no best language. The two most popular languages are Perl and JavaScript. Perl is very popular among Unix users, because it comes free with many Unix-based servers. Also, it has very strong string-manipulation capabilities. JavaScript is very popular among Windows and Mac users, because NT- and Mac-based servers install it. One can use any language to write a CGI script, as long as it can compile and execute on the Web server that is supposed to handle the name/value pairs of HTML forms.

Q: What are the downside risks of including forms in Web pages?

A: We can identify two potential problems. First, Web pages with forms can bog down the Web server by draining its computational power and memory resources. If the server is not configured properly to handle the load of responding to every form input by executing the CGI script, the response time degrades considerably. Web surfers will have to wait too long for a response from the server. Second, the CGI script can pose serious security problems to the Web site if the script has undiscovered flaws in it.

Q: What are the types of buttons that HTML can create?

A: HTML allows the creation of three types of buttons: submit, reset, and push. The submit and reset buttons are always used with forms. The push buttons are usually used in Web pages that use JavaScript to process their clicks. Clicking push buttons only does not generate any name/value pairs — thus, the CGI script has no way of telling which push button the user clicks — but these clicks can be handled via what are called event handlers in JavaScript. Interested readers should consult JavaScript books.

Q: How can I control the positions and layout of form elements in a form?

A: When you create a form with its elements, the only control you have seen so far in this book is either to center an element, by wrapping a <CENTER> tag around its <INPUT> tag, or to display it on a new line, by using the <BR> tag prior to its <INPUT> tag. Instead, you can use tables for formatting, as we will discuss in chapter 16 of this book. HTML tables provide such a versatile formatting tool that they are always used to format, not only form elements, but also entire Web pages.

Q: I have created a form. It runs fine in my browser. I made changes to it. When I click the `Reload` button of Netscape Communicator or the `Refresh` button of MS IE, neither browser displays the newly edited form as I expect. What is the problem? How can I fix it?

A: First, make sure that you have saved your last changes. If the old form is still displayed, the problem is your browser. In many cases, the browser opts to display the form from its cache instead of loading the latest version from your computer hard disk. This depends on how your browser is configured. The safest way to make sure that the browser loads your latest HTML code is to open the file explicitly by using the browser `File` menu (`File => Open` for MS IE or File => Open Page for Netscape Communicator), or to simply drag the HTML file and drop it in the browser window.

Q: I am supposed to create three checkboxes and two radio buttons in a Web page. Instead, the browser displays two checkboxes followed by a text field, and one radio button followed by another text field. I checked the HTML code over and over. I could not find anything wrong. What is the problem? How do I fix it?

A: The problem is very simple. If you check the <INPUT> tags carefully, for the third checkbox and the second radio button, you will find out that you have forgotten to close the quotes in the TYPE attribute. Make sure they read TYPE = "checkbox" and TYPE = "radio". You have the choice to use no quotes, single quotes, or double quotes to specify values of attributes of tags, as discussed in chapter 7; however, once you use them, you must be consistent. As for why you got text fields in place of a checkbox and a radio button, it is because the browser could not know the type of the form element you requested. Therefore, it used the default type, which is a text field.

Q: What is a good example of using the hidden element of a form?

A: Hidden fields are a way of passing information to a Web server. Such information is usually not relevant to the Web surfer who fills the form. It is not a secret, either, because the surfer can view it by simply clicking View => Page Source for Netscape Communicator, or View => Source for MS IE. This information helps Web authors to manage their forms. The CGI script decodes it to take relevant actions. Let us assume that we need to send an e-mail message to thank a surfer who fills in a form. We use the following hidden elements:

<INPUT TYPE = "hidden" NAME = "SendTo" VALUE = "zeid@coe.neu.edu">

<INPUT TYPE = "hidden" NAME = "Subject" VALUE = "Thank you for your time">

<INPUT TYPE = "hidden" NAME = "Message" VALUE = "http://www.neu.edu/thankYou.html">

A CGI script can decode the three name/value pairs that correspond to these three hidden fields and send an automatic e-mail message to the above e-mail address, with the above subject, and with the body defined in the thankYou.html file.

Q: Why would I want to send a file by using a form? Is one unable to simply e-mail it as an attachment?

A: Yes, you could e-mail it; however, when you send it by using a form, you can send it over a secure connection between the Web server and your computer. If the file has sensitive information, you should not e-mail it. With e-mail, you run the risk of someone's breaking into your account and reading your e-mail messages.

Q: I use a textarea as a front end GUI for a database. The database cannot accept more than 250 characters of user input. How can I create a text area that controls the user input to be within this limit?

A: Let us say you define the textarea in your Web page to have 10 rows, with each being 25 characters wide. You must use the WRAP attribute of the <TEXTAREA> tag to control the user input in the text area. This attribute (with values of HARD or SOFT) guarantees you lines of text with maximum length of 25 characters. It does not guarantee you a maximum of 10 rows, but you can enforce this limit easily by displaying the text area in the form with an initial text that reads something like this: `"Please input up to 10 lines of text as your feedback and comments. Any additional lines beyond the first ten are ignored by our database. Thank you for your cooperation!"`

14.8 Summary

Introduction

•HTML forms are a simple but powerful concept that allows Web surfers to communicate with Web sites and servers. Forms make Web pages interactive.

•The collected information is bundled (encoded) by the browser into name/value pairs according to a Common Gateway Interface (CGI) protocol (formats). These pairs are sent for processing to the Web server hosting the form.

•A CGI script, installed on the server, decodes the name/value pairs and extracts the values that the user has input while filling in the form. These values are used to process the user's order. CGI scripts can be written in any programming or scripting language, such as C, C++, Java, JavaScript, and so forth.

•A form consists of a collection of elements organized in a certain layout.

•Information collected from a form can be processed in different ways, such as by writing it to a file or a database, by submitting it to a database for requests, or by e-mailing it to someone.

•There is no limit on the number of forms per Web page, but, practically, each page should have one form only.

Form Structure And Communication Cycle

•A form has two main distinct parts: the visible and the invisible.

•The visible part is the form itself that Web surfers see on the computer screen and fill in.

•The invisible part is the CGI script that is responsible for processing form information and data received from a filled form, once it is submitted by a Web surfer. The CGI script decodes the name/value pairs that are sent to it by the surfer's browser.

•Web authors must develop both the visible and the invisible parts of a form for it to work successfully. Without the CGI script, information filled in by form users is never processed and gets lost. Form users never receive any warnings, either.

•A form CGI script has two main functions. First, it extracts form input by decoding the name/value pairs. Second, it processes the input.

•The communication cycle of a form is as follows. A Web surfer fills the form and clicks its submit button. The browser encodes the name/value pairs and sends them to a CGI script installed on the form Web server. The script reads the name/value pairs and extracts the user input. The input is then used by the CGI script to make decisions. The decisions result in generating a response that is sent to the user.

•The link between a form and its CGI script takes place in the <FORM> tag, through its ACTION attribute.

Form Elements

•The elements of an HTML form are similar to those of traditional paper forms. Form elements are text fields, checkboxes, radio buttons, passwords, hidden fields, images, buttons, submit buttons, reset buttons, menus, and text areas.

•Text fields are typically used when one line of text is needed as input, such as is the case with names, addresses, ID numbers, phone numbers, and so forth. A text field is displayed as a rectangle and has a size and a maximum length. Each is specified as a number of characters.

•Checkboxes provide users with multiple choices. Therefore, they are mutually inclusive. Checkboxes are displayed as squares. Selecting and deselecting them happens with a mouse click. Checkboxes that are already selected (checked) are shown with a checkmark inside.

•Radio buttons provide users with single choices. Therefore, they are mutually exclusive. Radio buttons are displayed as circles. Selecting and deselecting them happens with a mouse click. Radio buttons that are already selected are shown with a filled circle inside.

•Passwords are special text fields, in that they do not display what the user types. Instead, they display an echo character, usually an asterisk.

•Hidden fields are elements that are never displayed on the screen; however, Web surfers can find them if they view the source of the Web page using them. Hidden fields are used by Web authors for tracking purposes.

•Images can be used as submit buttons in forms. They are displayed as image hyperlinks.

•Buttons are also known as push buttons. Buttons do not generate name/value pairs when they are clicked. Instead, they generate events. Event-handling scripts are needed to process the events.

•Submit and reset buttons are special buttons. Each form must have only one of each. Clicking the submit button activates the browser to send the form contents as name/value pairs to a CGI script installed on the form Web server for processing. Clicking the reset button erases all the form input and replaces it by the form default values.

•Menus can allow users to choose either only one item or multiple items at the same time. Other names that are frequently used for an HTML menu are option list or menu, select list or menu, and drop-down list or menu.

•Text areas allows form users to input multiple lines of text. Each text area has a width (number of columns) and a height (number of rows). Both parameters are specified as numbers of characters.

Form Layout and Design

•The HTML form elements are standard, but the layout and design of a form makes it unique. Each form must have a submit button and a reset button.

•When designing forms, Web authors must keep them short, simple, and well organized to encourage Web surfers to use them.

Form Tags

•The form tags are <FORM>, <INPUT>, <SELECT>, <OPTION>, and <TEXTAREA>.

•The <FORM> tag acts as a container for the form. It controls the form layout. Its attributes are NAME, ACTION, METHOD, ENCTYPE, ACCEPT-CHARSET, and ACCEPT. NAME specifies the form name. ACTION specifies the CGI script of the form. METHOD specifies the way to send name/value pairs to the CGI script. Its value POST should always be used. The last three attributes are used less commonly.

•The <INPUT> tag creates the following form elements; text fields, checkboxes, radio buttons, password fields, hidden fields, images, buttons, submit buttons, and reset buttons. The <INPUT> tag has several attributes, including TYPE, VALUE, and NAME. TYPE specifies the form element to be created. VALUE specifies the initial value of the element. NAME specifies the element name.

•The <SELECT> and <OPTION> tags are used together to create menus.

•The <SELECT> tag has three attributes: NAME (menu name), SIZE (number of visible menu items on the screen), and MULTIPLE (allows selection of more than one item). The Web surfer must hold down the CTRL or SHIFT key on the keyboard and click the desired rows to achieve multiple selections.

•The <OPTION> tag has three attributes: SELECTED, VALUE, and LABEL. The first attribute specifies the default menu item. The last two attributes are seldom used.

•The <TEXTAREA> tag creates a textarea. Its attributes are NAME (name of textarea), ROWS (number of text lines), COLS (number of characters per line), and WRAP (forces text to wrap after the specified number of characters per line is reached).

Quick reference of the HTML tags covered in this chapter

:

Table 14.1   Summary of HTML form tags.

Tag	Close	Attribute	Value	Example	Chpt. page
<FORM>	Yes	NAME	text	`<FORM NAME = "myForm">`	475 476
		ACTION	text	`<FORM ACTION = "CGI Script">`	
		METHOD	POST	`<FORM METHOD = "post">`	
			GET	`<FORM METHOD = "get">`	
		ENCTYPE	text	not widely used	
		ACCEPT-CHARSET	text	not widely used	
		ACCEPT	text	not widely used	

Table 14.1 Summary of HTML form tags.

Tag	Close	Attribute	Value	Example	Chpt. page
\<INPUT\>	No	NAME	text	\<INPUT NAME ="myElement"\>	477 478
		TYPE	text	\<INPUT TYPE = "text"\>	
			checkbox	\<INPUT TYPE = "checkbox"\>	
			radio	\<INPUT TYPE = "radio"\>	
			password	\<INPUT TYPE = "password"\>	
			hidden	\<INPUT TYPE = "hidden"\>	
			image	\<INPUT TYPE = "image"\>	
			button	\<INPUT TYPE = "button"\>	
			submit	\<INPUT TYPE = "submit"\>	
			reset	\<INPUT TYPE = "reset"\>	
		VALUE	text	\<INPUT VALUE = "test"\>	
		SIZE	number	\<INPUT SIZE = 10\>	
		MAX-LENGTH	number	\<INPUT MAXLENGTH = 15\>	
		CHECKED	N/A	\<INPUT CHECKED\>	
		SRC	file name	\<INPUT SRC = "myImg.jpg"\>	

Table 14.1   Summary of HTML form tags.

Tag	Close	Attribute	Value	Example	Chpt. page
<SELECT>	Yes	NAME	text	`<SELECT NAME = "myMenu">`	488 489
		SIZE	number	`<SELECT SIZE = 3>`	
		MULTIPLE	N/A	`<SELECT MULTIPLE>`	
<OPTION>	No	SELECTED	N/A	`<OPTION SELECTED>`	489
		VALUE	text	`<OPTION VALUE= "myText">`	
		LABEL	text	`<OPTION LABEL= "myLab">`	
<TEXTAREA>	Yes	NAME	text	`<TEXTAREA NAME="myArea">`	491 492
		ROWS	number	`<TEXTAREA ROWS = 10>`	
		COLS	number	`<TEXTAREA COLS = 25>`	
		WRAP	soft	`<TEXTAREA WRAP = "soft">`	
			hard	`<TEXTAREA WRAP = "hard">`	

PROBLEMS

Exercises

14.1 Combine examples 14.1 and 14.2 to create a book order form.

14.2 Combine examples 14.1 and 14.3 to create a college survey form.

14.3 Write the HTML code to generate the pizza order form shown in figure 14.17.

14.4 Write the HTML code to generate the bug report form shown in figure 14.18.

14.5 Write the HTML code to generate the evaluation form shown in figure 14.19. The items for the select list shown in the figure are Doctorate, Master, Bachelor, High school, and None of the above.

Homework

In problems 14.6 – 14.12, write an HTML document and save it in an HTML file.

14.6 Write a Web page to create a stock survey form.

14.7 Write a Web page to create a car service form.

14.8 Users of databases may have to use Structured Query Language (SQL) to query them. They use SQL commands to receive results from the database. Many applications develop very easy-to-use GUIs that novice customers can use to shield them from using SQL. For a bank database, write a Web page to create a bank database query form. The form can have such information as customer information (name, address, account number, etc.), deposits, withdrawals, balances, and so forth.

14.9 Write the HTML code to generate the college survey form shown in figure 14.20.

14.10 Write the HTML code to generate the file access form shown in figure 14.21.

14.11 Write the HTML code to generate the survey shown in figure 14.22.

14.12 Write the HTML code to generate the dog adoption form shown in figure 14.23. The two select lists shown in figure 14.23 allow multiple selections. The list for available breeds has the items shown, plus the following ones: Golden Retriever, Wire-haired Fox Terrier, Mala mute, Dalmatian, Pug, Mixed-breed (large), and Mixed-breed (small). The list for dog age has the items shown, plus the following ones: 1 to 3 years, 3 to 5 years, 5 to 7 years, 7 to 9 years, and over 9 years.

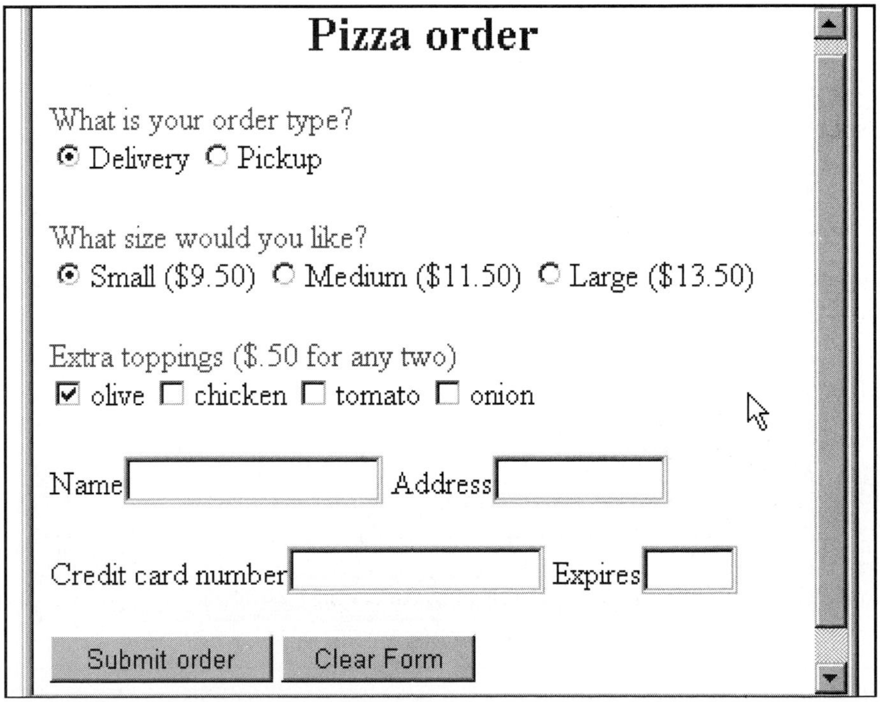

Figure 14.17   Problem 14.3.

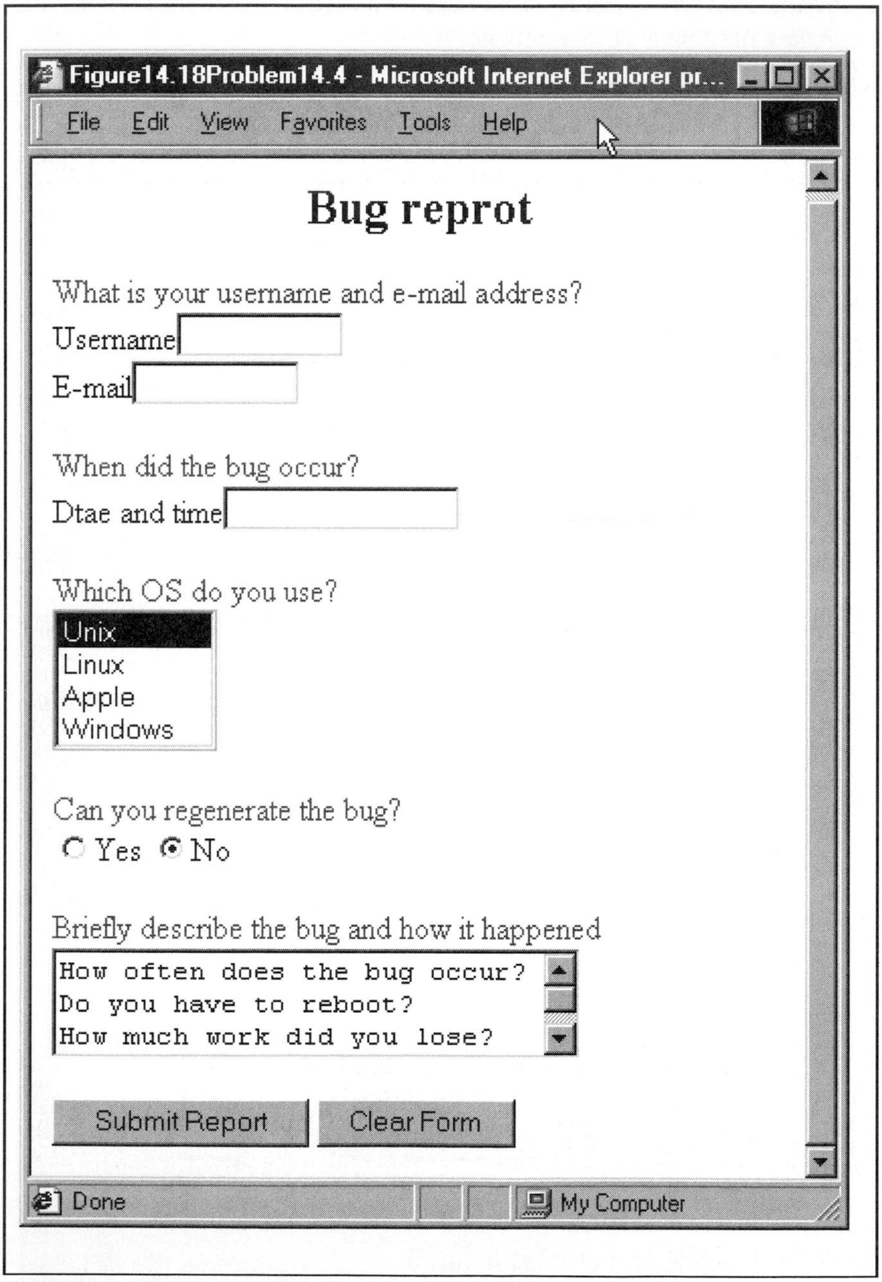

Figure 14.18 Problem 14.4.

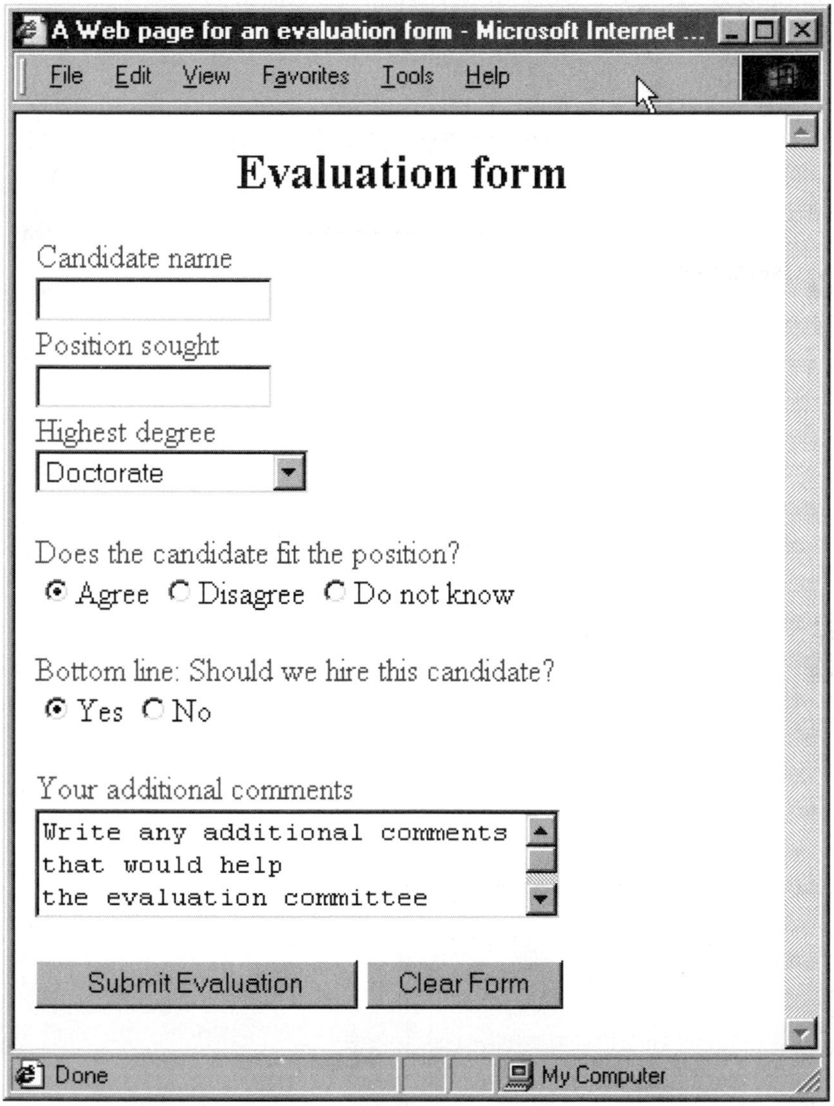

Figure 14.19 Problem 14.5.

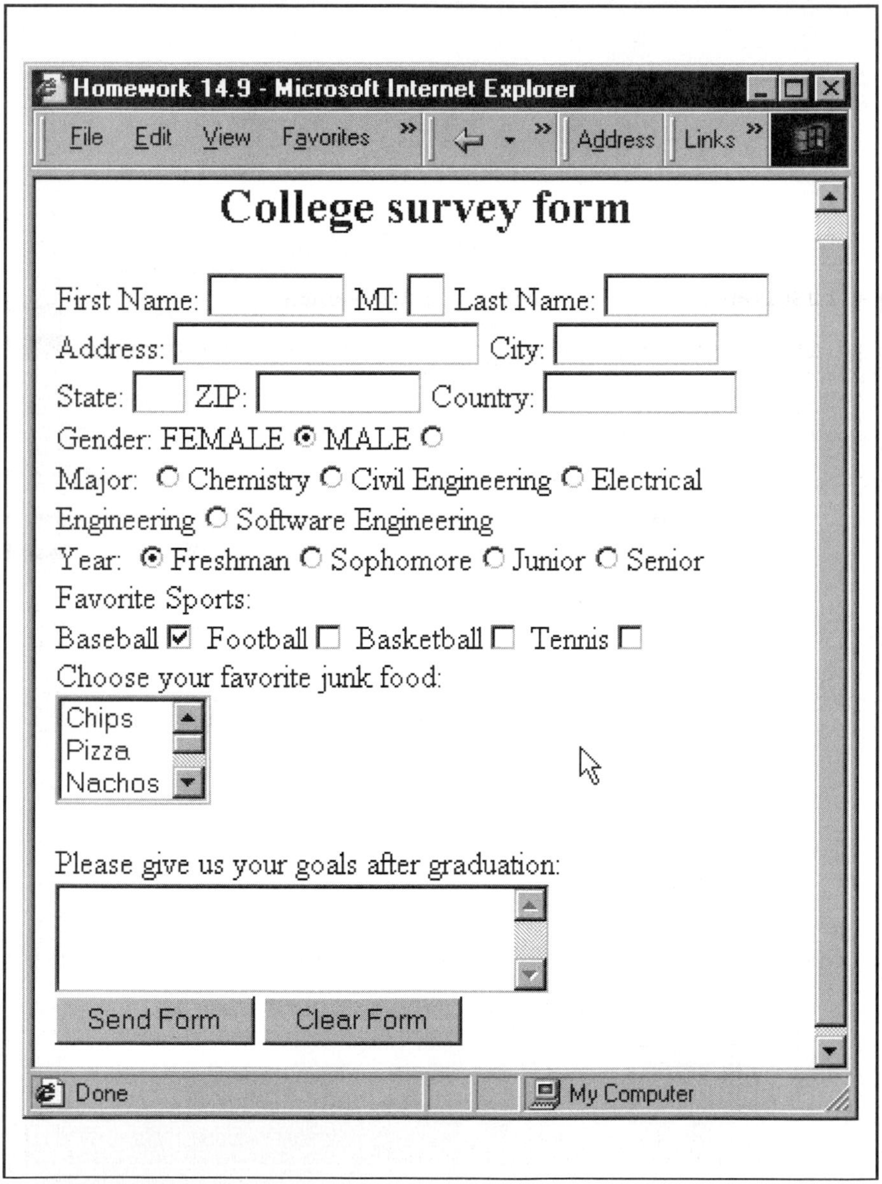

Figure 14.20 Problem 14.9.

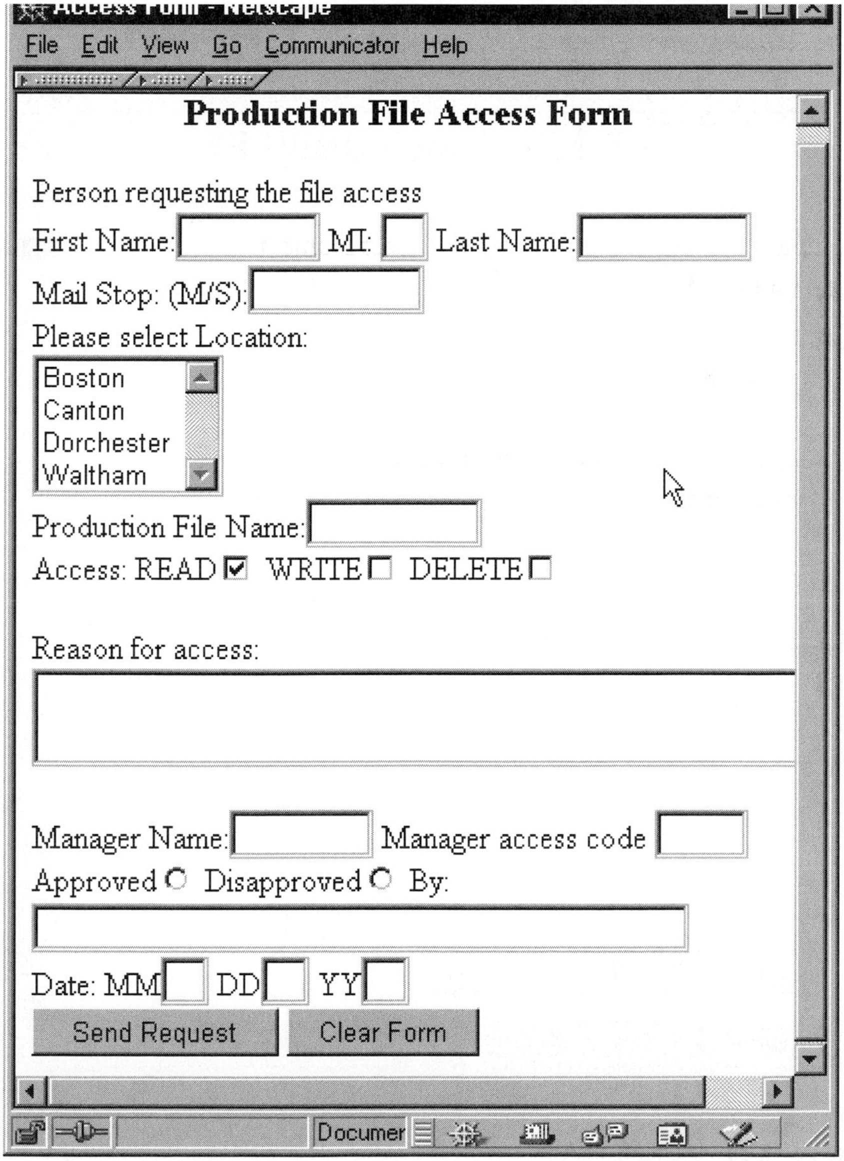

Figure 14.21 Problem 14.10.

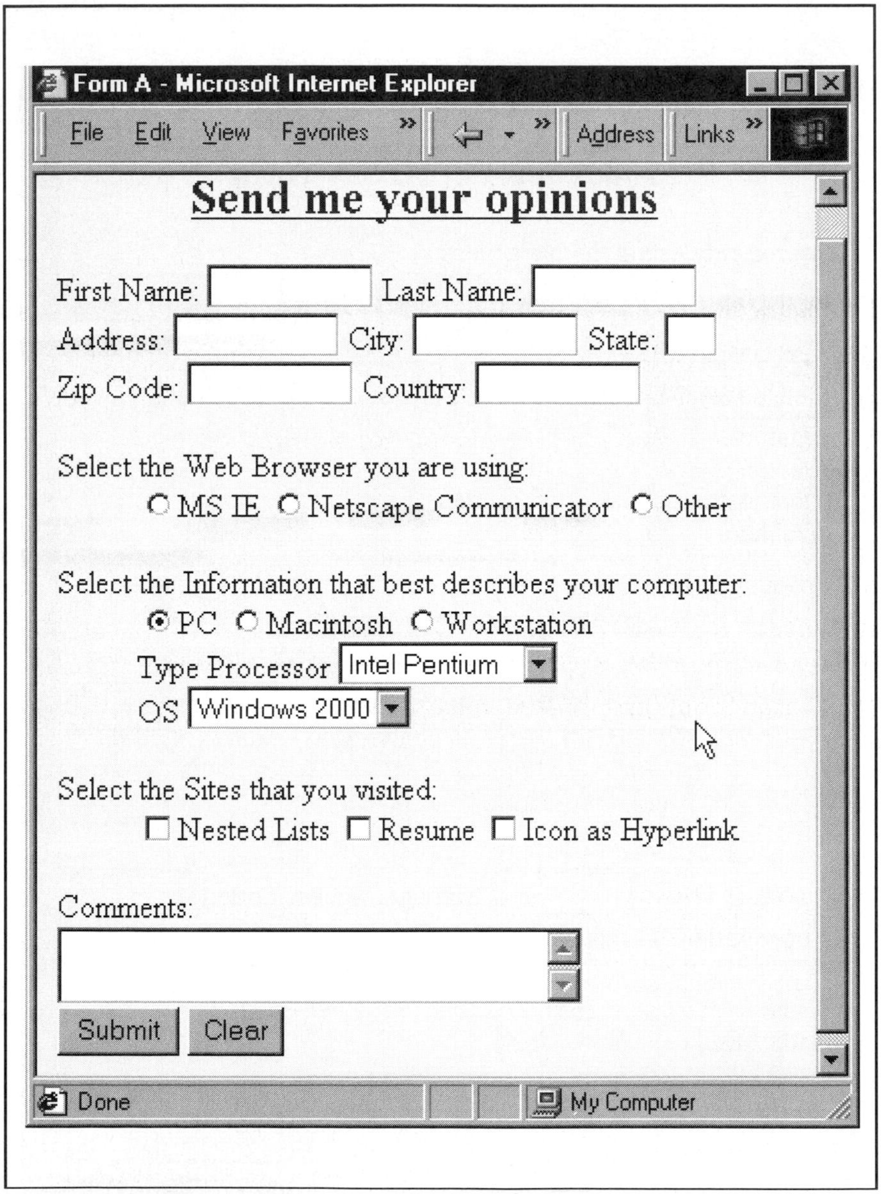

Figure 14.22 Problem 14.11.

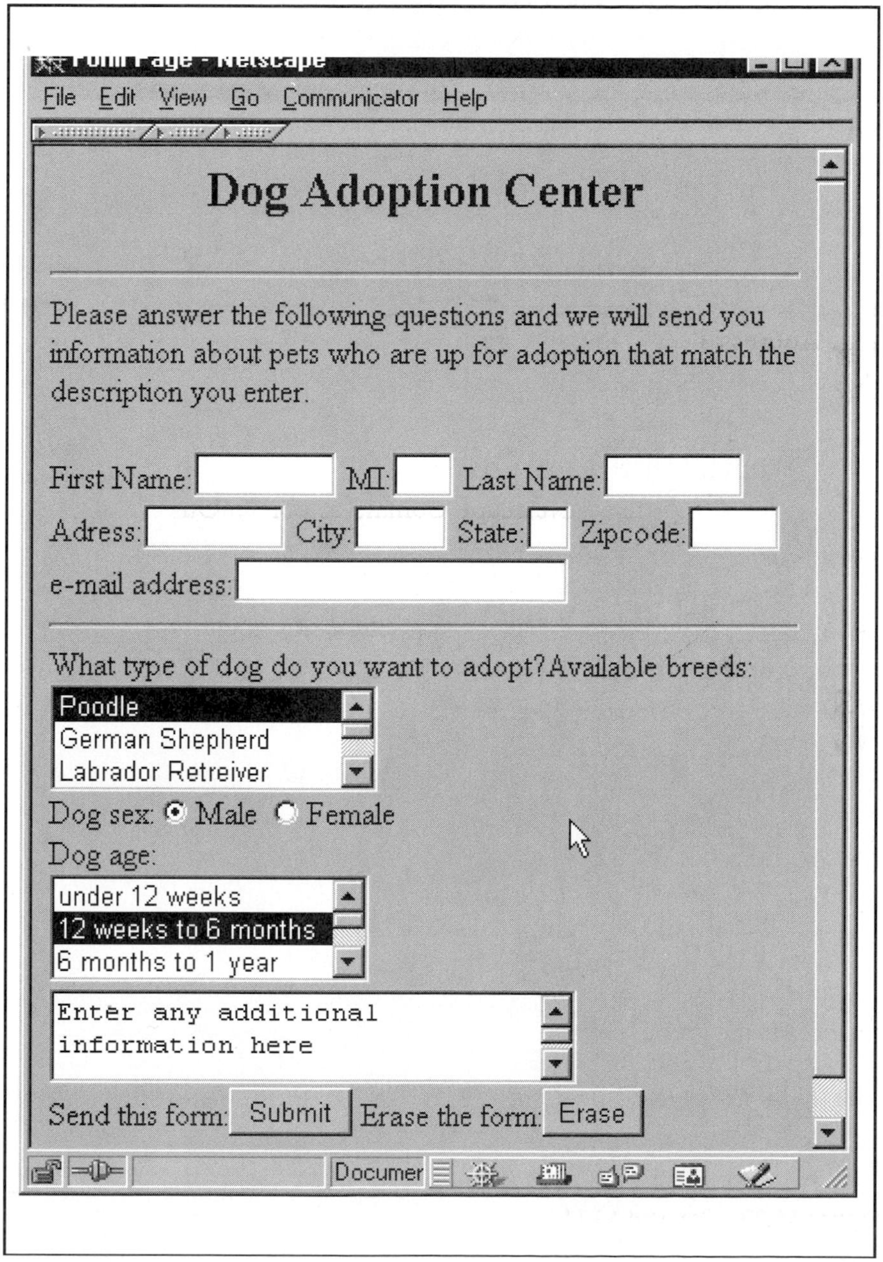

Figure 14.23 Problem 14.12.

Frames and Frame Tags

T his chapter covers the concept of HTML frames and its use in designing and developing Web pages. Frames provide Web authors with an effective design tool to utilize the Web page space effectively, by dividing it and using each division (frame) to display different Web information. Web authors can use frames for a wide range of needs in Web page design. One idea is to use a frame as a table of contents (TOC), and another to display the related information for each item on the TOC. After introducing frames and their importance, the chapter covers their layout and design. It then covers frame sets and their nesting, which can produce complex Web pages. It also covers the frame tags and their attributes. Following this coverage, the chapter discusses target frames and windows, which make using frames very efficient. At the end, the chapter presents tutorials that illustrate the use of frames in Web pages and FAQs, a summary of the important topics covered in the chapter, and problems.

15.1 Introduction

Web pages that do not use frames or tables in their layout tend to be left-side heavy, or left-justified. That means that most of the contents are concentrated on the left. This is a direct outcome of HTML tags. Very few tags can right-justify page contents. The <CENTER> tag centers page contents. As a result, the right sides of Web pages, and consequently of computer screens in terms of text, are very sparse and are not effectively utilized.

There is another Web page design issue. During navigation, an element in a Web page may force the display of a new Web page, thus forcing a Web surfer to use the history (Back) button of the browser to go back to the page originally displayed prior to the navigation. Consider the case of using image or clickable maps in Web pages, discussed in chapter 11. When a Web surfer clicks a map region or a hot spot, the browser displays the corresponding HTML file in a new

Web page. The Web page that has the map itself becomes invisible. The surfer must click the browser `Back` button to gain access to the map again to click another region or hot spot. This is obviously annoying to the Web surfer. This problem can be quite easily solved by using frames, as discussed in the tutorials at the end of this chapter.

HTML frames enable Web authors to display HTML documents in multiple views. These views are rendered by the browser in its same window. In essence, frames allow Web authors to display multiple Web pages on the screen in the same browser window at the same time. Each Web page is displayed in its own frame. A browser can display multiple frames simultaneously, with each frame displaying its own Web page. Therefore, frames are used to divide a browser window into regions or areas, with each region having its own Web page.

Displaying multiple frames simultaneously offers Web page designers a way to keep certain information visible while other information is scrolled or replaced. In the case of an image map, one frame can hold the map and its clickable hot spots while another frame displays the target clicked. When a Web surfer clicks a hot spot in one frame, the corresponding Web page is displayed in the other frame. Thus, the Web surfer has access to the map all the time while viewing the resulting information.

In addition to the use of frames in conjunction with image maps, there are several other innovative uses of frames. A Web author can use three frames (or more) in one Web page. One frame might display a static advertising banner; a second frame might display a navigation menu with hyperlinked menu items or images; and a third frame might hold the main Web page that can be scrolled or replaced by navigating the menu in the second frame.

Frames can also be used to provide a table of contents. A Web author can split a browser window vertically into two frames. The left frame is narrow and holds the TOC. The TOC can also be thought of as a menu. The items of the TOC are either text or image hyperlinks. The right frame is wide and holds Web pages that result from the clicking of items in the TOC. The contents of the left frame do not change, yet the contents of the right frame keep changing every time a Web surfer clicks a link in the left frame. For each click in the left frame, a Web page is displayed in the right frame.

Forms can be used effectively with frames. A Web site that is heavily involved in e-commerce and online shopping may have multiple forms, one per product. As with the TOC, a Web author uses the left frame as an entry point to any form display in the right frame. Thus, the left frame lists all the products that the Web site sells. Each hyperlink item of the product list invokes a Web page with an order form in the right frame. When an online shopper fills in a form and submits it, the shopper can access another product form by clicking the corresponding link.

Frames provide an effective and simple way to design Web sites. All that is needed is to design a Web site and its related Web pages is HTML. Another Web page design idea that is similar to using frames is using tabs instead. Such design is much more complicated and may require using JavaScript. A Web site may have its Web page with a GUI that has labeled tabs at the top. When a Web surfer clicks a tab, the corresponding Web page is displayed below the tabs area. The tabs area never disappears from the browser window. In comparison to using frames, the tabs area serves as the TOC frame, and the area below it serves as the second frame. Readers are encouraged to surf the Web to find Web sites that use this tabs design concept. As a matter of fact, these sites could be using image maps, with the tabs as the hot spots.

In the early days, during the development of Web browsers, earlier versions of these browsers did not support frames. Therefore, Web authors that used frames had to provide alternative, non-frame versions of their Web pages, to accommodate these earlier versions. This is a much less critical issue today, when all modern browsers support frames. With browsers being free, almost all Web surfers all over the world have the latest version of these browsers. The only impediment could be the operating system version that runs on a client computer. However, it is hard to believe that anyone is not running an OS that supports the latest versions of popular Internet browsers.

15.2 Frame Layout and Design

When Web authors need to create frames, they think in terms of the number of independent regions they need to subdivide a browser window into. The layout and design of a Web page with frames are what distinguish one Web page from another; however, there is a common theme for frame layout and design. First, each frame is a rectangle that has a width and height. Second, each frame has a location on the computer screen, left or right, top or bottom. Third, each frame has a Web page associated with it. Beyond this common theme, each frame has a unique content which results from its Web page HTML code. Figure 15.1 shows the generic layout of a Web page with two frames. As shown in the figure, the two frames divide the browser window vertically. The size of each frame is set at the time of its creation. Web surfers can be made able to adjust a frame size; this is very uncommon, though.

What decides the layout and the location of frames inside a browser window? A collection of frames is referred to as a *frame set*. Every frame set has a *frame container* that controls the layout of its frames. For example, figure 15.1 shows a frame set that has two frames. Thus, the frame container holds both frames. A frame set and its container are created via an HTML tag known as <FRAMESET>. This tag and its attributes are covered in more detail later in this chapter. Once a frame set is created and displayed on the screen, its layout cannot be changed. Only the contents of each frame in the set can change.

The frame set and its container are defined by an HTML document. This document has a different makeup from that of an HTML document without frames. A standard document has one HEAD section and one BODY section. A frameset document has a HEAD section, but a FRAMESET section in place of the BODY section. Thus, a frameset HTML document never has a <BODY> tag. This tag is replaced by the <FRAMESET> tag. The FRAMESET section of an HTML document defines the layout of the frames inside the frame container, as shown in figure 15.1. In addition, the FRAMESET section may contain a <NOFRAMES> tag, to provide alternate content to browsers that do not support frames or are configured not to display frames.

Almost always, Web authors do not have to worry about using the <NOFRAMES> tag. In addition, Web authors must never use before the first <FRAMESET> tag any HTML tags that normally appear inside the <BODY> tag, otherwise the <FRAMESET> tag will be ignored.

There are many useful tips and rules that Web authors usually follow to design HTML frames. They are mostly simple and logical and follow common sense. Here is a partial list of these tips (readers can augment it at need):

1. **Keep the frame set simple.** A Web page should not use more than two or three frames, at the most. Beyond this number, frames become distracting to Web surfers, and frame size becomes too small. Also, frame layout should be kept simple and easy to follow.

2. **Keep the frame contents short.** Web authors need to keep Web pages that are displayed in frames short, so that Web authors do not have to scroll the frames excessively to view all their contents.

3. **Keep the frames organized.** Web authors should clearly distinguish the "driver" frame from the other frames. A driver frame is one that holds all the links to the other frames. Examples include the TOC frame or the frame that holds an image map. Web authors may displays messages in other frames, informing Web surfers how to navigate the displayed frames.

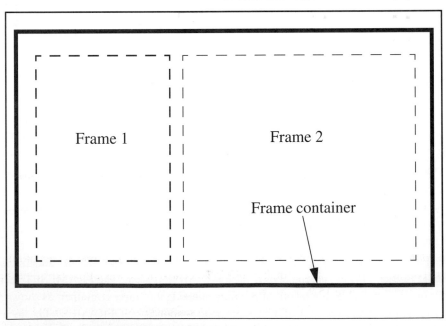

Figure 15.1 Frame layout.

4. **Surf the Web for existing design ideas.** Web authors may want to go online and surf the Web, looking for Web pages with frames so that they can learn from them.

15.3 Frame Sets and Nesting

HTML defines the rules that browsers and Web authors follow to create frames and frame sets. While these rules are simple, Web authors need to understand them clearly. These rules are related to the layout and design of frame sets. A frame set consists of multiple frames. Each frame must be sized and placed within the container of the frame set. Each frame is a rectangle. Thus, the size of a frame is determined by its width and height. A frame width is specified by the number of columns (COLS) in HTML. A frame height is specified by the number of rows (ROWS). Figure 15.2 shows a frame with its parameters. The units of ROWS and COLS are either pixels or a percentage of the browser window. The examples and tutorials show specific cases.

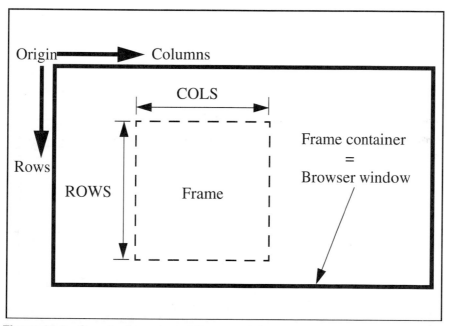

Figure 15.2   Coordinate system of frame container.

In addition to its size, a frame is placed in the container of its frame set according to the following coordinate system. The container origin is located at the top left corner of the browser window, as shown in figure 15.2. The container is effectively the browser window. The horizontal axis is the columns axis, and it points to the right. The vertical axis is the rows axis, and it points downwards. Using this coordinate system, the browser creates frames left-to-right for columns and top-to-bottom for rows. Consider the two frame sets shown in figure 15.3. The three frames in the horizontal frame set extend the entire width of the frame container (browser window), because no columns are set for any frame. Similarly, the frames in the vertical frameset extend the entire height of the container, because no rows are specified.

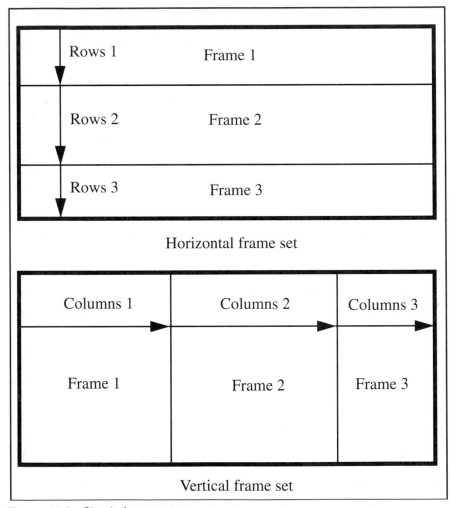

Figure 15.3 Simple frame sets.

The two frame sets shown in figure 15.3 are considered simple, because the browser window is divided in one direction only, either horizontally or vertically. Frame sets become complex when the window is divided in both directions multiple times. Such division creates nested frame sets. Nested frame sets are created left-to-right in the top row, left-to-right in the second row, and so forth. Consider the two nested frame sets shown in figure 15.4. The top set is created by using the rows-columns combination; the bottom set is created by using the columns-row-columns combination. To create the top set, the frame container is first divided into two rows. Then, the top row is divided into two columns. To create the bottom set, the container is first divided into two columns. Second, the right column is divided into two rows. Third, the bottom row is further divided into two columns.

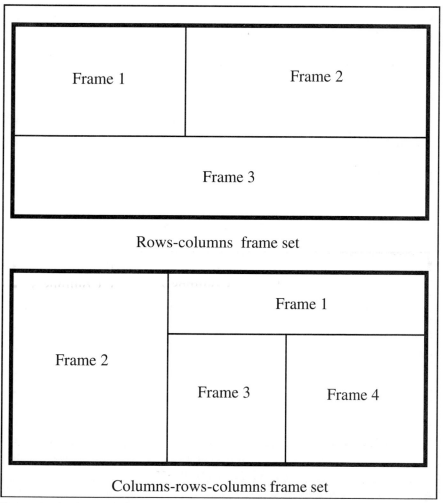

Figure 15.4 Complex frame sets.

HTML does not have a limit on the depth of frame nesting. A Web author can nest frames deep enough to divide a browser window into squares, each with a size of $1 inch \times 1 inch$, to create a checkerboard or a board for a monopoly game. However, one or two levels of nesting is all that is needed in practice.

15.4 Frame Tags

HTML provides Web authors with tags for creating and using frames. Web authors must be able to specify the sizes and locations of frames, initialize them, and nest them if needed. Four HTML tags are available. They are <FRAMESET>, <FRAME>, <IFRAME>, and <NOFRAMES>. The <FRAMESET> tag creates the frame container and the layout of frames inside it. It also creates nested frames. Nesting frame sets is equivalent to nesting <FRAMESET> tags. The <FRAME> tag creates the contents of each frame. The <IFRAME> tag creates in-line frames. The <NOFRAMES> tag provides alternatives to display frame contents. The details of each tag are discussed next.

15.4.1 <FRAMESET> Tag

This tag specifies the layout of the browser window in terms of frames. Frames are either rectangles or squares. This tag must close. The attributes of this tag are ROWS and COLS. Here are their details:

•The ROWS attribute defines the height of the frame, as shown in figure 15.2. It also specifies the layout of horizontal frames. The height can be specified as a number of pixels (e.g., ROWS = 200), as a percentage of the browser window (e.g., ROWS = 30%), or as a variable (e.g., ROWS = *). The default percentage is 100%, meaning one full row. We can use the three methods of height specification to define the horizontal frame set shown in figure 15.3, as follows: <FRAMESET ROWS = "100, 40%, *">. In this tag, the height of frame 1 is 100 pixels, the height of frame 2 is 40% of the total height of the browser window, and the height of frame 3 is the remainder of the window height. The variable * (asterisk is known as the *wild card*, in computer jargon) is very useful, because we do not know the height of the browser window a priori. Thus, the variable * is a way of telling the browser to use whatever is left as the frame height. This variable can be used for any frame. For example, we can write a tag as <FRAMESET ROWS = "*, 40%, 100">, <FRAMESET ROWS = "40%, *, 100">, or any other way.

•The COLS attribute is identical in meaning and behavior to the ROWS attribute, except that it defines the frame width, as shown in figure 15.2. It also specifies the layout of vertical frames. The width can be specified as a number of pixels (e.g., COLS = 200), as a percentage of the browser window (e.g., COLS = 30%), or as a variable (e.g., COLS = *). The default percentage is 100%, meaning one full column. We can define the vertical frame set shown in figure 15.3 as follows: <FRAMESET COLS = "*, *, 150">. In this tag, the widths of frame 1 and frame 2 are equal, and the width of frame 3 is 150 pixels.

If the ROWS and COLS attributes are set simultaneously, a frame grid is created. For example, the tag <FRAMESET ROWS = "*, *, *" COLS = "*, *, *, *"> creates a frame grid of size $3rows \times 4columns$, producing twelve equal frames. The frames in this grid are not nested frames. Nested frames are generated only if the <FRAMESET> tag is nested, as we show in the next section. It worth mentioning that the <FRAMESET> tag cannot be used by itself. It does not produce any visible results on the screen. It must be used with the <FRAME> tag, covered in the next section.

15.4.2 <FRAME> Tag

After the <FRAMESET> tag creates a certain frame set, the <FRAME> tag is used to define the contents and appearance of a single frame in the layout. It also controls the frame behavior, such as scrolling and resizing. The <FRAME> tag is always used inside the <FRAMESET> tag. This tag does not close. The attributes of this tag are NAME, SRC, NORE-SIZE, SCROLLING, FRAMEBORDER, MARGINWIDTH, MARGINHEIGHT, and LONG-DESC. These attributes are as follows:

•The NAME attribute assigns a name to the current frame. This name may serve as the target of other links.

•The SRC attribute specifies the HTML document (HTML file name and path) that is displayed in the frame initially upon its creation.

•The NORESIZE attribute is a boolean. When it is used, Web surfers cannot resize the frame by dragging its edges that neighbor other frames in the frame set.

•The SCROLLING attribute specifies, to the browser displaying the frame, whether to provide scroll bars for the frame. It has three values: AUTO, YES, and NO. AUTO is the default value, and it gives the browser the control of providing scroll bars whenever needed. YES forces the browser to provide scroll bars. While NO forbids providing them. Unless Web authors are sure that contents fit well within a frame, they should use the AUTO value.

•The FRAMEBORDER attribute is a binary attribute with two values: 0, or 1 (the default value). If it takes the value 1, the browser displays a border (separator) between the frame and every adjacent frame to it. The 0 value prevents the browser from displaying borders. However, if an adjacent frame uses borders, the effect of the 0 value is lost.

•The MARGINWIDTH attribute specifies the left and right margins of the frame, in pixels. These margins are the white space between the frame contents and its borders. If this attribute is not used, the browser rendering the frame uses its own default values.

•The MARGINHEIGHT attribute specifies the top and bottom margins of the frame, in pixels. These margins are the white space between the frame contents and its borders. If this attribute is not used, the browser rendering the frame uses its own default values.

•The LONGDESC attribute specifies a link to a long description of the frame.

Example 15.1 Develop a Web page that illustrates the use of frames.

Solution This example creates a Web page with a frame grid. The grid has four frames. We use most of the attributes of both the <FRAMESET> and the <FRAME> tag. Using a text editor, type the code that follows, and save it as *example15.1.html*. Figures 15.5 and 15.6 show the resulting Web page. Figure 15.5 shows the frame set as rendered by MS IE; figure 15.6 shows the result in Netscape Communicator.

```
<HTML>
<HEAD>
<TITLE>A Web page with a frame grid</TITLE>
</HEAD>
<FRAMESET ROWS = "5*, 2*" COLS = "50%, *">
<FRAME SRC = "" NAME = "myFrame1" FRAMEBORDER = 0>
<FRAME SRC = "" NAME = "myFrame2">
<FRAME SRC = "" SCROLLING = "no">
<FRAME SRC = ""  NORESIZE MARGINWIDTH = 10 MARGINHEIGHT = 10>
</FRAMESET>
</HTML>
```

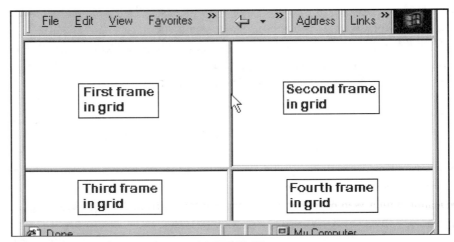

Figure 15.5   Rendering a frame grid via MS IE.

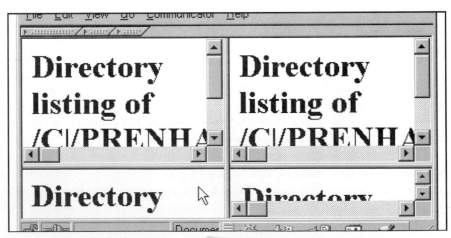

Figure 15.6   Rendering a frame grid using Netscape Communicator.

Here are several comments about this example HTML code:

•The example creates a grid of four frames, each with no contents, because no HTML file is specified in the SRC attribute.

•There is (and should be) no <BODY> tag in the HTML file defining the frame set.

•The order of the grid frames as specified in the code and created by the two browsers, is shown in figure 15.5. We have labeled the frames for ease of following.

•The ratio between the heights of the top and the bottom rows is 5 to 2, as shown by the ROWS attribute. The width of the frames is the same, as shown by the COLS attribute.

•The two browsers render empty frames differently. MS IE renders the frames with empty contents. Netscape Communicator looks for an index.html to use as the contents for each frame. If it does not find it, it displays the contents of the directory of the frameset HTML file. In this example, it shows the contents of the directory where the example15.1.html file resides.

•The first frame shows no border, as a result of the FRAMEBORDER attribute. The apparent border is that of the neighboring frames; however, if you pay close attention to figure 15.5, you can see that no border comes from the first frame.

•The third frame does not have scroll bars, as is shown in figure 15.6. This is a result of the SCROLLING attribute.

•The fourth frame is the only one using the NORESIZE attribute, so none of the other three frames can be resized. This is an outcome of this attribute.

•The MARGINWIDTH and MARGINHEIGHT attributes have no effect in this example, as there are no contents for any frame.

•Dealing with a Web page that has frames is different from dealing with a page that does not have them. For example, you cannot use the browser Print button to print the page. You can print only one frame at a time. To do so, right click anywhere inside the frame window, and choose Print from the pop-up menu. You do the same if you want to view the source code of the frame. If you use the View menu of the browser to view the source, the browser displays the HTML code of the frame set and not the HTML code of the contents of any frame.

Example 15.2 Develop a Web page that illustrates the use of nested frames.

Solution This example creates a Web page with three nested frames by using two <FRAMESET> tags. The first tag (the outer tag in the example code) divides the browser window into two columns. The second (inner) tag subdivides the left column into two rows. The contents of each frame come from a corresponding HTML file, as shown in the SRC attribute. In this example, we need four HTML files. One file creates the frame container that holds the frame set and its frames. We call it *example15.2.html*. The other three files are *myFrame1.html*, *myFrame2.html*, and *myFrame3.html*. They define the contents of the three frames. The file that creates the frame container is considered the "driver" or "main". It should have a unique name. It may also be a good idea to create a subdirectory or a folder to hold all the files of the frame set. If the set has *n* frames, we would need *n* + 1 files to create the frame set.

Using a text editor, type the following code and save it. Figure 15.7 shows the resulting Web page.

example15.2.html:

```
<HTML>
<HEAD>
<TITLE>A Web page with nested frames</TITLE>
</HEAD>
<FRAMESET COLS = "*, *">
<FRAMESET ROWS = "*, *">
<FRAME SRC = "myFrame1.html">
<FRAME SRC = "myFrame2.html">
</FRAMESET>
<FRAME SRC = "myFrame3.html">
</FRAMESET>
</HTML>
```

myFrame1.html:

```
<HTML>
<HEAD>
<TITLE>A Web page for frame 1</TITLE>
</HEAD>
<BODY>
<FONT COLOR = "blue"><H2>Hello from frame 1</H2></FONT>
</BODY>
</HTML>
```

myFrame2.html is the same as the above file, but replacing 1 by 2 and blue by red. Similarly, *myFrame3.html* uses 3 instead of 2, and green instead of blue.

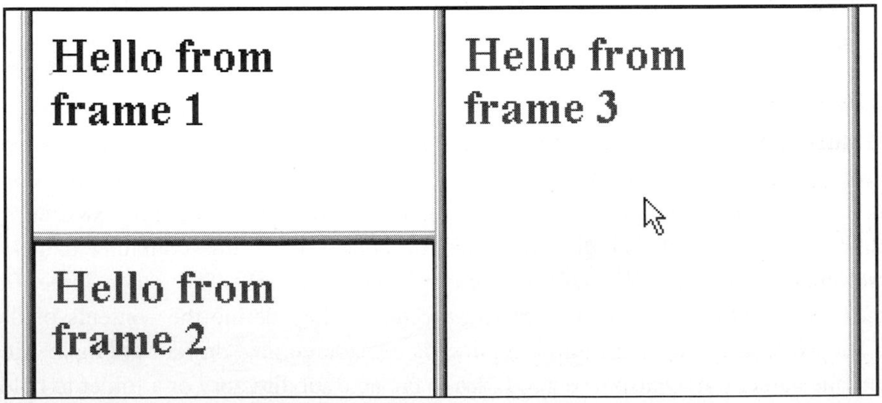

Figure 15.7   A Web page with a nested frame set.

Example 15.3 Rewrite the HTML code for example 15.2 so that the right column shown in figure 15.7 is divided into two rows, instead of the left column.

Solution This example shows the rule that the browser uses to divide nested frames. It divides frames from left to right, then top to bottom, unless the frame is already assigned an HTML file. Consider example 15.2 and its frameset code. The browser executes HTML code from top to bottom in the HTML file. Thus, the browser executes the first <FRAMESET> tag and divides its window into two columns. Next tag to execute is the second <FRAMESET> tag. This tag calls for dividing a column into two rows. The browser has to make a decision whether to divide the left or the right column. The browser divides the left column, because both columns are still available (neither has an HTML file assigned to it yet), and it uses the left-to-right rule. In order to force the browser to divide the right column, we could assign the left column an HTML file before we use the second <FRAMESET> tag. Thus, we need to move the first <FRAME> tag from its current location, shown in example 15.2, and insert it between the <FRAMESET> tags, as shown below. The browser executes it before the second <FRAMESET> tag. Now, the browser has no choice but to divide the right column into two rows, as requested by the second <FRAMESET> tag. We also must move the </FRAMESET> tag to after the last <FRAME> tag, to provide enough frames for the second <FRAMESET> tag.

Using a text editor, type the following code, and save it as *example15.3.html*.

```
<HTML>

<HEAD>

<TITLE>A Web page with nested frames</TITLE>

</HEAD>

<FRAMESET COLS = "*, *">

<FRAME SRC = "myFrame1.html" MARGINWIDTH = 50 MARGINHEIGHT =75>

<FRAMESET ROWS = "*, *">

<FRAME SRC = "myFrame2.html">

<FRAME SRC = "myFrame3.html">

</FRAMESET>

</FRAMESET>

</HTML>
```

Figure 15.8 shows the resulting Web page. Notice that we have used the MARGIN-WIDTH and the MARGINHEIGHT attributes in the first <FRAME> tag to center the contents of this frame. The other three HTML files remain the same as in example 15.2.

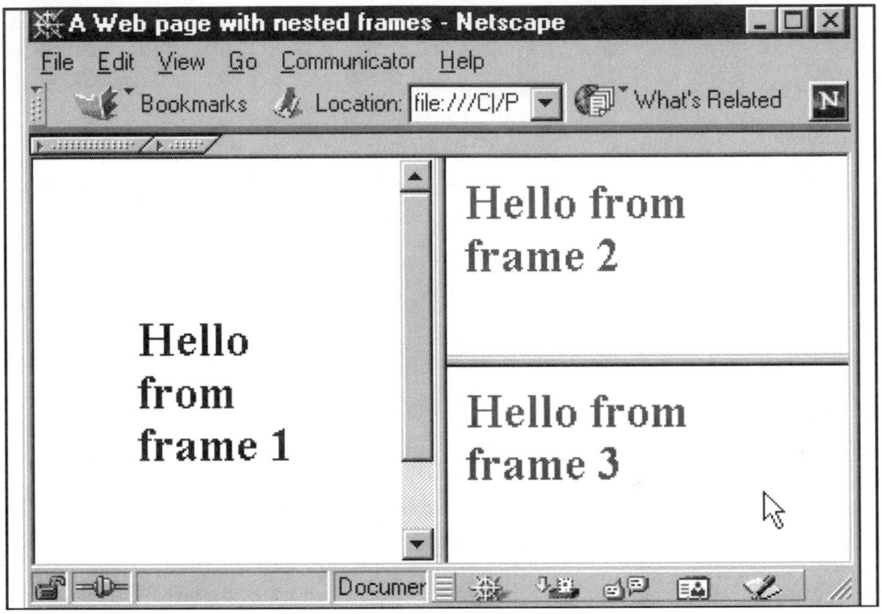

Figure 15.8   Dividing the right column in a nested frame set.

15.4.3 <IFRAME> Tag

The <IFRAME> tag creates inline frames. Inline frames are a different type of frame. An inline frame is a frame that is embedded inside a document (Web page). Unlike with normal frames, no frame sets are required to create inline frames. The <IFRAME> tag allows Web authors to create inline frames. The concept of inline frames was introduced by Microsoft into its Internet Explorer version 4 and higher. The <IFRAME> tag is part of the HTML 4.0 specification, yet it is not supported by Netscape Communicator. Thus, Web authors who want to guarantee compatibility between all browsers for the users of their Web sites should avoid using this tag. The Netscape browser ignores the tag without any warnings to the Web surfer.

Unlike the <FRAME> tag, the <IFRAME> tag is used inside the <BODY> tag of an HTML document, like any other tag. It must close. However, its attributes are similar to those of the <FRAME> tag. They are NAME, SRC, SCROLLING, FRAMEBORDER, MARGIN-WIDTH, MARGINHEIGHT, LONGDESC, ALIGN, WIDTH, and HEIGHT. If you compare these attributes with those of the <FRAME> tag, you find out that the NORESIZE is absent. This makes sense, as the inline frame size must be fixed once it is inserted in a Web page. In addition, three more attributes are added to control the placement (ALIGN) and the size (WIDTH and HEIGHT) of the inline frame. The ALIGN attribute controls the flow of the text surrounding the inline frame.

Example 15.4 Develop a Web page that illustrates the use of inline frames.

This example shows how to use the <IFRAME> tag. We create a Web page with an inline frame, some text, and a hyperlink. An IFRAME-compatible browser renders every tag, including the <IFRAME> tag, but it ignores the text inside the tag, as it should. On the other hand, a browser that does not support inline frames ignores the <IFRAME> tag and renders the text inside it. Using a text editor, type the code that follows, and save it as *example15.4.html*. Figures 15.9 and 15.10 show the resulting Web page, as rendered by MS IE and Netscape Communicator, respectively.

```
<HTML>
<HEAD>
<TITLE>A Web page with inline frames</TITLE>
</HEAD>
<BODY>
<FONT COLOR = "blue"><H2 ALIGN = "center">A Web page using inline
frames</H2></FONT>
<IFRAME   SRC = "statement.html"  WIDTH = 350 HEIGHT = 90>
This Web page uses the IFRAME tag.<BR>
This tag is only supported by MS IE.<BR>
Browsers that are not IFRAME compatible ignores the tag.<BR>
Instead, they render any tags and text enclosed by the IFRAME tag
as the case with this browser.
</IFRAME>
<P>
This Web page uses inline frames.<BR>
Text flows around these frames.<BR>
<A HREF = "http://www.neu.edu" Check the latest programs at NU</A>
</BODY>
</HTML>
```

The code for the *statement.html* file that is used in the SRC attribute in the preceding code is listed here:

```
<HTML>
<HEAD>
<TITLE>A Web page with inline frames</TITLE>
</HEAD>
<BODY>
<FONT COLOR = "red"><H2 ALIGN = "cennter">This is an inline frame
created with the IFRAME tag</H2></FONT>
</BODY>
</HTML>
```

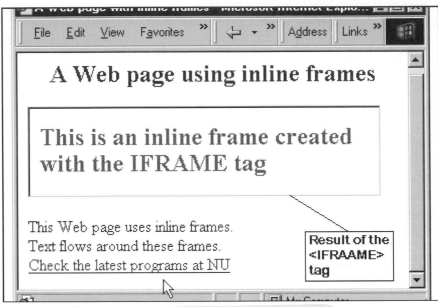

Figure 15.9   Rendering the <IFRAME> tag using MS IE.

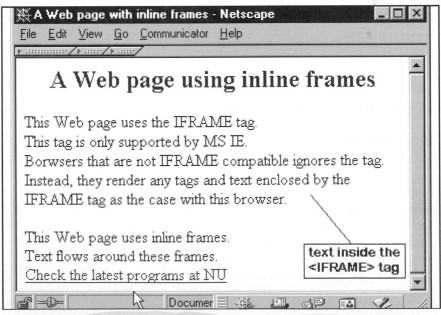

Figure 15.10   Rendering the <IFRAME> tag using Netscape Communicator.

15.4.4 <NOFRAMES> Tag

This tag must close. It does not have any attributes. The tag specifies alternative contents for a Web page that should be rendered by a browser that does not, or is configured not to, support frames. This tag is enclosed inside the <FRAMESET> tag. Thus, browsers that support frames render the <FRAMESET> tag and all the other tags that it encloses *except* the <NOFRAMES> tag and what is inside it. By contrast, browsers that do *not* support frames render *only* the <NOFRAMES> tag (and all the other tags that it encloses). In effect, a Web author writes the Web page twice in the same HTML code, once inside the <FRAMESET> tag and once inside the <NOFRAMES> tag.

Let us modify the HTML code of example 15.3 to show how to use the <NOFRAMES> tag:

```
<HTML>
<HEAD>
<TITLE>Welcome to our Web site</TITLE>
</HEAD>
<FRAMESET COLS = "*, *">
<FRAME SRC = "myFrame1.html" MARGINWIDTH = 50 MARGINHEIGHT =75>
<FRAMESET ROWS = "*, *">
<FRAME SRC = "myFrame2.html">
<FRAME SRC = "myFrame3.html">
</FRAMESET>
<NOFRAMES>
Any tags that are normally used inside the <BODY> tag go here
</NOFRAMES>
</FRAMESET>
</HTML>
```

15.5 Target Frames and Windows

Frames are typically used to optimize the use of a Web page layout and to facilitate navigation. For optimum navigation, a Web author may use one frame to hold, say, hyperlinks and then use another frame to display the results of clicking these hyperlinks. In this case, the contents of the first frame never change, while the contents of the second frame change for each mouse click. The advantage here is that the first frame always displays the hyperlinks for the convenience of the Web surfer. If frames are not used, navigating becomes a cumbersome task, as in the case of using a TOC or an image map. Whenever the surfer clicks a hyperlink, the contents of the page are replaced, thus removing the hyperlinks themselves from the screen. This forces the surfer to click the Back button of the browser to access these links again.

Frames that receive contents from other frames are known as target frames. Let us refer to frames that hold the TOC as source frames. Figure 15.11 shows the relationship between source frames and target frames. When a Web surfer clicks a hyperlink in the source frame, the contents of the corresponding Web page are displayed in the target frame.

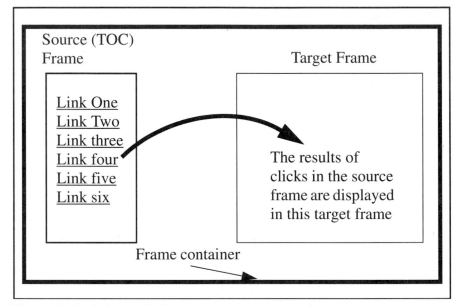

Figure 15.11   Relationship between source and target frames.

Target frames are not especially different from other frames. The only requirement is to name them at the time of their creation. Thus, their corresponding <FRAME> tags must use the NAME attribute. Assigning a name to a frame allows such a frame to be used as the target of other links, image maps, and forms. Any HTML tag that has the TARGET attribute can use the frame as a target. We can think of the TARGET attribute as the curved arrow shown in figure 15.11, or as the link between the source and the target frames. If, say, an <A> tag in the source frame uses the <TARGET> attribute with a value equal to the name of the target frame, the browser displays in the target frame, the contents of the destination anchor (discussed in chapter 7) of the <A> tag. Consequently, the contents of target frames are dynamically modified by the targets that use them. Contrarily, source frames almost always maintain their initial contents.

When many links in the same HTML document use the same target frame, Web authors may use the <BASE> tag to specify the target frame once for all; that eliminates the repetition of using the TARGET attribute. This is done by setting the TARGET attribute of this tag. In essence, Web authors factor out the target information, by defining it in the <BASE> tag and removing it from other tags needing a target frame, such as the <A> tag.

Browsers employ the following precedence rules (starting with the highest priority) to determine the target frame used in a tag:

1. If the TARGET attribute of the tag specifies a known frame, the browser uses it to display the HTML contents designated by the tag.
2. If the tag does not have a TARGET attribute set, the browser uses the frame set by the TARGET attribute of the <BASE> tag, if there is one.
3. If no TARGET attribute at all is specified, the browser uses the frame of the tag itself to display the designated HTML contents. In other words, the browser replaces the original contents of the tag frame.
4. If a TARGET attribute refers to an unknown frame, the browser creates a new instance of itself, with a frame that holds the unknown frame. This happens in many cases during browsing and surfing. A surfer clicks a link that results in opening a new browser window on top of the existing one. The surfer can kill the new browser window after being done with it and continue using the old window.

Example 15.5 Develop a Web page that illustrates the use of target frames.

Solution This example creates a Web page with two frames. The left frame acts as a TOC. It has four hyperlinks. Each one of them uses the right frame as a target frame. The initial contents of the target frame are used to instruct users on how to use the frame set. This example requires three HTML documents. One document is *example15.5.html*, and it defines the frame set. This document is also the main, or the driver. The second document is *tableOfContents.html*, and it defines the contents of the left frame. The third document is *initialContents.html*, and it defines the initial contents of the right frame. Using a text editor, type the code (following this paragraph) for the three files, and save them. Figure 15.12 shows the frameset definition, while figure 15.13 shows the target frame with designated HTML contents after clicking the second <A> tag. Observe that the second and the third <A> tags use the HTML files of examples 15.2 and 15.3 respectively, to ease the reproducing of this example by the readers, if the need arises.

Code for *example15.5.html*:

```
<HTML>
<HEAD>
<TITLE>A Web page with a target frame</TITLE>
</HEAD>
<FRAMESET COLS = "160, *">
<FRAME SRC = "tableOfContents.html">
<FRAME SRC = "" NAME = "myTarget">
</FRAMESET>
</HTML>
```

Code for *tableOfContents.html*:

```
<HTML>
<HEAD>
```

```
<TITLE>Contents of the TOC frame</TITLE>
</HEAD>
<BODY>
<A HREF = "http://www.neu.edu" TARGET ="myTarget" TITLE = "NU Web
page">NU propgrams</A><BR>
<A HREF = "example15.2.html" TARGET ="myTarget" TITLE = "Another
frame set">Another frame set</A><BR>
<A HREF = "example15.3.html" TARGET ="myTarget" TITLE = "More frame
sets">More frame sets</A><BR>
<A HREF = "http://www.prenhall.com" TARGET ="myTarget" TITLE =
"Prentice Hall Web page">Prentice Hall books</A>
</BODY>
</HTML>
```

Code for *initialContents.html*:

```
<HTML>
<HEAD>
<TITLE>Instructions to use target frames</TITLE>
</HEAD>
<BODY>
<FONT COLOR ="blue"><H2 ALIGN = "center">Click any link in the left
frame to display its designated HTML contents in this frame </H2>
</FONT>
</BODY>
</HTML>
```

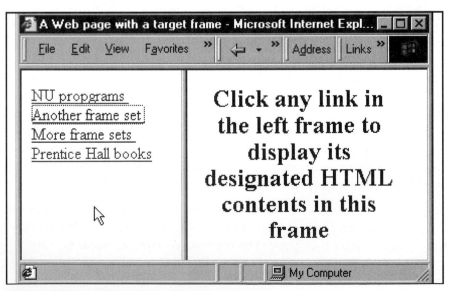

Figure 15.12   A Web page using a target frame.

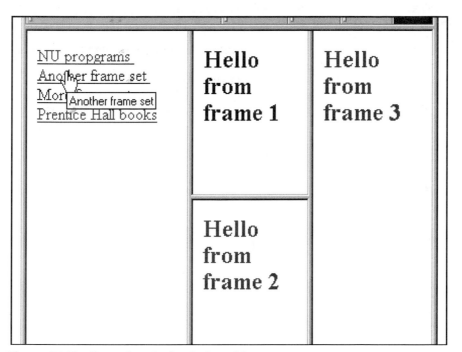

Figure 15.13   Current contents of a target frame.

Example 15.6 Rewrite the HTML code for example 15.5 so that it uses the <BASE> tag to define target frame.

Solution The code of the *tableOfContents.html* file in example 15.5 shows we have to repeat the name of the target frame in each hyperlink that needs it. Thus, the TARGET = "myFrame" has been used four times for the four links. Repeating the TARGET attribute like this becomes inefficient. This example shows how to use the <BASE> tag to eliminate this repetition and yet continue to define target frames. This tag has its own TARGET attribute, which is used to define target frames once. When this tag is used in a Web page, the browser follows the second precedence rule stated in this section.

The only change we need to do to the three files of example 15.5 is to remove the TARGET = "myFrame" from the four <A> tag in the *tableOfContents.html* file and add the <BASE> tag instead, as shown in the code below. This tag is always enclosed inside the <HEAD> tag as discussed in chapter 7. The other two files work the same. The resulting Web page, shown in figure 15.12, remains unchanged. If the user clicks the second or third link, the new browser window looks like figure 15.13.

```
<HTML>
<HEAD>
<TITLE>Contents of the TOC frame</TITLE>
<BASE TARGET ="myTarget">
</HEAD>
<BODY>
<A HREF = "http://www.neu.edu" TITLE = "NU Web page">NU propgrams
</A><BR>
<A HREF = "example15.2.html" TITLE = "Another frame set">Another
frame set</A><BR>
<A HREF = "example15.3.html" TITLE = "More frame sets">More frame
sets</A><BR>
<A HREF = "http://www.prenhall.com" TITLE = "Prentice Hall Web
page">Prentice Hall books</A>
</BODY>
</HTML>
```

Example 15.7 Rewrite the HTML code for example 15.5 so that it uses new browser windows.

Solution We modify the TARGET attribute of, say, the second and third <A> tags in the *tableOfContents.html* file in example 15.5 to specify an unknown name for a target frame. We use the name myUnknownTarget. This name is not defined in the *example15.5.html* file. This file defines the myTarget frame only. When a user clicks the first or the fourth link, the browser displays the corresponding HTML contents in the myTarget frame. However, if the user clicks the second or third link, the browser opens a new window of its own, and displays the contents of the corresponding HTML file in it. This new window is now called myUnknown-Target. The browser uses the fourth precedence rule stated in this section when it decides to open its new window. If another TARGET attribute uses it, the browser recognizes it. Thus, if a user clicks the second or the third link again, the browser displays results in its already opened window. The browser keeps track of the names of all its currently opened windows, although the browser users do not see them.

The only change we need to make to the three files of example 15.5 is to replace the TARGET = "myFrame" in the second and third <A> tags in the *tableOfContents.html* file by TARGET = "myUnknownTarget", as shown in the code that follows. The other two files are the same. The resulting Web page, shown in figure 15.12, remains unchanged. The new browser window looks the same, as shown in figure 15.7 or 15.8 (depending on which link the user clicks).

```
<HTML>
<HEAD>
<TITLE>Contents of the TOC frame</TITLE>
</HEAD>
<BODY>
```

```
<A HREF = "http://www.neu.edu" TARGET ="myTarget" TITLE = "NU Web
page">NU programs</A><BR>
<A HREF = "example15.2.html" TARGET ="myUnknownTarget" TITLE =
"Another frame set">Another frame set</A><BR>
<A HREF = "example15.3.html" TARGET ="myUnknownTarget" TITLE =
"More frame sets">More frame sets</A><BR>
<A HREF = "http://www.prenhall.com" TARGET ="myTarget" TITLE =
"Prentice Hall Web page">Prentice Hall books</A>
</BODY>
</HTML>
```

15.6 Tutorials

This section focuses on using the frame tags covered in this chapter. Any Web browser can be used to display the corresponding Web pages. It is a good idea to create a directory structure to save HTML files. This helps Web authors to organize HTML files and makes it easy to find them.

15.6.1 Using Ordered Lists in a TOC Frame

This tutorial creates a TOC as an ordered list with hyperlink items. In this tutorial, we create a course description Web page. The page has a frame set that consists of two vertical frames. The left frame holds the course links that make up the items of the ordered list. The right frame displays the course description for each user's choice. Using a text editor, type the code that follows and save it as shown. View the page in a browser. Figure 15.14 shows the resulting Web page for the HTML course description.

tutorial15.6.1.html:

```
<HTML>
<HEAD>
<TITLE>A Web page with course descriptions</TITLE>
</HEAD>
<FRAMESET COLS = "165, *">
<FRAME SRC = "tableOfContents.html">
<FRAME SRC = "initialContents.html" NAME = "myTarget">
</FRAMESET>
</HTML>
```

intialContents.html:

```
<HTML>
<HEAD>
<TITLE>Instructions to access course description</TITLE>
</HEAD>
```

```
<BODY>
<FONT COLOR ="blue"><H2 ALIGN = "center">Choose any link in the
left frame to display the corresponding course description here </
H2></FONT>
</BODY>
</HTML>
```

tableOfContents.html:

```
<HTML>
<HEAD>
<TITLE>Contents of the TOC frame</TITLE>
</HEAD>
<BODY>
<FONT COLOR = "red"><CENTER>List of courses</CENTER></FONT>
Choose a course for a full description.
<OL>
<LI><A HREF = "clientServerCourse.html" TARGET ="myTarget" TITLE =
"client/server">Client/server</A>
<LI><A HREF = "htmlCourse.html" TARGET ="myTarget" TITLE =
"HTML">Basic HTML</A>
<LI><A HREF = "xmlCourse.html" TARGET ="myTarget" TITLE =
"XML">Basic XML</A>
<LI><A HREF = "javaCourse.html" TARGET ="myTarget" TITLE =
"Java">Java</A>
</OL>
</BODY>
</HTML>
```

htmlCourse.html (the other course description files follow a similar format):

```
<HTML>
<HEAD>
<TITLE>Basic HTML Course description</TITLE>
</HEAD>
<BODY>
<FONT COLOR ="blue"><H2 ALIGN = "center">Basic HTML</H2></FONT>
This course covers the basic concepts of HTML.<BR>
It explains the HTML 4.0 tags and their attributes.<BR>
It briefly discusses good tips useful for  Web page design.<BR>
It provides ample examples and tutorials for hands-on experience.
</BODY>
</HTML>
```

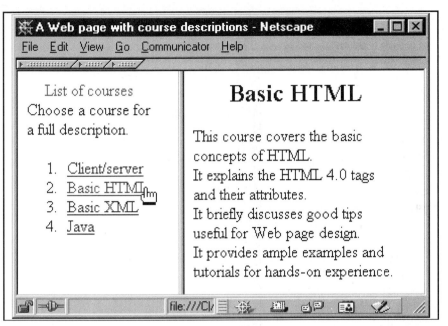

Figure 15.14 Using an ordered list in a TOC frame.

15.6.2 Using Image Maps with Frames

This tutorial uses an image map in a two-frame Web page to facilitate its navigation. The two frames are vertical. The left frame holds the image map with its hot spots. The right frame displays the contents of the HTML file that corresponds to a hot spot selected by the user. This tutorial builds on tutorial 11.7.3. In this tutorial, we use all the files of tutorial 11.7.3. We modify the main file, *tutorial11.7.3.html*, by adding the TARGET = "display" attribute to each of the three <AREA> tags. (We could have used the <BASE TARGET = "display"> tag instead.) We also change its name to *imageMap.html*. In addition, we create a new HTML file that defines the frame set. The name of this new file is *tutorial15.6.2.html*. The contents of these two files are listed following this paragraph. Figure 15.15 shows the image map when the `rectangle hot spot` is selected by the user.

tutorial15.6.2.html:

```
<HTML>
<HEAD>
<TITLE>A Web page with an image map</TITLE>
</HEAD>
<FRAMESET COLS = "165, *">
```

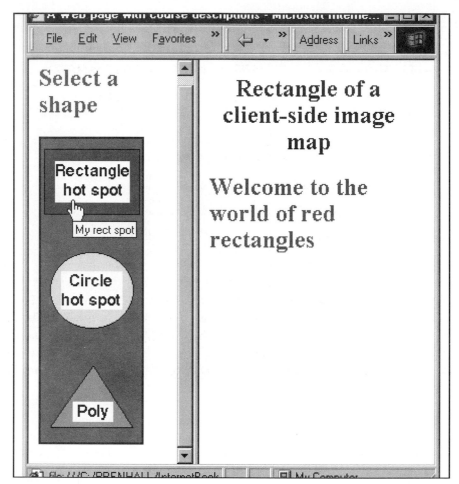

Figure 15.15   Using an image map in a frame set.

```
<FRAME SRC = "imageMap.html">
<FRAME SRC = "" NAME = "display">
</FRAMESET>
</HTML>
```

imageMap.html:

```
<HTML>
<HEAD>
<TITLE>A Web page with a client-side vertical image map</TITLE>
</HEAD>
```

```
<BODY>
<H2><B><FONT COLOR = "red">Select a shape</FONT></CENTER></B></H2>
<! Specify the map image>
<IMG SRC = "verticalMapImage.gif" ALT = "My vertical image map"
USEMAP = "#myVerticalMap">
<! Create the hot spots>
<FONT COLOR = "black"><MAP NAME = "myVerticalMap"></FONT>
<AREA SHAPE = "rect" COORDS = "3, 10 95, 75" ALT = "My rect spot"
HREF = "map/rectSpot.html" TARGET = "display">
<AREA SHAPE = "circle" COORDS = "50, 150 40" ALT = "My circle spot"
HREF = "map/circleSpot.html" TARGET = "display">
<AREA SHAPE = "poly" COORDS = "10, 285 90, 285 50, 225" ALT = "My
poly spot" HREF = "map/polySpot.html" TARGET = "display">
</MAP>
</BODY>
</HTML>
```

15.6.3 Using Forms with Frames

Tutorial 15.6.1 can be adapted to use forms. The left frame can be used to show the different forms available on a Web site. The right frame displays the form that corresponds to a user's selection in the left frame. We use the three forms developed in tutorials 14.6.1, 14.6.2, and 14.6.3. In addition to these three HTML files, we need to develop two more files. The first file has the name *tutorial15.6.3.html*, and it defines the frame set. The second file defines the contents of the TOC frame and has the name *forms.html*. The code of these two files follows this paragraph. Figure 15.16 shows the Web page when the user selects the customer survey link.

tutorial15.6.3.html:

```
<HTML>
<HEAD>
<TITLE>A Web page with forms</TITLE>
</HEAD>
<FRAMESET COLS = "185, *">
<FRAME SRC = "forms.html">
<FRAME SRC = "" NAME = "display">
</FRAMESET>
</HTML>
```

forms.html:

```
<HTML>
<HEAD>
<TITLE>Contents of the TOC frame</TITLE>
<BASE TARGET = "display">
</HEAD>
<BODY>
```

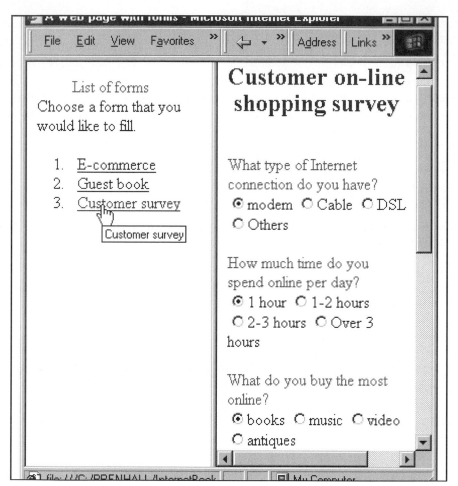

Figure 15.16   Using forms in a frame set.

```
<FONT COLOR = "red"><CENTER>List of forms</CENTER></FONT>
Choose a form that you would like to fill.
<OL>
<LI><A HREF = "ecommerceForm.html" TITLE = "E-commerce">E-com-
merce</A>
<LI><A HREF = "guestBookForm.html" TITLE = "Guest book">Guest
book</A>
<LI><A HREF = "customerSurveyForm.html" TITLE = "Customer sur-
vey">Customer survey</A>
</OL>
</BODY>
```

```
</HTML>
```

15.7 FAQs

Q: What happens if I create a frame without using the ROWS and COLS attributes?

A: The browser creates a frame that takes up its entire window. In effect, you do not need a frame.

Q: What is wrong with this code? I am trying to create three horizontal frames with a heading that reads "A horizontal frame set" in blue. The browser displays the heading only; it ignores the frame set all together.

```
<HTML>
<HEAD>
<TITLE>A Web page with a horizontal frame set</TITLE>
</HEAD>
<CENTER><FONT COLOR = "blue"><H2>A horizontal frame set</H2></FONT>
</CENTER><BR>
<FRAMESET ROWS = "100, 40%, *">
<FRAME SRC = "">
<FRAME SRC = "">
<FRAME SRC = "">
</FRAMESET>
</HTML>
```

A: You cannot use any HTML tags that go inside the <BODY> tag before the <FRAMESET> tag. If you do, as in this case, the browser ignore the <FRAMESET> tag. You must always remember that the two tags are mutually exclusive.

Q: What is wrong with this code? I am trying to create a frame container with three empty frames. The browser does not display any frames in its window.

```
<HTML>
<HEAD>
<TITLE>A Web page with a horizontal frame set</TITLE>
</HEAD>
<FRAMESET ROWS = "100, 40%, *">
</FRAMESET>
</HTML>
```

A: There is nothing wrong with the code syntax. Unless you use the three expected <FRAME> tags, the browser does not show any frames. Use the following code instead:

```
<HTML>
<HEAD>
<TITLE>A Web page with a horizontal frame set</TITLE>
```

```
</HEAD>
<FRAMESET ROWS = "100, 40%, *">
<FRAME SRC = "">
<FRAME SRC = "">
<FRAME SRC = "">
</FRAMESET>
</HTML>
```

Q: Why is the browser unable to display the latest changes I just made to an HTML file, although I made sure to save the code a couple of times? I used the browser's `Reload` button.

A: The problem is not yours. It the browser's. When you use the `Reload` button, the browser loads the HTML version it has saved in its cache, instead of loading the latest version you have just saved on your hard disk. To force the browser to load from the hard disk, drag the HTML file and drop it in the browser, or use the browser's `File => Open` sequence; or, simply place the mouse cursor in the browser URL bar, click it to bring the focus to the bar, and hit `Enter` on your keyboard, or yet hold down the `Shift` key on the keyboard and click the browser's `Reload` button simultaneously.

Q: What does the following frameset definition mean: <FRAMESET ROWS = "4*, 300, 1*">?

A: The browser window is divided into 3 rows. The middle row has a fixed height of 300 pixels. The first row receives 80% of the remaining space, and the last row receives 20% of the remaining space. The fixed-height frame could be useful for holding an image of a known size.

Q: What does the following frameset definition mean assuming a browser window that is 1000 pixels wide: <FRAMESET COLS = "30%, 400, 2*, *">?

A: The first frame is alloted 300 pixels. The width of the second frame is already specified to be exactly 400 pixels. That leaves 300 pixels for the remaining two frames. The width of the third frame is twice that of the last frame. Thus, the third frame becomes 200 pixels wide, and the last frame receives 100 pixels for its width.

Q: What happens if a Web author underspecifies or overspecifies the allocation of a browser window's height or width when defining a frame set?

A: The browser should adjust the heights and widths of the set frames to match exactly its window's height and width, respectively. When the set is underspecified (or overspecified), remaining (or lacking) space should be alloted (or reduced) proportionally to each frame.

Q: Why does my browser not display all the frames I expect, although the code of the frame set is correct?

A: This is an issue of space allocation that depends on the size of the currently displayed browser window. Let us assume that the size of the window is 300 pixels wide by 200 pixels high. If you request two rows of frames, and the first is 400 pixels high, you will not see the second row in this window size. If you enlarge the browser window to fill the entire screen, you should see all the frames, unless you are using very large sizes. It is usually recommended to use the wild card (*) to describe sizes of frames, to give the browser full freedom at the display time.

Q: Why does the browser not show the latest changes I made to my frame set?

A: Do not use the browser `Relaod` button. Force the browser to load the latest file , either by dragging and dropping it in the browser window or by using the `File` menu of the browser to open the file.

Q: Does a frameset definition ever change, once it is created?

A: A frameset definition refers to its layout and to the initial contents of each of its frames. Such a definition never changes after the creating of the frameset; however, the contents of some or all of its frames may later change. Changing frame contents does not change the frameset definition. Once the content of a frame changes, the frameset definition no longer reflects the current state of its frames.

Q: Which frame does a browser utilize if I use the TARGET attribute both in an <A> tag and in a <BASE> tag in a Web page?

A: The browser uses the frame specified by the TARGET attribute of the <A> tag. It ignores the TARGET attribute of the <BASE> tag. The browser follows the four precedence rules discussed in section 15.5 of this chapter.

Q: Should frames be used in Web pages?

A: Because early browsers did not support frames or had problems updating them, many existing design guidelines for Web pages state that frames should not be used in Web pages. This advice used to be true in the early days of browsers and the Web, but it is no longer true today. Web authors should decide whether to use frames on the basis of the design needs of their pages only. All browsers today fully support normal frames, and inline frames are supported by Microsoft Internet Explorer.

Q: How can I make a hyperlink in a frame open in a new browser window, to avoid browsing the Web from the frame itself (which is only part of the entire browser window)?

A: Use the TARGET attribute, in the <A> tag that creates the hyperlink, as follows: **<A HREF** = "..." **TARGET** = "_top">. The value of the TARGET attribute is a standard name that the browser understands. This value tells the browser to open a new window of itself to display the Web page specified in the hyperlink.

15.8 Summary

Introduction

•Frames help Web authors in Web page design/layout and navigation.

•Web page design/layout can be enhanced by dividing a browser window into frames.

•Web page navigation can be enhanced by using target frames, where a user navigates in one frame and the navigation results are displayed in the target frame.

•HTML frames enable Web authors to display multiple HTML documents (multiple Web pages) in multiple views rendered by the browser on its same window. Each frame displays a Web page.

Frame Layout and Design

•One of the popular Web page designs that uses frames is a two-frame layout. One frame serves as a TOC or navigation menu, and the other displays the navigation results. The two-frame layout is effective for navigating hyperlinks, image maps, and forms.

•A three-frame layout for a Web page may be used, where the third frame can be used for advertising to display banners.

•The use of forms with frames is effective if a Web site has multiple forms that Web surfers can choose from.

•All browsers today support frames.

Frame Sets and Nesting

•The design and layout of Web pages using frames follow a common theme. That is, each frame has a shape/size, a screen location, and content. The shape is a rectangle that has a width and height. The screen location is left or right, top or bottom. The content is a Web page that is associated with the frame.

•Frames can divide a browser window vertically, horizontally, or both.

•A collection of frames is referred to as a frame set. Every frame set has a container that controls the layout of its frames.

•A frame set layout cannot be changed once it is displayed on the screen. Only the contents of each frame in the set can change.

•The HTML document that defines a frame set uses the <FRAMESET> tag in place of the <BODY> tag.

•The FRAMESET section of an HTML document defines the layout of the frames inside the frame container.

•When designing frames, keep the frame set simple, the frame contents short, and the frames organized.

•HTML defines the rules that browsers and Web authors follow to create frames and frame sets. Each frame must be sized and placed within the container of the frame set.

•A frame size is specified by the number of columns (COLS) and the number of rows (ROWS) in HTML. The units of ROWS and COLS could be either pixels or a percentage of the browser window.

•A browser places frames in its window left-to-right for columns and top-to-bottom for rows.

•There are two types of frame sets: simple and complex. Simple frame sets divide a browser window into rows or columns only. Complex sets create nested frames, by dividing the window both horizontally and vertically.

•Nested frame sets are created left-to-right in the top row, left-to-right in the second row, and so forth. HTML does not have a limit on the depth of frame nesting; in practice, however, one or two levels of nesting is all that is needed.

Frame Tags

•HTML frame tags are <FRAMESET>, <FRAME>, <IFRAME>, and <NOFRAMES>.

•The attributes of the <FRAMESET> tag are ROWS and COLS.

•The attributes of the <FRAME> tag are NAME, SRC, NORESIZE, SCROLLING, FRAMEBORDER, MARGINWIDTH, MARGINHEIGHT, and LONGDESC.

•The attributes of the <IFRAME> tag are NAME, SRC, SCROLLING, FRAMEBORDER, MARGINWIDTH, MARGINHEIGHT, LONGDESC, ALIGN, WIDTH, and HEIGHT.

•The <NOFRAMES> tag has no attributes.

Target Frames and Windows

•Without target frames, navigation with frames is difficult, because the Web surfer is forced to use the browser Back button.

•Target frames are defined as frames that receive contents from other frames.

•Target frames are little different from any other frames. The only extra requirement is to name them at the time of their creation, so that these names can be used in other HTML tags to refer to them.

•When many tags in the same HTML document use the same target frame, Web authors can use the <BASE> tag to specify the target frame once, for all of them, to eliminate the repetition involved in using the TARGET attribute of these tags.

•The <BASE> tag has its own TARGET attribute.

•Browsers follow the following precedence rules to determine the target frame used in an HTML tag. First, the browser looks for a TARGET attribute in the tag. If it does not find one, it looks for a TARGET attribute in the <BASE> tag. If it does not find one, it displays the HTML contents in the frame of the tag. Lastly, if a TARGET attribute uses an undefined frame name, the browser creates a new window of its own.

•Quick reference of the HTML tags covered in this chapter

Table 15.1   Summary of HTML frame tags.

Tag	Close	Attribute	Value	Example	Chpt. page
`<FRAMESET>`	Yes	ROWS	number	`<FRAMESET ROWS="100,2*,*">`	524
		COLS	number	`<FRAMESET COLS="30%,*,4*">`	
`<FRAME>`	No	NAME	text	`<FRAME NAME = "display">`	525
		SRC	file	`<FRAME SRC = "myFil.html">`	
		NORE-SIZE	none	`<FRAME NORESIZE>`	
		SCROLL-ING	auto (default)	`<FRAME>`	
			yes	`<FRAME SCROLLING = "yes">`	
			no	`<FRAME SCROLLING = "no">`	
		FRAME-BORDER	0 or 1	`<FARME FRAMEBORDER = 0>`	
		MAR-GIN-WIDTH	pixels	`<FRAME MARGINWIDTH = 10>`	
		MAR-GIN-HEIGHT	pixels	`<FRAME MARGINHEIGHT = 10>`	
		LONG-DESC	file	`<FRAME LONGDESC = "ff.html">`	

Table 15.1   Summary of HTML frame tags.

Tag	Close	Attribute	Value	Example	Chpt. page
<IFRAME>	Yes	The <IFRAME> tag has all the attributes of the <FRAME> tag except NORESIZE. In addition, it has the following attributes:			530
		ALIGN	top	`<IFRAME ALIGN = "TOP">`	
			middle	`<IFRAME ALIGN="MIDDLE">`	
			bottom	`<IFRAME ALIGN="BOTTOM">`	
		WIDTH	pixels	`<IFRAME WIDTH = 60>`	
		HEIGHT	pixels	`<IFRAME HEIGHT = 50>`	
<NOFRAMES>	Yes	None	N/A	`<NOFRAMES> HTML tags go here </NOFRAMES>`	533

PROBLEMS

Exercises

15.1 Create the two frame sets shown in figure 15.3. The ratio between the frame sizes for the horizontal set is 1:2:1, for the vertical set is 2:2:1. All frames are empty (i.e., holding no contents). Use all the attributes of the <FRAME> tag, with different values.

15.2 Create the nested frame sets shown in figure 15.4. The two rows and columns are of equal sizes for the set shown on the top of the figure. For the bottom set, use the following sizes. Width of Frame 2 is 40% of the width of the browser window. Height of Frame 1 is 30% of the height of the browser window. The width of Frame 3 is 35% of that of Frame 4. All frames are empty (i.e. holding no contents). Use all the attributes of the <FRAME> tag, with different values.

15.3 Rewrite the HTML code for example 15.2 so that the top row shown in figure 15.7 is divided into two columns and the bottom row has the full width of the browser window.

15.4 Rewrite the HTML code for example 15.2 so that the bottom row shown in figure 15.7 is divided into two columns and the top row has the full width of the browser window.

15.5 Rewrite the HTML code for example 15.4 so that the right frame shown in figure 15.10 is the TOC frame.

15.6 Rewrite the HTML code for example 15.4 so that a top frame is the TOC frame and a bottom frame is the target frame.

15.7 Rewrite the HTML code for exercise 15.5 so that it uses the <BASE> tag to define the target frame.

15.8 Rewrite the HTML code for exercise 15.6 so that it uses the <BASE> tag to define the target frame.

Homework

15.9 Create a Web page that uses nested and target frames to facilitate navigation of the page. The page design and layout is left up to you. Be imaginative.

15.10 Create a Web page that uses frames and uses unordered lists in its TOC frame.

15.11 Create a Web page uses frames and uses image maps in its TOC frame.

15.12 Create a Web page that uses frames and forms.

15.13 Create a two-frame set that displays food recipes. The TOC frame should list the names of the recipes, while the other frame displays their details.

15.14 Rewrite the HTML code for tutorial 15.6.1 so that it uses an unordered list instead of an ordered one.

15.15 Rewrite the HTML code for tutorial 15.6.2 so that it uses two horizontal frames and the horizontal image map created in example 11.1 in chapter 11.

15.16 Rewrite the HTML code for exercise 15.6.3 so that it uses horizontal frames instead of vertical ones.

15.17 Create the frame set shown in figure 15.17. The two columns are equal in size, the two rows in the left column are also equal in size, and the three rows in the right column are equal in size.

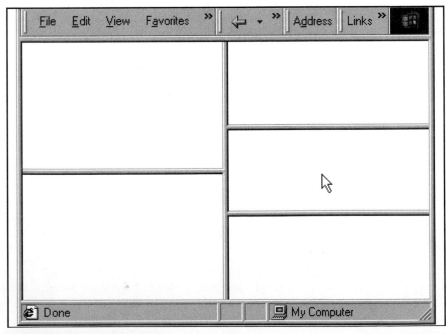

Figure 15.17   Problem 15.17.

Tables and Table Tags

This chapter covers the last HTML element that Web authors can use to develop Web pages and write HTML documents. It is tables and their tags. The use of HTML tables in Web pages goes beyond the tabulating of data, as in the case of traditional tables. They are frequently used to format Web pages and control their layout. Tables are especially used by HTML editors for formatting HTML documents. This chapter introduces the HTML table model. It begins by introducing tables and their importance. It then covers table structure and terminology. Layout and design of tables are introduced. The chapter also covers the table tags and their attributes. The calculations of table width and height and the sizes of its cells are covered. The chapter discusses nesting tables as an idea to control the layout and design of table cells. It also covers formatting Web pages via tables. At the end, the chapter presents tutorials that illustrate the use of tables in Web pages, FAQs, a summary of the important topics covered in the chapter, and problems.

16.1 Introduction

The formatting of Web pages has been an issue that we did not need or could ignore up until now. If the Web page is simple and has mainly text, formatting is not an issue. Web pages that have many HTML elements, including multimedia, would require formatting to arrange them properly in the pages. Frames, covered in chapter 15, offer limited formatting. They allow Web authors to divide a browser window into two or more frames; however, this is not really a solution to the formatting problem, because the original problem of arranging HTML in each Web page of each frame still exists.

Tables offer the optimal solution to the above formatting problem. A table is defined as a region that has rows and columns of small rectangles, called cells, that are arranged relative to each other in a certain way that makes up the table layout. Each cell holds its own data. When all the data of all the cells are displayed on the screen, the table layout, and therefore that of the data, is recognized. If the data of the table cells are such HTML elements as text, images, and so forth, Web authors can use tables to format their Web pages. As a matter of fact, we can even think of table cells as special frames. Thus, we can think of the table itself as a frame container that holds the cells' layout.

The HTML table model has been developed with the above formatting goal in mind. The model allows Web authors to include any HTML tag or combination of tags in a table cell. Thus, table cells can include text, hyperlinks, lists, images, colors, sound, video, forms, and so forth. In one extreme sense, we can include a full Web page in one table cell. Section 16.7 explores applying the HTML table model to formatting Web pages in more detail, with examples.

When tables are used to format Web pages, writing the HTML code of these pages becomes harder than writing without using tables. Thus, such code also becomes difficult to follow. Web authors would need to lay out the design of their Web pages with tables on paper, so that they can refer to it during the writing process of the HTML code. If this process of writing HTML code manually while using tables for formatting proves to be difficult for Web authors, they can use HTML editors, as covered in chapter 17.

HTML editors use tables for formatting when they implement the layouts of complex Web pages with many HTML elements. As a matter of fact, we use this observation to distinguish HTML code that is written manually (by hand) from code that is generated automatically by an HTML editor. During Web surfing, a Web surfer can tell whether a Web page was created manually or by an editor, simply by checking its source code. The surfer clicks `View => Page Source` or `View => Source` to view the HTML in Netscape Communicator or MS IE respectively. If the code has many tables and table tags all over the page code, then most likely it was created by an HTML editor. The Web surfer can check the <META> tag of the code for the editor name and version to be certain.

In addition to use in formatting Web pages, the HTML table model supports the more traditional use of tables. That is the of tabulating numerical data. Tables can be used to create matrices of data that describe, say, products, statistical results, and so forth. Let us assume that a company has many individual components that can be assembled in many ways to build products. The company can show a matrix of choices on its Web site. The matrix can show the product function, name, components, price, maintenance procedure, and delivery time. A non-profit organization may collect data about endangered species and tabulate it in tables published on its Web site. The table may include the name, the number, the geographical region, and the climate of each species.

When HTML tables are used for tabulating numerical data, they can follow the in footsteps of traditional tables. Web authors can create captions and headings for the tables. They can use different background colors for table cells. For example, a column or a row of a table may have a different color from another column or a row. A table may have horizontal or vertical headings, or both. One heading row goes across the table on the top, while a heading column goes along the table on the left. Web authors can control the size of tables. They can specify the width and the height of a table. Using this width and the height, the browser fits all the table cells, with their respective data, within the table display area.

One reason for the popularity of tables is attributed to organizing data in columns and rows, with little effort. Tables make data easy to understand. They reveal the correlation between data elements. They also reveal any trends that the data hold. Moreover, tables are easy to create in HTML.

HTML provides Web authors with table tags that they can use to add tables to their Web pages. The <TABLE>, <TH>, <TR>, and <TD> tags are the primary tags used to create tables. These tags have many attributes, as covered in section 16.4 of this chapter. The section also covers other tags.

How many tables can Web authors have in one Web page? Web authors can include as many tables as they need, if tables are used to tabulate data. Including more than one table makes the Web page multiple screens long — not a good idea from Web page design point of view. For formatting purposes, one table is usually enough to control the page layout. Such a table may include a nested table to offer finer control of table cells.

16.2 Table Structure and Variables

Tables are made out of grids of rows and columns. The grid elements are the table cells. HTML provides many variables that allow Web authors to control table structure. This is important if tables are to be used for formatting Web pages. For example, rows and columns can be grouped together. Such grouping affects the table rendering and display by browsers. Another example is that table cells may vary in size to accommodate different types of data. Consider the case of a table cell that holds an image. The cell may span multiple rows and columns to fit the image size correctly.

The HTML table variables may be grouped into two categories: non-cell and cell. Non-cell variables control the properties and structure of the table. These variables specify the table caption, summary, border, header, rows, columns, width, height, cells, and rules. Figure 16.1 shows these variables. The table caption is its title which provides a short description of the table's purpose. It can placed at the top of the table, as shown in the figure, or at the bottom. The table summary provides a longer description that may be used by people using speech or Braille-based browsers. The table border is its outside boundary. We can think of it as the table container.

The remaining non-cell variables are related to the table rows, columns, and cells. The table header is the first row in the table. Each cell in this row is a header for the column underneath it. It holds the title of the column. Table rows are the horizontal layout of the cells. Similarly, table columns are the vertical layout of the cells. The width and height of a table are a representation of the number of its rows and columns respectively. HTML allows Web authors to specify a table width and a height. When Web authors specify table width, the browser finds the width of a table cell by dividing the width of the page by the number of columns. If no width is specified, the browser uses a default value. Similarly, the browser finds the cell height by dividing the table height by the number of rows. If Web authors do not specify a table height, the browser uses a default value.

Cells are the basic units that make a table. Cells are arranged within the table border top-to-bottom, left-to-right. Thus, the cells' layout uses the top left corner of the table as the origin of the grid of the cells. As shown in figure 16.1, each cell location in the layout is defined by two counters to specify its horizontal and vertical positions. The first counter is the number of the cell row. The second counter is the number of the cell column. Thus, Cell (i, j) is located at row i and column j. Each cell holds its own data. Data could be any HTML element.

The horizontal and vertical lines that separate the cells from each other are known as rulings (or rules, as HTML calls them). Web authors can make these rules visible or invisible. They can remove them for a group of cells to create a connected area in the table. The thickness of these rules may be specified.

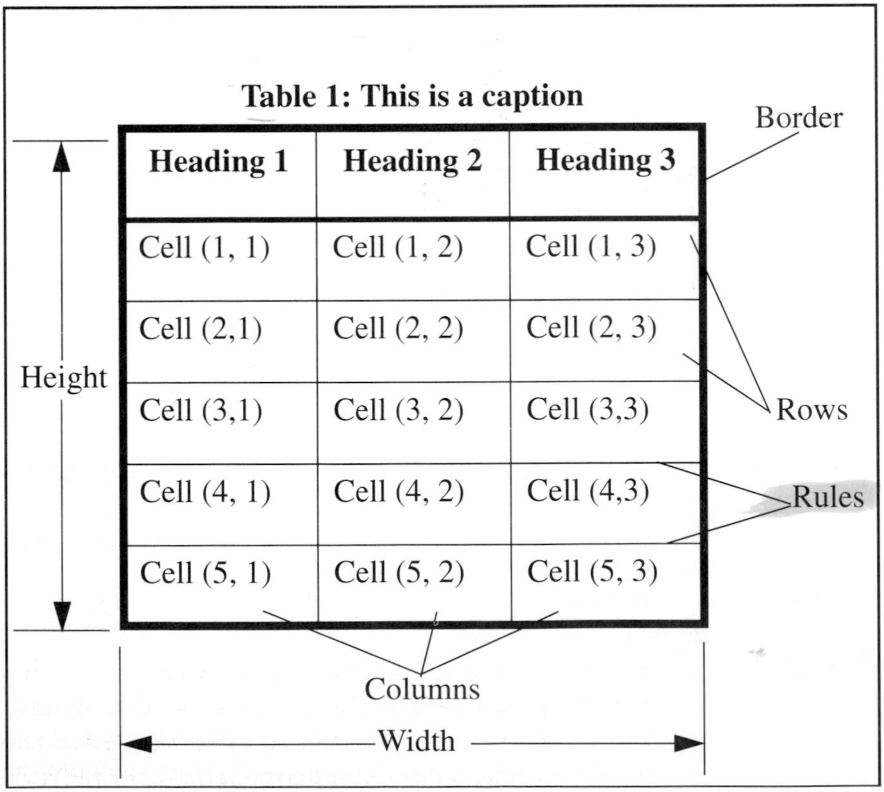

Figure 16.1 Table structure.

Cell variables control the properties and structure of individual cells. These variables specify the row span, column span, padding, spacing, and alignment of data within the cell. Figure 16.2 shows these variables. This figure shows a large cell in the center that spans four rows and two columns. This cell is surrounded by other cells that span one row and one column. The browser determines the smallest size (width and height) of a table cell by using the table width and height, together with the number of rows and columns of the table, as described above. Using this size as a basis, Web authors may specify a larger cell size if needed by using the row and column spans.

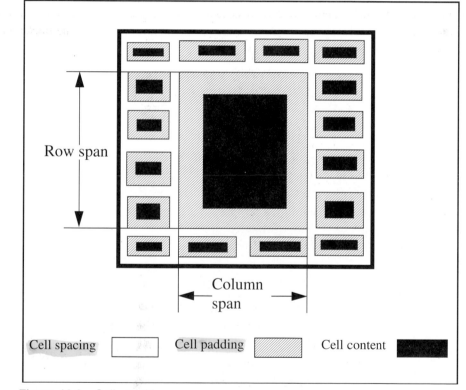

Figure 16.2 Cell variables.

Cell spacing describes the amount of the horizontal and vertical spacing between cells, as shown in figure 16.2. Web authors can use cell spacing to control the amount of white (or background color of Web page) space that is needed to separate the various data of the cells. Let us say that one cell holds an image and another cell holds a form. If Web authors use large enough cell spacing, the two elements could look as if each is in a separate frame.

Cell padding is equivalent to specifying top, bottom, left, and right margins for the cell. The padding describes the amount of horizontal and vertical spacing between cell content (data) and its borders. The color of the cell padding is the color of the cell background, which could be different from the background color of the Web page itself.

Cell content or data can be aligned within each cell both in the horizontal and vertical directions. Web authors have three choices to align data in either direction. Data could be aligned to the left (left justified), middle, or right (right justified) of the cell in the horizontal direction. In the vertical direction, data could be aligned to the top (top justified), middle, or bottom (bottom justified) of the cell. If the cell data fills the entire cell space, no effect of alignment is visible, as the data cannot move within the cell.

The table tags provide Web authors with many attributes that allow them to specify both the non-cell and cell variables discussed above. These tags and attributes are covered in section 16.4.

16.3 Table Layout and Design

The purpose of using a table determines its layout and design. If the table is used in the conventional way to tabulate data, three styles may be chosen from, depending on the table header. Figure 16.3 shows the three possible styles. The table header could be on the top or on the left side, or the table may have both top and left headers. The choice of a header depends on the data that is to be presented. Tables used for tabulating data usually have cells that span one row and one column each.

If tables are used for formatting Web pages, the table layout is dramatically different from tables displaying data. Headings are eliminated, as they are not needed. Sizes of cells are different. Some cells may span multiple rows and columns, while other cells are left empty to provide spacing between cell data. Table border and rules are eliminated to make the flow of the elements or content of a Web page smooth and seamless. A color may be assigned to the table background. Other different colors may be assigned to the background of cells. Cells could hold any of the MIME types of data, including images, lists, and hyperlinks.

Web authors must consider an important design issue of tables, regardless of whether the table is used for displaying data or for formatting Web pages. That is the size of the computer screen. A table may be designed with a large width and height for display on large screens. If this same table is displayed on smaller screens, it would fail to fit within them and so force the browsers to create scroll bars to view the full table. Such scrolling is a not a good idea. Web authors should use the width and height that fit the most common screen size. In some cases, the tables may be displayed in such a disarray that the Web surfers cannot read the Web page. Web authors should test their Web pages on multiple platforms with multiple screen sizes to ensure their correct display.

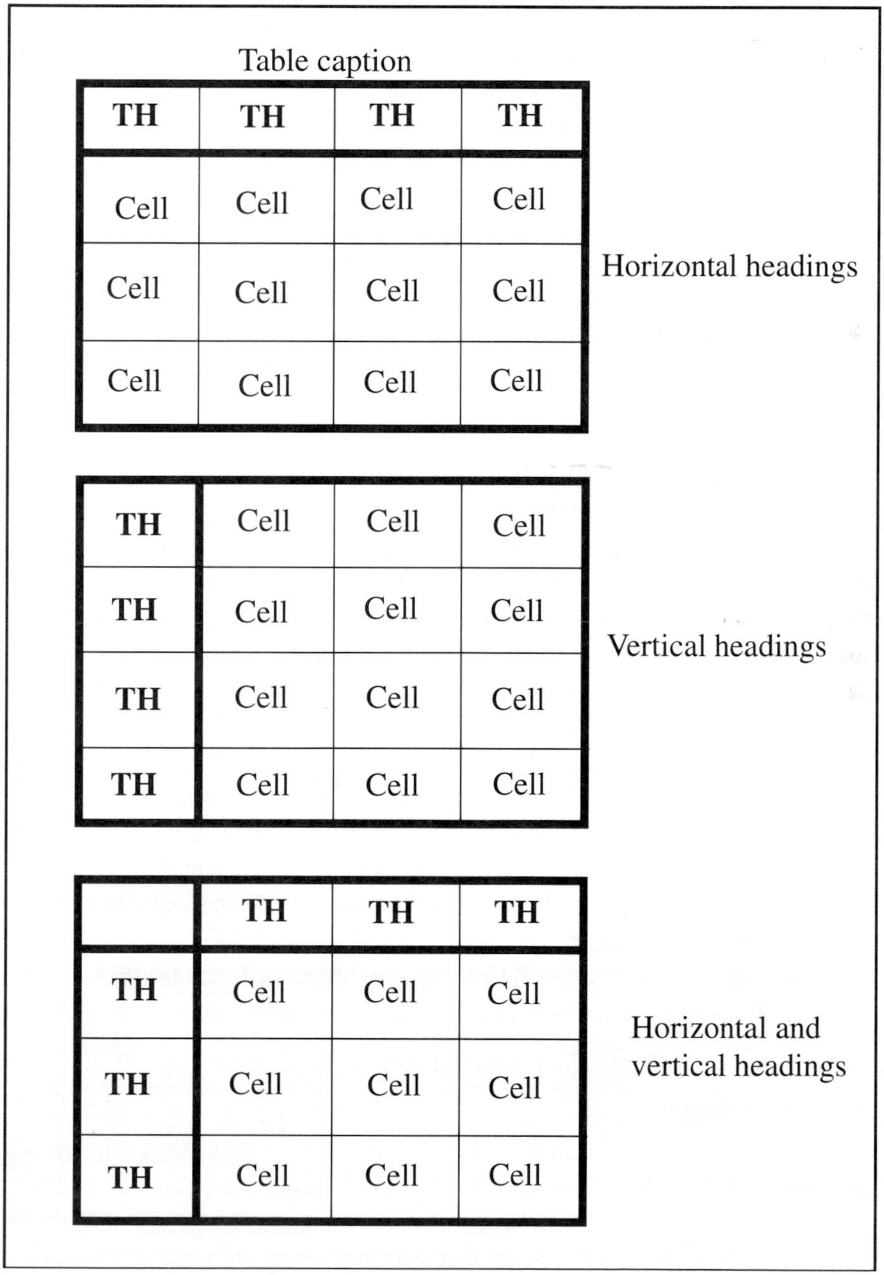

Figure 16.3 Table layout.

16.4 Table Tags

HTML provides all the tags necessary to create tables and control their structures. These tags and their attributes allow Web authors to design table layouts both for data display and for Web page formatting purposes. There are also enough tags at the cell level to control cell contents. The table tags covered in this section use all the concepts and variables introduced in section 16.2. The available table tags are <TABLE>, <CAPTION>, <TH>, <TR>, and <TD>. All these tags are covered here.

16.4.1 <TABLE> Tag

This is the master tag that encloses any other table tags. This tag must close. Thus, the end tag, </TABLE>, must always be used to tell the browser where a table ends. This is necessary when nesting tables. The attributes of this tag are SUMMARY, WIDTH, HEIGHT, BORDER, ALIGN, FRAME, RULES, CELLSPACING, and CELLPADDING. These attributes are described in the following list.

•The SUMMARY attribute provides a brief description of the table's purpose and structure. A browser uses this attribute when it renders the table to non-visual media for the disabled.

•The WIDTH and the HEIGHT attributes specify the entire width and height of the table respectively. They may be specified in pixels. If either or none of them is specified, the browser determines them automatically.

•The BORDER attribute specifies the thickness of the table border in pixels.

•The ALIGN attribute specifies the table position with respect to the documents. Its values are LEFT (left-justifies the table), CENTER (centers the table in the document), and RIGHT (right-justifies the table). LEFT is the default value.

•The FRAME attribute specifies the visibility of the sides of the frame that surrounds a table. Its values are VOID (no sides are shown), ABOVE (show top side only), BELOW (show bottom side only), LHS (show left-hand side only), RHS (show right-hand side only), HSIDES (show horizontal sides, i.e., top and bottom), VSIDES (show vertical sides, i.e., left and right), BOX (show all four sides), and BORDER (show all four sides). The default value is VOID. This attribute is rendered only by MS IE.

•The RULES attribute specifies which rules between cells are visible. Its values are NONE, GROUPS (rules appear between row groups and column groups only), ROWS (rules appear between rows only), COLS (rules appear between columns only), and ALL (rules appear between rows and columns). ALL is the default value. This attribute is rendered only by MS IE.

•The CELLSPACING attribute specifies the amount of space both between the table cells and between the cells and the table sides, as shown in figure 16.2. Its value is specified in pixels.

•The CELLPADDING attribute specifies the space between the contents of a cell and its border. Its value is specified in pixels or as a percentage of cell space. For example, CELLPADDING = "20%" means that the top and bottom margins of the cell are each 10% of the cell height, and the left and right margins of the cell are each 10% of the cell width.

Example 16.1 Develop a Web page that illustrates the use of tables.

Solution This example creates a Web page that uses the attributes of the <TABLE> tag. The example uses five attributes: ALIGN, BORDER, WIDTH HEIGHT, and CELLSPACING. The FRAME and RULES attributes are not used because not all browsers render them. The CELLPADDING attribute is used later in the chapter, when cells have more content. Using a text editor, type the code that follows, and save it as *example16.1.html*. Figure 16.4 shows the Web page. As shown in the figure, the browser uses a default cell spacing if none is specified.

```
<HTML>
<HEAD>
<TITLE>A Web page with tables</TITLE>
</HEAD>
<BODY>
<FONT COLOR = "red"><CENTER>This table uses no border</CENTER></
FONT>
<TABLE ALIGN = "center">
<TR><TD>Cell 1<TD>Cell 2<TD>Cell 3
<TR><TD>Cell 4<TD>Cell 5<TD>Cell 6
</TABLE>
<P>
<FONT COLOR = "red"><CENTER>This table has a border that is 4 pix-
els thick<CENTER></FONT>
<TABLE ALIGN = "center" BORDER = 4>
<TR><TD>Cell 1<TD>Cell 2<TD>Cell 3
<TR><TD>Cell 4<TD>Cell 5<TD>Cell 6
</TABLE>
<P>
<FONT COLOR = "red"><CENTER>This table has a width of 200 pixels, a
height of 100 pixels, and a border that is 4 pixels thick<CENTER>
</FONT>
<TABLE ALIGN = "center" BORDER = 4 WIDTH = 200 HEIGHT = 100>
<TR><TD>Cell 1<TD>Cell 2<TD>Cell 3
<TR><TD>Cell 4<TD>Cell 5<TD>Cell 6
</TABLE>
<P>
<FONT COLOR = "red"><CENTER>This table has a width of 200 pixels, a
height of 100 pixels, a border that is 4 pixels thick, and cell
spacing of 8 pixels</CENTER></FONT>
<TABLE ALIGN = "center" BORDER = 4 WIDTH = 200 HEIGHT = 100 CELL-
SPACING = 8>
<TR><TD>Cell 1<TD>Cell 2<TD>Cell 3
<TR><TD>Cell 4<TD>Cell 5<TD>Cell 6
</TABLE>
</BODY>
</HTML>
```

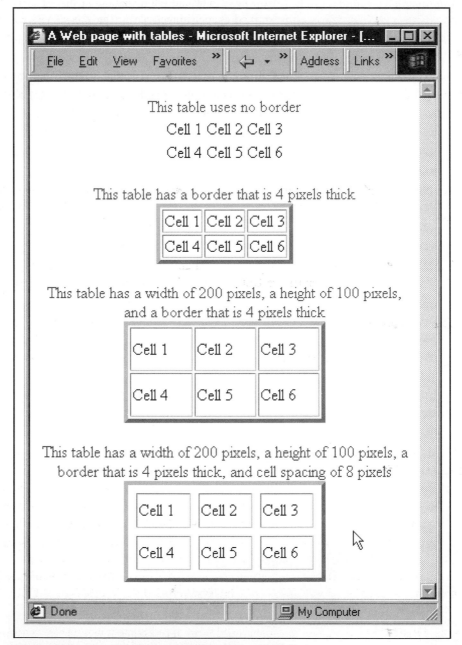

Figure 16.4   Results of the attributes of the <TABLE> tag.

16.4.2 <CAPTION> Tag

This tag assigns a caption or a title to a table. The caption text should be descriptive of the table nature and goal. This tag is not permitted except immediately after the <TABLE> tag. It comes before any other table tag is used. This tag cannot be used more than once. The tag must close. (It requires an end tag.)

The <CAPTION> tag has only one attribute, ALIGN. It has four possible values. The TOP value places the caption at the top of the table. This is the default value. BOTTOM, LEFT, and RIGHT place the caption at the bottom, left, and right of the table, respectively.

16.4.3 <TR> Tag

This tag creates the rows of a table. Its end tag is optional. Thus, it may or may not close. The number of rows in a table is equal to the number of occurrences of the <TR> tag inside the <TABLE> tag. The <TR> tag acts as a container for a row of table cells. The attributes of this tag are ALIGN and VALIGN. These attributes are described as follows:

•The ALIGN attribute specifies the horizontal alignment of cell content (within the cell) for all the cells of the row. Its values are LEFT (left-justify content), CENTER (center-justify content), and RIGHT (right-justify content). LEFT is the default value.

•The VALIGN attribute specifies the vertical alignment of cell content (within the cell) for all the cells of the row. Its values are TOP (content flush with the top of the cell), MIDDLE (center content vertically within the cell), and BOTTOM (content flush with the bottom of the cell). CENTER is the default value.

16.4.4 <TH> and <TD> Tags

These two tags create table cells. There are two types of cells, as indicated by these two tags. Heading cells display the headings of the table rows, columns, or both as shown in figure 16.3. The table heading tag, <TH>, creates this type of cells. The <TH> tag causes the headings to appear in bold font when they are rendered by a browser. Data cells hold and display the table data and content, as shown in figure 16.3. The table data tag, <TD>, creates data cells. Data cells may be empty (contain no data). In this case, they are used for formatting the Web page by providing empty spaces. The <TH> and <TD> tags are not different from each other, except in displaying headings in bold. Thus, they share the same attributes, which are ABBR, AXIS, HEADERS, SCOPE, ROWSPAN, COLSPAN, NOWRAP, ALIGN, VALIGN, and CELLPADDING. These attributes are described in the following list.

•The ABBR attribute provides an abbreviated form of cell content that may be rendered by browsers in place of the cell content when appropriate, such as for disabled Web surfers using speech synthesizers.

•The AXIS attribute specifies categories of cells. Each category forms an axis. A user may use this attribute to query a browser for all the cells that belong to a certain category. This may be done using a scripting language such as JavaScript.

•The HEADERS attribute is used to help non-visual Web surfers who use non-visual browsers. The attribute specifies header information for a data cell. This information is spoken prior to displaying the cell data.

•The SCOPE attribute may replace the HEADERS attribute for simple tables. It specifies the set of data cells for which the current header cell provides header information. The values of this attribute are ROW, COL, ROWGROUP, and COLGROUP. If we use, say, SCOPE = "row" for a cell, such a cell provides header information for the rest of the cells of this row.

•The ROWSPAN attribute specifies the number of rows that the cell spans. The default value is one (1). The value zero (0) means that the cell spans all rows from the current row to the last row of the table.

•The COLSPAN attribute is the companion of the ROWSPAN attribute. It performs the same functionality for columns instead of rows. Its value could be a number, 1, or 0 as above. Cells may span several rows and columns, as shown in figure 16.2. Cell definitions that span more than one row or column affect the definition of later cells.

•The NOWRAP attribute is a boolean attribute. Its use tells browsers to disable automatic text wrapping for a cell. This tag may result in excessively wide cells.

•The ALIGN attribute specifies the horizontal alignment of cell content within the cell. Its values are LEFT (left-justify content), CENTER (center-justify content), and RIGHT (right-justify content). LEFT is the default value. This attribute overrides the same attribute of the <TR> tag.

•The VALIGN attribute specifies the vertical alignment of cell content within the cell. Its values are TOP (content flush with the top of the cell), MIDDLE (center content vertically within the cell), and BOTTOM (content flush with the bottom of the cell). CENTER is the default value. This attribute overrides the same attribute of the <TR> tag.

•The CELLPADDING attribute works like the same attribute of the <TABLE> tag. If it is used with the <TH> or <TD> tag, it applies (locally to the cell only). If it is used with the <TABLE> tag, it applies globally to all table cells. The local value overrides the global one.

Example 16.2 Develop a Web page that illustrates the use of variable-size table cells.

Solution This example creates a Web page that uses some attributes of the <TD> tag. The example uses the ROWSPAN, COLSPAN, and ALIGN attributes. Using a text editor, type the following code and save it as *example16.2.html* (figures 16.5 shows the resulting Web page):

```
<HTML>
<HEAD>
<TITLE>A Web page with variable-size table cells</TITLE>
</HEAD>
```

```
<BODY>
<FONT COLOR = "red"><CENTER>This table uses equal size cells</CEN-
TER></FONT>
<TABLE ALIGN = "center" BORDER = 4>
<TR><TD>Cell 1<TD>Cell 2<TD>Cell 3<TD>Cell 4
<TR><TD>Cell 5<TD>Cell 6<TD>Cell 7<TD>Cell 8
<TR><TD>Cell 9<TD>Cell 10<TD>Cell 11<TD>Cell 12
</TABLE>
<P>
<FONT COLOR = "red"><CENTER>This table uses cell 5 that spans two
rows and three columns</CENTER></FONT>
<TABLE ALIGN = "center" BORDER = 4>
<TR><TD>Cell 1<TD>Cell 2<TD>Cell 3<TD>Cell 4
<TR><TD ROWSPAN = 2 COLSPAN = 3 ALIGN = "center">Cell 5<TD>Cell
6<TD>Cell 7<TD>Cell 8
<TR><TD>Cell 9<TD>Cell 10<TD>Cell 11<TD>Cell 12
</TABLE>
<P>
<FONT COLOR = "red"><CENTER>This table uses cell 5 that spans two
rows and three columns. The table also has a width of 200 pixels, a
height of 100 pixels, and cell spacing of 8 pixels</CENTER></FONT>
<TABLE ALIGN = "center" BORDER = 4 WIDTH = 200 HEIGHT = 100 CELL-
SPACING = 8>
<TR><TD>Cell 1<TD>Cell 2<TD>Cell 3<TD>Cell 4
<TR><TD ROWSPAN = 2 COLSPAN = 3 ALIGN = "center">Cell 5<TD>Cell
6<TD>Cell 7<TD>Cell 8
<TR><TD>Cell 9<TD>Cell 10<TD>Cell 11<TD>Cell 12
</TABLE>
</BODY>
</HTML>
```

The table shown in figure 16.5 has three rows and four columns, producing twelve cells. The example investigates the effect of the attributes of the <TD> tag on the table rendering. The first table shown in the figure does not use any attributes of the tag. The browser has full freedom to render the table cells. They all look equal in size, however, if a cell has larger text than do others, its size increases. The second table uses a cell that spans two rows and three columns. The browser must create Cell 5 with this size, yet it must create the other cells. The only way to meet both these constraints is to enlarge the table width.

If we add one more constraint, the browser must change the way the table looks. The third table shown in the figure is the same as the second table, but with a width and a height of 200 and 100 pixels, respectively. While the two labels have the same general layout, they look different.

The conclusion to make here is that the browser adjusts the cell size based on the cell content, its attributes, and the attributes of the <TABLE> tag that affect cells, such as table width, height, cell spacing, and so forth. Web authors must give careful thought to table rendering during the phase of table design. They may use an iterative approach to design tables. First, they build a simple table. Then, they start adding more attributes, to control the table size, the sizes of its cells, and the spacing between and within cells. Also, attention should be paid to cell layout. Usually, rows or columns of a table have the same number of cells. When Web authors begin using cells that span more than one row or column, they may want to reduce the number of cells compensatingly, to avoid having empty spacing in the table, as shown in figure 16.5. Web authors may eliminate cells 7, 8, 10, 11, and 12 to remove the empty space in the table.

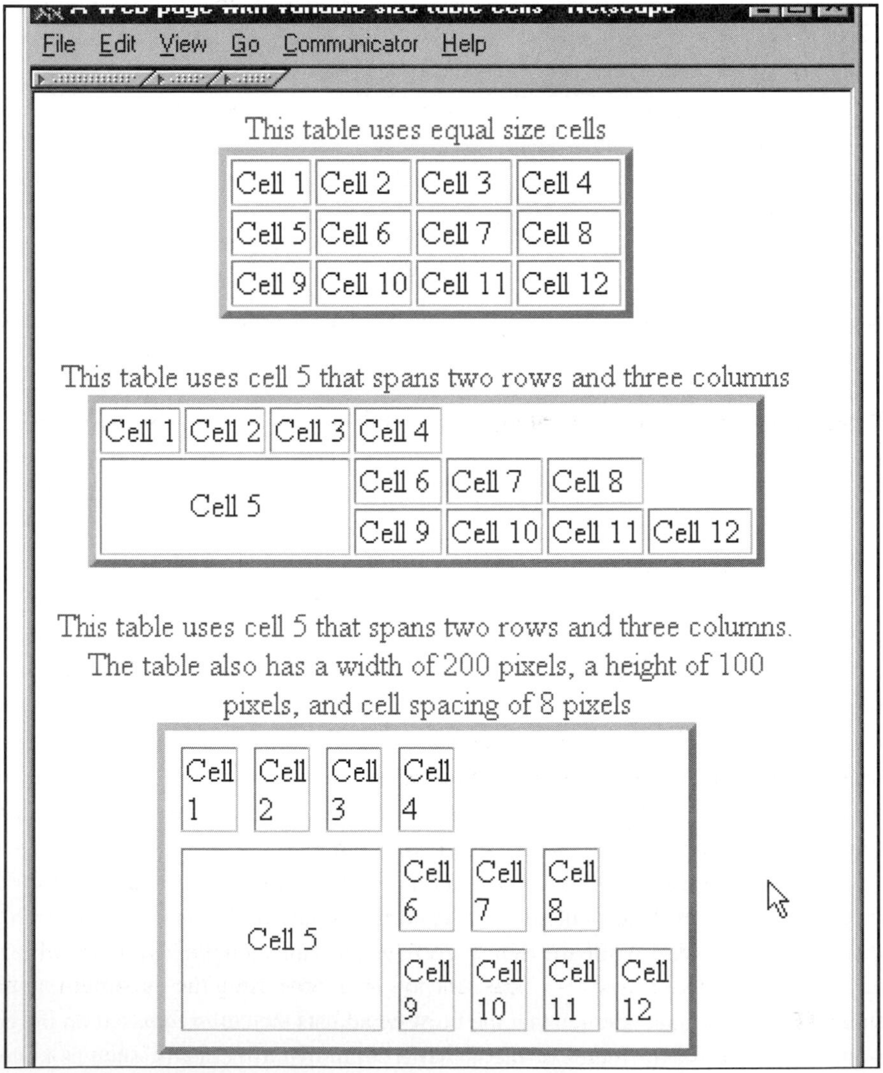

Figure 16.5   Results of the attributes of the <TD> tag.

16.5 Table Rendering and Calculations

As we have discussed in the previous sections, there are many conflicting variables and attributes of tables and their tags. There are variables at the table level (non-cell variables) and cell variables. Web authors may specify just rows and columns in the simplest case, to create a table; or they can specify rows, columns, table width and height, cell spans, and cell padding. In addition to all these variables, the browser still must ensure the proper display of cell contents that can range from simple text to images, lists, hyperlinks, and so forth.

How does a browser resolve all these conflicts? What are the basic issues in rendering tables? What are the precedence rules that a browser uses? The main issue in rendering tables is the display of cell contents. The content of each cell must be displayed properly and correctly. The browser uses all the table and cell variables entered by Web authors via attributes, to decide the table layout and the minimum cell size. During this decision process, the browser may ignore some variables, or variables may override each other. Once the minimum cell size is determined, the browser uses it as the common denominator to determine other cell sizes. For example, if a cell uses two row spans, its height is double the height of the minimum cell size.

While Web authors are not expected to fully understand the mathematical algorithms a browser uses to perform table calculations, they need to fully understand the effect of the tags and attributes they use to develop tables. Such understanding allows them to control table design and display. The following rules are used by browsers to render and calculate tables.

1. **Calculating table width and height.** Web authors must specify the number of columns and rows to create a table. In addition, they may also specify a table width, height, or both, as needed. If no table width or height is specified, the browser determines it. It first receives all the cell data, rows, and columns. Using all this information, it calculates the amount of horizontal and vertical space required by the table. If Web authors specify a table width and/or height, they can use one of two methods: fixed or percentage. A table width and/or height are specified via the WIDTH and HEIGHT attributes of the <TABLE> tag. A fixed specification is given in pixels (WIDTH = 600 HEIGHT = 500). A percentage specification is based on the screen width and/or height at the time of displaying the table (WIDTH = 70% HEIGHT = 60%).

2. **Calculating the number of columns in a table.** The browser uses the cells required by the table rows to calculate the maximum number of columns of the table. This number is equal to the number of columns required by the row with the most columns, including cells that span multiple columns. Once this maximum number is calculated by the browser, it becomes the number of columns for each row in the table. Any row that has fewer than this number of columns is padded by empty cells at its end. Under this method of calculations, there is always at least one row in a table using the maximum number of columns. Let us apply this method to the last two tables shown in figure 16.5. The last column has seven columns (cells): one cell that spans three columns and four additional cells. Thus, the maximum number of columns for this table is seven. Any row in the table must

therefore have seven columns. As a result, the browser uses three additional empty cells to render the first row and one extra empty cell to render the second rows.

3. **Calculating the size of a table cell.** After a browser calculates a table width and height and a number of columns, it uses these variables, together with cell content (data) and spacing, to determine the minimum cell size (width and height). If cell data fits within this minimum size, the browser uses it. If cell data needs more space for display, the browser increases the minimum cell size accordingly. The browser must also adjust other cells in the table to accommodate the larger cell size. To clarify this explanation, consider the second table shown in figure 16.5. All the cells of this table, except `Cell 5`, have an equal size, which is the minimum cell size. The data of each of these cells fits within this size. Let us force the data of, say, `Cell 7` to exceed this minimum size, by changing its content to `Cell 7777777777`. Figure 16.6 shows the results. The browser increases the size of `Cell 7` to accommodate the new cell content. As a result, all the cells in the same column as `Cell 7` assume the new size as well, to maintain the table integrity. In addition, comparing figures 16.5 and 16.6 shows that the minimum cell size has changed and that the table looks different.

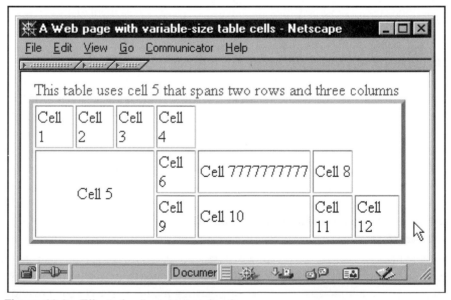

Figure 16.6   Effect of cell content on its size.

4. **Calculating cell spacing and padding.** Web authors may specify cell spacing and padding in two ways: fixed and percentage. The CELLSPACING and CELLPADDING attributes of the <TD> tag use a number of pixels in fixed specification (CELLSPACING = 10 CELLPADDING = 20). In the percentage specification, cell spacing is a percentage

of the table width or height. The browser calculates both and uses the smaller number. For example, if we specify CELLSPACING = 10% for a table whose width and height are 200 and 100 pixels respectively, the amount of cell spacing the browser uses is 10 pixels (10% of 100 pixels). This same percentage calculation applies to cell padding, but it uses the *cell* width and height. The browser waits to calculate the cell padding until it has already determined the cell width and height as described above. Unlike cell spacing, the actual margin space around cell boundaries is half the specified amount in the cell padding attribute. For example, using CELLPADDING = 20% results in an equal amount of 10% for each of the left, right, top, and bottom margins of the designated cell.

5. **Inheritance of alignment specifications.** The alignment of cell content can be specified at two levels: cell, or row. Cell content can be aligned horizontally or vertically within the cell via the ALIGN or VALIGN attributes. If cell-level control is needed, these attributes are used with the <TH> and/or <TD> tags. If row-level control (applies to all row cells) is needed, these attributes are used with the <TR> tag. What happens if Web authors specify both levels of control at the same time? The browser uses a precedence rule. It always applies cell-level control, and ignores row-level control, if both levels are specified. If cell-level control is absent, the browser applies row-level control to all cells of the row. If neither level is specified, the browser uses the default values of alignment, as specified by the ALIGN and VALIGN attributes.

16.6 Nesting Tables

Web authors may nest tables to achieve certain design goals of their Web pages. When tables are used to format Web pages (as discussed in section 16.7), table nesting may be used to control the formatting. Table nesting makes the HTML code quite complex and difficult to follow and understand, unless Web authors knows how the nesting is achieved. In general, nesting one object into another bigger object always happens at the level of a basic unit of the bigger object. Consider nesting frames, discussed in chapter 15. When we nest one frame set into another, the basic unit is a frame (row or column). The browser uses an available frame and inserts another entire frame set into it. The frames of the inserted frame set constitute the contents of the original frame.

How do browsers nest tables? The basic unit in a table is the cell. A cell is the smallest component a table can have. Thus, a cell content could be an entire table. Or, it could be a combination of a table and other data. For example, a cell could have text followed by a table. Web authors who wish to create a nested table in a certain cell location simply add the HTML code (that creates the inner table), after the <TD> tag of the cell. Therefore, this code is inserted between two subsequent <TD> tags of the outer table. Web authors may create an entire row of nested tables by using the <TABLE> tag after each <TD> tag of the row cells. Once you know how to create nested tables, reading HTML code that uses them is the reverse process. One would follow the code cell by cell, using the <TD> tags. Whenever a <TABLE> tag is encountered, it means that the related cell holds a nested table. The outer <TABLE> tag defines the table holding all the others.

When Web authors use nested tables, they should pay close attention to their rendering. For example, most likely they would not need to use their BORDER attributes, as they want them to blend seamlessly with the cells and boundaries of the outer table holding them. Actually, borders are usually not used if tables are used for formatting.

Nesting tables may produce awkward results. The sizes of table cells may vary greatly. The locations of empty cells may not be acceptable to Web authors. Moreover, the outer table proportions may not be optimal. The outer table may be wide and skinny, or tall and thin. We can overcome this problem by specifying the width and height of the outer table. The most general rule that Web authors should follow when dealing with nested tables is trial and error. Start by creating the nested table set as nearly as possible. Use a browser to display the set. Evaluate the display, change the code, and display again. Repeat this process as many times as is necessary, until the best design and layout of the table set is achieved.

Example 16.3 Develop a Web page that illustrates the use of nested tables.

Solution This example uses the Web page of example 16.2. It adds a nested table to each of the three tables shown in figure 16.5. We create a nested table within the top table in the Cell 2 location. The nested table has one row and three columns. As shown in the code below, and in figure 16.7, the content of Cell 2 of the outer table is text that reads Nested Table, followed by the nested table itself. The same table is nested two more times, once within the middle table in the Cell 7 location, and once within the bottom table in the Cell 11 location. In the last two nestings, the text preceding the table is removed to show different results. Using a text editor, type the following code and save it as *example16.3.html* (figures 16.7 shows the resulting Web page):

```
<HTML>
<HEAD>
<TITLE>A Web page with nested tables</TITLE>
</HEAD>
<BODY>
<FONT COLOR = "red"><CENTER>Cell 2 is an entire table</CENTER></
FONT>
<TABLE  ALIGN = "center" BORDER = 4>
<TR><TD>Cell 1<TD>Nested table
<TABLE ROWS =2 COLS = 3>
<TR><TD>T21<TD>T22<TD>T23
</TABLE>
<TD>Cell 3<TD>Cell 4
<TR><TD>Cell 5<TD>Cell 6<TD>Cell 7<TD>Cell 8
<TR><TD>Cell 9<TD>Cell 10<TD>Cell 11<TD>Cell 12
</TABLE>
```

```
<FONT COLOR = "red"><CENTER>Cell 7 is an entire table<CENTER></
FONT>
<TABLE  ALIGN = "center" BORDER = 4 CELLSPACING = 10%>
<TR><TD>Cell 1<TD>Cell 2<TD>Cell 3<TD>Cell 4
<TR><TD ROWSPAN = 2 COLSPAN = 3>Cell 5<TD>Cell 6<TD>
<TABLE ROWS =2 COLS = 3 BORDER = 5>
<TR><TD>T21<TD>T22<TD>T23
</TABLE>
<TD>Cell 8
<TR><TD>Cell 9<TD>Cell 10<TD>Cell 11<TD>Cell 12
</TABLE>
<FONT COLOR = "red"><CENTER>Cell 11 is an entire table</CENTER></
FONT>
<TABLE   ALIGN = "center" BORDER = 4 WIDTH = 200 HEIGHT = 100 CELL-
SPACING = 10>
<TR><TD>Cell 1<TD>Cell 2<TD>Cell 3<TD>Cell 4
<TR><TD ALIGN = "center" ROWSPAN = 2 COLSPAN = 3>Cell 5<TD>Cell
6<TD>Cell 7<TD>Cell 8
<TR><TD>Cell 9<TD>Cell 10<TD>
<TABLE ROWS =2 COLS = 3 BORDER = 5>
<TR><TD>T21<TD>T22<TD>T23
</TABLE>
<TD>Cell 12
</TABLE>
</BODY>
</HTML>
```

As shown in figure 16.7, the names of the cells of the nested table are T21, T22, and T23. The first digit indicates the table number (we use number 2 for the nested table; 1 being the number of the outer table), and the second digit indicates the cell number of the nested table. The figure also shows how the nested table flows after the text of the cell in the top table. While we have nested the same table into the three other tables, the resulting nested tables look different from each other. In all the tables, the cells of the column that holds the nested table have been stretched to accommodate the table.

16.7 Formatting Via Tables

On of the ultimate goals of using tables in HTML is to use them to format Web pages. Without tables, the formatting of Web pages would be limited to using a limited set of HTML tags, such as <CENTER>, and to using frames. If we examine carefully all the Web pages that we have created in the previous chapters of this book, we realize that they are all left-justified. Most, if not all, of the Web pages that are available on the Web are formatted via tables. One can simply check the HTML code by viewing the page source code to confirm this observation.

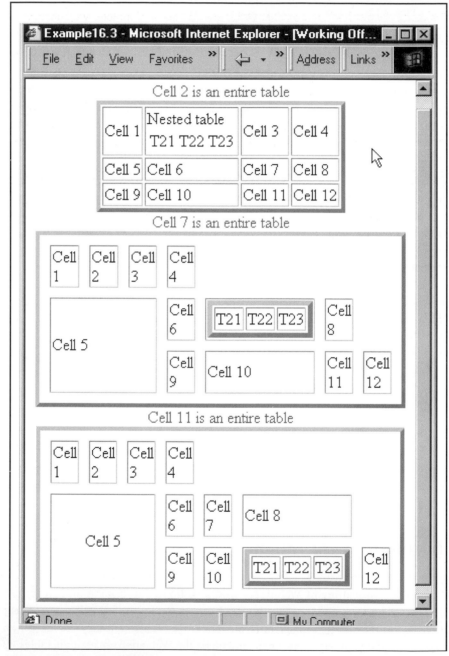

Figure 16.7 Nested tables.

Formatting Web pages by using tables is based on the same idea of nesting tables, covered in the previous section. Each table cell can be viewed as an independent screen that can hold any HTML content. Thus, we may begin the design of a Web page layout by dividing it into regions, where every region holds some contents. After the design is complete, we substitute for each region a table cell. We create an outer table that holds all these cells. We refrain from using a border for the table. When we write the HTML code while using these ideas, a well formatted Web page results.

As we design the Web page layout, we must keep the table structure in mind. A table must have rows and columns. As we create the various regions, we make sure that these regions from a grid structure that defines the rows and columns. If finer control over the grid structure is required, we can use nested tables. When the design and layout become more and more complex, HTML editors (chapter 17) may be used to create the Web pages.

The HTML content of any cell in the table could be any HTML data. We can think of each cell as an independent Web page. Thus, a cell can hold text, lists, hyperlinks, images, colors, sounds, forms, and so forth. We can assign a background color to a cell by using the BGCOLOR attribute of the <BODY> tag. This attribute is applicable to the <TD> tag.

Example 16.4 Develop a Web page that illustrates formatting with tables.

Solution This example creates a Web page that is formatted via a table. The design of the page layout is shown in figure 16.8. We need here a table with two rows. Each row has two columns. A total of four cells is needed to create the Web page. We use a different color for each cell. The cell that holds the hyperlinks also uses different link colors. Using a text editor, type the code that follows, and save it as *example16.4.html*. Figure 16.9 shows the resulting Web page. As shown in the code and the figure, each cell has its own background color. The table has no border. What seems to be a border in figure 16.9 is due to how the browser renders the page.

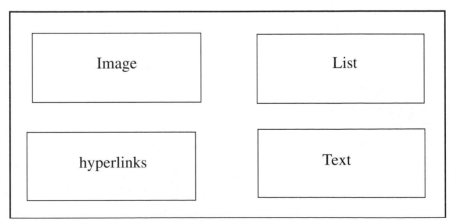

Figure 16.8   Design of a Web page layout.

```
<HTML>
<HEAD>
<TITLE>Formatting a Web page with tables</TITLE>
</HEAD>
<BODY>
<TABLE ALIGN = "center" BORDER =0>
<TR VALIGN = "top">
<TD BGCOLOR = "yellow">
<IMG SRC = "myImage.gif">
</TD>
<TD BGCOLOR = "green">
What to eat for a midnight snack?
<UL>
<LI>Pizza
<LI>Nachos
<LI>Ice cream
<LI>Pretzels
</TD>
</TR>
<TR VALIGN = "top">
<TD BGCOLOR = "gray">
Here are some Web sites to visit
<A HREF = "http://www.neu.edu">Check latest NU offerings<BR>
<A HREF = "http://www.prenhall.com">Prentice Hall latest books<BR>
<A HREF = "example16.1.html">Various types of tables
</TD>
<TD BGCOLOR = "purple">
It is once said that physical fitness and
exercises are very important to maintain a healthy life. We all
must eat well balanced meals, work out at least three times a week,
45 minutes each time.
</TD>
</TABLE>
</BODY>
</HTML>
```

Note that in the above HTML code, we use BORDER = 0 to tell the browser explicitly that we do not need a table border. Figure 16.9 reveals that the layout of the page is not very efficient; there is much empty space wasted in the page. If we swap the location of the image and the hyperlinks, we can save all that space. Modifying the above code, we move the <TD> tag that creates the image to the beginning of the second <TR> tag. We also move the first <TD> tag of that second <TR> tag to the beginning of the first <TR> tag. If we save the file and display the page again in a browser, it looks much better. Readers are encouraged to implement this change as an exercise. Readers may pursue other ideas of their own to experiment with formatting this page.

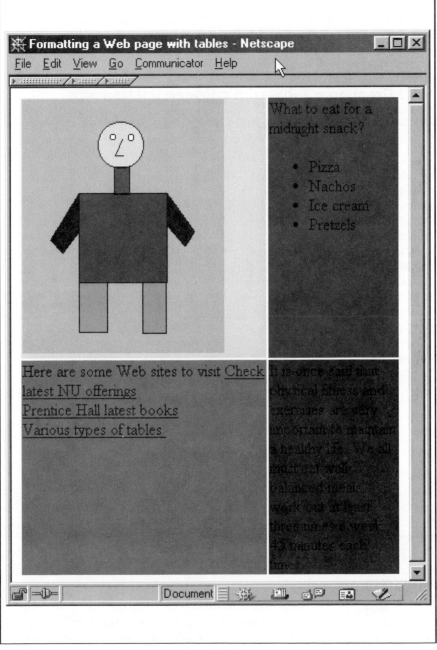

Figure 16.9 Formatting a Web page with tables.

16.8 Tutorials

This section covers the two main objectives of using tables: data presentation and formatting. Some tutorials cover tabulating data, others cover formatting. The section also focuses on using the table tags covered in this chapter. Any Web browser can be used to display the corresponding Web pages. It is a good idea to create a directory structure to save HTML files. This helps Web authors to organize HTML files and makes it easy to find them.

16.8.1 Creating a Table with a Horizontal Heading

This tutorial creates a Web page with a table that has a horizontal heading. The table is used like traditional tables. It tabulates the customer information of a fictitious bank. Using a text editor, type the code that follows, and save it as *tutorial16.8.1.html*. View the page in a browser. Figure 16.10 shows the resulting Web page.

```
<HTML>
<HEAD>
<TITLE>A Web page with horizontal heading</TITLE>
</HEAD>
<BODY>
<TABLE BORDER = 5 ALIGN = "center">
<CAPTION><FONT COLOR = "blue"><H2>Customer information of a bank</
H2></FONT></CAPTION>
<TR BGCOLOR = "red">
<TH>Account Number</TH>
<TH>First Name</TH>
<TH>Last Name</TH>
<TH>Account Balance</TH>
</TR>
<TR BGCOLOR = "yellow">
<TD>00057</TD>
<TD>John</TD>
<TD>Doe</TD>
<TD>1234.56</TD>
</TR>
<TR BGCOLOR = "yellow">
<TD>00100</TD>
<TD>Lisa</TD>
<TD>Stones</TD>
<TD>5329.78</TD>
</TR>
<TR BGCOLOR = "yellow">
<TD>00200</TD>
<TD>Joe</TD>
<TD>Ellis</TD>
<TD>25.00</TD>
</TR>
```

```
<TR BGCOLOR = "yellow">
<TD>00225</TD>
<TD>Kathy</TD>
<TD>Doherty</TD>
<TD>10258.94</TD>
</TR>
<TR BGCOLOR = "yellow" ALIGN = "center">
<TD>00316</TD>
<TD>Marilyn</TD>
<TD>Walsh</TD>
<TD>359.37</TD>
</TR>
<TR BGCOLOR = "yellow" ALIGN = "right">
<TD>00439</TD>
<TD>Anna</TD>
<TD>Clinton</TD>
<TD>2483.33</TD>
</TR>
</TABLE>
</BODY>
</HTML>
```

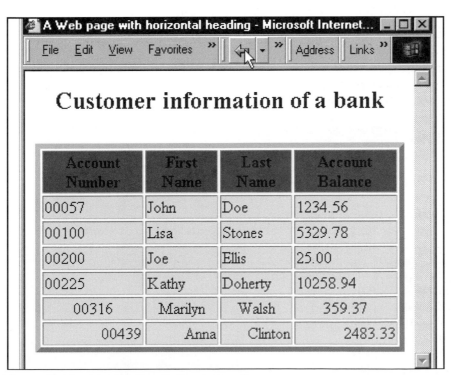

Figure 16.10   A table with a horizontal heading.

Here are some comments about this tutorial:

•The table is created row by row. We define the row cells by using the <TD> tags within the <TR> tags.

•The code is displayed as shown above, for ease of following.

•The <TR> and <TD> tags are closed, although their closing is optional. Closing them gives the HTML more structure and makes it easy to follow it.

•We use any tags we need within the <CAPTION> tag. Here, we use the <FONT> and <H2> tags.

•We use the BGCOLOR attribute within the <TR> tags. We use a red color for the heading cells and a yellow color for the data cells.

•The ALIGN attribute is used with the last two <TD> tags for illustration purposes.

16.8.2 Creating a Table with a Vertical Heading

This tutorial converts the table we have created in the above tutorial into a table with a vertical heading. In tutorial 16.8.1, we created seven rows: one header, and six data rows. Each row has four columns. This produces a total of 24 data cells. In this tutorial, we create the same cells in a different way. We create four rows. Each row has seven columns. The first cell in each row is a header. We have to use the BGCOLOR attribute differently to maintain the red color for the heading cells and the yellow color for the data cells. The tutorial uses the attribute in the most efficient way, by using it in the <TR> tag and overriding it in the <TH> tag. Using the attribute in each and every <TD> tag is very inefficient. We also used the ALIGN and VALIGN attributes in two data cells, to show their effect. Using a text editor, type the code that follows, and save it as *tutorial16.8.2.html*. View the page in a browser. Figure 16.11 shows the resulting Web page.

```
<HTML>
<HEAD>
<TITLE>A Web page with vertical heading</TITLE>
</HEAD>
<BODY>
<TABLE BORDER = 5 ALIGN = "center">
<CAPTION><FONT COLOR = "blue"><H2>Customer information of a bank</
H2></FONT></CAPTION>
<TR BGCOLOR = "yellow">
<TH BGCOLOR = "red">Account Number</TH>
<TD>00057</TD>
<TD>00100</TD>
<TD>00200</TD>
<TD>00225</TD>
<TD>00316</TD>
<TD>00439</TD>
</TR>
```

```
<TR BGCOLOR = "yellow">
<TH BGCOLOR = "red">First Name</TH>
<TD>John</TD>
<TD>Lisa</TD>
<TD>Joe</TD>
<TD>Kathy</TD>
<TD>Marilyn</TD>
<TD ALIGN = "center" VALIGN = "top">Anna</TD>
</TR>
<TR BGCOLOR = "yellow">
<TH BGCOLOR = "red">Last Name</TH>
<TD>Doe</TD>
<TD>Stones</TD>
<TD>Ellis</TD>
<TD>Doherty</TD>
<TD>Walsh</TD>
<TD ALIGN = "right" VALIGN = "bottom">Clinton</TD>
</TR>
<TR BGCOLOR = "yellow">
<TH BGCOLOR = "red">Account Balance</TH>
<TD>1234.56</TD>
<TD>5329.78</TD>
<TD>25.00</TD>
<TD>10258.94</TD>
<TD>359.37</TD>
<TD>2483.33</TD>
</TR>
</TABLE>
</BODY>
</HTML>
```

16.8.3 Creating a Table with a Dual Heading

This tutorial redesigns the table of tutorial 16.8.3 to have a dual heading. It has both horizontal and vertical headings. We show one possible design here. Readers are encouraged to find and implement other designs. We have eliminated one entry in the table, to make it fit within the limits of the page width. The HTML shows us using empty cells with white background to maintain the row and column structure of the table. We also make the second cell in the top row span six columns. Using a text editor, type the code that follows, and save it as *tutorial16.8.3.html*. View the page in a browser. Figure 16.12 shows the resulting Web page.

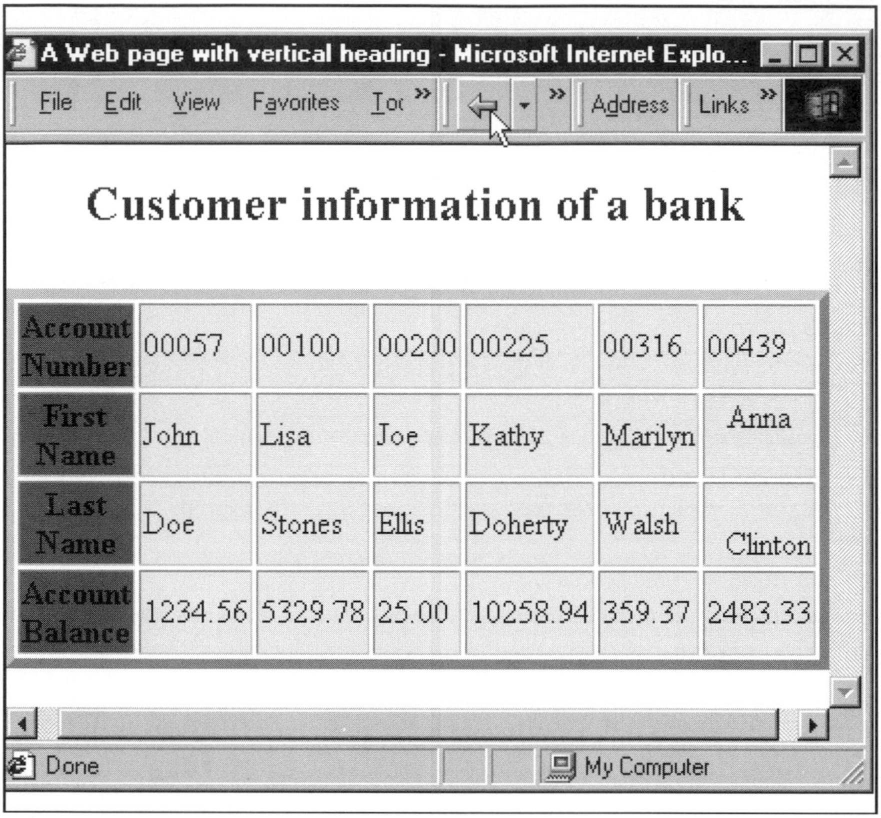

Figure 16.11   A table with a vertical heading.

```
<HTML>
<HEAD>
<TITLE>A Web page with dual heading</TITLE>
</HEAD>
<BODY>
<TABLE BORDER = 5 ALIGN = "center">
<CAPTION><FONT COLOR = "blue"><H2>Customer information of a bank</
H2></FONT></CAPTION>
<TR>
<TD></TD>
<TH BGCOLOR = "red" COLSPAN = 6>Customer name</TH>
</TR>
<TR BGCOLOR = "yellow">
<TD BGCOLOR = "white"></TD>
<TD>John Doe</TD>
```

```
<TD>Lisa Stones</TD>
<TD>Joe Ellis</TD>
<TD>Kathy Doherty</TD>
<TD>Marilyn Walsh</TD>
</TR>
<TR BGCOLOR = "yellow">
<TH BGCOLOR = "red">Account number</TH>
<TD>00057</TD>
<TD>00100</TD>
<TD>00200</TD>
<TD>00225</TD>
<TD>00316</TD>
</TR>
<TR BGCOLOR = "yellow">
<TH BGCOLOR = "red">Account balance</TH>
<TD>1234.56</TD>
<TD>5329.78</TD>
<TD>25.00</TD>
<TD>10258.94</TD>
<TD>359.37</TD>
</TR>
</TABLE>
</BODY>
</HTML>
```

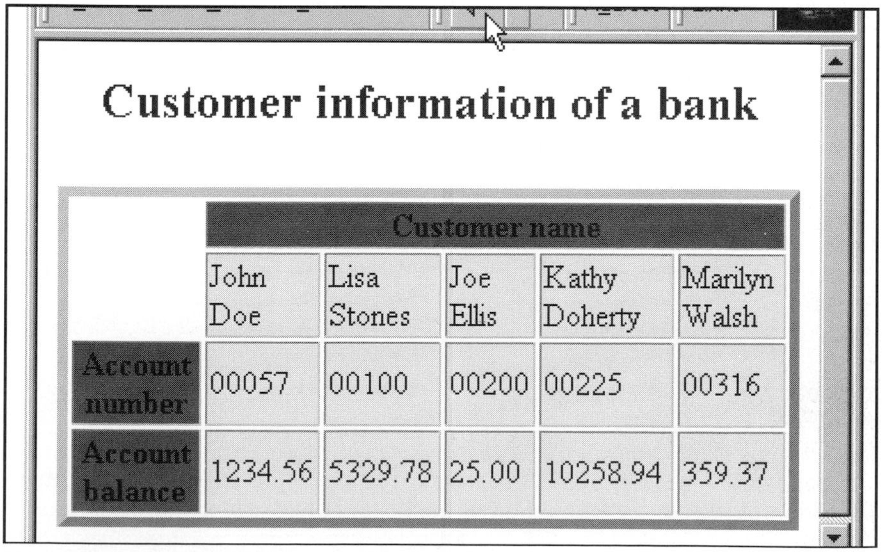

	Customer name				
	John Doe	Lisa Stones	Joe Ellis	Kathy Doherty	Marilyn Walsh
Account number	00057	00100	00200	00225	00316
Account balance	1234.56	5329.78	25.00	10258.94	359.37

Figure 16.12 A table with a dual heading.

16.8.4 Formatting a Form via a Table

Chapter 14 covers the details of creating forms. One problem common to all the forms created in that chapter is that their elements do not align properly. We would like, say, to make text fields align vertically. This tutorial shows how to use tables to format forms so that they appear well structured on Web pages. The common theme in formatting a form via a table is that each form element is a data cell. Thus, begin by enclosing each form tag in a <TD> tag. Use a browser to display the form. If some form element wraps around even though there is still enough space left on a line, use the COLSPAN attribute of the <TD> tag. As a common rule, a group of checkboxes or radio buttons can fit on one line if their enclosing <TD> tag has a large enough value for its COLSPAN attribute. Readers are encouraged to investigate this issue by changing the code of this tutorial. Using a text editor, type the code that follows, and save it as *tutorial16.8.4.html*. View the page in a browser. Figure 16.13 shows the resulting Web page.

```
<HTML>
<HEAD>
<TITLE>Formatting a form via tables</TITLE>
</HEAD>
<BODY>
<TABLE ALIGN = "center">
<CAPTION><FONT COLOR = "blue"><H2>Please fill this survey form</
H2></FONT></CAPTION>
<FORM>
<TR>
<TD>First Name:</TD><TD><INPUT TYPE = "text" NAME = "first" SIZE =
10 MAXLENGTH = 15></TD>
<TD>MI:</TD><TD><INPUT TYPE = "text" NAME = "mi" SIZE = 1></TD>
<TD>Last Name:</TD><TD><INPUT TYPE = "text" NAME = "last" SIZE = 10
MAXLENGTH = 18></TD>
</TR>
<TR>
<TD>City:</TD><TD><INPUT TYPE = "text" NAME = "ccityt" SIZE = 10
MAXLENGTH = 13></TD>
<TD>State:</TD><TD><INPUT TYPE = "text" NAME = "state" SIZE = 2></
TD>
<TD>Zip code:</TD><TD><INPUT TYPE = "text" NAME = "code" SIZE =
5></TD>
</TR>
<TR>
<TD COLSPAN = 2>Choose a sport:</TD>
</TR>
<TR>
<TD COLSPAN = 4>Basketball:<INPUT TYPE = "checkbox" CHECKED> Foot-
ball:<INPUT TYPE = "checkbox">Hockey:<INPUT TYPE = "checkbox"></TD>
</TR>
<TR>
```

```
<TD COLSPAN = 2>Choose a year:</TD>
</TR>
<TR>
<TD COLSPAN = 6>Freshman:<INPUT TYPE = "radio" NAME = "year"
CHECKED> Sophomore:<INPUT TYPE = "radio">Junior:<INPUT TYPE =
"radio" NAME = "year">Senior:<INPUT TYPE = "radio" NAME = "year"></
TD>
</TR>
<TR>
<TD COLSPAN = 3>Choose your favorite junk food:</TD>
</TR>
<TR>
<TD><SELECT MULTIPLE> <OPTION>Chips<OPTION>Pizza<OPTION>Nachos</
SELECT></TD>
</TR>
<TR>
<TD COLSPAN = 5><TEXTAREA ROWS = 5 COLS = 15 WRAP = "soft">Please
let us know your comments</TEXTAREA></TD>
</TR>
<TR>
<TD><INPUT TYPE = "submit" VALUE = "Send it"></TD>
<TD><INPUT TYPE = "reset" VALUE = "Clear it"></TD>
</TR>
</TABLE>
</BODY>
</HTML>
```

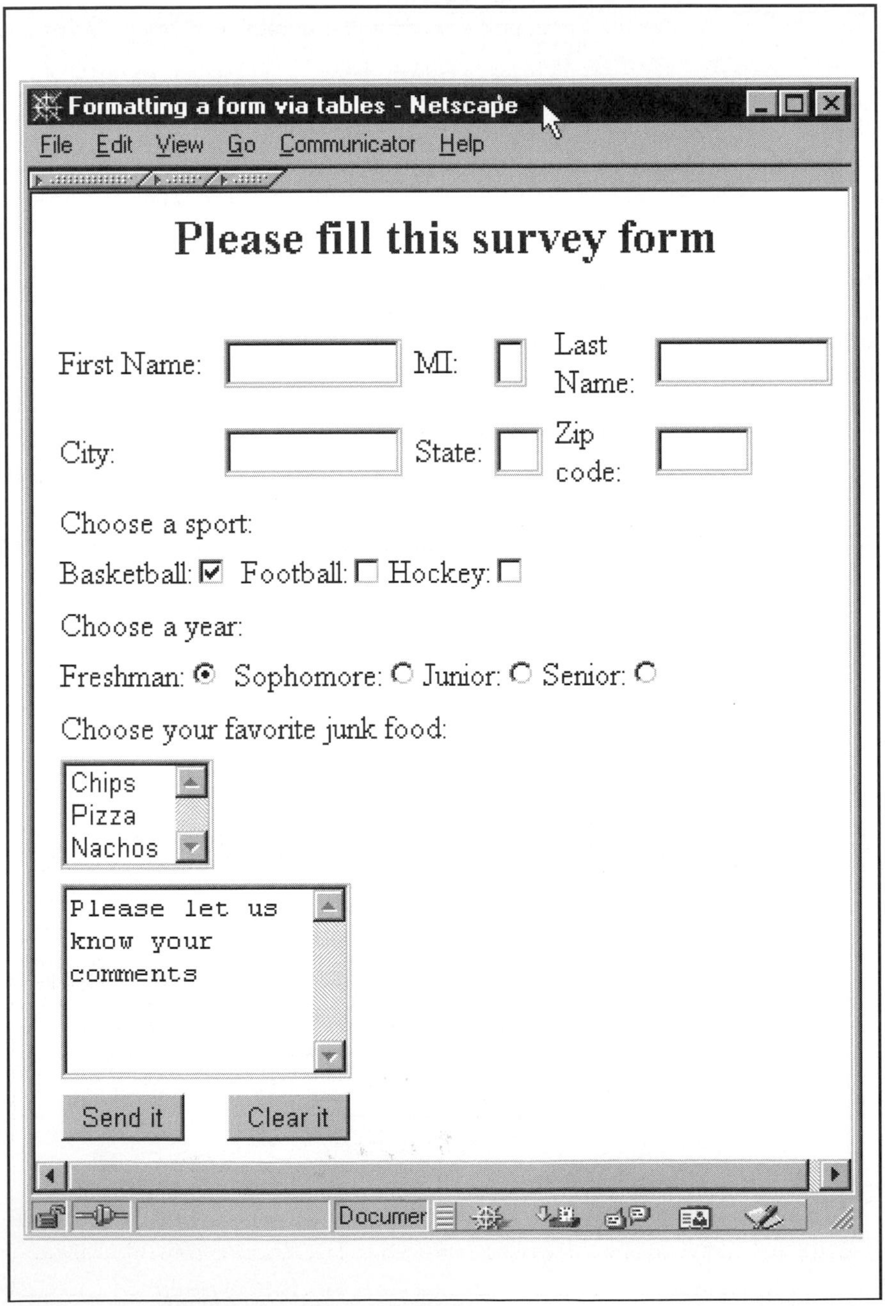

Figure 16.13 Formatting a form via tables.

16.9 FAQs

重叠（操作），覆盖．

Q: What happens if a table has overlapping cells?

A: Defining overlapping cells in tables is an error that should be avoided. Different browsers may render the table differently. One possibility is that a browser will render the overlapping parts of cells more than once, thus displaying cell contents that are hard to interpret. The following HTML code forces the overlapping of table cells 3 and 5. Cell 3 has its text repetitions of the character y, and cell 5 has the character x. Figure 16.14 shows the contents of the two cells overlapping.

```
<HTML>
<HEAD>
<TITLE>A Web page with overlapping cells</TITLE>
</HEAD>
<BODY>
<TABLE ALIGN = "center" BORDER = 2 WIDTH = 200>
<TR><TD ALIGN = "center">Cell 1<TD>Cell 2<TD  ALIGN = "center"
VALIGN = "top" ROWSPAN = 2>Cell 3 yy<BR>yyyyyy<BR>yyyyy
<TR><TD ALIGN = "center">Cell 4<TD COLSPAN = 2>Cell 5 xxxxxxxxxx
</TABLE>
</BODY>
</HTML>
```

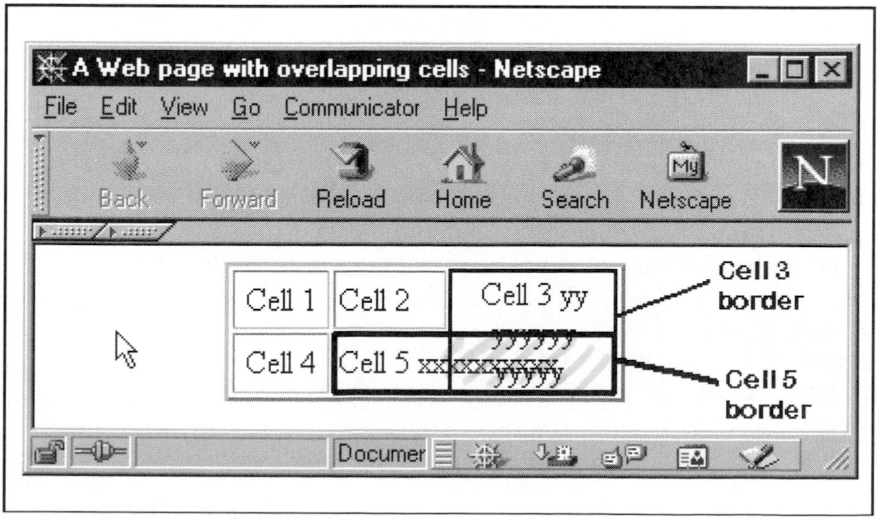

Figure 16.14 Overlapping of table cells.

Q: Do the FRAME and RULES attributes of the <TABLE> tag work?

A: MS IE browser recognizes the FRAME and RULES attributes of the <TABLE> tag with all their values. Netscape Communicator ignores their use in the tag and does not render them. Both browsers recognize the BORDER attribute. Thus, for consistent appearance of Web pages in all browsers, Web authors can only use the BORDER attribute of the <TABLE> tag.

Q: Does the <CAPTION> tag replace the SUMMARY attribute of the <TABLE> tag?

A: No. The <CAPTION> tag provides a very brief, one-statement description of a table. The SUMMARY attribute of the <TABLE> tag provides much more information about the table structure and purpose, to help disabled Web surfers to understand the table.

Q: Do browsers render all the values of the ALIGN attribute of the <CAPTION> tag correctly?

A: No. The only two values that browsers consistently render correctly are TOP and BOTTOM. Browsers give different results for LEFT and RIGHT values. Netscape Communicator ignores both of them. MS IE recognizes them by left- or right-justifying the table caption at the top of the table.

Q: What is a table directionality? Do all browsers support it?

A: A table directionality is how the cells of table rows are laid. They can be laid left-to-right or right-to-left. The former is the default. For a left-to-right table, the top left corner of the table is its origin. Thus, row zero is at the top, and column zero is on the left side. This is why the empty spacing (which is extra empty row cells) in the tables shown in figure 16.5 is added to the right of the table. For a right-to-left table, the top right corner is the origin of the table. Row zero is still at the top, but column zero is on the right side. Extra empty row cells are added to the left of the table for right-to-left tables. The table directionality also affects the flow direction of text within table cells.

To specify a right-to-left table, the DIR attribute is used in the <TABLE> tag. Its values are LTR (left to right) and RTL (right to left). LTR is the default value. Thus, we use <TABLE DIR = "rtl"> ... </TABLE> to create a right-to-left table. This attribute can also be used with cell tags such as <TH> and <TD> to make the text flow in the direction opposite to the table direction, if needed.

MS IE recognize the DIR attribute and renders it. Netscape Communicator ignores it. The following code creates the last table shown in figure 16.5 with right-to-left directionality. It also reverses this directionality for Cell 9. Figure 16.15 shows the resulting table.

```
<HTML>
<HEAD>
<TITLE>A Web page with right-to-left table</TITLE>
</HEAD>
<BODY>
<FONT COLOR = "red"><CENTER>This table is the same as the last
table shown in figure 16.5, but with right-to-left directional-
ity.<BR> Cell 9 uses left-to-right directionality to control its
```

```
text flow.</CENTER></FONT>
<TABLE ALIGN = "center" BORDER = 4 WIDTH = 200 HEIGHT = 100 CELL-
SPACING = 8 DIR = "rtl">
<TR><TD>Cell 1<TD>Cell 2<TD>Cell 3<TD>Cell 4
<TR><TD ROWSPAN = 2 COLSPAN = 3 ALIGN = "center">Cell 5<TD>Cell
6<TD>Cell 7<TD>Cell 8
<TR><TD DIR = "ltr">Cell 9<TD>Cell 10<TD>Cell 11<TD>Cell 12
</TABLE>
</BODY>
</HTML>
```

Q: If I use CELLSPACING = 10% in a <TD> tag, in a table whose width and height I did not specify, how does a browser calculate the spacing?

A: The browser first calculates the table width and height according to the methods explained in section 16.5. It then calculates 10% of each, and uses the smallest amount as the cell spacing to render the table. The browser uses the same approach to calculate cell padding, if it is given as a percentage of the cell size.

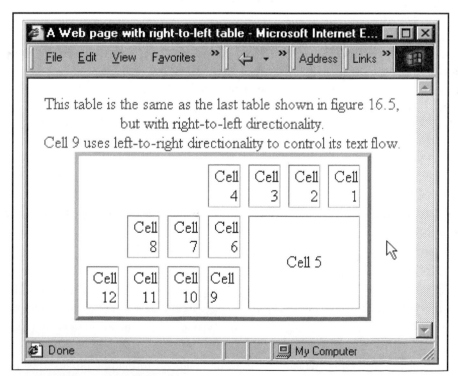

Figure 16.15 A right-to-left table.

Q: What is a good way to debug HTML code while using tables to format Web pages?

A: Use the BORDER attribute of the <TABLE> tag to get an idea of how the browser is creating the table rows, columns, and cells that you have designed. These borders should help you immensely in deciding what to change to finalize the formatting. Once you like the final layout of the page, simply remove the BORDER attribute.

Q: How do I assign different colors to cell text?

A: You need to use spot colors. The <FONT> tag should allow you to control the colors of a cell text.

Q: What are row and column groups for tables? What are their tags? Should I use them?

A: HTML allows Web authors to group table rows into a table head, a table foot, and one or more table bodies by using the <THEAD>, <TFOOT>, and <TBODY> tags. This division enables browsers to scroll table bodies independent of the table head and foot. HTML also allows Web authors to group table columns into column groups by using the <COLGROUP> and <COL> tags. This grouping enables authors to assign attributes to columns once per group instead of repeating them for each column or cell individually. For example, we could use the attribute VALIGN = "top" once for one column group. The content of each cell in the column group is printed starting at the top of the cell. If we do not use column groups, we would have to code this attribute for each cell individually. We do not recommend using these tags, because they are not universally supported by browsers. MS IE supports them; Netscape Communicator does not.

16.10 Summary

Introduction

•A table is defined as a region that has rows and columns of small rectangles, called cells, that are arranged relative to each other in a certain way that makes up the table layout.

•Each cell holds its own content (data). Cell data could be any HTML elements, such as text, hyperlinks, images, and so forth.

•HTML tables can, like traditional tables, be used to tabulate data and to create matrices that describe, say, products, statistical results, and so forth.

•Tables can also be used to format Web pages. The HTML table model has been developed to allow Web authors to include any HTML tag or combination of tags in a table cell.

•When tables are used to format Web pages, Web authors would need to lay out the design of their Web pages on paper and then translate it to table cells.

•If writing HTML code manually when using tables for formatting proves to be difficult, Web authors can use HTML editors, as covered in chapter 17.

•When HTML tables are used for tabulating data, they can use different background colors for table cells. A table may have horizontal or vertical headings, or both. It may also have a width and a height.

•Web authors can include as many tables as they need if tables are used to tabulate data. Including more than one table makes the Web page multiple screens long, and that is not a good idea.

•For formatting purposes, one table is usually enough to control the page layout. Such a table may include a nested table to offer finer control of table cells.

Table Structure and Variables

•The HTML table variables may be grouped into two categories: non-cell, and cell.

•Non-cell variables control the properties and structure of the table; they are the table caption, summary, border, header, rows, columns, width, height, cells, and rules. The table caption is a title that provides a short description of the table purpose. It can placed at the top of the table or at the bottom.

•The table summary provides a longer description that can be used by people using speech- or Braille-based browsers.

•The table border is its outside boundary. We can think of it as the table container.

•The table header is the first row in the table. Each cell in this row is a header for the column underneath it. It holds the title of the column.

•Table rows are the horizontal layout of the cells. Similarly, table columns are the vertical layout of the cells.

•The width and height of a table are a representation of the number of its rows and columns respectively. If no width is specified, the browser uses a default value. Similarly, the browser finds the cell height by dividing the table height by the number of rows. If Web authors do not specify a table height, the browser uses a default value.

•Cells are the basic units that make a table. Cells are arranged within the table border top-to-bottom and left-to-right.

•The horizontal and vertical lines that separate the cells from each other are known as rules. Web authors can make these rules visible or invisible by using the <BORDER> tag.

•Cell variables are the row span, column span, padding, spacing, and alignment of data within the cell. A cell may span more than one column and /or one row.

•Cell spacing describes the amount of the horizontal and vertical white spacing between cells.

•Cell padding is equivalent to specifying top, bottom, left, and right margins for the cell. It describes the amount of horizontal and vertical spacing between cell content (data) and its borders.

•The color of a cell padding is the color of the cell background, which could be different from the background color of the Web page itself.

•Cell content or data can be aligned within each cell in both the horizontal and the vertical directions. Data could be aligned to the left (left-justified), middle, or right (right-justified) of the cell in the horizontal direction. In the vertical direction, data could be aligned to the top (top-justified), middle, or bottom (bottom-justified) of the cell.

Table Layout and Design

•The purpose of a table determines its layout and design. If the table is used in the conventional way, to tabulate data, it will always have heading cells.

•If tables are used for formatting Web pages, headings are eliminated. Sizes of cells are different. Some cells may span multiple rows and columns, while other cells are left empty to provide spacing between cell data. Table border and rules are eliminated, to make the flow of the elements or content of a Web page smooth and seamless. A color may be assigned to the table background.

•Web authors must consider table width and height to ensure that the table fits on one computer screen, whether the screen is large or small. It may be a good idea to let the browser determine the table width and height at the time of display.

Table Tags

•The table tags are <TABLE>, <CAPTION>, <TH>, <TR>, and <TD>.

•The attributes of the <TABLE> tag are SUMMARY, WIDTH, HEIGHT, BORDER, ALIGN, FRAME, RULES, CELLSPACING, and CELLPADDING.

•The only attribute of the <CAPTION> tag is ALIGN.

•The attributes of the <TR> tag are ALIGN, VALIGN, and BGCOLOR.

•The attributes of <TH> and <TD> tags are ABBR, AXIS, HEADERS, SCOPE,   ROW-SPAN, COLSPAN, NOWRAP, WIDTH, HEIGHT, ALIGN, VALIGN, CELLPADDING, and BGCOLOR.

Table Rendering and Calculations

•Browsers use all table non-cell and cell variables to calculate cell sizes. They resolve any conflict they find between these variables. Each cell must be large enough to hold its content.

•Browsers use the following rules to render and calculate tables: A browser first calculates the table width and height, regardless of whether they are given. It then uses the cells required by the table rows to calculate the maximum number of columns of the table. This number is equal to the number of columns required by the row with the most columns, including cells that span multiple columns. After a browser calculates table width and height and the number of columns, it uses these variables together with cell content (data) and spacing to determine the minimum cell size (width and height). If cell data fits within this minimum size, the browser uses it. If cell data needs more space for display, the browser increases the cell minimum size accordingly. After that, the browser calculates the cell spacing and padding, if any are specified. The last step for the browser is to determine alignment of cell content. The browser uses the alignment specified by the <TD> and/or <TH> tags. If there is none, it uses what is specified by the <TR> tag. If both tags specify alignment, the <TD> and/or <TH> tags override the <TR> tag.

Nesting Tables

•Web authors may nest tables to achieve certain design goals of their Web pages. Table nesting makes the HTML code quite complex and difficult to follow and understand.

•HTML nests tables at the cell level. Web authors can create an entire table within a cell of another table.

•Nesting tables may produce awkward results. The sizes of table cells may vary greatly. The locations of empty cells may not be desirable or acceptable by Web authors. Moreover, the outer table proportions may not be optimal. Web authors should always render their nested tables during their development, to receive feedback from the browser.

Formatting via Tables

•Formatting Web pages with tables is based on the same idea of nesting tables. Each table cell can be viewed as an independent screen that can hold any HTML content. Web authors can divide Web page layout into regions (cells). These regions make up the table rows and columns.

•Quick reference of the HTML tags covered in this chapter

Table 16.1   Summary of HTML table tags.

Tag	Close	Attribute	Value	Example	Chpt. page
`<TABLE>`	Yes	SUM-MARY	text	`<TABLE SUMMARY "...">`	560
		WIDTH	pixels	`<TABLE WIDTH = 400>`	
		HEIGHT	pixels	`<TABLE HEIGHT = 200>`	
		BORDER	pixels	`<TABLE BORDER = 5>`	
		ALIGN	left	`<TABLE ALIGN = "left">`	
			center	`<TABLE ALIGN = "center">`	
			right	`<TABLE ALIGN = "right">`	
		CELL-SPACING	pixels	`<TABLE CELLSPACING = 10>`	
		CELLPAD-DING	pixels	`<TABLE CELLPADDING = 20>`	
`<CAPTION>`	Yes	ALIGN	top	`<CAPTION ALIGN = "top">`	563
			bottom	`<CAPTION ALIGN = "bottom">`	
			left	`<CAPTION ALIGN = "left">`	
			right	`<CAPTION ALIGN = "right">`	

Table 16.1 Summary of HTML table tags.

Tag	Close	Attribute	Value	Example	Chpt. page
`<TR>`	Optional	ALIGN	left	`<TR ALIGN = "left">`	563
			center	`<TR ALIGN = "center">`	
			right	`<TR ALIGN = "right">`	
`<TH>/<TD>`	Optional	ROWSPAN	number	`<TD ROWSPAN = 3>`	563
		COLSPAN	number	`<TD COLSPAN = 2>`	
		NOWRAP	none	`<TD NOWRAP>`	
		ALIGN	left	`<TD ALIGN = "left">`	
			center	`<TD ALIGN = "center">`	
			right	`<TD ALIGN = "right">`	
		VALIGN	top	`<TD VALIGN = "top">`	
			middle	`<TD VALIGN = "middle">`	
			bottom	`<TD VALIGN = "bottom">`	
		CELLPAD-DING	pixels	`<TD CELLPADDING = 10>`	

PROBLEMS

Exercises

16.1 Create the table shown in figure 16.1

16.2 Create the table shown in figure 16.2. Use a cell spacing of 10 pixels and a cell padding of 20 pixels.

16.3 Create the top table shown in figure 16.3.

16.4 Create the middle table shown in figure 16.3.

16.5 Create the bottom table shown in figure 16.3.

16.6 Change example 16.1 so that `Cell 1` spans two columns and `Cell 3` spans two rows in the three tables shown in figure 16.4.

16.7 Change example 16.2 so that `Cell 12` spans three rows and `Cell 6` spans two rows and thee columns. Make the change to the three tables.

16.8 Change example 16.3 so that the nested table occupies `Cell 5`.

16.9 Change example 16.4 so that you swap the locations of the cell of the image and that of the hyperlinks.

Homework

16.10 Create a Web page that uses tables. The page and table design and layout is left up to you. Be imaginative.

16.11 Rewrite the HTML code for tutorial 16.8.1 so that you reverse the order of the rows and columns shown in figure 16.10.

16.12 Rewrite the HTML code for tutorial 16.8.2 so that you reverse the order of the rows and columns shown in figure 16.11.

16.13 Rewrite the HTML code for exercise 16.8.3 so that you reverse the order of the rows and columns shown in figure 16.12.

16.14 Rewrite the HTML code for exercise 16.8.4 so that the select list and the text area belong to one table cell.

16.15 Create the table shown in figure 16.16. The cells in the last row use bold text and have a background color of #CEEFBD.

16.16 Create the dual-heading table shown in figure 16.17.

16.17 Create the flower order form shown in figure 16.18. The form is formatted via tables.

16.18 Create a monthly calendar, with your daily activities, by using a table.

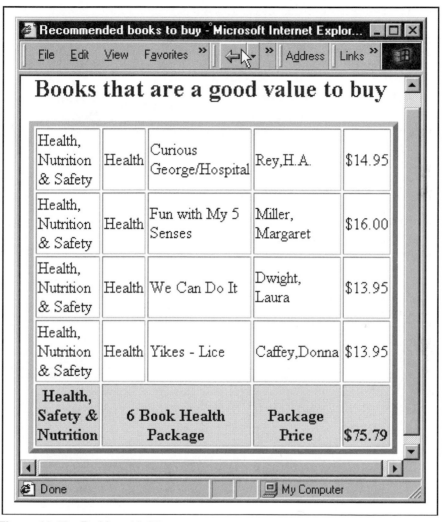

Figure 16.16 Problem 16.15.

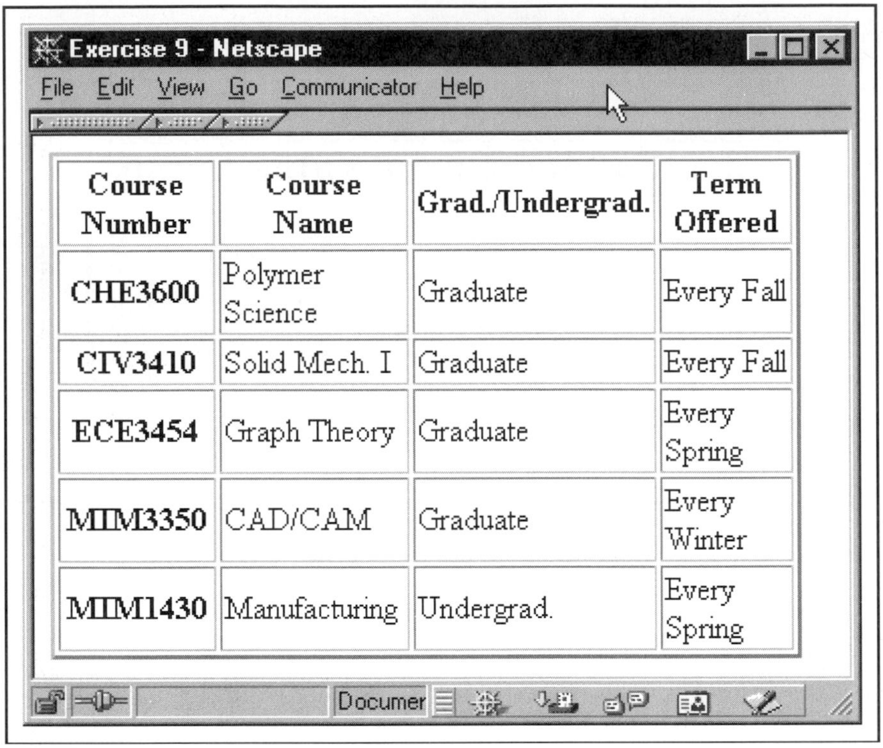

Course Number	Course Name	Grad./Undergrad.	Term Offered
CHE3600	Polymer Science	Graduate	Every Fall
CIV3410	Solid Mech. I	Graduate	Every Fall
ECE3454	Graph Theory	Graduate	Every Spring
MIM3350	CAD/CAM	Graduate	Every Winter
MIM1430	Manufacturing	Undergrad.	Every Spring

Figure 16.17 Problem 16.16.

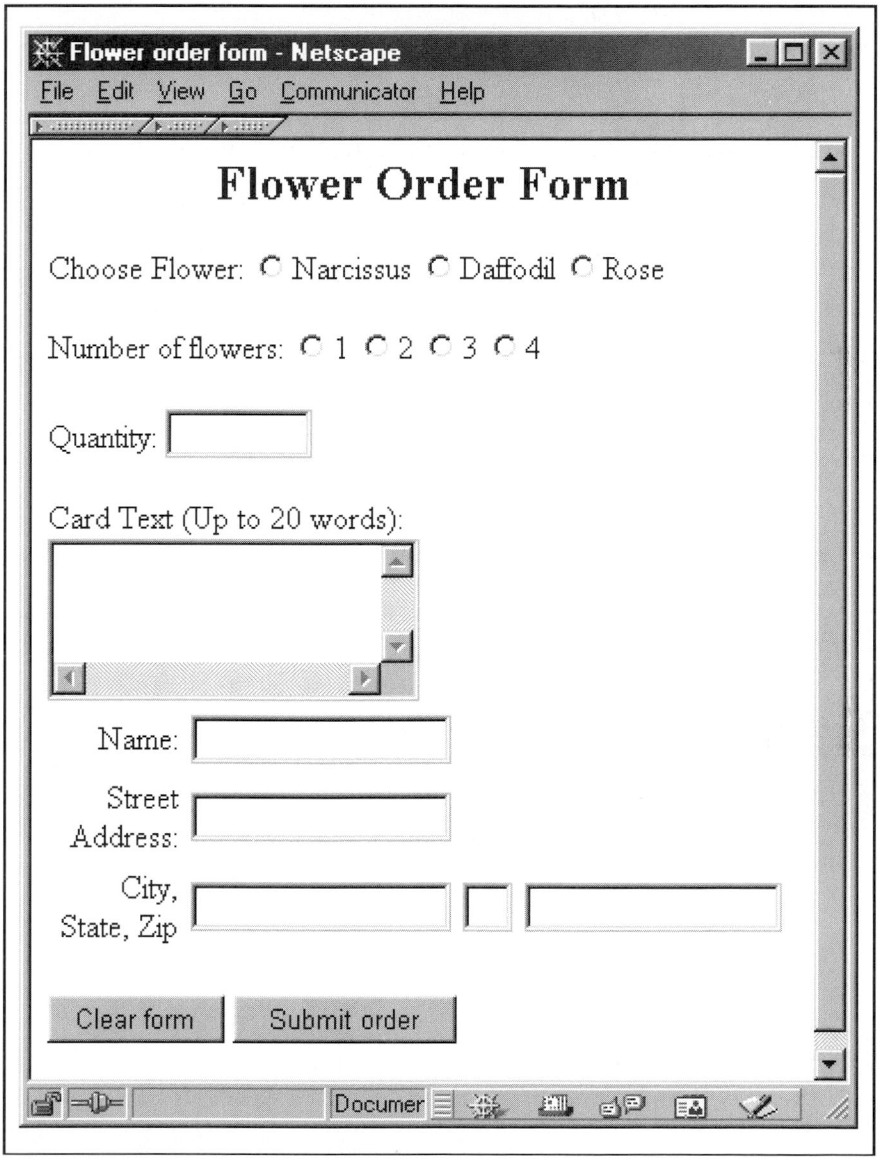

Figure 16.18 Problem 16.17.

CHAPTER 17

HTML Editors

This chapter covers the use of HTML editors as an automation tool to write and generate Web pages. These editors provide an alternative to the manual approach to developing HTML code. These editors free Web authors from the HTML tags and their syntax and allow them to focus on Web page design and layout. Using the editors without a good knowledge of HTML and its syntax is, however, not recommended — for two reasons: First, Web authors would not fully understand all the functions offered by these editors. Second, editors may not be able to provide Web authors with all the tools they need. In such cases, authors would need to add the extra HTML code manually. This chapter covers some issues related to HTML editors. It also covers the tasks performed by HTML editors. It then provides an overview of editors and their GUI structure. The chapter presents the HTML editor (known as the Composer) of Netscape Communicator as a sample editor. Following this coverage, it presents tutorials, FAQs, a summary, and problems.

17.1 Introduction

We have covered all the HTML concepts, tags, and syntax that Web authors need to write HTML code to implement the design and layout of their Web pages. Thus far, we have focused on writing the code manually. The development environment for manual code generation is a text editor and a browser. We use the text editor to write the code, then save it in a file with *html* extension. We test the code by running the file in the browser. We inspect the resulting Web page. If there are problems due to syntax or design, we go back to the text editor, edit the HTML file, save it, and finally test it again by running it in the browser. We repeat this development cycle until we are satisfied with the page final layout and design. This cycle depends mainly on visual inspection and foresight, because as HTML is not a compiled programming language. It is a scripting code.

Many programming languages such as Java, C++, and Visual Basic, have what is known as an IDE (Integrated Development Environment). These IDEs are tools that allow programmers to write programs, compile them, test them, and debug them in an efficient way. The tools make this development cycle faster, and more productive. For example, these tools report the compilation errors in a more friendly and easy-to-understand way. They also make the code easy to follow by using different colors for code parentheses and keywords. If the language uses the `class` keyword, the IDE may use a special color for it.

The idea of using IDEs for programming languages has been applied to HTML in the form of HTML editors. A Web author may use an HTML editor to develop a Web page and its code instead of following the manual approach. An editor is a tool that allows the author to choose the HTML element (e.g., a hyperlink, an image, etc.) to be created, from among the editor's GUI icons. The editor guides the author to create the element by presenting a series of requests for the data required to define the element. After the author inputs the data, the editor creates the elements in the Web page and generates its HTML code. Now the author evaluates the element as it looks on the Web page. If not satisfied, the author can delete it and then either create it again or create a new element.

Consider the case of creating a hyperlink. The HTML editor asks the Web author to input the link name that appears in the Web page. This is the source anchor (covered in chapter 7). The editor also asks for the Web site of the link. This is the destination anchor. After inputting all the data, the browser displays the hyperlink in the Web page in the location chosen by the author.

What do HTML editors really do when it comes to developing Web pages? To answer this question, let us contrast them against the manual approach of writing HTML code. In both approaches, the Web author has a design and layout of a Web page that needs to be implemented. In the manual approach, the author writes the HTML code first and then views the resulting page in a browser. Only then can the author find out whether the code is written incorrectly. If it is, the author follows the manual development cycle described earlier in this section.

In the editor's approach, the author does not deal with HTML code directly. The author builds the HTML elements of the page one by one as they appear in it. While doing so, the author uses the menus, icons, and other tools provided by the editor. Every time the author creates an element in the page, the editor generates the corresponding HTML code and places it in an html file specified by the author. At the end, the Web page is fully displayed in the editor's window, and the HTML code is stored in the html file.

In conclusion, the manual approach works opposite to the editor's approach. In the former, we start with HTML code and end with the Web page. In the latter, we start with the Web page and end with HTML code. The net outcome of both approaches is, however, the same: a Web page and an HTML file. Some Web authors may prefer not to get involved with HTML code; they argue that their main goal is the look and appeal of their Web pages and sites to their potential online customers, not the writing of HTML code. In such a case, they use HTML editors.

Other Web authors may use a hybrid approach. They use editors to develop the bulk of their Web pages and sites, then use the manual approach to fine-tune and finalize the development.

Is the HTML code generated by editors for a Web page the same as, or close to what the manual code would be? In general, the editor's code is more complex and cumbersome than manually written code. The code can be full of tags that may not be necessary. The editors act as an automation tool for code generation, so they use and apply the same algorithms equally to the same problems. Editors, like any other automation tools, cannot precisely generate the most compact code. They use the approach of "one size fits all" — in addition, editors use tables all the time to format Web pages according to design and layout needs of Web pages.

Should Web authors use HTML editors? We can ask this question differently. What are the pros and cons of using HTML editors? This is a traditional question. Different people can argue for or against using HTML editors. What we need to accomplish here is to bring out the facts and let each reader decide. Conventional wisdom suggests that the black-box approach is not a good idea. This approach defeats the purpose of using an automation tool, such as HTML editors, because users are not able to use the tool efficiently. They end up using trial and error to accomplish their tasks, thus spending more time when using the tool than by using the manual approach. If Web authors are not familiar at all with HTML concepts, they are not able to fully understand the editor's functions and icons. Therefore, Web authors need to be proficient in HTML concepts and tags and the writing of code manually, before using editors.

In some applications, Web authors do not use HTML editors at all. The best example is e-commerce. Authors write the HTML code manually, because they need to control the source code and every tag of their Web pages for security reasons. The code of these pages may also contain JavaScript code and/or Java applets that they must write.

The remainder of this chapter provides an overview of HTML editors and their tasks. It covers the details of Netscape's editor, the Composer. There are other editors such as MS FrontPage. The reason we cover the Composer only is that it is part of Netscape Communicator. Therefore, readers who want to experiment with editors before buying one can use it as a start.

17.2 Editor's Tasks

The main goal of using an HTML editor is to speed and automate the creation process of Web pages. This reduces the cycle time (from designing a page to posting it on the Web). Using an editor should also make page creation easier, especially if the editor user knows HTML. Knowledge of HTML enables users to understand all the editor's functions.

The use of an HTML editor is an iterative process. The process begins with a blank Web page or a template and ends with a filled page having all the required HTML elements. During the process, Web authors add elements, evaluate the page, make adjustments, change the design, and so forth. This loop of adding elements and evaluating the resulting Web page continues until Web authors are satisfied with the final page design and layout.

During the process of generating Web pages, Web authors can use all the functions an HTML editor provides them. When using editors, authors can drag and drop HTML building blocks to build the page. Blocks can include hyperlinks, forms, and tables. Some editors provide *split-view editing*, where authors write and edit HTML code in one window and view the resulting Web page in another window. While the functions and tasks of different editors may be different, there is a common set that all editors support and provide. Here is a list of common editor tasks:

1. **Design and write Web pages.** This is the core and essential task of an editor. Editors provide Web authors with either blank pages or default templates. The templates may be used to jump-start page design and layout. Authors may also design and save their own customized templates. There are many editor's activities that support this task. These activities support the creation of all the HTML elements covered in this part of the book. An editor's user interface shows all these elements as icons. Web authors create text, links, images, forms, frames, tables, and so forth. They can also import images, already existing to insert in pages. They may use different fonts, colors, clip art work, backgrounds, and special characters.

2. **Upload and download pages.** After authors finish their Web pages, editors enable them to use FTP to upload or download them for distribution on the Web. In this task, an editor guides authors to define the URL of the hosting server and of the server directory to store the pages. Some editors allow Web authors to publish their Web pages on free Internet hosts and servers or on any ISP where they have accounts.

3. **Save code for reuse.** Web authors, like other programmers, quite often reuse the same code many times. Towards this goal, editors allow them to save snippets of their generated code separately from Web pages, for reuse in the future. This is a useful way of saving, say, CGI scripts. Take the example of a page counter that keeps track of the number of hits (visitors to a page). If authors write such a code once, they can save it for reuse.

4. **Provide code components.** The software industry promotes the concept of software components. The idea here is to provide off-the-shelf software components that can be reused while developing new software products. This concept is similar to buying standard auto parts in the automotive industry. Java Beans from Sun Microsystems and ActiveX objects from Microsoft allow software developers to write reusable software components. HTML editors provide canned (pre-written) code and scripts to enhance and activate Web pages. If editors provide the script already, authors can just use it. Some editors provide CGI scripts for counting page hits or visits. This spares authors the time and the knowledge needed to write such scripts.

5. **Provide e-mail links.** Some editors provide wizards that Web authors can use to add e-mail links to their Web pages. Web authors and webmasters use them to receive feedback from Web surfers.

6. **Provide time and date stamp.** This function is very useful when a Web page is frequently updated. Editors provide an automatic insertion stamp for time and date that is normally displayed as part of a page footer.

7. **Use directory structures.** Editors allow the use of the directory structure found on Web servers. This helps authors to place their pages in the allowed space for their pages.

8. **Provide Help function.** As with any software, online help provides Web authors with instant access to editor's documentation. Web authors read about any editor's command or function.

9. **Provide spelling checking.** This is a useful function, as many of us overlook wrong spelling, no matter how hard we check. Editors also allow their users to customize the spelling checking by adding their own words and acronyms.

10. **Highlight HTML errors.** Editors usually use color codes to highlight HTML tags, attributes, text, and so forth. They also highlight errors associated with HTML tags and attributes, to make it easier for Web authors to spot the errors and correct them.

11. **Support *do* and *undo* functions.** These are useful universal functions supported by many HTML editors.

12. **Search for words and strings.** Some of the common search text functions are offered by editors for Web authors. They include `Find`, `Find Again`, and `Find/Change` functions.

13. **Perform concurrent page development.** Some editors allow their users to work on and test multiple pages at the same time. This is particularly useful if Web authors would like to compare different design ideas for the same page. Contrasting the different designs on the screen side by side offers the best comparison methodology.

14. **Import code files.** Some editors support importing files into the code of Web pages. This is useful for editing code to be included in Web pages, such as CGI scripts and Java applets. Some Web pages may require, say, JavaScript code that is already stored in a file. A Web author can define an insertion point in the HTML code, and import the file.

17.3 Overview of Editors

There are many HTML editors in existence. Some are more sophisticated than others. Sample editors are `CoffeeCup` (www.coffeecup.com), `HotDog Pro` (www.sausage.com), `HotMetal Pro` (www.softquad.com), Netscape `Composer` (comes with the Communicator), Microsoft `FrontPage` (www.microsoft.com), and Adobe `PageMill` (www.adobe.com).

HTML editors may be categorized in three groups. The first group is known as *What You See Is What You Get* (WYSIWYG) *editors*. This group includes the `Composer`, `FrontPage`, `CoffeeCup`, and `PageMill`. Any editor that belongs to the WYSIWYG group allows Web authors to set up and insert the elements of a Web page in the editor which, in turn, generates the HTML code automatically. This group is restrictive and might not allow Web authors the flexibility they need to use HTML tags freely.

The second group is known as *HTML tag editors*. This group includes HotDog Pro. Web authors who use editors in this group still use HTML tags and their attributes, as we have done in the previous chapters of this book. However, they do not use a text editor. HTML editors provide them with menus of tags. When they choose a tag, editors present them with the available attributes. Moreover, these editors provide them with far more functions and tasks to facilitate code writing than do WYSIWYG editors.

The third group is known as *hybrid* or *semi-WYSIWYG editors*. This group is a mix of the preceding two groups. This group includes HotMetal Pro. These editors can be used by all Web authors, regardless of whether they know HTML tags. The final product of the editors of this group, like the other groups, is the Web page and its HTML code.

An HTML editor has a general structure for its user interface, regardless of its type. Figure 17.1 shows a generic structure for an editor's GUI. There are three bars at the top of the editor's window. The Menu bar holds menus such as File, Edit, and so forth. The Elements bar contains icons of all the HTML elements that Web authors need to create their Web pages. These elements are text, hyperlinks, images, image maps, forms, frames, and tables. The Formatting bar contains icons for fonts, colors, lists, headings, and text justification. Specific HTML editors implement the information of these three bars in different ways. The next section covers Netscape Composer as an example. The remainder of the editor's window is the space that holds the Web page under development. That space may have other subwindows, to provide authors with more gadgets and choices.

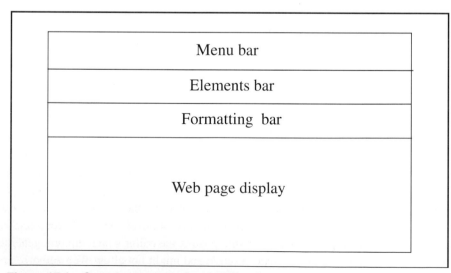

Figure 17.1   Generic structure of an HTML editor.

17.4 Netscape Composer

Netscape Composer is one of the many available HTML editors. It comes bundled with Netscape Communicator. It is automatically installed with the Communicator. It can be invoked by clicking the Composer icon on the bottom right corner of the Communicator window shown in figure 3.13. It can also be invoked by clicking the Communicator menu (figure 3.13) and then clicking the Composer menu item.

Figure 17.2 shows the Composer GUI. The GUI has four bars: Title, Menu, Composition, and Formatting. The Title bar holds the title of the currently opened page in the Composer, just as when we open a Web page in the Communicator. In addition to showing the page title, the Title bar shows the name of the HTML file, with its full path, of the Web page. When the user invokes the Composer, it opens with a blank page. The user can save the page by clicking this sequence; File (on the Menu bar) => Save As => input desired name of HTML file. After the user finishes this sequence, the Composer asks for a title for the page. The default value is the same as the name of the HTML file. After inputting the title, the Composer saves the page HTML code in the file. The user can view this code by clicking View (on the Menu bar) => Page Source. Here is the HTML code after saving the blank page with the title Just Testing (we explain this code later in the tutorials section):

```
<!doctype html public "-//w3c//dtd html 4.0 transitional//en">
<html>
<head>
   <meta http-equiv="Content-Type" content="text/html; charset=iso-
8859-1">
   <meta name="Author" content="Abe Zeid">
   <meta name="GENERATOR" content="Mozilla/4.6 [en] (Win98; I)
[Netscape]">
   <title>Just Testing</title>
</head>
<body>
 </body></html>
```

17.4.1 Menu Bar

The Menu bar holds several useful menus. The File menu has several items. Some of them are repeated in the Composition Toolbar (and are covered then). Others are self-explanatory. The New submenu let users open a new browser window (Navigator Window), an e-mail window (Message), blank page (Blank Page), a local user's template (Page from Template), or a Netscape's template (Page from Wizard). The last two menu items of the New submenu are what we use to create Web pages. Users must be online if they need to use a template from Netscape's Wizard, because the Wizard's templates are stored on Netscape's server (home.netscape.com). Templates are useful because they speed up the process of creating Web pages. They also provide uniformity among Web pages that use them.

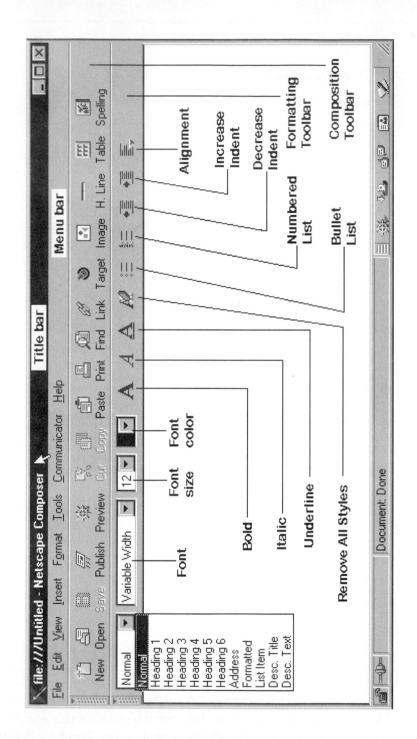

Figure 17.2 GUI of Netscape Composer.

The Edit menu has the most common edit functions we are familiar with, in addition to some specific to HTML. The common functions are Undo, Cut, Copy, Paste, Delete, and Select All. The HTML-related functions are Delete Table, Remove Link, Select Table, Find in Page, Find Again, HTML Source, and Preferences. A user can select a table (or a link), and delete it. The Composer allows the user to delete an entire table, one row, one column, or a cell. A user can search for certain text in a page by using the Find function. The Composer provides the HTML Source function (because it is a WYSIWYG editor) if a user needs to edit the page HTML code. Using this function invokes a browser window with the page displayed in it. The user can, in turn, view the page source. The Preferences menu item invokes the Preferences window of the browser; which was covered in chapter 3.

The View menu has two submenus (Show and Character Set) and six menu items (Reload, Show Images, Refresh, Stop Loading, Page Source, and Page Info). The Show submenu enables the user to turn on or off the display of the Composer bars and the paragraphs marks in the Web page. The Character Set submenu allows the user to choose a set that corresponds to the page language. The Page Source menu item allows users to view the code of the page. The Page Info menu item displays such page information as its location, security, and so forth. The other menu items are self explanatory, and we encourage readers to experiment with them.

The Insert menu allows the user to insert HTML elements into the Web page under construction. The menu repeats the same elements found on the Composition Toolbar. They are Link, Target, Image, H. Line, and Table. It is more convenient to access these elements from the Toolbar. The last three menu items of the Insert menu are additional (and useful). The HTML Tag item allows the user to insert any tag in the page. This item is useful if a tag is not listed on the Composition or the Formatting Toolbar. The other two items (New Line Break, and Break below Image(s)) are useful for formatting.

The Format menu repeats all the same elements found on the Formatting Toolbar. All these menu items are covered in section 17.4.3. It also has four extra menu items. They are the last four items. Three of them enable users to view and change the properties of characters, tables, and page colors. The Character Properties menu item provides control of the properties of characters, links, and paragraphs. When the user clicks this item, the Character Properties window shown in figure 17.3 pops up. The window has three tabs to control the properties of characters, links, and paragraphs. Similarly, the Page Colors and Properties menu item provides control of page title, author, and colors and of the <META> tag. When the user clicks this item, the Page Properties window shown in figure 17.4 pops up. The window has three tabs to control the page properties. Readers are encouraged to experiment with all these tabs.

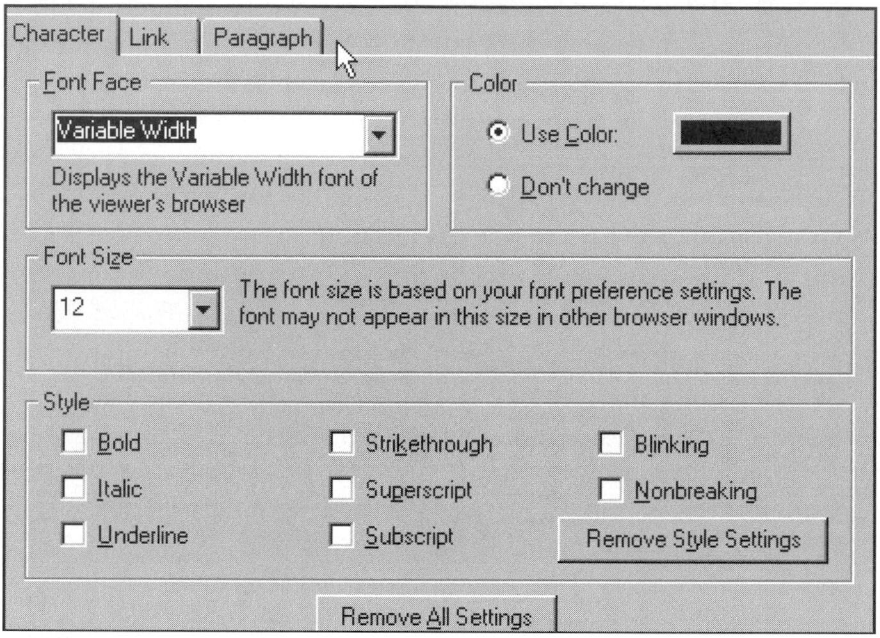

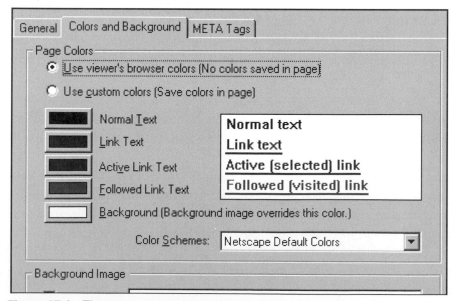

Figure 17.3   The `Character Properties` window of the Composer.

Figure 17.4   The `Page Properties` window of the Composer.

The `Tools` menu provides a spelling checking function that enables users to check the spelling of page text. It also provide three interesting submenus, as is shown in figure 17.5. The `Character Tools` submenu has the three menu items shown in figure 17.5. When the user clicks the `Insert Special Character` menu item, the special character window shown in figure 17.6 pops up. The user clicks a character, say `euro`, and the browser inserts it in the page in the current location. The `Rainbow Colorize` menu item allows a color spectrum, as in a rainbow. The text shown in figure 17.5 has a rainbow color that starts as red and fades gradually into a mix of yellow and red. The `Small Caps` menu item converts text into small caps. The user highlights the desired text and clicks this item. Figure 17.5 shows an example.

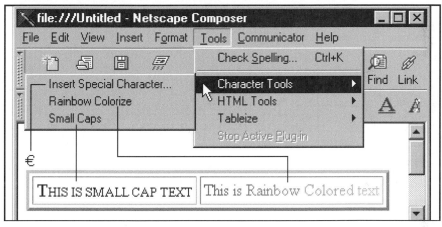

Figure 17.5 The `Tools menu` of the Composer.

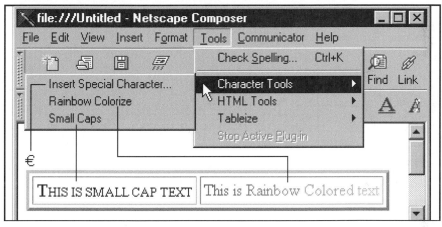

Figure 17.6 The special characters of the Composer.

The HTML Tools submenu of the Edit menu has one menu item, Edit HTML Source. When it is selected, an Edit HTML Source window is displayed with the HTML code of the current page, as shown in figure 17.7. If the user knows HTML, the user can insert any tag in the code and click the Apply button to view the changes in the page immediately. If not satisfied, the user can delete the inserted code and try something different. When done, the user clicks the OK button, which kills the window upon exit.

The last submenu of the Tools menu is Tableize, which allows users to include text in table cells. Cell text is identified by either a comma or a space as delimiter. The user highlights the text and chooses the By Commas or By Spaces menu item of the Tableize submenu. The Composer creates table cells that surround the text as shown in figure 17.5. The figure shows two table cells. The Composer creates all the necessary table tags.

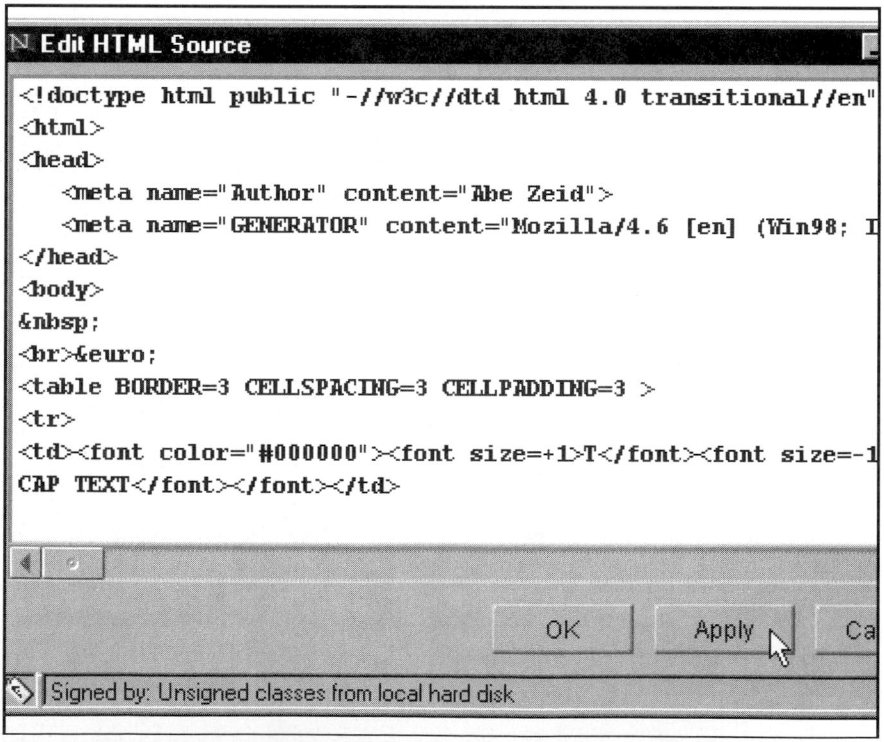

```
Edit HTML Source

<!doctype html public "-//w3c//dtd html 4.0 transitional//en"
<html>
<head>
   <meta name="Author" content="Abe Zeid">
   <meta name="GENERATOR" content="Mozilla/4.6 [en] (Win98; I
</head>
<body>
 
<br>&euro;
<table BORDER=3 CELLSPACING=3 CELLPADDING=3 >
<tr>
<td><font color="#000000"><font size=+1>T</font><font size=-1
CAP TEXT</font></font></td>
```

OK   Apply   Ca

Signed by: Unsigned classes from local hard disk

Figure 17.7 The Edit HTML Source window of the Composer.

The last two menus on the Menu bar are Communicator and Help. These two menus are the same as for the browser itself. Their details were covered in chapter 3.

17.4.2 Composition Toolbar

The Composition Toolbar shown in figure 17.2 is the main bar of the Composer GUI. It has all the HTML elements that users need to create their Web pages. The icons of this bar can be grouped into three categories. The first category deals with the Web page file and includes New, Open, Save, Publish, and Preview. The first four are found in the File menu of the Menu bar. When the user clicks the New icon, a window pops up. It provides the user with the same options (blank, template, or wizard), discussed in section 17.4.1, to create a new page. The Open icon opens an existing Web page. The Save icon saves the current page.

The Publish icon help the user publish the Web page. When the user clicks it, the Publish window shown in figure 17.8 pops up. The user fills in the information as shown. The location of the page on the server is defined by the server URL and the directory on the server that will hold the page. In figure 17.8, we use *courses* as the directory to which the page is downloaded. Observe that the user must have an account (user name and a password) on the server to publish the page, unless it is a free server. After filling in the information, the user clicks the OK button. The Composer downloads the page. The user must be online for a successful download. The Preview icon allows the user to view the Web page in a browser window for a final check before publishing or saving.

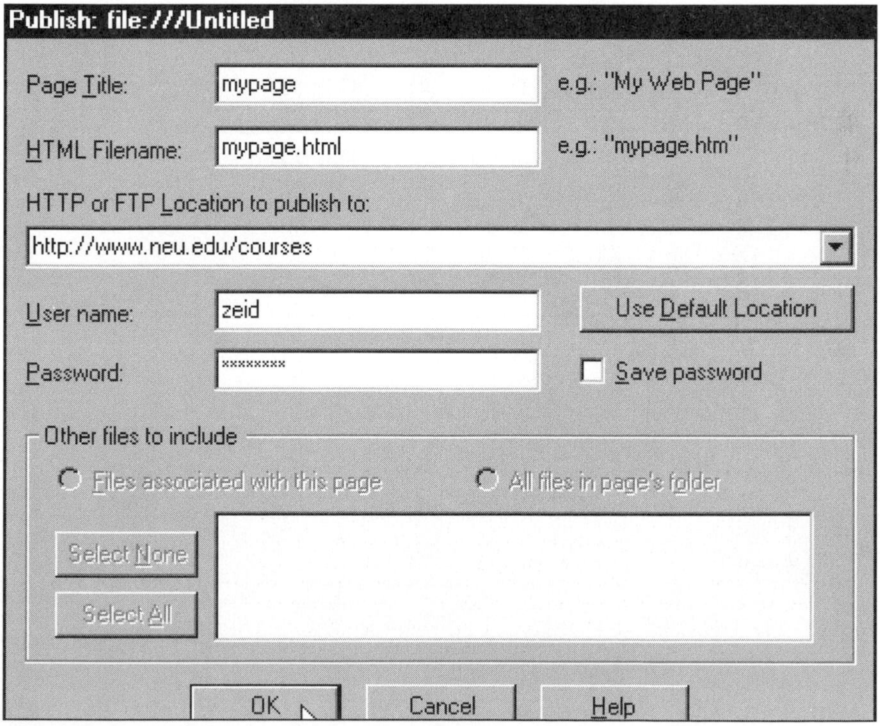

Figure 17.8 The Publish window of the Composer.

The second category of icons on the `Composition` Toolbar deals with the page text. The icons are `Cut`, `Copy`, `Paste`, `Print`, `Find`, and `Spelling`. These icons are used in the same way that we always use them in word processors and text editors.

The third category of icons deals with the creation of HTML elements. The icons are `Link`, `Target`, `Image`, `H. Line`, and `Table`. The tag of each one of these elements has been covered in its respective chapter. These elements are created at the current position of the screen cursor in the Web page. Whenever the user clicks an element, the `Composer` requests all the information required by the element tag and its attributes, by displaying a window with fields to fill in. For example, to insert a hyperlink in a page, the user clicks the `Link` icon, which invokes the `Character Properties` window (figure 17.3) with the `Link` tab displayed, as shown in figure 17.9. Comparing this figure with figure 7.5 shows where to input the <A> tag information. When the user clicks the `OK` button, the `Composer` displays the link in the page and inserts the <A> tag in the page code that is being generated in the background. Similarly, the `Target` icon creates the name that can be used later with the `Link` icon to create an intradocument link as discussed in section 7.9.2. The `H. Line` icon inserts a horizontal line in the page.

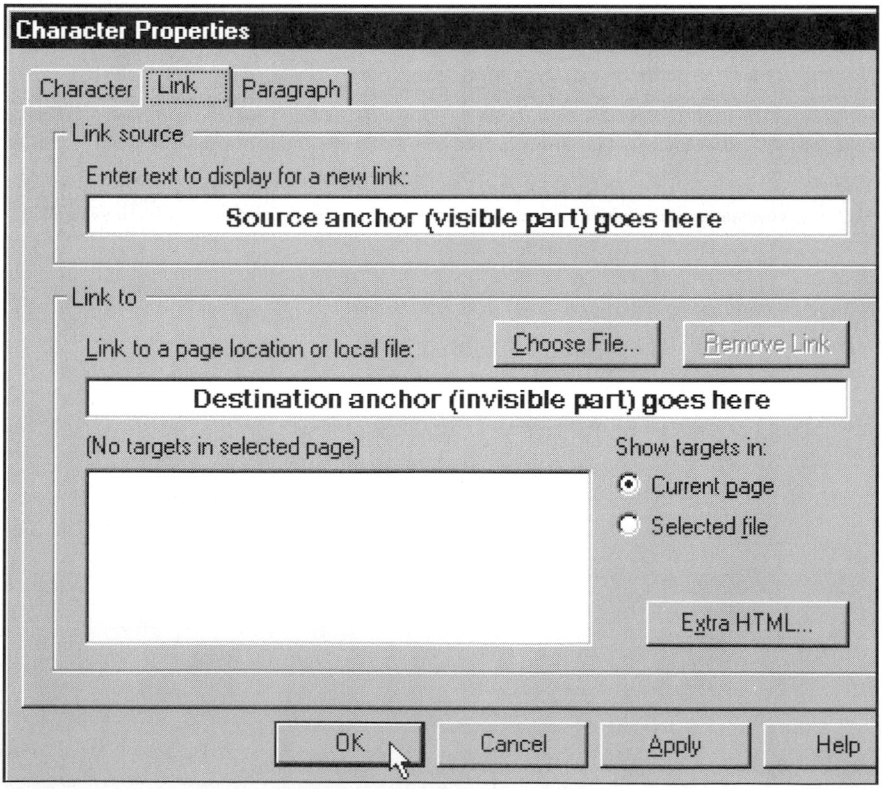

Figure 17.9   Insert a hyperlink in the Composer.

The `Image` icon inserts an image into the Web page. Clicking it displays the window shown in figure 17.10. The information requested in this window implements the <IMG> tag and its attributes, which were covered in section 10.4.1. The top `Image location` text field of figure 17.10 asks for the image file to be used with the SRC attribute. The `Text align-ment` section of this figure implements the ALIGN attribute. The `Dimensions` section imple-ments the WIDTH and the HEIGHT attributes. The `Space around image` section implements the HSPACE and VSPACE attributes.

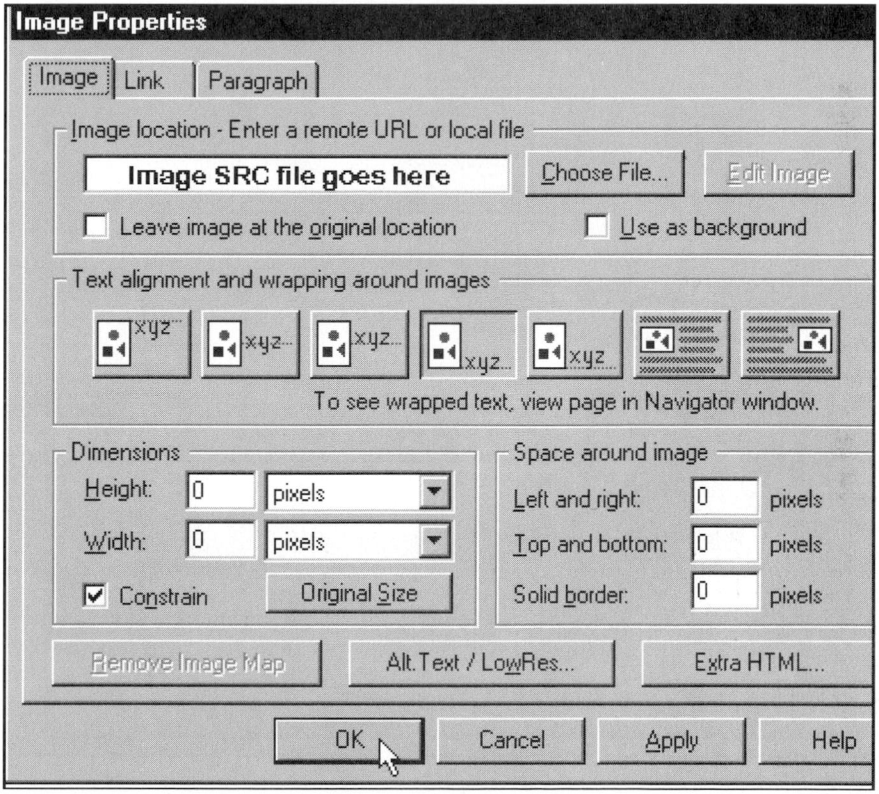

Figure 17.10   Insert an image in the Composer.

The `Table` icon inserts a table in the Web page. When the user clicks it, the window shown in figure 17.11 is displayed. All the fields and sections of this window implement the <TABLE> tag and its attributes. The number of rows (columns) implements the ROWS (COLS) attribute. The `Table Alignment` section implements the ALIGN attribute. The middle sec-tion implements CELLSPACING and CELLPADDING. In addition, the WIDTH, HEIGHT, and BGCOLOR are implemented in the last section of the window.

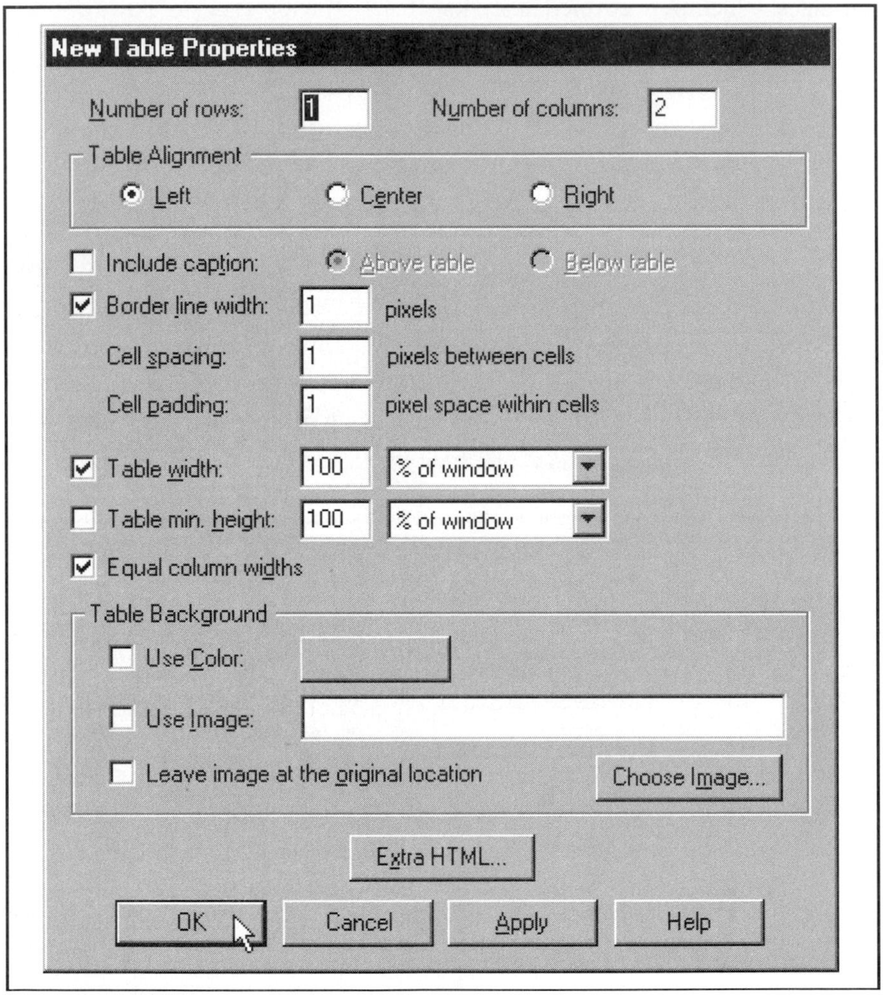

Figure 17.11   Insert a table in the `Composer`.

17.4.3 Formatting Toolbar

The `Formatting` Toolbar shown in figure 17.2 holds all the icons needed to format text in a Web page. The Toolbar has four drop lists. It begins with the `Paragraph style` drop list, which implements the heading tags, the <ADDRESS> tag, and others, as shown in the figure. The user chooses the style, by clicking it, and then begins typing the text. The next (`Font`) drop list is to choose text fonts. All the system fonts are usually available. The `Font Size` drop list allows the choice of a desired size. The user can also type any other size. The `Font`

`Color` drop list allows the user to choose the text (foreground) color. Clicking this list displays a color palette. The user clicks the desired color. This color becomes the default until the user changes it.

The next four icons (figure 17.2) deal with text appearance. There are three of them, to create bold, italic, and underlined text. These three icons are mutually inclusive; that is, they are selectable at the same time. For example, the user may click the bold and italic icons before typing to produce bold italic text. The fourth icon deals with styles and is not covered here.

The following two icons (figure 17.2) create lists. One creates a bullet (unordered) list, and the other creates a numbered (ordered) list. The user clicks, say, the `Bullet List` icon to create an unordered list. Upon clicking the icon, the paragraph style changes automatically to `List Item` in the first (left) drop list shown in figure 17.2. This is important to realize for the following reason. Upon finishing the creation of all the list items, the user clicks this same drop list, and selects the `Normal` style to exit the list mode. The user may, instead, click the `Bullet List` icon once to turn it off. List items are created by hitting the `Enter` key on the keyboard after inputting the text of each item. To create nested lists, the user indents before creating the inner list items, by using the indent icons shown in figure 17.2.

The two indent icons of the `Formatting` Toolbar, shown in figure 17.2, are used to indent text or to create nested lists (as just described). One icon increases indents by moving the cursor position to the right. The other icon decreases indents by moving the cursor position to the left.

The last icon of the Formatting Toolbar, shown in figure 17.2, is the `Alignment` icon. This icon allows the user to left- or right-justify or to center text in the Web page. The user chooses the type of alignment before or after typing the text, and the `Composer` adjusts the text accordingly.

17.5 The Composer Tasks

Section 17.2 discusses, in general terms, the tasks that an HTML editor can perform. We have covered some of the tasks in section 17.4, for Netscape `Composer` as an HTML editor. In this section, we focus on tasks related to page creation, formatting, and inserting raw HTML tags.

17.5.1 Creating, Saving, and Viewing Web Pages

To create or open a Web page, the user can use different starting points, as follows:

•**Start from a blank page.** Click the following sequence: `File` (menu of Netscape browser) => `New` => `Blank Page`. A `Composer` window containing a blank page opens up.

•**Start from a template.** Click the following sequence; `File` (menu of Netscape browser) => `New` => `Page From Template`. This sequence opens a dialog box that which provides three choices for a template, as shown in figure 17.12. Type the template name, choose a local file, or use Netscape templates that reside on the Netscape server.

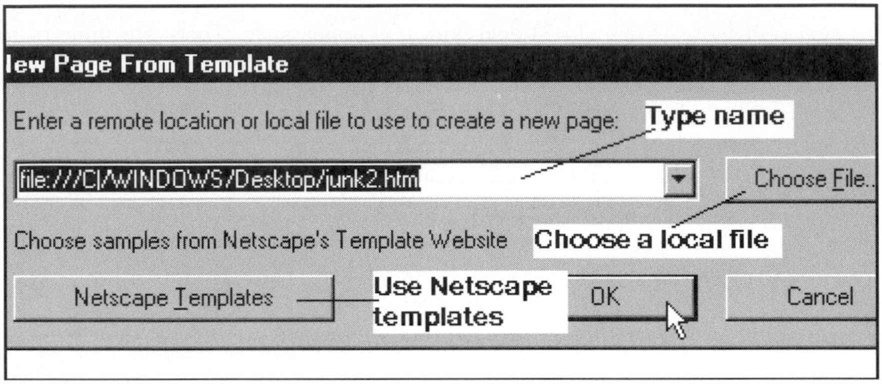

Figure 17.12   Choose a template file.

•Start from Netscape Wizard. Click the following sequence: `File` (menu of Netscape browser) => `New` => `Page From Wizard`. Follow instructions to open a template in `Composer`. You must be online to access the wizard.

•Start from the Web page you are currently browsing. Click this sequence: `File` (menu of Netscape browser) => `Edit Page`. A `Composer` window opens, with the current page in it.

Once a page is created or opened in the `Composer`, the user may perform various activities and insert various HTML elements. One common activity to do is spelling checking of the page text. The user clicks `Tools` (menu on `Composer` window) => `Check Spelling`. This sequence checks the entire text of the page. The user may select words or part of the page text to check. Spelling checking allows the user to add new vocabulary to the `Composer` dictionary. The window of the spelling checking is easy to follow.

When all editing activities are done, the user saves the page code in an HTML file by clicking `File` (menu of `Composer`) => `Save As` (or `Save`) => input file name. At this point, the `Composer` asks the user for a file name and for a title for the Web page. It uses this title in the page <TITLE> tag.

After saving the page in the composer, the user may view it in the browser. The user may click the `Preview` icon on the `Composition` Toolbar of the `Composer` (figure 17.2). Alternatively, the user may use a browser window directly and click `File` (menu of Netscape browser) => `Open Page`. The user can switch back and forth between the `Composer` and the browser until the page is fully developed.

17.5.2 Formatting Paragraphs

Users may format their Web pages in different ways. Formatting activities include the following: inserting horizontal lines; formatting paragraphs; changing text color, style, and font; and inserting raw HTML tags. To insert a horizontal line in a page, the user clicks the location where the line should appear. The user then clicks the `H. Line` on the Formatting Toolbar. Alternatively, the user may click `Insert` (menu of `Composer`) => `Horizontal Line`.

To format a paragraph, click the sequence `Format` (menu on `Composer` window) => `Character Properties`. The window shown in figure 17.9 pops up. Figure 17.13 shows the window with its `Paragraph` tab. The user can choose the paragraph style and alignment. The `Paragraph style` drop list of figure 17.13 is the same as the one shown in figure 17.2. The list has 12 items: `Normal`, `Heading 1 – Heading 6` (`<H1>` – `<H6>` tags), `Address` (`<ADDRESS>` tag), `Formatted` (useful for code examples), `List Item` (used to create bullet and numbered lists), `Desc. Title`, and `Desc. Text` (used to create definition lists).

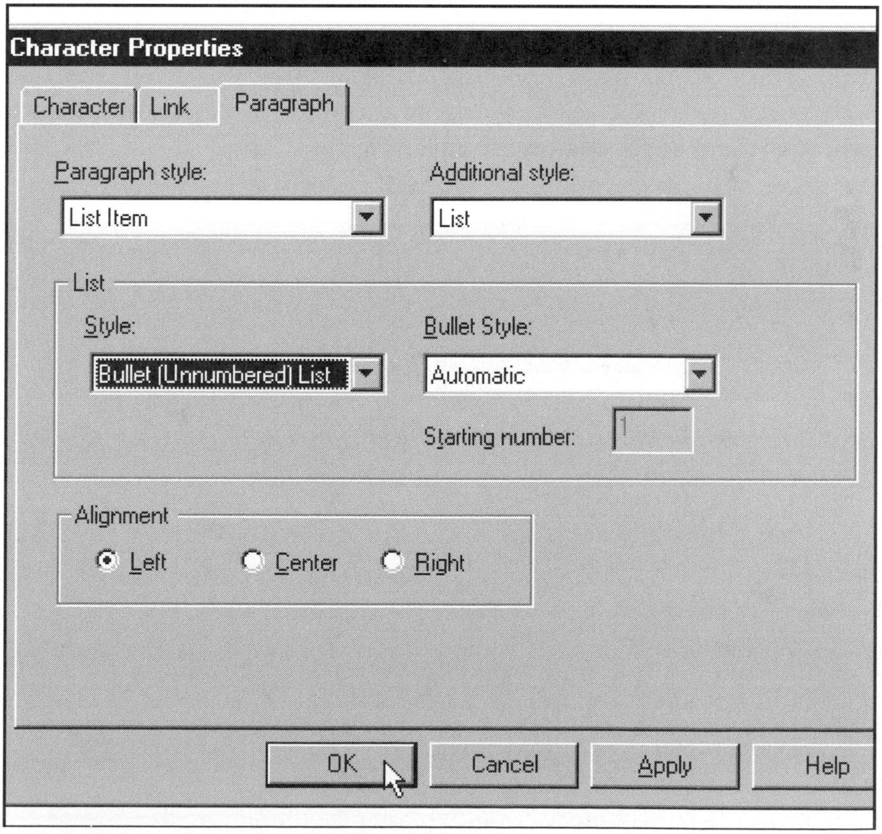

Figure 17.13 `Composer` window to format paragraphs.

The `Additional style` drop list enables users to use the `Block Quote` option to indent text, or the `List` option to create lists. If the `List` option is chosen, the `List` section shown in figure 17.13 is activated as shown. The `Style` drop list in the List section has five options; to create bullet, numbered, menu, directory, and description lists. The first three types of list have been covered in the book. The directory list makes short items appear horizontally in columns, as in a DOS directory listing. The description list is another name for a definition list. The `Bullet Style` drop list in the `List` section allows users to choose the type of bullet (solid or open circle, or solid square) for bullet lists. The `Starting number` text field in the `List` section allows the user to specify the first number in a numbered list.

The last section in the paragraph window shown in figure 17.13 is `Alignment`. Users can use it to align selected or new paragraphs at the left, center, or right of the page.

17.5.3 Formatting Characters

To change text color, style, and font, the user needs to highlight the existing text first. The user clicks the `Character` tab shown in figure 17.13. The window with the contents of this tab is shown in figure 17.14. The window has four sections. The `Font Face` section has a drop-down list to select a new font. The `Color` section has a color button, which displays a color palette to choose from if the user clicks the button. The `Font Size` section has a drop-down list to choose a size. The `Style` section has several checkboxes to specify the style. Multiple checkboxes can be chosen to use multiple styles.

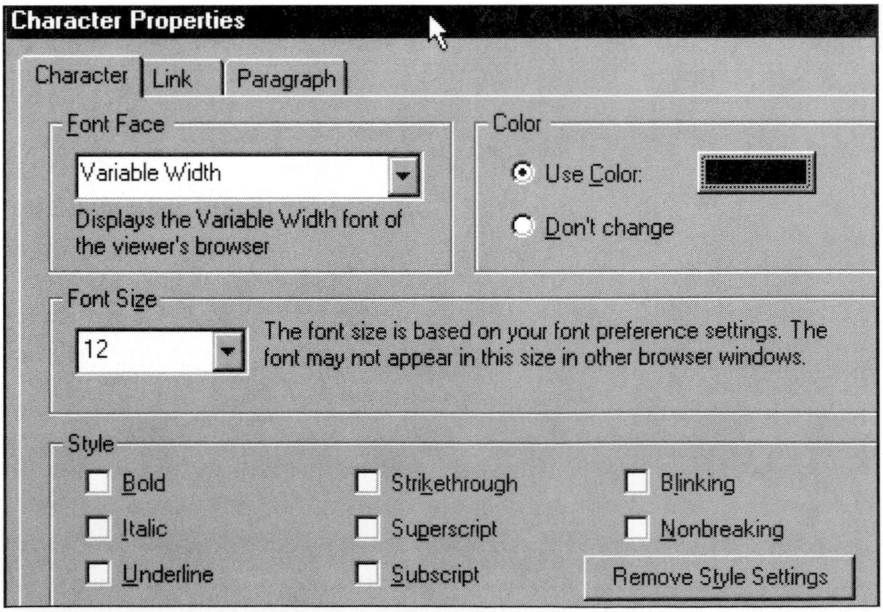

Figure 17.14 `Composer` window to format characters.

17.5.4 Inserting Raw HTML Tags

To insert a raw HTML tag at a location in a page, the user clicks `Insert` (menu of `Composer`) => `HTML Tag` to open the tag window shown in figure 17.15. The user uses this window to add HTML tags to the page. Let us assume that we need to insert the following tag at the current cursor location in the page: <A HREF="test.html">Just testing</A>. We type the first half of the tag as shown in the figure and click `OK`. The HTML window disappears, and the `Composer` inserts a yellow symbol in the page as shown in figure 17.16. This symbol indicates the beginning of an HTML tag. We now type "Just testing" next to the symbol. We then open the HTML tag window again by clicking `Insert` => `HTML tag`. We type </A>, and click `OK`. The window disappears again, and a closing yellow symbol is inserted in the page to indicate the completion of the tag, as shown at the bottom of figure 17.16. We repeat this procedure as many times as we need to insert tags. Observe that we can type only tags in the HTML window. No text is allowed in the window. Text outside the tags is typed in the page. If, say, we type <A HREF = "test.html">Just testing</A> all at once, the `Composer` returns an error that reads `Premature close of tag`.

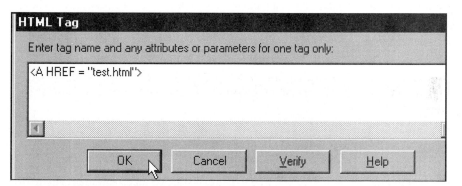

Figure 17.15 `HTML Tag` window of the `Composer`.

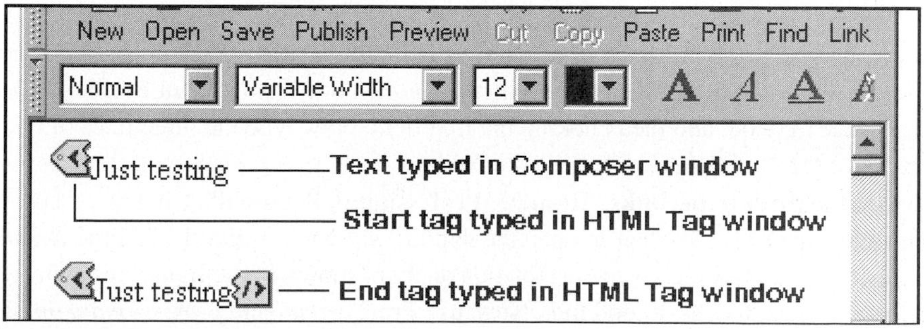

Figure 17.16 Inserting an HTML tag using the `Composer`.

17.6 Tutorials

This section focuses on using Netscape Composer as an HTML editor to design and develop Web pages. As we add elements in the Composer, it generates the page HTML code automatically. We list the generated code here, and contrast it with the manual code that we could have written to develop the same Web page. Any Web browser can be used to display the corresponding Web pages. It is a good idea to create a directory structure to save HTML files. This helps Web authors to organize HTML files and makes it easy to find them.

17.6.1 Creating a Web Page with Text and Links

In this tutorial, we create the same Web page we have created manually in tutorial 7.14.1, as shown in figure 7.14. We keep this figure in mind as we write the following steps to create the page by using Netscape Composer:

1. **Open a blank page.** Click File (browser menu) => Blank Page. This step opens up the Composer window.
2. **Write the first line of text, which reads "Welcome to my Web page".** This text has a style of <H2>, is centered in the page, and has a red color. Click the Font Color drop list on the Formatting Toolbar, and click a red box from the color palette. This sequence allows you to choose a red color. Click the Alignment icon on the Formatting Toolbar, and click the middle item. This sequence centers the text in the Web page. Click the Paragraph style drop list on the Formatting Toolbar => Heading 2. This sequence effectively chooses the <H2> tag. Now type the line of text. Hit Enter to advance to the next line.
3. **Write the next three lines of text, which read "Name goes here; Address goes here; Phone number goes here".** These lines are centered, have red color, and have normal size. After finishing step 2 above, hit Enter on the keyboard. The color and center settings from step 2 are still in effect. The paragraph style changes automatically to Normal, which is what we need. Now type the three lines of text. You need to hit Enter after entering a line. Also, hit Enter after the last line to leave a blank line.
4. **Write the following three lines of text.** This text is normal size, left-justified, and black in color. Change the red color to black by clicking the Font Color drop list and then clicking the black box. Change the center alignment to left alignment by clicking the Alignment icon, and then clicking the first item. Now type the three lines of text. Hit Enter after the last line, to leave a blank line.
5. **Create the three hyperlinks "Resume, Professional, Personal".** Click the Link icon on the Composition Toolbar to open the window shown in figure 17.9. Type *Resume* and *resume.html* for the source and destination anchors shown in the figure, respectively. Hit Enter. Repeat for the second link. Now, use *Professional* and *professional.html*. Hit Enter. Use *Personal* and *personal.html* for the third link. Hit *Enter* twice.

6. **Create the page address.** Click the Paragraph Style drop list on the Formatting Toolbar => Address. This sequence effectively chooses the <ADDRESS> tag. Now type *Copyright* followed by a space. To insert the copyright symbol, click Tools (Composer menu) => Character Tools => Insert Special Characters => click the copyright symbol. The symbol should show in the page now. Hit the space bar on the keyboard to leave a space. Type *2000* to finish off the first address line. Hit Enter. Type the second address line (Abe Zeid) and hit Enter. The third line is the e-mail link. Click the Link icon and follow sequence from step 5 above. Use *Please e-mail me* and *zeid@coe.neu.edu* for the anchors. Hit Enter. Type the last address line (Revised — January 2000). To finish the page off, hit *Enter* twice.

7. **Save the HTML code of the Web page in a file.** Click File (Composer menu) => Save As => type *tutorial17.6.1.html* as the file name. Now, the Composer asks for a page title. Type *My personal Web page* for the title, and click OK. Figure 17.17 shows the page as it appears in the Composer window. You can view the Web page in the browser by clicking the Preview icon of the Composer Composition Toolbar.

Figure 17.17 Web page of tutorial 7.14.1, created by using the Composer.

We have saved the HTML code that the Composer generated for this Web page in a file with the name *tutorial17.6.1.html*. The listing of this code is shown below.

```
<!doctype html public "-//w3c//dtd html 4.0 transitional//en">
<html>
<head>
   <meta http-equiv="Content-Type" content="text/html; charset=iso-
8859-1">
   <meta name="Author" content="Abe Zeid">
   <meta name="GENERATOR" content="Mozilla/4.6 [en] (Win98; I)
[Netscape]">
   <title>My personal Web page</title>
</head>
<body>
<center>
<h2>
<font color="#FF0000">Welcome to my Web page</font></h2></center>
<center><font color="#FF0000">Name goes here</font>
<br><font color="#FF0000">Address goes here</font>
<br><font color="#FF0000">Phone number goes he</font></center>
<p><font color="#000000">Let me introduce myself. I have mastered
HTML.</font>
<br><font color="#000000">I have been working with many people.
This is my personal Web page, in case you want to know more about
me.</font>
<p> <a href="../../../../../../resume.html">Resume</a>
<br> <a href="../../../../../../professional.html">Profes-
sional</a>
<br> <a href="../../../../../../personal.html">Personal</a>
<br> 
<address>
Copyright &copy; 2000</address>
<address>
Abe Zeid</address>
<address>
 <a href="../../../../../../zeid@coe.neu.edu">Please e-mail
me</a></address>
<address>
Revised - January 2000</address>
</body>
</html>
```

Here are some comments about the preceding code:

•HTML editors in general insert the first line in the file, which is a comment that describes that the document type is an HTML file generated using HTML 4.0.

•Editors also use the <META> tag to describe the Web page, its content, and the editor that created it. This help Web authors and search engines to index the page. The details of the <META> tag have been covered in chapter 7.

•The `Composer` inserts a <P> tag for every line space we create.

•The `Composer` uses the * * throughout the code. This is the symbol for non-breaking space. It is equivalent to hitting the space bar on the keyboard once.

•The rest of the HTML code may be compared with its manual counterpart written in tutorial 7.14.1. The comparison shows that the code generated by the editor is more clumsy than the manual code. There is a lot of repetition of the tags. The paths to the files of the links are hard to read. It will be interesting to use another HTML editor to create the same Web page and compare the code to see if it comes out any better.

17.6.2 Creating a Web Page with Lists

In this tutorial, we create the same Web page as in example 8.6, shown in figure 8.8. Follow the these steps:

1. **Open a blank page.** Click `File` (browser menu) => `Blank Page`.
2. **Write the first line of text, which reads "Creating non-text list items".** Follow step 2 in tutorial 17.6.1 to create this text that is <H2>, centered, and blue. Hit `Enter` to go to next line.
3. **Write the second line of text, which reads "Here are my non-text list items".** Follow step 2 in tutorial 17.6.1 to create this text that is normal, left-justified, and black. Hit `Enter` twice to leave a line space.
4. **Write the third line of text, which reads "This is a traditional list".** Follow step 3 above, but use instead of blue. Hit `Enter`.
5. **Create the bullet list.** Click the `Bullet List` icon on the `Formatting` Toolbar of the `Composer`. Change the color to black by clicking the `Font Color` icon on the `Formatting` Toolbar and then clicking the black box. Type *Traditional list item*. Hit `Enter`. Repeat twice to create the other two list items.
6. **Write the line of text that reads "List with hyperlinks".** We must convert the current cursor position from a bullet item to normal text. This requires two steps. Click the `Paragraph style` drop list on the `Formatting` Toolbar, and click `Normal`. Then click the `Decrease Indent` icon on the same Toolbar, to position the cursor at the left edge of the page. Now, change the color to red. Then type *List with hyperlinks*. Hit `Enter`.
7. **Create the numbered list.** Click the `Numbered List` icon on the Formatting Toolbar. Then, click the `Link` icon on the `Composition` Toolbar. Type *Northeastern University* and *http://www.neu.edu* for the source and destination anchors. Click OK. Now you should see the link in the page. Hit `Enter`. Repeat for the other two list items. Type *Prentice Hall publishing* and *http://www.prenhall.com* for the second item. Hit `Enter`. Type *Use a*

search engine and *http://altavista.com* for the third item. Hit `Enter`. Notice that the numbered list items use a pound sign (#) instead of a number in the `Composer` window. When you view the page in a browser window, you should see the numbers instead.

8. **Write the line of text that reads "Mix text and non-text list items".** Follow the details of step 6 above.

9. **Create the last bullet list.** Follow step 5 above to invoke the bullet list and to change the color to black. We need to change the list symbol from a solid circle to a solid square. Click `Format` (`Composer` menu) => `Paragraph Properties` => `Paragraph` (tab) => `Solid square` from the `Bullet Style` drop list => OK. Type *Traditional list item* for the first list item. Hit `Enter`. Click the `Link` icon to create the second list item. Use *Example 7.1 Web page* and *example7.1.html* for the anchors. Hit `Enter`. Type *Traditional list item* for the third list item. Hit `Enter`. Create the last link item. Use *Example 7.2 Web page* and *example7.2.html* for the anchors.

10. **Save the HTML code of the Web page in a file.** Follow step 7 in tutorial 17.6.1, and save the code in a file with the name *tutorial17.6.2.html*. Use *Non-text list items* for the page title. Figure 17.18 shows the page as it appears in the `Composer` window. View the Web page in the browser.

Here is a list of the generated HTML code:

```
<!doctype html public "-//w3c//dtd html 4.0 transitional//en">
<html>
<head>
   <meta http-equiv="Content-Type" content="text/html; charset=iso-
8859-1">
   <meta name="Author" content="Abe Zeid">
   <meta name="GENERATOR" content="Mozilla/4.6 [en] (Win98; I)
[Netscape]">
   <title>Non-text list items</title>
</head>
<body>
<center>
<h2>
<font color="#3333FF">Creating non-text list items</font></h2></
center>
<font color="#333333">Here is my non-text list items</font><font
color="#333333"></font>
<p><font color="#FF0000">This is a traditional list</font>
<ul>
<li>
<font color="#333333">Traditional list item</font></li>
<li>
<font color="#333333">Traditional list item</font></li>
<li>
<font color="#333333">Traditional list item</font></li>
```

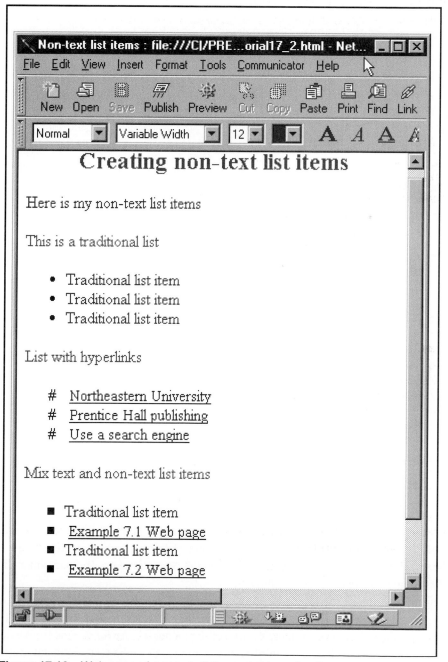

Figure 17.18 Web page of example 8.6, created by using the `Composer`.

```
</ul>
<font color="#FF0000">List with hyperlinks</font>
<ol>
<li>
 <a href="http://www.neu.edu">Northeastern University</a></
li>
<li>
 <a href="http://www.prenhall.com">Prentice Hall publishing</
a></li>
<li>
 <a href="../../../../../../http//www.altavista.com">Use a
search engine</a></li>
</ol>
<font color="#FF0000">Mix text and non-text list items</font>
<ul TYPE=SQUARE>
<li>
<font color="#333333">Traditional list item</font></li>
<li>
 <a href="../../../../../../example7.1.html">Example 7.1 Web
page</a></li>
<li>
<font color="#333333">Traditional list item</font></li>
<li>
 <a href="../../../../../../example7.2.html">Example 7.2 Web
page</a></li>
</ul>
<font color="#333333"></font>
</body>
</html>
```

17.6.3 Creating a Web Page with Images

In this tutorial, we use the `Composer` to create a Web page with an image. This Web page is the same page we created in example 10.2, aa shown in figure 10.4. Follow these steps:

1. **Open a blank page.** Click `File` (browser menu) => `Blank Page`.
2. **Write the first line of text, which reads "Web page with scaled image".** This text is `<H2>`, centered, and blue. Follow step 2 in tutorial 17.6.1 to create it. Hit `Enter` to go to the next line. Click the `Alignment` icon on the `Formatting` Toolbar, and click the first item to move the cursor to the left.
3. **Insert the image.** Click the `Image` icon on the `Composition` Toolbar to open the `Image Properties` window shown in figure 17.10. Fill in all the fields with the image values, as shown in figure 17.19. All the values we use here come from example 10.2. Make sure to choose the third button from the left in the text alignment section. We need it to write the text in the next step. Also, uncheck the `Constraint` checkbox, to be

able to input the width and height of the image independently. Click the `Apply` button. You should see the image in the Web page now. Click the `Close` button to close the `Image Properties` window.

4. **Write the remaining text.** Write the three lines of text that are shown in figure 10.4. Hit `Enter` after each line.

5. **Save the HTML code of the Web page in a file.** Follow step 7 in tutorial 17.6.1, and save the code in a file with the name *tutorial17.6.3.html*. Use *A Web page with scaled images* as the page title. View the Web page in a browser.

Figure 17.20 shows the resulting page in the `Composer`. The generated HTML code is also shown following figure 17.19.

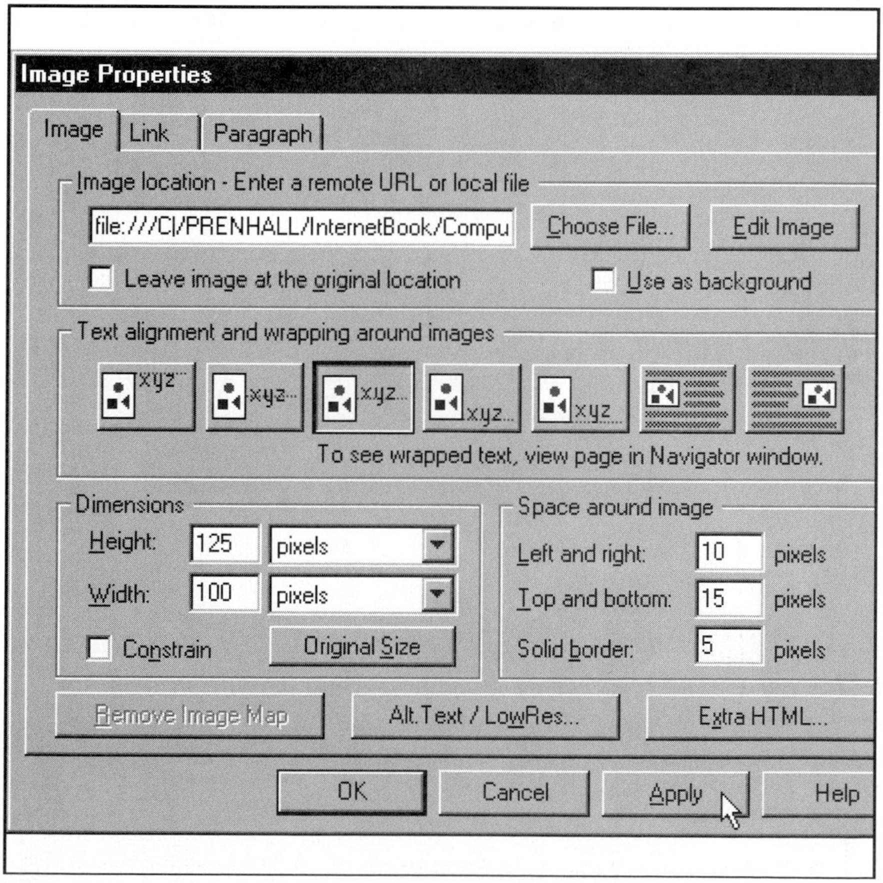

Figure 17.19 Image values for tutorial 17.6.3.

```
<!doctype html public "-//w3c//dtd html 4.0 transitional//en">
```

```html
<html>
<head>
   <meta http-equiv="Content-Type" content="text/html; charset=iso-
8859-1">
   <meta name="Author" content="Abe Zeid">
   <meta name="GENERATOR" content="Mozilla/4.6 [en] (Win98; I)
[Netscape]">
   <title>A Web page with scaled images</title>
</head>
<body>
<center>
<h2>
<font color="#3333FF">Web page with scaled image</font></h2></cen-
ter>
<img SRC="myImage.gif" HSPACE=10 VSPACE=15 BORDER=5 height=125
width=100 align=CENTER>Text aligned middle
<br>This text is placed 15 pixels
<br>below the image
</body>
</html>
```

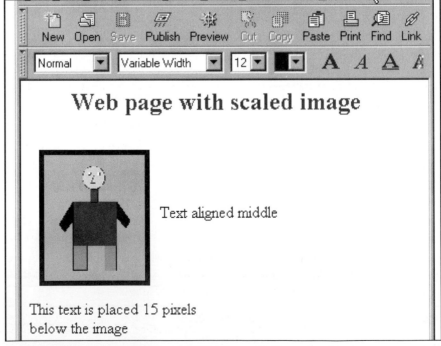

Figure 17.20   Web page of example 10.2, created by using the `Composer`.

17.6.4 Creating a Web Page with a Table

Let us create the three tables of example 16.2, as shown in figure 16.5. Here are the steps we follow when using the Composer:

1. **Open a blank page.** Click File (browser menu) => Blank Page.

2. **Write the first line of text, which reads "This table uses equal size cells".** This text is normal, centered, and red. Hit Enter.

3. **Create the first table.** Click the Table icon on the Composer Toolbar to open the table window shown in figure 17.11. In this window, input 3 and 4 for the number of rows and columns respectively. Click the Center alignment for the table. Enter 4 for Border line width. Also, uncheck the Table width and Equal column widths checkboxes. Click the Apply button, followed by the Close button. The table should show in the Composer window. To fill the cells, click in any cell and type its text, say, Cell 1. Hit the Tab button on the keyboard to advance the cursor from one cell to the next. If you need to delete an entire table or some of its elements, right click on the table and choose Delete from the popup menu. After you finish typing the text for the last cell, position the cursor in the line under the table by clicking there. Hit Enter to leave a line space.

4. **Write the text ahead of the second table.** Follow step 2 above. Hit Enter.

5. **Create the second table.** Repeat step 3 above. To change the size of Cell 5, right click on the cell to open the Table Properties window shown in figure 17.21. Click the Cell tab (figure 17.11). Change the horizontal alignment to Center. Enter 2 (rows) and 3 (columns) for the cell spans. Click the Apply button, followed by the Close button. You should see the table on the screen now. Position the cursor underneath the table, and hit Enter to leave a line space.

6. **Write the text ahead of the third table.** Follow step 2 above. Hit Enter.

7. **Create the third table.** Follow steps 3 and 5 above. In addition to the input values we have used in step 3, we need to input the table width and height and its cell spacing. Enter 8 for cell spacing. Input 200 for the table width, and select the pixels item from the drop list on the same line. Input 100 for the table height, and select the pixels item from the drop list on the same line. After you click the Apply and Close buttons, you should see the table.

8. **Save the HTML code of the Web page in a file.** Follow step 7 in tutorial 17.6.1, and save the code in a file with the name *tutorial17.6.4.html*. Use *A Web page with variable-size table cells* as the page title. View the Web page in a browser.

Figure 17.22 shows the resulting page in the Composer. The generated HTML code is also shown right after the figure.

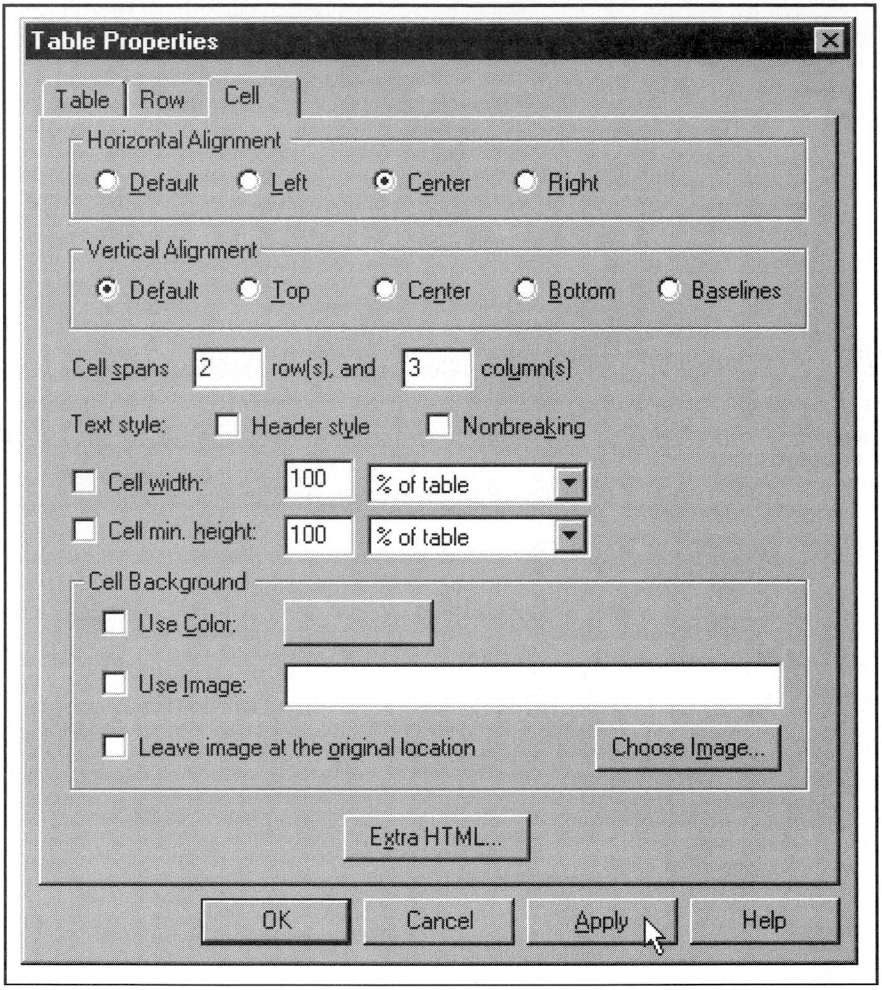

Figure 17.21 `Table Properties` window of the `Composer`.

```
<!doctype html public "-//w3c//dtd html 4.0 transitional//en">
<html>
<head>
   <meta http-equiv="Content-Type" content="text/html; charset=iso-
8859-1">
   <meta name="Author" content="Abe Zeid">
   <meta name="GENERATOR" content="Mozilla/4.6 [en] (Win98; I)
[Netscape]">
   <title>A web page with variable-size table cells</title>
```

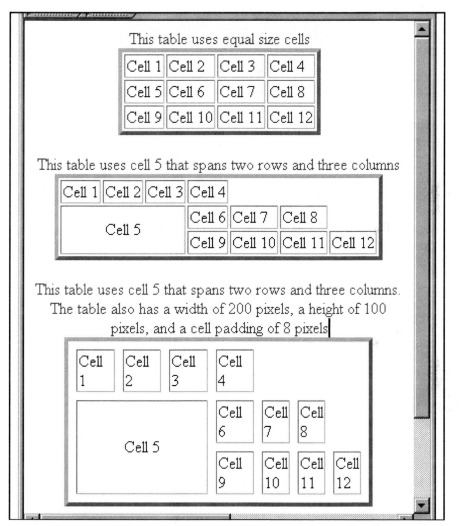

Figure 17.22 Web page of example 16.2, created by using the `Composer`.

```
</head>
<body>
<center><font color="#FF0000">This table uses equal size cells</
font></center>
<center><table BORDER=4 >
<tr>
<td>Cell 1</td>
<td>Cell 2</td>
```

```
<td>Cell 3</td>
<td>Cell 4</td>
</tr>
<tr>
<td>Cell 5</td>
<td>Cell 6</td>
<td>Cell 7</td>
<td>Cell 8</td>
</tr>
<tr>
<td>Cell 9</td>
<td>Cell 10</td>
<td>Cell 11</td>
<td>Cell 12</td>
</tr>
</table></center>
<center>
<p><font color="#FF0000">This table uses cell 5 that spans two rows and
three columns</font></center>
<center><table BORDER=4 >
<tr>
<td>Cell 1</td>
<td>Cell 2</td>
<td>Cell 3</td>
<td>Cell 4</td>
</tr>
<tr>
<td ALIGN=CENTER COLSPAN="3" ROWSPAN="2">Cell 5</td>
<td>Cell 6</td>
<td>Cell 7</td>
<td>Cell 8</td>
</tr>
<tr>
<td>Cell 9</td>
<td>Cell 10</td>
<td>Cell 11</td>
<td>Cell 12</td>
</tr>
</table></center>
<center>
<p><font color="#FF0000">This table uses cell 5 that spans two rows and
three columns. The table also has a width of 200 pixels, a height of 100
pixels, and a cell padding of 8 pixels</font></center>
<center><table BORDER=4 CELLSPACING=8 COLS=4 WIDTH="200"
HEIGHT="100" >
```

```
<tr>
<td>Cell 1</td>
<td>Cell 2</td>
<td>Cell 3</td>
<td>Cell 4</td>
</tr>
<tr>
<td ALIGN=CENTER COLSPAN="3" ROWSPAN="2">Cell 5</td>
<td>Cell 6</td>
<td>Cell 7</td>
<td>Cell 8</td>
</tr>
<tr>
<td>Cell 9</td>
<td>Cell 10</td>
<td>Cell 11</td>
<td>Cell 12</td>
</tr>
</table></center>
<font color="#FF0000"></font>
</body>
</html>
```

17.6.5 Web Page Formatting in the Composer

We have covered the use of tables to format Web pages in chapter 16. HTML editors make this task easier, as they keep track of the table structure and tags for Web authors during Web page development. In this tutorial, we create the Web page of example 16.4 in the `Composer`. Here are the steps to create the page.

1. **Open a blank page.** Click `File` (browser menu) => `Blank Page`.
2. **Create a table with two rows and two columns.** Follow step 3 in tutorial 17.6.4 to create the table with its rows and columns. Input 0 as the value for the `Border line width` item. The `Composer` shows the table with dashed borders, to help us follow the table structure.
3. **Insert the image.** Position the cursor in the first cell in the first row. Choose a yellow background color for the cell, as follows: Right click inside the cell. Click `Table Properties` from the popup menu. Check the `Use Color` checkbox. Click the blank button next to the checkbox. Click the yellow box from the color palette that pops up. Click the `Image` icon on the `Composition` Toolbar to insert the image in the cell. Specify only the image file name in the image window; we do not need to adjust any other parameters. The `Composer` displays the image in the cell and positions the cursor in the second cell of the first row.

4. **Create the bullet list.** Position the cursor in the second cell in the first row. Follow step 3 (preceding) to change the background color to green. Also, change the vertical alignment for the cell to Top by using the window shown in figure 17.21. Type this text: *What to eat for a midnight snack*. Hit `Enter` on the keyboard. Click the Bullet List icon on the Formatting Toolbar, and create the four list items: *Pizza*, *Nachos*, *Ice cream*, and *Pretzels*.

5. **Create the hyperlinks.** Position the cursor in the first cell in the second row. Change the background color to gray, and change the vertical alignment to `Top`. Type this text: *Here are some Web sites to visit*. Click the `Link` icon on the `Composition` Toolbar and create one of the three links. Hit `Enter`. Repeat for the other two links. Use *Check latest NU offerings* and *www.neu.edu* as the source and destination anchors, respectively, for the first link. For the second link, use *Prentice Hall latest books* and *www.prenhall.com*. For the third link, use *Various types of tables* and *example16.1.html*.

6. **Create the text in the last cell.** After positioning the cursor in the second cell of the second row, change the background color to purple, and type this text: *It is once said that physical fitness and exercises are very important to maintain a healthy life. We all must eat well balanced meals, work out three times a week, 45 minutes each time.*

7. **Save the HTML code of the Web page in a file.** Save the code in a file with the name *tutorial17.6.5.html*. Use *Formatting a Web page with tables* as the page title. View the Web page in a browser.

Figure 17.23 shows the resulting page in the `Composer`. The generated HTML code is as follows:

```
<!doctype html public "-//w3c//dtd html 4.0 transitional//en">
<html>
<head>
   <meta http-equiv="Content-Type" content="text/html; charset=iso-
8859-1">
   <meta name="Author" content="Abe Zeid">
   <meta name="GENERATOR" content="Mozilla/4.6 [en] (Win98; I)
[Netscape]">
   <title>Formatting a Web page with tables</title>
</head>
<body>
 
<center><table BORDER=0 >
<tr>
<td BGCOLOR="#FFFF00"><img SRC="myImage.gif" height=250
width=200></td>
<td VALIGN=TOP BGCOLOR="#009900">What to eat for a midnight snack?
<ul>
<li>
Pizza</li>
```

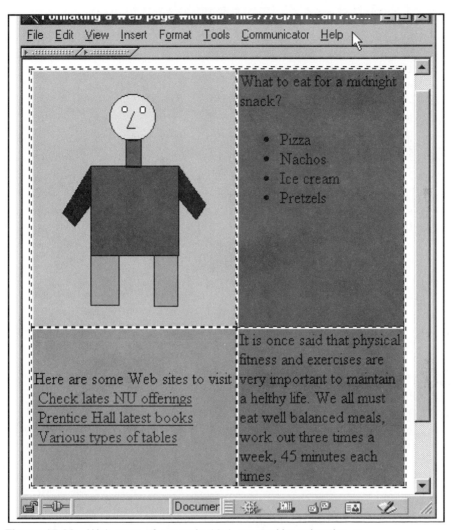

Figure 17.23   Web page of example 16.4, created by using the `Composer`.

```
<li>
Nachos</li>
<li>
Ice cream</li>
<li>
Pretzels</li>
</ul>
</td>
```

```
</tr>
<tr>
<td BGCOLOR="#999999">Here are some Web sites to visit
<br> <a href="http://www.neu.edy">Check lates NU offerings</
a> 
<br> <a href="http://www.prenhall.com">Prentice Hall latest
books</a> 
<br> <a href="../../../../../../example.16.1.html">Various
types of
tables</a> 
<br> </td>
<td VALIGN=TOP BGCOLOR="#CC33CC">It is once said that physical fit-
ness
and exercises are very important to maintain a helthy life. We all
must
eat well balanced meals, work out three times a week, 45 minutes
each times.</td>
</tr>
</table></center>
 
</body>
</html>
```

17.7 FAQs

Q: How do we know whether a Web page was developed manually or by using an HTML editor?

A: View the page source in a browser. In Netscape, use `View => Page Source`. In MS IE, use `View => Source`. There are two clues you should look for when you view the page source code. Check the code complexity and the <META> tag. If the code looks complex and uses tables for formatting, most likely the page was developed by using an editor. To double-check, inspect the <META> tag at the top of the page. If it shows a generator name, version, date, and other information, this confirms that the stated editor has been used.

Q: Can I use MS Word to create HTML documents?

A: Yes. MS Word allows you to take a Word document and save it as an HTML document. Use this sequence; `File => Save as HTML =>` input file name. Word inserts all the required tags into the document automatically, and assigns the html extension to the file. You can later view the document in a browser. Thus, you can have two versions of the same document: Word and HTML. This approach is useful if you have existing Word documents that you need to convert into HTML or embed in other HTML documents. An example is your resume.

Q: How can I create forms when using Netscape Composer?

A: The Composer does not have a direct way to create forms. One way is to use tables and raw HTML tags to create forms.

17.8 Summary

Introduction

•There are two approaches to writing HTML code: manual and automatic.

•HTML editors provide Web authors with an automation tool to write HTML code with.

•When using HTML editors, Web authors can focus on page design and layout while the editor generates the code automatically. The editor generates the needed tags for every HTML element the Web author inserts into the page.

•The HTML code generated by an HTML editor is usually more complex and cumbersome than manually written code. The code can be full of tags that may not be necessary.

•It is recommended that Web authors be familiar with basic HTML tags before using HTML editors, to fully understand their functions and what they offer.

•Some e-commerce applications may, for security reasons, not use HTML editors.

Editor's Tasks

•HTML editors perform and support many tasks. These tasks include Web page creation, uploading/downloading of Web pages, saving HTML code for reuse, providing e-mail links, adding a time and date stamp to pages, importing code files, highlighting HTML errors, searching for words and strings, performing concurrent page development, supporting do/undo functions, and providing Help functions and spelling checking.

Overview of Editors

•Sample editors are CoffeeCup (www.coffeecup.com), HotDog Pro (www.sausage.com), HotMetal Pro (www.softquad.com), Netscape Composer (comes with the Communicator), Microsoft FrontPage (www.microsoft.com), and Adobe PageMill (www.adobe.com).

•HTML editors can be categorized in three groups: What You See Is What You Get (WYSIWYG) editors, HTML tag editors, and hybrid editors.

•The WYSIWYG group includes the Composer, FrontPage, CoffeeCup, and PageMill. These editors show the page as the Web author creates it. The HTML tags are hidden.

•The HTML tag editors include HotDog Pro. These editors provide Web authors with menus of HTML tags and their attributes, to develop their Web pages.

•The hybrid editors are a mix of the above two groups and include HotMetal Pro. These editors allow authors to use HTML tags, if they need to.

•The general structure of the user interface of an HTML editor has a menu bar, a bar that holds HTML elements, and a bar that holds formatting functions. The menu bar contains menus such as File, Edit, and so forth. HTML elements include links, images, and so forth. Formatting elements include lists, horizontal lines, and such text formatting as bolding, justifying, and so forth.

Netscape Composer

•The GUI of the Netscape Composer has a Tile bar, a Menu bar, a Composition Toolbar, and a Formatting Toolbar. It comes bundled with Netscape Communicator. It can be invoked by clicking the Composer icon on the bottom right corner of the Communicator window shown in figure 3.13. It can also be invoked by clicking the Communicator menu (see figure 3.13) followed by clicking the Composer menu item.

•The Title bar holds the title and the file name of the currently opened page in the Composer.

•The Menu bar holds several menus: File, Edit, View, Insert, Format, Tools, Communicator, and Help.

•The File menu has several items. Some of them are repeated in the Composition Toolbar. Others are self-explanatory. Web authors can use the New submenu to open a blank or an existing Web page.

•The Edit menu has the following functions: Undo, Cut, Copy, Paste, Delete, Select All, Delete Table, Remove Link, Select Table, Find in Page, Find Again, HTML Source, and Preferences.

•The View menu has two submenus (Show and Character Set) and six menu items (Reload, Show Images, Refresh, Stop Loading, Page Source, and Page Info).

•The Insert menu repeats the elements found on the Composition Toolbar.

•The Format menu repeats all the elements found on the Formatting Toolbar.

•The Tools menu provides a spelling checking function and three submenus. The Character Tools submenu has three menu items: Insert Special Character, Rainbow Colorize, and Small Caps. The HTML Tools submenu has one menu item, Edit HTML Source. The Tableize submenu has two menu items: By Commas, and By Spaces.

•The Composition Toolbar has all the HTML elements that users need to create their Web pages. The icons of this bar are New, Open, Save, Publish, Preview, Cut, Copy, Paste, Print, Find, Link, Target, Image, H. Line, Table, and Spelling.

•The Formatting Toolbar holds all the icons needed to format text in a Web page. The Toolbar has four drop lists: Paragraph style, Font, Font Size, and Font Color. It also has these icons: Bold, Italic, Underline, Bullet List, Numbered List, Decrease Indent, Increase Indent, and Alignment.

The Composer Tasks

•The Composer performs many tasks including the creating/saving/viewing of Web pages, the formatting paragraphs and characters, and the insertion of raw HTML tags into Web pages.

Summary of Using Netscape Composer

•To open a blank page, click File (menu of Netscape browser) => New => Blank Page.

•To open a template page, click File (menu of Netscape browser) => New => Page From Template.

•To open a page from Netscape Wizard, click File (menu of Netscape browser) => New => Page From Wizard.

•To open the Web page you are currently browsing, click File (menu of Netscape browser) => Edit Page.

•To save a page, click File (menu of Composer) => Save As (or Save) => input file name and page title.

•To preview a page, click the Preview icon on the Composition Toolbar.

•To insert HTML elements, in a page, such as links, images, and so forth, click the icons on the Composition Toolbar.

•To format paragraphs and characters, click Format (menu on Composer window) => Character Properties; or click the drop lists and icons on the Formatting Toolbar.

•To insert a raw HTML tag at a location in a page, click Insert (menu of Composer) => HTML Tag.

PROBLEMS

Use an HTML editor such as Netscape Composer to create the following Web pages that we have created in previous chapters of this book. Compare the editor's HTML code with the manual code whenever possible.

Exercises

17.1 Web page of example 7.5, shown in figure 7.7 (hyperlinks).
17.2 Web page of example 8.1, shown in figure 8.1 (unordered lists).
17.3 Web page of example 8.2, shown in figure 8.3 (ordered lists).
17.4 Web page of example 8.3, shown in figure 8.5 (definition lists).
17.5 Web page of example 10.3, shown in figure 10.5 (image hyperlinks).
17.6 Web page of example 16.3, shown in figure 16.7 (nested tables).
17.7 Web page of example 7.5, shown in figure 7.7 (link tags).
17.8 Change example 16.3 so that the nested table occupies Cell 5.
17.9 Change example 16.4 so that you swap the locations of the cell of the image and that of the hyperlinks, as shown in figure 16.9.

Homework

17.10 Web page of example 7.6, shown in figure 7.8 (anchors).
17.11 Web page of tutorial 7.14.2, shown in figure 7.15 (anchors).
17.12 Web page of example 8.4, shown in figure 8.6 (nested lists).
17.13 Web page of tutorial 8.6.3, shown in figure 8.11 (nested lists).

17.14 Web page of problem 8.15, shown in figure 8.18 (nested lists).

17.15 Web page of example 10.4, shown in figure 10.6 (multiple use of images).

17.16 Web page of tutorial 16.8.1, shown in figure 16.10 (table with horizontal headings).

17.17 Web page of tutorial 16.8.3, shown in figure 16.12 (table with dual heading).

17.18 Web page of problem 16.15, shown in figure 16.16 (table with cell spacing).

CGI Scripting

This chapter covers Common Gateway Interface (CGI) scripting and the server-side processing of HTML data, such as form input. CGI scripts provide the necessary communications between clients (computers that Web surfers use) and servers (computers of Web sites that store Web pages). The chapter covers the necessity for making Web pages interactive. Interactivity is the beginning step toward performing e-commerce to buy and sell goods on the Internet. The popular client/server model of communication is described, because it forms the basis for interactivity. The chapter also covers the different elements of CGI. It follows that by covering some universal CGI scripts, such as page-hit counters and decoders of name/value pairs. The basics of CGI servers are discussed. Then, the chapter presents Apache server as an example CGI server. The chapter ends by presenting tutorials, FAQs, a summary, and problems.

18.1 Introduction

Thus far, this book has concentrated on the client side. All the Web pages and their HTML code have been tested on the client computer without having to be online or to connect to a Web site or server over the Internet. Even with forms, we were able to test without having to be online, because we ignored their CGI scripts. In this chapter, we move from the client side to the server side of an Internet connection and show how CGI facilitates the communication between both sides. We also show how we can install and set up a Web server on the same client computer, to allow us to practice the server-side concepts covered in this chapter.

The interaction between Internet clients and servers is accomplished via browsers that run on the client side. Web s send a request through a browser to a server by clicking buttons or hyperlinks that they see on a Web page. This server is the Web site that hosts the Web page. The browser bundles (encodes) the information of the request as name/value pairs, according to the rules of CGI, and sends them across the Internet to the server. The server usually holds many CGI scripts. The script requested by the Web page is automatically executed as part of the CGI rules. When this CGI script runs, it reads all the encoded name/value pairs, decodes them, extracts the data from them, processes the data, and finally sends the results to the browser according to the CGI rules. As soon as the browser receives the results, it displays them on the screen for the Web surfer. CGI scripts could send back Web pages, files, or any other type of MIME documents. Figure 18.1 shows this loop of communication.

The above communication loop is necessary to make Web pages interactive. Interactivity is the key to performing all transactions on the Web. Buying goods and services online requires Web surfers first to place their orders by filling in forms. Upon the submission of a form to the Web server that hosts the Web page of the form, the CGI script of the form processes the name/value pairs. It then sends a confirmation to the surfer that the order has been received and that the product is about to be shipped for delivery.

What is a CGI script? A CGI script is a computer program that a Web author writes to process the data and input of an interactive element in a Web page. Such an element is usually a form. It is known ahead of time that the data and input are sent to the Web server of the page as name/value pairs, so the CGI script is written accordingly. The CGI script performs three main functions. First, it parses and decodes the name/value pairs and extracts the data that is input by a Web surfer. Second, it makes a decision based on the data. Third, it sends a response back to the surfer based on its processing of the data.

Which programming language should we use to write CGI scripts? Any programming language is acceptable, although some are more popular than others. For example, many CGI scripts are written in Perl or JavaScript. There are three groups of languages to choose from. The first group is the *interpreted scripting languages*. These languages do not require compilation. The scripts are written and stored in ASCII files. These languages are executed by using an interpreter. These interpreters could be the browser itself or the operating system. Sample scripting languages are AppleScript (developed by Apple), Perl, Tool Command Language (TCL), and Unix Shell script. Perl is popular on Unix systems, because it comes as part of the Unix operating system. Perl is now available for other major operating systems, such as Windows and Mac. Windows and Mac users have to download a Perl interpreter from the Web and install it on their computers. Perl has powerful string manipulation functions. It has also evolved as a full programming language.

The second group is the compiled languages. Compiled programs run faster than interpreted programs. Also, the size of a compiled script is smaller than the size of an interpreted script. Another advantage to compiled scripts is their security. No one can read machine code, in case hackers break into a system and get access to its scripts. Sample languages are C, C++, Visual Basic, Fortran, and so forth. The problem with compiled languages is that the script has to be compiled on every hardware platform that it is expected to run on.

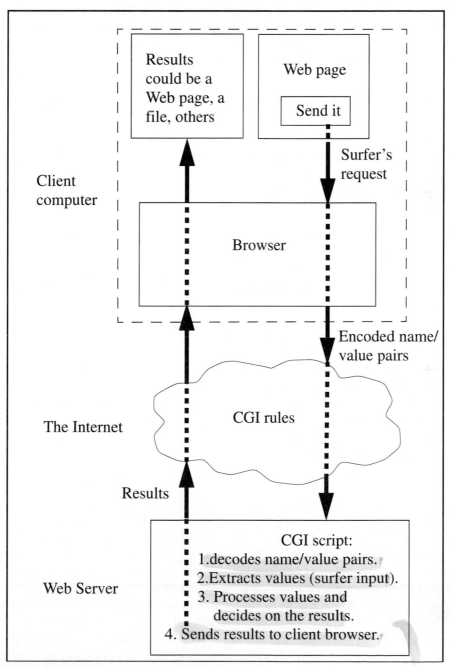

Figure 18.1 CGI loop of communication.

The third group is the interpreted compiled programming languages. In essence, this group is a mix of the other two groups. The script or program that is written in one of these languages can be compiled. It requires a compiler and interpreter to run. Sample languages are JavaScript (developed by Netscape), VBScript (developed by Microsoft), and Java (developed by Sun). JavaScript and VBScript programs do not require compilation, but Java programs must be compiled before being run. The big advantage of JavaScript, VBScript, and Java is that scripts written in them run on the client side. More specifically, a browser installed on the client runs them. The browser becomes a virtual compiler, and the interpreter, for scripts written in JavaScript and VBScript. In the case of Java, the program is compiled first and then runs in the browser, which has a *Java virtual machine* with an interpreter embedded in it.

Which of all the above languages is the best to use? There is really no single choice. It all depends on the Web server and its configuration. The most widely used languages are JavaScript and Perl. JavaScript is supported by both Netscape Communicator and MS IE on all platforms. Perl is popular on Unix Web servers. JavaScript has client-side and server-side parts of the language. The client-side JavaScript is included in the Netscape Communicator. The webmaster who is in charge of the Web server installs the Netscape server-side suite of applications (including JavaScript) known as the LiveWire product.

Which programming language should a Web author use to write CGI scripts? The simple answer is that Web authors can use a language they already know. Web surfers do not see the content of a CGI script, and they do not care. Web authors do not have to devote many resources to learning new languages, just to write CGI scripts. Web authors with Unix background would prefer to use Perl. Web authors with Visual Basic background would prefer to use VBScript; however, they should know that Netscape Communicator does not run VBScript on the client side, although MS IE runs both VBScript and JavaScript. Other Web authors may prefer to use Java or JavaScript. Some Web authors may have no choice, because they have to use languages supported by their Web servers. For example, Perl, C, and Java come free with Unix servers. Webmasters may not support JavaScript, because they would have to buy the Netscape LiveWire suite of applications.

CGI programmers should ensure that their scripts are both platform- and server-independent, to make them more universal and portable. Platform independence requires that programmers choose a common script language, such as C, Java, or Perl, and avoid platform-specific code. A programming language should be available on all platforms, such as Unix, Windows, Linux, and Mac. Programmers may also refrain from using specialized platform-specific system libraries. Server independence is easy to achieve. Programmers should not assume the existence of any system environments, such as local paths to files, or of privileges that may not be available on other servers. Also, programmers should not assume a certain network configuration when they develop and write their scripts. The issue of platform and server independence is important for two reasons. First, it protects against obsolescence of CGI scripts if Web servers are updated or replaced completely — a very common event in the fast-changing Web technology. Second, it makes CGI scripts a valuable free shareware for others to use.

18.2 Client/Server Model

The client/server model of computing is the pervasive model of modern computing. With the popularity of the Internet and the Web, this model is even more important than ever. One of the most important commercial applications of this model is access to the databases of companies, by customers, clients, and suppliers. Figure 18.1 shows an example of using this model in the CGI application. Many CGI applications access databases, and, therefore, are database applications. These CGI scripts may serve as some sort of front-end applications in order to see and use the data stored in databases.

There are three types of architectures of client/server models. They are the single-tier, the two-tier, and the three-tier models. All three models access a database stored on a server via an application program, such as a CGI script. The difference among these three models depends on how many layers are between the database and the application. If both the database and the application reside on the same computer, we have a single-tier model. Thus, one computer serves as the client and the server at the same time. Figure 18.2A shows a single-tier model. We use this model in section 18.6, when we set up the Apache server to practice CGI scripting.

If the application resides on a client while the database resides on a server, we have a two-tier model. Both the two-tier and the three-tier models have become possible with the development of server technology, communication protocols, and LAN and WAN networks. Figure 18.2B shown the two-tier model. The client application is connected to the database via a socket connection. Client applications (programs) send requests to the database server. The server returns the results to the client.

The three-tier model uses a middle layer (tier) to separate the database from the client application, as shown in figure 18.2C. This middle layer resides on an intermediate server. This layer can handle multiple client requests and can manage the connection to one or more database servers; thus it can support multiple protocols such as HTTP or TCP/IP. The three-tier model offers several advantages over the two-tier model. First, it supports multithreading which allows managing multiple client connections simultaneously. Second, the middle layer can be programmed to set access and manipulation rules of database data. Third, the database system is isolated from the client application. This enables switching database systems without affecting the client application.

The choice of one out of the above types of client/server model is up to the design of the Web server and the anticipated load it may receive. It is part of network design. Webmasters concern themselves with client/server configurations. In this book, we focus on CGI scripting and its communication with a server. We assume that the choice of a configuration has already been made for us.

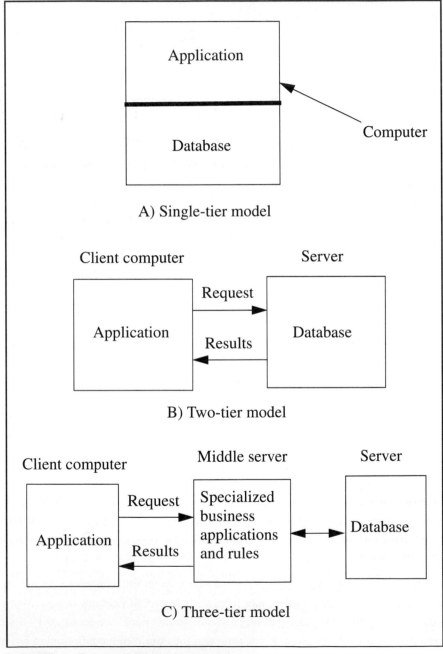

Figure 18.2   Types of client/server models.

18.3 Basics of CGI Scripting

CGI scripts follow a certain structure, perform certain tasks, and use certain standard environment variables and server setups, regardless of their programming languages. A CGI script receives input from the browser through the Web server in the form of name/value pairs, processes the input, and then produces an output that can go back to the Web surfer or to a file.

18.3.1 Script Structure and Tasks

The general structure of a CGI script has three main parts. The first part checks, receives, and parses the name/value pairs from the client. This part uses standard environment variables that are discussed later in this section. The second part decodes the name/value pairs and extracts the values. These values are the Web surfer's input in, say, a form. Using these values, the script does further processing to find what the Web surfer needs. The third part of the script prepares the output that should be sent to the Web surfer as a response. The output could be a Web page, a file, an image, or any other MIME type. The script sends the output to the client browser, which, in turn, formats it and displays it on the screen for the surfer's review.

We can identify four generic tasks that any CGI script may perform. They are initialization, parsing, decoding, and output. During the initialization task, the script may set initial values of its variables, determine how it is invoked by the client request, and read the client input. The variables that the script may initialize include loop counters, strings, and so forth. The method of invoking the script determines how the client data is read, as will be discussed in section 18.3.3. Once the script knows this method, it reads the client input by using a standard environment variable, as will be discussed in section 18.3.3.

The parsing and the decoding tasks form the heart of the script. The client input comes to the script as name/value pairs that are encoded according to the standard rules of CGI (covered in section 18.3.2). The script separates and isolates the name/value pairs from each other. Finishing this ends the parsing task. The decoding task extracts all the values of all the names. These are the values that a Web surfer has input in, say, a form. The script now knows the value for each name or variable of the form. It uses these values to make decisions about how to process the surfer's input or request.

The last task of a CGI script is producing its output. The output is based on the decisions that the script makes in the previous task. The type of output is determined by the design of the original Web page that has originated the request that the script just processed. This output may be another Web page, or an image, or a file, and so forth. The script has to format the output in such a way that the client browser can understand it. The browser needs to know what type of MIME output it is receiving from the script, so that it can display it on the client screen. There is a standard generic structure that CGI scripts use to structure and format their output. Section 18.3.4 covers the details of this structure and format.

Once the script sends its output to the browser, it does any cleaning up after itself, such as releasing system and memory resources before it terminates.

18.3.2 Encoding and Decoding Name/Value Pairs

The Common Gateway Interface is a standard method of communication between clients and Web servers that ensures that both understand each other in a clear, unambiguous manner. When the client sends information, the server knows what to do with it. When the server sends back a response, the client handles it correctly. A CGI script is a program that is executed in real time. It outputs dynamic information based on user input. A CGI script allows Web surfers to query Web servers all the time, as long as the server is up and running.

Part of the CGI is the format that a client browser uses to send user input or a request to a Web server. The browser uses this format to encode the input as name/value pairs, before sending it to a CGI script on the server for processing. The following string of name/value pairs was generated, by MS IE for the form input shown in figure 14.5:

```
firstName=John&middleInitial=K&lastName=Smith&address=12345+AAAAA+
street&city=My+City&state=My+State&zipCode=00000&country=My+Coun-
try&submitButton=Submit+Query
```

A close investigation of this string reveals a pattern. There are equal (=) signs, plus (+) signs, and ampersands (&). The CGI format separates the name/value pairs by ampersands. It separates each name from its value with an equal sign. It replaces each space in a user input by a plus sign. It also does one more thing that is not shown in this string (because it is not needed). It replaces special characters (non-unicode characters) by their hexadecimal values. A hex value xx is represented by %xx in the CGI format. The format uses the hex value for any character that is not part of a-z, A-Z, and 0-9. For example, if a user input includes a question mark (?) or a hyphen, the format replaces it by its hex value. Script programmers do not have to know the hex code for every character. Scripting languages have functions that enable them to convert between unicode (formerly, known as ASCII code) and hex code. Converting from unicode to hex code is known as *escaping* the character. The opposite process (hex code to unicode) is known as *unescaping*. For example, JavaScript has two functions: escape(), and unescape(), for these two conversions.

Knowing the above format makes the implementation of the parsing and decoding tasks of a CGI script that are covered in section 18.3.1 simple. The CGI programmer has a loop in the CGI script that scans the string of the name/value pairs and dissects it at the & signs to collect the pairs. Thus, the result of the parsing task of the above string are the following   pairs:
firstName=John,   middleInitial=K,   lastName=Smith, address=12345+AAAAA+street, city=My+City, state=My+State, zipCode=00000, country=My+Country, and submitButton=Submit+Query.

The decoding task of a CGI script starts with the above pairs. The CGI programmer has a another loop that scans each pair and splits it at the equal (=) sign, to separate the name from the value. The loop also replaces each plus (+) sign by a space. If there are % signs, the loop converts the hex code to unicode. Thus, the result of the decoding task is all the values that a Web surfer used to fill in the form. The result of task of decoding the above pairs is as follows: The names are `Name`, `middleIntial`, `lastName`, `address`, `city`, `state`, `zipCode`, `country`, and `submitButton`. The values are respectively `John`, `K`, `Smith`, `12345 AAAAA street`, `My City`, `My State`, `00000`, `My Country`, and `Submit Query`.

Now that all the mystery has been taken away from the string of the name/value pairs, the CGI programmer and the script know exactly how to process the input, make the right decisions, and send the right response to the surfer.

The names in the name/value pairs are the names that are assigned to the form elements as attributes of the <INPUT> tags during the creation of the form, as shown in chapter 14. Thus, the Web author who is also the CGI programmer has control over both the front end and the back end of a form. The Web author uses the names of the form input elements in the CGI script, knowing ahead of time what to expect.

18.3.3 Standard Environment Variables

In addition to defining the decoding format for the name/value pairs, The CGI defines a standard set of environment variables, to provide a standard method of communication between the client browser and the Web server. All that is left now is for the CGI programmers to use these variables in their scripts to establish client/server communications. The communication is simply a request from a client to a server. Therefore, there are three groups of variables: server, request, and client.

The server variables identify the server parameters. These variables are `GATEWAY_INTERFACE`, `SERVER_NAME`, `SERVER_PORT`, `SERVER_PROTOCOL`, and `SERVER_SOFTWARE`. The `GATEWAY_INTERFACE` shows the CGI version that the Web server complies with. The format is *CGI/version*. The `SERVER_NAME` is the server IP address or URL (host name), such as www.xxx.com. The `SERVER_PORT` is the server port that receives HTTP requests. It is port 80 for most servers. The `SERVER_PROTOCOL` is the name and version of the protocol that the server uses to process user requests. The format is *protocol/version*. The `SERVER_SOFTWARE` provides the name and version of the software of the Web server. The server information specified by these variables rarely changes, unless a new version of the software is installed.

The request variable hold all the information in a request. These variables are `AUTH_TYPE`, `CONTENT_FILE`, `CONTENT_LENGTH`, `CONTENT_TYPE`, `OUTPUT_FILE`, `PATH_INFO`, `PATH_TRANSLATED`, `QUERY_STRING`, `REMOTE_ADDR`, `REMOTE_USER`, `REQUEST_LINE`, `REQUEST_METHOD`, and `SCRIPT_NAME`. The `AUTH_TYPE` shows the authentication type used by the server. The `CONTENT_FILE` specifies a file name, if the CGI scripts needs one. The `CONTENT_LENGTH` holds the length of the string of name/value pairs, if a form uses the POST method in the <FORM> tag. The `CONTENT_LENGTH` is set to the number of URL-encoded bytes being sent to the standard input (`STDIN`) stream. The `CONTENT_TYPE` describes the type (e.g., `text/plain`) of data being sent to the server. In the case of form data, its value is `application/x-www-form-urlecncoded`. The `OUTPUT_FILE` specifies the name of an output file, if the script needs one. The `PATH_INFO` hold additional path information. The PATH_TRANSLATED provides the absolute path of the relative path specified in PATH_INFO. The QUERY_STRING holds name/value pairs if the GET method is used in the <FORM> tag or in any other tag. As we have discussed in chapter 14, it is not recommended to use the GET method; data may get lost or truncated. The REMOTE_ADDR is the IP address of the client originating the request. The REMOTE_UESR is the username, if one was used, of the person originating the request. The REQUEST_LINE shows the full request line provided to the server by the client. The REQUEST_METHOD specifies whether the POST or the GET method is used in the request. The SCRIPT_NAME specifies the name of the script that is used to process the request.

There are three request variables, out of all the above variables, that are very important to any CGI script. They are REQUEST_METHOD, CONTENT_LENGTH, and QUERY_STRING. The CGI script reads the value of the REQUEST_METHOD variable. If it is POST, the script uses the CONTENT_LENGTH to read all the user input and data that is stored in it. If the value is GET, the script uses the QUERY_STRING instead to read the user input and data.

The client variables have all the information about the client. They are ACCEPT, REFERER, and USER_AGENT. The ACCEPT variable specifies the MIME type that is accepted as a response by this request. The REFERER specifies the URL of the document that has a link that triggered the current document requesting information from the script. The USER_AGENT specifies the client browser software name and version. This is a very important variable. Web pages usually display best on only one browser. There are also some HTML tags that are specific to one browser. In this case, Web authors develop, say, two versions of the same page. When a Web surfer requests the page, a CGI script can check for the browser name sending the request by reading the value of the USER_AGENT variable. Depending on whether it is Netscape Communicator or MS IE, the script sends the correct page to prevent displeasing the surfer.

18.3.4 Output Structure

The ultimate goal of a CGI script is to send its response or results to fulfill the original request of the Web surfer. There are three different types of outputs that a script can send: a document (also known as content type), a location, or a status. The script must tell the browser what type of output it is receiving, so that the browser can format it and display it accordingly. Thus, the script output has a certain structure.

The output structure has two main sections: output header, and output data. The two sections must be separated by an empty line. The output header specifies to the browser what type of output data to expect. The output header specifies only one of the above three types. Thus, the first line in the script output is the header statement. The second line is empty. The third and the subsequent lines are the output data, if there is any.

If the output is a document, the output header looks something like this: Content-type: text/html. This line tells both the Web server and the client browser that the CGI script is sending an HTML file with MIME content. This output header is case-insensitive. The type of the MIME content is what comes after the colon in the output header. Here is the `Content-type` for the common MIME types: Use the content types text/html, text/plain, image/gif, image/jpeg, application/postscript, and video/mpeg to send HTML, text, GIF, JPEG, PostScript, and MPEG documents respectively.

The output data section must match the content type specified in the output header section. If the header specifies an HTML type, then the output data should be HTML code. The following sample pseudocode shows the structure of an output of a CGI script sending an HTML document as its response:

```
Content-type: text/html

<HEAD>
<TITLE>CGI script output</TITLE>
</HEAD>
<BODY>
<H1>Output form a CGI script</H1>
...
</BODY>
```

Notice the empty line separating the header from the data. This code looks exactly like the HTML code we have been writing. The difference is that this code is not stored in any file. It is part of the CGI script code. The script sends it, as its response, to the client browser, to display. Thus, this is like displaying a Web page on the fly.

How is the CGI script going to send this HTML code to the client browser? The idea here is to let the script pretend to print this code as an output stream to the screen. The Web server intercepts this stream with the code in it and sends it to the browser which displays the corresponding page. Thus, the script prints anything it needs to send to the client browser. The syntax of the print statement that the script uses depends on its programming language. In all languages, the print statement requires enclosing the string that is to be printed in single or double quotes. Thus, the above HTML code is used, as is, in the print statements of the script. For example, let us assume that a language uses `print ()` as its statement. The above code is therefore written as follows:

```
print ("Content-type: text/html");
print ("");
print ("<HEAD>");
print ("<TITLE>CGI script output</TITLE>");
print ("</HEAD>");
print ("<BODY>");
print ("<H1>Output form a CGI script</H1>");
...
print ("</BODY>");
```

The CGI script output does not have to be a stream of data. It could be just a remote or a local location. In this case, the script header specifies a location, followed by an empty line, as follows:

```
Location: http://www.xxx.com
```

When this header is sent to the browser, the browser retrieves the corresponding document and displays it.

In some cases, the script does not have to send a response to the client. In this case, the script sends a status regarding the client request. There are standard status codes, defined by HTML standards. These codes can be found in this document: http://www.w3.org/Protocols/HTTP/HTRESP.html. One response that is common is 204 No Response. This response occurs when the server is down or has ceased to exist. The output header to send such a status is the following line, followed by an empty line:

```
Status: 204 No Response
```

18.4 Universal CGI Scripts

CGI scripts can be thought of as universal tools that can be used over and over. The tasks that these scripts perform and the environment variables that they use are standard. Thus, we expect to write a script only once and then use it in many Web pages. For example, we need to write a script that processes form input by parsing and decoding name/value pairs only once. Every Web author who needs it can use it. Other example scripts include page-hit counters, the sending of automatic e-mails, and so forth. Here, we present the pseudocode of a form CGI script. The tutorial section (18.7) shows the implementation in some programming languages.

The script is based on section 18.3. Let us assume that we use the POST method in the <FORM> tag. Let us also assume that the script sends its output to the client as an HTML document that displays the name/value pairs as items of an unordered list. Let us also assume that the script name is pageQuery. Here is the pseudo code of the pageQuery script:

```
declare and initialize variables;
print ("Content-type: text/html");
if the environment variable REQUEST_METHOD is NOT equal to POST,
then
        print ("This script should be referenced with a METHOD of
        POST");
exit script;
if the enviornment variable CONTENT_TYPE is NOT equal to
        application/x-www-form-urlencoded, then
        print ("This script can only be used to decode form
        results");
```

```
exit script;
retrieve the value of the environment variable CONTENT_LENGTH;
        if CONTENT_LENGTH is greater than zero, then read
        CONTENT_LENGTH bytes from STDIN stream;
        parse and decode the name/value pairs;
        print ("<H1>Query Results</H1>");
        print ("You submitted the following name/value pairs");
        print ("<UL>");
        loop over all the pairs
            print ("<LI>" name of form element " = " value of form
            element);
        end loop
        print ("</UL>");
end script
```

The statements describing the parsing and decoding of the name/value pairs shown in the above pseudocode would require a bit of work to implement. One or more function would need to be written. We need to break the CONTENT_LENGTH variable at the Ampersand (&) to separate the name/value pairs. Then we need to break each name/value pair at the equal (=) sign to extract the value. Finally, we need to unescape any hex code. These details are shown in section 18.7

18.5 Web Servers

A Web server is a software program. A Web server runs on a networked fast computer with a large hard disk and a large amount of memory (RAM). In this chapter, we refer to the software and the hardware of a Web server as a unit, for ease of communication. The Web server is the gateway to the Internet and the outside world. In addition to the hardware, there is the special server software that allows the running of multi-user applications at the same time. The server software performs many tasks, such as hosting Web pages and CGI scripts, guarding against unauthorized users (by using firewalls), managing incoming and outgoing e-mail, supporting newsgroups, supporting FTP and Telnet tasks, and responding to Web surfers' requests. The server, by being connected to the Internet, Intranets, and/or Extranets, can respond to requests from client browsers. These requests are sent to the server under the HTTP protocol. When the server receives a request, it sends back a response in the form of a Web page or a location, as discussed in section 18.3.

There are many types of Web servers. Each type is related directly to the tasks that the server is intended to be used for. There are e-mail, newsgroup, application, proxy, FTP, and Telnet servers. E-mail servers are set up to handle a very large number of e-mail messages. They are also set up to respond to some messages automatically. Some of the busiest e-mail servers may handle hundreds of millions of e-mail messages daily. Newsgroup servers are set up to handle multiple newsgroups, with many threads within each group, as discussed in Chapter 5. Application servers are usually utilized to support database applications. A server hosts the database and responds to client requests to access the database. An example is a bank server that allows the bank customers to access their accounts online to perform different transactions.

A proxy server is an intermediary between an enterprise network (and its workstations), and the Internet. Thus, a proxy server could be part of the enterprise Intranet or Extranet. The proxy server allows the enterprise to ensure the security and administrative control of its network. A proxy server receives requests from the Internet. Each request must pass filtering requirements, set up by the webmaster, before the server can respond to the request. Proxy servers are invisible to Web clients.

FTP and Telnet servers allow clients to establish sessions, as we have discussed in Chapter 5. FTP servers have files and shareware that Web surfers can download. Most FTP servers are anonymous. Telnet servers allow users to connect to perform different tasks. Most Telnet servers require users to have accounts.

A Web server, regardless of its type and what it should do, needs to be set up. Many operating systems (OS) require that Web server software run on a stand-alone dedicated computer. Web servers host the high-traffic Web sites. A computer OS determines the type of Web server software to use. Both free and commercial server software are available for all existing OS, including Unix, Windows, Linux, Macintosh, and OS/2. The setup of a Web server includes tasks such as configuring it and optimizing its utilization. HTTP services handled by Web servers are not CPU-intensive but frequency-intensive. There are many hits, or requests, that a server receives per minute, and they come randomly. This makes the load on the server variable. All Web servers have peaks, where the number of hits is maximum. Other setup tasks of a Web server include creating a firewall, if one is needed, setting up e-mail accounts, creating directories for different Web sites and pages, creating user accounts, installing software, and creating directories for CGI scripts.

Some Web servers must be set up to be secure. Secure Web servers are used in all e-commerce applications. These servers use encryption techniques to protect against hackers' accessing users' sensitive or personal data transmitted across the Web, such as credit card numbers, all types of IDs, and so forth. Secure Web servers use Secure Sockets Layer (SSL) to support encryption. SSL creates a secure, encrypted channel between the server and the client browser by using certificate authentication. There are companies such as VeriSign that provide server certificates for a fee, to allow using SSL.

Web servers typically house and run CGI scripts. Each Web server has a designated directory to store CGI scripts for security reasons. This directory is usually know as the cgi-bin directory. CGI scripts could be a drain on a server's resources, especially if it has heavy traffic. Every time a server executes a CGI script, it must spawn a new task or a process. The server must both monitor all these tasks and listen for new tasks or requests, at the same time. The server has an HTTP daemon (HTTPd) that enables it to listen to requests from different clients concurrently. Spawning a task usually takes system resources; specifically, memory and disk space and processor time. These resources are usually minimal for a single spawning task, but they add up very quickly if the server attempts to handle dozens of hits or tasks simultaneously. The result could be a very slow server. This is why it is very crucial for the success of a Web server of a Web site to be configured properly to handle its peak load. Otherwise, Web surfers shy away from using it.

There are many Web servers in existence. Some are free, some charge a cost. The majority of them support all major OSs, such as Unix (in all its flavors), Windows, Macintosh, and IBM OS/2. Unix flavors include Sun Solaris, IBM AIX, HP-UX, SGI IRIX, Linux, FreeBSD (Berkeley Software Distribution, or Berkeley Software Design — it is a form of Unix OS), and NetBSD. Sample servers are AOLserver (offered free by AOL at www.aolserver.com), Apache (offered free by the Apache Group at www.apache.org), Lotus Domino (offered by Lotus, www.lotus.com), CommerceServer/400 (offered by I/NET Inc., www.inetmi.com), Enterprise Server (offered by Novonyx, www.novnyx.com), Java Web Server (offered by Sun Microsystems, www.sun.com), Microsoft Personal Web Server (PWS) — (offered free by Microsoft at www.microsoft.com), Microsoft Internet Information Server (IIS) — offered free by Microsoft, NCSA HTTPd (offered free by NCSA at www.hoohoo.ncsa.uiuc.edu), Netscape Enterprise Server (offered by Netscape, home.netscape.com), Netscape Fast Track Server, Oracle Web Application Server (offered by Oracle, www.oracle.com/products), and Spyglass MicroServer (offered by Spyglass, www.spyglass.com).

We here overview some of these servers briefly. The Apache server is covered in more detail in section 18.6, when we use it in this chapter to gain hands-on experience with CGI scripting.

The IBM Internet Connection Secure Server (ICSS) is designed to run on IBM OS/2 OS. However, there are versions of it for AIX, HP-UX, Sun Solaris, and Windows NT. The server is easy to configure from a browser. This server allows user login and supports SSL, CGI, and Java. It also allows the publishing of HTML documents on an Intranet or securely over the Internet.

The Lotus Domino server is the best choice for organizations that already use Lotus Notes. This server is an excellent tool to move Notes collaborative applications to the Web. The Domino server is more than a Web server. In addition to supporting HTML and Web capabilities, it provides e-mail, scheduling, discussion groups, project tracking, and groupware applications features. Users can access all these features via a standard Web browser, instead of regular Notes client software. Domino's best feature is its ability to publish information stored in Notes databases over the Web. The server has robust administrative features, such as for adding new users and groups and assigning different privileges to access different databases. The Windows NT version of Domino is integrated with NT's User Manager.

The Microsoft IIS is built for Windows NT OS. IIS comes with many useful tools built into it, such as Active Server Pages (for building dynamic Web pages), and the FrontPage HTML editor. The server supports services such WWW and FTP. It also supports ActiveX components, Java and database access. In addition, it supports CGI scripting with VBScript and JavaScript. Building on Windows NT security, IIS has its own additional security levels. It allows webmasters to restrict access to a directory or URL by user, by group, or by IP address.

The Netscape Enterprise Server (ES) is suitable for medium-size to large-scale Web sites that require sophisticated control over the server and site content. The server offers many content management tools and a robust Web development platform. It runs under many OSs, such as WIndows NT, SGI IRIX, and Sun Solaris. The server is fairly easy to install and can be configured to fit the needs of any Web site. Webmasters can manage the server remotely from a client browser or platform. They can use it to view server documents organized by such categories as title and author. ES supports creating hardware and software virtual servers for large Web sites. ES also supports CGI, JavaScript, and Java. It offers an open development platform. Its LiveWire module has many features and comes with Site Manager and Application Manager. The Site Manager is similar to Microsoft FrontPage. It has tools to track site elements and verify site hyperlinks. The Application Manager lets Web authors create, debug, and modify Web applications, such as the writing of JavaScript code. For database connectivity, LiveWire provides JavaScript methods for accessing various data. Moreover, ES supports encryption and SSL to secure Web sites.

The Sun Java Web Server (JWS) unites the features of the Java Programming language with those of the Internet. The server is based on Java and uses the Java servlets (server-side programs similar to CGI scripts). The server runs under Windows (NT, 98, 2000) and Solaris OSs. JWS naturally supports and runs all the available Java applications. It is easy to install, configure, and use. It is also secure (SSL-compliant) and platform-independent. The server has several features. For one, it supports dynamic server pages, by allowing server code (Java servlets) to be embedded in HTML files to create Web pages on the fly. Another feature of the server is session tracking that allows webmasters to track how Web surfers use and navigate the Web site supported by the server. JWS comes with presentation templates that Web authors can use as a start to develop web pages.

18.6 Apache Server

The Apache server is one of the most widely used Web servers on the Internet. It offers a customizable approach to Web servers. It comes with the source code. Apache is a Unix-based server, but Windows-based and Mac-based versions are available. In this chapter, we install and use Apache under Windows 98 to allow us to develop, run, and test CGI scripts. Webmasters who use Apache must be very experienced with Unix, in order to be able to customize it and fine-tune it; however, the Windows version can be used as an out-of-the-box product. Its installation is easy. Readers who need to customize the Apache server further are encouraged to read the documentation that comes with the software.

Apache was originally based on the HTTP server of the National Center for Supercomputing Applications (NCSA) at the University of Illinois at Urbana Champaign; however, it is a far different system today, one that can compete easily against other existing Unix-based servers. Apache was created by a non-profit group called the Apache Group. It is based on the volunteer work of software engineers and programmers who simply want a server that can behave well and is easy to customize. Apache has been tested thoroughly by both its developers and its users.

The name Apache comes from "A PAtCHy server" — to reflect its start as some patches and existing code put together. It is also a name of an American Indian tribe that has adapted with time. This adaptation reflects the nature of Apache software as well. The Apache Group does not offer official support for Apache. There are three newsgroups, one for each of the three OSs (Unix, Windows, and Mac). Their names are listed in the FAQs section of this chapter. There is also a FAQs section in the Apache user's guide that comes with the software. In addition, the Apache Web site (www.apache.org) provides links to Apache-specific articles and books.

For Apache, future plans are to continue as an open-source and free-HTTP server that implements the latest in technology. The remainder of this section covers downloading, installing, and using Apache to run CGI scripts. We show how and where to install and use these scripts. This section does not provide an in-depth coverage of how to customize Apache or of how to configure it as an efficient Web server. Such in-depth coverage is beyond the scope of this book.

18.6.1 Downloading

To download the latest version of the Apache server, access the Web page of the Apache Group by typing www.apache.org in the browser URL bar. Click the following link sequence: `Apache Server` (a hyperlink) `=> Download` (a hyperlink) `=> apache 1 3 9 win32.exe`. (Scroll down to see this hyperlink.) This sequence downloads Apache version 1.3.9 for Windows (95/98/2000/NT). After the last click, the browser displays a `Save As` dialog box, as shown in figure 18.3, with a default name (`apache_1_3_9_win32.exe`). Upon the clicking of the `Save` button of this dialog box, a `Saving Location` dialog box with a progress meter is displayed, as shown in figure 18.4. The box also displays the directory and the file name we have chosen. When downloading has finished, the dialog box will close.

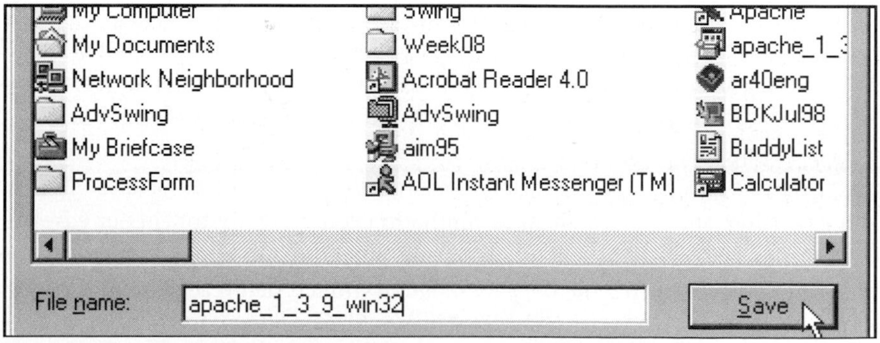

Figure 18.3 Downloading Apache server 1.3.9: save options.

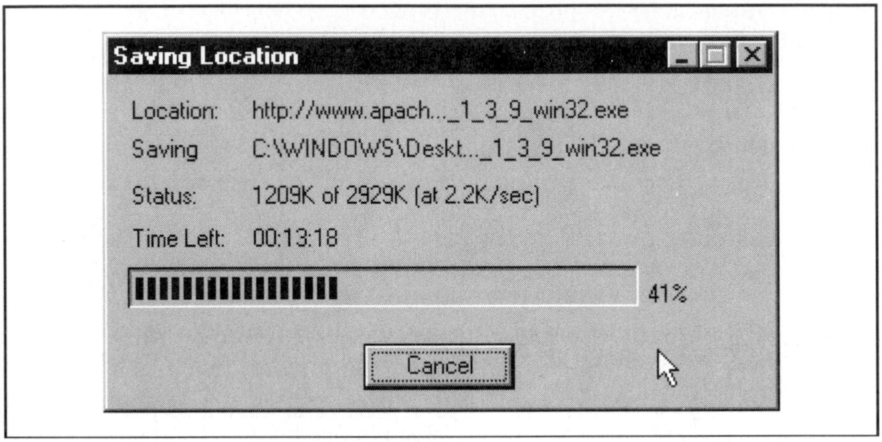

Figure 18.4   Downloading Apache server 1.3.9: progress meter.

18.6.2 Installing

The installation procedure for the Apache server is simple. We cover the procedure for Windows here. The installation begins with a double-clicking of the downloaded executable, apache_1_3_9_win32.exe. This executable is a self-extracting file. A series of setup dialog windows is displayed. Read them, and respond to them. For successful installation, click the following sequence: Next (after reading Welcome) => Yes (accept license agreement) => Next (after reading Readme information) => Next (accept default destination directory) => Next (accept Typical as the type of setup) => Next (accept default program folder) => Finish (restart computer). Figures 18.5 – 18.11 show screen captures of the displayed dialog boxes corresponding to this sequence.

During installation, Apache configures itself for the current OS by using the files in its conf directory. The root folder (directory) for Apache is the Apache Group. The next folder underneath the root is Apache. This folder includes all the other remaining subfolders of the Apache server, as shown in figure 18.12. Three folders of particular interest to users are cgi-bin, htdocs, and conf. We use the first two folders in section 18.6.3. The conf folder has three configuration files. They are access.conf.default, httpd.conf.default, and srm.conf.default. During installation, Apache makes copies of these files, removes the default extension, and changes them to configure itself correctly for (in our case) Windows 98. The three files are ASCII files and can be read and edited in a text editor (e.g., Notepad). Apache uses the httpd.conf file only for Windows. Interested readers could use this file to do custom configuration.The Apache folder also has the executable. It is an icon with the shape of a feather and the name of Apache (figure 18.12). Double clicking this icon starts the server.

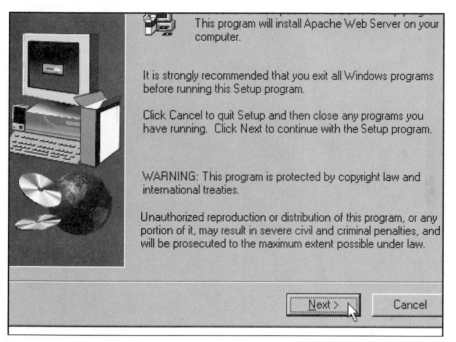

Figure 18.5 Installing Apache server 1.3.9: continue after reading Welcome.

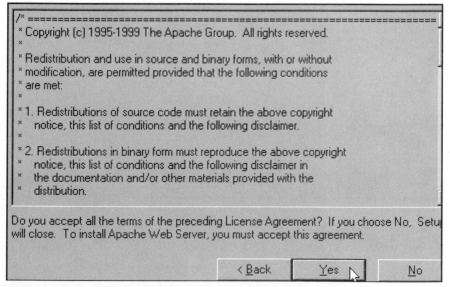

Figure 18.6 Installing Apache server 1.3.9: accept license agreement.

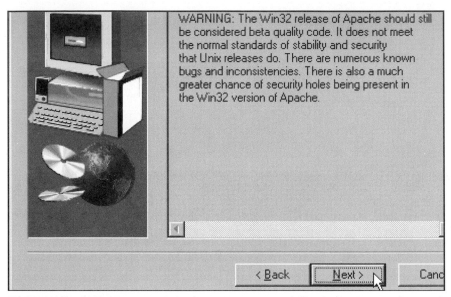

Figure 18.7   Installing Apache server 1.3.9: reading information.

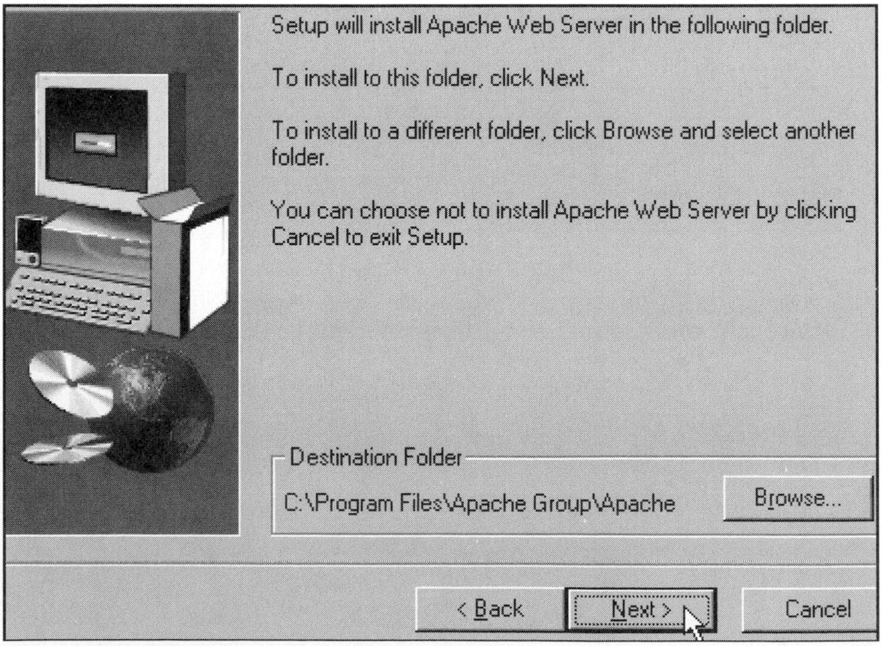

Figure 18.8   Installing Apache server 1.3.9: accept default destination folder.

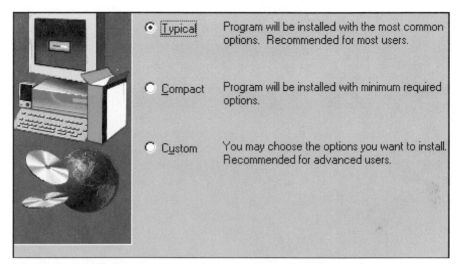

Figure 18.9 Installing Apache server 1.3.9: accept `Typical` as setup.

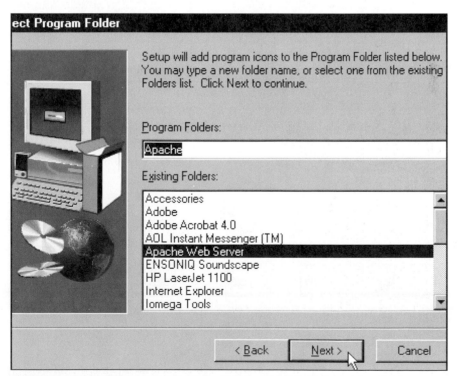

Figure 18.10 Installing Apache server 1.3.9: accept default program folder.

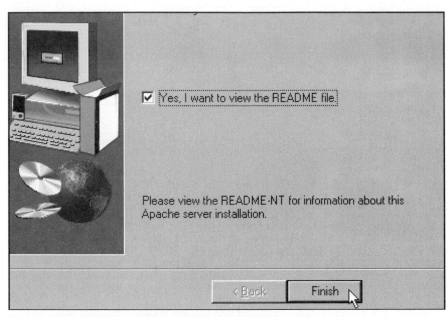

Figure 18.11   Installing Apache server 1.3.9: finish setup.

Figure 18.12   Apache folders.

18.6.3 Running and Using

TCP/IP protocol must be set up and running on the intended computer in order to install and run Apache. If TCP/IP is not running, Apache will crash Windows. A quick test to find out is to ping some IP address, or you can ping yourself. A PC IP address is 127.0.0.1. Thus, type *ping 127.0.0.1* in a DOS window. If TCP/IP is installed and working, you receive a message like the one shown in figure 18.13.

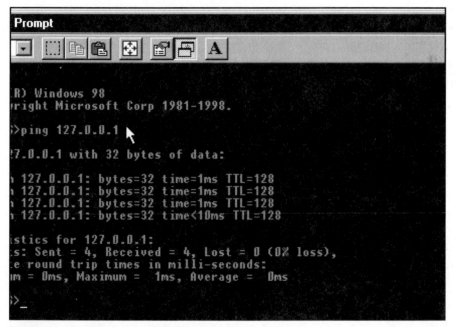

Figure 18.13   Testing for TCP/IP protocol using ping.

There are three ways to run Apache in Windows. The first method is to click the following sequence, Start (Windows start menu on bottom left corner of screen) => Programs => Apache Web Server => Start Apache as console app. The second method is to double click a shortcut of the executable. To create a shortcut, drag the executable (the feather) shown in figure 18.12 and drop it on the desktop of the computer. The third method is to run the Apache server from a DOS window, by typing the command apache -s at the DOS prompt. In order for the third method to work, we need to add the following statement to the *autoexec.bat* file: *SET PATH=C:\Progra~1\Apache~1\Apache*. This statement uses the DOS names of the Apache folders.

Regardless of which method is used, Apache opens its own DOS window, shown in Figure 18.14, and starts running inside it. This window remains open and active until we stop it. To stop Apache while it is running, click this sequence; Start (Windows menu) => Programs => Apache Web Server => Shutdown Apache console app. We can also stop it from a DOS window, by typing the command apache -k shutdown at the DOS prompt.

While running, the Apache daemon is listening to port 80 (unless Apache is configured to use a different one), in real time, for any requests from a client through the HTTP protocol. Port 80 is the default port that Apache uses. In order to establish a client/server communication (session), we invoke a browser's window. In the browser's URL bar, we type http://localhost. (Localhost is the same as the 127.0.0.1 IP address.) If Apache is running, it sends a message to the browser indicating that communication has been established. If nothing happens, or if Apache generates an error, it saves it in the error_log file in the logs folder (figure 18.12). Now, we are running a Web server (Apache) and a client (a browser) on the same computer. This is all that we need to develop and test CGI Scripts. Figure 18.15 shows the responseof Apache to the browser when we type the above URL: a welcome page, with a link to the Apache manual.

Figure 18.14   Apache running in its DOS window.

Figure 18.15   Apache/browser communication.

Once a Web server/browser connection is established, we begin running CGI scripts as follows. The Apache server has two default folders (directories) for this purpose. They are `cgi-bin` and `htdocs`, as shown in figure 18.12. The `cgi-bin` folder holds the CGI scripts we intend to use and run. The `htdocs` folder holds the documents we intend to load in client browsers. These documents are usually the HTML files of the Web pages we display on client browsers. Let us consider running a Web page with a form. The <FORM> tag uses a CGI script in its ACTION attribute. Here are the steps we need to run the form CGI script from the same computer, when using Apache:

1. Place the CGI script in the Apache `cgi-bin` folder. Assume that the name of the CGI script is *myScript.exe*.

2. Place the HTML file of the page in the Apache `htdocs` folder. Assume that the name of the HTML file is *myForm.html*.

3. Run the Apache server.

4. Invoke a browser window.

5. Use the browser to open the HTML file. The full name of the file is *C:\Program Files\Apache Group\Apache\myForm.html*. In using this name, we assume we have used all the default settings during the installing of Apache.

6. Redirect the browser to the Apache server. Step 5 displays the form in the browser window. The browser URL bar shows the full name. We must change it to point to the Apache server, by replacing it by *http://localhost:80/myForm.html*. This name tells the browser to contact the Apache server to download the Web page.

7. Fill in the form. When done, click the form submit button.

After step 7 is complete, the browser encodes the form data as name/value pairs and sends them to the Apache server. Apache looks in its `cgi-bin` directory, finds the CGI script specified in the ACTION attribute of the <FORM> tag, and runs it. After the script finishes running, Apache sends its results to the browser, which displays them in its window. This cycle simulates a client/server communication and allows us to test CGI scripts successfully. The tutorials of the chapter show more specific examples, to help us understand this process further.

18.7 Tutorials

This section shows how we write CGI scripts and use them to process input and data from forms. We also show how to print the values of the CGI environment variables covered in section 18.3.3. We will write the same script in different languages, hoping that the readers find the script in their favorite language and make use of it in their own Web pages.

18.7.1 Using a C Program as a CGI Script

In this tutorial, we write a C program to implement the pseudocode covered in section 18.4. We also write an HTML file that creates a Web page with a form. The <FORM> tag in this page uses the C program as its script. We display the Web page in a browser. We fill in the form and submit it to the Apache Server that runs the script and returns the results to the browser. Here are the steps we need to follow:

1. **Type and save the HTML code.** Using a text editor, type the HTML code (shown following this paragraph) of the Web page. Save the code in a file called *myForm.html*. This file must reside in the `htdocs` folder of Apache. The ACTION attribute of the <FORM> tag uses the `posttest.exe` as the CGI script. This script must reside in the Apache `cgi-bin` folder. The "../" in front of `cgi-bin` tells the browser to go one level up in the directory tree structure to find `cgi-bin` relative to the directory (folder) of the *myForm.html* file, which is `htdocs`. Both `cgi-bin` and `htdocs` reside inside the `Apache` directory.

```
<HTML>
<HEAD>
<TITLE> Post a Form </TITLE>
</HEAD>
<BODY>
<FONT SIZE = 4 COLOR = "red"><B>Post a Form</B></FONT>
<FORM ACTION = "../cgi-bin/posttest.exe" METHOD = "POST">
fill in the box<INPUT TYPE = "text" NAME = "textbox1"><BR>
fill in the box<INPUT TYPE = "text" NAME = "textbox2"><BR>
check the box<INPUT TYPE = "checkbox" NAME = "checkbox1">
check in the button<INPUT TYPE = "radio" NAME = "radio1"><BR>
check the box<INPUT TYPE = "checkbox" NAME = "checkbox2">
check the button<INPUT TYPE = "radio" NAME = "radio2"><BR>
click the box<INPUT TYPE = "submit" VALUE = "submit data"><BR>
</FORM>
</BODY>
<HTML>
```

2. **Type and save the C code of the CGI script.** Using a text editor, type the C program that follows this paragraph. This program is the CGI script we need to process the data of the form created in step 1. Save the program code in a file called *pageQuery.c*. Compile this program, and create an executable with the name `posttest.exe`. This executable must reside in the `cgi-bin` folder of Apache, as indicated in step 1 above. The C program is an implementation of the pseudocode covered in section 18.4.

```
#include <stdio.h>
#include <stdlib.h>
#include <string.h>
```

```
#define PAIR_DELIM_STRING "&"
#define VALUE_DELIM_CHAR '='
char hex2char(char *what);
void RemoveEscapeSequences(char *url);
void plus2space(char *str);
//////////////////////////////////////////////////////////////
// Purpose of this program is to simply parse the query string
// that is passed from a POST operation.
//
// the program will output a page to the client that shows:
// 1. the original query string
// 2. a list of the name-value pairs that were submitted
//////////////////////////////////////////////////////////////
void main(int argc, char *argv[])
{
    int cl;// length of the query string
        char*buf;// pointer to the query string buffer
        char*name;// pointers used to parse query string
        char*value;//    and extract name-value pairs
// start by sending the html header string
    printf("Content-type: text/html\n\n");

// check to make sure that the page that is being received
// from the client is in correct format
    if( (!getenv("REQUEST_METHOD")) ||
        (strcmp(getenv("REQUEST_METHOD"),"POST")))
        {
        printf("This script should be referenced with a METHOD of
POST.\n");
        exit(1);
    }
    if( (!getenv("CONTENT_TYPE")) ||
        (strcmp(getenv("CONTENT_TYPE"),"application/x-www-form-
urlencoded")))
        {
        printf("This script can only be used to decode form
results.\n");
        exit(1);
    }
// get length of query string
        cl = atoi(getenv("CONTENT_LENGTH"));
// alloc an input buffer and read the query string
        buf = (char *) malloc(sizeof(char) * (cl + 1));
        if (cl != (signed)fread(buf, sizeof(char), cl, stdin))
        {
        printf("Read of query data failed.\n");
        exit(1);
    }
```

```
        buf[cl] = '\0';
// let the client know what the original query string was
// and write heading for parsed section of page
    printf("<H1>Raw Query Results</H1>");
    printf("You submitted the following %i character
string:<br><br>%s",cl, buf);
    printf("<H1>Parsed Query Results</H1>");
    printf("You submitted the following name/value pairs:<p>\n");
    printf("<ul>\n");
// let's start processing the query string by putting in
// blanks where the +'s have been used
    plus2space(buf);
// the parsing of the query string involves:
// 1. finding a name-value pair - deliminated by "&"
// 2. removing any escape sequences in this string - %xx
// 3. splitting the name and value - deliminated by "="
// 4. printing the name and value
// 5. and then repeating until we run out of pairs
    name = strtok(buf, PAIR_DELIM_STRING);
        while(name)
        {
        RemoveEscapeSequences(name);
        value = strchr(name, VALUE_DELIM_CHAR);
        *value = '\0';// terminate the name string
        value++;// point to start of value string
        printf("<li> <code>%s = %s</code>\n",name, value);
        name = strtok(NULL, PAIR_DELIM_STRING);
    }
// finish up the page and cleanup
    printf("</ul>\n");
        free (buf);
}
//////////////////////////////////////////////////////////////
// Utility routine that takes the next 2 Hex characters from the
// input character string and converts them to binary character
// Routine assumes that the characters are either 0-9, A-F or a-f
//////////////////////////////////////////////////////////////
char hex2char(char *what)
{
    char digit;
// convert the first hex character
// if it's >='A' then its either A-F or a-f
// so convert to upper case (mask of 0xdf)
// and subtract 'A' and add result to 10
// if digit is 0-9 then just subtract '0'
    digit = (what[0] >= 'A' ? ((what[0] & 0xdf) - 'A')+10 : (what[0]
- '0'));
// shift hex digit to upper nibble of result
```

```
    digit *= 16;
// convert the second hex digit and place it in the lower nibble
    digit += (what[1] >= 'A' ? ((what[1] & 0xdf) - 'A')+10 :
(what[1] - '0'));
    return(digit);
}
/////////////////////////////////////////////////////////////////
// Utility routine that searches the input character string
// for Hex escape sequences and replaces them with binary character
/////////////////////////////////////////////////////////////////
void RemoveEscapeSequences(char *url)
{
    int x,y;
// iterate through the character string
    for(x=0,y=0;url[y];++x,++y) {
// if we find an escape character then
// then replace it with the binary representation
// of the next 2 hex digits and adjust the pointers
        if((url[x] = url[y]) == '%') {
            url[x] = hex2char(&url[y+1]);
            y+=2;
        }
    }
// append the null termination since we never moved it
    url[x] = '\0';
}
/////////////////////////////////////////////////////////////////
// Utility routine that replaces all the +'s in the input
// string with blanks
/////////////////////////////////////////////////////////////////
void plus2space(char *str) {
    int x;
// simply iterate over the string and replace all +'s
    for(x=0;str[x];x++)
        if(str[x] == '+')
        str[x] = ' ';
}
```

3. **Run the Apache server on the client computer.** Click this sequence: Start (Windows menu) => Programs => Apache Web Server => Start Apache as console app.

4. **Run the browser on the same client computer.** Simply double click the browser icon on the desktop. We use Netscape Communicator in this tutorial.

5. **Load the Web page created in step 1 into the browser.** Click this sequence: File => Open Page => Choose File. The file we need is *myForm.html*, whivh resides in Apache htdocs folder, as discussed in step 1. The full absolute path to this file is *C:\Program*

Files\Apache Group\Apache\htdocs. After choosing the file, click the Open button of the browser Open Page popup window. At this point, the browser displays the Web page with a form in its window.

6. **Redirect the browser to the Apache server.** At this point, the browser sees the Web page as a local file in the directory *C:\Program Files\Apache Group\Apache\htdocs*. This is obvious if we look at the page URL shown in the browser URL bar. We need to tell the browser that this is a Web page that resides on the Apache server that also happens to be installed on the same client computer. The redirection requires changing the page URL to the following: *http://localhost:80/myForm.html*. Now that we know what is going on, we can replace steps 5 and 6 by simply typing *http://localhost:80/myForm.html* in the browser URL bar directly, instead of using its Open menu.

7. **Fill in the form and submit it for processing.** At the end of step 6, all the pieces needed to fill in the form and process its data are in place. The Apache server is running and listening to any HTTP requests that might come its way from port 80. The CGI script, posttest.exe, needed to process the page is waiting to be invoked by the server. The Web page of the form is using this script in the ACTION attribute of the <FROM> tag. We fill in the form as shown in figure 18.16. After filling in the form elements and selecting the checkboxes and buttons, we click the Submit data button.

8. **Wait for the CGI script to send the results.** Upon completing step 7, the browser sends the query to the Apache server. The server, in turn, finds that posttest.exe is the script that is needed by the query. It therefore invokes it. The executable runs and sends the results back to the browser. The browser interprets the results and displays them as shown in figure 18.17.

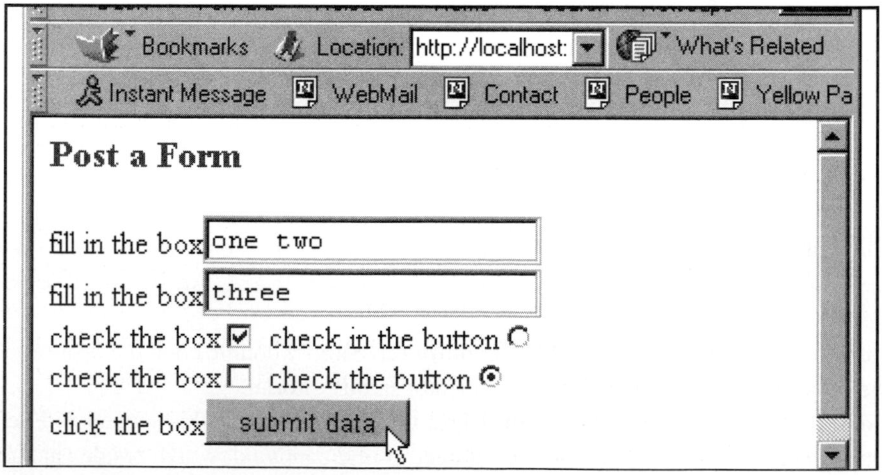

Figure 18.16   Submit form data to the Apache server.

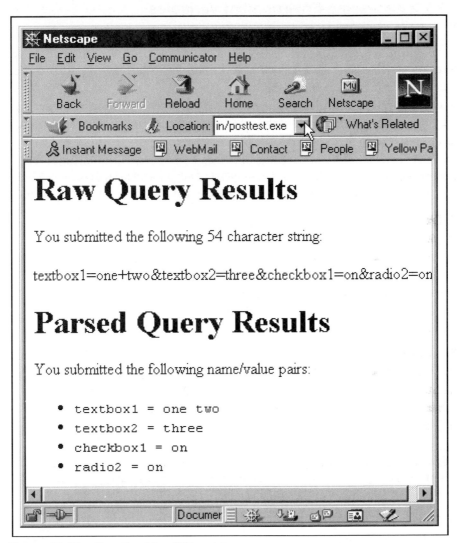

Figure 18.17 Results of the CGI script.

Figures 18.16 and 18.17 shows how the name/value pairs are generated, parsed, and decoded. The form input data is encoded according to the CGI format, as the raw query string in figure 18.17 shows. When this string is sent to the CGI script, it parses it first, to extract each name/value pair. It then decodes each name/value pair to extract the name and the value. The name of each name/value pair is the name that is given to the form element in the HTML code of *myForm.html* file, shown in step 1. The names of the two text fields are *textbox1* and *textbox2*. The name of the checkboxes are *checkbox1* and *checkbox2*. The names of the two radio buttons are *radio1* and *radio2*. Figure 18.17 shows the names of the selected checkbox and button.

18.7.2 Accessing Environment Variables

In this tutorial, we write a C program that displays all the environment variables that we have discussed in section 18.3.3. The program accesses and prints the three sets of variables. These are the server, request, and client variables. After we compile the code, we use the executable as the CGI script in a form. We write an HTML file to create this form. In this case, we can submit the form without filling it in, because the CGI script does not parse the form data. We are interested only in printing the values of the environment variables. We must run both the Apache server and a browser on the computer. Here are the detailed steps:

1. **Type and save the HTML code.** Using a text editor, type the HTML code (shown following this paragraph) of the Web page. Save the code in a file called *myForm1.html*. This file must reside in the htdocs folder of Apache. The ACTION attribute of the <FORM> tag, shown below, uses envvar.exe as the CGI script. This script must reside in the Apache cgi-bin folder.

```
<HTML>
<HEAD>
<TITLE>Print environment variables</TITLE>
</HEAD>
<BODY>
<FONT SIZE = 4 COLOR = "red"><B>Post a Form</B></FONT>
<FORM ACTION = "../cgi-bin/envvar.exe" METHOD = "POST">
fill in the box<INPUT TYPE = "text" NAME = "abox"><BR>
</FORM>
</BODY>
</HTML>
```

2. **Type and save the C code of the CGI script.** Using a text editor, type the C program that follows this paragraph. Save the program code in a file called *envvir.c*. Compile this program, and create an executable with the name envvir.exe. This executable must reside in the cgi-bin folder of Apache, as indicated in step 1 above.

```
#include <stdio.h>
#include <stdlib.h>
//////////////////////////////////////////////////////////////
// Purpose of this program is to print the values of the
// environment variables established by the apache server
// when it launches this program
//////////////////////////////////////////////////////////////
void main(int argc, char *argv[])
{
        intindx1 = 0;// a couple of indexes for the
        intindx2 = 0;//  array processing
// the list of Server Variables to be displayed
```

```
         char*sv[] = {"GATEWAY_INTERFACE",
            "SERVER_NAME",
            "SERVER_PORT",
            "SERVER_PROTOCOL",
            "SERVER_SOFTWARE",
            NULL };
// the list of Request Variables to be displayed
            char*rv[] = {"AUTH_TYPE",
            "CONTENT_FILE",
            "CONTENT_LENGTH",
            "CONTENT_TYPE",
            "OUTPUT_FILE",
            "PATH_INFO",
            "PATH_TRANSLATED",
            "QUERY_STRING",
            "REMOTE_ADDR",
            "REMOTE_USER",
            "REQUEST_LINE",
            "REQUEST_METHOD",
            "SCRIPT_NAME",
            NULL};
// the list of Client Variables to be displayed
            char*cv[] = {"ACCEPT",
            "REFERER",
            "USER_AGENT",
            NULL};
// one more list
// containing the title to display on the page
// and the address of the list that follows
            struct LIST
            {
            char *title;
            char **envVarName;
            };
            struct LIST list[] = {"SERVER VARIABLES", sv,
              "REQUEST VARIABLES", rv,
              "CLIENT VARIABLES", cv,
              NULL, NULL};
// ok all that setup is done...
// start by sending the html header string
        printf("Content-type: text/html\n\n");
// now loop through all the groups; until we hit the NULL
            while (list[indx1].title)
            {
            char**varNames;
            char*value;
// print each heading with a little flair
            printf("<BR><FONT SIZE=4 COLOR=\"RED\"><B>%s"
```

```
             "</B><BR>------------------------------</FONT>",
             list[indx1].title);
// get the address of the list of variables
// and loop through the list until we hit NULL
       varNames = list[indx1].envVarName;
       while (varNames[indx2])
       {
// print the variable we're looking for and
// if the variable has been set...print the value
// then go to the next entry in the variable list
       printf("<BR>%s = ", varNames[indx2]);
       if (value = getenv(varNames[indx2]))
       printf("%s", value);
       indx2++;
       }
// print 1 extra blank line between groups
// and set up the indexes for the next group and variable list
       printf("<BR>\n");
       indx2 = 0;
       indx1++;
       }
}
```

3. **Run the Apache server and the browser on the same computer.** Click this sequence to run Apache: `Start` (Windows menu) => `Programs` => `Apache Web Server` => `Start Apache as console` app. Double click the browser icon on the desktop. We use MS IE.

4. **Load the Web page created in step 1 into the browser.** In the browser URL bar, type the page URL as http://localhost:80/myForm1.html. The browser asks the Apache server to send the Web page. The browser loads the page in its window, as shown in figure 18.8.

5. **Fill in the form and submit it.** The form shown in figure 18.18 is trivial. All that we need is to invoke the `envvir.exe` executable. Type any text in the text filed, and hit `Enter` on the keyboard. At the end of this step (5), all the pieces needed to fill in the form and process its data are in place.

6. **Wait for the CGI script to send the results.** The browser sends the query to the Apache server. The server, in turn, invokes the `envvir.exe`. The executable runs and sends the results back to the browser. The browser interprets the results and displays them, as shown in figure 18.19.

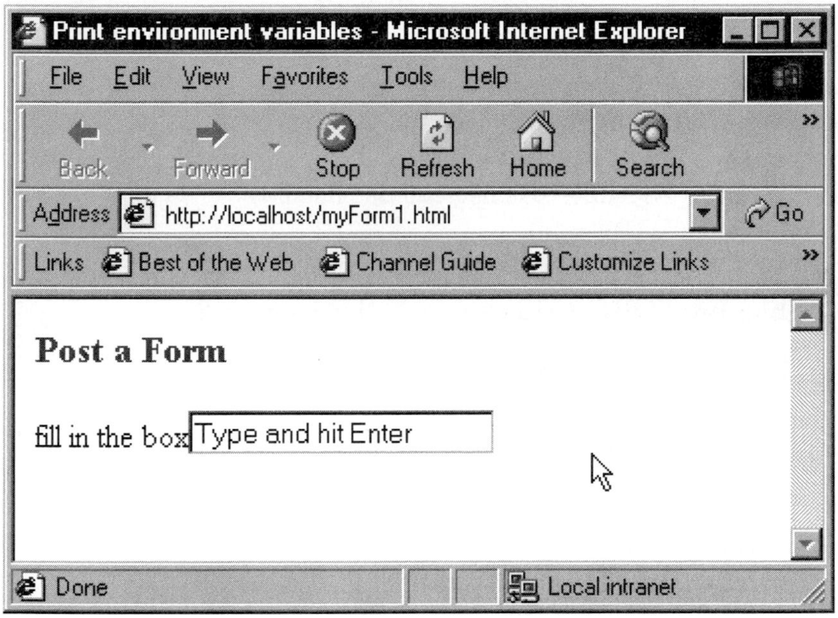

Figure 18.18   Form to invoke the CGI script that prints CGI environment variables.

Figure 18.9 shows the three sets of CGI variables. Only the server variables have values, because the script is running on the server side. The server variables show the expected values about the server. The request variables have values only for the variables that apply to the form submitted. For example, the value of the CONTENT_LENGTH variable is 23. This is equal to the length (including spaces in the string) of the string that holds the submitted name/value pair, which should read abox=Type and hit Enter. The name abox is used in the HTML code shown in step 1. The value of the QUERY_STRING is null, because the method used in the form is POST, not GET. The value of the CONTENT_TYPE is what is expected from a form, as was explained in section 18.3.3. The REMOTE_ADDR variable is the address of the server. This corresponds to the name localhost that we have been using in the URLs. The values of REQUEST_METHOD and SCRIPT_NAME are what we expect.

There are no values to all the client variables. If we need client values, we need to run a client script to find these values and send them to the server. This is ouside the scope of this chapter.

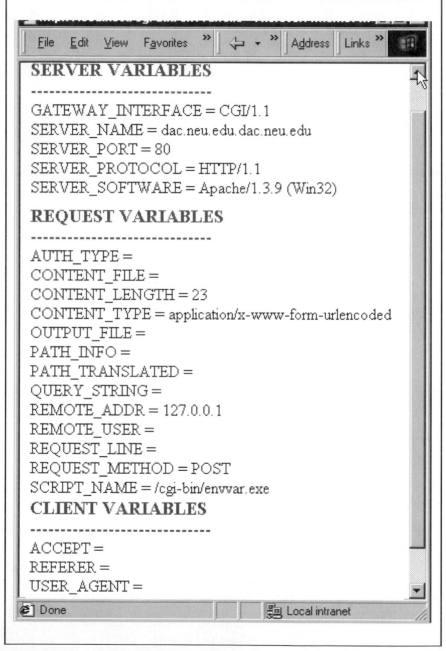

Figure 18.19   CGI environment variables.

18.8 FAQs

Q: What are some of the tasks that CGI scripts can perform?

A: CGI scripts can be written for various reasons. They can be viewed as small application programs. CGI scripts let users communicate with Web servers to obtain customized information, build interactivity between clients and servers, search databases, provide feedback to users, and send replies to users that are based on their requests.

Q: Are there any limitation to what CGI scripts can do?

A: No. A Web daemon on a Web server executes a CGI script to transmit (receive) information to (from) a client. There is no limit to what you can hook up to the Web. The only requirement is that the CGI do its job very quickly; otherwise, the Web surfer will just move on to doing something else.

Q: When I use CGI scripts written in a given programming language, do I need the language compiler and runtime environment?

A: Not necessarily. It all depends on the language you use. For example, if you use already-existing executables written in C or another compiled language, you do not need to install anything on your computer. The executables are machine code and should run fine. If you use scripts written in Java, you would need to install the Java virtual machine (VM). You can download the JDK from the Sun Web site, java.sun.com. If you use scripts written in JavaScript, you need a browser that has a JavaScript interpreter. Above all, if you write and compile your own scripts, you would need the language compiler and runtime machine.

Q: Why do Web servers use the cgi-bin directory for CGI scripts?

A: A CGI script is an executable running on a Web server. This is equivalent to letting the entire world, including hackers, run a program on your Web server. This raises security issues. A webmaster must implement precautions when it comes to using CGI scripts. Webmasters designate a special directory, usually with the name cgi-bin, that stores all CGI scripts. They set up all types of security restrictions on this directory. This directory is under their direct control. They prevent an average user from creating CGI programs in it. CGI programmers must give them their scripts to post them. The outside world is allowed only "execute" access to this directory on the Web server and so cannot sneak to any other resources of the Web server.

Q: Why does the browser not use the latest CGI script that I specify in the ACTION attribute of the <FORM> tag of my form?

A: This is a browser cache problem. Kill the browser cache, both Memory and Disk. For Netscape Communicator, click Edit (menu of Netscape).

Q: Can I use a batch file to write CGI scripts?

A: Yes. The batch file for Windows is like a Unix Shell script for Unix. If you need a simple script to test your client/server communication during development, you can write the CGI script using batch (DOS) commands and save it in a batch file with a name, say, *myCGIFile.bat*. Use this name in the ACTION attribute of a <FORM> tag, just like any other executable. The batch file idea is particularly useful if you have both the server and the client running on the same computer. You can actually include any DOS-level commands in the batch file. For example, if you want to run a Java application, use the command *java MyApplication*, where *Myapplication* is the class to run; or, if you want to run an applet, use *appletviewer myApplet.html*, where *myApplet.html* is the file that has the applet class. A batch file that runs the application may look as follows:

```
@echo off
java MyApplication
echo .
```

The first line says "do not echo the commands of this file onto the screen". The second line runs the Java application. The third line leaves a blank line.

Q: What are No-Parse-Header (NPH) CGI scripts?

A: In some cases, the script programmer may want the script not to rely on the Web server to process its output, to reduce overhead on the server. In these cases, the programmer has to do more work to specify the output header followed by the output data. The name of an NPH script should begin with a nph- prefix. This makes the HTTPd connect script's output stream directly to the requesting client. Here is the format for an NPH script:

```
HTTP/1.0 script results follow
Server: MyServer
Content-type: text/html

<HEAD>
<TITLE>CGI script output</TITLE>
</HEAD>
<BODY>
<H1>Output form a CGI script</H1>
...
</BODY>
```

Q: Can I run more than one invocation of Apache on Windows simultaneously?

A: No. The latest invocation overrides the previous one and gives a message that the previous run was not shut down cleanly. If you need multiple servers running, you can create as many virtual servers as you need — see the last FAQ in this section.

Q: Where can I find the Apache manual in the Apache folders?

A: There is a folder called `manual` in *C:\Program Files\Apache Group\Apache\htdocs*. Double click this folder. You should find the *index.html* file in there. When you run this file in a browser, you see the manual's table of contents as hyperlinks. When you click any link, you get the details. You may print all the Web pages of the manual to generate a hard copy.

Q: Why does my system not understand Apache commands, such as
`apache -k shutdown`, when I type them in a DOS window?

A: This problem means that you have not set up the path to the Apache directory in your *autoexec.bat* file. Edit the file, and add this statement to it:

```
SET PATH=C:\;C:\Progra~1\Apache~1\Apache
```
This statement specifies the path to the Apache directory. The above path is *Program Files\Apache Group\Apache*, but using the DOS names. If you have installed Apache differently, use the path you have defined. To find this path, simply keep opening folders until you reach the Apache directory. The path is the names of all folders you have opened in order, separated by backslashes. Also, if you do not know where the *autoexec.bat* file is, search for it using `Start` (Windows menu on bottom left corner of screen) => `Find` => `Files or Folders`.

Q: Can I stop Apache by pressing CTRL-C, from the keyboard, in the Apache console window?

A: Yes — but you should not, because it does not let Apache end any current transactions correctly. If you run Apache again, it gives a message that it was not shut down properly before.

Q: Are there any newsgroups for Apache?

A: Yes. There is a separate newsgroup for eah of the three OSs: Unix, Windows, and Mac. Their names are respectively comp.infosystems.www.servers.unix, comp.infosystems.www.servers.ms-windows, and comp.infosystems.www.servers.mac. These newsgroups are important because Apache is free, and its developer, the Apache Group, does not offer any formal support. Many Apache users field their questions to these groups. They can also read the posted messages to learn from them. A newsreader is needed. Refer to Chapter 5 to refresh your memory on how to subscribe to newsgroups and on how to read their threads and messages.

Q: How can I create multiple virtual hosts (servers of IP addresses) on an Apache server?

A: Hosting (creating) multiple addresses on an Apache server is simple. The `httpd.conf` file (full path is C:\Program Files\Apache Group\Apache\conf\httpd.conf) contains two directives (`Listen` and `VirtualHost`) that enable Apache to support multiple virtual hosts (servers). The `Listen` directive tells Apache which port to use (listen to) for a given IP address. The `VirtualHost` directive provides Apache with the host name, root directory, server name, and separate logging information for the server.

18.9 Summary

Introduction

•The interaction between Internet clients and servers is accomplished via browsers that run on the client side. The client browser sends a request, as name/value pairs, to the server, which in turn processes the request using CGI scripts and sends the results back to the client.

•The server usually holds many CGI scripts. The script requested by a Web page is automatically executed.

•When a browser receives results from CGI scripts, it displays them on the screen. CGI scripts could send back Web pages, files, or any other type of MIME document.

•A CGI script is a computer program that is written on the basis of the CGI standard environment variables.

•A CGI script performs three main functions. First, it parses and decodes the name/value pairs, to extract the input data. Second, it makes a decision based on the data. Third, it sends a response (back to the surfer) based on the processing of the data.

•A CGI script may be written in any programming language, whether it is compiled (such as C, C++, Java, etc.) or interpreted (such as JavaScript, Perl, TCL, Unix Shell, etc.). CGI scripts should be both platform- and server-independent, to make them more nearly universal and portable.

Client/server Model

•The client/server model is the one most widely used over the Internet.

•There are three types of architecture for a client/server model. They are the single-tier, the two-tier, and the three-tier models. The single-tier model uses the same computer for both the client and the server. The two-tier model uses one computer for each. The three-tier model uses one client computer and two server computers.

Basics of CGI Scripting

•The general structure of a CGI script has three main parts. The first part checks, receives, and parses the name/value pairs from the client. The second part decodes the name/value pairs and extracts the values. The third part of the script prepares and sends the script output.

•The main generic tasks of a script are initialization, parsing, decoding, and output.

•The encoding and decoding of name/value pairs is done according to the rules of the Common Gateway Interface. The CGI format separates the name/value pairs by ampersands (&). It separates each name from its value by an equal (=) sign. It replaces each space in a user input by a plus (+) sign. It also replaces special characters (non-unicode characters) by their hexadecimal values. A hex value *xx* is represented by *%xx* in the CGI format.

•The parsing task of a CGI script entails chopping off the name/value pairs at the ampersand signs. The decoding task entails separating the names from the values at the equal signs, replacing the pluses by spaces, and converting the hex codes.

•The CGI standard environment variables includes three groups: server, request, and client. The server variables are `GATEWAY_INTERFACE`, `SERVER_NAME`, `SERVER_PORT`, `SERVER_PROTOCOL`, and `SERVER_SOFTWARE`.

•The request variables are `AUTH_TYPE`, `CONTENT_FILE`, `CONTENT_LENGTH`, `CONTENT_TYPE`, `OUTPUT_FILE`, `PATH_INFO`, `PATH_TRANSLATED`, `QUERY_STRING`, `REMOTE_ADDR`, `REMOTE_USER`, `REQUEST_LINE`, `REQUEST_METHOD`, and `SCRIP_NAME`.

•The client variables are `ACCEPT`, `REFERER`, and `USER_AGENT`.

•The output structure of a script has two main sections: output header, and output data. The two sections must be separated by an empty line. The output header specifies to the browser what type of output data to expect.

•If the CGI script output is a document, the output header is `Content-type: text/html`. If it is a location, the output header is, say, `Location: http://www.xxx.com`. If no output is expected, the output header is, say, `Status: 204 No Response`.

Universal CGI Scripts

•CGI scripts can be thought of as universal tools that can be used over and over. The tasks that these scripts perform, and the environment variables that they use, are standard. Thus, we expect to write a script once and use it in many Web pages.

Web Servers

•A Web server is a software program. A Web server runs on a networked fast computer with a large hard disk and a large amount of memory (RAM). The server software performs many tasks, such as the hosting Web pages and CGI scripts.

•There are e-mail, newsgroup, application, proxy, FTP, and Telnet servers. Each type of server is configured to execute its tasks efficiently.

•A computer OS determines the type of Web server software to use. Both free and commercial server software are available for all existing OSs. The setup of a Web server includes tasks such as configuring it and optimizing its utilization.

•Some Web servers must be set up to be secure. These servers use Secure Sockets Layer (SSL) to support encryption.

•Web servers typically house and run CGI scripts. Each Web server has a designated directory to store CGI scripts for security reasons. This directory is usually know as the cgi-bin directory. Running CGI scripts could be a drain on a server's resources, especially if it has heavy traffic.

•Sample Web servers are AOLserver (offered free by AOL, www.aolserver.com), Apache (offered free by the Apache Group, www.apache.org), Lotus Domino (offered by Lotus, www.lotus.com), CommerceServer/400 (offered by I/NET Inc., www.inetmi.com), Enterprise Server (offered by Novonyx, www.novnyx.com), Java Web Server (offered by Sun Microsystems, www.sun.com), Microsoft Personal Web Server (PWS) — offered free by Microsoft (www.microsoft.com), Microsoft Internet Information Server (IIS) — offered free by Microsoft, NCSA HTTPd (offered free by NCSA, www.hoohoo.ncsa.uiuc.edu), Netscape Enterprise Server (offered by Netscape, home.netscape.com), Netscape Fast Track Server, Oracle Web Application Server (offered by Oracle, www.oracle.com/products), and Spyglass MicroServer (offered by Spyglass, www.spyglass.com).

Apache Server

•The Apache server is one of the Web servers most widely used on the Internet. Apache was created as a Unix-based server; however, Windows-based and Mac-based versions are now available.

•To download the latest version of the Apache server, type www.apache.org in the browser URL bar. Click the following link sequence: `Apache Server` (a hyperlink) => `Download` (a hyperlink) => `apache 1 3 9 win32.exe`. (Scroll down to see this hyperlink.)

•To install Apache, double click the executable `apache_1_3_9_win32.exe`. Then, click the following sequence: `Next` (after reading Welcome) => `Yes` (accept license agreement) => `Next` (after reading `Readme` information) => `Next` (accept default destination directory) => `Next` (accept `Typical` as the type of setup) => `Next` (accept default program folder) => `Finish` (restart computer).

•TCP/IP protocol must be set up and running on the intended computer in order to install and run Apache. Type ping 127.0.0.1 in a DOS window. If TCP/IP is installed and working, you will receive some messages.

•There are three methods to run Apache in Windows. The first method is to click the following sequence: `Start` (Windows start menu on bottom left corner of screen) => `Programs` => `Apache Web Server` => `Start Apache as console app`. The second method is to double click a shortcut of the executable. The third method is to run the Apache server from a DOS window, by typing the command `apache -s` at the DOS prompt.

•While running, Apache uses its own DOS window. This window remains open and active until we stop Apache. To stop Apache while it is running, click this sequence; `Start` (Windows menu) => `Programs` => `Apache Web Server` => `Shutdown Apache console app`. We can also stop it from a DOS window, by typing the command `apache -k shutdown` at the DOS prompt.

•In order to establish a client/server communication (session), we invoke a browser's window. In the browser's URL bar, we type http://localhost. If Apache is running, it sends a message to the browser, indicating that communication has been established.

•Once a Web server/browser connection is established, we begin running CGI scripts as follows: Scripts must reside in the Apache `cgi-bin` folder. HTML files must reside in the Apache `htdocs` folder. We run Apache. We open a browser window. We type http://localhost:80/xxx.html in the browser URL bar. The *xxx.html* is the Web page we need to run. It uses a CGI script that resides in the Apache `cgi-bin` folder. When the script finishes running, it sends its results to the browser, which displays them.

PROBLEMS

Exercises

18.1 Fill the form of example 14.6.1. Use *posttest.exe* as its CGI script. Capture the screen that displays the script results.

18.2 Repeat problem 1.1 for example 14.6.2.

18.3 Repeat problem 1.1 for example 14.6.3.

18.4 Repeat problem 1.1 for example 14.6.4.

18.5 Repeat problem 1.1 for example 14.6.5.

18.6 Repeat problem 1.1 for example 14.6.6.

18.7 Repeat problem 1.1 for example 14.6.7.
18.8 Repeat problem 1.1 for example 14.6.8.

Homework

18.9 Repeat problem 1.1 for tutorial 14.6.1.
18.10 Repeat problem 1.1 for tutorial 14.6.2.
18.11 Repeat problem 1.1 for example 14.6.3.

Glossary

T his appendix serves as a quick reference to many of
the terms and abbreviations that are widely used with the Internet, the World Wide Web, and
HTML. This appendix is a compilation of all the important terms and abbreviations that are used
throughout the book. The appendix provides an alphabetical listing of these terms and abbreviations.

address book

Browsers provide their users with address books to allow them to store all their e-mail
addresses in one location and use them to send mail to individuals or mailing lists.

ADSL (Asynchronous Digital Subscriber Line)

This is a technology that allows Internet users to connect into the Internet over an ordinary phone line.

alink (active link)

During the time between when the user presses the mouse button and holds it down on
the link and when the user releases it, the link is said to be active and is called active link.

Apache server

The Apache server is one of the most widely used Web servers on the Internet. Apache
is a Unix-based server; however, Windows-based and Mac-based versions are available.

ARPA (Advanced Research Projects Agency)

This is a research agency within the U.S. Department of Defense. It is responsible for
advancing technology by supporting new research innovations and ideas.

ARPAnet
This is the first network that was established by ARPA in an effort to connect together the U.S. Defense Department networks and computers. In 1969, four client computers were connected together via ARPAnet. ARPAnet was the nucleus of the Internet.

ATM (Asynchronous Transfer Mode)
A method of transferring data over the Internet.

Big Seven
Originally the Usenet groups were divided into seven subgroups, which are still called the Big Seven. They are comp, sci, rec, news, talk, soc, and misc.

B-ISDN (broadband ISDN)
This is broadband ISDN. B-ISDN lines use fiber optics instead of twisted-pair copper wires. B-ISDN is much faster than ISDN.

bookmarks
Browsers provide their users with the concept of bookmarks, to allow them to save for future use URLs they have visited.

Boolean search
Some search engines provide their users with advanced search features, such as Boolean search. These features help users to focus their search results. Boolean searches are based on the classical Boolean operations found in the mathematics and science fields. Boolean operations are performed via Boolean operators. The most commonly available Boolean operators are union (OR operator), intersection (AND operator) and subtraction (NOT operator).

cache
Browsers, like other applications, use the cache concept to improve document access. A cache is a storage location. A browser uses two types of caching schemes: memory and disk. The memory cache is a portion of the computer's RAM that the browser uses to store the most recently downloaded Web pages during the current session of surfing the Internet. The disk cache is a portion of the computer's hard disk that the browser uses to store previously downloaded Web pages.

CATV (Cable Access TV)
Cable TV companies provide Internet access. They act as service providers.

CDPD (cellular digital packet data)

This is the protocol, similar to TCP/IP, that is used to transmit data over wireless (cellular) Internet connections that use cellular phones.

CERN (French acronym)

This is European Laboratory for Particle Physics in Geneva, Switzerland where, Berners-Lee conceived the World Wide Web.

CGI (Common Gateway Interface) script

A CGI script is a computer program that a Web author writes to process the data and input of a form in a Web page. A CGI script runs on a Web server.

cgi-bin directory

Webmasters designate a special directory, usually with the name cgi-bin, that stores all CGI scripts. They set up all types of security restrictions on this directory. This directory is under their direct control.

channels

Channels are directories of such general topics as sports, travel, shopping, and so forth. They categorize information to make it easy for surfers to locate. After choosing a generic topic, such as computers, the user is transported to the computer channel with dozens of links to related resources for buying, using, and researching computers. Channels are offered by AOL (Netscape), Microsoft and others.

checkbox

This is a form element. Checkboxes are mutually inclusive, allowing a user to select multiple boxes simultaneously. Checkboxes are displayed as squares. Selecting and deselecting them happens with a mouse click. Checkboxes that are already selected (checked) are shown with checkmarks inside them.

CIX (Commercial Internet Exchange)

In 1991, the CIX (Commercial Internet Exchange) Association was formed by Internet service providers to commercialize the Internet and to establish the legitimate uses of the Internet for business and profit.

CMY (cyan, magenta, and yellow) color model

This model is the complement to the RGB model — the cyan, magenta, and yellow are the complements of red, green, and blue respectively. The CMY model is a subtractive model, because the primary colors are subtracted from white to form different colors in the model.

codecs

Video compression schemes use codec (**co**mpression/**dec**ompression) algorithms. These algorithms compress the video, to store and transmit it, and decompress it, to play it.

color palette and lookup table

The available colors are usually known as the color palette, and the mappings from pixel values to colors are stored in the monitor color lookup table. The browser-safe color palette uses 216 colors.

Common Gateway Interface (CGI)

The Common Gateway Interface is a standard method of communication that between clients and Web servers that ensures that each understands the other in a clear, unambiguous manner. When the client sends information, the server knows what to do with it. When the server sends back a response, the client handles it correctly.

dial-up connection

A dial-up connection typically uses a PC, a modem, and a phone line to connect to the Internet via a phone call.

digital certificate

Digital certificates are used for digital signature. A digital certificate is an electronic ID similar to, say, a credit card or driver's license. It is issued by a certification authority. The certificate includes the person's name, expiration date, and public key and the digital signature of the issuer of the certificate. These certificates are kept in registries, so that their owners can look up their public keys, like a deed of a house.

digital sound

Sound as generated by computers and used over the Internet is known as digital sound.

digital-to-analog (D/A) converter

Such a converter converts the continuous natural (analog) sound into digital sound.

digital video

Video as generated by computers and used over the Internet is known as digital video.

dithering

Dithering can be thought of as a method of interpolation to resolve missing colors. The method is used by browsers during the rendering of Web pages.

DNS (Domain Name System)

This is application software that provides name-to-address translation. For example, the name ftp.netscape.com corresponds to the 198.95.249.66 IP address. It is easier and more logical to use names as Internet addresses. The IP addresses are the ones used to send the packets through the Internet. There are DNS servers that maintain lists of domain name/IP adress correspondences. A DNS server maps a domain name to its IP address.

DoD (Department of Defense)

This is the U.S. government entity that is responsible for the national security of the United States of America.

DSL (Digital Subscriber Line)

A DSL connection is one of the methods to connect to the Internet. It allows Internet users to connect into the Internet over an ordinary phone line

e-commerce (electronic commerce)

e-commerce is a common term that means doing business activities on the Internet. Web surfers can buy goods and services over the Intenret. Also, businesses can buy and sell to each other over the Internet. The business-to-business (B2B) e-commerce market is very large.

e-mail (electronic mail) address

Each node, computer, or user on the Internet has a unique e-mail address. This is like a social security number. This address is used to send and receive e-mail messages and files.

encryption/decryption

Encryption/decryption uses complex computer and mathematical algorithms to scramble data and content for secure transmission across the Internet.

Ethernet

A network that was developed by Xerox during the 1970s. It provides open-architecture networking. It is popular today.

Extranet

An Extranet is a network outside an organization. It facilitates intercompany relationships. Extranets typically link companies and businesses with their customers, suppliers, and partners over the Internet. An Extranet may be viewed as an intermediate network between the Internet and the Intranet.

form

An HTML form consists of a collection of elements organized in a certain layout.

frame differencing

This is a method used by many codecs to compress video.

frame rate

Frame rate (also known as refresh rate) is defined as the number of frames that is displayed per second. In TV video, the frame rate is 30 frames per second.

frame size

Frame size is defined as the pixel size of the video image. In TV video, the frame size is the size of the TV screen itself, unless the screen is split between multiple channels.

FTP (File Transfer Protocol)

FTP is the Internet tool you want to use when you know that the information you seek is stored in a large file in a given location. FTP lets you download a copy of the file from a remote host to your local computer. FTP can transfer ASCII and binary files. FTP is a client/server application.

HDTV (High Definition)

HDTV is a digital TV that can receive both digital broadcast programs and Internet data. HDTV provides high-quality video and audio, both in digital streaming formats. One of the most distinguishing features of HDTV is its 16:9 aspect ratio.

helper applications

These are external applications that a browser launches that can open or save files that the browser cannot handle on its own.

hidden field

This is form element. Hidden fields are elements that are never displayed on the screen. Hidden fields are used by Web authors for tracking purposes.

HSB (hue, saturation, and brightness) color model

The HSB (hue, saturation, and brightness) color model creates colors by mixing three values, one for each primary signal. The value for each signal is between 0 and 1.

HTML (HyperText Markup Language)

This is a simple and easy-to-use scripting language for writing code to format and create Web pages. The code is stored in HTML documents. The two main characteristics of HTML are its markup and hyperlinks.

HTML document structure

A well-structured HTML document should have three parts: header, body and footer. The header identifies the document as HTML, establishes its title, and includes its <META> tag. The body contains the content of the Web page. The footer has the Web-site address information that Web surfers can use to get in touch with the site's webmaster.

HTML editor

This is an editor that generates HTML code and tags automatically. HTML editors provide Web authors with an automation tool for writing HTML code. By using HTML editors, Web authors can focus on page design and layout while the editor generates the code automatically.

HTML frame

HTML frames enable Web authors to display multiple HTML documents (multiple Web pages) in multiple views rendered by the browser on its one window. Each frame displays a Web page.

HTML frame set

A collection of HTML frames is referred to as a frame set.

HTML frame size

A frame size is specified by the number columns (COLS) and the number of rows (ROWS) in HTML. The units of ROWS and COLS could be pixels or a percentage of the browser window.

HTML hybrid editor

The hybrid editors are a mix of WYSIWYG and tag editors. They include HotMetal Pro. These editors allow authors to use HTML tags if they need to.

HTML nested frames

There are two types of frame sets: simple and complex. Simple frame sets divide a browser window into rows or columns only. Complex sets create nested frames by dividing the window horizontally and vertically.

HTML tags

HTML tags are special keywords enclosed in brackets (< and >). Web authors use them to format Web pages. Browsers execute them and display the Web pages.

HTML tag editor

This is a type of HTML editor. The HTML tag editors include `HotDog Pro`. These editors provide Web authors with menus of HTML tags and their attributes, to develop their Web pages.

HTML target frames

Target frames are defined as frames that receive contents from other frames.

HTML WYSIWYG (What You See Is What You Get) editor

These editors show the page as the Web author creates it. The HTML tags are hidden during the editing session. Sample editors are Netscape `Composer` and MS `FrontPage`.

HTTP (HyperText Transport Protocol)

The protocol that is used to transfer Web pages from Web sites or servers to client browsers, so that Web surfers can view them.

hyperlinks

Hyperlinks create hypertext. Hyperlinks produce two effects when Web authors include them in Web pages. First, they link other Web pages and files to the current Web page. Second, the reader of an HTML document can click any link in the page, at any time, at random. Despite its simplicity, the link has been one of the driving forces behind the success of the Web.

IAB (Internet Architecture Board)

The IAB (Internet Architecture Board) sets up such details of Internet operation as how IP addresses are assigned and how TCP/IP packets are interpreted.

ICANN (Internet Corporation for Assigned Names and Numbers)

The ICANN, based in California and run by a board of 19 members from around the world is responsible for running the Internet, particularly the entire system of assigning and managing IP addresses and domain names, such as those ending with .com, .net, etc.

image hyperlink

Images can be used as hyperlinks. Instead of text, an image is used as the link. As with text hyperlinks, the mouse cursor changes to a hand when a surfer moves the mouse over the image hyperlink.

IMAP (Internet Message Access Protocol)

Incoming mail servers use the IMAP protocol to receive e-mail messages.

image formats

Among the many image formats, three are supported by browsers by default. They are Graphics Interchange Format (GIF), Joint Photographic Experts Group (JPEG or JPG), and Portable Network Graphics (PNG).

image (clickable) map

An image map is defined as a single image that links to multiple URLs or HTML documents. The image is divided into regions, sometimes known as "hot spots" or "hotlinked" regions.

Internet

The Internet is a giant network. It is known as the information superhighway. It consists of computers located all over the world that communicate with each other.

interdocument links

Hyperlinks that connect external Web pages to a particular Web page are known as interdocument links.

Intradocument links (anchors)

Hyperlinks that connect different sections within the same Web page are known as intradocument links, or anchors.

Intranet

An Intranet is a network that is contained within an organization; that is, it is an internal or private network.

IP address

This is an identification number that is assigned to a computer that is connected to a network. Without IP addresses, the Internet would not work. IP addresses allow successful communication between the different networks, servers, and computers that make up the Internet. An IP address is a 32-bit number. A typical IP address is 129.10.1.13.

ISDN (integrated service digital network) Line

This is a fast Internet connection. An ISDN connection operates at speed of 128-144 Kbps.

ISOC (Inetnet SOCiety)

ISOC sets the rules by which the Internet operates.

ISO Latin-1 (8859-1) Character set

This contains the Latin characters. It represents each character by a unique code. It allows Web authors to include Latin characters in their Web pages.

IPS (Internet Service Provider)

ISPs offer direct Internet connections as well as dial-up access for individual and home users. They do not offer content. They offer only access. Sample ISPs are AT&T WorldNet, IBM Internet Connection, MCI Internet, MindSpring Enterprises, and Prodigy Internet.

Kbps (KiloBits Per Second)

A measuring unit that show how fast data is transmitted throughout the Internet.

LAN (Local Area Network)

A network that connects computers. The computers must be within a certain physical distance for the network to work. Ethernet LANs are quite popular.

lists

These are HTML elements that can be used in a Web page to organize its contents in a list or bullet form. Three types of lists exist. They are bullet (unordered), numbered (ordered), and definition lists. Lists can be nested to support different hierarchical levels.

listserv

Listserv discussion groups combine elements of e-mail and Usenet news.

Mbps (MegaBits Per Second)

A measuring unit that shows how fast data is transmitted throughout the Internet.

menu

This is a form element. Menus allow users to choose one or multiple items at the same time. Other names that are frequently used for an HTML menu are option list or menu, select list or menu, and drop-down list or menu.

MES (Mobile End System)

A special CDPD (cellular digital packet data) telephone that is used to connect to the Internet via a wireless (cellular) connection.

metadata

Metadata is data about an HTML document rather than the document content. Browsers do not render metadata. Such data is used by search engines for indexing and ranking page hits in a given search.

metasearch engine

This is a search engine that searches several other search engines at once for every search request — that is, it performs a multi-engine search. Metasearch engines speed the searching of the Web.

MIME (multipurpose Internet mail extension)

A variety of audio, video, and animation formats, collectively known as MIME data types, is now found on a large number of Web sites. There are seven main MIME types. They are text, application, image, audio, video, multipart, and message. All browsers support them and their formats.

Mosaic

The first graphically-oriented browser, it was developed at the National Center for Supercomputing Applications (NCSA) at the University of Illinois at Urbana-Champaign (UIUC) in 1992.

MP3 sound format

MP3 format allows playing near-CD-quality digital music and songs over the Internet and on PCs.

name/value pairs

When a Web surfer fills in a form in a Web page, the browser encodes the data into name/value pairs before sending it to the server for processing via a CGI script. The name is the name of the form element, and the value is what the Web surfer inputs in this form element.

NC (Network Computer)

A network computer, sometimes known as a thin client, is a stripped-down version of a PC. The idea is to use it as an inexpensive computer to connect to the Internet. NCs do not have much memory or hard disk.

NCSA (National Center for Supercomputing Applications)

A computing center at the University of Illinois at Urbana-Champaign. It developed the first Web browser, known as Mosaic.

newsgroups (discussion groups)

Practically, discussion groups and newsgroups refer to the same thing. Discussion groups are groups of people who are interested in certain topics and usually share opinions and ideas about these topics. Newsgroups are the collections of the messages that the discussion groups post to a news server about a given topic or subject. Newsgroups are also known as Net-news.

newsreader

Newsreader is software (e.g., a browser) that helps users deal with newsgroups and their messages.

NGI (Next Generation Internet)

The NGI initiative is led by the federal government; the Internet2 initiative program is led by U.S. universities. Both NGI and Internet2 were established in October 1996, and they are working together in many areas to improve the future of the Internet.

NNTP (Net News Transport Protocol)

Usenet software uses the NNTP protocol to organize messages and distribute copies and replies of these messages to users.

NSFnet

The NSFnet network replaced ARPAnet in 1990, with a well-developed set of regional and metropolitan area networks feeding into the NSF backbone. The NSFnet major objective was to serve educational, research, and government networking needs.

NTSC (National Television System Committee)

A standard transmission code that transmits analog video signals. NTSC is used mostly in North America and Japan.

online service providers

These providers serve the end-user dial-up Internet-connectivity market. They offer content and connection (access). Sample commercial online services are AOL and the Microsoft Network (MSN).

PAL (Phase Alteration Line)

A standard transmission code that transmits analog video signals. PAL is used mostly in Western Europe, England, and the Middle East.

playback video

Playback video is video created, stored in files, and included in Web pages as video clips.

plug-ins

A plug-in is a program that, after installation, runs within the browser window, extending its capabilities. Even though it is a separate program, a plug-in appears to be part of the browser. Plug-ins are better to use than helper applications.

POP (Point Of Presence or Post Office Protocol)

This is an access point to the Internet with an IP address. Service providers have many POP locations in various geographical locations, to allow customers to connect to the Internet vial local phone calls.

POP3

POP3 is a popular mail -erver type.

PPP (Point-to-Point Protocol)

This protocol allows connecting two hosts, say your PC and an Internet server, over a direct link such as a telephone connection. The connection is know as a PPP connection.

public and private keys

These two keys are used as part of encryption/decryption technology. The public and private keys are used to encrypt and decrypt data, respectively. The two keys are a set of two numbers that are generated randomly. The private key is used to decrypt data that has been encrypted by the public key. The keys come in pairs that are not interchangeable.

radio button

This is a form element. Radio buttons are mutually exclusive, allowing a user only one choice at a time. Radio buttons are displayed as circles. Selecting and deselecting them happen with a mouse click. A radio button that is already selected is shown with a filled circle inside.

reset button

This is a form element. Each form must have this button. Clicking the reset button erases all the form input and replaces it by the form default values.

RGB (red, green, and blue) color model

This color model is used to create colors in Web pages. It generate colors additively by mixing its three primary colors: red, green, and blue.

router

This is a network device that controls traffic on the network. It finds the fastest route along which to deliver Internet content and information.

search engine

This is an application software that allows Web surfers to search and navigate the Internet and the Web.

SECAM (Systeme Electronic Pour Coleur Avec Memoire)

This is standard transmission code that transmits analog video signals. SECAM is used in France and Russia.

SGML (Standard Generalized Markup Language)

This is the superset that defines HTML tags. HTML is a subset of SGML.

signature file

The signature file is a file that you develop yourself in a word processor such as Word. The file usually contains your affiliation, including name, company name and address, phone and fax numbers, e-mail address, and company logo. The browser appends your signature file automatically to every e-mail message you send out. Thus, you save time by not typing that same information over and over. In other words, your signature file acts as a rubber stamp for you.

single-tier client/server model

The single-tier model uses one computer as both the client and the server.

SLIP (Serial Line Interface Protocol)

This protocol, similar to the PPP protocol, connects two hosts over the Internet. The PPP protocol is better and faster than this protocol.

smart browsing

Smart browsing provides intelligent and fast access to information. It is supported by Netscape Communicator.

SMTP (Simple Mail Transfer Protocol)

Outgoing mail servers use the SMTP protocol to communicate with client computers. The SMTP protocol allows the sender to identify him/herself, specify a recipient, and transfer an e-mail message.

sound formats

The available sound formats are AU (Sun), WAV (Microsoft), MIDI, and AIFF. The file extensions (types) for these formats are .au, .wav, .mid, and .aif, respectively.

SSL (Secure Sockets Layer)

Both Web servers and browsers use SSL technology, which was developed by Netscape, to manage the security of data transmission between them.

static sound

Static sound is sound stored in files and included in Web pages as sound clips.

streaming sound

Streaming sound is the broadcast sound coming from broadcast stations operating on the Internet. This sound is similar to that of real audio and conventional radio stations.

streaming video

Streaming video is real-time video. Streaming video allows Web surfers to view video as it is downloaded. Web surfers can use streaming video to watch live events from all over the world. Video cards that come with PCs can play streaming video if the software that can handle streaming video is installed.

submit button

This is a form element. Each form must have this button. Clicking the submit button activates the browser to send the form contents as name/value pairs to a CGI script installed on the form Web server for processing.

T1 and T3 lines

They provide dedicated access to the Internet. A T1 line provides a bandwidth of 1.5 million bits per second. A T3 line has a bandwidth of 45 Mbps.

table

A table is defined as a region that has rows and columns of small rectangles, called cells, that are arranged relative to each other in a certain way that makes up the table layout.

table caption

The table caption is its title which provides a short description of the table purpose. It can placed at the top of the table or at the bottom.

table cell

This is the basic unit of a table. Each table cell holds its own content (data). Cell data could be any HTML elements, such as text, hyperlinks, images, and so forth.

table cell padding

Cell padding is equivalent to specifying top, bottom, left, and right margins for the cell. It describes the amount of horizontal and vertical spacing between cell content (data) and its borders.

table cell spacing

Cell spacing describes the amount of the horizontal and vertical white spacing between cells.

table directionality

A table directionality describes how the cells of table rows are laid. They can be laid left-to-right or right-to-left. The former is the default.

table header

The table header is the first row in the table. Each cell in this row is a header for the column underneath it. It holds the title of the column.

table nesting

This implies embedding an entire table inside another table. Web authors may nest tables to achieve certain design goals and layouts of their Web pages.

table rows and columns

Table rows are the horizontal layout of the cells. Similarly, table columns are the vertical layout of the cells.

table summary

The table summary provides a longer description that may be used by people using speech or Braille-based browsers.

table border

The table border is its outside boundary. We can think of it as the table container.

table width and height

The width and height of a table are a representation of the number of its rows and columns respectively.

TCP/IP (Transmission Control Protocol/Internet Protocol)

This is the communication method that the Internet uses to transmit content and information from one location to another. TCP/IP can be viewed as Internet rules similar to the postal service rules.

TCP and IP packets

The TCP/IP protocol breaks the data to be transmitted, say an e-mail message, into chunks (called TCP packets) of a maximum size of 1500 bytes each. These packets are enclosed in IP packets. The IP packets travel through the telephone lines and/or the fiber-optic cables of the Internet to their final destinations.

Telnet

Telnet is an important tool for accessing the resources of the Internet. Rather than providing a method to obtain files, it provides a way to obtain computing services from the hosts that can be reached on the Internet. Telnet allows you to log into a remote computer (host) and use it. You must be a valid user and have an account on that computer. When you telnet to a host from a remote location, it asks you for your username and password.

tiling

An image can be used as a background for a Web page. In this case, the browser uses the image and repeats it horizontally and vertically across the page to create a pattern. This pattern is known as tile or tiling effect.

textarea

This is a form element. Textareas allows form users to input multiple lines of text. Each textarea has a width (number of columns) and a height (number of rows). Both parameters are specified as numbers of characters.

text field

This is a form element. Text fields are typically used when one line of text is needed as input. A text field is displayed as a rectangle, and has a size and a maximum length.

three-tier client/server model

The three-tier model uses one client computer and two server computers. One server is intermediate. It is used for security reasons.

two-tier client/server model

The two-tier model uses two computers, one for the client and one for the server.

URL (Uniform Resource Locator)

The name that corresponds to an IP address in the DNS is known as a URL or an Internet name. A URL identifies a node on the Internet uniquely. The Internet DNS follows a standard format to assign a URL (IP address) to any of its nodes.

Usenet

The network of computers (news servers) that exchange Netnews is known as Usenet. News servers are maintained by companies, groups, and individuals and can host thousands of newsgroups.

vCard

This is an electronic business card that users can create and use in their e-mail messages. E-mail tools such Netscape e-mail or Microsoft Outlook Express use vCards. The e-mail tool attaches the vCard at the end of each e-mail message a user sends.

video formats

There are many video formats available for producing playback video. The available common formats are AVI (Audio Video Interleave), QuickTime, MPEG (Moving Picture Experts Group), and MJPEG (Motion JPEG). The file extensions (types) for these formats are `.avi`, `.mov`, `.mpg`, and `.mjpg`, respectively.

vlink (visited link)

After the user clicks a link and releases the mouse button, the link becomes a visited link.

WAN (Wide Area Network)

A network that connects computers. The computers must be within a certain physical distance for the network to work. WANs cover a much larger geographical area than LANs do.

Web browser

A Web browser is an application that has a GUI (Graphical User Interface) that allows its users to read their e-mail, participate in discussion groups, display Web pages, search the Internet, run Java applets, and so forth.

Web page

This is the outcome of displaying, in a browser, a document that is written in HTML. A Web page can contain hyperlinks which lead to other Web pages. The formatting of a Web page is achieved by HTML tags.

Web portals

"Web portal" (also portal site or just portal) is a metaphor used to describe Web sites that work as gateways, launching pads, or starting points to the Internet. They act as tables of contents (information meccas) to the Web. Web portals aggregate a lot of content in one place for users' convenience. They offer a variety of online services, such as travel, chat rooms, news, forums, e-mail, weather forecasts, stock quotes, sports, shopping, search engines, and so forth.

Web server

A Web server is a software program. A Web server runs on a networked fast computer with a large hard disk and a large amount of memory (RAM). The server software performs many tasks, such as hosting Web pages and CGI scripts.

WebTV

A WebTV is a television set that allows you to connect to the Internet. It is also supposed to enhance TV programs with online content.

Winsock (Windows socket) protocol

Winsock is the Windows Sockets API (Application Programming Interface). It allows Windows to work with the Internet. It allows Windows-based PCs to be connected to the Internet. The protocol became available in 1993.

World Wide Web (WWW)

The World Wide Web (WWW or W3) is the section of the Internet that features such multimedia capabilities as video, audio, images, graphics, and text. In 1989, the World Wide Web was conceived by Berners-Lee of the European Laboratory for Particle Physics, or CERN (an acronym for the group's original name in French), in Geneva, Switzerland. The Web began to take off after graphical Web viewers, called browsers, were developed in 1993.

World Wide Web Consortium (W3C)

This is the group that manages the HTML standards. To find out what is current for HTML, visit their Web site at www.w3.org.

Summary of HTML Tags

T his appendix serves as a quick reference to the HTML tags that are used throughout the book. The appendix compiles all the HTML tables that are found in the summary sections of the book chapters, to make it convenient for Web authors and book users to find any tag quickly. The tables are listed here in their order of appearance in the book.

B.1 HTML Document Structure, Text, Link, Anchor, and Meta Tags

Table B.1   Summary of HTML document structure, text, link, anchor, and meta tags.

Tag	Close	Attribute	Value	Example	Page
<HTML>	Yes	None	N/A[a]	<HTML>...</HTML>	236
<!....>	No	None	N/A	<! This is a comment>	235
<HEAD>	Yes	PROFILE	url	<HEAD PROFILE = "http:// www.xxx.com/myProfile"> ...</HEAD>	236
<TITLE>	Yes	None	N/A	<TITLE> Page one</TITLE>	236
<BODY>	Yes	See Cht. 9	See Chpt. 9	<BODY> Page content and tags go here </BODY>	236
<ADDRESS>	Yes	None	N/A	<ADDRESS> ... </ADDRESS>	237
<H1> – <H6>	Yes	ALIGN	left(def), center, right	<H1 ALIGH = "center"> ...</H1> <H2 ALIGN="right">.</H2>	239
<P>	Yes/ No	ALIGN	left center right	<P> Left is the default <P ALIGN = "center"> ... <P ALIGN = "right"> ...	240
<B>	Yes	None	N/A	<B> Tag bolds text </B>	242
<BASEFONT>	No	SIZE	1 – 7	<BASEFONT SIZE = 4>	242
<BIG>	Yes	None	N/A	<BIG>Big text here</BIG>	242

a.   Not applicable

Tag	Close	Attribute	Value	Example	Page
<BLOCKQUOTE>	Yes	None	N/A	<BLOCKQUOTE> Quote goes here </BLOCKQUOTE>	242
 	NO	None	N/A	Force a line break 	242
<CENTER>	Yes	None	N/A	<CENTER> Text </CENTER>	242
<CITE>	Yes	None	N/A	<CITE> Cite text </CITE>	242
<CODE>	Yes	None	N/A	<CODE>Comp. code</CODE>	242
<EM>	Yes	None	N/A	<EM>Important text</EM>	242
<FONT>	Yes	SIZE	1 – 7	<FONT SIZE=5>...</FONT>	242
		COLOR	name or hex code	<FONT COLOR="green"> Text goes here </FONT>	
<HR>	No	ALIGN	center, right	<HR ALIGN = "center">	242
		COLOR	name or hex code	<HR COLOR = "green">	
		NOSHADE	None	<HR NOSHADE>	
		SIZE	pixels	<HR SIZE = 15>	
		WIDTH	pixels or %	<HR WIDTH = 70>	
<I>	Yes	None	N/A	<I> Text goes heere </I>	242
<KBD>	Yes	None	N/A	<KBD> Text goes here </KBD>	242

Tag	Close	Attribute	Value	Example	Page
<SMALL>	Yes	None	N/A	<SMALL>Text here</SMALL>	242
<STRIKE>	Yes	None	N/A	<STRIKE> Text </STRIKE>	242
<STRONG>	Yes	None	N/A	<STRIKE> Text </STRIKE>	242
<U>	Yes	None	N/A	<U> Text goes here </U>	242
<A>	Yes	HREF	url	<A HREF="f.html">...</A>	244, 245
		TITLE	text	<A ...TITLE="tt">...</A>	
		NAME	text	<A ... NAME="nn">...</A>	
		CHARSET	set name	<A...CHARSET="..">...</A>	
		TYPE	mime	<A TYPE=text/html>..</A>	
		HRE-FLANG	lang.	<A HREFLANG="fr">...</A>	
		REL	file	<A .. REL="doc.">...</A>	
<LINK>	No	HREF	url	<LINK HREF = "f.html">	254
		TITLE	text	<LINK TITLE="Food page">	
		CHARSET	set name	<LINK CHAARSET="ISO...">	
		TYPE	MIME	<LINK TYPE="text/css">	

Tag	Close	Attribute	Value	Example	Page
		HRE-FLANG	lang.	`<LINK HREFLANG="fr">`	
		LANG	lang.	`<LINK LANG="fr">`	
		REL	file	`<LINK REL="alternate">`	
		REV	file	`<LINK REV="f.html>`	
		MEDIA	type	`<LINK MEDIA="print">`	
<BASE>	No	HREF	url	`<BASE HREF="www.xx.com">`	255
<META>	No	NAME	text	<META NAME = "keywords">	256
		CON-TENT	text	<META CONTENT="text/html">	
		HTTP-EQUIV	keyword	<META http-equiv="content-type">	
		SCHEME	keyword	<META SCHEME="ISBN">	

B.2 HTML List Tags

Table B.2   Summary of HTML list tags.

Tag	Close	Attribute	Value	Example	Page
<UL>	Yes	None	N/A	<UL> ... </UL>	292
<OL>	Yes	None	N/A	<OL> ... </OL>	295
<DL>	Yes	None	N/A	<DL> ...</DL>	299
<LI>	No	TYPE (for UL)	disk	<LI TYPE = "disc">	292 293
			square	<LI TYPE = "square">	
			circle	<LI TYPE = "circle">	
		TYPE (for OL)	letter	<LI TYPE = "A">	295 296
			roman	<LI TYPE = "I">	
		COM- PACT	boolean	<LI COMPACT= true>	
		START (for OL)	number	<LI START= 4>	
		VALUE (for OL)	number	<LI VALUE = 7>	
<DT>	No	None	N/A	<DT>Term 1	299
<DD>	No	None	N/A	<DD>Definition 1	299

B.3 HTML Color Tags

Table B.3   Summary of HTML color tags.

Tag	Close	Attribute	Value	Example	Page
<BODY>	Yes	TEXT	hex code	<BODY TEXT = "#FF0000">	333 334
		LINK	hex code	<BODY LINK= "#00FF00">	
		ALINK	hex code	<BODY ALINK = "#0000FF">	
		VLINK	hex code	<BODY VLINK = "#FFFF00">	
		BGCOLOR	hex code	<BODY BGCOLOR= "#FF0000">	
		BACK-GROUND	image file	See Chapter 10	
<FONT>	YES	COLOR	hex code	<FONT COLOR = "#ADEAEA">	334

B.4 HTML Image Tags

Table B.4   Summary of HTML image tags.

Tag	Close	Attribute	Value	Example	Page
<IMG>	No	SRC	img. file	`<IMG SRC="myImage.gif">`	345 346
		ALT	text	`<IMG ALT="image text">`	
		LONG-DESC	url	`<IMG longdesc="xx.html">`	
		BORDER	pixels	`<IMG BORDER=5>`	
		WIDTH	pixels	`<IMG WIDTH=100>`	
		HEIGHT	pixels	`<IMG HEIGHT=150>`	
		ALIGN	top	`<IMG ALIGN="top">`	
			middle	`<IMG ALIGN="middle">`	
			bottom	`<IMG ALIGN="bottom">`	
			left	`<IMG ALIGN="left">`	
			right	`<IMG ALIGN="right">`	
		HSPACE	pixels	`<IMG HSPACE=10>`	
		VSPACE	pixels	`<IMG VSPACE=15>`	
		USEMAP	anchor	See Chapter 11.	
		ISMAP	anchor	See Chapter 11.	

B.5 HTML Image Map Tags

Table B.5   Summary of HTML image map tags.

Tag	Close	Attribute	Value	Example	Page
\<IMG>	No	USEMAP	#name	`<IMG ... USEMAP = "#myImage">`	382
\<MAP>	Yes	NAME	name	`<MAP NAME = "myImage"> ...</MAP>`	382
\<AREA>	No	SHAPE	default	`<AREA ... SHAPE = "default">`	383
			rect	`<AREA ... SHAPE = "rect">`	
			circle	`<AREA .. SHAPE = "circle">`	
			poly	`<AREA ... SHAPE = "poly">`	
		COORDS	pixels	`<AREA ... COORDS =    "5,8 20,25">`	
		ALT	text	`<AREA ... ALT = "my hot spot">`	
		HREF	html file	`<AREA ... HREF = "myFile.html">`	

B.6 HTML Sound Tags

Table B.6   Summary of HTML sound tags.

Tag	Close	Attribute	Value	Example	Page
<EMBED>	Yes	SRC	name	<EMBED SRC="mySound.au">	418 419
		WIDTH	pixels	<EMBED WIDTH = 145>	
		HEIGHT	pixels	<EMBED HEIGHT = 60>	
		VOLUME	number	<EMBED VOLUME = 70>	
		AUTOSTART	boolean	<EMBED AUTOSTART = "true">	
		HIDDEN	boolean	<EMBED HIDDEN = "true">	
		LOOP	boolean	<EMBED LOOP = "true">	

B.7 HTML Video Tags

Table B.7 Summary of HTML video tags.

Tag	Close	Attribute	Value	Example	Page
<EMBED>	Yes	SRC	name	<EMBED SRC="mySound.au">	443 444
		WIDTH	pixels	<EMBED WIDTH = 400>	
		HEIGHT	pixels	<EMBED HEIGHT = 300>	
		VOLUME	number	<EMBED VOLUME = 70>	
		AUTOSTART	boolean	<EMBED AUTOSTART = "true">	
		HIDDEN	boolean	<EMBED HIDDEN = "true">	
		LOOP	boolean	<EMBED LOOP = "true">	

B.8 HTML Form Tags

Table B.8   Summary of HTML form tags.

Tag	Close	Attribute	Value	Example	Page
<FORM>	Yes	NAME	text	`<FORM NAME = "myForm">`	475 476
		ACTION	text	`<FORM ACTION = "CGIScript">`	
		METHOD	POST	`<FORM METHOD = "post">`	
			GET	`<FORM METHOD = "get">`	
		ENCTYPE	text	not widely used	
		ACCEPT-CHARSET	text	not widely used	
		ACCEPT	text	not widely used	

Table B.8 Summary of HTML form tags.

Tag	Close	Attribute	Value	Example	Page
<INPUT>	No	NAME	text	`<INPUT NAME = "myElement">`	477 478
		TYPE	text	`<INPUT TYPE = "text">`	
			checkbox	`<INPUT TYPE = "checkbox">`	
			radio	`<INPUT TYPE = "radio">`	
			password	`<INPUT TYPE = "password">`	
			hidden	`<INPUT TYPE = "hidden">`	
			image	`<INPUT TYPE = "image">`	
			button	`<INPUT TYPE = "button">`	
			submit	`<INPUT TYPE = "submit">`	
			reset	`<INPUT TYPE = "reset">`	
		VALUE	text	`<INPUT VALUE = "test">`	
		SIZE	number	`<INPUT SIZE = 10>`	
		MAX-LENGTH	number	`<INPUT MAXLENGTH = 15>`	
		CHECKED	N/A	`<INPUT CHECKED>`	
		SRC	file name	`<INPUT SRC = "myImg.jpg">`	

Table B.8   Summary of HTML form tags.

Tag	Close	Attribute	Value	Example	Page
<SELECT>	Yes	NAME	text	<SELECT NAME = "myMenu">	488 489
		SIZE	number	<SELECT SIZE = 3>	
		MULTIPLE	N/A	<SELECT MULTIPLE>	
<OPTION>	No	SELECTED	N/A	<OPTION SELECTED>	489
		VALUE	text	<OPTION VALUE= "myText">	
		LABEL	text	<OPTION LABEL= "myLab">	
<TEXTAREA>	Yes	NAME	text	<TEXTAREA NAME="myArea">	491 492
		ROWS	number	<TEXTAREA ROWS = 10>	
		COLS	number	<TEXTAREA COLS = 25>	
		WRAP	soft	<TEXTAREA WRAP = "soft">	
			hard	<TEXTAREA WRAP = "hard">	

B.9 HTML Frame Tags

Table B.9   Summary of HTML frame tags.

Tag	Close	Attribute	Value	Example	Page
<FRAMESET>	Yes	ROWS	number	`<FRAMESET ROWS="100,2*,*">`	524
		COLS	number	`<FRAMESET COLS="30%,*,4*">`	
<FRAME>	No	NAME	text	`<FRAME NAME = "display">`	525
		SRC	file	`<FRAME SRC = "myFil.html">`	
		NORE-SIZE	none	`<FRAME NORESIZE>`	
		SCROLL-ING	auto (default)	`<FRAME>`	
			yes	`<FRAME SCROLLING = "yes">`	
			no	`<FRAME SCROLLING = "no">`	
		FRAME-BORDER	0 or 1	`<FRAME FRAMEBORDER = 0>`	
		MARGIN-WIDTH	pixels	`<FRAME MARGINWIDTH = 10>`	
		MARGIN-HEIGHT	pixels	`<FRAME MARGINHEIGHT = 10>`	
		LONG-DESC	file	`<FRAME LONGDESC = "ff.html">`	

Table B.9   Summary of HTML frame tags.

Tag	Close	Attribute	Value	Example	Page
<IFRAME>	Yes	<IFRAME> tag has the same attributes as <FRAME> tag except NORESIZE. In addition, it has the following attributes:			530
		ALIGN	top	<IFRAME ALIGN = "TOP">	
			middle	<IFRAME ALIGN="MIDDLE">	
			bottom	<IFRAME ALIGN="BOTTOM">	
		WIDTH	pixels	<IFRAME WIDTH = 60>	
		HEIGHT	pixels	<IFRAME HEIGHT = 50>	
<NOFRAMES>	Yes	None	N/A	<NOFRAMES> HTML tags go here </NOFRAMES>	533

B.10 HTML Table Tags

Table B.10   Summary of HTML table tags.

Tag	Close	Attribute	Value	Example	Page
<TABLE>	Yes	SUM-MARY	text	<TABLE SUMMARY "...">	560
		WIDTH	pixels	<TABLE WIDTH = 400>	
		HEIGHT	pixels	<TABLE HEIGHT = 200>	
		BORDER	pixels	<TABLE BORDER = 5>	
		ALIGN	left	<TABLE ALIGN = "left">	
			center	<TABLE ALIGN = "center">	
			right	<TABLE ALIGN = "right">	
		CELL-SPACING	pixels	<TABLE CELLSPACING = 10>	
		CELLPAD-DING	pixels	<TABLE CELLPADDING = 20>	
<CAPTION>	Yes	ALIGN	top	<CAPTION ALIGN = "top">	563
			bottom	<CAPTION ALIGN = "bottom">	
			left	<CAPTION ALIGN = "left">	
			right	<CAPTION ALIGN = "right">	

Table B.10   Summary of HTML table tags.

Tag	Close	Attribute	Value	Example	Page
<TR>	Optional	ALIGN	left	<TR ALIGN = "left">	563
			center	<TR ALIGN = "center">	
			right	<TR ALIGN = "right">	
<TH>/<TD>	Optional	ROWSPAN	number	<TD ROWSPAN = 3>	563
		COLSPAN	number	<TD COLSPAN = 2>	
		NOWRAP	none	<TD NOWRAP>	
		ALIGN	left	<TD ALIGN = "left">	
			center	<TD ALIGN = "center">	
			right	<TD ALIGN = "right">	
		VALIGN	top	<TD VALIGN = "top">	
			middle	<TD VALIGN = "middle">	
			bottom	<TD VALIGN = "bottom">	
		CELLPAD-DING	pixels	<TD CELLPADDING = 10>	

Hexadecimal Codes of Colors

T his appendix provides a quick refrence to the hexadecimal codes of various colors that are shown in table 9.1 of chapter 9.

Table C.1   Color names and their hex codes

Color name	Hex code	Color name	Hex code	Color name	Hex code
Aqua	#00FFFF	Godzilla	#145F0A	Purple	#800080
Black	#000000	Green	#008000	Red	#FF0000
Blue	#0000FF	Hard Hat	#F6EF31	Scarlet	#8C1717
Blue Violet	#9F5F9F	Hedgehog	#A78424	Silver	#C0C0C0
Braindead	#4566C9	Hunter Green	#215E21	Spicy pink	#FF1CAE
Brass	#B5A642	Indian Red	#4E2F2F	Spring Green	#00FF7F
Brown	#A62A2A	Khaki	#9F9F5F	Steel Blue	#236B8E
Copper	#B87333	Lime	#00FF00	Succotash	#94BD44

Table C.1   Color names and their hex codes

Color name	Hex code	Color name	Hex code	Color name	Hex code
Coral	#FF7F00	Maroon	#800000	Summer Sky	38B0DE
Corn Dog	#F0C373	Navy	#000080	Tan	#DB9370
Dark Brown	#5C4033	Neon Blue	#4D4DFF	Teal	#008080
Dusty Rose	#856363	Neon Pink	#FF6FC7	The Family Rat	#827964
Fledspar	#D19275	Old Gold	#CFB53B	Thistle	#D8BFD8
Firebrick	#8E2323	Olive	#808000	Turquoise	#ADEAEA
Fuchsia	#FF00FF	Orange	#FF7F00	Wheat	#D8D8BF
Full Bladder	#FFC136	Pink	#BC8F8F	White	#FFFFFF
Gray	#808080	Plum	#EAADEA	Yellow	#FFFF00

Index